A FIRST LOOK AT
COMMUNICATION
THEORY

A FIRST LOOK AT
COMMUNICATION
THEORY

SEVENTH EDITION

EM GRIFFIN

Wheaton College

 **McGraw-Hill
Higher Education**

Boston   Burr Ridge, IL   Dubuque, IA   New York   San Francisco   St. Louis
Bangkok   Bogotá   Caracas   Kuala Lumpur   Lisbon   London   Madrid   Mexico City
Milan   Montreal   New Delhi   Santiago   Seoul   Singapore   Sydney   Taipei   Toronto

McGraw-Hill
Higher Education

Published by McGraw-Hill, an imprint of The McGraw-Hill Companies, Inc., 1221 Avenue of the Americas, New York, NY 10020. Copyright © 2009, 2006, 2003, 2000, 1997, 1994, 1991 by The McGraw-Hill Companies. All rights reserved. No part of this publication may be reproduced or distributed in any form or by any means, or stored in a database or retrieval system, without the prior written consent of The McGraw-Hill Companies, Inc., including, but not limited to, in any network or other electronic storage or transmission, or broadcast for distance learning.

This book is printed on acid-free paper.

1 2 3 4 5 6 7 8 9 0 QPD/QPD 0 9 8

ISBN 978-0-07-338502-0
MHID 0-07-338502-6

Editor in Chief: *Michael Ryan*
Publisher: *Frank Mortimer*
Executive Editor: *Katie Stevens*
Developmental Editor: *Jennie Katsaros*
Marketing Manager: *Leslie Oberhuber*
Media Project Manager: *Thomas Brierly*
Production Editor: *Leslie LaDow*
Production Service: *Matrix Productions*
Designer: *Ashley Bedell*
Production Supervisor: *Tandra Jorgensen*
Composition: *10/12 Palatino by Aptara*
Printing: *45# New Era Matte Plus by Quebecor World, Inc.*

Credits: The credits section for this book begins on page C-1 and is considered an extension of the copyright page.

Library of Congress Cataloging-in-Publication Data
Griffin, Emory A.
  A first look at communication theory / Em Griffin.—7th ed.
    p. cm.
  Includes bibliographical references and index.
  ISBN-13: 978-0-07-338502-0 (alk. paper)
  ISBN-10: 0-07-338502-6 (alk. paper)
  1. Communication—Philosophy.   I. Title.
P90G725 2008
302.201—dc22

                                    2008002862

The Internet addresses listed in the text were accurate at the time of publication. The inclusion of a Web site does not indicate an endorsement by the authors or McGraw-Hill, and McGraw-Hill does not guarantee the accuracy of the information presented at these sites.

www.mhhe.com

ABOUT THE AUTHOR

Em Griffin is Professor Emeritus of Communication at Wheaton College in Illinois, where he has taught for more than 35 years and has been chosen Teacher of the Year. He received his bachelor's degree in political science from the University of Michigan, and his M.A. and Ph.D. in communication from Northwestern University. His research interest centers on the development of close friendships.

Em is the author of three applied communication books: *The Mind Changers* analyzes practical techniques of persuasion; *Getting Together* offers research-based suggestions for effective group leadership; and *Making Friends* describes the way that quality interpersonal communication can create and sustain close relationships.

In addition to his teaching and writing, Em serves with Opportunity International, a microenterprise development organization that provides opportunities for people in chronic poverty around the world to transform their lives. He is also an active mediator at the Center for Conflict Resolution in Chicago and has his own mediation service, Communication First.

Em's wife, Jeanie, is an artist. They have two married, adult children, Jim and Sharon, and six grandchildren, Joshua, Amy, Sam, Kyle, Alison, and Dan.

CONTENTS

PREFACE FOR INSTRUCTORS

Instructors who are familiar with *A First Look at Communication Theory* and understand the approach, organization, and features of the book may want to jump ahead to the "Major Changes in the Seventh Edition" section. For those who are new to the text, reading the entire preface will give you a good grasp of what you and your students can expect.

A Balanced Approach to Theory Selection. *A First Look* is written for students who have no background in communication theory. It's designed for undergraduates enrolled in an entry-level course, whatever the students' classification. The trend in the field is to offer students a broad introduction to theory relatively early in their program. *A First Look* is written for those beginning students. Yet if a department chooses to offer its first theory course on the junior or senior level, the class will still be the students' first comprehensive look at theory, so the book will meet them where they are.

The aim of this text is to present 32 specific theories in a way that makes them both interesting and understandable. By the time readers complete the book they should have a working knowledge of theories that explain a wide range of communication phenomena. My ultimate goal is to help students see the relationship between different theoretical positions. The final chapter offers an integrative synthesis. But before students can integrate the leading theoretical ideas in our field, they need to have a clear understanding of what those theories are. The bulk of the book provides that raw material.

With the help of journal and yearbook editors, and the feedback of hundreds of communication theory professors, I've selected a wide range of theories that reflect the diversity within the discipline. Some theories are proven candidates for a Communication Theory Hall of Fame. For example, Aristotle's analysis of logical, emotional, and ethical appeals continues to set the agenda for many public-speaking courses. Mead's symbolic interactionism is formative for interpretive theorists who are dealing with language, thought, self-concept, or the effect of society upon the individual. The axioms of Watzlawick's interactional view continue to be debated by interpersonal scholars. And no student of mediated communication should be ignorant of Gerbner's cultivation theory, which explains why heavy television viewing cultivates fear of a mean and scary world.

It would be shortsighted, however, to limit the selection to the classics of communication. Some of the discipline's most creative approaches are its newest. For example, Leslie Baxter and Barbara Montgomery's theory of relational dialectics offers insight into the ongoing tensions inherent in personal relationships. Joe Walther's social information processing is one of the few fully developed and well-researched theories of computer-mediated communication. And Gerry Philipsen's speech codes theory upgrades the ethnography of communication from a methodology to a theory that can be used to explain, predict, and control discourse about discourse.

Organizational Plan of the Book. Each chapter introduces a single theory in 10–15 pages. I've found that most undergraduates think in terms of discrete packets of information, so the concentrated coverage gives them a chance to focus their thoughts while reading a single chapter. In this way, students can gain an in-depth understanding of important theories rather than acquire only a vague familiarity with a jumble of related ideas. The one-chapter–one-theory arrangement also gives teachers the opportunity to drop theories or rearrange the order of presentation without tearing apart the fabric of the text.

The opening chapter, "Launching Your Study of Communication Theory," provides working definitions of both *theory* and *communication*, and also prepares students for the arrangement of the chapters and the features within them. Chapter 2, "Talk About Theory," lays the groundwork for understanding the differences between objective and interpretive theory. Chapter 3, "Weighing the Words," presents two sets of criteria for determining a good objective or interpretive theory. I apply these standards to Bormann's symbolic convergence theory because he has dual scientific and rhetorical agendas. Based on the overall conception of Robert Craig at the University of Colorado, Chapter 4, "Mapping the Territory," introduces seven traditions within the field of communication theory.

Following this integrative framework, I present the 31 other theories in 31 self-contained chapters. Each theory is discussed within the context of a communication topic: interpersonal messages, relationship development, relationship maintenance, influence, group decision making, organizational communication, public rhetoric, media and culture, media effects, intercultural communication, and gender and communication. These communication context sections usually contain two or three theories. Each section has a brief introduction that outlines the crucial issues that the theorists address and places the subsequent chapters within that context. The placement of theories in familiar categories helps students recognize that theories are answers to questions they've been asking all along. The final chapter, "Common Threads in Comm Theories," offers a new form of integration that will help students discern order in the tapestry of communication theory that might otherwise seem chaotic.

Because all theory and practice has value implications, I briefly explore a dozen ethical principles throughout the book. Consistent with the focus of this text, each principle is the central tenet of a specific ethical theory. Other disciplines may ignore these thorny issues, but to discuss communication as a process that is untouched by questions of good and bad, right and wrong, virtue and vice, would be to disregard an ongoing concern in our field.

Features of Each Chapter. Most people think in pictures. Students will have a rough time understanding a theory unless they apply its explanations and interpretations to concrete situations. The typical chapter uses an extended example to illustrate the "truth" a theory proposes. I encourage readers to try out ideas by visualizing a first meeting of freshman roommates, responding to conflict in a dysfunctional family, trying to persuade other students to support a zero tolerance policy on driving after drinking, and many more. I also use the films *Bend It Like*

Beckham, Thank You for Smoking, Erin Brockovich, When Harry Met Sally, You've Got Mail, Blade Runner, and Toni Morrison's book *Beloved,* as well as speeches of Martin Luther King and Malcolm X to illustrate principles of the theories. The case study in each chapter follows the pedagogical principle of explaining what students don't yet know in terms of ideas and images already within their experience.

Some theories are tightly linked with an extensive research project. For example, the impact of cognitive dissonance theory was greatly spurred by Festinger's surprising finding in his now classic $1/$20 experiment. Philipsen's speech codes theory began with a three-year ethnographic study of what it means to speak like a man in Teamsterville. And Delia's constructivist research continues to be dependent on Crockett's Role Category Questionnaire. When such exemplars exist, I describe the research in detail so that students can learn from and appreciate the benefits of grounding theory in systematic observation. Thus, readers of *A First Look* are led through a variety of research designs and data analyses.

Students will encounter the names of Baxter, Berger, Burgoon, Burke, Deetz, Fisher, Giles, Kramarae, Pacanowsky, Pearce, Philipsen, Ting-Toomey, Walther, Wood, and many others in later communication courses. I therefore make a concerted effort to link theory and theorist. By pairing a particular theory with its originator, I try to promote both recall and respect for a given scholar's effort.

The text of each chapter concludes with a section that critiques the theory. This represents a hard look at the ideas presented in light of the criteria for a good theory outlined in Chapter 3. I usually provide a brief summary of the theory's strengths and then turn to the weaknesses, unanswered questions, and possible errors that still remain. I try to stimulate a "That makes sense, and yet I wonder . . ." response among students.

I include a short list of thought questions at the end of each chapter. Labeled "Questions to Sharpen Your Focus," these probes encourage students to make connections among ideas in the chapter and also to apply the theory to their everyday communication experience. As part of this feature, the words printed in italics remind students of the key terms of a given theory.

The end of every chapter also has a short list of annotated readings entitled "A Second Look." The heading refers to resources for students who are interested in a theory and want to go further than a 10- to 15-page introduction will allow. The top item is the resource I recommend as the starting point for further study. The other listings identify places to look for material about each of the major issues raised in the chapter. The format is designed to offer practical encouragement and guidance for further study without overwhelming the novice with multiple citations. The sources of quotations and citations of evidence are listed in an "Endnotes" section at the end of the book.

I believe professors and students alike will get a good chuckle out of the cartoons I've selected, but their main function is to illustrate significant points in the text. As in other editions, I'm committed to using "Calvin and Hobbes," "The Far Side," "Dilbert," "Cathy," "Zits," and quality art from the pages of *The New Yorker* and *Punch* magazines. Perceptive cartoonists are modern-day prophets—their humor serves the education process well when it slips through mental barriers or attitudinal defenses that didactic prose can't penetrate.

In 13 of the chapters, you'll see photographs of the theorists who appear in the video "Conversations with Communication Theorists." The text that accompanies each picture previews a few intriguing comments that the theorist makes so that students will watch the interview with a specific purpose in mind.

While no author considers his or her style ponderous or dull, I believe I've presented the theories in a clear and lively fashion. Accuracy alone does not communicate. I've tried to remain faithful to the vocabulary each theorist uses so that the student can consider the theory in the author's own terms, but I also translate technical language into more familiar words. Students and reviewers cite readability and interest as particular strengths of the text. I encourage you to sample a chapter dealing with a theory you regard as difficult so that you can decide for yourself.

If you are new to the book, there's one other feature you should know about. The Web site *www.afirstlook.com* offers a number of instructional aids that equip teachers to make studying theory exciting for students. These include information on movie clips to illustrate specific theories, student application log entries that show Kurt Lewin was right when he said that there's nothing as practical as a good theory, and a comparison of all major comm theory texts to see what theories are covered in each book. Many of you will be grateful for the theory archive, which contains 20 complete chapters from previous editions. This way you can assign one of your favorites if it isn't in the current edition. But by far the most popular resource on the site is the world-class instructor's manual prepared by Emily Langan and Glen McClish, which accounts for the vast majority of the 40,000 log-ins per month. Many of the visitors are students whose instructors have encouraged them to tap into the resources that they first discovered—all openly accessible except for exam questions.

Major Changes in the Seventh Edition. The expanded trim size of the book is the most obvious difference from previous editions. The change was made to provide room for key definitions in the margins—a request from students—while making sure that the breadth and depth of coverage for each theory is just as thorough—an instructor concern. Expanding the size of the margins became the win-win solution.

I've added two new theories in this edition. Howard Giles' *communication accommodation theory,* a well-established theory of intercultural and intergroup communication, is now the lead chapter in the intercultural communication section. And a greatly revised chapter on *media ecology* reintroduces the thoughts of Marshall McLuhan. Previously billed as *technological determinism*—a label McLuhan's detractors use—the new title reflects a distinct change in focus. Although a longer version has been online the past 3 years, few students have read it. In response to the request of many instructors, I'm pleased to bring a more user-friendly description of McLuhan's ideas to the media and culture section of the book.

As important as these two additions are, I regard the most significant change in this edition to be the expansion of theoretical integration. I've added two new "bookend" chapters that deal with metatheoretical issues. At the front end I walk students through the issues of what a theory is, and how to get their minds around the concept of communication. Since the text truly offers a first look at theories used within the communication discipline, I think it's no longer fair to assume that students enter the class knowing what a *theory* is or does. Nor do I think it's likely that they've thought much about the thorny issue of what *communication* is or isn't. The first chapter, "Launching Your Study of Communication Theory," starts that process.

In the new final chapter, I take a quite different approach to identifying similarities and differences among the theories by identifying 10 principles of communication that run through multiple theories. These principles cut across communication context, the objective-interpretive distinction, and traditions of communication theory—the ways that students have been classifying theories throughout the book. I refer to these principles as *threads*, because each strand connects theories that might otherwise seem unrelated. Hopefully my review of these common threads will help students to better understand the whole matrix of ideas they've studied during the course, and will also serve as a comprehensive review before the final exam. Glance at Figure 36-1 on page 484 to get a preview of this integrative project.

Chapters 2 and 3, "Talk About Theory" and "Weighing the Words," continue to lay out the distinction between objective and interpretive theories and how to evaluate them, but with new examples. In this edition, Glenn Sparks and Marty Medhurst analyze a humorous commercial featuring football star Peyton Manning as a diehard fan. At the end of Chapter 2, I not only describe an objective-interpretive scale, but also display the chart that classifies the location of every theory in the book on that continuum instead of waiting until the end of the book. Each theory chapter displays the appropriate slice of that chart on the opening page to flag students to its metatheoretical location. I continue to use Bormann's symbolic convergence theory to illustrate how to use scientific or interpretive criteria to evaluate a theory. But I've also added an extensive example of fantasy themes and fantasy chains that a communication professor recorded among the regular patrons at a cigar store as they resist antismoking pressure coming from others outside the group. I believe the ethnographic study makes symbolic convergence theory come alive for readers.

Acknowledgments. I am pleased to acknowledge the wisdom and counsel of many generous scholars whose intellectual capital is embedded in every page you'll read. They include Ron Adler, Santa Barbara City College; Jim Anderson, University of Utah; Ed Appel, Temple University; Judy Burgoon, University of Arizona; Brant Burleson, Purdue University; Tina Carroll, California State Polytechnic University, Pomona; Ken Chase, Wheaton College; Cliff Christians, University of Illinois; Lynn Cooper, Wheaton College; Bob Craig, University of Colorado; Thomas Duncanson, University of Illinois; Tom Feeley, SUNY Buffalo; Larry Frey, University of Colorado; John Greene, Purdue University; John W. Howard III, East Carolina University; Derek Lane, University of Kentucky; Andrew Ledbetter, Ohio University; W. Barnett Pearce, Fielding Graduate Institute; Chris Peiper, Center for Public Policy Priorities, Austin; Laura Prividera, East Carolina University; Russ Proctor, Northern Kentucky University; Linda Putnam, Texas A&M University; Art Ramerez, Ohio State University, Anthony Roberto, Ohio State University; Quentin Schultz, Calvin College; Lenny Shedletsky, University of Southern Maine; Nicole Steigerwald, Ohio State University; Scott Turcott, Indiana Wesleyan University; Steve Weiss, Northern Kentucky University; Robert Woods, Jr., Spring Arbor University. Without their help, this book would not exist. I also appreciate the willingness of many of the theorists featured in the book to engage in email exchanges, phone conversations, and face-to-face discussions in order to help make chapters up-to-date, accurate, and interesting. I don't take their participation for granted.

My relationships with the professionals at McGraw-Hill have been highly satisfactory. I am grateful for Philip Butcher, publisher Frank Mortimer, sponsoring editor Katie Stevens, design manager Ashley Bedell, production coordinator Leslie LaDow, and Merrill Peterson, an unflappable project manager at Matrix Productions. I'm especially thankful for my developmental editor, Jennie Katsaros, who has been my go-to person at McGraw-Hill for the last four editions. I've also been well-served by three outside contractors: Jenn Meyer, a commercial computer artist created and revised figures on 24-hours notice; Judy Brody achieved the impossible by making the extensive permissions process enjoyable; Robyn Tellefsen was my student research assistant for the fourth edition of the book, and enthusiastically agreed to proofread the entire text when I needed someone familiar with the content and I needed to work in sync with someone I trusted implicitly. Other authors are envious when they hear of my good fortune to work with these nine people.

Three other individuals have contributed in ways that are above and beyond what any author could expect. Emily Langan, my colleague and former student at Wheaton, and Glen McClish at San Diego State University have written an instructor's manual that is recognized as the gold standard by others in our field. Instructor's tell me that they walk into class with confidence after reading Glen and Emily's insights regarding a theory and of best practices on how to help students to grasp and appreciate it. Their ideas are also woven into what I've written in the book. My research assistant for this edition has been Kevin Sheehan, a communication honors student and computer whiz who started on the project in his senior year at Wheaton and then committed to working in the area for a year after graduation so he could help me. His work has included the Herculean task of constructing the index for the book in just a few weeks while the publishing deadline loomed. Kevin's expertise, dedication, suggestions, and cheerful helpfulness are greatly appreciated.

Finally, I gratefully recognize the continued encouragement, understanding, and loving support of my wife, Jean—not just on this project, but throughout 48 years of marriage. Her love, sense of humor, and parallel passion to create art and play glorious music have made it possible for me to throw myself into this project.

Em Griffin

DIVISION ONE

Overview

CHAPTER 1

Launching Your Study of Communication Theory

This is a book about theories—communication theories. After that statement you may already be stifling a yawn. Many college students, after all, regard theory as obscure, dull, and irrelevant. People outside the classroom are even less charitable. An aircraft mechanic once chided a professor: "You academic types are all alike. Your heads are crammed so full of theory, you wouldn't know which end of a socket wrench to grab. Any plane you touched would crash and burn. All Ph.D. stands for is 'piled higher and deeper.'"

The mechanic could be right. Yet it's ironic that even in the process of knocking theory, he resorts to his own theory of cognitive overload to explain what he sees as the mechanical stupidity of scholars. I appreciate his desire to make sense of his world. Here's a man who spends a big hunk of his life making sure that planes stay safely in the air until pilots are ready to land. When we really care about something, we should seek to answer the *why* and *what if* questions that always emerge. That was the message I heard from University of Arizona communication theorist Judee Burgoon when I talked with her in my series of interviews, *Conversations with Communication Theorists.*[1] If we care about the fascinating subject of communication, she suggested, we've got to "do theory."

WHAT IS A THEORY AND WHAT DOES IT DO?

In previous editions I've used *theory* as "an umbrella term for all careful, systematic, and self-conscious discussion and analysis of communication phenomena," a definition offered by University of Minnesota communication professor Ernest Bormann.[2] I like this definition because it's general enough to cover the diverse theories presented in this book. Yet the description is so broad that it doesn't give us any direction on how we might construct a theory, nor does it offer a way to figure out when thoughts or statements about communication haven't attained that status. If I call any idea a "theory," does saying it's so make it so?

In my discussion with Judee Burgoon, she suggested that a theory is nothing more than a "set of systematic hunches about the way things operate."[3] Since Burgoon is the most frequently cited female scholar in the field of communica-

tion, I was intrigued by her unexpected use of the nontechnical term *hunch.* Would it therefore be legitimate to entitle the book you're reading *Communication Hunches*? She assured me that it would, quickly adding that they should be "informed hunches." So for Burgoon, a theory consists of *a set of systematic, informed hunches about the way things work.* In the rest of this section I'll examine how these three core concepts provide a helpful definition of what a theory is, what it isn't, and how we might begin to create one.

Set of Hunches

If a theory is a set of hunches, it means we aren't yet sure we have the answer. When there's no puzzle to be solved or the explanation is obvious, there's no need to develop a theory. Theories always involve an element of speculation, or conjecture. Being a theorist is risky business because theories go beyond accepted wisdom. Once you become a theorist you probably hope that all thinking people will eventually embrace the trial balloon that you've launched, but when you first float your theory, it's definitely in the hunch category.

By referring to a plural "set of hunches" rather than a single "hunch," Burgoon makes it clear that a theory is not just one inspired thought or an isolated idea. The young theorist in the cartoon may be quite sure that dogs and bees can smell fear, but that isolated conviction isn't a theory. A developed theory offers some sort of explanation. For example, how are bees and dogs able to sniff out fright? Perhaps the scent of sweaty palms that comes from high anxiety is qualitatively different than the odor of people perspiring from hard work. A theory will also give some indication of scope. Do only dogs and bees possess this keen sense of smell, or do butterflies and kittens have it as well? Theory construction involves multiple hunches.

Informed Hunches

Bormann's description of creating communication theory calls for a careful, self-conscious analysis of communication phenomena, but Burgoon's definition asks for more. It's not enough simply to think carefully about an idea; a theorist's hunches should be *informed*. Working on a hunch that a penny thrown from the Empire State Building will become deeply imbedded in the sidewalk, the young theorist has a responsibility to check it out. Before developing a theory, there are articles to read, people to talk to, actions to observe, or experiments to run, all of which can cast light on the subject. At the very least, a communication theorist should be familiar with alternative explanations and interpretations of the type of communication they are studying. (Young theorist, have you heard the story of Galileo dropping an apple from the Leaning Tower of Pisa?)

Pepperdine University communication professor Fred Casmir's description of theory parallels Burgoon's call for multiple informed hunches:

> Theories are sometimes defined as guesses—but significantly as "educated" guesses. Theories are not merely based on vague impressions nor are they accidental by-products of life. Theories tend to result when their creators have prepared themselves to discover something in their environment, which triggers the process of theory construction.[4]

Hunches That Are Systematic

Most scholars reserve the term *theory* for an integrated *system* of concepts. A theory not only lays out multiple ideas, but also specifies the relationships among them. In common parlance, it connects the dots. The links among the informed hunches are clearly drawn so that a whole pattern emerges.

None of the young theories in the cartoon rise to this standard. Since most of the nine are presented as one-shot claims, they aren't part of a conceptual framework. One possible exception is the dual speculation that "adults are really Martians, and they're up to no good." But the connecting word *and* doesn't really show the relationship of grown-ups' unsavory activity and their hypothesized other-world origin. To do that, the young theorist could speculate about the basic character of Martians, how they got here, why their behavior is suspicious, and whether today's youth will turn into aliens when they become parents. A theory would then tie together all of these ideas into a unified whole. As you read about any theory covered in this book, you have a right to expect a set of *systematic*, informed hunches.

Images of Theory

In response to the question, *What is a theory?* I've presented a verbal definition. Many of us are visual learners as well and would appreciate a concrete image that helps us understand what a theory is and does. I'll therefore present three metaphors that I find helpful, but will also note how an over-reliance on these representations of theory might lead us astray.

Theories as Nets: Philosopher of science Karl Popper says that "theories are nets cast to catch what we call 'the world' . . . . We endeavor to make the mesh ever finer and finer."[5] I appreciate this metaphor because it highlights the ongoing labor of the theorist as a type of deep-sea angler. For serious scholars, theories are the tools of the trade. The term *the world* can be interpreted as everything that goes on under the sun—thus requiring a *grand* theory that applies to all communication, all the time. Conversely, catching the world could be construed as calling for numerous *special* theories—different kinds of small nets to capture distinct types of communication in local situations. Yet either way, the quest for finer-meshed nets is somewhat disturbing because the study of communication is about people rather than schools of fish. The idea that theories could be woven so tightly that they'd snag everything that humans think, say, or do strikes me as naive. The possibility also raises questions about our freedom to choose some actions and reject others.

Theories as Lenses: Many scholars see their theoretical constructions as similar to the lens of a camera or a pair of glasses as opposed to a mirror that accurately reflects the world out there. The lens imagery highlights the idea that theories shape our perception by focusing attention on some features of communication while ignoring other features, or at least pushing them into the background. Two theorists could analyze the same communication event—an argument, perhaps—and depending on the lens each uses, one theorist may view this speech act as a breakdown of communication or the breakup of a relationship, while the other theorist will see it as democracy in action. For me, the danger of the lens metaphor is that we might regard what is seen through the glass as so dependent on the theoretical stance of the viewer that we abandon any attempt to discern what is real or true.

Theories as Maps: I use this image when I describe the *First Look* text to others. Within this analogy, communication theories are maps of the way communication works. The truth they depict may have to do with objective behaviors "out there" or subjective meanings inside our heads. Either way we need to have theory to guide us through unfamiliar territory. In that sense this book of theories is like a scenic atlas that pulls together 32 must-see locations. It's the kind of travel guide that presents a close-up view of each site. I would caution, however, that the map is not the territory.[6] A static theory, like a still photograph, can never fully portray the richness of interaction between people that is constantly changing, always more varied, and inevitably more complicated than what any theory can chart. As a person intrigued with communication, aren't you glad it's this way?

WHAT IS COMMUNICATION?

To ask this question is to invite controversy and raise expectations that can't be met. Frank Dance, the University of Denver scholar credited for publishing the first comprehensive book on communication theory, cataloged over 120 definitions of *communication*—and that was almost 40 years ago.[7] Communication scholars have suggested many more since then, yet no single definition has risen to the top and become the standard within the field of communication. When it comes to defining what it is we study, there's little discipline in the discipline.

At the conclusion of his study, Dance suggested that we're "trying to make the concept of communication do too much work for us."[8] Other communication theorists agree, noting that when the term is used to describe almost every kind of human interaction, it's seriously overburdened. Michigan Tech University communication professor Jennifer Slack brings a splash of reality to attempts to draw definitive lines around what it is that our theories and research cover. She declares that "there is no single, absolute essence of communication that adequately explains the phenomena we study. Such a definition does not exist; neither is it merely awaiting the next brightest communication scholar to nail it down once and for all."[9]

Communication
The relational process of creating and interpreting messages that elicit a response.

Despite the pitfalls of trying to define *communication* in an all-inclusive way, it seems to me that students who are willing to spend a big chunk of their college education studying communication deserve a description of what it is they're looking at. Rather than giving the final word on what human activities can be legitimately referred to as *communication*, this designation would highlight the essential features of communication that shouldn't be missed. So for starters I offer this working definition:

> *Communication is the relational process of creating and interpreting messages that elicit a response.*

To the extent that there is redeeming value in this statement, it lies in drawing your attention to five different features of communication that you'll run across repeatedly as you read about the theories in the field. In the rest of this section I'll briefly flesh out these concepts.

Messages

Messages are at the very core of communication study. University of Colorado communication professor Robert Craig says that communication involves "talking and listening, writing and reading, performing and witnessing, or, more generally, doing anything that involves 'messages' in any medium or situation."[10]

When academic areas such as psychology, sociology, anthropology, political science, literature, and philosophy deal with human symbolic activity, they intersect with the study of communication. The visual image of this intersection of interests has prompted some to refer to communication as a *crossroads discipline*. The difference is that communication scholars are parked at the junction focusing on messages whereas other disciplines are just passing through on their way to other destinations. With possibly one exception, all of the theories covered in this book deal specifically with messages.

Communication theorists use the word *text* as a synonym for a message that can be studied, regardless of the medium. This book is a text. So is a verbatim transcript of a conversation with your instructor, a recorded presidential news conference, a silent YouTube video, or a Dixie Chicks' CD of "Not Ready to Make Nice." To illustrate the following four parts of the definition, suppose you received this brief instant message from a close, same-sex friend: "Pat and I spent the night together." You immediately know that the name Pat refers to a person with whom you have an ongoing romantic relationship. An analysis of this text and the context surrounding its transmission provides a useful case study for examining the essential features of communication.

Text
A record of a message that can be analyzed by others; for example, a book, film, photograph, or any transcript or recording of a speech or broadcast.

Creation of Messages

This phrase in the working definition indicates that the content and form of a text are usually *constructed, invented, planned, crafted, constituted, selected,* or *adopted* by the communicator. Each of these terms is used in one or more of the theories I describe, and they all imply that the communicator is usually making a conscious choice of message form and substance. For whatever reason, your friend sent an IM rather than meeting face-to-face, calling you on the phone, sending an email, or writing a note. Your friend also chose the seven words that were transmitted to your PDA. There is a long history of textual analysis in the field of communication, wherein the rhetorical critic looks for clues in the message to discern the motivation and strategy of the person who created the message.

There are, of course, many times when we speak, write, or gesture in seemingly mindless ways—activities that are like driving on cruise control. These are preprogrammed responses that were selected earlier and stored for later use. In like manner, our repertoire of stock phrases such as *thank you, no problem, whatever,* or a string of swear words were chosen sometime in the past to express our feelings, and over time have become habitual responses. Only when we become more mindful of the nature and impact of our messages will we have the ability to alter them. That's why consciousness-raising is a goal of five or six of the theories I'll present—they each seek to increase our communication choices.

Interpretation of Messages

Messages do not interpret themselves. The meaning that a message holds for both the creators and receivers doesn't reside in the words that are spoken, written, or acted out. A truism among communication scholars is that *words don't mean things, people mean things*. Symbolic interactionist Herbert Blumer states its implication: "Humans act toward people or things on the basis of the meanings they assign to those people or things."[11]

What is the meaning of your friend's instant message? Does "spent the night together" mean *talking until all hours? Pulling an all-night study session? Sleeping on the sofa? Making love?* If it's the latter, was Pat a *willing* or *unwilling partner* (perhaps drunk or the victim of acquaintance rape)? How would your friend characterize their sexual liaison? *Recreational sex? A chance hookup? Friends with benefits? Developing a close relationship? Falling in love? The start of a long-term commitment?* Perhaps of more importance to you, how does Pat view it? What emotional meaning is behind the message for each of them? *Satisfaction? Disappointment? Surprise? The morning-after-the-night-before blahs? Gratefulness? Guilt? Ecstasy?* And finally, what does receiving this message through an electronic channel mean for you, your friendship, and your relationship with Pat? None of these answers are in the message. Words and other symbols are polysemic—they're open to multiple interpretations.

A Relational Process

The Greek philosopher Heraclites observed that "one cannot step into the same river twice."[12] These words illustrate the widespread acceptance among communication scholars that communication is a *process*. Much like a river, the flow of communication is always in flux, never completely the same, and can only be described with reference to what went before and what is yet to come. This means that the text message "Pat and I spent the night together" is not the whole story. You'll probably contact both your friend and Pat to ask the clarifying questions raised earlier. As they are answered or avoided, you'll interpret the IM in a different way. That's because communication is a process, not a freeze-frame snapshot.

In the opening lines of her essay "Communication as Relationality," University of Georgia rhetorical theorist Celeste Condit suggests that the communication process is more about relationships than it is about content.

> Communication is a process of relating. This means it is not primarily or essentially a process of transferring information or of disseminating or circulating signs (though these things can be identified as happening within the process of relating).[13]

Communication is a relational process not only because it takes place between two or more persons, but also because it affects the nature of the connections among those people. It's obvious that the text message you received will influence the triangle of relationships among you, Pat, and your (former?) friend. But this is true in other forms of mediated communication as well. Television viewers and moviegoers have emotional responses to people they see on the screen. And as businesses are discovering, even the impersonal recorded announcement that "this call may be monitored for the purpose of quality control" has an impact on how we regard their corporate persona.

Messages That Elicit a Response

This final component of communication deals with the effect of the message upon people who receive it. For whatever reason, if the message fails to stimulate any cognitive, emotional, or behavioral reaction, it seems pointless to refer to it as *communication*. We often refer to such situations as a message "falling on deaf ears" or the other person "turning a blind eye." That nonresponse is different than the prison warden's oft-quoted line in Paul Newman's classic film, *Cool Hand Luke*.[14] When Luke repeatedly breaks the rules laid down by the warden, this man who insists on being called Boss drawls, "Luke, what we have here is a failure to communicate." He's wrong. Luke understands and actively resists the clearly stated rules; the Boss responds violently to Luke's insubordination and his attempts to escape. Both men respond to the message of the other.

In like manner, surely you would respond to your friend's cryptic message—one way or another. In fact, the text seems to be crafted and sent in a way to provoke a response. How closely your thoughts, feelings, words, or other reactions would match what your friend expected or intended is another matter. But whether successful or not, the whole situation surrounding the text and context of the instant message fits the working definition of communication that I hope will help you frame your study of communication theory: *Communication is the relational process of creating and interpreting messages that elicit a response.*

AN ARRANGEMENT OF IDEAS TO AID COMPREHENSION

Now that you have a basic understanding of what a communication theory is, knowing how I've structured the book and arranged the theories can help you grasp their content. That's because I've organized the text to place a given theory in a conceptual framework and situational context before I present it. After this chapter, there are three more integrative chapters in the "Overview" division. For Chapter 2, I've asked two leading communication scholars to analyze a highly acclaimed TV ad in order to illustrate how half the theories in the book are based on *objective* assumptions, while the other half are constructed using an *interpretive* set of principles. Chapter 3 presents criteria for judging both kinds of theory and applies them to *symbolic convergence theory*, a theory of group interaction that has both objective and interpretive goals. This chapter introduces the first of 32 theories while also preparing you to make an informed evaluation of a theory's worth rather than relying solely on a gut reaction. Finally, Chapter 4 describes seven traditions of communication theory and research. When you know the family tree of a theory, you can explain why it has a strong affinity with some theories but doesn't speak the same language as others.

Following this overview, there are 31 chapters that run 10–15 pages a piece, each concentrating on a single theory. I think you'll find that the one-chapter, one-theory format is user-friendly because it gives you a chance to focus on one theory at a time. This way they won't all blur together in your mind. These chapters are arranged into four major divisions according to the primary communication context that they address. The theories in Division II, "Interpersonal Communication," consider one-on-one interaction. Division III, "Group and Public Communication," deals with face-to-face involvement in collective settings. Division IV, "Mass Communication," pulls together theories that explore electronic and print media. Division V, "Cultural Context," explores systems of shared meaning that are so all-encompassing that we often fail to realize their impact upon us. These divisions are based on the fact that theories are tentative answers to questions that occur to people as they mull over practical problems in specific situations. It therefore makes sense to group them according to the different communication settings that prompt those questions.

This organizational plan I've described is like having four separately indexed file cabinets. Although there is no natural progression from one division to another, the plan provides a convenient way to classify and retrieve the 32 theories. The format also lends itself to further separation into topical concerns. For example, the interpersonal division is divided into sections on interpersonal messages, relationship development, relationship maintenance, and influence. When you read the two- to four-page introduction at the start of a section, the theories within it will make more sense to you than if you come to them with no background.

Finally, Division VI, "Integration," seeks to distill core ideas that are common to a number of theories. Ideas have power, and each theory is driven by one or more ideas that may be shared by other theories from different contexts. For example, there's at least one theory in each of the four divisions committed to the force of narrative. They each declare that people respond to stories and dramatic imagery with which they can identify. Reading about key concepts that cut across multiple theories wouldn't mean much to you now, but after you become familiar with a number of communication theories, it can be an eye-opening experience that also helps you review what you've learned.

CHAPTER FEATURES TO ENLIVEN THEORY

In most of the chapters ahead, I use an extended example from life on a college campus, a well-known communication event, or the conversations of characters in movies, books, or TV shows. The main purpose of these illustrations is to provide a mind's-eye picture of how the theory works. The imagery will also make the basic thrust of the theory easier to recall. But if you can think of a situation in your own life where the theory is relevant, that personal application will make it doubly interesting and memorable for you.

You might also want to see how others put the theories into practice. With my students' permission, I've posted accounts of application for each theory featured in the text. I'm intrigued by the rich connections these students make—ones that I wouldn't have thought of on my own. To access these accounts, go to the book's Web site, www.afirstlook.com, and click on the "Application Logs" option. The entries are indexed by theory within the four divisional contexts discussed earlier. At the same site you can click on "Movie Clips" to see an annotated list of brief feature film segments that illustrate the theories.

I make a consistent effort to link each theory with its author. It takes both wisdom and courage to successfully plant a theoretical flag. In a process similar to the childhood game king-of-the-hill, as soon as a theorist constructs a theory of communication, critics try to pull it down. That's OK, because the value of a theory is discerned by survival in the rough-and-tumble world of competitive ideas. For this reason I always include a section in theory chapters labeled "Critique." Theorists who prevail deserve to have their names associated with their creations.

There is a second reason for tying a theory to its author. Many of you will do further study in communication, and a mastery of names like Deetz, Giles, Walther, Baxter, Berger, and Burke will allow you to enter into the dialogue without being at a disadvantage. Ignoring the names of theorists could prove to be false economy in the long run.

Don't overlook the three features at the end of each chapter. The queries under the title "Questions to Sharpen Your Focus" will help you mull over key points of the theory. They can be answered by pulling together information from this text and from the text of your life. The italicized words in each question highlight terms that you need to know in order to understand the theory. Whenever you see a picture of the theorist, it's captured from one of my *Conversations with Communication Theorists* and shown alongside a brief description of what we talked about. You can view these 6–8 minute interviews at www.afirstlook com. And the feature entitled "A Second Look" offers an annotated bibliography of resources should you desire to know more about the theory. You'll find it a good place to start if you are writing a research paper on the theory or are intrigued with a particular aspect of it.

You've already seen the last feature I'll mention. In every chapter and section introduction I include a cartoon for your learning and enjoyment. Cartoonists are often modern-day prophets. Their incisive wit can illustrate a feature of the theory in a way more instructive and memorable than a few extra paragraphs. In addition to enjoying their humor, you can use the cartoons as minitests of comprehension. Unlike my comments on "Young Theories" earlier in this chapter, I usually don't refer to the art or the caption that goes with it. So if you can't figure out why a particular cartoon appears where it does, make a renewed effort to grasp the theorist's ideas.

Some students are afraid to try. Like travelers whose eyes glaze over at the sight of a road map, they have a phobia about theories that seek to explain human intentions and behavior. I sympathize with their qualms and misgivings, but I find that the theories in this book haven't dehydrated my life or made it more confusing. On the contrary, they add clarity and provide a sense of competence as I communicate with others. I hope they do that for you as well.

Every so often a student will ask me, "Do you really think about communication theory when you're talking to someone else?" My answer is "Yes, but not all the time." Like everyone else, I often say things while speaking on automatic pilot—words, phrases, sentences, descriptions rolling off my tongue without conscious thought. Old habits die hard. But when I'm in a new setting or the conversational stakes are high, I start to think strategically. And that's when the applied wisdom of theories that fit the situation comes to mind. By midterm, many of my students discover that they're thinking that way as well. That's my wish for you as you launch your study of communication theory.

QUESTIONS TO SHARPEN YOUR FOCUS

1. Suppose you share the aircraft mechanic's suspicion that scholars who create theories would be all thumbs working on a plane's ailerons or engine. What would it take to transform your *hunch* into a *theory*?

2. Which *metaphor* offered to capture the meaning of theory do you find most helpful—a theory as a *net*, a *lens*, or a *map*? Can you think of another image that you could use to explain to a friend what this course is about?

3. Suppose you wanted to study the effects of yawns during intimate conversations. Would your research fall under *communication* as defined as the *relational process of creating and interpreting messages to elicit a response*? If not, how would you change the definition to have it include your interest?

4. You come to this course with a vast array of communication experiences in *interpersonal, group and public, mass media,* and *intercultural contexts.* What are the communication *questions* you want to answer, *puzzles* you want to solve, *problems* you want fix?

A SECOND LOOK

Recommended resource: Gregory Shepherd, Jeffrey St. John, and Ted Striphas (eds.), *Communication as . . . Perspectives on Theory,* Sage, Thousand Oaks, CA, 2006.

Diverse definitions of communication: Frank E.X. Dance, "The Concept of Communication," *Journal of Communication,* Vol. 20, 1970, pp. 201–210.

Focus on messages: George Gerbner, "Mass Media and Human Communication Theory," in Frank E.X. Dance, *Human Communication Theory: Original Essays,* Holt, Rinehart and Winston, New York, 1967, pp. 40–60.

Communication as human symbolic interaction: Gary Cronkhite, "On the Focus, Scope and Coherence of the Study of Human Communication," *Quarterly Journal of Speech,* Vol. 72, No. 3, 1986, pp. 231–246.

Theories of communication as practical: J. Kevin Barge, "Practical Theory as Mapping, Engaged Reflection, and Transformative Practice," *Communication Theory,* Vol. 11, 2001, pp. 5–13.

Integration of scientific and humanistic theories: Karl Erik Rosengren, "From Field to Frog Ponds," *Journal of Communication,* Vol. 43, No. 3, 1993, pp. 6–17.

Multidimensional view of theory: James A. Anderson and Geoffrey Baym, "Philosophies and Philosophic Issues in Communication, 1995–2004," *Journal of Communication,* Vol. 54, 2004, pp. 589–615.

Differences in theoretical scope: Ernest Bormann, *Communication Theory,* Sheffield, Salem, WI, 1989, pp. 81–101.

CHAPTER 2

Talk About Theory

I met Glenn Sparks and Marty Medhurst my first year teaching at Wheaton College. Glenn and Marty were friends who signed up for my undergraduate persuasion course. As students, both men were interested in broadcast media. After graduating from Wheaton, both went on for a master's degree at Northern Illinois University. Each then earned a doctorate at a different university, and both are now nationally recognized communication scholars. Glenn is on the faculty at Purdue University; Marty is at Baylor University.

Behavioral scientist
A scholar who applies the scientific method to describe, predict, and explain recurring forms of human behavior.

Rhetorician
A scholar who studies the ways in which symbolic forms can be used to identify with people, or to persuade them toward a certain point of view.

Despite their similar backgrounds and interests, Glenn and Marty are quite different in their approaches to communication. Glenn calls himself a *behavioral scientist*, while Marty refers to himself as a *rhetorician*. Glenn's training was in empirical research; Marty was schooled in rhetorical theory and criticism. Glenn conducts experiments; Marty interprets texts.

To understand the theories ahead, you need to first grasp the crucial differences between the objective and interpretive approaches to communication. As a way to introduce the distinctions, I asked Glenn and Marty to bring their scholarship to bear on a television commercial that was first aired a few months before Super Bowl XLI. Both drams featured football star Peyton Manning.

TWO COMMUNICATION SCHOLARS VIEW A DIEHARD FAN

In 1998 Peyton Manning was drafted to play quarterback for the Indianapolis Colts. A year earlier, MasterCard had launched its "Priceless" campaign, which suggests that the credit card company has a sense of humor and the wisdom to realize that some of the best things in life can't be bought, no matter what your credit limit. Nine years later, Peyton and "Priceless" commercials were still going strong. Manning was poised to lead the Colts to a 2007 Super Bowl victory, and MasterCard was using his star power to project their image. *Adweek* sets the scene:

> Peyton Manning is one of the few superstar athletes who shows he can act in his commercials. We've seen his cheerleader-for-the-everyday guy before. This time he's rooting for the waitress who drops her tray, the latte guy who's burned by escaping steam, and the movers who let a piano escape down a hill. "That's okay guys. They're not saying 'boo,' they're saying mooooooovers.' "[1]

The fourth scene, captured in Figure 2–1, is Manning shouting encouragement to the paperboy who made an errant throw: "That's alright, Bobby. You've

supporting your team: priceless

FIGURE 2–1   Diehard Fan Peyton Manning Shouting Encouragement

still got the best arm in the neighborhood." All four scenes illustrate the spoken and written message of the ad: Support for your team is priceless—especially when they've screwed up. It's something money can't buy. "For everything else, there's MasterCard." Social scientist Glenn and rhetorical critic Marty take different theoretical approaches to analyze how the ad works.

Glenn: An Objective Approach

Objective approach
The assumption that truth is singular and is accessible through unbiased sensory observation; committed to uncovering cause-and-effect relationships.

The distinguishing feature of this commercial is football superstar Peyton Manning. The folks at MasterCard are obviously convinced that his celebrity appeal will rub off on the public image of their credit card. As a social scientist, I'd like to discover if they are right. The answer will help scholars and advertisers better predict what persuasive techniques really work. If this "branding" strategy proves effective, I would also want to find out *why* it does. Objective researchers want to *explain* as well as *predict*.

Theory is an essential tool in the scientific effort to predict and explain. For this type of commercial, I might turn to *source credibility theory,* proposed by Carl Hovland and Walter Weiss as part of the Yale Attitude project on persuasion.[2] They suggest that expertise and trustworthiness are the two main ingredients of perceived credibility. For football fans who watched the ad, there's no question that Peyton Manning is a highly competent quarterback. And cheering on ordinary people who are having a bad day may suggest that he's on our side and won't steer us wrong. The central premise of source credibility theory is that people we view as trusted experts will be much more effective in their attempts to persuade us than sources we distrust or regard as incompetent.

Source credibility
Perceived competence and trustworthiness of a speaker or writer that affects how the message is received.

Herbert Kelman's theory of opinion change also offers insight. Kelman said that when people forge a bond of *identification* with a highly attractive figure like Manning, they'll gladly embrace his persuasive pitch.[3] In contrast to many top

Identification
A perceived role relationship that affects self-image and attitudes; based on attractiveness of the role model and sustained if the relationship remains salient.

athletes who come across as surly, uptight, or egotistical, Manning is upbeat, relaxed, and encouraging as he cheers on people like us who don't have his fan base.

As a scientist, however, I can't just assume that this commercial is persuasive and the theories I applied are correct. Manning's expertise is football—not finance. Do viewers transfer his expertise from the gridiron to credit cards? I'd want an objective test to find out if celebrity appeals really work. I might find out if this ad campaign was followed by either an increase in new card applications or a spike in the number of charges made by MasterCard users. Or I could test whether the ad has the same effect on viewers who don't know who Manning is—he's never identified in the ad. Testing the audience response is a crucial scientific enterprise. Even though a theory might sound plausible, we can't be sure it's valid until it's been tested. In science, theory and research walk hand in hand.

Marty: An Interpretive Approach

Interpretive approach
The linguistic work of assigning meaning or value to communicative texts; assumes that multiple meanings or truths are possible.

Burke's dramatistic pentad
A five-pronged method of rhetorical criticism to analyze a speaker's persuasive strategy—act, scene, agent, agency, purpose.

I see this ad for MasterCard, starring NFL quarterback Peyton Manning, as an attempt to identify manliness with money. The ad achieves its effect by inviting the viewer to become part of the "team" being instructed by "Coach" Manning. To become part of the team, one must adopt the attitudes and actions of the coach. Kenneth Burke's theory of dramatism helps us understand the symbolic action.

Since we can consider this 30-second commercial to be a mini-drama, Burke's *dramatistic pentad* of act, scene, agent, agency, and purpose can help provide a framework for interpretation.[4] Peyton Manning is the coach—the agent. Everyday activities such as eating brunch, drinking coffee, moving furniture, and retrieving the morning paper are the background—the scene. Coaching people in the proper attitude is what Manning does in each scene—the act. Using the typical jargon and gestures of a football coach is the vehicle—the agency. And the goal is the acquisition and use of a MasterCard—the purpose.

Burke holds that as a drama develops, the symbolic action moves through different stages. He encourages critics to look at the symbolic forms as they move *"from what through what to what."*[5] In this ad, the symbolic action starts with confusion—Wendy dropping the tray of food. It moves through pain and destruction—Johnny scalded by steam, the mover dropping the piano, the paperboy breaking the window. And by the end, the drama arrives at manliness, money, and acceptance—football helmets crashing together (manliness), forming the MasterCard logo (money), Johnny's giving a thumbs-up signal (acceptance).

What's important to notice is that a symbolic transformation has taken place. Throughout most of the ad, Manning is "coaching" the right attitude. We hear it in his language ("You're the man; Rub some dirt on it; It's alright, Bobby"). We see it in his gestures (arms raised, palms up, clapping, pointing). Yet by the end of the ad the transformation is complete. It is Johnny who is doing the coaching, with a thumbs-up gesture that signals his acceptance of the right attitude and his adoption of the right action—getting a MasterCard. A symbolic equivalence has been established between being manly (like a pro football player) and being in the money (with MasterCard).

The message of this ad is clear. To be a man is to have the right attitude about the little trials of life; it is to be a part of the home team. Acquiring a MasterCard is a way of symbolically identifying with the tough guys and achieving victory over the obstacles that stand between a man and his goals.

OBJECTIVE OR INTERPRETIVE: A DIFFERENCE THAT MATTERS

Although both of these scholars focus on the role of Peyton Manning in promoting MasterCard, Glenn's and Marty's approaches to communication study clearly differ in starting point, method, and conclusion. Glenn is a social *scientist* who works hard to be *objective*. Throughout these introductory chapters I will use those terms interchangeably. Marty is a *rhetorical critic* who does *interpretive* study. Here the labels get tricky.

While it's true that all rhetorical critics do interpretive analysis, not all interpretive scholars are rhetoricians. Most (including Marty) are *humanists*, but a growing number of postmodern communication theorists reject that tradition. These scholars refer to themselves with a bewildering variety of brand names: hermeneuticists, poststructuralists, deconstructivists, phenomenologists, cultural studies researchers, and social action theorists, as well as combinations of these terms. Writing from this postmodernist perspective, University of Utah theorist James Anderson observes:

Humanistic scholarship Study of what it's like to be another person, in a specific time and place; assumes there are few important panhuman similarities.

> With this very large number of interpretive communities, names are contentious, border patrol is hopeless and crossovers continuous. Members, however, often see real differences.[6]

All of these scholars, including Marty, do interpretive analysis—scholarship concerned with meaning—yet there's no common term like *scientist* that includes them all. So from this point on I'll use the designation *interpretive scholars* or the noun form *interpreters* to refer to the entire group and use *rhetorician, humanist, critic,* or *postmodernist* only when I'm singling out that particular subgroup.

The separate worldviews of interpretive scholars and scientists reflect contrasting assumptions about ways of arriving at knowledge, the core of human nature, questions of value, the very purpose of theory, and methods of research. The rest of this chapter sketches these differences.

Why should you care whether the theorists I describe do objective or interpretive work—or a mix of both kinds? One reason is *they* care. When I did the interviews for *Conversations with Communication Theorists,*[7] I had a chance to see each scholar's passionate commitment to a specific worldview and explore how that grounding shaped the theory that he or she crafted. If you have a grasp of a theorist's basic assumptions, you'll be better able to appreciate his or her ideas. In addition, your understanding of the objective/interpretive choice-points I describe can help you decide the direction in which you want to go in your communication studies. Most important, the approach you end up favoring will definitely affect how you view your own communication. The distinction between objective and interpretive worldviews is a difference that makes a difference.

WAYS OF KNOWING: DISCOVERING TRUTH OR CREATING MULTIPLE REALITIES?

Epistemology The study of the origin, nature, method, and limits of knowledge.

How do we know what we know, if we know it at all? This is the central question addressed by a branch of philosophy known as *epistemology*. You may have been in school for a dozen-plus years, read assignments, written papers, and taken tests without ever delving into the issue "What is truth?" With or without in-depth study of the issue, however, we all inevitably make assumptions about the nature of knowledge.

Scientists assume that Truth is singular. They see a single, timeless reality "out there" that's not dependent on local conditions. It's waiting to be discovered through the five senses of sight, sound, touch, taste, and smell. Since the raw sensory data of the world is accessible to any competent observer, science seeks to be bias-free, with no ax to grind. The evidence speaks for itself. As Galileo observed, anyone could see through his telescope. Of course, no one person can know it all, so individual researchers pool their findings and build a collective body of knowledge about how the world works.

Scientists consider good theories to be those that are faithful representations of an underlying reality—mirrors of nature. They are confident that once a principle is discovered and validated, it will continue to hold true as long as conditions remain relatively the same. That's why Glenn believes the credibility of a message source can explain why other media messages succeed or fail.

Interpretive scholars seek truth as well, but many interpreters regard that truth as socially constructed through communication. They believe language creates social realities that are always in flux rather than revealing or representing fixed principles or relationships in a world that doesn't change. Knowledge is always viewed from a particular standpoint. A word, a gesture, or an act may have constancy within a given community, but it's dangerous to assume that interpretations can cross lines of time and space.

Texts never interpret themselves. Most of these scholars, in fact, hold that truth is largely subjective—that meaning is highly interpretive. Rhetorical critics like Marty are not relativists, arbitrarily assigning meaning on a whim. They do maintain, however, that objectivity is a myth; we can never entirely separate the knower from the known.

Convinced that meaning is in the mind rather than in the verbal sign, interpreters are comfortable with the notion that a text may have multiple meanings. Rhetorical critics are successful when they get others to view a text through their interpretive lens—to adopt a new perspective on the world. For example, did Marty convince you that the MasterCard ad was an attempt to equate manliness with money? As Anderson notes, "Truth is a struggle, not a status."[8]

HUMAN NATURE: DETERMINISM OR FREE WILL?

Determinism
The assumption that behavior is caused by heredity and environment.

One of the great philosophical debates throughout history revolves around the question of human choice.[9] Hard-line *determinists* claim that every move we make is the result of heredity ("biology is destiny") and environment ("pleasure stamps in, pain stamps out"). On the other hand, free-will purists insist that every human act is ultimately voluntary ("I am the master of my fate: I am the captain of my soul"[10]). Although few communication theorists are comfortable with either extreme, most tend to line up on one side or the other. Scientists stress the forces that shape human behavior; interpretive scholars focus on conscious choices made by individuals.

The difference between these two views of human nature inevitably creeps into the language people use to explain what they do. Individuals who feel like puppets on strings say, "I *had* to . . . ," while people who feel they pull their own strings say, "I *decided* to . . . ." The first group speaks in a passive voice: "I was distracted from studying by the argument at the next table." The second group speaks in an active voice: "I stopped studying to listen to the argument at the next table."

In the same way, the language of scholarship often reflects theorists' views of human nature. Behavioral scientists usually describe human conduct as occurring *because of* forces outside the individual's awareness. Their causal explanations tend not to include appeals to mental reasoning or conscious choice. They usually describe behavior as the response to a prior stimulus. Note that Kelman's theory of opinion change that Glenn cited suggests a cause-and-effect inevitability in the persuasion process. We *will* be swayed by those we find attractive.

In contrast, interpretive scholars tend to use explanatory phrases such as *in order to* and *so that* because they attribute a person's action to conscious intent. Their choice of words suggests that people are free agents who could decide to respond differently under an identical set of circumstances. Marty, for example, uses the language of voluntary *action* rather than knee-jerk *behavior* when he writes about the ad *inviting* the viewer to become part of the team and Johnny *adopting* the right attitude. The consistent interpreter doesn't ask why Johnny made that choice. As Anderson explains, "True choice demands to be its own cause and its own explanation."[11]

Human choice is therefore problematic for the behavioral scientist because as individual freedom goes up, predictability of behavior goes down. Conversely, the roots of humanism are threatened by a highly restricted view of human choice. In an impassioned plea, British author C. S. Lewis exposes the paradox of stripping away people's freedom and yet expecting them to exercise responsible choice:

> In a sort of ghastly simplicity we remove the organ and expect of them virtue and enterprise. We laugh at honor and are shocked to find traitors in our midst. We castrate and bid the geldings be fruitful.[12]

Lewis assumes that significant decisions are value laden; interpretive scholars would agree.

THE HIGHEST VALUE: OBJECTIVITY OR EMANCIPATION?

When we talk about values, we are discussing priorities, questions of relative worth.[13] Values are the traffic lights of our lives that guide what we think, feel, and do. The professional values of communication theorists reflect the commitments they've made concerning knowledge and human nature. Since most social scientists hold to a distinction between the "knower" and the "known," they place a high value on an objectivity that's not biased by ideological commitments. Because humanists and others in the interpretive camp believe that the ability to choose is what separates humanity from the rest of creation, they value scholarship that expands the range of free choice.

As a behavioral scientist, Glenn works hard to maintain his objectivity. He is a man with strong moral and spiritual convictions, and these may influence the topics he studies. But he doesn't want his personal values to distort reality or confuse what *is* with what he thinks *ought to be*. As you can see from Glenn's call for objective testing, he is frustrated when theorists offer no *empirical evidence* for their claims or don't even suggest a way in which their ideas could be validated by an independent observer. He is even more upset when he hears of researchers who fudge the findings of their studies to shore up questionable hypotheses. Glenn shares the research values of Harvard sociologist George Homans—to let the evidence speak for itself: "When nature,

Empirical evidence
Data collected through direct observation.

however stretched out on the rack, still has a chance to say 'no'—then the subject is science."[14]

Marty is aware of his own ideology and is not afraid to bring his values to bear upon a communication text under scrutiny. By pointing out the subtle equating of manliness with money, Marty creates an awareness that this is more than a humorous, feel-good spot. Although he doesn't take an overtly critical stance toward advertising or the capitalist system, his insight is a resource for viewers that enables them to laugh not only at Peyton's over-the-top support for his "team," but also at the underlying economic boosterism in the ad. Critical interpreters value socially relevant research that seeks to liberate people from oppression of any sort—economic, political, religious, emotional, or any other type. They decry the detached stance of scientists who refuse to take responsibility for the results of their work. Whatever the pursuit—a Manhattan Project to split the atom, a Genome Project to map human genes, or a class project to analyze the effectiveness of an ad—critical interpreters insist that knowledge is never neutral. "There is no safe harbor in which researchers can avoid the power structure."[15]

Emancipation
Liberation from any form of political, economic, racial, religious, or sexual oppression; empowerment.

In the heading above, I've contrasted the primary values of scientific and interpretive scholars by using the labels *objectivity* and *emancipation*. University of Colorado communication professor Stan Deetz frames the issue somewhat differently. He says that every general communication theory has two priorities—*effectiveness* and *participation*.[16] Effectiveness is concerned with successfully communicating information, ideas, and meaning to others. It also includes persuasion. Participation is concerned with increasing the possibility that all points of view will affect collective decisions and individuals being open to new ideas. It also encourages difference, opposition, and independence. The value question is *Which concern has higher priority?* Objective theorists usually foreground effectiveness and relegate participation to the background. Interpretive theorists tend to focus on participation and downplay effectiveness.

PURPOSE OF THEORY: UNIVERSAL LAWS OR INTERPRETIVE GUIDES?

Even if Glenn and Marty could agree on the nature of knowledge, the extent of human autonomy, and the ultimate values of scholarship, their words would still sound strange to each other because they use distinct vocabularies to accomplish different goals. As a behavioral scientist, Glenn is working to pin down universal laws of human behavior that cover a variety of situations. As a rhetorical critic, Marty strives to interpret a particular communication text in a specific context.

If these two scholars were engaged in fashion design rather than research design, Glenn would probably tailor a coat suitable for many occasions that covers everybody well—one size fits all. Marty might apply principles of fashion design to style a coat that makes an individual statement for a single client—a one-of-a-kind, custom creation. Glenn adopts a theory and then tests it to see if it covers everyone. Marty uses theory to make sense of unique communication events.

Since theory testing is the basic activity of the behavioral scientist, Glenn starts with a hunch about how the world works—perhaps the idea that source credibility enhances persuasion. He then crafts a tightly worded hypothesis that temporarily commits him to a specific prediction. As an empiricist, he can never completely "prove" that he has made the right gamble; he can only show in test after test that his behavioral bet pays off. If repeated studies uphold his hypothesis, he can more confidently predict which media ads will be effective, explain why, and make recommendations on how practitioners can increase their credibility.

The interpretive scholar explores the web of meaning that constitutes human existence. When Marty creates scholarship, he isn't trying to prove theory. However, he sometimes uses the work of rhetorical theorists like Kenneth Burke to inform his interpretation of the aural and visual texts of people's lives. Robert Ivie, former editor of the *Quarterly Journal of Speech,* suggests that rhetorical critics ought to use theory this way:

> We cannot conduct rhetorical criticism of social reality without benefit of a guiding rhetorical theory that tells us generally what to look for in social practice, what to make of it, and whether to consider it significant.[17]

RESEARCH METHODS: QUANTITATIVE OR QUALITATIVE?

Whether the quest is for a universal law that makes prediction possible or a guide for interpretation that helps makes sense of equivocal communication, theorists know that the task demands research. Because social scientists value the precise measurement that numerical scales and frequency counts offer, they usually employ *quantitative* research methods. But interpretive scholars are convinced that statistical averaging lops off important differences between people. They embrace *qualitative* research methods that study how humans use signs and symbols to create and infer meaning.

Quantitative research
Research in which the data is recorded in numerical form.

Qualitative research
Research in which the data is recorded in linguistic (non-numeric) form.

A leading textbook on communication inquiry presents four research strategies for the study of communication.[18] *Experiments* and *survey research* offer quantitative ways for the scientist to test theory. *Textual analysis* and *ethnography* provide qualitative tools that aid the interpretive scholar's search for meaning. I'll briefly describe the distinct features of the four methods and give examples of the kinds of research questions that each technique is designed to answer. All of the questions I list have been posed and explored by the theorists I introduce in later chapters.

1. Experiments

Experiment
A research method that manipulates a variable in a tightly controlled situation in order to find out if it has the predicted effect.

Working on the assumption that human behavior is not random, an experimenter tries to establish a cause-and-effect relationship by systematically manipulating one factor (the independent variable) in a tightly controlled situation to learn its effect on another factor (the dependent variable). Since Glenn suggested testing the effect of celebrity endorsement using the Peyton Manning ad, we can imagine that he would run an experiment to test the following hypothesis: *Viewers who perceive a celebrity in a commercial as competent and trustworthy will respond more favorably toward the corporate sponsor than viewers who perceive the celebrity as incompetent and untrustworthy.*

Given that the ad targeted football fans, Glenn could operationalize the independent variables by adapting standardized credibility scales to measure *competence* in football and the quarterback's *trustworthiness* to be supportive of others.[19] He could measure response to the corporate sponsor—the dependent variable—by giving people an opportunity to apply for a major brand credit card of their choice. Volunteers would be prescreened so as to limit the pool of subjects to those who didn't have a MasterCard. He might also determine which potential subjects recognized a picture of Peyton Manning and knew something of his football success, and which ones didn't. He would then assign them to one of three treatment groups:

Group A: People who recognize the football star and will see the ad

Group B: People who don't recognize the football star and will see the ad

Group C: Control group of people who do and do not recognize the football star and will see a humorous ad that has nothing to do with celebrity appeal or credit cards

Control group
Subjects in an experiment who experience no form of the independent variable; a no-treatment comparison group.

After showing the ad, Glenn would have subjects fill out the competency and trustworthiness scales in order to determine if Group A viewers really perceived Peyton as more credible than Group B viewers did, and more credible than Group C perceived the actor in the ad they watched. Finally, all subjects would have the opportunity to apply for a credit card. If Glenn found that a significantly greater proportion of viewers in Group A applied for a MasterCard than viewers in Group B and Group C, that result would be strong support for source credibility theory.

Fitting questions for experimental research

- What is the relationship between perceived similarity and interpersonal attraction?
- What conditions are necessary for small groups to make high-quality decisions?
- When does a violation of another person's nonverbal expectations cause a favorable response?

"Are you just pissing and moaning, or can you verify what you're saying with data?"

2. Surveys

Whether using questionnaires or conducting interviews, survey researchers rely on self-reported data to discover who people are and what they think, feel, or intend to do. Of the four research strategies discussed in this section, surveys are undoubtedly the best known and most widely used technique. In the MasterCard ad they could serve the sponsor well both before and after the spot first runs.

McCann Erickson/New York, MasterCard's advertising agency, already knew that typical viewers for their ad would be middle-class male football fans. They could survey a random sample of this target audience to discover attitudes toward Peyton Manning and the sponsor. If they found that the credit card company's reputation paled in comparison to ratings of Manning's skill and character, they could boost their client's public image by crafting an ad that rides on the quarterback's credibility.

After the ad first runs, survey research could explore whether the cost of future time-buys is justified. Usually a sponsor has little more to go on than anecdotal evidence such as a comment made by the marketing director's next-door neighbor or a cryptic *gr8 commercial* posted online by someone who saw it on YouTube. But a systematic phone survey could discover how many people remember seeing it, how many people liked it, how many people could name the sponsor, how many people already owned the credit card or what their next purchase might be, and if these were the "right" people—the ones the sponsor wanted to reach.

Survey research can also help social scientists validate theory. In the experiment sketched in the previous section, the dependent variable was a discrete behavior—applying for a MasterCard. But it would be hard to gauge people's attitudes toward the credit card company using an either/or measure that leaves no room for nuance or subtle change. Alternatively, we might find members of the target audience who had seen the commercial during a game, and then ask them to respond to two multi-item scales, one that that measures identification with Peyton Manning, the other that gauges an attitude toward MasterCard. A strong correlation between the twin scores across the entire sample would be added support for Kelman's processes of opinion change that Glenn introduced in his analysis of the ad.

Of course, there's no guarantee that a viewer's postgame behavior wasn't influenced by comments from friends and family members during or after the game. It's always difficult to support cause-and-effect relationships from correlational data. Yet unlike a highly controlled laboratory experiment, a well-planned survey gives the social scientist a chance to get inside the heads of people in a "real-life" situation. There's less rigor, but more vigor, than in an experiment.

Fitting questions for survey research

- How much do people differ in their need for cognitive clarity?
- Do people who watch a high amount of dramatic violence on TV hold an exaggerated belief in a mean and scary world?
- To what extent does media news coverage set the agenda for what people think about and believe?

3. Textual Analysis

The aim of *textual analysis* is to describe and interpret the characteristics of a message. Communication theorists use this term to refer to the intensive study

Textual analysis
A research method that describes and interprets the characteristics of any text.

of a single message grounded in a humanistic perspective. Rhetorical criticism is the most common form of textual research in the communication discipline. Marty's analysis of Manning's words and gestures in the ad is a good example.

An increasing number of interpretive scholars aren't content merely to interpret the intended meanings of a text. They want to expose and publicly resist the ideology that permeates the accepted wisdom of society. These *critical scholars* tend to reject any notion of permanent truth or meaning. To traditional thinkers, their activity looks like a few angry children in kindergarten knocking over other kids' blocks, but they are intentionally using theory to carve out a space where people without power can be heard. For example, a feminist scholar reviewing the same ad that Glenn and Marty saw might note that Wendy's pratfall is the only moment a woman is portrayed in the commercial, and that even in his "support," a paternalistic Peyton refers to her as a man. Feminists would also point out that under the guise of humor and social support, the ad clearly reinforces a "big boys don't cry" masculine stereotype. Cultural studies theorists would scoff at the idea that the sponsor really believes that some things are priceless. By listing the cost of a ruined brunch, latte, and piano, it's obvious that the commercial is about money.

Critical theorists
Scholars who use theory to reveal unjust communication practices that create or perpetuate an imbalance of power.

For theorists critical of the "culture industries," advertising is the linchpin of oppression and needs to be resisted by those who are aware that television imposes meaning on the viewer. Their form of textual analysis isn't a detached and impartial enterprise; it is a powerful tool in the service of a reformist agenda.

Fitting questions for textual analysis

- What does the speaker's choice of language reveal about her strategic intent?
- How did the metaphors that Martin Luther King, Jr. used in his "I Have a Dream" speech reflect the historical context of that time and place?
- In what way is this text an example of the ideology of corporately controlled media?

4. Ethnography

In the 1990 Academy Award–winning film *Dances with Wolves*, Kevin Costner plays John Dunbar, a nineteenth-century Army lieutenant alone on the Dakota plains.[20] Amidst some anxiety and with great tentativeness, Dunbar sets out to understand the ways of the Sioux tribe camped a short distance away. He watches carefully, listens attentively, appreciates greatly, and slowly begins to participate in the tribal rituals. He also takes extensive notes. That's ethnography!

Ethnography
A method of participant observation designed to help a researcher experience a culture's complex web of meaning.

Princeton anthropologist Clifford Geertz says that *ethnography* is "not an experimental science in search of law, but an interpretive [approach] in search of meaning."[21] As a sensitive observer of the human scene, Geertz is loath to impose his way of thinking onto a society's construction of reality. He wants his theory of communication grounded in the meanings that people within a culture share. Getting it right means seeing it from their point of view.

Most people have long regarded advertising as a world unto itself. A communication researcher could view the MasterCard commercial as an artifact of that particular subculture and seek to understand the web of meaning surrounding this creation and other television spots. An ethnographer would look for the rites, ceremonies, rituals, myths, legends, stories, and folklore that reflect the shared meanings and values of the advertising industry. With some concentrated effort you might find an ad agency or one of its corporate clients that would welcome you as an intern who was willing to assume a participant-observer role. Here are some of the questions that you might reasonably pursue in your ethnographic research:

Fitting questions for ethnographic research

- What significance does the CEO's open door have for middle managers within the company?
- How does the standpoint of women affect the value they place on caregiving?
- When a teenager and an elderly person interact, how do they typically alter their communication behavior to accommodate the style of the other?

PLOTTING THEORIES ON AN OBJECTIVE-INTERPRETIVE SCALE

In this chapter I've introduced five important areas of difference between objective and interpretive communication scholars and the theories they create. A basic appreciation of these distinctions will help you understand where like-minded thinkers are going and why they've chosen a particular path to get there. But once you grasp how they differ, it will be helpful for you to realize that not all theorists fall neatly into one category or the other. Many have a foot in both camps. It's more accurate to picture the *objective* and *interpretive* labels as anchoring the ends of a continuum, with theorists spread out along the scale.

Objective _____ **Interpretive**

Figure 2–2 displays my evaluation of where each theory I feature fits on an objective-interpretive continuum. For easier reference to positions on the scale, I've numbered the five columns at the bottom of the chart. In placing a theory, I've tried to factor in choices the theorists have made about ways of knowing, human nature, what they value most, the purpose of theory, and their research strategy. I've consulted a number of scholars in the field to get their "read" on appropriate placements. They didn't always agree, but in every case the discussion has sharpened my understanding of theory and the issues to be considered in the process of creating one. What I learned is reflected in the chapters ahead.

Of course, the position of each dot won't make much sense to you until you've read about the theory. But by looking at the pattern of distribution you can see that roughly half of the theories have an objective orientation, while the other half reflect an interpretive commitment. This 50–50 split matches the mix of scholarship I see in our field. When talking about relationships among the theories and the common assumptions made by a group of theorists, your instructor may frequently refer back to this chart. So for easy reference, I've reproduced the appropriate "slice" of the chart on the title page of each chapter.

Chapter 3 uses Ernest Bormann's symbolic convergence theory to introduce the way that standards for judging the quality of an objective theory differ from criteria for an interpretive one. The minigraphic above the title will show the reason I've chosen Bormann's theory for this purpose. The dot in the center of the scale indicates that its roots run deep into both approaches.

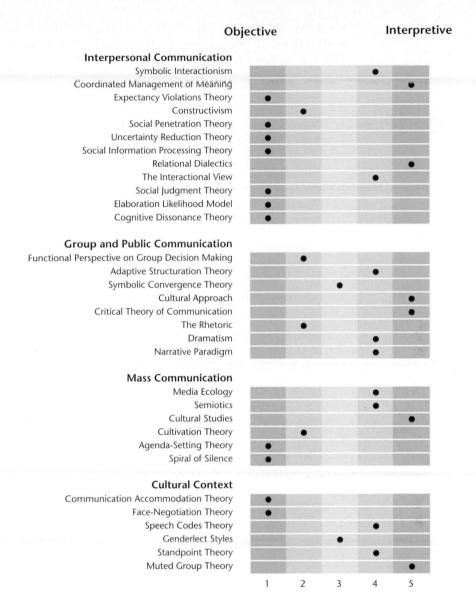

FIGURE 2–2 Classification of Communication Theories According to Objective/Interpretive Worldview

QUESTIONS TO SHARPEN YOUR FOCUS

1. Compare Glenn Sparks' and Marty Medhurst's approaches to the Master-Card commercial. Which analysis makes the most sense to you? Why?

2. How do scientists and interpretive scholars differ in their answers to the question *What is truth?* Which perspective do you find more satisfying?

3. Think of the communication classes you've taken. Did an *objective* or *interpretive* orientation undergird each course? Was this due more to the nature of the subject matter or to the professor's point of view?

4. Why are *experiments, surveys, textual analysis,* and ethnography fitting methods for answering the three bulleted *research questions?* For each question, can you select another research method that might be just as appropriate?

A SECOND LOOK

Recommended resource: James A. Anderson and Geoffrey Baym, "Philosophies and Philosophic Issues in Communication 1995–2004," *Journal of Communication,* Vol. 54, 2004, pp. 589–615.

Metatheoretical overview: James A. Anderson, *Communication Theory: Epistemological Foundations,* Guilford, New York, 1996, pp. 13–77.

Contemporary scientific scholarship: Charles Berger and Steven Chaffee, *Handbook of Communication Science, Sage,* Newbury Park, CA, 1987.

Contemporary rhetorical scholarship: Sonja Foss, Karen Foss, and Robert Trapp, *Contemporary Perspectives on Rhetoric,* 3rd ed., Waveland, Prospect Heights, IL, 2000.

Defense of empirical scholarship: Robert Bostrom and Lewis Donohew, "The Case for Empiricism: Clarifying Fundamental Issues in Communication Theory," *Communication Monographs,* Vol. 59, 1992, pp. 109–129.

Defense of interpretive scholarship: Arthur Bochner, "Perspectives on Inquiry II: Theories and Stories," in *Handbook of Interpersonal Communication,* 2nd ed., Mark Knapp and Gerald Miller (eds.), Sage, Thousand Oaks, CA, 1994, pp. 21–41.

Scientific research: Glenn Sparks, *Media Effects Research: A Basic Overview,* 2nd ed., Wadsworth, Belmont, CA, 2006.

Rhetorical analysis: Martin J. Medhurst, "Why Rhetoric Matters: George H.W. Bush in the White House," in *The Rhetorical Presidency of George H.W. Bush,* Martin J. Medhurst (ed.), Texas A&M University, College Station, 2006, pp. 3–18.

Critical approach to theory: Stanley Deetz, *Democracy in an Age of Corporate Colonization,* State University of New York, Albany, 1992, "The Role of Communication Studies," pp. 65–90.

Research methods: Lawrence R. Frey, Carl H. Botan, and Gary L. Kreps, *Investigating Communication: An Introduction to Research Methods,* 2nd ed., Allyn and Bacon, Boston, 2000.

Bridging science and interpretation: Charles Pavitt, "Answering Questions Requesting Scientific Explanations for Communication," *Communication Theory,* Vol. 10, 2000, pp. 379–404.

Relationship between theory and research: Robert Bostrom, "Theories, Data and Communication Research," *Communication Monographs,* Vol. 70, 2003, pp. 275–294.

For a historical perspective on the place of objective and interpretive theory
in the field of communication, select Talk About Communication
in the theory archive section at
www.afirstlook.com.

Weighing the Words

of Ernest Bormann's Symbolic Convergence Theory

In Chapter 2 we looked at two distinct approaches to communication theory—objective and interpretive. Because the work of social scientists and interpreters is so different, they often have trouble understanding and valuing their counterparts' scholarship. This workplace tension parallels the struggle between ranchers and farmers in Rodgers and Hammerstein's Broadway musical *Oklahoma!* One song calls for understanding and cooperation:

> The farmer and the cowman should be friends,
> Oh, the farmer and the cowman should be friends,
>> One man likes to push a plough,
>> The other likes to chase a cow,
> But that's no reason why they cain't be friends.[1]

The problem, of course, is that farmers and ranchers want to push a plough or chase a cow over the same piece of land. Daily disputes over fences, water, and government grants make friendship tough. The same can be said of the turf wars that are common between objective and interpretive scholars. Differences in ways of knowing, views of human nature, values, goals of theory building, and methods of research seem to ensure tension and misunderstanding.

Friendly attitudes between empiricists and critical interpreters are particularly hard to come by when each group insists on applying its own standards of judgment to the work of the other group. As a first-time reader of communication theory, you could easily get sucked in to making the same mistake. If you've had training in the scientific method and judge the value of every communication theory by whether it predicts human behavior, you'll automatically reject 50 percent of the theories presented in this book. On the other hand, if you've been steeped in the humanities and expect every theory to help unmask the meaning of a text, you'll easily dismiss the other half.

Regardless of which approach you favor, not all objective or interpretive communication theories are equally good. For each type, some are better than others. Like moviegoers watching one of Clint Eastwood's early Westerns, you'll want a way to separate the good, the bad, and the ugly. Since I've included theories originating in both the social sciences and the humanities, you need to have two separate lenses through which to view their respective claims. This chapter offers that pair of bifocals. I hope by the time you finish you'll be on friendly terms with the separate criteria that behavioral scientists and a wide range of interpretive scholars use to weigh the works and words of their colleagues.

A TEST CASE: ERNEST BORMANN'S SYMBOLIC CONVERGENCE THEORY

University of Minnesota professor Ernest Bormann developed a theory of communication that is unusual in that it has both interpretive and objective roots. The project started as a method of rhetorical criticism, a long-honored tradition in humanistic study. Bormann called his method *fantasy theme analysis*, and he used it to study a type of communication that takes place in small groups.

Bormann soon discovered a link between the dramatic imagery members use when they talk to each other and the degree of group consciousness and solidarity. In standard social science fashion, he defined his terms and then crafted a cause-and-effect hypothesis, which he now believes holds for all groups regardless of where they meet, who they are, or why they get together. Simply stated, Bormann's symbolic convergence theory maintains that "the sharing of group fantasies creates symbolic convergence."[2]

Fantasy
The creative and imaginative interpretation of events that fulfills a psychological or rhetorical need; depicts events outside of the group or in its past or future.

Some people restrict the term *fantasy* to children's literature, sexual desire, or things "not true." Bormann, however, uses the word to refer to "the creative and imaginative interpretation of events that fulfills a psychological or rhetorical need."[3] In a small-group setting, this definition includes any reference to events in the group's past, speculation about what might happen in the future, and any talk about the world outside the group. The term does not cover comments about actions taking place "here and now" within the group. Fantasies are expressed in the form of stories, jokes, metaphors, and other imaginative language that interprets or places a spin on familiar events. Voiced fantasies become vehicles to share common experiences and invest them with an emotional tone.

For example, University of Kentucky communication professor Alan DeSantis asks us to picture a group of Kentucky-born, middle-aged white guys sitting around a cigar store smoking hand-rolled imported cigars. As the topic shifts from college basketball to the risk of smoking, the owner tells the story of a heart surgeon who came into the shop after having been on duty for 36 hours. After lighting up, the doctor blew out a big mouthful of smoke and said, "This is the most relaxed I have felt in days. Now how can that be bad for you?"[4]

Whether or not the doctor really said this isn't the issue. Symbolic convergence theory is concerned with the group's response to the tale. Does the account fall flat or do these regular patrons chuckle in appreciation, nod in agreement, or say "You've got it!" to punctuate the narrative? Do others lose their self-consciousness and vie to tell their own stories that dismiss the harm of cigar smoking, a pastime that they consider a benign hobby? Bormann says that we can spot a *fantasy chain reaction* by increased energy within the group, by an upbeat tempo in the conversation, and especially through a common response to the imagery.

Most fantasies don't chain out; they fall on deaf ears. But when one catches the imagination of members within the group, the same *fantasy theme* will run throughout multiple narratives—à la *Seinfeld*. Perhaps the hero of every man's account is a famous cigar smoker who lived into old age without ill effects— George Burns, Winston Churchill, Fidel Castro, or Milton Berle. Or maybe each image reflects a meddling government bureaucrat who wants to limit their right to enjoy a cigar in a public place. Whatever the theme, Bormann believes that by sharing common fantasies, a collection of individuals is transformed into a cohesive group. He calls the process *symbolic convergence*.

Symbolic convergence
The linguistic process by which group members develop a sense of community or closeness; cohesiveness, unity, solidarity.

Through symbolic convergence, individuals build a sense of community or a group consciousness. References to *I, me,* and *mine* give way to pronouns that assume a joint venture—*we, us,* and *ours.* Groups draw even closer when members share a cluster of fantasy themes. Along with examples of octogenarian smokers, group stories might focus on the difference between cigars and cigarettes, safety in moderation, inconsistent scientific findings concerning cancer, the greater risks of everyday living, and the health benefit of relaxation that comes from smoking a good cigar. When the same set of integrated fantasy themes is voiced repeatedly across many groups, Bormann describes people's view of social reality as a *rhetorical vision*.

Rhetorical vision
A composite drama that catches up multiple groups of people into a common symbolic reality.

The concept of rhetorical vision moves symbolic convergence theory beyond its original small-group context. A coherent rhetorical vision can be spread and reinforced through recurring media messages. This occured in the United States soon after *Cigar Aficionado* magazine was launched in late 1992. The glossy periodical lauded the sophisticated pleasure of smoking premium tobacco, while repeatedly elaborating the cluster of fantasy themes mentioned above. The following year cigar smoking in the country increased 50 percent.[5]

The entire master script of a rhetorical vision can be triggered by a single code word, slogan, or nonverbal symbol. In the Kentucky smoke shop where these fantasy themes were voiced, any mention of criticism of cigar smoking from family or friends was enough to set off a new round of protest among store regulars. Their emotional reaction was captured on a T-shirt sold at the store that satirized the Surgeon General's cautionary statement: "Warning—Harassing me about my smoking can be hazardous to your health."[6] Bormann is convinced that symbolic convergence explains the meeting-of-minds and sense of communion taking place among the men.

Now that you have a thumbnail sketch of fantasy themes, symbolic convergence, and rhetorical visions, let's take a look at the distinct criteria that objective or interpretive scholars use to judge the quality of Bormann's theory. We'll start with the wisdom of science.

WHAT MAKES AN OBJECTIVE THEORY GOOD?

Symbolic convergence theory is credible because it fulfills what a leading text on social research methods calls the "twin objectives of scientific knowledge." The theory *explains* the past and present, and it *predicts* the future. Social scientists of all kinds agree on three additional criteria a theory must meet to be good—*relative simplicity, testability,* and *usefulness.* As I discuss the standards, I will use the terms *objective* and *scientific* interchangeably.

Scientific Standard 1: Explanation of the Data

A good objective theory explains an event or human behavior. Philosopher of science Abraham Kaplan says that theory is a way of making sense out of a disturbing situation.[7] A good objective theory brings clarity to an otherwise jumbled situation; it draws order out of chaos.

The idea of symbolic convergence helps researchers make sense of chaotic group discussion. Even though a leader urges members to *speak one at a time* and *stick to the point*, participants will often interrupt each other and go off on verbal tangents. According to symbolic convergence theory, graphic digressions and boisterous talk aren't signs of a flawed process. Rather, they are evidence that the group is coming together. As Bormann says, "the explanatory power of the fantasy chain analysis lies in its ability to account for the development, evolution, and decay of dramas that catch up groups of people and change behavior."[8]

A good theory synthesizes the data, focuses our attention on what's crucial, and helps us ignore that which makes little difference. Bormann's theory organizes these verbal inputs into a coherent whole. His focus on the cohesive effect of chained fantasy goes beyond the raw data. It explains what's happening.

A good theory also explains *why*. When Willie Sutton was asked why he robbed banks, the Depression-era bandit replied, "'cuz that's where they keep the money." It's a great line, but as a theory of motivation, it lacks explanatory power. There's nothing in the words that casts light on the internal processes or environmental forces that led Sutton to crack a safe while others tried to crack the stock market.

Symbolic convergence explains the causal process as well as the result. Bormann suggests that group members often voice fantasies as a way to relieve tensions within the group.[9] The atmosphere may be charged with interpersonal conflict, the group as a whole may be frustrated by its inability to come up with a good solution, or perhaps individuals import their own brand of stress as each walks in the door. Whatever the reason, a joke, story, or vivid analogy provides welcome relief.

Of course, most group members really don't care how fantasy chains work; they're just thankful to have a pleasant diversion. In like manner, you can be a skillful public speaker without understanding why the audience likes what you say. But when you take a course in communication *theory*, you've lost your amateur status. The *reason* something happens becomes as important as the fact that it does.

Scientific Standard 2: Prediction of Future Events

A good objective theory predicts what will happen. Prediction is possible only when we are dealing with things we can see, hear, touch, smell, and taste over and over. As we repeatedly notice the same things happening in similar situations, we begin to speak of invariable patterns or universal laws. In the realm of the physical sciences, we are seldom embarrassed. Objects don't have a choice about how to respond to a stimulus.

The social sciences are another matter. While theories about human behavior often cast their predictions in cause-and-effect terms, a certain humility on the part of the theorist is advisable. Even the best theory may be able to talk about people in general, rather than about specific individuals, and these only in terms of probability and tendencies—not absolute certainty. That's the kind of soft predictive power Bormann claims for symbolic convergence theory.

Bormann believes that rhetorical visions contain motives that prompt or propel true believers to act out a fantasy. When ethnographer Alan DeSantis first describes the core group of cigar shop patrons, they were experiencing angst at the premature death of their friend Greg. Like the rest of the regulars who sat around the store smoking, Greg had scoffed at the health risks of their practice. Now they were confronted with the sobering fact of his heart attack. Within a week of the funeral, however, his smoking buddies had constructed a verbal collage of images depicting Greg's stressful lifestyle. The store owner voiced their consensus: "Smoking had nothing to do with his death. He lived, drank and played hard and it took a toll on him at the end."[10]

Bormann has had little success predicting when a fantasy will ignite and trigger a chain reaction. Members with rhetorical skill seem to have a better chance of providing the spark, but there's no guarantee that their words will ignite others. Even when a skillful image-maker sparks a fantasy chain, he or she has little control over where the conversation will go. Fantasy chains seem to have a life of their own. You can see why most social scientists want more predictive power than Bormann's theory offers. Yet once a fantasy chain catches fire, the theory predicts that the group will become more cohesive and of one mind, which is exactly what happened in the cigar shop.

Scientific Standard 3: Relative Simplicity

A good objective theory is as simple as possible—no more complex than it has to be. A few decades ago a cartoonist named Rube Goldberg made people laugh by sketching plans for complicated machines that performed simple tasks. His "better mousetrap" went through a sequence of 15 mechanical steps that were triggered by turning a crank and ended with a bird cage dropping over a cheese-eating mouse.

Goldberg's designs were funny because the machines were so needlessly convoluted. They violated the scientific principle called Occam's razor, so named because philosopher William of Occam implored theorists to "shave off" any assumptions, variables, or concepts that aren't really necessary to explain what's

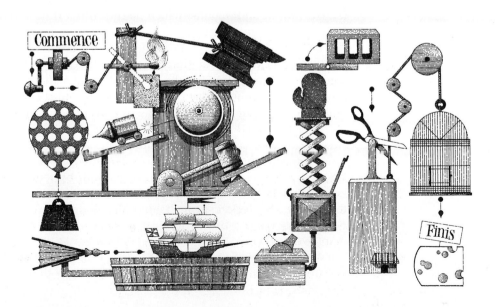

Rule of parsimony (Occam's razor)
Given two plausible explanations for the same event, we should accept the simpler version.

going on.[11] When you've concentrated on a subject for a long time, it's easy to get caught up in the grandeur of a theoretical construction. (Why say it simply when you can say it elaborately?) Yet the *rule of parsimony*—another label for the same principle—states that given two plausible explanations for the same event, we should accept the simpler version.

College professors often criticize others for offering simple solutions to complex questions. It's a jungle out there, and we're quick to pounce on those who reduce the world's complexity to a simplistic "me Tarzan, you Jane." But every so often a few explorers will cut through the underbrush and clear a straight path to a truth, which they announce in simple, direct, concise terms. Consider Bormann's summary statement, cited earlier: "The sharing of group fantasies creates symbolic convergence."[12] Simplicity is a virtue of his theory.

Scientific Standard 4: Hypotheses That Can Be Tested

Falsifiability
The requirement that a scientific theory must be stated in a way that it can be tested and disproved if it is indeed wrong.

A good objective theory is testable. If a prediction is wrong, there ought to be a way to demonstrate the error. Karl Popper called this requirement *falsifiability*, and saw it as the defining feature of scientific theory.[13] Some theories are so loosely stated that it's impossible to imagine empirical results that could disprove their hypotheses. But if there is no way to prove a theory false, then the claim that it's true seems hollow. A boyhood example may help illustrate this point.

When I was 12 years old, I had a friend named Mike. We spent many hours shooting baskets in his driveway. The backboard was mounted on an old-fashioned, single-car garage whose double doors opened outward like the doors on a cabinet. In order to avoid crashing into them on a drive for a layup, we'd open the doors during play. But since the doors would only swing through a 90-degree arc, they extended about 4 feet onto the court along the baseline.

One day Mike announced that he'd developed a "never-miss" shot. He took the ball at the top of the free-throw circle, drove toward the basket, then cut to the right corner. When he got to the baseline, he took a fade-away jump shot, blindly arching the ball over the top of the big door. I was greatly impressed as the ball swished through the net. When he boasted that he never missed, I challenged him to do it again—which he did. But a third attempt was an air ball—it completely missed the rim.

Before I could make the kind of bratty comment junior high school boys make, he quickly told me that the attempt had not been his never-miss shot. He claimed to have slipped as he cut to the right and therefore jumped from the wrong place. Grabbing the ball, he drove behind the door and again launched a blind arching shot. Swish. That, he assured me, was his never-miss shot.

I knew something was wrong. I soon figured out that any missed attempt was, by definition, not the ballyhooed never-miss shot. When the ball went in, however, Mike heralded the success as added evidence of 100 percent accuracy. I now know that I could have called his bluff by removing the net from the basket so that he couldn't hear whether the shot went through. This would have forced him to declare from behind the door whether the attempt was of the never-miss variety. But as long as I played by his rules, there was no way to disprove his claim. Unfortunately, some theories are stated in a similar fashion. They are presented in a way that makes it impossible to prove them false. They shy away from the put-up-or-shut-up standard—they aren't testable.

Symbolic convergence theory is vulnerable at this point. Since Bormann claims that shared fantasies create cohesive groups, an empirical researcher's first task is to measure these variables separately. This is not as easy as it sounds. Because most groups already have a history, it's difficult to know whether a fantasy chain is a trigger for new solidarity among members or merely a reflection of a group consciousness that's already in place. Indeed, leading advocates of the theory seem to confound the two variables, often treating the presence of a fantasy chain as proof of group cohesiveness. Note, for example, how the two concepts merge in the following passage: "For a fantasy theme to chain out, a saga to exist, a symbolic cue to convey meaning, or a rhetorical vision to evolve, there must be a shared group consciousness within a rhetorical community."[14] You can see why many outside observers consider symbolic convergence theory a never-miss shot—it's not falsifiable.

Scientific Standard 5: Practical Utility

A good objective theory is useful. Since an oft-cited goal of social science is to help people have more control over their daily lives, objective theories should offer practical advice for those facing thorny social situations. Symbolic convergence theory does this well. Bormann and his followers have used fantasy theme analysis to advise small groups, improve organizational communication, conduct market research, and assess public opinion. To illustrate the pragmatic value of the methodology, John Cragan (Illinois State University) and Donald Shields (University of Missouri–St. Louis) require students in their applied research classes to analyze the way that high school seniors talk about college.

Symbolic convergence theory claims that most rhetorical visions employ one of three competing master analogues—a righteous vision, a social vision, or a pragmatic vision. That's what Cragan's and Shields' students typically find.[15] Potential applicants who embrace a *righteous* vision are interested in a school's academic excellence, the reputation of its faculty, and special programs that it offers. Those who adopt a *social* vision view college as a way to get away from home, meet new friends, and join others in a variety of social activities. High school seniors who buy into a *pragmatic* vision are looking for a marketable degree that will help them get a good job. (What was your vision when you entered college?) Knowledge of these distinct visions could help admissions officers develop a strategy to appeal to graduates who would most appreciate the character of their campus.

In Chapter 1, I cited Lewin's claim that there is nothing as practical as a good theory. This final standard—one of utility—suggests that social science theories that aren't helpful aren't good. As you read about theorists who work from an objective perspective, let usefulness be a crucial test of each theory. If a theory offers practical advice, act on it; if it offers no pragmatic insight for your life, discard it. There is one caution, however. Most of us can be a bit lazy or short-sighted. We have a tendency to consider as unimportant anything that's hard to grasp or can't be applied to our lives right now. Before dismissing a theory as irrelevant, make certain you understand it and consider how others have made use of its advice. I'll try to do my part by presenting each theory as clearly as possible and suggesting possible applications.

WHAT MAKES AN INTERPRETIVE THEORY GOOD?

Unlike scientists, interpretive scholars don't have an agreed-on, five-point set of criteria for evaluating their theories. But even though there is no universally approved model for interpretive theories, rhetoricians, critical theorists, and other interpreters repeatedly urge that theories should accomplish some or all of the following functions: *create understanding, identify values, inspire aesthetic appreciation, stimulate agreement,* and *reform society.* The rest of this chapter examines these often-mentioned ideals.

Interpretive Standard 1: New Understanding of People

Interpretive scholarship is good when it offers fresh insight into the human condition. Rhetorical critics, ethnographers, and other humanistic researchers seek to gain new understanding by analyzing the activity that they regard as uniquely human—symbolic interaction. As opposed to social science theories that attempt to identify communication patterns common to all people, an interpretive scholar typically examines a one-of-a-kind speech community that exhibits a specific language style. By analyzing this group's communication practice, the researcher hopes to develop an understanding of local knowledge or members' unique rules for interaction. Interpretive theories are tools to aid this search for situated meaning. DeSantis' use of Bormann's symbolic convergence theory to understand what's going on among a core group of cigar store regulars is a good example.

Suppose that an interpretive scholar wanted to study the public communication of politicians whose reputations are on the line. He or she would start by selecting one or more texts—George W. Bush's announcement of a troop surge as a last-ditch attempt to quell violence in Iraq, Dick Cheney's belated explanation of shooting a friend on a quail hunt, Bill Clinton's presidential news conferences and White House communiqués on the Monica Lewinsky affair, or any other text that could shed light on political crisis communication.

When an interpretive theory is good, it helps the critic understand the text. For example, a Burkean analysis of Bush's plan to send more troops to Iraq would offer insight as to why he emphasized that he was the sole agent responsible for the decision—"I am the decider." Fisher's narrative paradigm might help the critic understand why Cheney's account of the hunting accident didn't hang together or ring true for most Americans. Or Pacanowsky's cultural approach to organizations could suggest that Clinton's responses to the press revealed a White House culture that had its own rites, rituals, and myths. You'll read about these theories in the pages to come. To the extent that they help you make sense out of complex communication, they fulfill the first interpretive standard for a good theory.

Some critics fear that by relying on rhetorical theory, we will read our preconceived ideas into the text rather than letting the words speak for themselves. They suggest that there are times when we should "just say no" to theory. But Bormann notes that rhetorical theory works best when it suggests universal patterns of symbol-using: "A powerful explanatory structure is what makes a work of humanistic scholarship live on through time."[16]

Bormann's claim is akin to the behavioral scientist's insistence that theory explains why people do what they do. But the two notions are somewhat different. Science wants an objective explanation; humanism desires subjective understanding. Klaus Krippendorff of the Annenberg School of Communication at the University of Pennsylvania urges us to recognize that we, as theorists, are both the cause and the consequence of what we observe. His *self-referential imperative* for building theory states: "Include yourself as a constituent of your own construction."[17]

Self-referential imperative
Include yourself as a constituent of your own construction.

To the extent that Krippendorff's imperative means abandoning a detached and dispassionate stance, Bormann's fantasy theme analysis is self-referential. In his preface to *The Force of Fantasy*, Bormann describes the personal thrill of discovery and creation:

> Mulling over the materials for my book in the history of religious and reform speaking at the same time as I was caught up in these exciting new developments in small group communication resulted in one of those exhilarating moments of illumination when it seemed clear to me that the force of fantasy is just as strong in mass communication as it is in small group interaction. Merging the discoveries in group fantasies with recent developments in rhetorical criticism provided me with my critical method—the fantasy theme analysis of rhetorical visions.[18]

This is not the account of a detached observer. However, inasmuch as the self-referential imperative implies that scholars can and should affect the communication they study, fantasy theme analysis seems to remain a spectator sport.

Interpretive Standard 2: Clarification of Values

A good interpretive theory brings people's values into the open. The theorist actively seeks to acknowledge, identify, or unmask the ideology behind the message under scrutiny. Since fantasy theme analysis is based on the assumption that meaning, emotion, and motive for action are manifest in the content of a message, value clarification is a particular strength of symbolic convergence theory.

Interpretive theorists should also be willing to reveal their own ethical commitments. As Texas A&M University communication professor Eric Rothenbuhler notes, "Theoretical positions have moral implications, and when we teach them, advocate their use by others, or promote policies based upon them they have moral consequences."[19] Of course, not all interpretive scholars occupy the same moral ground, but there are core values most of them share. For example, humanists usually place a premium on individual liberty. Krippendorff wants to make sure that scholars' drive for personal freedom extends to the people they study. His *ethical imperative* directs the theorist to "grant others that occur in your construction the same autonomy you practice constructing them."[20] When theorists follow this rule, scholarly monologue gives way to collegial dialogue, wherein people have a say in what's said about them. This kind of communal assessment requires reporting multiple voices rather than relying on one or two informants.

Ethical imperative
Grant others that occur in your construction the same autonomy you practice constructing them.

Many interpretive scholars value equality as highly as they do freedom. This commitment leads to a continual examination of the power relationships inherent in all communication. Critical theorists, in particular, insist that scholars can no longer remain ethically detached from the people they are studying or from the political and economic implications of their work. "There is no safe harbor in which researchers can avoid the power structure."[21]

As for symbolic convergence theory, Bormann's method of analyzing group fantasies seems to be ethically neutral. On the other hand, his commentary on nineteenth-century romantic pragmatism suggests that he is a man who applauds restoring the American dream of freedom, equal opportunity, hard work, and moral decency.[22] I get the impression that he'd be more in sympathy with the rhetorical vision of the African-American Million Man March on Washington to pledge self-reliance than with the ideology of the cigar shop that DeSantis describes as a unique form of civil libertarianism—"Keep your government off my liquor, pornography, guns, and cigars."[23] But in symbolic convergence theory, Bormann isn't explicit about where he stands.

Interpretive Standard 3: Aesthetic Appeal

The way a theorist presents ideas can capture the imagination of a reader just as much as the wisdom and originality of the theory he or she has created. As with any type of communication, both content and style make a difference. Objective theorists are constrained by the standard format for acceptable scientific writing—propositions, hypotheses, operationalized constructs, and the like. But interpretive theorists have more room for creativity, so aesthetic appeal becomes an issue. Although the elegance of a theory is in the eye of the beholder, clarity and artistry seem to be the two qualities necessary to satisfy this aesthetic requirement.

No matter how great the insights the theory contains, if the essay describing them is disorganized, overwritten, or opaque, the theorist's ideas will come across as murky rather than clear. One student of mine who fought through a theorist's monograph filled with esoteric jargon likened the experience to "scuba diving in fudge." Bormann writes better than this. Readers can easily grasp his key concepts of fantasy chains, rhetorical visions, and group cohesiveness. Bormann and his followers may not write with the lucidity or wit of an essayist for *The Atlantic* or *The New Yorker*, but they aren't afraid to support their key ideas with the words of people who do. For example, Bormann underscores the importance of fantasy with Robert Frost's observation that "society can never think things out; it has to see them acted out by actors."[24]

According to Unversity of Washington professor Barbara Warnick, a rhetorical critic can fill one or more of four roles—artist, analyst, audience, and advocate.[25] As an artist, the critic's job is to spark appreciation. Along with clarity, it's another way to construct an interpretive theory with aesthetic appeal. By artfully incorporating imagery, metaphor, illustration, and story into the core of the theory, the theorist can make his or her creation come alive for others.

I'm intrigued by Bormann's descriptions of fantasy themes that emerge from Harley-Davidson bikers, unwed mothers, and *The Big Book* of Alcoholics Anonymous. His analysis of AA literature reveals a rhetorical vision that is best characterized as "Fetching Good Out of Evil," a felicitous expression introduced by Bormann.[26] It takes only a few such apt turns of phrase to heighten the aesthetic appeal of the theory.

Interpretive Standard 4: A Community of Agreement

We can identify a good interpretive theory by the amount of support it generates within a community of scholars who are interested and knowledgeable about the same type of communication. Interpretation of meaning is subjective, but whether the interpreter's case is reasonable is decided ultimately by others in the field. Their acceptance or rejection is an objective fact that helps verify or vilify a theorist's ideas.

Sometimes interpretive theorists present a controversial thesis to an audience restricted to true believers—those who already agree with the author's position. But an interpretive theory can't meet the community of agreement standard unless it becomes the subject of widespread analysis. For example, former National Communication Association president David Zarefsky warns that rhetorical validity can be established only when a work is debated in the broad marketplace of ideas. For this Northwestern University rhetorical critic, sound arguments differ from unsound ones in that

> sound arguments are addressed to the general audience of critical readers, not just to the adherents of a particular "school" or perspective. . . . They open their own reasoning process to scrutiny.[27]

John Stewart is the editor of *Bridges, Not Walls*—a collection of humanistic articles on interpersonal communication. As the book has progressed through 10 editions, Stewart's judgment to keep, drop, or add a theoretical work has been made possible by the fact that interpretive scholarship is "not a solitary enterprise carried out in a vacuum." It is instead, he says, "the effort of a community of scholars who routinely subject their findings to the scrutiny of editors, referees, and readers."[28]

When it comes to widespread scrutiny, Bormann has done it right. He's published his ideas in major journals that are open to rhetorical scholarship—*Quarterly Journal of Speech, Communication Theory,* and *Journal of Communication* among them. While not all communication scholars find value in his theory, the majority do. When confronted by critics, Bormann has responded publicly and convincingly.[29]

Fantasy theme analysis has become a standard method of symbolic study. Based on the human nature assumption that people are symbol-users in general, and storytellers in particular, the approach squares neatly with several other theories in this book.[30] As you can see, the community of agreement that supports Bormann's theory is both wide and articulate.

Interpretive Standard 5: Reform of Society

A good interpretive theory often generates change. Contrary to the notion that we can dismiss calls for social justice or emancipation as *mere rhetoric,* the critical interpreter is a reformer who can have an impact on society. Kenneth Gergen, a Swarthmore College social psychologist, states that theory has

> the capacity to challenge the guiding assumptions of the culture, to raise fundamental questions regarding contemporary social life, to foster reconsideration of that which is "taken for granted," and thereby to generate fresh alternatives for social action.[31]

Fantasy theme analysis reliably documents rhetorical visions that contain motives to go public, gain converts, and use the mass media to spread their truth. Yet symbolic convergence theory itself has no reform agenda for society. Scholars trying to identify fantasy chains prefer to investigate rather than instigate.

Bormann is trying to achieve a more modest change. As was stressed in Chapter 2, social scientists and interpreters in our discipline have typically gone their separate ways. Bormann would like it otherwise. He's crafted a theory that considers fantasy theme analysis "a liberal and humanizing art, a scholarly endeavor which aims to illuminate the human condition."[32] Definitely interpretive. On the other hand, his claim that a chain of fantasies (whatever they might be) draws together people (whoever they might be) is a universal prediction. Definitely scientific. Inasmuch as Bormann's joint venture between interpretive and objective approaches to communication is a model that encourages rhetoricians and empiricists to work in harmony, it may occasion a modest reform among the society of scholars who have difficulty appreciating the value of the other group's work.

COMMON GROUND AMONG OBJECTIVE AND INTERPRETIVE CRITERIA

Throughout this chapter I have urged using separate measures for weighing the merits of objective and interpretive theories. Yet a side-by-side comparison of the two lists in Figure 3–1 suggests that the standards set by scientists and the evaluative criteria used by interpretive theorists may not be as different as first thought. Work down through the chart line by line and note the conceptual overlap between each pair of terms on the same line. Here are the commonalities that I see:

1. An *explanation* of communication behavior can lead to further *understanding* of people's motivation.
2. Both *prediction* and *value clarification* look to the future. The first suggests what *will* happen; the second, what *ought* to happen.
3. For many students of theory, *simplicity* has an *aesthetic appeal*.
4. *Testing hypotheses* is a way of achieving a *community of agreement*.
5. What could be more *practical* than a theory that *reforms* unjust practices?

For teachers and students of communication, the parallels I've cited suggest that social scientists and interpreters could be friends. At the very least, they should have a familiarity with each other's work. That's one reason I've elected to discuss both objective and interpretive theories in this book.

Scientific Theory	Interpretive Theory
Explanation of Data	Understanding of People
Prediction of Future	Clarification of Values
Relative Simplicity	Aesthetic Appeal
Testable Hypotheses	Community of Agreement
Practical Utility	Reform of Society

FIGURE 3–1   Summary of Criteria for Evaluating Communication Theory

You'll find that I often refer to these requirements for good theory in the critique sections at the end of each chapter. As you might expect, the 32 theories stack up rather well—otherwise I wouldn't have picked them in the first place. But constructing theory is difficult, and most theories have an Achilles' heel that makes them vulnerable to criticism. All of the theorists readily admit a need for fine-tuning their work, and some even call for major overhauls. I encourage you to weigh their words by the standards you think are important before reading my critique at the end of each chapter.

QUESTIONS TO SHARPEN YOUR FOCUS

1. Ernest Bormann's *symbolic convergence* theory has both *objective* and *interpretive* features. Does it seem to be a better scientific or interpretive theory? Why?

2. How can we call a scientific theory good if it is *capable of being proved wrong*?

3. How can we decide when a *rhetorical critic* provides a *reasonable interpretation*?

4. All theories involve trade-offs; no theory can meet every standard of quality equally well. Of the 10 criteria discussed, which two or three are most important to you? Which one is least important?

A SECOND LOOK

Recommended resource: Ernest Bormann, John Cragan, and Donald Shields, "Three Decades of Developing, Grounding, and Using Symbolic Convergence Theory," in *Communication Yearbook 25*, William Gudykunst (ed.), Lawrence Erlbaum, Mahwah, NJ, 2001, pp. 271–313.

Scientific evaluation: Steven Chaffee, "Thinking About Theory" and Michael Beatty, "Thinking Quantitatively," in *An Integrated Approach to Communication Theory and Research*, Michael Salwen and Don Stacks (eds.), Lawrence Erlbaum, Mahwah, NJ, 1996, pp. 15–32, 33–43.

Interpretive evaluation: Klaus Krippendorff, "On the Ethics of Constructing Communication," in *Rethinking Communication*, Vol. 1, Brenda Dervin, Lawrence Grossberg, Barbara O'Keefe, and Ellen Wartella (eds.), Sage, Newbury Park, CA, 1989, pp. 66–96.

Interpretive analysis: Ernest Bormann, "Fantasy Theme Analysis and Rhetorical Theory," in *The Rhetoric of Western Thought*, 5th ed., James Golden, Goodwin Berquist, and William Coleman (eds.), Kendall/Hunt, Dubuque, IA, 1992, pp. 365–384.

Empirical research: Ernest Bormann, Roxann Knutson, and Karen Musolf, "Why Do People Share Fantasies? An Empirical Investigation of a Basic Tenet of the Symbolic Convergence Communication Theory," *Communication Studies*, Vol. 48, 1997, pp. 254–276.

Applied research: John Cragan and Donald Shields, *Symbolic Theories in Applied Communication Research: Bormann, Burke, and Fisher*, Hampton, Cresskill, NJ, 1995, chapters 2 and 6.

Progress in scientific research: Franklin Boster, "On Making Progress in Communication Science," *Human Communication Research*, Vol. 28, 2002, pp. 473–490.

Validity in interpretive research: David Althede and John Johnson, "Criteria for Assessing Interpretive Validity in Qualitative Research," in *Collecting and Interpreting Qualitative Materials,* Norman Denzin and Yvonna S. Lincoln (eds.), Sage, Thousand Oaks, CA, 1998, pp. 283–312.

Cigar shop ethnography: Alan D. DeSantis, "Smoke Screen: An Ethnographic Study of a Cigar Shop's Collective Rationalization," *Health Communication,* Vol. 14, 2002, pp. 167-198.

Critique and response: Ernest Bormann, John Cragan, and Donald Shields, "Defending Symbolic Convergence Theory from an Imaginary Gunn," *Quarterly Journal of Speech,* Vol. 89, 2003, pp. 366–372.

For more discussion of these standards,
go to *www.afirstlook.com,*
choose the Instructor's Manual link,
then click on "Weighing the Words."

CHAPTER 4

Mapping the Territory

(Seven Traditions in the Field of Communication Theory)

In Chapter 1, I presented working definitions for the concepts of *communication* and *theory*. In Chapters 2 and 3, I outlined the basic differences between objective and interpretive communication theories. These distinctions should help bring order out of chaos when your study of theory seems confusing. And it may. University of Colorado communication professor Robert Craig describes the field of communication theory as awash with hundreds of unrelated theories that differ in starting point, method, and conclusion. He suggests that our field of study resembles "a pest control device called the Roach Motel that used to be advertised on TV: Theories check in, but they never check out."[1]

My mind conjures up a different image when I try to make sense of the often baffling landscape of communication theory. I picture a scene from the film *Raiders of the Lost Ark* in which college professor Indiana Jones is lowered into a dark vault and confronts a thick layer of writhing serpents covering the floor—a tangle of communication theories. The intrepid adventurer discovers that the snakes momentarily retreat from the bright light of his torch, so he's able to secure a safe place to stand. It's my hope that the core ideas of Chapters 1–3 will provide you with that kind of space. The fantasy nature of the film is such that I could even imagine Indiana Jones emerging from the cave with all the snakes straightened like sticks of kindling wood, bound together in two bundles—the objective batch held in his right hand and the interpretive batch held in his left. But that's an oversimplistic fantasy. Craig offers a more sophisticated solution.

Craig agrees that the terrain is confusing if we insist on looking for some kind of grand theoretical overview that brings all communication study into focus—a top-down, satellite picture of the communication theory landscape. He suggests, however, that communication theory is a coherent field when we understand communication as a practical discipline.[2] He's convinced that our search for different types of theory should be grounded where real people grapple with everyday problems and practices of communication. Craig explains that "all communication theories are relevant to a common practical lifeworld in which *communication* is already a richly meaningful term."[3] Communication theory is the systematic and thoughtful response of communication scholars to questions posed as humans interact with each other—the best thinking within a practical discipline.

Craig thinks it's reasonable to talk about a *field of communication theory* if we take a collective look at the actual approaches that researchers have used to study communication problems and practices. He identifies seven established traditions of communication theory that include most, if not all, of what theorists have done. These already established traditions offer "distinct, alternative vocabularies" that describe different "ways of conceptualizing communication problems and practices."[4] This means that scholars within a given tradition talk comfortably with each other but often take potshots at those who work in other camps. As Craig suggests, we shouldn't try to smooth over these between-group battles. Theorists argue because they have something important to argue about.

In the rest of the chapter I'll outline the seven traditions that Craig describes. Taken together, they provide a helpful survey of the field of communication theory. The classification will also help you understand why some theories share common ground, while others are effectively fenced off from each other by conflicting goals and assumptions. As I introduce each tradition, I'll highlight how its advocates tend to define communication, suggest a practical communication problem that this kind of theory addresses, and describe an early theorist or school of theorists who helped set the agenda for those who followed.[5]

THE SOCIO-PSYCHOLOGICAL TRADITION

Communication as Interpersonal Interaction and Influence

The socio-psychological tradition epitomizes the scientific or objective perspective described in Chapter 2. Scholars in this tradition believe there are communication truths that can be discovered by careful, systematic observation. They look for cause-and-effect relationships that will predict when a communication behavior will succeed and when it will fail. When they find such causal links, they are well on the way to answering the ever-present question of relationship and persuasion practitioners: *What can I do to get them to change?*

When researchers search for universal laws of communication, they try to focus on what *is* without being biased by their personal view of what *ought to be.* As empiricists, they heed the warning of the skeptical newspaper editor: "You think your mother loves you? Check it out—at least two sources." For communication theorists in the socio-psychological tradition, checking it out usually means designing and running a series of controlled experiments.

Psychologist Carl Hovland was one of the "founding fathers" of experimental research on the effects of communication.[6] Hovland headed up a group of 30 researchers at Yale University who sought to lay a "groundwork of empirical propositions concerning the relationships between communication stimuli, audience predisposition, and opinion change" and to provide "an initial framework for subsequent theory building."[7]

Attitude
A predisposition to respond, composed of beliefs, feelings, and intended actions.

Working within a framework of "*who* says *what* to *whom* and with what *effect*," the Yale Attitude Studies explored three separate causes of persuasive variation:

Who—source of the message (expertise, trustworthiness)

What—content of the message (fear appeals, order of arguments)

Whom—audience characteristics (personality, susceptibility to influence)

The main *effect* they measured was opinion change as revealed by attitude scales given before and after the message. Although the Yale researchers plowed new ground in many areas, their work on source credibility attracted the most interest.

Source credibility
Audience perception of the competence and trustworthiness of a speaker or writer.

Hovland and his colleagues discovered that a message from a high-credibility source produced large shifts in opinion compared to the same message coming from a low-credibility source. For example, an article on cures for the common cold carried more weight when it was attributed to a doctor writing in the *New England Journal of Medicine* than when it was attributed to a staff reporter from *Life* magazine. Once this overall effect was firmly established, they began to test specific variables, one by one.

The Yale researchers found two types of credibility—*expertness* and *character.* Experts were those who seemed to know what they were talking about; audiences judged character on the basis of perceived sincerity. Expertness turned out to be more important than character in boosting opinion change, but the persuasive effects didn't last. Within a few weeks the difference between high- and low-credibility sources disappeared. Hovland and his colleagues found that, over time, people forget where they heard or read about an idea. By reestablishing a link between the source and the message, credibility would still make a significant difference. In terms of generating theory, the socio-psychological tradition is by far the predominant of the seven traditions Craig names, and that disciplinary fact of life is reflected in the theories I discuss in the book. For example, the relational development, influence, media effects, and intercultural communication sections each feature three theories—11 of the 12 theories were crafted within the socio-psychological tradition.

THE CYBERNETIC TRADITION

Communication as a System of Information Processing

MIT scientist Norbert Wiener coined the word *cybernetics* to describe the field of artificial intelligence.[8] The term is a transliteration of the Greek word for "steersman" or "governor," and it illustrates the way feedback makes information processing possible in our heads and on our laptop computers. During World War II, Wiener developed an antiaircraft firing system that adjusted future trajectory by taking into account the results of past performance. His concept of feedback anchored the cybernetic tradition, which regards communication as the link connecting the separate parts of any system, such as a computer system, a family system, an organizational system, or a media system. Theorists in the cybernetic tradition seek to answer the question *How can we get the bugs out of this system?*

Cybernetics
The study of information processing, feedback, and control in communication systems.

The idea of communication as information processing was firmly established by Claude Shannon, a Bell Telephone Company research scientist who developed a mathematical theory of signal transmission. His goal was to get maximum line capacity with minimum distortion. Shannon showed little interest in the meaning of a message or its effect on the listener. His theory merely aimed at solving the technical problems of high-fidelity transfer of sound.

Since Bell Laboratories paid the bill for Shannon's research, it seems only fair to use a telephone call you might make to explain his model, shown in Figure 4–1. Shannon would see you as the information source. You speak your message into

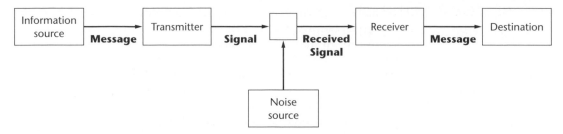

FIGURE 4–1   Shannon and Weaver's Model of Communication
Adapted from Shannon and Weaver, *The Mathematical Theory of Communication*

the telephone mouthpiece, which transmits a signal through the telephone-wire channel. The received signal has picked up static noise along the way, and this altered signal is reconverted to sound by the receiver in the earpiece at the destination. Information loss occurs every step of the way, so that the message received differs from the one you sent. The ultimate aim of information theory is to maximize the amount of information the system can carry.

Information

The reduction of uncertainty; the less predictable a message is, the more information it carries.

Most of us are comfortable with the notion that information is simply "stuff that matters or anything that makes a difference."[9] For Shannon, however, *information* refers to the reduction of uncertainty. The amount of information a message contains is measured by how much it combats chaos. If you phone home and tell your family that you've just accepted a public relations internship in Chicago for the summer, you've conveyed lots of information because your message reduces a great amount of your folks' uncertainty about your immediate future. The less predictable the message, the more information it carries. There are, however, many fine things that can be said over a communication channel that don't qualify as information. Perhaps your phone call is merely an "I just called to say I love you" reminder. If the person on the other end has no doubt of your love, the words are warm ritual rather than information. When the destination party already knows what's coming, information is zero.

Noise is the enemy of information because it cuts into the information-carrying capacity of the channel between the transmitter and the receiver. Shannon describes the relationship with a simple equation:[10]

$$\text{Channel Capacity} = \text{Information} + \text{Noise}$$

Every channel has an upper limit on the information it can carry. Even if you resort to a fast-talking monologue, a three-minute telephone call restricts you to using a maximum of 600 words. But noise on the line, surrounding distractions, and static in the mind of your listener all suggest that you should devote a portion of the channel capacity to repeating key ideas that might otherwise be lost. Without a great amount of reiteration, restatement, and redundancy, a noisy channel is quickly overloaded. On the other hand, needless duplication is boring for the listener and wastes channel capacity. Shannon regards communication as the applied science of maintaining an optimal balance between predictability and uncertainty. His theory of signal transmission is an engineer's response to everyday problems of technical glitches, system overloads, and equipment failure. Therefore, its usefulness in describing face-to-face communication is questionable.

THE RHETORICAL TRADITION

Communication as Artful Public Address

Greco-Roman rhetoric was the main source of wisdom about communication well into the twentieth century. In the fourth century B.C., Demosthenes raged against the sea with pebbles in his mouth in order to improve his articulation when he spoke in the Athenian assembly. A few hundred years later, Roman statesman Cicero refined and applied a system for discovering the key issue in any legal case. In 1963 Martin Luther King, Jr., crafted his moving "I Have a Dream" speech using such stylistic devices as visual depiction, repetition, alliteration, and metaphor. These three men, and thousands like them, perpetuated the Greco-Roman tradition of oratory that began with the Sophists in the ancient city-states of the Mediterranean and continues today. Whether talking to a crowd, a legislative assembly, a jury, or a single judge, orators seek practical advice on how to best present their case.

Rhetoric
The art of using all available means of persuasion, focusing upon lines of argument, organization of ideas, language use, and delivery in public speaking.

There are a half-dozen features that characterize this influential tradition of rhetorical communication:

- A conviction that speech distinguishes humans from other animals. Of oral communication, Cicero asks: "What other power could have been strong enough either to gather scattered humanity into one place, or to lead it out of its brutish existence in the wilderness up to our present condition of citizens, or, after the establishment of social communities, to give shape to laws, tribunals, and civic rights?"[11]

- A confidence that public address delivered in a democratic forum is a more effective way to solve political problems than rule by decree or resorting to force. Within this tradition, the phrase "mere rhetoric" is a contradiction in terms.

- A setting where a single speaker attempts to influence an audience of many listeners through explicitly persuasive discourse. Public speaking is essentially one-way communication.

- Oratorical training as the cornerstone of a leader's education. Speakers learn to develop strong arguments and powerful voices that carry to the edge of a crowd without electronic amplification.

- An emphasis on the power and beauty of language to move people emotionally and stir them to action. Rhetoric is more art than science.

- Oral public persuasion as the province of males. Until the 1800s, women had virtually no opportunity to have their voices heard. So a key feature of the women's movement in America has been the struggle for the right to speak in public.

Within the rhetorical tradition, there has been an ongoing tension in regard to the relative value of study and practice in the development of effective public speakers. Some speech coaches believe there is no substitute for honing skills before an audience. "Practice makes perfect," they say. Other teachers insist that practice merely makes permanent. If speakers don't learn from the systematic advice of Aristotle (see Chapter 21) and others in the Greco-Roman tradition, they are doomed to repeat the same mistakes whenever they speak. The fact that this debate continues suggests that both factors play an important role in artful public address.

THE SEMIOTIC TRADITION

Communication as the Process of Sharing Meaning Through Signs

Semiotics
The study of verbal and nonverbal signs that can stand for something else, and how their interpretation impacts society.

Symbols
Arbitrary words and nonverbal signs that bear no natural connection with the things they describe; their meaning is learned within a given culture.

Semiotics is the study of signs. A *sign* is anything that can stand for something else. High body temperature is a <u>sign</u> of infection. Birds flying south <u>signal</u> the coming of winter. A white cane <u>signifies</u> blindness. An arrow <u>designates</u> which direction to go.

Words are also signs, but of a special kind. They are *symbols*. Unlike the examples I've just cited, most symbols have no natural connection with the things they describe. There's nothing in the sound of the word *kiss* or anything visual in the letters *h-u-g* that signifies an embrace. One could just as easily coin the term *snarf* or *clag* to symbolize a close encounter of the romantic kind. The same thing is true for nonverbal symbols like *winks* or *waves*. Most theorists grounded in the semiotic tradition are trying to explain and reduce the misunderstanding created by the use of ambiguous symbols.

Cambridge University literary critic I. A. Richards was one of the first in the semiotic tradition to systematically describe how words work. According to Richards, words are arbitrary symbols that have no inherent meaning. Like chameleons that take on the coloration of their environment, words take on the meaning of the context in which they are used. He therefore railed against the semantic trap that he labeled "the proper meaning superstition"—the mistaken belief that words have a precise definition. For Richards and other semiologists, meanings don't reside in words or other symbols; meanings reside in people.

Together with his British colleague C. K. Ogden, Richards created his semantic triangle to show the indirect relationship between symbols and their supposed referents. Figure 4–2 illustrates the iffy link between the word *dog* and the actual hound that may consume the majority of your groceries.

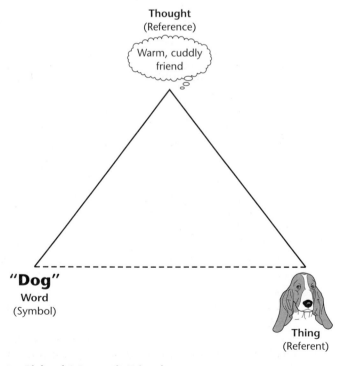

FIGURE 4–2   Richards' Semantic Triangle
Adapted from Ogden and Richards, *The Meaning of Meaning*

The top of the semantic triangle shows some thoughts that you might have when observing the Hush Puppy pictured at the lower right. Once you perceive the actual animal, thoughts of warmth and faithful friendship fill your mind. Since there is a direct or causal relationship between the referent and the reference, Richards connected the two with a solid line.

Your thoughts are also directly linked with the *dog* symbol at the lower left of the triangle. Based on childhood language learning, using the word *dog* to symbolize your thoughts is quite natural. Richards diagrammed this causal relationship with a solid line as well.

But the connection between the word *dog* and the actual animal is tenuous at best. Richards represented it with a dotted line. Two people could use that identical word to stand for completely different beasts. When you say *dog*, you might mean a slow-moving, gentle pet who is very fond of children. When I use the word, I might mean a carnivorous canine who bites anyone—and is very fond of children. (Note the slippery use of the term *fond* in this example.) Unless we both understand that ambiguity is an inevitable condition of language, you and I are liable to carry on a conversation about dogs without ever realizing that we're talking about two very different breeds.

Although Richards and Ferdinand de Saussure (the man who coined the term *semiology*) were fascinated with language, many researchers in the semiotic tradition focus on nonverbal emblems and pictorial images. For example, French semiologist Roland Barthes analyzed the emotional and ideological meanings created by print and broadcast media (see Chapter 25). But whether the signs are a few pictures or thousands of words, scholars in this tradition are concerned with the way signs mediate meaning, and how they might be used to avoid misunderstanding rather than create it.

THE SOCIO-CULTURAL TRADITION

Communication as the Creation and Enactment of Social Reality

The socio-cultural tradition is based on the premise that as people talk, they produce and reproduce culture. Most of us assume that words reflect what actually exists. However, theorists in this tradition suggest that the process often works the other way around. Our view of reality is strongly shaped by the language we've used since we were infants.

We've already seen that the semiotic tradition holds that most words have no necessary or logical connection with the ideas they represent. For example, the link between black marks on a page that spell **g-r-e-e-n** and the color of the lawn in front of the library is merely a convention among English-speaking people. Although socio-cultural theorists agree that the term *green* is arbitrary, they also claim that the ability to *see* green as a distinct color depends on having a specific word to label the 510–560 nanometer band of the electromagnetic wave spectrum.[12] English offers such a word, but many Native American languages don't. Within these cultures, yellow is described as merging directly into blue. We might be tempted to label these speakers "color-blind," yet they really aren't. Linguists in the socio-cultural tradition would say that these language users inhabit a different world.

University of Chicago linguist Edward Sapir and his student Benjamin Lee Whorf were pioneers in the socio-cultural tradition. The Sapir–Whorf hypothesis of linguistic relativity states that the structure of a culture's language shapes what people think and do.[13] "The 'real world' is to a large extent unconsciously built

Sapir-Whorf hypothesis of linguistic relativity
The claim that the structure of a language shapes what people think and do; the social construction of reality.

upon the language habits of the group."[14] Their theory of linguistic relativity counters the assumptions that all languages are similar and that words merely act as neutral vehicles to carry meaning.

Consider the second-person singular pronoun that English speakers use to address another person. No matter what the relationship, Americans use the word *you*. German speakers are forced to label the relationship as either formal (*Sie*) or familiar (*du*). They even have a ceremony (*Bruderschaft*) to celebrate a shift in relationship from *Sie* to *du*. Japanese vocabulary compels a speaker to recognize many more relational distinctions. That language offers 10 alternatives—all translated "you" in English—yet only one term is proper in any given relationship, depending on the gender, age, and status of the speaker.

While most observers assume that English, German, and Japanese vocabularies *reflect* cultural differences in relationship patterns, the Sapir–Whorf hypothesis suggests that it works the other way around as well. Language actually structures our perception of reality. As children learn to talk, they also learn what to look for. Most of the world goes unnoticed because it is literally *unremarkable*.

Contemporary socio-cultural theorists claim that it is through the process of communication that "reality is produced, maintained, repaired, and transformed."[15] Or stated in the active voice, *persons-in-conversation co-construct their own social worlds*.[16] When these perceptual worlds collide, the socio-cultural tradition offers help in bridging the culture gap that exists between "us" and "them."

THE CRITICAL TRADITION

Communication as a Reflective Challenge of Unjust Discourse

The term *critical theory* comes from the work of a group of German scholars known as the "Frankfurt School" because they were part of the independent Institute for Social Research at Frankfurt University. Originally set up to test the ideas of Karl Marx, the Frankfurt School rejected the economic determinism of orthodox Marxism yet carried on the Marxist tradition of critiquing society.

The leading figures of the Frankfurt School—Max Horkheimer, Theodor Adorno, and Herbert Marcuse—were convinced that "all previous history has been characterized by an unjust distribution of suffering."[17] They spotted the same pattern of inequality in modern Western democracies where the "haves" continued to exploit the "have nots." Frankfurt School researchers offered thoughtful analyses of discrepancies between the liberal values of freedom and equality that leaders proclaimed and the unjust concentrations and abuses of power that made those values a myth. These critiques offered no apology for their negative tone or pessimistic conclusions. As Marcuse noted, "Critical theory preserves obstinacy as a genuine quality of philosophical thought."[18] When Hitler came to power in Germany, that obstinacy forced the Frankfurt School into exile—first to Switzerland, then to the United States.

What types of communication research and practice are critical theorists *against?* Although there is no single set of abuses that all denounce, critical theorists consistently challenge three features of contemporary society:

1. *The control of language to perpetuate power imbalances.* Critical theorists condemn any use of words that inhibits emancipation. For example, feminist scholars point out that women tend to be a muted group because men are the gatekeepers of language. The resultant public discourse is shot through with metaphors drawn from war and sports—traditionally masculine arenas with their own in-group lingo. This concept of muted groups is not new. Marcuse claimed that "the avenues of entrance are closed to the meaning of words and ideas other than the established one—established by the publicity of the powers that be, and verified in their practices."[19]

2. *The role of mass media in dulling sensitivity to repression.* Marx claimed that religion was the opiate of the masses, distracting working-class audiences from their "real" interests. Critical theorists see the "culture industries" of television, film, CDs, and print media as taking over that role. Adorno was hopeful that people might rise in protest once they realized their unjust repression. Yet he noted that "with populations becoming increasingly subject to the power of mass communications, the pre-formation of people's minds has increased to a degree that scarcely allows room for an awareness of it on the part of the people themselves."[20] Marcuse was even more pessimistic about social change coming from the average citizen who is numbed by the mass media. He claimed that hope for change in society comes from "the outcasts and outsiders, the exploited and persecuted of other races and other colors, the unemployed and the unemployable."[21]

3. *Blind reliance on the scientific method and uncritical acceptance of empirical findings.* Horkheimer claimed that "it is naïve and bigoted to think and speak only in the language of science."[22] *Naïve* because science is not the value-free pursuit of knowledge that it claims to be. *Bigoted* because survey researchers assume that a sample of public opinion is a true slice of reality. Adorno contends that "the cross-section of attitudes represents, not an approximation to the truth, but a cross-section of social illusion."[23] These theorists are particularly critical of leaders in government, business, and education who use the empirical trappings of social science to validate an unjust status quo—to "bless the mess" that obviously favors them.

Critical theorists are less specific about what they are *for.* Their essays are filled with calls for liberation, emancipation, transformation, and consciousness raising, but they are often vague on how to achieve these worthy goals. They do, however, share a common ethical agenda that considers solidarity with suffering human beings as our minimal moral responsibility. That's why Adorno declared, "To write poetry after Auschwitz is barbaric."[24] Most critical theorists hope to move beyond feelings of sympathy and stimulate *praxis,* a term Craig defines as "theoretically reflective social action."[25]

Culture industries
Entertainment businesses that reproduce the dominant ideology of a culture and distract people from recognizing unjust distribution of power within society; e.g., film, television, music, and advertising.

THE PHENOMENOLOGICAL TRADITION

Communication as the Experience of Self and Others Through Dialogue

Although *phenomenology* is an imposing philosophical term, it basically refers to the intentional analysis of everyday life from the standpoint of the person who is living it. Thus, the phenomenological tradition places great emphasis on people's perception and interpretation of their own subjective experience. For the phenomenologist, an individual's story is more important—and more authoritative—than any research hypothesis or communication axiom. As psychologist Carl Rogers asserts, "Neither the Bible nor the prophets—neither Freud nor research—neither the revelations of God nor man—can take precedence over my own direct experience."[26]

The problem, of course, is that no two people have the same life story. Since we cannot experience another person's experience, we tend to talk past each other and then lament, "Nobody understands what it's like to be me." Can two

Phenomenology
Intentional analysis of everyday experience from the standpoint of the person who is living it; explores the possibility of understanding the experience of self and others.

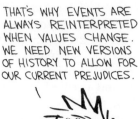

people get beyond surface impressions and connect at a deeper level? Based on years of nondirective counseling experience, Carl Rogers was confident that personal and relational growth is indeed possible.

Rogers believed that his clients' health improved when his communication created a safe environment for them to talk. He described three necessary and sufficient conditions for personality and relationship change. If clients perceived a counselor's (1) congruence, (2) unconditional positive regard, and (3) empathic understanding, they could and would get better.[27]

Congruence is the match or fit between an individual's inner feelings and outer display. The congruent counselor is genuine, real, integrated, whole, transparent. The noncongruent person tries to impress, plays a role, puts up a front, hides behind a facade. "In my relationship with persons," Rogers wrote, "I've found that it does not help, in the long run, to act as though I was something I was not."[28]

Unconditional positive regard is an attitude of acceptance that isn't contingent on performance. Rogers asked, "Can I let myself experience positive attitudes toward this other person—attitudes of warmth, caring, liking, interest, and respect?"[29] When the answer was *yes*, both he and his clients matured as human beings. They also liked each other.

Empathic understanding is the caring skill of temporarily laying aside our views and values and entering into another's world without prejudice. It is an active process of seeking to hear the other's thoughts, feelings, tones, and meanings as if they were our own. Rogers thought it was a waste of time to be suspicious or to wonder, *What does she really mean?* He believed that we help people most when we accept what they say at face value. We should assume that they describe their world as it really appears to them.

Although Rogers' necessary and sufficient conditions emerged in a therapeutic setting, he was certain that they were equally important in all interpersonal relationships. Jewish philosopher and theologian Martin Buber reached a similar conclusion. He held out the possibility of authentic human relationships through dialogue—an intentional process in which the only agenda both parties have is to understand what it's like to be the other. The ideas of Rogers, Buber, and others in the phenomenological tradition have permeated the textbooks and teaching of interpersonal communication. They offer their theories to answer two

Congruence
The match between an individual's inner feelings and outer display; authenticity, genuineness.

questions: *Why is it so difficult to establish and sustain authentic human relationships? How can this be done?*

FENCING THE FIELD OF COMMUNICATION THEORY

The seven traditions I've described have deep roots in the field of communication theory. Team loyalties run strong, so theorists, researchers, and practitioners working within one tradition often hear criticism from those in other traditions that their particular approach has no legitimacy. In addition to whatever arguments each group might muster to defend their choice, they can also claim "squatters' rights" because scholars who went before had already established the right to occupy that portion of land. Taking the real estate metaphor seriously, in Figure 4–3 I've charted the seven traditions as equal-area parcels of land that collectively make up the larger field of study. A few explanations are in order.

First, it's important to realize that the location of each tradition on the map is far from random. My rationale for placing them where they are is based on the distinction between objective and interpretive theories that was outlined in Chapter 2. According to the scientific assumptions presented in that chapter, the socio-psychological tradition is the most objective, and so it occupies the far left position on the map—solidly rooted in objective territory. Moving across the map from left to right, the traditions become more interpretive and less objective. I see the phenomenological tradition as the most subjective, and so it occupies the position farthest to the right—firmly grounded in interpretive territory. The order of presentation in this chapter followed the same progression—a gradual shift from objective to interpretive concerns. Scholars working in adjacent traditions usually have an easier time appreciating each others' work. On the map they share a common border. Professionally, they are closer together in their basic assumptions.

Second, hybrids are possible across traditions. You've seen throughout this chapter that each tradition has its own way of defining communication and its

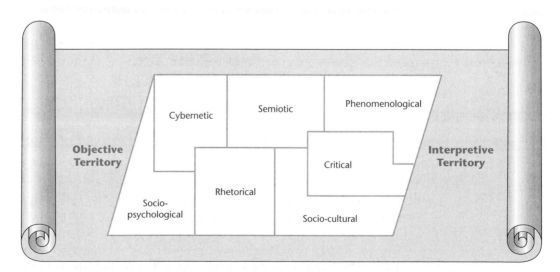

FIGURE 4–3   A Survey Map of Traditions in the Field of Communication Theory

own distinct vocabulary. Thus, it's fair to think of the dividing lines on the map as fences built to keep out strange ideas. Scholars, however, are an independent bunch. They climb fences, read journals, and fly to faraway conferences. This cross-pollination sometimes results in theory grounded in two or three traditions.

Finally, the seven charted traditions might not cover every approach to communication theory. Craig recently suggested the possibility of a *pragmatist tradition*—a pluralistic land where different perspectives on truth could all be legitimate in different ways. He pictures it as a tradition that "orients to practical problems, and evaluates ideas according to their usefulness rather than by an absolute standard of truth."[30] It would be a location where he sees his own work fitting in well. Craig's openness to considering new territories leads me to offer a quite different stream of theory running through the field of communication. My candidate is an *ethical tradition*.

Pragmatism
An applied approach to knowledge; the philosophy that true understanding of an idea or situation has practical implications for action.

THE ETHICAL TRADITION

Communication as People of Character Interacting in Just and Beneficial Ways

More than most academic disciplines, the field of communication has been concerned with ethical responsibility. Since the time of Plato and Aristotle, communication scholars have grappled with the obligations that go along with the opportunities we have to communicate. Contemporary discussions of morality are increasingly beleaguered by the rise of ethical relativism.[31] Yet despite the postmodern challenge to all claims of Truth, the National Communication Association (NCA) recently adopted a "Credo for Communication Ethics" (see Appendix C).[32] Like most attempts to deal with communication ethics, it addresses the problem of what is ethical and starts with the issue of honesty versus lying. I'll cite three of the creed's nine principles in order to illustrate the major streams of thought within the ethical tradition:[33]

1. *We advocate truthfulness, accuracy, honesty, and reason as essential to the integrity of communication.* This principle centers on the *rightness* or *wrongness* of a communication act regardless of whether it benefits the people involved. It speaks to questions of *obligation*. Is it *legitimate* to use emotional appeals to short-circuit rational thought? Is falsehood *fair* or *just*? Is it always our *duty* to be honest?

2. *We accept responsibility for the short- and long-term consequences of our own communication and expect the same of others.* This principle is concerned with the *good* or *bad* results that our words produce. It raises questions of *outcomes*. Do our words *benefit* or *harm* people? Can a lie promote *well-being* or prevent *injury*?

3. *We strive to understand and respect other communicators before evaluating and responding to their messages.* This principle focuses on the *character* of communicators rather than the act of communication. It bids all of us to look at our *motives* and *attitudes*. Do I *value* the other as a fellow human being? Do I have the *courage* to try to see the world through his or her eyes? Do I seek to be a person of *integrity* and *virtue*?

These are difficult questions to answer, and some readers might suggest that they have no place in a communication theory text. But to deal with human intercourse as a mechanical process separate from values would be like discussing sex using ground rules that prohibit any reference to love. And within the ethical tradition, communication theorists do offer answers to these questions. Many of these theorists come out of the rhetorical or critical traditions. Others are spread across the objective-interpretive landscape I've drawn in Figure 4–3, so I won't try to locate the ethical tradition in any single spot. I have, however, encapsuled the thoughts of a dozen ethical theorists into 12 brief summary statements. I refer to them as *ethical reflections* and place each one alongside a theory with which it naturally resonates.

With or without my addition of an ethical tradition, Craig's framework can help make sense of the great diversity in the field of communication theory. As you read about a theory in the section on media effects, remember that it may have the same ancestry as a theory you studied earlier in the section on relationship development. On the first page of the next 31 chapters, I'll tie each theory to one or more traditions. Hopefully this label will make it easier for you to understand why the theorist has made the choices he or she has made. After four chapters of introduction and integration, let's begin.

QUESTIONS TO SHARPEN YOUR FOCUS

1. Considering the differences between *objective* and *interpretive* theory, can you make a case that the *rhetorical* tradition is less objective than the *semiotic* one or that the *socio-cultural* tradition is more interpretive than the *critical* one?

2. Suppose you and your best friend have recently been on an emotional rollercoaster. Which of the seven highlighted *definitions of communication* offer the most promise of helping you achieve a stable relationship? Why?

3. Craig characterizes communication as a *practical discipline*. What kind of communication problems would the *socio-psychological* tradition help resolve? The *cybernetic* tradition? The *phenomenological* tradition?

4. The map in Figure 4–3 represents seven traditions in the field of communication theory. In which region do you feel most at home? What other areas would you like to explore? Where would you be uncomfortable? Why?

A SECOND LOOK

Recommended resource: Robert T. Craig, "Communication Theory as a Field," *Communication Theory,* Vol. 9, 1999, pp. 119–161.

Communication as a practical discipline: Robert T. Craig, "Communication as a Practical Discipline," in *Rethinking Communication,* Vol. 1, Brenda Dervin, Lawrence Grossberg, Barbara O'Keefe, and Ellen Wartella (eds.), Sage, Newbury Park, CA, 1989, pp. 97–122.

Anthology of primary resources for each tradition: Heidi L. Muller and Robert T. Craig (eds.) *Theorizing Communication: Readings Across Traditions,* Sage, Los Angeles, 2007.

Socio-psychological tradition: Carl Hovland, Irving Janis, and Harold Kelley, *Communication and Persuasion,* Yale University, New Haven, CT, 1953, pp. 1–55.

Cybernetic tradition: Norbert Wiener, *The Human Use of Human Beings,* Avon, New York, 1967, pp. 23–100.

Rhetorical tradition: Thomas M. Conley, *Rhetoric in the European Tradition,* Longman, New York, 1990, pp. 1–52.

Semiotic tradition: C. K. Ogden and I. A. Richards, *The Meaning of Meaning,* Harcourt, Brace & World, New York, 1946, pp. 1–23.

Phenomenological tradition: Carl Rogers, "The Characteristics of a Helping Relationship," *On Becoming a Person*, 1961, pp. 39–58.

Socio-cultural tradition: Benjamin Lee Whorf, "The Relation of Habitual Thought and Behaviour to Language," in *Language, Culture, and Personality: Essays in Memory of Edward Sapir*, University of Utah, Salt Lake City, 1941, pp. 123–149.

Critical tradition: Raymond Morrow with David Brown, *Critical Theory and Methodology*, Sage, Thousand Oaks, CA, 1994, pp. 3–34, 85–112.

Ethical tradition: Richard L. Johannesen, "Communication Ethics: Centrality, Trends, and Controversies," in *Communication Yearbook 25*, William B. Gudykunst (ed.), Lawrence Erlbaum, Mahwah, NJ, 2001, pp. 201–235.

Critique of Craig's model and his response: David Myers, "A Pox on All Compromises: Reply to Craig (1999)," and Robert T. Craig, "Minding My Metamodel, Mending Myers," *Communication Theory*, Vol. 11, 2001, pp. 218–230, 231–240.

For full-chapter treatments of Shannon's information theory,
Richards' meaning of meaning, and Rogers' existential approach,
go to the theory archive section of
www.afirstlook.com.

DIVISION TWO

Interpersonal Communication

Communication theorists often use the image of a game to describe interpersonal communication. Various scholars refer to *language games, rules of the game, game-like behavior,* and even *game theory.* Most of us have played games of all sorts since we were kids, so I'll use three specific game metaphors to illustrate what interpersonal communication *is,* and what it *is not.*[1]

Communication as Bowling The bowling model of message delivery is likely the most widely held view of communication. I think that's unfortunate.

This model sees the bowler as the sender. He or she addresses the pins (the target audience). The bowler then delivers the ball, which is the message. As it rolls down the lane (the channel), clutter on the boards (noise) may deflect the ball (the message). Yet if it is aimed well, the ball strikes the passive pins (the audience) with a predictable effect.

In this one-way model of communication, the speaker (bowler) must take care to select a precisely crafted message (ball) and practice diligently to deliver it the same way every time. Of course, that makes sense only if target listeners are interchangeable, static pins waiting to be bowled over by our words—which they aren't. Communication theory that emphasizes message content to the neglect of relational factors simply isn't realistic.

The bowling analogy also fails because the pins don't roll the ball back at the bowler. Real-life interpersonal communication is sometimes confusing, is often unpredictable, and always involves more than just the speaker's action. This realization has led some observers to propose an interactive model for interpersonal communication.

Communication as Ping-Pong Unlike bowling, Ping-Pong is not a solo game. This fact alone makes it a better analogy for interpersonal communication. One party puts the conversational ball in play, and the other gets into position to receive. It takes more concentration and skill to receive than to serve because while the speaker (server) knows where the message is going, the listener (receiver) doesn't. Like a verbal or nonverbal message, the ball may appear straightforward yet have a deceptive spin.

Ping-Pong is a back-and-forth game; players switch roles continuously. One moment the person holding the paddle is an initiator; the next second the same player is a responder, gauging the effectiveness of his or her shot by the way the ball comes back. The repeated adjustment essential for good play closely parallels the feedback process described in a number of interpersonal communication theories. There are, however, three inherent flaws in the table-tennis analogy.

In the first place, Ping-Pong is played in a controlled environment where the platform is stable, the bounce is true, and the ball is not deflected by the wind. In contrast, most face-to-face communication occurs in a storm of distraction.

The second defect is that the game is played with one ball, which at any given time is headed in a single direction. A true model of interpersonal encounters would have people sending and receiving balls at the same time.

The third problem is that table tennis is a competitive game—someone wins and someone loses. In successful dialogue, both people win.

Communication as Charades   The game of charades better captures the simultaneous and cooperative nature of interpersonal communication. A charade is neither an action, like bowling a strike, nor an interaction, like a rally in Ping-Pong. It's a *transaction*.

Charades is a mutual game. Although a team of two or more may compete against others, the actual play is cooperative. One member draws a title or slogan from a batch of possibilities and then tries to act it out visually for teammates in a silent minidrama. The goal is to get at least one partner to say the exact words that are on the slip of paper. Of course, the actor is prohibited from talking out loud.

Suppose you drew the saying "God helps those who help themselves." That sentiment might not square with your idea of "amazing grace," but that's not the point. Your job is to create mental pictures for others that will cause them to utter those identical words. For *God* you might try folding your hands and gazing upward. For *helps* you could act out offering a helping hand or giving a leg-up boost over a fence. By pointing at a number of real or imaginary people you may elicit a response of *them*, and by this point a partner may shout out, "God helps those who help themselves." Success.

Like charades, interpersonal communication is a mutual, ongoing process using verbal and nonverbal messages with another person to create and alter

the images in both of our minds. Communication between us begins when there is some overlap between two images, and is effective to the extent that overlap increases. But even if our mental pictures were congruent, communication would be partial as long as we interpreted them differently. The idea that "God helps those who help themselves" could strike one person as a hollow promise, while the other might regard it as a divine stamp of approval for hard work.

All four theories in the following section reject a simplistic, one-way bowling analogy and an interactive Ping-Pong model of interpersonal communication. Instead, they view interpersonal communication in a way more akin to charades—a complex transaction in which overlapping messages simultaneously affect and are affected by the other person and other multiple factors.

Chapter 5 presents George Herbert Mead's *symbolic interactionism*, a wide-ranging theory that links language with meaning, thinking, self-concept, and society. Mead regarded the ability to communicate with words as the essence of being human. He was interested in the way we attach labels to people and their actions—especially our own.

Similar to Mead, Barnett Pearce and Vernon Cronen believe that through communication, people create their own social reality. Chapter 6 presents their theory entitled *coordinated management of meaning (CMM)*, which suggests that all of us use communication to coordinate our actions with the behavior of others and to make sense of that interaction.

Chapter 7 traces the development of Judee Burgoon's *expectancy violations theory*, which forecasts how others will respond when a communicator acts in inappropriate ways. Her early model included the surprising prediction that there are times when talking at a distance "too close" to or "too far" from another person may actually help you achieve a communication goal. She later expanded the theory to include a variety of nonverbal behaviors such as touch, eye contact, and facial expression, and she now uses it to explain the effects of verbal violations as well.

Chapter 8 describes Jesse Delia's *constructivism*, a cognitive theory of message production. Delia and his colleagues suggest that individual differences in cognitive complexity affect a person's ability to craft an effective message for a specific interpersonal audience. They believe that people who have this mental ability are better at understanding, informing, persuading, comforting, and entertaining others—valuable communication skills in a game of charades and the game of life.

Symbolic Interactionism

of George Herbert Mead

Jodie Foster received a best actress Oscar nomination for her 1994 portrayal of a backwoods Appalachian woman raised in almost total isolation. The film, *Nell*, covers a three-month period of the young woman's life immediately following the death of her mother.[1] Nell is discovered by Jerry Lovell, a small-town doctor who is quickly joined by Paula Olsen, a psychologist from a big-city university medical center. Both are appalled and fascinated by this grown-up "wild child" who cowers in terror and makes incomprehensible sounds.

Nell is based on the play *Idioglossia*, a Greek term meaning a personal or private language. As Jerry and Paula come to realize, Nell's speech is not gibberish. Her language is based on the King James Version of the Bible, which her mother read to her out loud for over 20 years. Yet because the mother had suffered a stroke that left one side of her face paralyzed, the words Nell learned were unintelligible to anyone else.

Early in the film Paula labels Nell "autistic" and tries to have her committed to a psych ward for observation. Jerry, on the other hand, treats Nell as a frightened human being and tries to get to know her by learning her language. Although fiction, the movie is an intriguing story about the civilizing influence of language. As such, it could easily have been scripted by a symbolic interactionist. I'll use scenes from the film to illustrate the key ideas of George Herbert Mead, his student Herbert Blumer, and others who adopt an interactionist approach.

Mead was a philosophy professor at the University of Chicago for the first three decades of the twentieth century. As a close personal friend of renowned pragmatist John Dewey, he shared Dewey's applied approach to knowledge. Mead thought that the true test of any theory is whether it is useful in solving complex social problems. He was a social activist who marched for women's suffrage, championed labor unions in an era of robber-baron capitalism, and helped launch the urban settlement house movement with pioneer social worker Jane Addams.

Although Mead taught in a philosophy department, he is best known by sociologists as the teacher who trained a generation of the best minds in their field. Strangely, he never set forth his wide-ranging ideas in a book or systematic treatise. After he died in 1931, his students pulled together class notes and conversations with their mentor and published *Mind, Self, and Society* in his name. It was only then that his chief disciple, Herbert Blumer at the University of

Symbolic interaction
Communication through symbols; people talking to each other.

California, Berkeley, coined the term *symbolic interactionism*. The words capture what Mead claimed is the most human and humanizing activity that people can engage in—talking to each other.

Blumer stated three core principles of symbolic interactionism that deal with *meaning, language,* and *thought*.[2] These premises lead to conclusions about the creation of a person's *self* and socialization into a larger *community*. The rest of this chapter discusses these five related topics one by one. As you will see, all of these themes are prominent in the story of Nell.

MEANING: THE CONSTRUCTION OF SOCIAL REALITY

Blumer starts with the premise that *humans act toward people or things on the basis of the meanings they assign to those people or things.* The viewer of *Nell* can see this principle played out in the radically different responses that Jodie Foster's character elicits from the people she meets. The county sheriff regards Nell as crazy and suggests she be put in a padded cell. His chronically depressed wife sees Nell as a free spirit and joins her in a lighthearted game of patty-cake. The chief psychiatrist at the medical center views this child-of-the-wild case as a chance to make research history and insists the patient be brought to the center for study. And because a group of sleazy guys in a pool hall are convinced that Nell will mindlessly mimic any action she sees, they approach her as easy sexual prey. As for the doctor who found her, Jerry assumes Nell is fully human and seeks to become her friend. She in turn calls Jerry her guardian angel.

Which of these interpretations is correct? Who is the *real* Nell? From Mead's pragmatic standpoint, the answer doesn't make much difference. Once people define a situation as real, it's very real in its consequences.[3] And with the possible exception of Jerry, all of the people in the story initially regard Nell as totally other than themselves—an oddity to be explored or exploited.

In Jane Wagner's one-woman play *The Search for Signs of Intelligent Life in the Universe,* Trudy the bag lady views society from her perspective on the street. Her words underscore the interactionist position that meaning-making is a community project:

> It's my belief we all, at one time or another,
> secretly ask ourselves the question,
> "Am *I* crazy?"
> In my case, the answer came back: A resounding
> YES!

> You're thinkin': How does a person know if they're crazy or not? Well, sometimes you don't know. Sometimes you can go through life suspecting you *are* but never really knowing for sure. Sometimes you know for sure 'cause you got so many people tellin' you you're crazy that it's your word against everyone else's. . . .

> After all, what is reality anyway? Nothin' but a collective hunch.[4]

LANGUAGE: THE SOURCE OF MEANING

Blumer's second premise is that *meaning arises out of the social interaction that people have with each other.* In other words, meaning is not inherent in objects; it's not preexistent in a state of nature. Meaning is negotiated through the use of *language*—hence the term *symbolic interactionism.*

As human beings, we have the ability to name things. We can designate a specific object *(person)*, identify an action *(scream)*, or refer to an abstract idea *(crazy)*. Occasionally a word sounds like the thing it describes *(smack, thud, crash)*, but usually the names we use have no logical connection with the object at hand. Symbols are arbitrary signs. There's nothing inherently small, soft, or lovable in the word *kitten*.[5] It's only by talking with others—symbolic interaction—that we come to ascribe that meaning and develop a universe of discourse.

Mead believed that symbolic naming is the basis for human society. The book of Genesis in the Bible states that Adam's first task was to name the animals—the dawn of civilization.

Interactionists claim that the extent of knowing is dependent on the extent of naming. Although language can be a prison that confines us, we have the potential to push back the walls and bars as we master more words. You know from your experience of taking the SAT or ACT college entrance exams that half the questions center on linguistic aptitude. The construction of the test obviously reflects agreement with the interactionist claim that human intelligence is the ability to symbolically identify much of what we encounter. When Paula realizes the extent of Nell's personal vocabulary, she can no longer treat Nell as incompetent or ignorant.

But symbolic interaction is not just a means for intelligent expression; it's also the way we learn to interpret the world. A symbol is "a stimulus that has a learned meaning and value for people."[6] Consider the puzzle posed by the following story:

> A father and his son were driving to a ball game when their car stalled on the railroad tracks. In the distance a train whistle blew a warning. Frantically, the father tried to start the engine, but in his panic, he couldn't turn the key, and the car was hit by the onrushing train. An ambulance sped to the scene and picked them up. On the way to the hospital, the father died. The son was still alive but his condition was very serious, and he needed immediate surgery. The moment they arrived at the hospital, he was wheeled into an emergency operating room, and the surgeon came in, expecting a routine case. However, on seeing the boy the surgeon blanched and muttered, "I can't operate on this boy—he's my son."[7]

How can this be? How do you explain the surgeon's dilemma? If the answer isn't immediately obvious, I encourage you to close the book and think it through.

This puzzle is the opening paragraph of an article that appears in a fascinating book of readings that is my recommended resource for symbolic interactionism. Douglas Hofstadter, the man who poses the problem, is adamant that readers think it through until they figure out the answer. There's no doubt, he assures us, that we'll know it when we get it.

I first heard this puzzle in a slightly different form about a decade ago. I'm ashamed to admit that it took me a few minutes to figure out the answer. My chagrin is heightened by the fact that my doctor is the wife of a departmental colleague and my daughter-in-law is a physician as well. How could I have been taken in?

Hofstadter's answer to my question is that the words we use have *default assumptions*. Since the story contains no reference to the doctor's gender, and the majority of physicians in America are men, we'll likely assume that the surgeon in the story is male. While such an assumption may have some basis in fact, the subtle tyranny of symbols is that we usually don't consciously think about the mental jump we're making. Unless we're brought up short by some obvious glitch in our taken-for-granted logic, we'll probably conjure up a male figure every time we read or hear the word *surgeon*. What's more, we'll probably assume that the way we think things are is the way they ought to be. That's how most of the "normal" people in *Nell* operated. They labeled Nell *strange, weird,* or *deviant*—assuming that those who are different are also demented.

In the first paragraph of this chapter I introduced the main characters in the movie *Nell*. Other than the typical masculine spelling of Jerry Lovell's first name, I made no reference as to whether the doctor is a man or a woman. If you had heard the name rather than read it, would you have consciously held open the possibility that Jerry (or Geri) is female? If so, symbolic interactionists would say, "good for you."

THOUGHT: THE PROCESS OF TAKING THE ROLE OF THE OTHER

Minding
An inner dialogue used to test alternatives, rehearse actions, and anticipate reactions before responding; self-talk.

Blumer's third premise is that *an individual's interpretation of symbols is modified by his or her own thought processes.* Symbolic interactionists describe thinking as an inner conversation. Mead called this inner dialogue *minding.*

Minding is the pause that's reflective. It's the two-second delay while we mentally rehearse our next move, test alternatives, anticipate others' reactions. Mead says we don't need any encouragement to look before we leap. We naturally talk to ourselves in order to sort out the meaning of a difficult situation. But first, we need language. Before we can think, we must be able to interact symbolically.

Lion King and *Lassie* movies aside, Mead believed that animals act "instinctively" and "without deliberation."[8] They are unable to think reflectively because, with few exceptions, they are unable to communicate symbolically. The human animal comes equipped with a brain that is wired for thought. But that alone is not sufficient for thinking. Interactionists maintain that "humans require social stimulation and exposure to abstract symbol systems to embark upon conceptual thought processes that characterize our species."[9] Language is the software that activates the mind.

Throughout the first half of *Nell*, Jerry and Paula are hard-pressed to explain Nell's ability to reflect rather than merely react. They understand that Nell interacted with her mother but are puzzled as to how communication with a single reclusive and taciturn adult would offer the social stimulation that learning a language requires.[10] According to interactionist principles, there's no way that a person who has had almost zero human contact would be able to develop a language or think through her responses. Yet through cinematic flashbacks, viewers learn that Nell had a twin sister, who was her constant companion during her early childhood development. Until her sister died, Nell's life was rich in social stimulation, twin-speak, and shared meaning. As her past comes to light, Jerry and Paula gain an understanding of Nell's capacity to think. Symbolic interaction has activated cognitive processes that, once switched on, won't shut down.

Mead's greatest contribution to our understanding of the way we think is his notion that human beings have the unique capacity to *take the role of the other.* Early in life, kids role-play the activities of their parents, talk with imaginary friends, and take constant delight in pretending to be someone else. As adults, we continue to put ourselves in the place of others and act as they would act,

Taking the role of the other
The process of mentally imagining that you are someone else who is viewing you.

although the process may be less conscious. Mead was convinced that thought is the mental conversation we hold with others.

In Harper Lee's novel *To Kill a Mockingbird,* Scout stands on Boo Radley's porch and recalls her father's words, "you never really know a man until you stand in his shoes and walk around in them."[11] That's a clear statement of what symbolic interactionism means by role-taking. The young, impulsive girl takes the perspective of a painfully shy, emotionally fragile man. Note that she doesn't *become* him—that would be *Invasion of the Body Snatchers.* She does, however, look out at the world through his eyes. More than anything else, what she sees is herself.

THE SELF: REFLECTIONS IN A LOOKING GLASS

Looking-glass self
The mental self-image that results from taking the role of the other; the objective self; me.

Once we understand that *meaning, language,* and *thought* are tightly interconnected, we're able to grasp Mead's concept of the *self.* Mead dismissed the idea that we could get glimpses of who we are through introspection. He claimed, instead, that we paint our self-portrait with brush strokes that come from *taking the role of the other*—imagining how we look to another person. Interactionists call this mental image the *looking-glass self* and insist that it's socially constructed. Mead borrowed the phrase from sociologist Charles Cooley, who adapted it from a poem by Ralph Waldo Emerson. Emerson wrote that each close companion . . .

> Is to his friend a looking-glass
> Reflects his figure that doth pass.[12]

Symbolic interactionists are convinced that the self is a function of language. Without talk there would be no self-concept. "We are not born with senses of self. Rather, selves arise in interaction with others. I can only experience myself in relation to others; absent interaction with others, I cannot be a self—I cannot emerge as someone."[13] To the extent that we interact with new acquaintances or have novel conversations with significant others, the self is always in flux. We can only imagine the wrenching change in self-concept that a real-life Nell would experience when thrust into interviews with psychologists, reporters, and lawyers.

I
The spontaneous driving force that fosters all that is novel, unpredictable, and unorganized in the self.

According to Mead, the self is an ongoing process combining the "I" and the "me." The "I" is the spontaneous, driving force that fosters all that is novel, unpredictable, and unorganized in the self. For those of you intrigued with brain hemisphere research, the "I" is akin to right-brain creativity. Nell's dancelike movements that simulated trees blowing in the wind sprang from the "I" part of self. So did Jerry's spur-of-the-moment musical accompaniment. (Surely if he'd thought about it ahead of time, he'd have selected a song other than Willie Nelson's "Crazy.") When Paula goes ballistic over his lack of professionalism, he can only respond that sometimes people do things on impulse. Like Jerry, we know little about the "I" because it's forever elusive. Trying to examine the "I" part of the self is like viewing a snowflake through a lighted microscope. The very act causes it to vanish.

Me
The objective self; the image of self seen when one takes the role of the other.

The "me" is viewed as an object—the image of self seen in the looking glass of other people's reactions. Do you remember in grammar school how you learned to identify the personal pronoun *me* in a sentence as the *object* of a verb? Because of the role-taking capacity of the human race, we can stand outside our bodies and view ourselves as objects. This reflexive experience is like having the Goodyear blimp hover overhead, sending back video images of ourselves while

THREE-WAY MIRROR

It might be time to start thinking about a *little skirt*, dear.

Hey, honey! How about one of those Brazilian thong deals?

Seriously, Mom — who's going to be looking at *YOU?*

we act. Mead described the process this way: "If the 'I' speaks, the 'me' hears."[14] And "the 'I' of this moment is present in the 'me' of the next moment."[15]

An early turning point in the film comes when Jerry is with Nell in her cabin. She runs to a wardrobe mirror and reaches out to her reflected image and says, "May," a word Jerry understands to mean "me." She then pulls back and hugs herself while saying, "Tay," a word he interprets as "I." In the next scene, therapists viewing Paula's videotape of the sequence are impressed by this perfect case of Nell seeing her objective self as distinct from her subjective self. As a result of her actions, they have little doubt about Nell's humanity and sanity. She has an intact self.[16]

COMMUNITY: THE SOCIALIZING EFFECT OF OTHERS' EXPECTATIONS

If Nell's only human contacts were with her mother, her twin sister, and Jerry, her "me" would be formed by the reflected views of those three significant others. But once she leaves her remote mountain cabin, Nell plunges into a community of other people. In order to survive and thrive within that community,

Generalized other
The composite mental image a person has of his or her self based on community expectations and responses.

Nell needs to figure out what they are doing, what their actions mean, and what they expect of her. Mead and other symbolic interactionists refer to the composite mental image she puts together as her *generalized other.*

The generalized other is an organized set of information that the individual carries in her or his head about what the general expectation and attitudes of the social group are. We refer to this generalized other whenever we try to figure out how to behave or how to evaluate our behavior in a social situation. We take the position of the generalized other and assign meaning to ourselves and our actions.[17]

Unlike most sociologists, Mead saw the community as consisting of individual actors who make their own choices. Yet they align their actions with what others are doing to form health care systems, legal systems, economic systems, and all the other societal institutions that Nell soon encounters. It is unclear from *Mind, Self, and Society* whether Mead regarded the *generalized other* as (1) an overarching looking-glass self that we put together from the reflections we see in everyone we know or (2) the expectations of society that influence every conversation that takes place in people's minds. Either way, the generalized other shapes how we think and interact within the community.

To summarize, there is no "me" at birth. The "me" is formed only through continual symbolic interaction—first with family, next with playmates, then in institutions such as schools. As the generalized other develops, this imaginary composite person becomes the conversational partner in an ongoing mental dialogue. In this way, kids participate in their own socialization. The child gradually acquires the roles of those in the surrounding community. Mead would have us think of the "me" as the organized community within the individual.

Although *Nell* consistently portrays Mead's interactionist concepts, there's one discordant note at the end of the film. The final scene shows Nell five years later with the people she first met. Nell has obviously changed their lives. For example, Jerry and Paula are now married and have a daughter, who reminds the viewer of Nell as a child. The sheriff's wife is no longer depressed, and she attributes her transformation to Nell. Despite the fact that Nell has been thrust into a wider world of lawyers, reporters, and salesclerks who label her behavior as deviant and insist that she conform to societal roles, she seems strangely unaffected by their judgment or expectations. The character that Jodie Foster plays radiates an inner peace and contentment. The community in the form of her generalized other has not held sway. Of course, symbolic interactionists would remind us that the story of Nell is fiction.

A SAMPLER OF APPLIED SYMBOLIC INTERACTION

Since Mead believed that a theory is valuable to the extent that it is useful, I've pulled together six separate applications of symbolic interactionism. Not only will this provide a taste of the practical insights the theory has generated, it will give you a chance to review some of the theoretical ideas covered in the chapter.

Creating Reality. Shakespeare wrote, "All the world's a stage, and all the men and women merely players."[18] In his book *The Presentation of Self in Everyday Life,* University of California, Berkeley, sociologist Erving Goffman develops the metaphor of social interaction as a dramaturgical performance.[19] Goffman claims that we are all involved in a constant negotiation with others to publicly define our identity and the nature of the situation. He warns that "the impression of reality fostered by a performance is a delicate, fragile thing that can be shattered by minor mishaps."[20] His colleague, Joan Emerson, outlines the cooperative effort required to sustain the definition of a gynecological exam as a routine medical procedure.[21] The doctor and nurse enact their roles in a medical setting to assure patients that "everything is normal, no one is embarrassed, no one is thinking in sexual terms." The audience of one is reassured only when the actors give a consistent performance.

Meaning-ful Research.   Mead advocated research through participant observation, a form of ethnography. Like Jerry in the movie *Nell*, researchers systematically set out to share in the lives of the people they study. The participant observer adopts the stance of an interested—yet ignorant—visitor who listens carefully to what people say in order to discover how they interpret their world. Mead had little sympathy for tightly controlled behavioral experiments or checklist surveys. The results might be quantifiable, but the lifeless numbers are void of the meaning the experience had for the person. Mead would have liked the wrangler who said that the only way to understand horses is to smell like a horse, eat from a trough, and sleep in a stall. That's participant observation! Undoubtedly, *Seabiscuit's* trainer and *The Horse Whisperer* were symbolic interactionists.

Generalized Other.   The sobering short story "Cipher in the Snow" tells the true account of a boy who is treated as a nonentity by his parents, his teachers, and other children. Their negative responses gradually reduce him to what they perceive him to be—nothing. He eventually collapses and dies in a snowbank for no apparent reason. The interactionist would describe his death as symbolic manslaughter.[22]

Naming.   Here's a partial list of epithets heard in public places over a one-year period; they were all spoken in a demeaning voice: *dummy, ugly, slob, fag, nigger, retard, fundamentalist, liberal, Neanderthal, slut, liar.* Sticks and stones can break my bones, but names can *really* hurt me. Name-calling can be devastating because the epithets force us to view ourselves in a warped mirror. The grotesque images aren't easily dismissed.

Self-Fulfilling Prophecy.   One implication of the looking-glass self idea is that each of us has a significant impact on how others view themselves. That kind of interpersonal power is often referred to as a *self-fulfilling prophecy*, the tendency for our expectations to evoke responses in others that confirm what we originally anticipated. The process is nicely summed up by Eliza Doolittle, a woman from the gutter in George Bernard Shaw's play *Pygmalion:* "The difference between a lady and a flower girl is not how she behaves, but how she's treated."[23]

Symbol Manipulation.   Saul Alinsky was a product of the "Chicago School" of sociology at a time when Mead was having his greatest influence. But instead of pursuing a life of scholarship, Alinsky became a community organizer and applied what he learned to empower the urban poor. For example, in the early 1960s he helped found The Woodlawn Organization (TWO) to oppose his alma mater's complicity in substandard neighborhood housing. He searched for a symbol that would galvanize Woodlawn residents into united action and stir the

Participant observation
A method of adopting the stance of an ignorant yet interested visitor who carefully notes what people say and do in order to discover how they interpret their world.

Self-fulfilling prophecy
The tendency for our expectations to evoke responses that confirm what we originally anticipated.

sympathies of other Chicago residents. He earlier described his technique for selecting a symbolic issue:

> You start with the people, their traditions, their prejudices, their habits, their attitudes and all of those other circumstances that make up their lives. It should always be remembered that a real organization of the people . . . must be rooted in the experiences of the people themselves.[24]

Alinsky found his symbol in the rats that infested the squalid apartments. TWO's rallying cry became "Rats as big as cats." Not only did the city start to crack down on slum landlords, but for the first time Woodlawn residents gained a sense of identity, pride, and political clout.

CRITIQUE: A THEORY TOO FLUID?

Most readers of *Mind, Self, and Society* are struck by the baffling array of concepts that Mead tries to cover. The theory's fluid boundaries, vague concepts, and undisciplined approach don't lend themselves to an easy summary. There are no *CliffsNotes* for this one. Perhaps Mead was precise when he presented his ideas in class, but their exact meaning was blurred in the years before his students compiled the manuscript. Whatever the explanation is, the theory suffers from a lack of clarity.

Symbolic interactionism may also suffer from overstatement. Mead repeatedly declared that our capacity for language—the ability to use and interpret abstract symbols—is what distinguishes humans from other animals. My former graduate assistant is the mother of a son who has a permanent peripheral nerve disorder. His eyes, ears, and other sense receptors work fine, but the messages they send get scrambled on the way to his brain. Doctors say that he is, and always will be, unable to talk or interact with others on a symbolic level. After reading an early draft of this chapter, she asked, "So this means that Caleb is less than human?" Her haunting question serves as a caution to any theorist who claims to have captured the essence of humanity.

Issues of clarity and human nature aside, symbolic interactionism is a remarkable endeavor. University of California, Riverside, sociologist Randall Collins has labeled Mead "America's greatest sociological thinker."[25] Mead crafted an interconnecting network of ideas that has greater breadth than any other theory discussed in this book. I could have easily presented his ideas in the section on relationship development, intercultural communication, or gender and communication.

Although Mead's ideas are best known by students of sociology, symbolic interactionism offers great insight into the creation of symbolic messages and their impact on the one who speaks and the one who hears. Most of the interpretive communication theorists I feature in this book owe an intellectual debt to Mead's thinking. Look for ideas from symbolic interaction in Bormann's symbolic convergence theory, Pearce and Cronen's coordinated management of meaning, Geertz and Pacanowsky's cultural approach to organizations, Burke's dramatism, Fisher's narrative paradigm, Philipsen's speech codes theory, Harding and Wood's standpoint theory, and Kramarae's muted group theory. That impressive list of significant others could give a boost to any theorist's looking-glass self.

QUESTIONS TO SHARPEN YOUR FOCUS

1. Blumer's three core *premises of symbolic interactionism* deal with *meaning, language,* and *thought.* According to Blumer, which comes first? Can you make a case for an alternative sequence?

2. What do interactionists believe are the crucial differences between *human beings* and *animals*? What would you add to or subtract from the list?

3. As Mead used the terms, is a *looking-glass self* the same thing as a person's *me*? Why or why not?

4. Think of a time in your life when your concept of *self* changed significantly. Do you believe that *self-fulfilling prophecy* played a major role in the shift?

SELF-QUIZ

For chapter self-quizzes, go to the book's Online Learning Center at
www.mhhe.com/griffin7.

A SECOND LOOK

Recommended resource: Jodi O'Brien (ed.), *The Production of Reality,* 4th ed., Pine Forge, Thousand Oaks, CA, 2005.

Original statement: George Herbert Mead, *Mind, Self, and Society,* University of Chicago, Chicago, 1934.

Development of Mead's ideas: Herbert Blumer, *Symbolic Interactionism,* Prentice-Hall, Englewood Cliffs, NJ, 1969, pp. 1–89.

Summary statement: Herbert Blumer, "Symbolic Interaction: An Approach to Human Communication," in *Approaches to Human Communication,* Richard W. Budd and Brent Ruben (eds.), Spartan Books, New York, 1972, pp. 401–419.

Basic concepts of symbolic interactionism: John Hewitt, *Self and Society: A Symbolic Interactionist Social Psychology,* 10th ed., Allyn and Bacon, Boston, 2006, pp. 36–81.

Empirical support for looking-glass self: King-To Yeung and John Martin, "The Looking Glass Self: An Empirical Test and Elaboration," *Social Forces,* March 2003, pp. 843–879.

Dramaturgical metaphor: Erving Goffman, *The Presentation of Self in Everyday Life,* Doubleday Anchor, Garden City, NY, 1959.

Effects of social isolation: Kingsley Davis, "Final Note on a Case of Extreme Isolation," *American Journal of Sociology,* Vol. 3, 1947, pp. 432–437.

Applied interactionist activism: Donald Reitzes and Dietrich Reitzes, "Saul D. Alinsky: An Applied Urban Symbolic Interactionist," *Symbolic Interaction,* Vol. 15, 1992, pp. 1–24.

The self as a social construction: Susan Harter, "Symbolic Interactionism Revisited: Potential Liabilities for the Self Constructed in the Crucible of Interpersonal Relationships," *Merrill-Palmer Quarterly,* Vol. 45, 1999, pp. 677–703.

Communication issues: Bruce E. Gronbeck, "Symbolic Interactionism and Communication Studies: Prolegomena to Future Research," in *Communication and Social Structures,* D. R. Maines and C. J. Couch (eds.), Charles C Thomas, Springfield, IL, 1988, pp. 323–340.

Critique: Peter Hull, "Structuring Symbolic Interaction: Communication and Power," *Communication Yearbook 4,* Dan Nimmo (ed.), Transaction Books, New Brunswick, NJ, 1980, pp. 49–60.

Coordinated Management of Meaning (CMM)

of W. Barnett Pearce & Vernon Cronen

Barnett Pearce (The Fielding Graduate University) and Vernon Cronen (University of Massachusetts) believe that communication is the process by which we collectively create the events and objects of our social world.[1] Their theory, the coordinated management of meaning (CMM), starts with the assertion that *persons-in-conversation co-construct their own social realities and are simultaneously shaped by the worlds they create.* Stating this another way, every conversation has an *afterlife.* Tomorrow's social reality is the afterlife of how we interact today. That's why Pearce and Cronen find it useful to ask, *What are we making together? How are we making it? How can we make better social worlds?*

Pearce and Cronen present CMM as a practical theory crafted to help make life better for real people in a real world.[2] Unlike some objective theorists, they don't claim to have discovered ironclad principles of communication that hold true for everyone in every situation. Instead, CMM consists of a set of concepts and models to help parents, therapists, social workers, mediators, teachers, consultants, and others enhance their understanding and act more effectively in a wide range of communication situations. For its creators, the ultimate test of CMM lies not in the truthfulness of its claims, but rather in its usefulness in helping us identify critical moments in our conversations and helping us act wisely in those moments. They deem their theory successful when it helps us create the kind of social world in which we want to live.

CMM IN ACTION—STORIES FROM THE FIELD

I've paraphrased three brief reports from CMM advocates so that you can catch a glimpse of their theory in practice. These first-person narratives provide a context for you to understand Pearce and Cronen's coordinated management of meaning and the reason they chose that title. Throughout the chapter I'll refer back to these stories to illustrate some of the analytical tools that CMM practitioners use as they try to construct a more supportive social environment.

Mediation

From Jonathan Shailor, Professor of Communication, University of Wisconsin, Parkside

In my mediation work, I act in the roles of practitioner, researcher, and trainer. In all of these roles I use the CMM concept of levels of meaning to tease out disputants' and mediators' constructions of episodes, relationships, identities, and cultural patterns. For example, what story does she tell about the *episode* that answers the question *Why did we come to mediation?* What story does she voice about her *relationship* with the other disputant? How does she construct her *identity?* Do *cultural narratives* come into play?

Peter and Anne were a young couple who fell into a pattern of angry fighting, which culminated with Anne obtaining a restraining order that forced Peter to move out of the apartment. A judge approved the order on the condition that the couple attend mediation and then return to court for futher review. In the mediation session, Peter framed this sequence as the story of "Anne's betrayal," a detailed series of events in which Anne's actions were interpreted as attacks and cold-blooded manipulations. Peter explained his own actions as necessary acts of self-defense, ignoring all other aspects of their relationship.

Anne constructed an autobiographical narrative that linked her history of family abuse with her sense of being "endangered" by Peter. In that context, a continued relationship with Peter was seen as dangerous. For Anne, any agreement in mediation that might compromise her physical or economic security would define her as a "victim."

Peter demanded that Anne pay for the rent during the two weeks that he was prevented from living in the apartment. This demand made sense, of course, within the subsystem of contextual meanings that Peter had assembled. But Anne interpreted this demand within her own subsystem of meanings and was determined not to play the part of the victim. Her refusal to pay confirmed Peter's construction of Anne as his persecutor and obligated him to press for retribution by looking for concessions on other issues, which she then refused, and so on.

After the mediation was over, CMM helped me describe to the two mediators the reflexive process of action and interpretation that they were co-constructing with Peter and Anne. By focusing their attention on the disputants' enactments of episodes, relationships, identities, and cultural patterns, I was able to help them see how mediator communication can either open up or shut down opportunities for empowerment.[3]

Family Therapy

From John Burnham, Consultant Family Therapist, Parkview Clinic, Birmingham, England

A father and mother came to me to talk about their 14-year-old son who was diagnosed with Asperger's syndrome, a mild form of autism. Halfway through the session it hit me that the boy and his parents were trapped in a repetitive pattern of behavior that CMM calls a *strange loop* (see Figure 6–1). If the parents accepted the diagnosis of Asperger's, they acted toward their son in a compassionate, patient, and forgiving way. Yet when they treated him this way, the boy improved to such an extent that it led them to think, *This is not Asperger's.* Under their altered belief they began to be less forgiving toward their son. He in turn deteriorated, which led them to think, *This is Asperger's,* and so on.

Strange loop
An unwanted repetitive communication pattern— "Darn, we did it again."

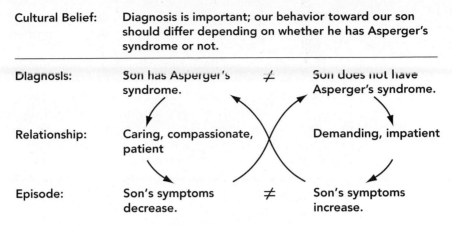

Cultural Belief:	Diagnosis is important; our behavior toward our son should differ depending on whether he has Asperger's syndrome or not.

FIGURE 6–1 **A Strange Loop of Diagnosis and Behavior**
Courtesy of W. Barnett Pearce

When I described this never-ending loop, the parents acted as if a light had been turned on. As long as they treated the question of whether this was Asperger's, the family continued to retrace the closed-circuit, figure-eight path. But the diagram of the loop that they were in helped me suggest a different question: *What relationship do you want with your son?* By focusing on what they were making together rather than what their son had or didn't have, their chances of escaping from this loop were increased. This approach worked well for the parents and their son, and they began to report many positive changes in their relationships with each other. They then moved on to ask, *When is it useful to think of this odd behavior as Asperger's, and when is it not?* I now use CMM's idea of strange loops in my work with other families whose children have been diagnosed as having a specific mental disorder. I tell this story because, like the parents, I learned that labeling a disease has significant consequences.[4]

Cupertino Community Project

From W. Barnett Pearce and Kimberly A. Pearce, Public Dialogue Consortium

In 1996, the Public Dialogue Consortium[5] approached the city manager of Cupertino, California, and offered to introduce a productive form of communication to discuss the most pressing issue within the community—*ethnic diversity*. Many residents privately described race relations as a "powder keg waiting to go off," yet were unwilling to speak of it publicly for fear of providing the spark.

Our task was to change the form of communication, showing people that they could hold onto and express their deeply held convictions in a form of communication that promoted reciprocal understanding. The first phase of the project consisted of structuring situations in which people with all sorts of views could speak in a manner that made others want to listen, and listen in a manner that made others want to speak. We call this *dialogic communication*. When key members of the community gained confidence in this type of communication, it was time to focus on specific issues. Working with the city government and an independent citizens' group, we invited all community members to a "Diversity Forum" in order to give them an opportunity to discuss the way Cupertino handled three flashpoint issues—a Mandarin immersion program in the schools, public signs written only in Chinese, and a multicultural Fourth of July celebration.

The centerpiece of the forum consisted of numerous small-group discussions facilitated by members of the community. Each facilitator received at least 10 hours of training from the Public Dialogue Consortium.[6] The challenge the facilitators faced was to help participants communicate dialogically beyond what they were initially willing or able to do. To accomplish this task, we trained each facilitator to (a) frame the forum as a special event in which unusual forms of communication would occur; (b) remain neutral by actively aligning oneself with all participants; (c) help people tell their own stories by expressing curiosity and asking questions; (d) enable people to tell even better stories through appreciative reframing and the weaving together of diverse stories; and (e) provide "in-the-moment" coaching and intervention.

The dialogic communication that they stimulated transformed the social environment of Cupertino. A year after the forum only 2 percent of the residents mentioned race or ethnic diversity as a problem. The city manager interpreted this response to mean that people had finished "working through" the issue and that increased diversity was "an accomplished fact of life."

In the Cupertino Project we were particularly well served by CMM's insistence that communication creates the events and objects of our social world. We reaffirmed that dialogue requires remaining in the tension between holding our own perspective and being profoundly open to others who are unlike us, and enabling others to act similarly.[7]

Dialogic communication
Conversation in which people speak in a manner that makes others want to listen, and listen in a way that makes others want to speak.

PERSONS-IN-CONVERSATION: CREATING BONDS OF UNION

The CMM users who tell these stories refer to themselves as *social constructionists*. From their stories you can spot that they share the core conviction that our social environment is not something we find or discover. Instead, we create it. As was stated at the start of the chapter, they're convinced that **persons-in-conversation co-construct their own social realities and are simultaneously shaped by the worlds they create.**

Figure 6–2 presents artist M. C. Escher's 1955 lithograph *Bond of Union*, which is a striking picture of CMM notions about persons-in-conversation. The unusual drawing illustrates the following tenets of the theory:

Social constructionists
Language theorists who believe that persons-in-conversation co-construct their own social realities and are simultaneously shaped by the worlds they create.

1.   The experience of persons-in-conversation is the primary social process of human life. Pearce says that this core concept runs counter to the prevailing intellectual view of "communication as an odorless, colorless vehicle of thought that is interesting or important only when it is done poorly or breaks down."[8] He sees the ribbon in Escher's drawing as representing the process of communication. It isn't just one of the activities the pair does or a tool that they use to achieve some other end. On the contrary, their communication literally forms who they are and creates their relationship. The Cupertino Community Project radically altered the face of the community, not by changing what citizens wanted to talk *about* but by changing the *form* of their communication.

2.   The way people communicate is often more important than the content of what they say. The mood and manner that persons-in-conversation adopt plays

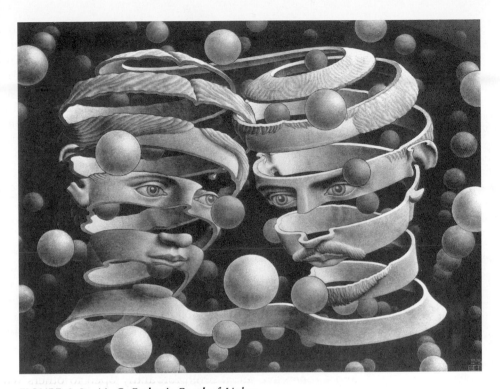

FIGURE 6–2   M. C. Escher's *Bond of Union*

a large role in the social construction process. Pearce points out that the faces in *Bond of Union* have no substance; they consist in the twists and turns of the spiraling ribbon:

> Were the ribbon straightened or tied in another shape, there would be no loss of matter, but the faces would no longer exist. This image works for us as a model of the way the process of communication (the ribbon) creates the events and objects of our social worlds (the faces) not by its substance but by its form.[9]

The parties in mediation, therapy, or ethnic disputes are often stuck in a destructive pattern of interaction. They call each other racists, liars, or jerks; they describe the other person's actions as criminal, cruel, or crazy. Since Pearce regards language as "the single most powerful tool that humans have ever invented for the creation of social worlds,"[10] he thinks it's tragic when people in conflict are caught up in a language game that they are bound to lose. MRI scans show that interpersonal distress affects the brain the same way as a punch in the stomach.[11]

CMM theorists speak of a *logic of meaning and action* that is made in the give-and-take of conversation. Consider this all-too-familiar sequence: You say something, and I respond. That response makes you feel that you must instruct me about the error of my ways, but I don't feel that I should take instruction from you. So I inform you that you are not qualified to have an opinion on this topic, and that information conflicts with your self-concept as an intelligent, knowledgeable person, so you lash out with a bitter insult. In just

Logical force
The moral pressure or sense of obligation a person feels to respond in a given way to what someone else has just said or done—"I had no choice."

Reflexivity
The process by which the effects of our words and actions on others bounce back and affect us.

five turns, we've moved into an escalating pattern in which we are competing to see who can say the most hurtful things to the other. By this time, the original topic of conversation is irrelevant. We can continue this feud forever, fueled only by the *logical force* of the interaction. When informed by CMM, mediators, therapists, consultants, and teachers become attuned to the logic of meaning and action generated by the way the turns in a conversation are connected. Armed with this understanding, they are equipped to intervene, breaking the destructive cycle and creating an opportunity for better patterns of communication to emerge.

3.   The actions of persons-in-conversation are reflexively reproduced as the interaction continues. Reflexivity means that our actions have effects that bounce back and affect us. The endless ribbon in *Bond of Union* loops back to *re*form both people. If Escher's figures were in conflict, each person would be wise to ask, "If I win this argument, what kind of person will I become?"

Escher's spheres suspended in space can be seen as worlds or planets of the social universe that is also co-constructed by the intertwined actors. "When we communicate," writes Pearce, "we are not just talking about the world, we are literally participating in the creation of the social universe."[12] For years, environmentalists have stressed that we have to live in the world that we produce. By fouling the air we breathe, we pollute the quality of our lives—as residents of Bangkok, Bucharest, and Mexico City know all too well. In like fashion, Pearce and Cronen are social ecologists who alert us to the long-term effects of our communication practices.

Do the persons-in-conversation shown in Figure 6–2 realize that they are creating the social universe in which they talk and act? If they're like the parents who went to the family therapist to discuss their son's Asperger's syndrome, probably not. Yet that's the task that CMM practitioners have set for themselves—to get people to first ask and then answer the question *What are we making together?*

4.   As social constructionists, CMM researchers see themselves as curious participants in a pluralistic world. They are *curious* because they think it's folly to profess certainty when dealing with individuals acting out their lives under ever-changing conditions. They are *participants* rather than spectators because they seek to be actively involved in what they study. They live in *pluralistic worlds* because they assume that people make multiple truths rather than find a singular Truth. So Escher's *Bond of Union* is an apt representation of persons-in-conversation even when one of the parties is a CMM researcher.

Pearce regards Australian Ernest Stringer's *community-based action research* as a model for doing research. Action research is a "collaborative approach to investigation that seeks to engage community members as equal and full participants in the research process."[13] That research bond goes way beyond the "participant observation" approach favored by symbolic interactionists (see Chapter 5). Action researchers work together with people to build a picture of what's going on. They then develop a shared minitheory as to why relationships are the way they are. Finally, they enact a cooperative plan to change things for the better. That's exactly the approach taken by the Public Dialogue Consortium in Cupertino.

The *Bond of Union* lithograph helps us grasp what Pearce and Cronen mean when they say that persons-in-conversation co-construct their own social realities. But the drawing doesn't show that *stories* are the basic means that people use to pursue these social joint ventures. Since all of us perceive, think, and live our lives in terms of characters, roles, plots, and narrative sequences, CMM theorists say we shouldn't be surprised that the social worlds we create take on the shape of story.

STORIES TOLD AND STORIES LIVED

CMM theorists draw a distinction between *stories lived* and *stories told*. Stories lived are the co-constructed actions that we perform with others. *Coordination* takes place when we fit our stories lived into the stories lived by others in a way that makes life better. Stories told are the narratives that we use to make sense of stories lived.[14]

Pearce and Cronen note that the stories we tell and the stories we live are always tangled together yet forever in tension. That's because one is the stuff of language and the other of action. In stories told, a cocky young man can envision being faster than a speeding bullet and able to leap over tall buildings in a single bound. But in stories lived, inertia, gravity, and the witness of other people impose lower limits on what he can do. This tension is why Pearce and Cronen call their theory the *management of meaning;* we have to adjust our stories told to fit the realities of our stories lived—or vice versa. They put the term *coordinated* in the title because we have to constantly make these adjustments through interactions with others. As practical theorists, they want to help people interpret what's said and coordinate what's done so that the social environment they create is one in which they can survive and thrive. They use CMM's concepts and models as ways of displaying the complexity of communication processes. Each layer of complexity provides a potential opening for strategic action.

Making and Managing Meaning Through Stories Told

The stories we tell are open to many interpretations. Pearce and Cronen offer a variety of communication models to help people figure out what's going on in a conversation. In Figure 6–3, I've combined two of them—the *hierarchy model of meaning* and the *serpentine model*—into a single drawing.[15] You'll find it helpful to think of this hierarchical-serpentine model as a schematic diagram of the communication process taking place in Escher's *Bond of Union.*

Hierarchy of meaning
A rank order of the relative significance of contexts—episode, relationship, identity, and culture—that encompass a given story as an aid to interpretation.

According to the hierarchy model of meaning, storytelling is the central act of communication, but every story is embedded within multiple contexts, or frames. No matter what the speaker says, the words of a story will make sense only if they are understood within the framework of a specific *episode,* the *relationship* between the parties, the self-*identity* of the speaker, and the *culture* from which he or she comes. These contexts rarely have equal significance when we try to figure out what another person means, so Pearce suggests that we rank-order their importance for interpreting a specific *speech act*—giving most weight to the overarching frame that encompasses all others.

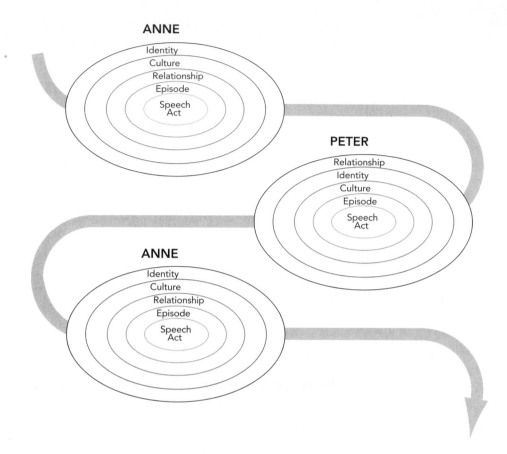

FIGURE 6–3   Hierarchical-Serpentine Model

Speech act
Any verbal or nonverbal message as part of an interaction; the basic building block of the social universe people create; threats, promises, insults, compliments, etc.

For example, consider the way that many high school seniors talk about "The Prom." The stories they tell often elevate the *episode* to mythic proportions, yet their descriptions seem to downplay a romantic *relationship* with their prom date. The hierarchy of meaning that we construct makes a big difference. If the prom event has the most importance, there might be several partners who could serve equally well as satisfying dates. But if a specific relationship is the most important to you, you could probaby find other things to do that would be equally as enjoyable as the prom—and certainly less expensive.

Since Jonathan Shailor employs these four contexts in his analysis of communication patterns in mediation, I'll illustrate their place in the hierarchical-serpentine model referring to the dispute between Peter and Anne. Assume that Peter's *speech act* in the figure is his story of Anne's betrayal told during their court-appointed mediation.

Episode
A "nounable" sequence of speech acts with a beginning and an end that are held together by story; an argument, interview, wedding, mediation, etc.

Episode.   An episode is a sequence of speech acts with a beginning and an end that are held together by story. Pearce and Cronen say that such sequences are "nounable." The noun used to designate an episode should answer the question *What does he think he's doing?* The term *mediation* labels the episode that Shailor described. Mediators hope that their participation as a neutral third party will elicit patterns of speech acts that are part of the solution rather than part of the problem. But the fact that both Peter and Anne were locked into their separate stories of "betrayal" and "endangerment" suggests that the mediation episode had little impact on the hostile social world that they were making.

Relationship. Pearce says that relationships emerge from the dynamic dance over coordinated actions and managed meanings. And just as punctuation provides a context for the printed word, the relationship between persons-in-conversation suggests how a speech act might be interpreted. This is especially true for Peter, who is fixated on Anne's betrayal in a way that blots out everything else. Without exacting some kind of retribution, he can't get on with his life. As for Anne, the relationship is important only if it doesn't end. She's in court to make sure that it does.

Identity. CMM holds that our identities are continually crafted through the process of communication, and in turn our self-images become a context for how we manage meaning. For Anne, Peter's demand for money is less about their broken relationship than it is about a potential threat to her self-identity. She's unwilling to do anything that suggests she is a passive victim. By asking the judge for a restraining order and refusing to pay rent for the apartment, she sees herself as actively rewriting her personal life script. Regarding Peter's self-concept, the story is mute.

Culture. Since the term *culture* describes webs of shared meanings and values, people who come from different cultures won't interpret messages exactly the same way. Although Shailor's mediation story doesn't suggest that Anne's ethnic or national background differs from Peter's, the history of abuse in her family of origin makes it difficult for her to make or manage meaning cooperatively with anyone who hasn't experienced a similar subculture of violence. Peter doesn't seem able to relate to her background of physical and verbal abuse.

The two identical sets of concentric ellipses on the left side of Figure 6–3 display my perception of Anne's hierarchy of meaning. The all-encompassing concern for her personal identity relegates the other contexts to lesser importance. As for Peter, I see his fixation with their relationship as the overarching frame that encompasses all other contexts. My judgment is depicted in the set of ovals on the right-hand side of the model. The interpretive trick, of course, is to figure out which context is dominant in any particular conversation. That's one reason a CMM analysis of communication is more art than science.

The *serpentine flow of conversation* is the other CMM model blended into Figure 6–3. Similar to Escher's *Bond of Union*, the diagram suggests that what one person says affects—and is affected by—what the other person says. The contexts for what they're saying co-evolve even as they speak. So it's foolish to try to interpret Anne's first message because we don't know what was said before. It's equally hard to decipher the meaning of Anne's second message because we don't know what follows. As the parents in therapy suddenly grasped, any comment about their son's mental health was both the result and the cause of other statements within the family. Perhaps this is the most striking feature of the serpentine model; it leaves no room for isolated acts of speech. Everything in a conversation is connected to everything else. Understanding how others make and manage meaning is possible only when we perceive the flow of conversation.

Do you get the impression from the hierarchical-serpentine model that even a brief conversation is a process that's incredibly complex and open-ended? If so, Pearce would be pleased. He thinks it's impossible to explain in a simple declarative sentence what a statement means—even when it's your own statement. For that reason, Pearce finds it difficult to give a straight answer when someone in a discussion asks him, "What does that mean?" Consistent with CMM thinking, he's tempted to reply, "I'm not completely sure yet. We haven't finished our conversation."[16]

Coordination—The Meshing of Stories Lived

Coordination

The process by which persons collaborate in an attempt to bring into being their vision of what is necessary, noble, and good and to preclude the enactment of what they fear, hate, or despise.

According to CMM, *coordination* refers to the "process by which persons collaborate in an attempt to bring into being their vision of what is necessary, noble, and good and to preclude the enactment of what they fear, hate, or despise."[17] This intentional meshing of stories lived does not require people to reach agreement on the meaning of their joint action. They can decide to coordinate their behavior without sharing a common interpretation of the event. For example, conservative activists and radical feminists could temporarily join forces to protest a pornographic movie. Although they have discrepant views of social justice and different reasons for condemning the film, they might agree on a unified course of action. As the *Calvin and Hobbes* cartoon on the next page suggests, parties can coordinate effectively without much mutual understanding.

Like many other students of communication, CMM theorists enjoy reading descriptions of the rules for meaning and action in families, organizations, and cultures (see Chapters 13, 19, and 33). In light of these descriptions of how real groups of people coordinate their behavior, "Calvinball" no longer looks so strange.

CMM began as an interpretive theory, its authors attempting to describe and understand recurring patterns of communication.[18] As the theory evolved, however, it developed a critical edge. CMM advocates today aren't satisfied with simply describing patterns of communication or providing tools for understanding how people interpret their social worlds. They want to function as *peacemakers*, "providing a way of intelligently joining into the activity of the world so as to enrich it."[19] If any of us are tempted to dismiss the significance of helping others coordinate the way they talk with each other, CMM reminds us that communication has the power to create a social universe of alienation, anger, and malice—or one of community, tolerance, and generosity.

As a case in point, Pearce believes that the polarization of the electorate in the United States is both the cause and the product of communication patterns that he describes as *reciprocated diatribe*.[20] He claims that what President George W. Bush labeled the "war on terror" is reproduced and sustained by patterns of communication that dismiss and demonize the other.[21] The president's address to the nation on the night of the 9/11 attack set the tone. The speech, Pearce notes, "created an after life that magnified the effects of the terrorist attack and deteriorated the quality of life around the world."[22] A CMM view of the conflict between al-Qaeda and the United States suggests that *both* sides are acting morally according to their own understanding of the universe. Yet it's no surprise that each side calling the other "evil" isn't likely to resolve the conflict. As a way of expressing his own sense of horror and sadness at what he perceived as a missed opportunity to make the world a better place, Pearce wrote an alternative

response that he wished the president had made that evening. One portion of Pearce's version goes as follows:

> If we are to understand why people hate us so much, we will have to understand how the world looks from their perspective. And if we are to respond effectively to protect ourselves, we must understand those whose sense of history and purpose are not like our own.
>
> It is tempting to see this vicious attack as the result of madmen trying to destroy civilization, and our response as a war of "good" against "evil." But if we are to understand what happened here today, and if we are to act effectively in the days to come, we must develop more sophisticated stories than these about the world, about our place in it, and about the consequences of our actions.
>
> This is a terrorist attack. If we are in a state of war, it is a different kind of war than we have ever fought before. Terrorists are not capable of occupying our country or meeting our armies on the field of battle. They hope to destroy our confidence; to disrupt our way of life. They hope that we will destroy ourselves by the way we respond to the atrocities that they commit. Our first reaction, that of wanting revenge, to lash out at those who have injured us so, is almost surely the wrong response because it makes us accomplices of what they are trying to achieve.[23]

COSMOPOLITAN COMMUNICATION: DISAGREE, YET COORDINATE

Cosmopolitan communication
Coordination with others who have different backgrounds, values, and beliefs without trying to change them.

CMM theorists advocate an uncommon form of communication they believe will create a social world where we can live with dignity, honor, joy, and love.[24] Over the last three decades Pearce has used a number of terms to describe the communication style that he values. He started by calling it *cosmopolitan communication*.[25] When applied to individuals, the label calls to mind a citizen of the world who interacts comfortably with people who come from diverse cultural backgrounds, hold different values, and express discrepant beliefs. Pearce's cosmopolitan communicators assume that there is no single truth, or if there is, that it has many faces. So they try to find ways of coordinating with others with whom they do not—and perhaps should not—agree.

Although he still likes the concept of cosmopolitan communication, Pearce also uses the term *dialogue* in the same way that Jewish philosopher Martin Buber does—to describe what he believes is the optimum form of interaction. (See the section that follows.) For Buber, *dialogic communication* "involves remaining in the tension between holding our own perspective while being profoundly open to the other."[26] This, of course, could be dangerous. As happened in Cupertino, we might learn something new that will change what we think, or even who we are.[27]

In the hierarchical-serpentine model displayed in Figure 6–3, Pearce would represent a pair who are communicating dialogically as holding an equal concern for their own *identities* and the *relationship* between them. He might resort to computer art to capture the tension between matters of "I" and "we" that each person would experience. Perhaps two same-sized, superimposed ovals that reciprocally expand and contract would best show that neither concern for one's own identity nor concern for the relationship becomes fixed as the context for the other. Pearce labels this kind of beneficial relationship a *charmed loop,* as opposed to a *strange loop,* which, as you'll recall, locks parties into behaviors that no one really wants.[28]

ETHICAL REFLECTION: MARTIN BUBER'S DIALOGIC ETHICS

Martin Buber was a German Jewish philosopher and theologian who immigrated to Palestine before World War II and died in 1965. His ethical approach focuses on relationships between people rather than on moral codes of conduct. "In the beginning is the relation," Buber wrote. "The relation is the cradle of actual life."[29]

Buber contrasted two types of relationships—*I-It* versus *I-Thou*. In an I-It relationship we treat the other person as a thing to be used, an object to be manipulated. Created by monologue, an I-It relationship lacks mutuality. Parties come together as individuals intent on creating only an impression. Deceit is a way to maintain appearances.

In an I-Thou relationship we regard our partner as the very one we are. We see the other as created in the image of God and resolve to treat him or her as a valued end rather than as a means to our own end. This implies that we will seek to experience the relationship as it appears to the other person. Buber says we can do this only through dialogue.

For Buber, *dialogue* is a synonym for ethical communication. Dialogue is mutuality in conversation that creates the *between*, through which we help each other to be more human. Dialogue is not only a morally appropriate act, it is also a way to discover what is ethical in our relationship. It thus requires self-disclosure to, confirmation of, and vulnerability with the other person.

Buber used the image of the *narrow ridge* to picture the tension of dialogic living. On one side of the moral path is the gulf of relativism, where there are no standards. On the other side is the plateau of absolutism, where rules are etched in stone:

Narrow ridge
A metaphor of I-Thou living in the dialogic tension between ethical relativism and rigid absolutism; standing your own ground while being profoundly open to the other.

> On the far side of the subjective, on this side of the objective, on the narrow ridge, where I and Thou meet, there is the realm of the Between.[30]

Duquesne University communication ethicist Ron Arnett notes that "living the narrow-ridge philosophy requires a life of personal and interpersonal concern, which is likely to generate a more complicated existence than that of the egoist or the selfless martyr."[31] Despite that tension, many interpersonal theorists have carved out ethical positions similar to Buber's philosophy. Consistent with CMM's foundational belief that persons-in-conversation co-construct their own social realities, Pearce is attracted to Buber's core belief that dialogue is a joint achievement, which cannot be produced on demand, yet occurs among people who seek it and are prepared for it.

CRITIQUE: ASTUTE INTERPRETATIONS THAT ARE HARD TO GRASP

In almost every way, CMM meets the standards of a good interpretive theory as outlined in Chapter 3 ("Weighing the Words"). By offering such tools as the hierarchical and serpentine models of communication, its authors provide analytical tools to promote *a better understanding of people* and of the social worlds created by their conversation. Pearce and Cronen's description of the ideal cosmopolitan communicator *makes it clear that they value* curiosity, participation, and an appreciation of diversity rather than the detached aloof certainty of someone interacting in a my-way-is-Yahweh style.

Pearce writes that CMM "can function as a ladder for the 'upward' evolution of society."[32] If *reforming society* seems a bit of a stretch, recall that by teaching residents to speak in a dialogic way, Pearce and his associates changed the social world of Cupertino, California. And although many objectivist theorists ignore or dismiss CMM because of its social constructivist assumptions, CMM has generated widespread interest and *acceptance within the community* of interpretive communication scholars.

Despite meeting these four standards with ease, lack of clarity has seriously limited CMM's *aesthetic appeal*. CMM has a reputation of being a confusing mix of ideas that are hard to pin down because they're expressed in convoluted language. When Pearce asked longtime CMM practitioners what changes or additions they thought should be made to the theory, the most frequent plea was for user-friendly explanations expressed in easy-to-understand terms. The following story from the field underscores why this call for clarity is so crucial:

> My counseling trainees often find CMM ideas exciting, but its language daunting or too full of jargon. Some trainees connect with the ideas but most feel intimidated by the language and the concepts—diminished in some way or excluded! One trainee sat in a posture of physically cringing because she did not understand. This was a competent woman who had successfully completed counselor training three years ago and was doing a "refresher" with us. I don't think she found it too refreshing at that moment. CMM ideas would be more useful if they were available in everyday language—perhaps via examples and storytelling. (Gabrelle Parker, Dance Movement Therapist)[33]

Pearce responds that he can train people to use CMM concepts, but not by asking them to read. He first asks them to describe something going on in their lives and then *shows* them rather than tells them how to use the ideas and models that the theory offers. Because that interactive option isn't available to us, I've tried to heed Parker's advice while writing this chapter. Hopefully, you haven't cringed. But in order to reduce the wince factor, I've had to leave out many of the valued terms, tools, and models that are the working vocabulary of this complex theory. You haven't read about constitutive rules, regulative rules, reconstructed contexts, gamemastery, grammars, the daisy model, or the LUUUTT model—just to name a few. Pearce introduces these concepts, as well as the ones I covered, in *Making Social Worlds: A Communication Perspective*, a book written in a relatively readable style.

What I have stressed is Pearce and Cronen's rock-solid belief that persons-in-conversation co-construct their social realities. While many theorists today hold that the joint use of language creates, shapes, and limits the diverse social worlds in which we live, the coordinated management of meaning is the most comprehensive statement of social construction crafted by communication scholars. Your evaluation of CMM's worth will ultimately hinge on whether or not you share their worldview. Therefore, I urge you to think through your answer to question #1 in the following "Questions to Sharpen Your Focus."

QUESTIONS TO SHARPEN YOUR FOCUS

1. *Social constructionists* see themselves as curious participants in a pluralistic world. Are you willing not to strive for certainty, a detached perspective, and a singular view of Truth so that you can join them?

2. Can you provide a rationale for placing this chapter on CMM immediately after the chapter on *symbolic interactionism?*

3.   CMM suggests that we can take part in joint action without shared under-standing—*coordination* without *coherence*. Can you think of examples from your own life?

4.   Pearce and Cronen claim that CMM is a *practical theory*. What *consequences* do you foresee had President Bush delivered the speech Pearce wrote after the 9/11 attack? What aspects of *dialogic communication* do you see in Pearce's version?

CONVERSATIONS

View this segment online at www.mhhe.com/griffin7 or www.afirstlook.com.

As you watch my conversation with Barnett Pearce, you might think of us as the persons-in-conversation pictured in Escher's *Bond of Union*. What kind of social world do you see us creating as we talk? I like to think that our conversation displays a few examples of cosmopolitan communication. If so, is Pearce right in thinking that you'll find this kind of talk contagious? At one point I repeat my "Questions to Sharpen Your Focus" query about how social constructionists must give up claims of certainty, objectivity, and truth. I then ask if that's a fair question. See if you agree with Pearce's response and the reason he gives.

A SECOND LOOK

Recommended resource: W. Barnett Pearce, *Making Social Worlds: A Communication Perspective*, Blackwell, Malden, MA, 2008.

Brief overview with extended example: W. Barnett Pearce, "The Coordinated Management of Meaning (CMM)," in *Theorizing About Intercultural Communication,* William Gudykunst (ed.), Sage, Thousand Oaks, CA, 2004, pp. 35–54.

Early statement of theory: W. Barnett Pearce and Vernon E. Cronen, *Communication, Action, and Meaning: The Creation of Social Realities,* Praeger, New York, 1980; also www.cios.org/www/opentext.htm.

Social constructionism: W. Barnett Pearce, "A Sailing Guide for Social Constructionists," in *Social Approaches to Communication,* Wendy Leeds-Hurwitz (ed.), Guilford, New York, 1995, pp. 88–113.

Coordination and coherence: W. Barnett Pearce, *Communication and the Human Condition,* Southern Illinois University, Carbondale, IL, 1989, pp. 32–87.

Intellectual heritage: Vernon E. Cronen, "Coordinated Management of Meaning: The Consequentiality of Communication and the Recapturing of Experience," in *The Consequentiality of Communication,* Stuart Sigman (ed.), Lawrence Erlbaum, Hillsdale, NJ, 1995, pp. 17–65.

Peacemaking: W. Barnett Pearce and Stephen W. Littlejohn, *Moral Conflict: When Social Worlds Collide,* Sage, Thousand Oaks, CA, 1997.

Dialogic communication: W. Barnett Pearce and Kimberly A. Pearce, "Combining Passions and Abilities: Toward Dialogic Virtuosity," *Southern Communication Journal,* Vol. 65, 2000, pp. 161–175.

CMM as a critical theory: Victoria Chen, "The Possibility of Critical Dialogue in the Theory of Coordinated Management of Meaning," *Human Systems,* Vol. 15, 2004, pp. 179–192.

Research review of CMM: J. Kevin Barge and W. Barnett Pearce, "A Reconnaissance of CMM Research," *Human Systems,* Vol. 15, 2004, pp. 193–203.

To access an inventory of scenes from feature films that illustrate CMM, click on Movie Clips at *www.afirstlook.com.*

Expectancy Violations Theory

of Judee Burgoon

Early in my teaching career, I was walking back to my office, puzzling over classroom conversations with four students. All four had made requests. Why, I wondered, had I readily agreed to two requests but just as quickly turned down two others? Each of the four students had spoken to me individually during the class break. Andre wanted my endorsement for a graduate scholarship, and Dawn invited me to eat lunch with her the next day. I said yes to both of them. Belinda asked me to help her on a term paper for a class with another professor, and Charlie encouraged me to play water polo that night with guys from his house, something I had done before. I said no to those requests.

Sitting down at my desk, I idly flipped through the pages of *Human Communication Research (HCR)*, a relatively new behavioral science journal that had arrived in the morning mail. I was still mulling over my uneven response to the students when my eyes zeroed in on an article entitled "A Communication Model of Personal Space Violations."[1] "That's it," I blurted out to our surprised department secretary. I suddenly realized that in each case my response to the student may have been influenced by the conversational distance between us.

I mentally pictured the four students making their requests—each from a distance that struck me as inappropriate in one way or another. Andre was literally in my face, less than a foot away. Belinda's 2-foot interval invaded my personal space, but not as much. Charlie stood about 7 feet away—just outside the range I would have expected for a let's-get-together-and-have-some-fun-that-has-nothing-to-do-with-school type of conversation. Dawn offered her luncheon invitation from across the room. At the time, each of these interactions had seemed somewhat strange. Now I realized that all four students had violated my expectation of an appropriate interpersonal distance.

Consistent with my practice throughout this book, I've changed the names of these former students to protect their privacy. In this case, I've made up names that start with the letters *A, B, C,* and *D* to represent the increasing distance between us when we spoke. (Andre was the closest; Dawn, the farthest away.) Figure 7–1 plots the intervals relative to my expectations.

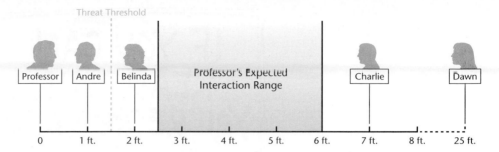

FIGURE 7–1   Expectancy Violations in a Classroom Setting

Judee Burgoon, a communication scholar at the University of Arizona, wrote the journal article that stimulated my thinking. The article was a follow-up piece on the *nonverbal expectancy violations model* that she had introduced in *HCR* two years earlier. Since my own dissertation research focused on interpersonal distance, I knew firsthand how little social science theory existed to guide researchers studying nonverbal communication. I was therefore excited to see Burgoon offering a sophisticated theory of personal space. The fact that she was teaching in a communication department and had published her work in a communication journal was value added. I eagerly read Burgoon's description of her nonverbal expectancy violations model to see whether it could account for my mixed response to the various conversational distances chosen by the four students.

PERSONAL SPACE EXPECTATIONS: CONFORM OR DEVIATE?

Personal space
The invisible, variable volume of space surrounding an individual that defines that individual's preferred distance from others.

Burgoon defined *personal space* as the "invisible, variable volume of space surrounding an individual that defines that individual's preferred distance from others."[2] She claimed that the size and shape of our personal space depend on our cultural norms and individual preferences, but it's always a compromise between the conflicting approach-avoidance needs that we as humans have for affiliation and privacy.

The idea of personal space wasn't original with Burgoon. In the 1960s, Illinois Institute of Technology anthropologist Edward Hall coined the term *proxemics* to refer to the study of people's use of space as a special elaboration of culture.[3] He entitled his book *The Hidden Dimension* because he was convinced that most spatial interpretation is outside our awareness. He claimed that Americans have four proxemic zones, which nicely correspond with the four interpersonal distances selected by my students:

Proxemics
The study of people's use of space as a special elaboration of culture.

1. Intimate distance: 0 to 18 inches (Andre)
2. Personal distance: 18 inches to 4 feet (Belinda)
3. Social distance: 4 to 10 feet (Charlie)
4. Public distance: 10 feet to infinity (Dawn)

Hall's book is filled with examples of "ugly Americans" who were insensitive to the spatial customs of other cultures. He strongly recommended that in order to be effective, we learn to adjust our nonverbal behavior to conform to the communication rules of our partner. We shouldn't cross a distance boundary uninvited.

Cartoon by Peter Steiner. Reprinted with permission.

In his poem "Prologue: The Birth of Architecture," poet W. H. Auden echoes Hall's analysis and puts us on notice that we violate his personal space at our peril:

> Some thirty inches from my nose
> The frontier of my Person goes,
> And all the untilled air between
> Is private pagus or demesne.
> Stranger, unless with bedroom eyes
> I beckon you to fraternize,
> Beware of rudely crossing it:
> I have no gun, but I can spit.[4]

Burgoon's nonverbal expectancy violations model offered a counterpoint to Hall and Auden's advice. She didn't argue with the idea that people have definite expectations about how close others should come. In fact, she would explain Auden's 30-inch rule as based on well-established American norms plus the poet's own idiosyncracies. But contrary to popular go-along-to-get-along wisdom, Burgoon suggested that there are times when it's best to break the rules. She believed that under some circumstances, violating social norms and personal expectations is "a superior strategy to conformity."[5]

AN APPLIED TEST OF THE ORIGINAL MODEL

Whether knowingly or not, each of the four students making a request deviated from my proxemic expectation. How well did Burgoon's initial model predict my responses to these four different violations? Not very well. So that you can capture the flavor of Burgoon's early speculation and recognize how far her current theory has come, I'll outline what the model predicted my responses would be and in each case compare that forecast to what I actually did.

Threat threshold
The hypothetical outer boundary of intimate space; a breach by an uninvited other occasions fight or flight.

Andre. According to Burgoon's early model, Andre made a mistake when he crossed my invisible *threat threshold* and spoke with me at an intimate eyeball-to-eyeball distance. The physical and psychological discomfort I'd feel would hurt his cause. But the model missed on that prediction, since I wrote the recommendation later that day.

Belinda. In the follow-up article I read that day, Burgoon suggested that noticeable deviations from what we expect cause us to experience a heightened state of arousal. She wasn't necessarily referring to the heart-pounding, sweaty-palms reaction that drives us to fight or flight. Instead, she pictured violations stimulating us to review the nature of our relationship with the person who acted in a curious way. That would be good news for Belinda if I thought of her as a highly rewarding person. But every comment she made in class seemed to me a direct challenge, dripping with sarcasm. Just as Burgoon predicted, the narrow, 2-foot gap Belinda chose focused my attention on our rocky relationship, and I declined her request for help in another course. Score one for the nonverbal expectancy violations model.

Charlie. Charlie was a nice guy who cared more about having a good time than he did about studies. He knew I'd played water polo in college, but he may not have realized that his casual attitude toward the class was a constant reminder that I wasn't as good a teacher as I wanted to be. In her 1978 *HRC* article, Burgoon wrote that a person with "punishing power" (like Charlie) would do best to observe proxemic conventions or, better yet, stand slightly farther away than expected. Without ever hearing Burgoon's advice, Charlie did it right. He backed off to a distance of 7 feet—just outside the range of interaction I anticipated. Even so, I declined his offer to swim with the guys.

Dawn. According to this nonverbal expectancy violations model, Dawn blew it. Because she was an attractive communicator, a warm, close approach would have been a pleasant surprise. But her decision to issue an invitation from across the room would seem to guarantee a poor response. The farther she backed off, the worse the effect would be. There's only one problem with this analysis: Dawn and I had lunch together in the student union the following day.

Obviously, my attempt to apply Burgoon's original model to conversational distance between me and my students didn't meet with much success. The theoretical scoreboard read:

> Nonverbal expectancy violations model: **1**
> Unpredicted random behavior: **3**

Burgoon's first controlled experiments didn't fare much better. But where I was ready to dismiss the whole model as flawed, she was unwilling to abandon *expectancy violation* as a key concept in human interaction. At the end of her journal article she hinted that some of her basic assumptions might need to be tested and reevaluated.

Of course that was then; this is now. Over the last three decades Judee Burgoon and her students have crafted a series of sophisticated laboratory experiments and field studies to discover and explain the effects of expectancy violations. One of the reasons I chose to write about her theory is that the current version is an excellent example of ideas continually revised as a result of empirical disconfirmation. As she has demonstrated, in science failure can lead to success.

A CONVOLUTED MODEL BECOMES AN ELEGANT THEORY

Arousal, relational
A heightened state of awareness, orienting response, or mental alertness that stimulates a review of the relationship.

When applied to theories, the term *elegant* suggests "gracefully concise and simple; admirably succinct."[6] That's what expectancy violations theory has become. Burgoon has dropped concepts that were central in earlier versions, yet never panned out. Early on, for example, she abandoned the idea of a "threat threshold." Even though that hypothetical boundary made intuitive sense, repeated experimentation failed to confirm its existence.

Burgoon's retreat from *arousal* as an explanatory mechanism has been more gradual. She originally stated that people felt physiologically aroused when their proxemic expectations were violated. Later she softened the concept to "an orienting response" or a mental "alertness" that focuses attention on the violator. She now views arousal as a side effect of a partner's deviation and no longer considers it a necessary link between expectancy violation and communication outcomes such as attraction, credibility, persuasion, and involvement.

By removing extraneous features, Burgoon has streamlined her model. By extending its scope, she has produced a complete theory. Her original nonverbal expectancy violations model was concerned only with spatial violations—a rather narrow focus. But by the mid-1980s, Burgoon had realized that proxemic behavior is part of an interconnected system of nonlinguistic cues. It no longer made sense to study interpersonal distance in isolation. She began to apply the model to a host of other nonverbal variables—facial expression, eye contact, touch, and body lean, for example. Burgoon continues to expand the range of expectancy violations. While not losing interest in nonverbal communication, she now applies the theory to emotional, marital, and intercultural communication as well. Consistent with this broad sweep, she has dropped the *nonverbal* qualifier and refers to her theory as "expectancy violations theory" and abbreviates it EVT. From this point on, so will I.

What does EVT predict? Burgoon sums up her empirically driven conclusions in a single paragraph. It is my hope that my long narrative account of the theory's development will help you appreciate the 30 years of work that lie behind these simple lines.

> Expectancies exert significant influence on people's interaction patterns, on their impressions of one another, and on the outcomes of their interactions. Violations of expectations in turn may arouse and distract their recipients, shifting greater attention to the violator and the meaning of the violation itself. People who can assume that they are well regarded by their audience are safer engaging in violations and more likely to profit from doing so than are those who are poorly regarded. When the violation act is one that is likely to be ambiguous in its meaning or to carry multiple interpretations that are not uniformly positive or negative, then the reward valence of the communicator can be especially significant in moderating interpretations, evaluations, and subsequent outcomes. . . . In other cases, violations

have relatively consensual meanings and valences associated with them, so that engaging in them produces similar effects for positive- and negative-valenced communicators.[7]

CORE CONCEPTS OF EVT

A close reading of Burgoon's summary suggests that EVT offers a "soft determinism" rather than hard-core universal laws (see Chapter 2). The qualifying terms *may*, *more likely*, *can be*, and *relatively* reflect her belief that too many factors affect communication to allow us ever to discover simple cause-and-effect relationships. She does, however, hope to show a link among surprising interpersonal behavior and attraction, credibility, influence, and involvement. These are the potential outcomes of expectancy violation that Burgoon and her students explore. In order for us to appreciate the connection, we need to understand three core concepts of EVT: *expectancy*, *violation valence*, and *communicator reward valence*. I'll illustrate these three variables by referring back to my students' proxemic behavior and to another form of nonverbal communication—touch.

Expectancy

When I was a kid, my mother frequently gave notice that she *expected* me to be on my best behavior. I considered her words to be a wish or a warning rather than a forecast of my future actions. That is not how Burgoon uses the word. She and her colleagues "prefer to reserve the term *expectancy* for what is predicted to occur rather than what is desired."[8] Figure 7–1 shows that I anticipated conversations with students to take place at a distance of 2½ to 6 feet. How did this expectation arise? Burgoon suggests that I processed the context, type of relationship, and characteristics of the others automatically in my mind so that I could gauge what they might do.

Expectancy
What people predict will happen, rather than what they desire.

Context begins with cultural norms. Three feet is too close in England or Germany yet too far removed in Saudi Arabia, where you can't trust people who won't let you smell their breath. Context also includes the setting of the conversation. A classroom environment dictates a greater speaking distance than would be appropriate for a private chat in my office.

Relationship factors include similarity, familiarity, liking, and relative status. In one study, Burgoon discovered that people of all ages and stations in life anticipate that lower-status people will keep their distance. Because of our age difference and teacher–student relationship, I was more surprised by Andre and Belinda's invasion of my personal space than I was by Charlie and Dawn's remote location.

Communicator characteristics include all of the age/sex/place-of-birth demographic facts asked for on application forms, but they also include personal features that may affect expectation even more—physical appearance, personality, and communication style. Dawn's warm smile was a counterpoint to Belinda's caustic comments. Given this difference, I would have assumed that Dawn would be the one to draw close and Belinda the one to keep her distance. That's why I was especially curious when each woman's spatial "transgression" was the opposite of what I would have predicted.

We can do a similar analysis of my expectation for touch in that classroom situation. Edward Hall claimed that the United States is a "noncontact culture," so I wouldn't anticipate touch during the course of normal conversation.[9] Does this mean that Latin American or Southern European "contact cultures" wouldn't have tight expectations for nonverbal interaction? By no means; Burgoon is convinced that all cultures have a similar *structure* of expected communication behavior but that the *content* of those expectations can differ markedly from culture to culture. Touch is fraught with meaning in every society, but the who, when, where, and how of touching are a matter of culture-specific standards and customs.

As a male in a role relationship, it never occurred to me that students might make physical contact while voicing their requests. If it had, Dawn would have been the likely candidate. But at her chosen distance of 25 feet, she'd need to be a bionic woman to reach me. As it was, I would have been shocked if she'd violated my expectation and walked over to give me a hug. (As a lead-in to the next two sections, note that I didn't say I would have been disturbed, distressed, or disgusted.)

Violation Valence

Violation valence
The perceived positive or negative value assigned to a breach of expectations, regardless of who the violator is.

The term *violation valence* refers to the positive or negative value we place on a specific unexpected behavior, regardless of who does it. Do we find the act itself pleasing or distressing, and to what extent? With her commitment to the scientific method, Burgoon may have borrowed the concept of valence from chemistry, where the valence of a substance is indicated by a number and its sign (+3 or −2, for example). The term *net worth* from the field of accounting seems to capture the same idea.

We usually give others a bit of wiggle room to deviate from what we regard as standard operating procedure. But once we deal with someone who acts outside the range of expected behavior, we switch into an evaluation mode. According to Burgoon, we first try to interpret the meaning of the violation, and then figure out whether we like it.

The meaning of some violations is easy to spot. As a case in point, no one would agonize over how to interpret a purposeful poke in the eye with a sharp stick. It's a hostile act, and if it happened to us, we'd be livid. Many nonverbal behaviors are that straightforward. For example, moderate to prolonged eye contact in Western cultures usually communicates awareness, interest, affection, and trust. A level gaze is welcome; shifty eyes are not. With the exception of a riveting stare, we value eye contact. Even Emerson, a man of letters, wrote, "The eyes of men converse as much as their tongues, with the advantage that the ocular dialect needs no dictionary. . . ."[10]

When a behavior has a socially recognized meaning, communicators can usually figure out whether to go beyond what others expect. If the valence is negative, do less than expected. If the valence is positive, go further. Burgoon validated this advice when she studied the effect of expectancy on marital satisfaction.[11] She questioned people about how much intimate communication they expected from their partner compared to how much focused conversation they actually got. Not surprisingly, intimacy was ranked as positive. Partners who received about as much intimacy as they expected were moderately satisfied with their marriages. But people were highly satisfied with their marriages when they had more good talks with their husbands or wives than they originally thought they would.

On the other hand, many expectancy violations are ambiguous and open to multiple interpretations. For example, the meaning of unexpected touch can be puzzling. Is it a mark of total involvement in the conversation, a sign of warmth and affection, a display of dominance, or a sexual move? Distance violations can also be confusing. Andre isn't from the Middle East, so why was he standing so close? I don't bark or bite, so why did Dawn issue her invitation from across the room? According to EVT, it's at times like these that we consider the reward valence of the communicator as well as the valence of the violation.

Before we look at the way communicator reward valence fits into the theory, you should know that Burgoon has found few nonverbal behaviors that are ambiguous when seen in a larger context. A touch on the arm might be enigmatic in isolation, but when experienced along with close proximity, forward body lean, a direct gaze, facial animation, and verbal fluency, almost everyone interprets the physical contact as a sign of high involvement in the conversation.[12] Or consider actor Eric Idle's words and nonverbal manner in a *Monty Python* sketch. He punctuates his question about Terry Gilliam's wife with a burlesque wink, a leering tone of voice, and gestures to accompany his words: "Nudge nudge. Know what I mean? Say no more . . . know what I mean?"[13] Taken alone, an exaggerated wink or a dig with the elbow might have many possible meanings, but as part of a coordinated routine, both gestures clearly transform a questionable remark into a lewd comment.

There are times, however, when nonverbal expectancy violations are truly equivocal. The personal space deviations of my students are cases in point. Perhaps I just wasn't sensitive enough to pick up the cues that would help me make sense of their proxemic violations. But when the meaning of an action is unclear, EVT says that we interpret the violation in light of how the violator can affect our lives.

Communicator Reward Valence

EVT is not the only theory that describes the human tendency to size up other people in terms of the potential rewards they have to offer. *Social penetration theory* suggests that we live in an interpersonal economy in which we all "take stock" of the relational value of others we meet (see Chapter 9). The questions *What can you do for me?* and *What can you do to me?* often cross our minds. Burgoon is not a cynic, but she thinks the issue of reward potential moves from the background to the foreground of our minds when someone violates our expectation and there's no social consensus as to the meaning of the act. She uses the term *communicator reward valence* to label the results of our mental audit of likely gains and losses.

Communicator reward valence
The sum of positive and negative attributes brought to the encounter plus the potential to reward or punish in the future.

The reward valence of a communicator is the sum of the positive and negative attributes that the person brings to the encounter plus the potential he or she has to reward or punish in the future. The resulting perception is usually a mix of good and bad and falls somewhere on a scale between those two poles. I'll illustrate communicator characteristics that Burgoon frequently mentions by reviewing one feature of each student that I thought about immediately after their perplexing spatial violations.

Andre was a brilliant student. Although writing recommendations is low on my list of fun things to do, I would bask in reflected glory if he were accepted into a top graduate program.

Belinda had a razor-sharp mind and a tongue to match. I'd already felt the sting of her verbal barbs and thought that thinly veiled criticism in the future was a distinct possibility.

Charlie was the classic goof-off—seldom in class and never prepared. I try to be evenhanded with everyone who signs up for my classes, but in Charlie's case I had to struggle not to take his casual attitude toward the course as a personal snub.

Dawn was a beautiful young woman with a warm smile. I felt great pleasure when she openly announced that I was her favorite teacher.

My views of Andre, Belinda, Charlie, and Dawn probably say more about me than they do about the four students. I'm not particularly proud of my stereotyped assessments, but apparently I have plenty of company in the criteria I used. Burgoon notes that the features that impressed me also weigh heavily with others when they compute a reward valence for someone who is violating their expectations. Status, ability, and good looks are standard "goodies" that enhance the other person's reward potential. The thrust of the conversation is even more important. Most of us value words that communicate acceptance, liking, appreciation, and trust. We're turned off by talk that conveys disinterest, disapproval, distrust, and rejection.

Why does Burgoon think that the expectancy violator's power to reward or punish is so crucial? Because puzzling violations force victims to search the social context for clues to their meaning.[14] Thus, an ambiguous violation embedded in a host of relationally warm signals takes on a positive cast. An equivocal violation from a punishing communicator stiffens our resistance.

Now that I've outlined EVT's core concepts of expectancy, violation valence, and communicator reward valence, you can better understand the bottom-line advice that Burgoon's theory offers. Should you communicate in a totally unexpected way? If you're certain that the novelty will be a pleasant surprise, the answer is yes. But if you know that your outlandish behavior will offend, don't do it.

When you aren't sure how others will interpret your far-out behavior, let their overall attitude toward you dictate your verbal and nonverbal actions. So if like Belinda and Charlie you have reason to suspect a strained relationship, and the meaning of a violation might be unclear, stifle your deviant tendencies and do your best to conform to expectations. But when you know you've already created a positive personal impression (like Andre or Dawn), a surprise move not only is safe, it probably will enhance the positive effect of your message.

INTERACTION ADAPTATION—ADJUSTING EXPECTATIONS

As evidence of its predictive power, EVT has been used to explain and predict attitudes and behaviors in a wide variety of communication contexts. These include students' perceptions of their instructors, patients' responses to health care providers, and individuals' actions in romantic relationships. For example, Arizona State University communication professor Paul Mongeau has studied men and women's expectations for first dates and compares those expectations with their actual experiences.[15] He discovered that men are pleasantly surprised when a woman initiates a first date and that they usually interpret such a request as a sign that she's interested in sexual activity. But there's a second surprise in store for most of these guys when it turns out that they have less physical intimacy than they do on the traditional male-initiated first date. We might expect that the men's disappointment would put a damper on future dates together, but surprisingly it doesn't.

For Mongeau, EVT explains how dating partners' expectations are affected by who asks out whom. Yet unlike early tests of EVT, Mongeau's work considers how one person's actions might reshape a dating partner's perceptions after their time together—a morning after the night-before adjustment of expectations. In the same way, Burgoon has reassessed EVT's single-sided view and now favors a dyadic model of adaptation. That's because she regards conversations as more akin to duets than solos. Interpersonal interactions involve synchronized actions rather than unilateral moves. Along with her former students Lesa Stern and Leesa Dillman, Burgoon has crafted *interaction adaptation theory* as an extension and expansion of EVT.[16]

Burgoon states that human beings are predisposed to adapt to each other. That's often necessary, she says, because another person's actions may not square with the thoughts and feelings that we bring to our interaction. She sees this initial *interaction position* as made up of three factors: requirements, expectations, and desires. *Requirements* (R) are the outcomes that fulfill our basic needs to survive, be safe, belong, and have a sense of self-worth. These are the panhuman motivations that Abraham Maslow outlined in his hierarchy of needs.[17] As opposed to requirements that represent what we need to happen, *expectations* (E) as defined in EVT are what we think really will happen. Finally, *desires* (D) are what we personally would like to see happen. These RED factors coalesce or meld into our interaction position of what's needed, anticipated, and preferred. I'll continue to use touch behavior to show how Burgoon uses this composite mindset to predict how we adjust to another person's behavior.

I'm a "people person" who places a high value on close relationships—a requirement. When I get together with my friend Bob, we usually greet each other with a simultaneous clasp of each other's elbow or a side-by-side shoulder hug, physical contact more intimate than a formal handshake—an expectation. I'd like our nonverbal behavior to convey the enjoyment I think we both feel when we get together—a personal desire. Suppose Bob were to walk up to me with widespread arms to give me a bear hug for the first time in our relationship. This move would be somewhat discrepant from my interaction position, so I'd need to adapt my response in some way. What would I do?

Because I regard Bob's action as more positive than the sum of my RED factors, interaction adaptation theory predicts I would either reciprocate his warm approach or at least adjust my behavior in the direction of more intimacy. That means that I'd make the bear hug mutual, or perhaps give an enthusiastic shoulder hug that's longer and firmer than usual. Conversely, if I liked my interaction position better than Bob's effusive action, I'd compensate by merely going through the motions in a half-hearted way or back off completely. The same principle of compensation would apply if Bob greeted me without any physical touch. I'd try to reestablish our previous level of nonverbal closeness, or at least move to shake his hand.

About a decade ago Burgoon outlined two shortcomings of expectancy violations theory that she found particularly troubling:

> First, EVT does not fully account for the overwhelming prevalence of reciprocity that has been found in interpersonal interactions. Second, it is silent on whether communicator valence supersedes behavior valence or vice versa when the two are incongruent (such as when a disliked partner engages in a positive violation).[18]

Interaction adaptation theory
A systematic analysis of how people adjust their approach when another's behavior doesn't mesh with what's needed, anticipated, or preferred.

Interaction position
A person's initial stance toward an interaction as determined by a blend of personal requirements, expectations, and desires (RED).

Reciprocity
A strong human tendency to respond to another's action with similar behavior.

Interaction adaptation theory is Burgoon's attempt to address these problems within the broader framework of ongoing behavioral adjustments. There's obviously more to the theory than I've been able to present, but hopefully this brief sketch lets you see that for Burgoon, one theory leads to another.

CRITIQUE: A WELL-REGARDED WORK IN PROGRESS

I have a friend who fixes my all-terrain cycle whenever I bend it or break it. "What do you think?" I ask Bill. "Can it be repaired?" His response is always the same: "Man made it. Man can fix it!"

Judee Burgoon shows the same resolve as she seeks to adjust and redesign an expectancy violations model that never quite works as well in practice as its theoretical blueprint says it should. Almost every empirical test she runs seems to yield mixed results. For example, her early work on physical contact suggested that touch violations were often ambiguous. However, a sophisticated experiment she ran in 1992 showed that unexpected touch in a problem-solving situation was almost always welcomed as a positive violation, regardless of the status, gender, or attractiveness of the violator.

Do repeated failures to predict outcomes when a person stands far away, moves in too close, or reaches out to touch someone imply that Burgoon ought to trade in her expectancy violations theory for a new model? Does interaction adaption theory render EVT obsolete? From my perspective, the answer is no.

Taken as a whole, Burgoon's expectancy violations theory continues to meet four of the five criteria of a good scientific theory, as presented in Chapter 3. Her theory advances a reasonable explanation for the effects of expectancy violations during communication. The explanation she offers is relatively simple and has actually become less complex over time. The theory has testable hypotheses that the theorist is willing to adjust when her tests don't support the prediction. Finally, the model offers practical advice on how to better achieve important communication goals of increased credibility, influence, and attraction. Could we ask for anything more? Of course.

We could wish for predictions that prove more reliable than the *Farmer's Almanac* long-range forecast of weather trends. A review of recent expectancy violations research suggests that EVT may have reached that point. For example, a comparative empirical study tested how well three leading theories predict interpersonal responses to nonverbal immediacy—close proximity, touch, direct gaze, direct body orientation, and forward lean.[19] None of the theories proved to be right all of the time, but EVT did better than the other two. And based on what a revised EVT now predicts, the scoreboard for my responses to the proxemic violations of Andre, Belinda, Charlie, and Dawn would show four hits and no misses.

ETHICAL REFLECTION: KANT'S CATEGORICAL IMPERATIVE

EVT focuses on what's *effective*. Before we knowingly violate another's expectation we should consider what's *ethical*. German philosopher Immanuel Kant believed that any time we speak or act, we have a moral obligation to be truthful. He wrote that "truthfulness in statements which cannot be avoided is the formal duty of an individual to everyone, however great may be the disadvantage accruing to himself or another."[20] Others might wink at white lies, justify deception for the other's own good, or warn of the dire consequences that can result from total honesty. But from

Kant's perspective, there are no mitigating circumstances. Lying is wrong—always. So is breaking a promise. He'd regard nonverbal deception the same way.

Kant came to this absolutist position through the logic of his *categorical imperative*, a term that means duty without exception. He stated the categorical imperative as a universal law: "Act only on that maxim which you can will to become a universal law."[21] In terms of EVT, Kant would have us look at the violation we are considering and ask, *What if everybody did that all the time?* If we don't like the answer then we have a solemn duty not to do the deed.

The categorical imperative is a method for determining right from wrong by thinking through the ethical valence of an act, regardless of motive. Suppose we're thinking about touching someone in a way he or she doesn't expect and hasn't clearly let us know is welcome. Perhaps the other might be pleasantly surprised. But unless we can embrace the idea of everyone—no matter what their communication reward valence—having that kind of unbidden access to everybody, the categorical imperative says don't do it. No exceptions. In the words of a sports-minded colleague who teaches ethics, "Kant plays ethical hardball without a mitt." If we say, *I "Kant" play in that league,* what ethical scorecard will we use in place of his categorical imperative?

Categorical imperative
Duty without exception; act only on that maxim which you can will to become a universal law.

QUESTIONS TO SHARPEN YOUR FOCUS

1. What *proxemic* advice would you give to communicators who believe they are seen as *unrewarding?*

2. Except for ritual handshakes, *touch* is often *unexpected* in *casual relationships.* If you don't know someone well, what is the *violation valence* you ascribe to a light touch on the arm, a brief touch on the cheek, or a shoulder hug?

3. EVT suggests that *communicator reward valence* is especially important when the *violation valence* is equivocal. What verbal or nonverbal expectancy violations would be confusing to you even when experienced in context?

4. EVT and coordinated management of meaning (see Chapter 6) hold diverse assumptions about the nature of *knowledge, reality,* and *communication research.* Can you draw the distinctions?

CONVERSATIONS

View this segment online at www.mhhe.com/griffin7 or www.afirstlook.com.

A few minutes into my discussion with Judee Burgoon, you'll notice that one of us violates a communication expectation of the other. See if you think the violation is accidental or strategic. How does this event affect the rest of the conversation? Burgoon's love of theory is apparent throughout the segment. Do you think her enthusiasm is bolstered by a view of theories as systematic hunches rather than timeless principles chiseled in stone? As a scientist, Burgoon believes that much of human behavior is genetically programmed, yet she insists that communication is also a choice-driven, strategic behavior. As you watch, decide whether you think these beliefs are compatible.

A SECOND LOOK

Recommended resource: Judee K. Burgoon and Jerold Hale, "Nonverbal Expectancy Violations: Model Elaboration and Application to Immediacy Behaviors," *Communication Monographs,* Vol. 55, 1988, pp. 58–79.

Original model: Judee K. Burgoon, "A Communication Model of Personal Space Violations: Explication and an Initial Test," *Human Communication Research,* Vol. 4, 1978, pp. 129–142.

Expectancy: Judee K. Burgoon and Beth A. LePoire, "Effects of Communication Expectancies, Actual Communication, and Expectancy Disconfirmation on Evaluations of Communicators and Their Communication Behavior," *Human Communication Research,* Vol. 20, 1993, pp. 67–96.

Expectation and valence of touch: Judee K. Burgoon, Joseph Walther, and E. James Baesler, "Interpretations, Evaluations, and Consequences of Touch," *Human Communication Research,* Vol. 19, 1992, pp. 237–263.

Communicator reward valence: Judee K. Burgoon, "Relational Message Interpretations of Touch, Conversational Distance, and Posture," *Journal of Nonverbal Behavior,* Vol. 15, 1991, pp. 233–259.

Extension of the theory: Walid A. Afifi and Judee K. Burgoon, "The Impact of Violations on Uncertainty and the Consequences for Attractiveness," *Human Communication Research,* Vol. 26, 2000, pp. 203–233.

Nonverbal persuasion: Judee K. Burgoon, Norah E. Dunbar, and Chris Segrin, "Nonverbal Influence," in *The Persuasion Handbook: Developments in Theory and Practice,* James Dillard and Michael Pfau (eds.), Sage, Thousand Oaks, CA, 2002, pp. 445–473.

Interaction adaptation theory: Judee K. Burgoon, Lesa Stern, and Leesa Dillman, *Interpersonal Adaptation: Dyadic Interaction Patterns,* Cambridge University, Cambridge, 1995.

Kant's categorical imperative: Immanuel Kant, *Groundwork of the Metaphysics of Morals,* H. J. Paton (trans.), Harper Torchbooks, New York, 1964, pp. 60–88.

Cultural violations: Judee K. Burgoon and Amy Ebesu Hubbard, "Cross-Cultural and Intercultural Applications of Expectancy Violations Theory and Interaction Adaptation Theory," in *Theorizing About Intercultural Communication,* William B. Gudykunst (ed.), Sage, Thousand Oaks, CA, 2004, pp. 149–171.

To access a chapter on Hall's proxemic theory that appeared
in a previous edition, click on Theory Archive at
www.afirstlook.com.

Constructivism

of Jesse Delia

Constructivism is a communication theory that seeks to explain individual differences in people's ability to communicate skillfully in social situations. You probably don't need to be convinced that some people are better at understanding, attracting, persuading, informing, comforting, or entertaining others with whom they talk. In fact, you may be taking communication courses so that you can become more adept at reaching these communication goals. Although some might suspect that communication success is simply a matter of becoming more assertive or outgoing, Jesse Delia believes that there is a crucial behind-the-eyes difference in people who are interpersonally effective. His theory of constructivism offers a cognitive explanation for communication competence.

Delia is the former chair of the department of speech communication at the University of Illinois at Urbana-Champaign and now serves as associate chancellor of the school. Along with a network of constructivist researchers, he uses Walter Crockett's open-ended Role Category Questionnaire (RCQ) to help us "get inside our head."[1] So that you fully understand the theory and what it says about your communication, take 10 minutes to respond to the RCQ before you become sensitized to what the survey is measuring.

ROLE CATEGORY QUESTIONNAIRE INSTRUCTIONS

Think of people about your age whom you know well. Select one person you like and pick someone you dislike. Once you have two specific people in mind, spend a moment to mentally compare and contrast them in terms of personality, habits, beliefs, and the way they treat others. Don't limit yourself to similarities and differences between the two; let your mind play over the full range of characteristics that make them who they are.

Now take a piece of paper and for about five minutes describe the person you enjoy so that a stranger would understand what he or she is like. Skip physical characteristics, but list all of the attributes, mannerisms, and reactions to others that identify who he or she is.

When you've finished the description, do the same thing for the person you don't like. Again, write down all the personal characteristics or actions that you associate with that person. Spend about five minutes on this description.

INTERPERSONAL CONSTRUCTS AS EVIDENCE OF COGNITIVE COMPLEXITY

Interpersonal constructs
The cognitive templates or stencils we fit over social reality to order our impressions of people.

The core assumption of constructivism is that "persons make sense of the world through systems of personal constructs."[2] *Constructs* are the cognitive templates or stencils we fit over reality to bring order to our perceptions. The Role Category Questionnaire is designed to sample the interpersonal constructs in our mental toolbox that we bring to the construction site of meaning—the central processing function of our minds. Much like sets of opposing terms (warm-cool, good-bad, fast-slow), constructs are contrasting features that we have available to classify other people.

A police artist has an identification kit with which an eyewitness can construct the face of a suspect. By systematically altering the shape of the chin, size of the nose, distance between the eyes, line of the hair, and so forth, the witness can build a likeness of the person in question. However, the RCQ doesn't bother with physical features. It centers on the categories of personality and action that we use to define the character of another person.

Role Category Questionnaire (RCQ)
A free-response survey designed to measure the cognitive complexity of a person's interpersonal perception.

The arena of politics offers a familiar example of the way we use constructs to describe another individual. All of us have our own bipolar dimensions of judgment that we apply to politicians. Some typical scales are liberal-conservative, steadfast-flexible, competent-inept. The politically astute observer may draw on dozens of these interpretive orientations to describe shades of difference. There are *conservatives*, and there are *social* conservatives. Then there are *articulate* social conservatives. Some of them are *belligerent*, and so forth. On the other hand, those who are politically unsophisticated may use only one value-laden construct as they watch the six o'clock news. They see only winners and losers.

An Index of Social Perception Skills

Cognitive complexity
The mental ability to distinguish subtle personality and behavior differences among people.

Researchers who rely on the RCQ are trying to determine our degree of *cognitive complexity* as we form impressions of other people and analyze social situations. They are convinced that people with a large set of interpersonal constructs have better *social perception skills* than those whose set of mental templates is relatively small. Those skills include figuring out others' personality traits, where they stand in relationship to us, what they are doing, and why they are doing it. As you will see in Walther's *social information processing theory*, impression formation is the crucial first step in relational development (see Chapter 11). Cognitively complex people have a definite advantage in that process. They also are better able to "take the role of the other," the mental perspective-taking that makes humans unique, according to Mead (see Chapter 5). Brant Burleson (Purdue University), a long-time colleague of Delia in the constructivism project, maintains that those who have high levels of cognitive complexity are comparative experts when it comes to understanding the people and events in their social world.[3]

Cognitive theorists like Delia and Burleson distinguish between mental *structures* and mental *processes*. What you know about word processing on your computer may help you understand the different roles of structure and process in the mind. The computer hardware is the structure. What the software does when we strike a function key is the process. A four-year-old boy at a playground explained to me the difference between mental structure and mental process without ever using those terms. "My brain is like a jungle gym," he said. "Thinking is like climbing all over it."

Delia and Burleson are more concerned with the *structure* of our constructs than with the actual judgments we make. Consistent with that focus, it's been said that there are two kinds of people in the world—those who think there are two kinds of people in the world and those who don't. Constructivists believe that the first kind of person is cognitively immature because he or she is able to see others only in terms of black and white. But the second type of person has developed into a sophisticated observer of the human scene, capable of distinguishing subtle differences among people. When it comes to thinking about these differences, the Role Category Questionnaire is designed to gauge how intricate the jungle gym in your head might be.

SCORING THE RCQ FOR CONSTRUCT DIFFERENTIATION

Differentiation
The main component of cognitive complexity as measured by the number of separate personal constructs used on the RCQ.

Although the RCQ can be scored in different ways, most constructivist researchers cull the descriptions of liked and disliked peers for the amount of construct differentiation. *Differentiation* is defined as the number of separate personality constructs used to portray the person in question. I'll take you through a shorthand version of the scoring procedure so that you can see how constructivists might rate you on cognitive complexity.

Let's assume you wrote about the personal characteristics of a friend named Chris and a co-worker named Alex. Add up the number of different descriptions you used to describe both people. As a rule of thumb, consider that each new term represents an additional mental construct. Seeing Chris as both *sharp* and *competent* would earn two points. So would a judgment that Alex is *hurried* and *never has time.* But there are exceptions to the one-term-equals-one-construct rule.

Adjectives and adverbs that merely modify the extent of a characteristic don't reflect additional constructs. Score just one point if you wrote that Chris is *totally sincere.* Since idioms such as *good ole boy* have a single referent, they get a single point as well. On their own, physical descriptions (*tall*) and demographic labels (*Irish*) say nothing about character, so skip over them. Apart from these rules, close calls should get the benefit of the doubt and score an extra point.

Constructivists regard the combined number of constructs for both descriptions as an index of cognitive complexity. The higher your score, the more elaborate is the structure within your mind over which your interpersonal perceptions play. I've seen individual scores as low as 6 and as high as 45, but about 70 percent of college students score between 15 and 25, with a mean of 20. Burleson interprets any score over 25 as a reliable indicator of high interpersonal cognitive complexity.

Are RCQ scores really an accurate measure of cognitive complexity? Delia makes a good case for their validity. His claim that cognitive complexity develops with a child's chronological age is reflected in progressively higher scores as youngsters grow older. He also believes that individual differences between adults should be relatively stable over time. That standard has been met through good test-retest reliability.

Finally, Delia notes that a pure test of personality shouldn't be confounded by other character traits or extraneous factors. Research has established that RCQ scores are independent of IQ, empathy, writing skill, and extroversion. Some critics charge that it's merely a measure of loquacity, or wordiness, but constructivists maintain that high scores on this free-response test take more than the gift of gab. What's required is a wide range of interpersonal constructs.

PERSON-CENTERED MESSAGES—THE INTERPERSONAL EDGE

Now that you have an idea of what's involved in cognitive complexity, we'll consider the main hypothesis of constructivism. Delia and his colleagues claim that people who are cognitively complex in their perceptions of others have a communication advantage over those with less developed mental structures. These fortunate individuals have the ability to produce person-centered messages that give them a better chance to achieve their communication goals.

Person-centered message
A tailor-made message for a specific individual and context; reflects the communicator's ability to anticipate response and adjust accordingly.

As Delia uses the phrase, *person-centered messages* refers to "messages which reflect an awareness of and adaptation to subjective, affective, and relational aspects of the communication contexts."[4] In other words, the speaker is able to anticipate how different individuals might respond to a message, and adjust his or her communication accordingly.

The study by Ruth Ann Clark and Delia of second- to ninth-grade schoolchildren is a prototype of constructivist research that links person-centered messages to cognitive complexity.[5] It focused on the children's ability to adapt persuasive appeals to different target listeners. After taking the RCQ orally, the kids were given the role-play task of convincing a woman they didn't know to keep a lost puppy.

Naturally, the quality of messages differed. Some children showed no realization that the woman's perspective on the matter might be different from their own. Other kids recognized the difference but failed to adapt their message to this reality. A more sophisticated group took notice of the difference and were able to imagine what the woman was thinking. ("My husband will think I'm a sucker for every stray in town.") They then could make an attempt to refute the counterarguments they knew their appeal would raise. The most sophisticated messages also stressed the advantages that would come to her if she complied with the request. ("Having a dog for a companion will take away some of the loneliness you feel at night when your husband is out of town. He'll also feel better when he knows you've got a furry friend.")

Constructivists assume that strategic adaptation is a developmentally nurtured skill. Consistent with their belief, Clark and Delia found that the quality of messages improved as the age of the children increased. But differences in construct differentiation that weren't due to chronological age also had a significant impact. Cognitively complex students were two years ahead of their same-age classmates in the ability to encode person-centered messages. Thus, the older kids who possessed cognitive complexity beyond their years were best able to take the perspective of the other and tailor the message to the individual listener.

Scholars who study communication use different terms to describe the capacity to create person-centered messages: *rhetorical sensitivity, taking the role of the other, identification, self-monitoring, audience awareness, listener adaptation.* Whatever we call it, the creation of person-centered messages is a *sophisticated communication skill.* Constructivists say that cognitively complex people can do it better. Note that constructivists don't claim that such people *always* do it, only that they have a capacity that others don't. The way constructivists put it is that cognitive complexity is a "necessary but not sufficient condition" of person-centered messages."[6] Fatigue, the effects of alcohol, or pressure to conform to a fixed style of communication can mute the advantage. There are also many routine or mundane communication situations where this adaptive skill is neither called for nor particularly helpful. But when the stakes are high and emotions run deep, people who can craft person-centered messages are way ahead of the game.

Sophisticated communication
A person-centered message that accomplishes multiple goals.

MESSAGE PRODUCTION: CRAFTING GOAL-BASED PLANS FOR ACTION

Early versions of constructivism couldn't pin down the reason high construct differentiation usually leads to more effective communication. Like a terse bumper sticker, the theory proclaimed COGNITIVELY COMPLEX PERSONS CAN DO IT BETTER, but Delia wasn't sure why. By the late 1980s, however, other cognitive theorists had begun to develop models of *message production* that constructivists could use to explain the thought processes that tie cognitive structures to speech acts. Delia and his colleagues now consider the basic mental sequence that cognitive scientists outline as the missing link that connects mental complexity with person-centered messages.

Message production
A three-stage process of *goals* assessed, *plans* selected, and tactics enacted (*action*).

For example, consider the workplace plight of a young single woman named Laura, whose married male boss suggests meeting together to talk about her career. At their business lunch he comes on to her—suggesting a sexual affair. Through no fault of her own, Laura's been placed in a tough communication situation.[7] In order to understand her thought process, we'll work through a *goals-plans-action model* of message production outlined by Pennsylvania State University communication professor James Dillard.[8]

Goals

What does Laura want to accomplish? If her sole aim is to stop her employer's sleazy suggestions once and for all, she might adopt a simple plan of attack that creates a message expressing the repulsion she feels:

> You are the most rude and disgusting man I have ever met. You're nothing but a dirty old man. Where do you get off thinking you could force me to have an affair with you? You make me sick.[9]

But she may have another goal that's equally important to her, such as keeping her job. If so, she would have two primary persuasive goals, which she has to juggle. In other situations, she might have different primary communication goals—to inform, advise, comfort, entertain, gain assistance, or alter a relationship. These goals are called *primary* because they "set into motion an ensemble of lower-level cognitive processes that occur in parallel and align with the overall aim represented by the primary goal."[10]

The adoption of multiple primary goals usually prompts the rise of secondary goals. These additional but less important aims often conflict with the primary goals. In Laura's case, stopping the harassment and protecting her job require that she find a way to save face for both her boss and herself. She needs to keep a good working relationship with him while preserving her professional identity and reputation. If, in fact, Laura does simultaneously pursue multiple interpersonal goals, it's a sign of her cognitive complexity. Burleson says that "people with high levels of interpersonal cognitive complexity . . . tend to develop more complex and sophisticated goals for many social situations, especially those that appear challenging or demanding."[11] The number and variety of her interpersonal constructs also equip her to develop a multifaceted plan that can pull it off.

Plans

Once Laura knows what she wants her response to accomplish, she'll devise a message plan using *procedural records* that are stored in her long-term memory.[12] According to John Greene, a colleague of Burleson at Purdue, a procedural record is a recollection of an action taken in a specific situation paired with its consequences—how things turned out. I think of it as a memory that has *if-when-then* implications for future actions. For example, suppose when Laura hears the unwanted sexual proposition from her boss, a long-dormant image pops into her conscious mind. She was 12 years old when the high school guy who lived next door suggested he give her kissing lessons. Confused and troubled by his offer, she laughed and treated the whole thing as a joke, although she knew he was quite serious. If she and her teenage neighbor maintained a casual, nonromantic relationship after the incident, the procedural record filed away in her long-term memory might take this form:

> *If* I want to avoid getting physical and not offend a guy (goals),
>
> *When* he makes an improper sexual suggestion (situation),
>
> *Then* I should pretend he's just kidding (action).

Laura may have over a million procedural records in her long-term memory, but most of them aren't applicable to the problem posed by her employer's indecent proposal. The ones that will be activated and affect her message plan are the memories of times when she had similar goals in somewhat similar circumstances. Although not a perfect fit, the procedural record of how she handled her neighbor's proposal is a close match and will probably inform her response to her boss. If she has lots of memories of successfully feigning ignorance of questionable motives in a variety of situations, this approach could become the top-down strategy that dictates all the other tactics in her message plan.

In an article describing his basic goals-plans-action model of message production, Dillard addresses a number of frequently asked questions about constructing a cognitive plan.[13] Perhaps you'll find that format helpful to better understand the thought process that Laura and the rest of us go through before we speak.

- *What do we do first?* We search our long-term memory for tried-and-true, boilerplate plans that are likely to achieve our primary goal(s).

- *What if none of these prepackaged plans seem promising?* We'll make an existing plan more complete by fleshing out the details, or we'll make it more complex by adding steps to cover many contingencies.

Procedural record
The recollection of an action taken in a specific situation paired with its consequences; an *if-when-then* memory.

- *Are we consciously aware that we're engaged in this mental process?* Most of this mental activity takes place below our level of consciousness. Yet if someone asked us to reflect on why we said what we did, we'd be able to identify the goals our plan was meant to serve.
- *How long does it take for goals to activate procedural records and to assemble them into a message plan?* Usually it's a matter of milliseconds. But if we decide to create a novel message plan rather than adopting or adapting an existing one, the mental process will take more time and effort.
- *Can we change the plan in midconversation?* Definitely—and we usually do if we aren't getting our hoped-for response. Berger's hierarchy hypothesis (see Chapter 10) suggests that we will alter low-level elements of the plan such as word choice or facial expression—changes that won't demand wholesale reorganization. If, however, we change our *goals* midstream, we automatically discard the original plan and adopt or create another one.

Action

Person-centered messages are the form of communication that Delia wants to explain, predict, and promote. Because cognitively complex people have the social perception to see the necessity of pursuing multiple goals and the skills to develop message plans to achieve them, they are the fortunate folks who can communicate skillfully when the situation demands it.

Most people regard the communication context as a factor that limits a speaker's options. It certainly seems that Laura is trapped in a no-win situation as the man who has power over her tries to use it to leverage sexual favors. But as a cognitively complex person, Laura has the ability to use context as a resource. The message she crafts parries her boss's unwelcome advances, salvages her job, and saves face both for herself *and* for him:

> We've got a great working relationship now, and I'd like us to work well together in the future. So I think it's important for us to talk this out. You're a smart and clear-thinking guy and I consider you to be my friend as well as my boss. That's why I have to think you must be under a lot of unusual stress lately to have said something like this. I know what it's like to be under pressure. Too much stress can really make you crazy. You probably just need a break.[14]

Some readers are bothered by this response. In their minds, Laura's words let her lecherous boss off the hook. These folks believe that a clear threat of exposure would be the appropriate way to block his sexual advances and possible retaliation for rejecting them. But from Laura's perspective, a person-centered message is the best way to meet her multiple concerns in this complex situation. By framing her employer's proposition as one that springs from stress rather than from sleaze, Laura is able to achieve *all* of her goals.

I've used the words spoken by a woman to illustrate a person-centered message. That choice is appropriate because women display this crucial communication skill more than men do. You therefore won't be surprised that the average female scores three points higher for construct differentiation on the RCQ than her male counterpart. It turns out to be a difference that makes a difference when a sophisticated interpersonal message is called for. Burleson suggests that we can spot the reason for this gender discrepancy through the social life of children and adolescents. When guys get together they typically talk about others in terms of external *behaviors*—the sports they play, the cars they drive, the battles they fight. Conversely, girls tend to talk about *people*—their perceptions of internal motives, attitudes, traits, and personalities. As you'll see by the end of the chapter, it's by becoming sensitive to the inner life of others that a person's set of interpersonal constructs grows.

BENEFICIAL EFFECTS OF PERSON-CENTERED MESSAGES

Figure 8–1 portrays the linkages that constructivists have forged. High cognitive complexity facilitates sophisticated message plans, which in turn produce person-centered messages. Those links of the chain are well-established. Constructivist researchers have now turned to exploring the positive effects of person-centered messages on every conceivable form of communication outcome. We've already seen that these messages can be more persuasive. In this section I'll highlight the findings in three other areas of research that my students have found particularly interesting.

Social support messages try to ease the emotional distress experienced by others. Burleson has developed a nine-stage hierarchical scale to code the degree of comfort a message of support offers. At the bottom end are messages that dismiss the thoughts and feelings of the person who is hurting: "You shouldn't be so upset about losing your boyfriend. After all, there are lots of fish in the

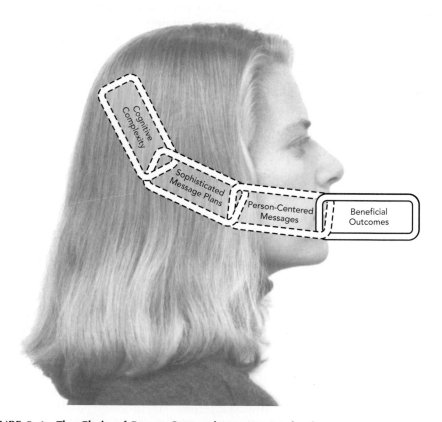

FIGURE 8–1 The Chain of Person-Centered Message Production

sea." Midlevel messages take the other's distress seriously: "Gee, I'm sorry you guys broke up. I guess things like this happen, though. Breaking up just seems to be a part of relationships." Top-of-the-line, sophisticated support messages explicitly validate the other's feelings and often add an additional perspective to the situation: "I know it must hurt. I know you're feeling a lot of pain and anger right now. And that's OK, 'cause I know you were really involved; you guys were together a long time and you expected things to work out differently. I'm here whenever you want to talk about things."[15]

As you might suspect, sophisticated messages are usually experienced as more comforting than clumsy attempts at social support. You hope that's reward enough for the friend who offers well-chosen words in a time of need. But Burleson notes that other positive outcomes accrue to the sensitive comforter:

> Compared to persons using less sophisticated comforting strategies, users of sophisticated strategies are better liked and more positively evaluated by both message recipients and observers. Further, users of sophisticated comforting strategies report feeling better both about themselves and those they try to help.[16]

Relationship maintenance is a process distinct from relationship development. As discussed in Chapters 9 through 11, voluntary relationships usually begin through mutual attraction, self-disclosure, and reduction of uncertainty. Once the relationship is established, however, its ongoing health requires periodic affirmation, conflict resolution, and the type of comforting communication that Burleson describes. As with any interpersonal skill, some people are better at relationship maintenance than others. Burleson and Wendy Samter of Bryant College figured that people with sophisticated communication skills would be especially good at sustaining close friendships. It turns out they were only partially right.[17]

To test their hypothesis, Burleson and Samter reviewed their own previous studies on friendship as well as the work of other researchers. They discovered a consistent pattern, which they labeled the *similar skills model*. To their surprise, individuals' ability to give ego-support, resolve conflict, and provide comfort in times of stress did little to guarantee that their close personal relationships would survive and thrive. But the degree of similarity with their partner did. Friendships tended to last when partners possessed matching verbal skills—high or low. Apparently, highly refined communication skills are an advantage in friendship only when the other has the sophistication to appreciate them. And a person with few of these abilities may be more comfortable spending time with someone who likes the same activities, can tell a good story, and isn't always "talking about feelings" or "pushing that touchy-feely crap."[18]

Organizational effectiveness isn't determined by a single, sophisticated message. According to constructivist theory, high performance and promotion reflect a continual use of person-centered communication that seeks to achieve multiple goals with customers and co-workers. Employees who do it better should climb the corporate ladder faster.

Beverly Sypher (Purdue University) and Theodore Zorn (University of Waikato, New Zealand) conducted a longitudinal study of 90 white-collar workers at a large Eastern insurance company.[19] At the start of the study they measured cognitive complexity with the RCQ, tested for perspective-taking ability, and gauged communication skill by asking employees to write a charitable fundraising appeal. As expected, workers with highly developed social constructs wrote letters that were more persuasive. Four years later, Sypher and Zorn

Similar skills model
A hypothesis that relationships fare better when parties possess the same level of verbal sophistication.

checked each employee's progress within the company. Cognitively complex workers had better-paying jobs and were moving up through the ranks of the company faster than were their less complex colleagues. Anytime we deal with people, cognitive complexity seems to play a significant role.

SOCIALIZING A NEW GENERATION OF SOPHISTICATED SPEAKERS

In early editions of this text, I chided constructivists for not addressing the question of how cognitively complex thinkers get that way. That's no longer a fair criticism. Burleson, Delia, and James Applegate of the University of Kentucky have marshaled evidence that complex thinking is a culturally transmitted trait. Specifically, they suggest that parents' capacity for complex social thinking is re-created in their children through complex messages of nurture and discipline.[20] Their claim is an extension of the truism that culture is produced and reproduced through the communication of its members.

Suppose, for example, a 5-year-old boy picks a flower from a neighbor's yard without permission and presents it to his mother. Almost any parent can scold the kid for stealing. ("Taking people's things without asking is wrong. Now go and apologize for taking the flower.") But it requires a mother with a complex set of interpersonal constructs to create a sophisticated message that encourages reflection and helps her son focus on the motivation, feelings, and intentions of others—mental exercises that increase the child's own cognitive complexity. After warmly thanking her son for the gift, such a mom might say:

> When people work hard to have things (flowers), they usually want to keep them to appreciate them. Mrs. Jones might have given you a flower if you'd asked, but taking things from people without asking upsets them a lot.

Who is most likely to use this form of sophisticated socialization? According to Burleson, Delia, and Applegate, parents from more advantaged socioeconomic backgrounds are likely candidates. They inhabit a world of intricate work environments, role systems, and social expectations. This more complicated social world stimulates the development of more complex ways of thinking and communicating. And once developed, complex ways of thinking and acting tend to perpetuate themselves. The **culture → complexity → communication** path seems to ensure that, cognitively speaking, the rich get richer. This cognitive fact of life was obvious to me in a paper submitted by Jane, a 40-year-old grad student in my interpersonal communication class. She recorded the precocious words of her 7-year-old daughter, Sunny, a child raised in the midst of sophisticated adult conversation.

> Mom, is nonverbal communication like when you don't point your face at me when we're talking about my day? Or when you say "Uh-huh" and "Really?" but your face doesn't move around like you really care what we're talking about? When you walk around cooking or Dad writes while we're talking, I feel like I'm boring. Sometimes when you guys talk to me it sounds like you're just teaching, not talking.

Constructivists would note that Sunny can reflect on her social world because communication from mother Jane has been anything but plain.

CRITIQUE: SECOND THOUGHTS ABOUT COGNITIVE COMPLEXITY

Delia launched what he called an interpretive theory of cognitive differences in the 1970s, when most communication scientists were trying to discover laws of behavior that applied equally to everyone. While these empirical researchers were assessing communication effectiveness by crunching the numbers from standardized attitude scales, Delia called for "free-response data" that could reflect subtle differences in mental processes. He believed that open-ended responses would also force researchers to become theoretically rigorous. Constructivist analysis of person-centered messages clearly meets that goal.

Constructivists' total reliance on the RCQ to gauge cognitive complexity is another story. It's difficult to accept the notion that a single number adequately reflects the intricate mental structures that exist behind the eyes. Doesn't it seem curious to ask respondents for their perceptions of two other people and then reduce their rich narratives to a mere frequency count of constructs? The total number may predict interesting communication differences, but explanatory depth is lacking.

A prophetic ethical voice also seems to be missing. If cognitive complexity is the key to interpersonal effectiveness, and if construct differentiation is enhanced by a privileged upbringing, advocates of the theory should devote some effort to creating reflective settings for disadvantaged kids. That way black-and-white thinkers could develop the ability to see shades of gray. There are precedents for such a reform agenda.

Once medical researchers discovered the brain-deadening effects of lead poisoning, they were quick to mount a public campaign to stop the use of lead-based paint. Likewise, teachers lobbied for "Project Head Start" when they realized that food for the stomach was a prerequisite of food for thought. Obviously poverty, peeling paint, and poor nutrition are linked, and constructivist research suggests that a childhood devoid of reflection-inducing communication is part of the same vicious circle. Constructivism is open to the charge of elitism unless the theorists devise a plan for remedial efforts that will help narrow the gap between the "haves" and the "have-nots." Burleson is keenly aware of this weakness:

> As a communication researcher and educator, I find this situation embarrassing and unacceptable. We researchers now know a lot about cognitive complexity and advanced social perception and communication skills, but thus far there have been few efforts to translate what we know into proven programs that effectively enhance these skills.[21]

More than most scholars, constructivists are capable of spearheading a reform movement to shape public policy. Early on, Delia made a strong call for a "reflective analysis of the implicit assumptions and ordering principles underlying research questions and methods."[22] He launched a research program that models that commitment, and others have enlisted in the cause. As one of the best known theories about communication to spring from within the discipline, constructivism is worth thinking about.

QUESTIONS TO SHARPEN YOUR FOCUS

1. How many points for *differentiation* would the phrase "humorous and totally funny" score on the *Role Category Questionnaire*?

2. Look at the *Calvin and Hobbes* cartoon on page 100. How would *constructivists* explain Calvin's success in getting a horsey ride from his father?

3. Sometimes during an argument, one kid will chide another with the words "Aw, grow up!" According to constructivists, the phrase offers good advice in a way that's ineffective. Why?

4. Osama bin Laden constructed a highly effective terrorist campaign that reflects *sophisticated message plans*. Can you explain why the successful achievement of his goals does not necessarily show that he is *cognitively complex* as Delia uses the term?

CONVERSATIONS

View this segment online at www.mhhe.com/griffin7 or www.afirstlook.com.

In this discussion, Jesse Delia (right) is joined by Brant Burleson (center) and Jim Applegate (left), the other leading theorists on the constructivist research team. They link our ability to communicate effectively with our mental constructs, our degree of cognitive complexity, the way we process information, and the way we form impressions of others. The theorists then describe the advantages of crafting person-centered messages that are designed to accomplish multiple goals. How well do you think Delia, Burleson, and Applegate adapt their messages to their audience—students of communication theory? Do you think the theorists are pursuing multiple goals? If so, do they succeed?

A SECOND LOOK

Recommended resource: Brant R. Burleson, "Constructivism: A General Theory of Communication Skill," in *Explaining Communication: Contemporary Theories and Exemplars,* Bryan Whaley and Wendy Samter (eds.), Lawrence Erlbaum, Mahwah, NJ, 2007, pp. 105–128.

Early statement: Jesse Delia, Barbara J. O'Keefe, and Daniel O'Keefe, "The Constructivist Approach to Communication," in *Human Communication Theory,* F. E. X. Dance (ed.), Harper & Row, New York, 1982, pp. 147–191.

Classic research study: Brant R. Burleson, "The Constructivist Approach to Person-Centered Communication: Analysis of a Research Exemplar," in *Rethinking Communication,* Vol. 2, Brenda Dervin, Lawrence Grossberg, Barbara J. O'Keefe, and Ellen Wartella (eds.), Sage, Newbury Park, CA, 1989, pp. 29–36.

Comprehensive research review: Brant R. Burleson and Scott Caplan, "Cognitive Complexity," in *Communication and Personality: Trait Perspectives,* James McCroskey, John Daly, and Matthew Martin (eds.), Hampton Press, Cresskill, NJ, 1998, pp. 233–286.

Role Category Questionnaire: Brant R. Burleson and Michael S. Waltman, "Cognitive Complexity: Using the Role Category Questionnaire Measure," in *A Handbook for the Study of Human Communication,* Charles Tardy (ed.), Ablex, Norwood, NJ, 1988, pp. 1–35.

Message production in the mind: James Price Dillard, "The Goals-Plans-Action Model of Interpersonal Influence," in *Perspectives on Persuasion, Social Influence, and Compliance Gaining,* John Seiter and Robert Gass (eds.), Pearson, Boston, 2003, pp. 185–206.

Social support: Wendy Samter, "How Gender and Cognitive Complexity Influence the Provision of Emotional Support: A Study of Indirect Effects," *Communication Reports,* Vol. 15, 2002, pp. 5–16.

Relationship maintenance: Brant R. Burleson and Wendy Samter, "A Social Skills Approach to Relationship Maintenance," in *Communication and Relationship Maintenance,* Daniel Canary and Laura Stafford (eds.), Academic Press, San Diego, 1994, pp. 61–90.

Developing cognitive complexity: Brant R. Burleson, Jesse Delia, and James Applegate, "The Socialization of Person-Centered Communication: Parental Contributions to the Social-Cognitive and Communication Skills of Their Children," in *Perspectives in Family Communication,* Mary Anne Fitzpatrick and Anita Vangelisti (eds.), Sage, Thousand Oaks, CA, 1995, pp. 34–76.

Review and critique: John Gastil, "An Appraisal and Revision of the Constructivist Research Program," in *Communication Yearbook 18,* Brant R. Burleson (ed.), Sage, Thousand Oaks, CA, 1995, pp. 83–104.

To access a chapter on Greene's action assembly theory that appeared in a previous edition, click on Theory Archive at *www.afirstlook.com.*

Think about your closest personal relationship. Is it one of "strong, frequent and diverse interdependence that lasts over a considerable period of time?"[1] That's how UCLA psychologist Harold Kelley and eight co-authors define the concept of close relationship. Although their definition could apply to parties who don't even like each other, most theorists reserve the term *close* for relationships that include a positive bond. That's how I'll use the term in this section.

The close relationship you thought of likely falls into one of three categories: friendship, romance, or family. Each type has characteristics that set it apart from the other two.

Friendship is the most voluntary and least programmed of all close relationships.[2] The contrast with kinship is particularly stark. We don't choose our relatives, but we can pick our friends. And once we do, the course of friendship is free from the romantic rings, family responsibilities, and legal regulations that give society a stake in other types of relationships. Yet to say that friendship is free is not to suggest that it's random. Longtime friends usually share a rough equality of talents and social status; we typically select friends who are similar to ourselves in age, background, interests, and values. The very freedom and mutuality that make friendship attractive are also the qualities that render it fragile. Friends who become disaffected tend to drift apart because there's little community structure undergirding the relationship.

Romance is set apart from friendship and family by two qualities—sexual passion and exclusiveness. Although anyone who has recently "fallen in love" needs no convincing, Yale University psychologist Robert Sternberg concludes that a romantic relationship requires a combination of intimacy, passion, and commitment.[3] Intimacy by itself is the strong liking reflective of friendship. Passion alone is sexual infatuation, or being "in lust." Commitment without intimacy or passion is typical of an arranged marriage at the start, or a marriage of convenience near its end. But when two people experience intimacy, passion, and commitment together, the relationship is usually closer than friendship or kinship.

Family members have a history. Years of shared experience provide close relatives with a knowledge that allows them to predict the responses of their parents, children, or siblings. Self-disclosure may be crucial in a developing romance or friendship, but except in times of crisis, close relatives feel they already know what's going on inside other family members. Intimate communication within families often begins with words like "Remember when . . . ," rather than "Let me tell you about . . . ."

Not all memories are pleasant, however. Greater friction exists within the family than would be tolerated in most friendships. Hostility is normally expressed symbolically through sullen silence, dirty looks, sarcastic comments, or angry words. Yet even in the face of emotional or physical abuse, most people still return to family in times of trouble. As poet Robert Frost reminds us, "Home is the place where, when you have to go there, they have to take you in."[4]

Despite differences among friendship, romance, and family ties, the quality of closeness in each of these relationships is remarkably similar. All three types of intimacy can provide enjoyment, trust, sharing of confidences, respect, mutual assistance, and spontaneity.[5] The question is, *How do we develop a close relationship?*

Two distinct approaches have dominated the theory and practice of relational development. One tradition is the *phenomenological approach* typified by humanistic psychologist Carl Rogers (see Chapter 4). Rogers believed that people draw close to others when (1) their outward behavior is congruent with their inner feelings; (2) they unconditionally accept others for who they are, not for what they do; and (3) they listen to what others say with the aim of understanding what it's like to be them. Rogers' thoughts have permeated the textbooks and teaching of interpersonal communication.[6] The topics of self-disclosure, nonverbal warmth, empathic listening, and trust are mainstays in the introductory course.

The other approach assumes that relationship behavior is shaped by the *rewards and costs of interaction.* In 1992 University of Chicago economist Gary Becker won the Nobel Prize in economics on the basis of his application of supply-and-demand market models to predict the behavior of everyday living, including love and marriage. News commentators expressed skepticism that matters of the heart could be reduced to cold numbers, but the economic metaphor has dominated social science discussions of interpersonal attraction for the last four decades. The basic assumption of most relational theorists is that people interact with others in a way that maximizes their personal benefits and minimizes their personal costs.

Numerous parallels exist between the stock market and relationship market:

Law of supply and demand. A rare, desirable characteristic commands higher value on the exchange.

"I've done the numbers, and I will marry you."

Courting a buyer. Most parties in the market prepare a prospectus that highlights their assets and downplays their liabilities.

Laissez-faire rules. Let the buyer beware. All's fair in love and war. It's a jungle out there.

Expert advice. Daily newspapers around the country carry syndicated advice columns by Michelle Singletary ("The Color of Money") and Abigail Van Buren ("Dear Abby"). Whether the topic is money or love, both columnists suggest cautious risk taking.

Investors and traders. Investors commit for the long haul; traders try to make an overnight killing.

Even from these brief summaries, you can tell that a humanistic model of relational development is quite different from an economic model of social exchange. Yet both models affect each of the theories presented in Chapters 9 through 11.

Altman and Taylor's *social penetration theory* suggests that people draw close to each other through the type of honest self-disclosure that occurs in Rogerian counseling. They use a social exchange analysis to predict whether parties will take that risk.

Berger's *uncertainty reduction theory* contends that we have a deep desire to know what we can expect from the other person before we invest in a relationship—a reliable market forecast, as it were. But the relational variables he considers crucial read like a list of humanistic values—nonverbal warmth, intimate self-disclosure, reciprocal vulnerability, liking, and so on.

Walther's *social information processing* (SIP) theory makes the surprising claim that people using computer-mediated communication can form relationships that are equally close as those developed face-to-face; it just takes longer. His hyperpersonal perspective—an extension of SIP—explains why online communication is at times more intimate than the relational communication that takes place when people are in each other's presence.

All three theories in this section regard communication as the means by which people can draw close to one another. Each theory considers instant intimacy a myth; relationships take time to develop and they don't always proceed on a straight-line trajectory toward that goal. In fact, most relationships never even get close. Yet some people do have deep, satisfying, long-lasting relationships. Why do they develop close ties when others don't? Each of these three theories offers an answer.

Social Penetration Theory

of Irwin Altman & Dalmas Taylor

A friend in need is a friend indeed.
Neither a borrower nor a lender be.

A soft answer turns away wrath.
Don't get mad, get even.

To know him is to love him.
Familiarity breeds contempt.

Proverbs are the wisdom of the ages boiled down into short, easy-to-remember phrases. There are probably more maxims about interpersonal relationships than about any other topic. But are these truisms dependable? As we can see in the pairings above, the advice they give often seems contradictory.

Consider the plight of Pete, a new freshman at a residential college, as he enters the dorm to meet his roommate for the first time. Pete has just waved good-bye to his folks and already feels a sharp pang of loneliness as he thinks of his girlfriend back home. He worries about how she'll feel about him when he goes home at Thanksgiving. Will she illustrate the reliability of the old adage "absence makes the heart grow fonder," or will "out of sight, out of mind" be a better way to describe the next few months?

Pete finds his room and immediately spots the familiar shape of a lacrosse stick. He's initially encouraged by what appears to be a common interest, but he's also fascinated by a campaign button that urges him to vote for a candidate for Congress who is on the opposite end of the political spectrum from Pete. Will "birds of a feather flock together" hold true in their relationship, or will "opposites attract" better describe their interaction?

Just then Jon, his roommate, comes in. For a few minutes they trade the stock phrases that give them a chance to size up each other. Something in Pete makes him want to tell Jon how much he misses his girlfriend, but a deeper sense of what is an appropriate topic of conversation when first meeting someone prevents him from sharing his feelings. On a subconscious level, perhaps even a conscious one, Pete is torn between acting on the old adage "misery loves company" or on the more macho "big boys don't cry."

Pete obviously needs something more than pithy proverbs to help him understand relational dynamics. More than a decade before Pete was born, social psychologists Irwin Altman and Dalmas Taylor proposed a *social penetration process* that explains how relational closeness develops. Altman is distinguished professor of psychology at the University of Utah, and Taylor, now deceased, was provost and professor of psychology at Lincoln University in Pennsylvania. They predict that Pete and Jon will end up best friends only if they proceed in a "gradual and orderly fashion from superficial to intimate levels of exchange as a function of both immediate and forecast outcomes."[1] In order to capture the process, we first have to understand the complexity of people.

Social penetration
The process of developing deeper intimacy with another person through mutual self-disclosure and other forms of vulnerability.

PERSONALITY STRUCTURE: A MULTILAYERED ONION

Altman and Taylor compare people to onions. This isn't a commentary on the human capacity to offend. Like the self-description that the ogre in *Shrek* shares with his donkey sidekick in the original film, it is a depiction of the multilayered *structure* of personality. Peel the outer skin from an onion, and you'll find another beneath it. Remove that layer and you'll expose a third, and so on. Pete's outer layer is his public self that's accessible to anyone who cares to look. The outer layer includes a myriad of details that certainly help describe who he is but are held in common with others at the school. On the surface, people see a tall, 18-year-old male business major from Michigan who lifts weights and gets lots of phone calls from home.

Personality structure
Onion-like layers of beliefs and feelings about self, others, and the world; deeper layers are more vulnerable, protected, and central to self-image.

If Jon can look beneath the surface, he'll discover the semiprivate attitudes that Pete reveals only to some people. Pete is sympathetic to liberal social causes, deeply religious, and prejudiced against overweight people.

Pete's inner core is made up of his values, self-concept, unresolved conflicts, and deeply felt emotions. This is his unique private domain, which is invisible to the world but has a significant impact on the areas of his life that are closer to the surface. Perhaps not even his girlfriend or parents know his most closely guarded secrets about himself.

CLOSENESS THROUGH SELF-DISCLOSURE

Pete becomes accessible to others as he relaxes the tight boundaries that protect him and makes himself vulnerable. This can be a scary process, but Altman and Taylor believe it's only by allowing Jon to penetrate well below the surface that Pete can draw truly close to his roommate.

There are many ways to show vulnerability. Pete could give up the territoriality that marks his desk and dresser drawers as his private preserve, share his clothes, or read a letter from his girlfriend out loud. Nonverbal paths to openness include mock roughhousing, eye contact, and smiling. But the main route to deep social penetration is through *self-disclosure*.

Self-disclosure
The voluntary sharing of personal history, preferences, attitudes, feelings, values, secrets, etc., with another person; transparency.

Figure 9–1 illustrates a wedge being pulled into an onion. It's as if a strong magnetic force were drawing it toward the center. The depth of penetration represents the degree of personal disclosure. To get to the center, the wedge must first separate the outer layers. Altman and Taylor claim that on the surface level this kind of biographical information exchange takes place easily, perhaps at the first meeting. But they picture the layers of onion skin tougher and more tightly wrapped as the wedge nears the center.

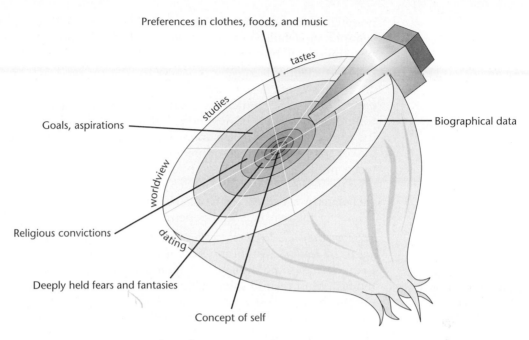

Preferences in clothes, foods, and music

tastes

studies

Goals, aspirations

worldview

Biographical data

Religious convictions

dating

Deeply held fears and fantasies

Concept of self

FIGURE 9–1   Penetration of Pete's Personality Structure

Recall that Pete was hesitant to share his longing for his girlfriend with Jon. If he admits these feelings, he's opening himself up for some heavy-handed kidding or emotional blackmail. In addition, once the wedge has penetrated deeply, it will have cut a passage through which it can return again and again with little resistance. Future privacy will be difficult. Realizing both of these factors, Pete may be extra cautious about exposing his true feelings. Perhaps he'll fence off this part of his life for the whole school term. According to social penetration theory, a permanent guard will limit the closeness these two young men can achieve.

THE DEPTH AND BREADTH OF SELF-DISCLOSURE

Depth of penetration
The degree of disclosure in a specific area of an individual's life.

The *depth of penetration* is the degree of intimacy. Although Altman and Taylor's penetration analogy strikes some readers as sexual, this was not their intent. The analogy applies equally to intimacy in friendship and romance. Figure 9–1 diagrams the closeness Jon has gained if he and Pete become friends during the year. In their framework of social penetration theory, Altman and Taylor have outlined the following four observations about the process that will have brought Pete and Jon to this point:

1. *Peripheral items are exchanged more frequently and sooner than private information.* When the sharp edge of the wedge has barely reached the intimate area, the thicker part has cut a wide path through the outer rings. The relationship is still at a relatively impersonal level ("big boys don't cry"). University of Connecticut communication professor Arthur VanLear analyzed the content of conversations in developing relationships. His study showed that 14 percent of talk revealed nothing about the speaker, 65 percent dwelled on public items, 19 percent shared semiprivate details, and only 2 percent disclosed intimate confidences.[2] Further penetration will bring Pete to the point where he can share deeper feelings ("misery loves company").

2. *Self-disclosure is reciprocal, especially in the early stages of relationship development.* The theory predicts that new acquaintances like Pete and Jon will reach roughly equal levels of openness, but it doesn't explain why. Pete's vulnerability could make him seem more trustworthy, or perhaps his initial openness makes transparency seem more attractive. It's also possible that the young men feel a need for emotional equity, so that a disclosure by Pete leaves Jon feeling uneasy until he's balanced the account with his own payment—a give-and-take exchange in which each party is sharing deeper levels of feeling with the other. Whatever the reason, social penetration theory asserts a *law of reciprocity*.

3. *Penetration is rapid at the start but slows down quickly as the tightly wrapped inner layers are reached.* Instant intimacy is a myth. Not only is there internal resistance to quick forays into the soul, but there are societal norms against telling too much too fast. Most relationships stall before a stable intimate exchange is established. For this reason, these relationships fade or die easily after a separation or a slight strain. A comfortable sharing of positive and negative reactions is rare. When it is achieved, relationships become more important to both parties, more meaningful, and more enduring.

4. *Depenetration is a gradual process of layer-by-layer withdrawal.* A warm friendship between Pete and Jon will deteriorate if they begin to close off areas of their lives that had earlier been opened. Relational retreat is a sort of taking back of what has earlier been exchanged in the building of a relationship. Altman and Taylor compare the process to a movie shown in reverse. Surface talk still goes on long after deep disclosure is avoided. Relationships are likely to terminate not in an explosive flash of anger but in a gradual cooling off of enjoyment and care.

Law of reciprocity
A paced and orderly process in which openness in one person leads to openness in the other; "You tell me your dream, I'll tell you mine."

Breadth of penetration
The range of areas in an individual's life over which disclosure takes place.

While depth is crucial to the process of social penetration, *breadth* is equally important. Note that in Figure 9–1 I have segmented the onion much like an orange to represent how Pete's life is cut into different areas—dating, studies, and so forth. It's quite possible for Pete to be candid about every intimate detail of his romance yet remain secretive about his father's alcoholism or his own minor dyslexia. Because only one area is accessed, the relationship depicted in the onion drawing is typical of a summer romance—depth without breadth. Of course, breadth without depth describes the typical "Hi, how are you?" casual relationship. A model of true intimacy would show multiple wedges inserted deeply into every area.

REGULATING CLOSENESS ON THE BASIS OF REWARDS AND COSTS

Will Pete and Jon become good friends? According to social penetration theory, it all depends on the cost-benefit analysis that each man performs as he considers the possibility of a closer relationship. Right after their first encounter, Pete will sort out the pluses and minuses of friendship with Jon, computing a bottom-line index of relational satisfaction. Jon will do the same regarding Pete. If the perceived mutual benefits outweigh the costs of greater vulnerability, the process of social penetration will proceed.

"Since we're both being honest, I should tell you I have fleas."

I previewed this kind of economic analysis in the introduction to the present section on relationship development. Altman and Taylor's version draws heavily on the *social exchange theory* of psychologists John Thibaut (University of North Carolina at Chapel Hill) and Harold Kelley (University of California, Los Angeles).[3] Throughout their lives, both researchers studied the key concepts of social exchange—relational outcome, relational satisfaction, and relational stability. Since Altman and Taylor believe that principles of *social exchange* accurately predict when people will risk self-disclosure, I'll describe these concepts in some detail.

Social exchange
Relationship behavior and status regulated by both parties' evaluations of perceived rewards and costs of interaction with each other.

Outcome: Rewards Minus Costs

Thibaut and Kelley suggest that people try to predict the *outcome* of an interaction before it takes place. Thus, when Pete first meets his roommate, he mentally gauges the potential rewards and costs of friendship with Jon. He perceives a number of benefits. As a newcomer to campus, Pete strongly desires someone to talk to, eat with, and just hang around with when he's not in class or studying. His roommate's interest in lacrosse, easy laugh, and laid-back style make Jon an attractive candidate.

Outcome
The perceived rewards minus the costs of interpersonal interaction.

Pete is also aware that there's a potential downside to getting to know each other better. If he reveals some of his inner life, his roommate may scoff at his faith in God or ridicule his liberal "do-gooder" values. Pete isn't ashamed of his convictions, but he hates to argue, and he regards the risk of conflict as real. Factoring in all the likely pluses and minuses, reaching out in friendship to Jon strikes Pete as net positive, so he makes the first move.

The idea of totaling potential benefits and losses to determine behavior isn't new. Since the nineteenth century, when philosopher John Stuart Mill first stated his principle of utility,[4] there's been a compelling logic to the *minimax principle of human behavior*. The minimax principle claims that people seek to maximize their benefits and minimize their costs. Thus, the higher we rate a relational outcome, the more attractive we find the behavior that might make it happen.

Social exchange theorists assume that we can accurately gauge the payoffs of a variety of interactions and that we have the good sense to choose the action that will provide the best result. Altman and Taylor aren't sure that the input we receive is always reliable, but that's not the issue. What matters to them is that we base our decision to open up with another person on the perceived benefit-minus-cost outcome.

Early in a relationship, we tend to see physical appearance, similar backgrounds, and mutual agreement as benefits ("birds of a feather flock together"). Disagreement and deviance from the norm are negatives. But as the relationship changes, so does the nature of interaction that friends find rewarding. Deeper friendships thrive on common values and spoken appreciation, and we can even enjoy surface diversity ("opposites attract").

Because Pete sees much more benefit than cost in a relationship with Jon, he'll start to reveal more of who he is. If the negatives outweighed the positives, he'd try to avoid contact with Jon as much as possible. Since they've just been assigned as roommates, Pete doesn't have the option to withdraw physically from Jon. But a negative assessment could cause him to hold back emotionally for the rest of the year.

Comparison Level (CL)—Gauging Relational Satisfaction

Evaluating outcomes is a tricky business. Even if we mentally convert intangible benefits and costs into a bottom-line measure of overall effect, its psychological impact upon us may vary. A relational result has meaning only when we contrast it with other real or imagined outcomes. Social exchange theory offers two standards of comparison that Pete and others use to evaluate their interpersonal outcomes. The first point of reference deals with relative *satisfaction*—how happy or sad an interpersonal outcome makes a participant feel. Thibaut and Kelley call this the *comparison level*.

A person's comparison level (CL) is the threshold above which an outcome seems attractive. Suppose, for example, that Pete is looking forward to his regular Sunday night phone call with his girlfriend. Since they usually talk for about a half hour, 30 minutes is Pete's comparison level for what makes a pleasing conversation. If he's not in a hurry, a 45-minute call will seem especially gratifying, while a 15-minute chat would be quite disappointing. Of course, the length of the call is only one factor that affects Pete's positive or negative feelings when he hangs up the phone. He also has developed expectations for the topics that they'll discuss, his girlfriend's tone of voice, and the warmth of her words when she says good-bye. These are benchmarks that Pete uses to gauge his relative satisfaction with the interaction.

Our CL for friendship, romance, or family ties is pegged by our relational history. We judge the value of a relationship by comparing it to the baseline of

Minimax principle of human behavior People seek to maximize their benefits and minimize their costs.

Comparison level (CL) The threshold above which an interpersonal outcome seems attractive; a standard for relational satisfaction.

past experience. If Pete had little history of close friendship in high school, a relationship with Jon would look quite attractive. If, on the other hand, he's accustomed to being part of a close-knit group of intimate friends, hanging out with Jon could pale by comparison.

Sequence plays a large part in evaluating a relationship. The result from each interaction is stored in the individual's memory. Experiences that take place early in a relationship can have a huge impact because they make up a large proportion of the total relational history. One unpleasant experience out of 10 is merely troublesome, but 1 out of 2 can end a relationship before it really begins. Trends are also important. If Pete first senses coolness from Jon yet later feels warmth and approval, the shift will raise Jon's attractiveness to a level higher than it would be if Pete had perceived positive vibes from the very beginning.

Comparison Level of Alternatives (CL$_{alt}$)—Gauging Relational Stability

Comparison level of alternatives (CL$_{alt}$)
The best outcome available in other relationships; a standard for relationship stability.

Thibaut and Kelley suggest that there is a second standard by which we evaluate the outcomes we receive. They call it the *comparison level of alternatives* (*CL$_{alt}$*), and its position vis-à-vis actual interpersonal outcomes shows the relative *stability* of the relationship. The level is pegged by the best relational outcome available outside the current relationship. The location of my CL$_{alt}$ answers the twin questions *Would my relational payoffs be better with another person?* and *What is the worst outcome I'll put up with and still stay in the present relationship?* As more attractive outside possibilities become available, or as existent outcomes slide below an established CL$_{alt}$, relational instability increases. Here again, a social exchange explanation reads like a stock-market analysis. That's why some advocates label a social exchange approach a *theory of economic behavior.*

Unlike the comparison level, the concept of CL$_{alt}$ doesn't indicate relationship satisfaction. It does explain, however, why people sometimes stay with an abusive partner. For example, social workers describe the plight of the battered wife as "high cost, low reward." Despite her anguish, the woman feels trapped in the distressing situation because the option of being alone in the world appears even worse. As dreadful as her outcomes are, she can't imagine a better alternative. She won't leave until she perceives an outside alternative that promises a better life.

The relative values of outcome, CL, and CL$_{alt}$ go a long way in determining whether a person is willing to become vulnerable in order to have a deeper relationship. The optimum situation is when both parties find

$$\text{Outcome} > \text{CL}_{alt} > \text{CL}$$

Using Pete as an example, this notation shows that he forecasts a friendship with Jon that will be more than *satisfying*. The tie with Jon will be *stable* because there's no other relationship on campus that is more attractive. Yet Pete won't feel trapped, because he has other satisfying options available should this one turn sour. We see, therefore, that social exchange theory explains why Pete is primed for social penetration. If Jon's calculations are similar, the roommates will begin the process of mutual vulnerability that Altman and Taylor describe, and reciprocal self-disclosure will draw them close.

ETHICAL REFLECTION: EPICURUS' ETHICAL EGOISM

Ethical egoism
The belief that individuals should live their lives so as to maximize their own pleasure and minimize their own pain.

The minimax principle that undergirds social exchange theory—and therefore social penetration theory as well—is also referred to as *psychological egoism*. The term reflects many social scientists' conviction that all of us are motivated by self-interest. Unlike most social scientists who limit their study to what *is* rather than what *ought* to be, *ethical egoists* claim we *should* act selfishly. It's right and it's good for us to look out for number one.

Epicurus, a Greek philosopher who wrote a few years after Aristotle's death, defined the good life as getting as much pleasure as possible: "I spit on the noble and its idle admirers when it contains no element of pleasure."[5] Although his position is often associated with the adage "Eat, drink, and be merry," Epicurus actually emphasized the passive pleasures of friendship and good digestion, and above all, the absence of pain. He cautioned that "no pleasure is in itself evil, but the things which produce certain pleasures entail annoyances many times greater than the pleasures themselves."[6] The Greek philosopher put lying in that category. He said that the wise person is prepared to lie if there is no risk of detection, but since we can never be certain our falsehoods won't be discovered, he didn't recommend deception.

A few other philosophers have echoed the Epicurean call for selfish concern. Thomas Hobbes described life as "nasty, brutish and short" and advocated political trade-offs that would gain a measure of security. Adam Smith, the spiritual father of capitalism, advised every person to seek his or her own profit. Friedrich Nietzsche announced the death of God and stated that the noble soul has reverence for itself. Egoist writer Ayn Rand dedicated her novel *The Fountainhead* to "the exultation of man's self-esteem and the sacredness of his happiness on earth."[7] Of course, the moral advice of Epicurus, Hobbes, Nietzsche, and Rand may be suspect. If their counsel consistently reflects their beliefs, their words are spoken for their own benefit, not ours.

Most ethical and religious thinkers denounce the selfishness of egoism as morally repugnant. How can one embrace a philosophy that advocates terrorism as long as it brings joy to the terrorist? When the egoistic pleasure principle is compared to a life lived to reduce the suffering of others, as with the late Mother Teresa, ethical egoism seems to be no ethic at all. Yet the egoist would claim that the Nobel Peace Prize winner was leading a sacrificial life because she took pleasure in serving the poor. If charity becomes a burden, she should stop.

A SIMPLE NOTION BECOMES MORE COMPLEX IN PRACTICE

Viewing increased self-disclosure as the path to intimacy is a simple idea—one that's easily portrayed in the onion model of Figure 9–1. It can also be summarized in less than 40 words:

> Interpersonal closeness proceeds in a gradual and orderly fashion from superficial to intimate levels of exchange, motivated by current and projected future outcomes. Lasting intimacy requires continual and mutual vulnerability through breadth and depth of self-disclosure.

But Altman later had second thoughts about his basic assumption that openness is the predominant quality of relationship development. He began to speculate that the desire for privacy may counteract what he first thought was a unidirectional quest for intimacy. He now proposes a *dialectical model*, which

Dialectical model
The assumption that people want both privacy and intimacy in their social relationships, they experience a tension between disclosure and withdrawal.

assumes that "human social relationships are characterized by openness or contact and closedness or separateness between participants."[8] He believes that the tension between openness and closedness results in cycles of disclosure or withdrawal.

Sandra Petronio, a communication theorist at the University of Indiana, Indianapolis, agrees that close relationships are much more complex than Altman and Taylor first thought. Based upon a wide range of empirical studies, her *communication privacy management theory* maps out the intricate ways people handle their conflicting desires for privacy and openness.

Communication Privacy Management Theory

Petronio claims that all people have personal boundary rules to guide whether or not they will disclose private information to someone else. If and when an individual decides to reveal something previously concealed, then the revealer and the person now in-the-know usually adopt collective boundary rules to regulate their disclosure to third parties. Petronio's theory describes (1) the way people form their personal rules for disclosure, (2) how those who disclose private information need to coordinate their privacy boundaries with the borders drawn by their confidants, and (3) the relational turbulence that occurs when parties have boundary rules that don't match. I'll illustrate how these three processes of privacy management play out by revisiting Pete's private fear that his girlfriend will become interested in another guy while he's away at college.

Privacy rules
Personal guides for privacy/disclosure decisions shaped by culture, gender, motive, context, and a risk-benefit ratio.

Privacy Rule Foundations.   Petronio claims that the personal rules that guide our privacy/disclosure decisions are based on five criteria. As always, *culture* is a major factor. For example, North Americans tend to be considerably more open about their feelings than Southeast Asians. Yet as the film *Bowling for Columbine* illustrates, people in the United States are more concerned about personal privacy than their Canadian neighbors. In terms of *gender* differences, women tend to disclose more than men, and when men do share their inner feelings, it's usually with a woman. The interpersonal *motives* of attraction and liking draw people toward disclosure, as does the insistent pull of reciprocity—relationally as strong as the law of gravity. The *context* of the conversation also makes a big difference. In the midst of crisis or after experiencing trauma, we need a sympathetic ear. But if, like Pete, we only face the possibility of loss, the pressure to disclose is less immediate. Finally, Petronio suggests that Pete will mentally calculate a *risk-benefit ratio* that's akin to the reward-cost analysis described by social exchange theory. She writes, "The choice to share the information or to keep it private often hinges on a risk-benefit ratio for those involved. We know that revealing exposes us to a certain amount of vulnerability, but so does concealing."[9]

Taking these five criteria into account, we can imagine Pete calling to mind rules that advise caution as he thinks about revealing his fear to Jon: *Go slow. I'll have only one chance to make a first impression. Big boys don't cry. It's none of his business.* If so, Pete will keep his qualms private during this initial conversation. Yet like other theorists who describe rule-based behavior, Petronio doesn't make a firm prediction as to whether Pete will either share or mask his fear. Her theory's aim is to help us understand the way we handle the tension between revealing and concealing private information.

Boundary coordination
The process through which the revealer and recipient agree on the same privacy rules for a given disclosure.

Boundary Coordination Operations.   If Pete decides to reveal his fear to his new roommate, he's probably hoping that Jon won't tell others. Will Jon respect that confidence? Petronio says that it depends on boundary linkage, boundary ownership, and boundary permeability. *Boundary linkage* refers to the strength of their relationship. Since Pete and Jon have just met, it's unlikely that the guys will automatically draw their privacy boundaries in the same place. Relational coordination takes work. *Boundary ownership* refers to a confidant's willingness to not spread the insider information that he or she now knows. If Jon becomes the co-owner of information that he didn't want to hear in the first place, he may feel no obligation to treat it as private. Finally, *boundary permeability* refers to the density of the privacy walls that parties erect. Jon may understand that news of Pete's anxiety is off-limits to the other guys in the dorm, yet he may be reluctant to keep that secret for long. We can see therefore that self-disclosure doesn't always draw people together. The closeness of the relationship between revealer and recipient is strongly affected by the extent to which they coordinate their privacy boundaries.

Boundary turbulence
The conflict that results from parties' failure to coordinate privacy rules and boundary management.

Boundary Turbulence.   Petronio says that boundary turbulence arises out of parties' inability to coordinate privacy rules and boundary management.[10] For example, Jon might violate a jointly held rule of confidentiality when he becomes frustrated with Pete. Maybe Jon doesn't realize what a big deal it is to Pete, or perhaps the secret slips out when Jon is drinking. Conversely, Pete may swear Jon to secrecy and then voice his fear to others. Whatever its cause, the existence of boundary turbulence is evidence that self-disclosure is not just about the self, nor does it always result in a closer relationship. If both parties don't draw their lines of confidentiality in the same place, the act of revealing private information can create confusion, conflict, or even chaos in their relationship.

CRITIQUE: PULLING BACK FROM SOCIAL PENETRATION

Social penetration theory is an established and familiar explanation of how closeness develops in friendships and romantic relationships. Altman and Taylor's image of multiple wedges penetrating deeply into a multilayered onion has proved to be a helpful model of growing intimacy. But just as these theorists describe friends and lovers continually reappraising their relationships in light of new experiences, it makes sense for us to reconsider the basic assumptions and claims of their theory. Social penetration theory has many critics.

Even though Altman praises Petronio's theoretical framework as "directly on target to guide us . . . through the maze of interpersonal communication in the twenty-first century,"[11] you may have noticed that her theory challenges two core assumptions of social penetration theory. Petronio thinks it's simplistic to equate self-disclosure with relational closeness. It can *lead* to intimacy, but a person may reveal private information merely to express oneself, to release tension, or to gain relational control. In none of these cases does the speaker necessarily desire nor achieve a stronger bond with the confidant. And if the listener is turned off or disgusted by what was said, depenetration can be swift.

Petronio also questions Altman and Taylor's view of personality structure. While the onion-layer model of social penetration theory posits fixed boundaries that become increasingly thick as one penetrates toward the inner core of personality,

Petronio claims that boundaries are personally created, often shifting, and frequently permeable.

Other personal relationship scholars are uncomfortable with Altman and Taylor's wholesale use of a reward-cost analysis to explain the differential drive for penetration. Can a complex blend of advantages and disadvantages be reduced to a single numerical index? And assuming that we can forecast the value of relational outcomes, are we so consistently selfish that we always opt for what we calculate is in our own best interest?

University of North Dakota psychologist Paul Wright believes that Pete and Jon could draw close enough that their relationship would no longer be driven by a self-centered concern for personal gain. When friendships have what Wright calls "an intrinsic, end-in-themselves quality," people regard good things happening to their friends as rewards in themselves.[12] When that happens, Jon would get just as excited if Pete had a successful employment interview as he would if he himself had been offered the job. This rare kind of selfless love involves a relational transformation, not just more self-disclosure.[13] Altman and Taylor's theory doesn't speak about the transition from *me* to *we*, but that apparently takes place only after an extended process of social penetration.

QUESTIONS TO SHARPEN YOUR FOCUS

1. The onion model in Figure 9–1 is sectioned into eight parts, representing the *breadth* of a person's life. How would you label eight regions of interest in your life?

2. Jesus said, "There is no greater love than this: to lay down one's life for one's friends."[14] Given the *minimax principle* of human behavior used in a *social exchange* analysis, how is such a sacrifice possible?

3. Social penetration theory is usually thought of as a theory of *self-disclosure*. What are some other ways of showing *vulnerability* in a relationship?

4. The romantic truism "to know her is to love her" seems to contradict the relational adage "familiarity breeds contempt." Given the principles of social penetration theory, can you think of a way both statements might be true?

SELF-QUIZ *www.mhhe.com/griffin7*

A SECOND LOOK

Recommended resource: Irwin Altman and Dalmas Taylor, *Social Penetration: The Development of Interpersonal Relationships,* Holt, New York, 1973.

Later developments: Dalmas Taylor and Irwin Altman, "Communication in Interpersonal Relationships: Social Penetration Processes," in *Interpersonal Processes: New Directions in Communication Research,* Michael Roloff and Gerald Miller (eds.), Sage, Newbury Park, CA, 1987, pp. 257–277.

Social exchange theory: John W. Thibaut and Harold H. Kelley, *The Social Psychology of Groups,* John Wiley & Sons, New York, 1952.

Dialectic revision: Irwin Altman, Anne Vinsel, and Barbara Brown, "Dialectic Conceptions in Social Psychology: An Application to Social Penetration and Privacy Regulation," in *Advances in Experimental Social Psychology,* Vol. 14, Leonard Berkowitz (ed.), Academic Press, New York, 1981, pp. 107–160.

Reward-cost analysis: Dalmas Taylor and Irwin Altman, "Self-Disclosure as a Function of Reward-Cost Outcomes," *Sociometry,* Vol. 38, 1975, pp. 18–31.

Self-disclosure reciprocity: C. Arthur VanLear, "The Formation of Social Relationships: A Longitudinal Study of Social Penetration," *Human Communication Research,* Vol. 13, 1987, pp. 299–322.

Cycles of self-disclosure: C. Arthur VanLear, "Testing a Cyclical Model of Communicative Openness in Relationship Development: Two Longitudinal Studies," *Communication Monographs,* Vol. 58, 1991, pp. 337–361.

Study of roommates: John Berg, "Development of Friendship Between Roommates," *Journal of Personality and Social Psychology,* Vol. 46, 1984, pp. 346–356.

Effects of environment on relationship closeness: Carol Werner, Irwin Altman, and Barbara B. Brown, "A Transactional Approach to Interpersonal Relations: Physical Environment, Social Context and Temporal Qualities," *Journal of Social and Personal Relationships,* Vol. 9, 1992, pp. 297–323.

Ethical egoism: Edward Gegis, "What Is Ethical Egoism?" *Ethics,* Vol. 91, 1980, pp. 50–62.

Managing privacy boundaries: Sandra Petronio, *Boundaries of Privacy: Dialectics of Disclosure,* State University of New York, Albany, 2002.

Boundary turbulence in stepfamilies: Tamara D. Afifi, "'Feeling Caught' in Stepfamilies: Managing Boundary Turbulence Through Appropriate Communication Privacy Rules," *Journal of Social and Personal Relationships,* Vol. 20, 2003, pp. 729–755.

Boundary management—state of the art: Mary Claire Morr and Sandra Petronio, "Communication Privacy Management Theory," in *Explaining Communication: Contemporary Theories and Exemplars,* Bryan Whaley and Wendy Samter (eds.), Lawrence Erlbaum, Mahwah, NJ, 2007, pp. 257–274.

To access a chapter on Thibant and Kelley's social exchange theory that appeared in a previous edition, click on Theory Archive at
www.afirstlook.com.

Uncertainty Reduction Theory

of Charles Berger

No matter how close two people eventually become, they always begin as strangers. Let's say you've just taken a job as a driver for a delivery service over the Christmas holidays. After talking with the other drivers, you conclude that your income and peace of mind will depend on working out a good relationship with Heather, the radio dispatcher. All you know for sure about Heather is her attachment to Hannah, a 100-pound Labrador retriever that never lets Heather out of her sight. The veteran drivers joke that it's hard to tell the difference between the voices of Heather and Hannah over the radio. With some qualms you make arrangements to meet Heather (and Hannah) over coffee and donuts before your first day of work. You really have no idea what to expect.

Chuck Berger believes that it's natural to have doubts about our ability to predict the outcome of initial encounters. Berger, a professor of communication at the University of California, Davis, notes that "the beginnings of personal relationships are fraught with uncertainties."[1] Unlike social penetration theory, which tries to forecast the future of a relationship on the basis of projected rewards and costs (see Chapter 9), Berger's uncertainty reduction theory focuses on how human communication is used to gain knowledge and create understanding.

> Central to the present theory is the assumption that when strangers meet, their primary concern is one of uncertainty reduction or increasing predictability about the behavior of both themselves and others in the interaction.[2]

Interpersonal ignorance is not bliss; it's frustrating! Berger contends that our drive to reduce uncertainty about new acquaintances gets an extra boost from any of three prior conditions:[3]

1. *Anticipation of future interaction:* We know we will see them again.
2. *Incentive value:* They have something we want.
3. *Deviance:* They act in a weird way.

Heather hooks you on all three counts. You know you're going to be dealing with her for the next few weeks, she can make you or break you financially

125

according to the routes she assigns, and she has this strange attachment to Hannah. According to Berger, when you add these three factors to your natural curiosity, you'll *really* want to solve the puzzle of who she is.

Berger believes that our main purpose in talking to people is to "make sense" out of our interpersonal world. That's why you're having breakfast with a stranger and her dog. If you brought your own hound to the meeting, chances are the two dogs would circle and sniff each other, trying to get some idea of what their counterpart was like. Humans are no different; we're just a bit more subtle as we use symbols instead of smells to reach our conclusions.

UNCERTAINTY REDUCTION: TO PREDICT AND EXPLAIN

Berger's focus on predictability is straight from Shannon and Weaver's information theory (see Chapter 4). "As the ability of persons to predict which alternative or alternatives are likely to occur next decreases, uncertainty increases."[4] He also owes a debt to Fritz Heider's view of people as intuitive psychologists. Heider, the father of *attribution theory*, believed that we constantly draw inferences about why people do what they do.[5] We need to predict *and* explain. If Heather's going to bark at you on the radio, you want to understand why.

Attribution theory
A systematic explanation of how people draw inferences about the character of others based upon observed behavior.

Berger notes that there are at least two kinds of uncertainty that you face as you set out for your first meeting with Heather. Because you aren't sure how you should act, one kind of uncertainty deals with *behavioral* questions. Should you shake hands? Who pays for the donuts? Do you pet the dog? Often there are accepted procedural protocols to ease the stress that behavioral uncertainty can cause. Good manners go beyond common sense.

Uncertainty reduction
Increased knowledge of what kind of person another is that provides an improved forecast of how a future interaction will turn out.

A second kind of uncertainty focuses on *cognitive* questions aimed at discovering who the other person is as a unique individual. What does Heather like about her job? What makes her glad, sad, or mad? Does she have other friends, or does she lavish all her attention on Hannah? When you first meet a person, your mind may conjure up a wild mix of potential traits and characteristics. Reducing cognitive uncertainty means acquiring information that allows you to discard many of these possibilities. That's the kind of uncertainty reduction Berger's theory addresses—cognitive rather than behavioral uncertainty.

AN AXIOMATIC THEORY: CERTAINTY ABOUT UNCERTAINTY

Berger proposes a series of axioms to explain the connection between his central concept of uncertainty and eight key variables of relationship development: *verbal communication, nonverbal warmth, information seeking, self-disclosure, reciprocity, similarity, liking,* and *shared networks*.[6] *Axioms* are traditionally regarded as self-evident truths that require no additional proof. (All people are created equal. The shortest distance between two points is a straight line. What goes up must come down.) Here are Berger's eight truths about initial uncertainty.

Axiom
A self-evident truth that requires no additional proof.

> *Axiom 1, Verbal Communication:* Given the high level of uncertainty present at the onset of the entry phase, as the amount of verbal communication between strangers increases, the level of uncertainty for each interactant in the relationship will decrease. As uncertainty is further reduced, the amount of verbal communication will increase.

When you first sit down with Heather, the conversation will be halting and somewhat stilted. But as words begin to flow, you'll discover things about each other that make you feel more confident in each other's presence. When your comfort level rises, the pace of the conversation will pick up.

> ***Axiom 2, Nonverbal Warmth:*** As nonverbal affiliative expressiveness increases, uncertainty levels will decrease in an initial interaction situation. In addition, decreases in uncertainty level will cause increases in nonverbal affiliative expressiveness.

When initial stiffness gives way to head nods and tentative smiles, you'll have a better idea of who Heather is. This assurance leads to further signs of warmth, such as prolonged eye contact, forward body lean, and pleasant tone of voice.

> ***Axiom 3, Information Seeking:*** High levels of uncertainty cause increases in information-seeking behavior. As uncertainty levels decline, information-seeking behavior decreases.

What is it about Heather that prompted the other drivers to warn you not to start off on the wrong foot? You simply have no idea. Like a bug with its antennae twitching, you carefully monitor what she says and how she acts in order to gather clues about her personality. But you become less vigilant after she explains that her pet peeve is drivers who complain about their assignments on the radio. Whether or not you think her irritation is justified, you begin to relax because you have a better idea of how to stay on her good side.

> ***Axiom 4, Self-Disclosure:*** High levels of uncertainty in a relationship cause decreases in the intimacy level of communication content. Low levels of uncertainty produce high levels of intimacy.

Like Altman and Taylor (Chapter 9), Berger equates intimacy of communication with depth of self-disclosure. Demographic data revealing that Heather was raised in Toledo and that you are a communication major are relatively nonintimate. They typify the opening gambits of new acquaintances who are still feeling each other out. But Heather's comment that she feels more loyalty from Hannah than from any person she knows is a gutsy admission that raises the intimacy level of the conversation to a new plane. Most people wait to express attitudes, values, and feelings until they have a good idea what the listener's response will be.

> ***Axiom 5, Reciprocity:*** High levels of uncertainty produce high rates of reciprocity. Low levels of uncertainty produce low levels of reciprocity.

Self-disclosure research confirms the notion that people tend to mete out the personal details of their lives at a rate that closely matches their partner's willingness to share intimate information.[7] Reciprocal vulnerability is especially important in the early stages of a relationship. The issue seems to be one of power. When knowledge of each other is minimal, we're careful not to let the other person one-up us by being the exclusive holder of potentially embarrassing information. But when we already know some of the ups and downs of a person's life, an even flow of information seems less crucial. Berger would not anticipate long monologues at your first get-together with Heather; future meetings might be a different story.

> ***Axiom 6, Similarity:*** Similarities between persons reduce uncertainty, while dissimilarities produce increases in uncertainty.

The more points of contact you establish with Heather, the more you'll feel you understand her inside and out. If you are a dog lover, the two of you will click. If, however, you are partial to purring kittens, Heather's devotion to this servile beast will cause you to wonder if you'll ever be able to figure out what makes her tick.

Axiom 7, Liking: Increases in uncertainty level produce decreases in liking; decreases in uncertainty produce increases in liking.

This axiom suggests that the more you find out about Heather, the more you'll appreciate who she is. It directly contradicts the cynical opinion that "familiarity breeds contempt" and affirms instead the relational maxim that "to know her is to love her."

Axiom 8, Shared Networks: Shared communication networks reduce uncertainty, while lack of shared networks increases uncertainty.

This axiom was not part of Berger's original theory, but his ideas triggered extensive research by other communication scholars who soon moved uncertainty reduction theory beyond the confines of two strangers meeting for the first time. Berger applauds this extension: "The broadening of the theory's scope suggests the potential usefulness of reconceptualizing and extending the original formulation."[8] For example, Malcolm Parks (University of Washington) and Mara Adelman (Seattle University) discovered that men and women who communicate more often with their romantic partners' family and friends have less uncertainty about the person they love than do those whose relationships exist in relative isolation.[9] Networking couples also tend to stay together. On the basis of these findings, Berger incorporated this axiom into his formal design.

THEOREMS: THE LOGICAL FORCE OF UNCERTAINTY AXIOMS

Theorem
A proposition that logically and necessarily follows from two axioms.

Once we grant the validity of the eight axioms, it makes sense to pair two of them together to produce additional insight into relational dynamics. The combined axioms yield an inevitable conclusion when inserted in the well-known pattern of deductive logic:

$$\text{If } A = B$$
$$\text{and } B = C$$
$$\text{then } A = C$$

Berger does this for all possible combinations, thereby generating 28 theorems—for example:

If similarity reduces uncertainty (axiom 6)
and reduced uncertainty increases liking (axiom 7)
then similarity and liking are positively related (theorem 21)

In this case, the result isn't exactly earthshaking. The connection between similarity and liking is a long-established finding in research on interpersonal attraction.[10] When viewed as a whole, however, these 28 logical extensions sketch out a rather comprehensive theory of interpersonal development—all based on the importance of reducing uncertainty in human interaction.

Instead of listing all 28 theorems, I've plotted the relationships they predict in Figure 10–1. The chart reads like a mileage table you might find in a road

	Ax 1 Verbal Communication	Ax 2 Nonverbal Warmth	Ax 4 Self-Disclosure	Ax 3 Information Seeking	Ax 5 Reciprocity	Ax 7 Liking	Ax 6 Similarity	Ax 8 Shared Networks
Ax 1 Verbal Communication		1 +	2 +	3 −	4 −	5 +	6 +	22 +
Ax 2 Nonverbal Warmth	1 +		7 +	8 −	9 −	10 +	11 +	23 +
Ax 4 Self-Disclosure	2 +	7 +		12 −	13 −	14 +	15 +	24 +
Ax 3 Information Seeking	3 −	8 −	12 −		16 +	17 −	18 −	25 −
Ax 5 Reciprocity	4 −	9 −	13 −	16 +		19 −	20 −	26 −
Ax 7 Liking	5 +	10 +	14 +	17 −	19 −		21 +	27 +
Ax 6 Similarity	6 +	11 +	15 +	18 −	20 −	21 +		28 +
Ax 8 Shared Networks	22 +	23 +	24 +	25 −	26 −	27 +	28 +	

FIGURE 10–1   Theorems of Uncertainty Reduction Theory

Adapted from Berger and Calabrese, "Some Explorations in Initial Interaction and Beyond"

atlas. Select one axiom along the top and another down the side. The intersection between the two shows the number of Berger's theorem and the type of correlation it asserts. A plus sign (+) shows that the two interpersonal variables rise or fall together. A minus sign (−) indicates that as one increases, the other decreases. Will the warmth of Heather's nonverbal communication increase as the intimacy of her self-disclosure deepens? Theorem 7 says it will. Suppose you grow fond of Heather as a friend. Will you seek to find out more about her? Theorem 17 makes the surprising prediction that you won't (more on this later).

MESSAGE PLANS TO COPE WITH UNCERTAIN RESPONSES

Ten years after introducing uncertainty reduction theory, Berger switched his research focus to the thought processes that people go through in order to produce the messages they speak. He concluded that most social interaction is goal-driven; we have reasons for saying what we say. Berger labeled his work "A Plan-Based Theory of Strategic Communication" because, like the cognitive theorists discussed in Chapter 8 (*constructivism*), he was convinced that we continually construct cognitive plans to guide our social action.[11] According to Berger, "*plans* are mental representations of action sequences that may be used to achieve goals."[12] Figure 10–2 offers a possible example of a strategic plan for your breakfast with Heather.

Your main reason for getting together with the dispatcher is to maximize your income over the Christmas holidays. Your overall strategy to reach that goal is to build a good working relationship with Heather, since she assigns the routes. The term *overall* is appropriate because Berger claims that plans are "hierarchically

Message plans

Mental representations of action sequences that may be used to achieve goals.

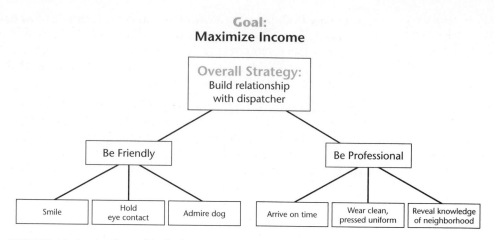

FIGURE 10–2   A Hierarchical Plan of Goal-Directed Communication

organized with abstract action representations at the top of the hierarchy and progressively more concrete representation toward the bottom."[13] In order to build that relationship, you intend to converse in a *friendly* and *professional* manner. In this case, friendly means smiling, admiring her dog, and holding eye contact when she speaks. You'll show professionalism by arriving on time; wearing a clean, pressed uniform; and revealing knowledge of the neighborhood.

If you switch strategies at the top—seeking pity for a poor, struggling college student, for example—the alteration will cascade down the hierarchy, requiring changes in many of the behaviors below. Thus, a top-down revision of an action plan requires great amounts of a person's cognitive capacity.

Even if you are a cognitively complex person (see Chapter 8), Berger claims you can't be sure that you'll reach your goal. You may have a great plan but execute it poorly. Heather may interpret words that you meant one way to mean something else. Or she may have her own goals and plans that will inevitably thwart yours. Berger has come to the conclusion that uncertainty is central to *all* social interaction: "The probability of perfect communication is zero."[14]

Although Berger originally considered uncertainty reduction theory and the study of plan-based message production as separate projects, he now sees an intersection between the two bodies of research. Berger asks, "How do individuals cope with the inevitable uncertainties they must face when constructing messages?" And again, "How can a person hedge against embarrassment, anger, rejection and other downside risks associated with deploying a given message?"[15] The following strategies are some of his answers.

Seeking Information.   Berger outlines three approaches we can use to find out how others might react to our messages. Using a *passive strategy*, we unobtrusively observe others from a distance. This fly-on-the-wall tactic works best when we spot others reacting to people in informal, or "backstage," settings. (The strategy sounds like normal "scoping" behavior on any college campus.) In an *active strategy*, we ask a third party for information. We realize that our mutual acquaintance will probably give a somewhat slanted view, but most of us have confidence in our ability to filter out the bias and gain valuable information. With an *interactive strategy*, we talk face-to-face with the other person and ask specific questions. This is the quickest route to reduce uncertainty, but continual probing

Passive strategy
Impression formation by observing a person interact with others.

Active strategy
Impression formation by asking a third party about a person.

Interactive strategy
Impression formation through face-to-face discussion with a person.

in social settings begins to take on the feel of a cross-examination, or "the third degree." Our own self-disclosure offers an alternative way to elicit information from others without seeming to pry. By being transparent, we create a safe atmosphere for others to respond in kind—something that the "law of reciprocity" suggests they will do (see Chapter 9).

Choosing Plan Complexity.   The complexity of a message plan is measured in two ways—the level of detail the plan includes and the number of contingency plans prepared in case the original one doesn't work. If it's crucial that you make top dollar in your holiday delivery job, you're likely to draw upon a plan from memory or create a new one far more complex than the sample shown in Figure 10–2. You're also likely to have a fallback plan in case the first one fails. On the other hand, you don't know much about Heather's goals or feelings, and high uncertainty argues for a less complex plan that you can adjust in the moment, once you get a feel for who she is and what she wants. This simpler approach is preferred for another reason. Enacting a complex plan takes so much cognitive effort that there's usually a deterioration in verbal and nonverbal fluency, with a resultant loss in credibility.

Plan complexity
A characteristic of a message plan based on the level of detail it provides and the number of contingencies it covers.

Hedging.   The possibility of plan failure suggests the wisdom of providing ways for both parties to save face when at least one of them has miscalculated. Berger catalogues a series of planned hedges that allow a somewhat gracious retreat. For instance, you may be quite certain about what you want to accomplish in your meeting with Heather yet choose words that are *ambiguous* so as not to tip your hand before you find out more about her. You might also choose to be equivocal in order to avoid the embarrassment that would come from a refusal of a specific request for preferred treatment in route assignment. *Humor* can provide the same way out. You could blatantly propose to use a portion of the saved time and good tips that come from prime assignments to stop at the butcher shop for a juicy bone for Hannah—but make the offer in a joking tone of voice. If Heather takes offense, you can respond, "Hey, I was just kidding."

Hedging
Use of strategic ambiguity and humor to provide a way for both parties to save face when a message fails to achieve its goal.

The Hierarchy Hypothesis.   What happens to action choices when plans are frustrated? Berger's *hierarchy hypothesis* asserts that "when individuals are thwarted in their attempts to achieve goals, their first tendency is to alter lower level elements of their message."[16] For example, when it's obvious the person we're talking to has failed to grasp what we are saying, our inclination is to repeat the same message—but this time louder. The tactic seldom works, but it takes less mental effort than altering strategic features higher up in the action plan. Berger describes people as "cognitive misers" who would rather try a quick fix than expend the effort to repair faulty plans.[17] There's no doubt that in-the-moment modifications are taxing, but when the issue is important, the chance to be effective makes it worth the effort. An additional hedge against failure is asking a "true friend" who will critique your action plan before you put it into effect.[18] As a Hebrew proverb warns, "Without counsel, plans go wrong."[19]

Hierarchy hypothesis
The prediction that when people are thwarted in their attempts to achieve goals, their first tendency is to alter lower-level elements of their message.

ANXIETY/UNCERTAINTY MANAGEMENT (AUM) THEORY

Inspired by Berger's theory, the late California State, Fullerton, communication professor William Gudykunst began to apply some of the axioms and theorems of uncertainty reduction theory to intercultural settings. In many ways, Berger's

AUM theory
An intercultural theory that claims high levels of uncertainty and anxiety lead to greater misunderstanding when strangers don't communicate mindfully.

original emphasis on the interaction of strangers was a natural for Gudykunst, who assumed that at least one person in an intercultural encounter is a *stranger*.[20] Through a series of initial crises, strangers undergo both anxiety and uncertainty—they don't feel secure and they aren't sure how to behave. He noted that strangers and in-group members experience some degree of anxiety and uncertainty in any new interpersonal situation, but when the encounter takes place between people of different cultures, strangers are hyperaware of cultural differences. They then tend to overestimate the effect of cultural identity on the behavior of people in an alien society, while blurring individuals' distinctions. Despite their common axiomatic format and parallel focus on the meeting of strangers, Gudykunst's *anxiety/uncertainty management theory* differs in five significant ways from Berger's uncertainty reduction theory.

Anxiety.   Whereas Berger treats *uncertainty* as the key communication variable, Gudykunst elevated *anxiety* to an equal status. He defined anxiety as "the feeling of being uneasy, tense, worried or apprehensive about what might happen."[21] As the title of his theory suggests, and Figure 10–3 depicts, Gudykunst believed that uncertainty and anxiety are the twin threats that must be managed to achieve effective communication. They are the basic cause of intercultural misunderstanding. His research shows that anxiety and uncertainty usually go together,[22] yet he saw them as different in that uncertainty is cognitive, whereas anxiety is affective—an emotion.

Anxiety
The feeling of being uneasy, tense, worried, or apprehensive about what might happen.

Effective Communication.   The end goal of AUM theory is *effective communication* rather than closeness or relational satisfaction. Gudykunst used the term to refer to the process of minimizing misunderstandings. He wrote that "communication is effective to the extent that the person interpreting the message attaches a meaning to the message that is relatively similar to what was intended by the person transmitting it."[23] Other authors use a variety of terms to convey the same idea—accuracy, fidelity, mutual understanding.[24]

Effective communication
The extent to which a person interpreting a message does so in a way that's relatively similar to what was intended; minimizing misunderstanding.

Multiple Causes of Anxiety/Uncertainty.   The third way AUM theory differs from Berger's theory is the vast array of axioms, not shown, which cluster under the seven categories on the left side of Figure 10–3. There are 34 of them,

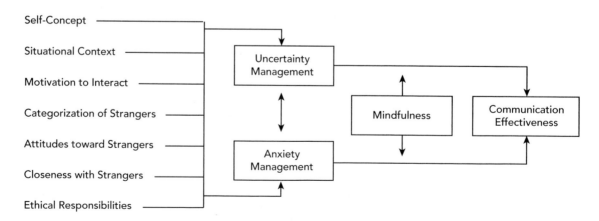

FIGURE 10–3   Basic Components of AUM Theory
Based on "An Anxiety/Uncertainty Management (AUM) Theory of Effective Communication"

each linking a separate variable to the rise or fall of anxiety and uncertainty. For example, a large measure of any of the following factors reduces anxiety and uncertainty: self-esteem, cognitive complexity, perceived similarity, positive expectations, interdependence, attraction, respect from the other, a sense of power, shared networks, and cooperative tasks to complete. When these personal and situational factors are in short supply, anxiety and uncertainty rise. This, of course, makes effective intercultural communication that much harder.

Lower and Upper Thresholds for Fear and Doubt. According to Gudykunst, anxiety and uncertainty aren't always bad—a small amount of both makes us more vigilant. He suggested that we have a minimum threshold of apprehension that will guarantee that adrenaline runs through our veins and prods us to communicate effectively. But there's also a threshold of high anxiety above which we become paralyzed with fear. Above that level of angst we can't concentrate on the message or the messenger, and fall back on negative stereotypes or simply withdraw from the conversation.

In like manner, the minimum threshold for uncertainty is the lowest amount of doubt we can have and yet not feel bored or overconfident about our predictions of strangers' behavior.[25] If we aren't curious about the stranger, we'll go on automatic pilot and likely misinterpret the words we hear. On the other hand, if uncertainty crosses the upper threshold, we lose all confidence that we can predict others' behavior and communication no longer seems worthwhile. Effective intercultural communication is possible only when participants' levels of doubt and fear fall somewhere between these upper and lower thresholds. Unfortunately, Gudykunst died before he could work out a way to measure where a person's thresholds lie.

Mindfulness
The process of thinking in new categories, being open to new information, and recognizing multiple perspectives.

Mindfulness. According to AUM theory, *mindfulness* is the way that in-group members and strangers can reduce their anxiety and uncertainty to optimum levels. We are mindful when we consciously think about our communication and continually work at changing what we do in order to become more effective. Following Harvard psychologist Ellen Langer's notion of *mindful learning*,[26] Gudykunst suggested that being mindful involves the creation of new categories rather than simply classifying people according to their ethnicity, gender, age, wealth, or rules (see Chapter 8). It also means being open to information and recognizing that the other person may have a different perspective than we do.

The concept of mindfulness provides a potential solution to the age-old dilemma concerning free will and determinism. Most theorists tacitly plant their flag somewhere on the continuum between the two extremes, but neither they nor their readers seem particularly comfortable with their selection. In what I regard as a potentially brilliant move, Gudykunst made it possible to embrace both sides of the scale. Each axiom that predicts a change in anxiety or uncertainty explicitly states that it holds only if the people involved aren't mindful. When they aren't, the axioms have the force of law, and doubt and fear in intercultural situations is inevitable (determinism). But when strangers are mindful about their encounter, their mindfulness trumps the axioms, therefore reducing anxiety and uncertainty to manageable levels (free will). It's an idea that transcends the cause-and-effect logic of Berger's uncertainty reduction theory.

Shrew People: quick, carnivorous, usually nocturnal; smaller but more vicious than the better-known Mole People; eat five times their own body weight every day; cannibals.

CRITIQUE: NAGGING DOUBTS ABOUT UNCERTAINTY

Berger's uncertainty reduction theory is an early prototype within the communication discipline of what an objective theory should be. His theory makes specific testable predictions, and offers the human need to reduce interpersonal uncertainty as the engine that drives its axioms. Although combining the axioms generates a slew of theorems, they are straightforward, logically consistent, and simple to understand. As for practical utility, readers interested in promoting interpersonal ties can regard the linkages the theorems describe as a blueprint for constructing solid relationships. There are, however, continuing questions about Berger's reliance on the concept of *uncertainty* and his assumption that we're motivated to reduce it.

In a state-of-the-art update on uncertainty reduction theory, Charles Berger admits that his original statement contained "some propositions of dubious validity."[27] Critics quickly point to theorem 17, which predicts that the more you like people, the less you'll seek information about them.

> Frankly, it is not clear why information-seeking would decrease as liking increased other than being required by deductive inference from the axiomatic structure of uncertainty reduction theory. In fact, it seems more reasonable to suggest that persons will seek information about and from those they like rather than those they dislike.[28]

That's the blunt assessment of Kathy Kellermann at the University of California, Santa Barbara, who originally participated in Berger's research program. We might be willing to dismiss this apparent error as only one glitch out of 28 theorems, but the tight logical structure that is the genius of the theory doesn't provide that option. Theorem 17 is dictated by axioms 3 and 7. If the theorem is wrong, the axioms are suspect. Kellermann targets the motivational assumption of axiom 3 as the problem.

Axiom 3 assumes that lack of information triggers a search for knowledge. But Kellermann and Rodney Reynolds at Pepperdine University studied motivation to reduce uncertainty in more than a thousand students at 10 universities, finding that "wanting knowledge rather than lacking knowledge is what promotes information-seeking in initial encounters with others."[29] The distinction is illustrated by the story of a teacher who asked a boy, "What's the difference between *ignorance* and *apathy?*" The student replied, "I don't know, and I don't care." (He was right!)

Kellermann and Reynolds also failed to find that anticipated future interaction, incentive value, or deviance gave any motivational kick to information seeking, as Berger claimed they would. Thus, it seems that Berger's suggestion of a universal drive to reduce uncertainty during initial interaction is questionable at best. Yet along with the suspect third axiom, it, too, remains part of the theory.

Another attack on the theory comes from Michael Sunnafrank at the University of Minnesota in Duluth. He challenges Berger's claim that uncertainty reduction is the key to understanding early encounters. Consistent with Altman and Taylor's social penetration model presented in the previous chapter, Sunnafrank insists that the early course of a relationship is guided by its *predicted outcome value.*[30] He's convinced that maximizing rewards is more important than figuring out personality. If this is true, you'll be more concerned with establishing a smooth working relationship with Heather at your first meeting than you will be in figuring out what makes her tick.

Predicted outcome value A forecast of future benefits and costs of interaction based on limited experience with the other.

Who's right—Berger or Sunnafrank? Berger thinks there's no contest. He maintains that any predictions you make about the payoffs of working with Heather are only as good as the quality of your current knowledge. To the extent that you are uncertain of how an action will affect the relationship, predicted outcome value has no meaning.

Even though the validity of Berger's theory is in question, his analysis of initial interaction is a major contribution to communication scholarship. Berger notes that "the field of communication has been suffering and continues to suffer from an intellectual trade deficit with respect to related disciplines; the field imports much more than it exports."[31] Uncertainty reduction theory was an early attempt by a scholar trained within the discipline to reverse that trend. His success at stimulating critical thinking among his peers can be seen in the fact that every scholar cited in this chapter is a member of a communication faculty.

Although some of Berger's axioms may not perfectly reflect the acquaintance process, his focus on the issue of reducing uncertainty is at the heart of communication inquiry. Appealing for further dialogue and modification rather than wholesale rejection of the theory, Berger asks:

> What could be more basic to the study of communication than the propositions that (1) adaptation is essential for survival, (2) adaptation is only possible through the reduction of uncertainty, and (3) uncertainty can be both reduced and produced by communicative activity?[32]

It's a sound rhetorical question.

QUESTIONS TO SHARPEN YOUR FOCUS

1. An *axiom* is a self-evident truth. Which one of Berger's axioms seems least self-evident to you?

2. Check out *theorem 13* in Figure 10–1. Does the predicted relationship between *self-disclosure* and *reciprocity* match the forecast of social penetration theory?

3. What is your goal for the class period when *uncertainty reduction theory* will be discussed? What is your *hierarchical action plan* to achieve that goal?

4. The relationship between *information seeking* and *liking* in *theorem 17* is only 1 out of 28 predictions. Why do critics take doubts about its validity so seriously?

CONVERSATIONS

View this segment online at www.mhhe.com/griffin7 or www. a firstlook.com.

Chuck Berger would not be surprised if you were confused by the midchapter switch from axioms of uncertainty reduction to plan-based strategic communication. In our conversation he describes why he originally viewed the two lines of research as separate but now sees them as tightly linked. Many students find this interview especially fascinating because of Berger's strongly stated opinions. For example, he dismisses CMM's idea of co-creation of social reality because it offers a "total amnesia model." He also criticizes social scientists who purposely create ambiguity so that they can never be proved wrong. Berger's explicit and forthright statements show that he's willing to risk being wrong.

A SECOND LOOK

Recommended resource: Charles R. Berger, "Communicating Under Uncertainty," in *Interpersonal Processes: New Directions in Communication Research,* Michael Roloff and Gerald Miller (eds.), Sage, Newbury Park, CA, 1987, pp. 39–62.

Original statement: Charles R. Berger and Richard Calabrese, "Some Explorations in Initial Interaction and Beyond: Toward a Developmental Theory of Interpersonal Communication," *Human Communication Research,* Vol. 1, 1975, pp. 99–112.

Strategies for uncertainty reduction: Charles R. Berger, "Beyond Initial Interaction: Uncertainty, Understanding, and the Development of Interpersonal Relationships," in

Language and Social Psychology, H. Giles and R. St. Clair (eds.), Blackwell, Oxford, 1979, pp. 122–144.

Further development: Charles R. Berger and J. J. Bradac, *Language and Social Knowledge: Uncertainty in Interpersonal Relations,* Arnold, London, 1982.

Theory update: Charles R. Berger and William B. Gudykunst, "Uncertainty and Communication," in *Progress in Communication Sciences,* Vol. 10, Brenda Dervin and Melvin Voigt (eds.), Ablex, Norwood, NJ, 1991, pp. 21–66.

Comparison with other uncertainty theories: Charles R. Berger, "Uncertainty and Information Exchange in Developing Relationships," in *A Handbook of Personal Relationships,* Steve Duck (ed.), John Wiley & Sons, New York, 1988, pp. 239–255.

Plan-based strategic communication: Charles R. Berger, *Planning Strategic Interaction,* Lawrence Erlbaum, Mahwah, NJ, 1997.

Planning messages when response is uncertain: Charles R. Berger, "Producing Messages Under Uncertainty," in *Message Production: Advances in Communication Theory,* John Greene (ed.), Lawence Erlbaum, Mahwah, NJ, 1997, pp. 221–244.

Goals and plans in message production: Charles R. Berger, "Message Production Skill in Social Interaction," in *Handbook of Communication and Social Interaction Skills,* John O. Greene and Brant R. Burleson (eds.), Lawrence Erlbaum, Mahwah, NJ, 2003, pp. 257–290.

Living with uncertainty: Dale Brashers, "Communication and Uncertainty Management," *Journal of Communication,* Vol. 51, No. 3, 2001, pp. 477–497.

Varied significance of uncertainty: Daena J. Goldsmith, "A Normative Approach to the Study of Uncertainty and Communication," *Journal of Communication,* Vol. 51, 2001, pp. 514–533.

Uncertainty reduction in close relationships: Leanne K. Knobloch and Denise H. Solomon, "Information Seeking Beyond Initial Interaction: Negotiating Relational Uncertainty Within Close Relationships," *Human Communication Research,* Vol. 28, 2002, pp. 243–257.

Anxiety/Uncertainty Management (AUM) theory: William B. Gudykunst, "An Anxiety/Uncertainty Management (AUM) Theory of Effective Communication: Making the Mesh of the Net Finer," in *Theorizing About Intercultural Communication,* William B. Gudykunst (ed.), Sage, Thousand Oaks, CA, 2005, pp. 281–322.

Critique: Kimberley A. Powell and Tamara D. Afifi, "Uncertainty Manager and Adoptees; Ambiguous Loss of Their Birth Parents," *Journal of Social and Personal Relationships,* Vol. 22, pp. 129–151.

Critique: Kathy Kellermann and Rodney Reynolds, "When Ignorance Is Bliss: The Role of Motivation to Reduce Uncertainty in Uncertainty Reduction Theory," *Human Communication Research,* Vol. 17, 1990, pp. 5–75.

To access a chapter on Heider's attribution theory
that appeared in a previous edition, click on Theory Archive at
www.afirstlook.com.

Social Information Processing Theory

of Joseph Walther

In 1992, I was working at home on the relationship development section of an early edition of this text when two computer-savvy friends dropped by. One of them asked what I was writing. About a minute into my description of *social penetration* and *uncertainty reduction,* the other friend blurted out, "I've got it. How 'bout a chapter on intimacy through email?" We all roared with laughter at this crazy idea and headed off to Starbucks for an enjoyable time chatting together over coffee.

Our derisive attitude toward building close relationships through computer-mediated communication (CMC) was shared by many in the early 1990s. CMC might be fine for task-related purposes such as information processing, news dissemination, and long-distance conferencing. But as a place to bond with others, cyberspace seemed be a relational wasteland—stark and barren. Scholars who studied new electronic media had already offered a variety of theories to explain the inherent differences between CMC and face-to-face communication. I'll mention three.

Social presence theory suggests that text-based messages deprive CMC users of the sense that other warm bodies are jointly involved in the interaction.[1] To the extent that we no longer feel that anyone is *there,* our communication becomes more impersonal, individualistic, and task-oriented.

Media richness theory classifies each communication medium according to the complexity of the messages it can handle efficiently.[2] For example, the theory suggests that face-to-face communication provides a rich mix of verbal and nonverbal cue systems that can convey highly nuanced emotions, and even double meanings. By contrast, the limited bandwidth of CMC makes it rather lean—appropriate for transacting everyday business, but not for negotiating social relations.

A third theory concentrates on the *lack of social context cues* in online communication.[3] It claims that CMC users have no clue as to their relative status, and norms for interaction aren't clear, so people tend to become more self-absorbed and less inhibited. The result is increased *flaming*—hostile language

CMC
Computer-mediated communication; text-based messages, which filter out most nonverbal cues.

Social presence theory
Suggests that CMC deprives users of the sense that another actual person is involved in the interaction.

Media richness theory
Purports that CMC bandwidth is too narrow to convey rich relational messages.

that zings its target and creates a toxic climate for relational growth on the Internet.

All of these theories share a *cues filtered out* interpretation of CMC.[4] They regard the absence of nonverbal cues as a permanent flaw of the medium, which limits its usefulness for developing interpersonal relationships. But the same year my friends and I laughed at the idea of intimacy through email, communication professor Joe Walther published a theory that countered this conventional wisdom. Now at Michigan State University, Walther claimed that CMC users can adapt to this restricted medium and use it effectively to develop close relationships. He argued that given the opportunity for a sufficient exchange of social messages and subsequent relational growth, *as goes face-to-face communication, so goes CMC.*

Cues filtered out
Interpretation of CMC that regards lack of nonverbal cues as a fatal flaw for using the medium for relationship development.

CMC VERSUS FACE-TO-FACE: A SIP INSTEAD OF A GULP

Walther labeled his theory *social information processing (SIP)* because he believes relationships grow only to the extent that parties first gain information about each other and use that information to form interpersonal impressions of who they are. In taking this view, SIP theory is consistent with *social penetration theory* and *uncertainty reduction theory* (see Chapters 9 and 10). With these more or less defined impressions in mind, the interacting parties draw closer if they both like the image of the other that they've formed. Walther's SIP focuses on the first link of the chain—the personal information available through CMC and its effect on the composite mental image of the other that each one creates.

Interpersonal Information → Impression Formation → Relationship Development

Impression formation
The composite mental image one person forms of another.

Walther acknowledges that nonverbal cues are filtered out of the interpersonal information that we send and receive through CMC. Physical context, facial expression, tone of voice, interpersonal distance, body position, appearance, gestures, touch, and smell are all missing. But unlike *cues filtered out* theorists, he doesn't think this loss is necessarily fatal or even injurious to a well-defined impression of the other or the relational development that it triggers. Walther highlights two features of CMC that provide a rationale for SIP theory.[5]

1. *Verbal cues.* When motivated to form impressions and develop relationships, communicators employ any cue system that's available. Thus, CMC users can create fully formed impressions of others based solely on the linguistic content of computer-mediated messages.

2. *Extended time.* The exchange of social information through CMC is much slower than it is face-to-face, so impressions are formed at a reduced rate. Yet given enough time, there's no reason to believe that CMC relationships will be weaker or more fragile than those developed with the benefit of nonverbal cues.

The *SIP* acronym suggests a liquid analogy that can help us understand Walther's thinking.[6] Suppose someone hands you a 12-ounce glass of water, cola, or beer—whatever drink you find refreshing. You could hoist the glass and chug the contents in a matter of seconds. That big gulp is similar to being face-to-face with someone you've just met and want to know better. The flood of verbal and nonverbal information makes it possible to form a vivid interpersonal impression that will affect your future interaction. But what if you had to drink your beverage through a straw—one *sip* at a time? You'd still be able to drain the entire 12 ounces, but it would take much longer. That's the situation for CMC users who are thirsty for social information. They end up with the same quantity and quality of interpersonal knowledge, but it accumulates at a slower rate.

You've Got Mail—A Case Study of Online Romance

Social information processing theory was a startling alternative to early CMC theories that seemed reasonable back when most Internet users were scientific researchers, corporate managers, technocrats, and self-described "computer geeks." But as field reports of close online relationships became common in the mid-1990s, Walther's ideas no longer seemed radical. By 1998, the movie *You've Got Mail* could portray a budding Internet romance that was believable and attractive to mainline audiences.

The film stars Meg Ryan as Kathleen Kelly, the owner of a small children's bookstore, and Tom Hanks as Joe Fox, the head of Fox Books—a Barnes & Noble–type superstore. Kathleen and Joe meet online in an over-30 chat room as "Shopgirl" and "NY152." Discovering a common love of books, music, and New York City, they exit chat and pursue their friendship through email. They decide not to reveal their real identities or life stories, a limitation that narrows their verbal channel of communication, the only one they have. Despite this constraint, the messages they send support SIP's contention that CMC text can convey rich relational information. I'll cite portions of Kathleen and Joe's emails throughout the rest of the chapter. Their words illustrate the *verbal cues* and *extended time* features of SIP theory, as well as Walther's subsequent thinking.

VERBAL CUES OF AFFINITY REPLACE NONVERBAL CUES

Walther claims that the human need for affiliation is just as active when people communicate online as when they are with each other face-to-face. But since computer-mediated communication eliminates the nonverbal cues that typically signal relational affinity, CMC users must rely on text-only messages to convey the same social information. He's convinced that verbal and nonverbal cues can be used interchangeably.

If Walther's claim strikes you as far-fetched, remember that prior to electronic communication, people developed pen-pal relationships by discovering similarities and expressing affection through the written word alone. Long-distance romantic relationships thrived as the casual exchange of friendly notes progressed to a stream of passionate love letters, and the same relational development can take place through CMC. The email messages in *You've Got Mail* demonstrate that people can express social information through a linguistic medium and that their words can carry the load.

You've Got Mail opens with Kathleen waking up in the morning and eagerly booting up her computer to check for an email from Joe. Viewers get a hint of earlier messages from their retrospective comments to friends, but the digital letter she opens provides an abundance of social information for her to process.

Joe: Brinkley is my dog. He loves the streets of New York as much as I do, although he likes to eat bits and pieces of bagel off the sidewalk, and I prefer to buy them. Frankly, he's a great catcher and was offered a tryout on a Mets farm team, but he chose to stay with me so that he could spend 18 hours a day sleeping on a large green pillow the size of an inner tube. Don't you love New York in the fall? Makes me want to buy school supplies. I would send you a bouquet of newly sharpened pencils if I knew your name and address. On the other hand, this not knowing has its charm.

Note that Joe's email is filled with self-disclosure. He presents himself as a regular guy—a dog lover who likes nothing better than playing fetch in the park with Brinkley. From Joe's words Kathleen can call up the warm image of a man typing a message to her with his furry friend sleeping contentedly nearby. He reminds her of their similar attitude—they both enjoy the sights, sounds, and tastes of the city. Even better, he has a delightful sense of humor. And best of all, he uses his wit to give her a creative virtual present—a bouquet of newly sharpened pencils. He obviously likes her and appreciates the mystery of their relationship. Although most of his message is about *him*, the last few lines are about *them*.

While Kathleen is reading Joe's message, he's reading her words, which take self-disclosure to a more intimate level. Her entire email consists of metacommunication—communication about their communication and the state of their relationship (see Chapter 12).

Kathleen: Dear friend, I like to start my notes to you as if we were already in the middle of a conversation. I pretend that we're the oldest and dearest friends as opposed to what we actually are, people who don't know each other's names and met in a chat room where we both claimed we'd never been before. "What will NY152 say today?" I wonder. I turn on my computer; I wait impatiently as it connects. I go online, and my breath catches in my chest until I hear three little words: "You've got mail." I hear nothing. Not even a sound on the streets of New York, just the beat of my own heart. I have mail. From you.

Experimental Support for a Counterintuitive Idea

Are the verbal strategies adopted by Joe and Kathleen typical of the way CMC users pursue their social goals? Can affinity for another person be expressed just as well through a digital medium as it can be face-to-face? Walther and two of his students ran a comparative study that suggests the answer to both questions is *yes*.[7]

Walther asked 28 pairs of students who didn't know each other to discuss moral dilemmas—a communication task used in many previous experiments. Half of the dyads talked face-to-face, while the other half interacted via CMC. In both media conditions, one member of each pair was a student accomplice who had been recruited ahead of time to pursue a specific communication goal. Half of these confederates were asked to interact in a friendly way that would create a positive impression, while the other half were told to interact in an unfriendly way that would leave a negative impression. Since Walther designed the experiment to find out what communication strategies people would use, he didn't specify any particular way that the confederates should act to accomplish their goal.

During the experiment, the face-to-face conversations were videotaped from behind a one-way mirror, and all computer messages were saved. Following the interaction, raters who were trained to code verbal and nonverbal behaviors categorized the different ways confederates communicated affect. Naïve participants rated their partners on the degree of affection expressed during the discussion period.

A core principle of SIP theory is that CMC users employ their verbal-only medium to convey a level of relational communication that eventually equals the affect that can be expressed face-to-face through multiple channels. The results of Walther's experiment confirmed that claim. The mode of communication made no difference in the emotional tone perceived by naïve participants. Any discrepancy in affect was due to the intention of each confederate. Regardless of the medium, positive affinity was successfully conveyed by those who made an effort to be nice, and negativity was communicated by those who tried to be mean.

What verbal behaviors did confederates use in CMC to show that they were friendly? A content analysis of their linguistic strategies matched up well with what Joe and Kathleen wrote to each other in *You've Got Mail.* As you might expect, self-disclosure, praise, and explicit statements of affection topped the list of effective ways they communicated warmth. These are core strategies of making an impression by reducing uncertainty and drawing close through social penetration (see Chapters 10 and 9). Yet surprisingly, indirect disagreement, a change of subject, and compliments offered while proposing a contrasting idea were also associated with friendliness. Each of these verbal techniques allows a partner to save face and defuse potential conflict. We see Kathleen taking this conciliatory approach after being stood up by Joe when she went to meet him in person for the first time:

> *Kathleen:* I've been thinking about you. Last night I went to meet you and you weren't there. I wish I knew why. I felt so foolish . . . I so wanted to talk to you. I hope you have a good reason for not being there last night. You don't seem like the kind of person who would do something like that. The odd thing about this form of communication is that you're more likely to talk about nothing than something, but I just want to say that all this nothing has meant more to me than so many somethings. So thanks.

The same verbal-channel cues used in CMC to establish a positive relationship in Walther's experiment could have been used by confederates who conversed with their partners face-to-face. Some of them were, especially self-disclosure. But *what* confederates said when physically present with their partners seemed insignificant compared to *how* they showed it nonverbally. Consistent with previous research, confederates relied on facial expression, eye contact, tone of voice, body position, and other nonverbal cues to convey how they felt about their partners.[8] In sum, the study supports Walther's claim that people meeting online can initiate a relationship just as effectively as if they had met face-to-face, but instead of forming their impressions of each other through nonverbal cues, they do so through the content of what they write.

EXTENDED TIME—THE CRUCIAL VARIABLE IN CMC

Walther is convinced that the length of time that CMC users have to send their messages is the key factor that determines whether their messages can achieve the level of intimacy that others develop face-to-face. Over an extended period, the issue is not the *amount* of social information that can be conveyed online; rather, it's the *rate* at which that information mounts up. Since typing is slower than talking, text-based messages take longer to compose. How much longer? Walther finds that any message spoken in person will take at least four times longer to say through CMC.[9]

This four-to-one time differential explains why many controlled lab studies seem to show that CMC is task-oriented and impersonal. With both modes of communication artificially limited to 15–20 minutes, CMC users don't have time to garner enough social information to form a distinct impression of their online partner. (They've had only a few sips, rather than a gulp of relational cues.) Walther says that a fair test for different channels of relational communication would extend the time limit for unacquainted online users so they could have the opportunity to send the same number of messages as strangers in the face-to-face condition. That's how he designed the content-cues experiment reported in the previous section. When comparing 10 minutes of face-to-face conversation with 40 minutes of CMC, there was no difference in partner affinity between the two modes.

In real life, there's usually no imposed time limit on electronic messaging, whether in length or frequency. Since CMC conveys social information more slowly than does face-to-face communication, Walther advises online users to make up for the rate difference by sending messages more often. Not only does this practice help impression formation in personal relationships, but it's also reassuring to virtual group partners who naturally wonder who their colleagues are, what they're thinking, and if they're going to do the work they've promised.

The pressures of daily living, job, school, family, or other relationship commitments may make online communication more difficult or less attractive, but we still have a choice. In *You've Got Mail,* two business owners with live-in partners choose to carve out time to send emails to each other on a daily basis. Kathleen and Joe's online correspondence spans at least eight months, so they more than meet the extended time requirement that Walther lays out for relational development through CMC. It comes as no surprise to the viewer that the pair slowly fall in love, sight unseen.

Two other temporal factors can contribute to intimacy on the Internet—anticipated future interaction and chronemic cues. *Anticipated future interaction* wasn't part of Walther's original conception of SIP, but he now sees it as a way of extending psychological time. Recall that Chuck Berger claims that our drive to reduce uncertainty about someone we've just met gets an added boost when we think we're going to see each other again (see Chapter 10). Through his empirical research, Walther's discovered that members of an online conference or task group start to trade relational messages when they are scheduled for multiple meetings. It's as if the "shadow of the future" motivates them to encounter others on a personal level.[10] Although Berger's prediction was made with a face-to-face context in mind, Walther finds that anticipation of future interaction is a better predictor of relational development than whether people meet online or in the flesh.

Chronemics is the label that nonverbal researchers use to describe how people perceive, use, and respond to issues of time in their interaction with others. Unlike tone of voice, interpersonal distance, or gestures (*vocalics, proxemics, kinesics*), time is the one nonverbal cue that's not filtered out in CMC. A recipient can note the time of day an email was sent and then gauge the

Anticipated future interaction

A way of extending psychological time; the likelihood of future interaction motivates CMC users to develop a relationship.

Chronemics
The study of people's systematic handling of time in their interaction with others.

elapsed time between messages. Does this knowledge really affect a relationship? Walther's research suggests that a late-night request sent to a teacher or boss will seem demanding, but a social message sent to a friend at the same hour will signal affection. As for time lag, Walther says that a prompt reply signals deference and liking in a new relationship or business context. On the other hand, "a delayed response to someone may indicate receptivity and liking in a more intimate relationship; partners who are comfortable with one another do not need to reply to each other quickly."[11] So you'd do well to send your email at a time that fits the relationship stage and the tone that you want to convey.

You now have the basic predictions of social information processing theory. SIP claims that Kathleen, Joe, and other CMC users can get to know each other and develop a mutual affinity by using the medium's available cues to manage their relational development. The process will probably take longer than is typical in face-to-face bonding, but there's no reason to believe that their relationship will be any less personal. After offering a similar summary, Walther asks, "Is this the best that one can hope to attain when communicating electronically—the mere potential for intimacy where time permits?"[12] His answer is *no—in a number of instances CMC actually surpasses the quality of relational communication that's available when parties talk face-to-face.* Walther's hyperpersonal perspective shows how this works.

HYPERPERSONAL PERSPECTIVE: CLOSER THROUGH CMC THAN IN PERSON

Hyperpersonal perspective
The claim that CMC relationships are often more intimate that those developed when partners are physically together.

Walther uses the term *hyperpersonal* to label CMC relationships that are more intimate than romances or friendships would be if partners were physically together. Under the familiar *sender-receiver-channel-feedback* categories, he classifies four types of media effects that occur precisely because CMC users aren't face-to-face and don't have a full range of communication cues with which to work. Specifically, Walther's hyperpersonal perspective depicts "how senders select, receivers magnify, channels promote, and feedback increases enhanced and selective communication behaviors in CMC."[13]

Sender: Selective Self-Presentation

Selective self-presentation
An online positive portrayal without fear of contradiction, which enables people to create an overwhelmingly favorable impression.

Walther claims that through *selective self-presentation,* people who meet online have an opportunity to make and sustain an overwhelmingly positive impression. That's because they can write about their most attractive traits, accomplishments, thoughts, and actions without fear of contradiction from their physical appearance, their inconsistent actions, or the objections of third parties who know their dark side. As a relationship develops, they can carefully edit the breadth and depth of their self-disclosure to conform to their cyber-image without worrying that nonverbal leakage will shatter their projected persona.

The comic force of *You've Got Mail* derives from the viewer knowing what Kathleen and Joe don't—that their virtual friend in cyberspace is a person they detest in real life. We can see selective self-presentation play out in the contrast between the sarcastic zingers Joe throws at Kathleen when they meet at a literary party as opposed to the warm emails he sends to Shopgirl. The limited cues conveyed by CMC and the anonymity that channel offers give Joe the chance to suppress his "Mister Nasty" tendency in early messages. As a result, even though Kathleen refers to the Joe Fox she knows and loathes as "The Enemy" and a "Bottom Dweller," she perceives her online friend to be a man who doesn't have "a cruel or careless bone in his body."

Parties who are getting to know each other online face an important question: *Should we swap pictures?* Given the availability of digital cameras, the ease of electronic transmission, and our natural curiosity, a photo exchange would seem to be a logical step in CMC relationship development. But the less-is-more assumption that undergirds Walther's hyperpersonal perspective suggests that instead of boosting relational closeness over time, the flood of social cues that photo-realism offers can have a dampening effect. Walther's research bears this out. He's discovered that "CMC partners with time on their side can achieve greater interpersonal outcomes through strictly text-based exchanges than can others using more bandwidth."[14] The implication is clear. If you're in a developing online relationship, resist the temptation or pressure to exchange photographs with each other.

Kathleen and Joe followed this verbal-only path. They became more than friends through the content of their words rather than being distracted by their physical appearance. That doesn't mean they didn't privately speculate. But as Joe told his best friend on the way to his first scheduled meeting with Kathleen,

> Kevin, this woman is the most adorable creature I've ever been in contact with, and if she turns out even to be as good looking as a mailbox, I'd be crazy not to turn my life upside down and marry her.

Of course, by most 30-year-old men's standards, Meg Ryan *looked* adorable. But the hyperpersonal perspective suggests that even if she didn't, after an extended period of selective self-presentation, it wouldn't have made any difference to Joe.

Receiver: Overattribution of Similarity

Attribution is a perceptual process whereby we observe what people do and then try to figure out what they're really like. Our basic interpretive bias is to assume that the specific action we see reflects the personality of the person who did it. People who *do* things like that *are* like that. But when it comes to reading a newsgroup post or email, we have very little to go on. Our only basis for judgment is the verbal behavior of the person who sent the message. Walther says that the absence of other cues doesn't keep us from jumping to conclusions. To the contrary, he's convinced that we'll likely overattribute the meager information we have and create an idealized image of the sender.

Walther draws on SIDE theory, developed by European social psychologists Martin Lea and Russell Spears, to explain this kind of over-the-top identification.[15] SIDE is their acronym for *social identity-deindividuation*. As the title implies, most CMC relationships start when parties meet in online groups that center on a common interest, problem, or passion. Whether participants discuss documentary films, breastfeeding, or the chances of the Chicago Cubs reaching the World Series, they assume that others visiting the site are like them in one important way. In the absence of cues that focus on individual differences, their commonality is all they have to go on as they form their impressions of each

Social identity-deindividuation (SIDE)
A theory that suggests CMC users overestimate their similarity with others they meet in online interest groups.

other. The result is an exaggerated sense of similarity and group solidarity. When this excessively positive image of others is paired with the anticipation of future interaction, virtual partners can SIP and SIDE into a hyperpersonal relationship.

A compelling attraction is especially likely when parties meet through online support groups. These are virtual networks of people who seek and offer information, acceptance, and encouragement centering on a common problem that drew them to the interactive site. For example, CMC users search the Web to find others who struggle to overcome chemical addiction, eating disorders, shyness, depression, cancer, or other problems. Many find that guaranteed anonymity, 24/7 access, and greater candor from those in the know make Internet support groups more attractive than their face-to-face counterparts.[16] So are the invisible fellow members who seem to understand and appreciate everything the sufferer is going through.

Channel: Communicating on Your Own Time

Most forms of interpersonal communication require that parties synchronize their schedules in order to talk with each other. Although face-to-face interaction and phone conversations offer a sense of immediacy, co-presence is achieved at

"I can't wait to see what you're like online."

a high price. One partner's desire to communicate often comes at a bad time for the other. An overture to talk that might be welcome one day can be an inconvenience, interruption, or intrusion the next. Parties may make a date to talk, of course, but locking in a time for communication raises expectations for significance that may be hard to meet. And relationships are at risk when appointments are frequently canceled, or worse, forgotten.

In contrast, computer communication is mediated through a channel that gives partners the opportunity to interact relationally without having to attend to each other at the same time. Walther refers to CMC as an *asynchronous* channel of communication, meaning that parties can use it nonsimultaneously. With time constraints relaxed, CMC users are free to write person-centered messages, knowing that the recipient will read the message at a convenient time. This is a big plus, especially when communicating across time zones or for people whose waking hours are out of sync.

Asynchronous channel
A nonsimultaneous medium of communication that each individual can use when he or she desires.

Walther notes an added benefit of nonsimultaneous CMC over face-to-face communication: "In asynchronous interaction one may plan, contemplate, and edit one's comments more mindfully and deliberatively than one can in more spontaneous, simultaneous talk."[17] This is a tremendous advantage when dealing with touchy issues, misunderstandings, or conflict between parties. In *You've Got Mail*, for example, Joe is hard-pressed to explain why he failed to show up to meet Shopgirl in person as they had carefully planned. Fearing that the truth will destroy their relationship, he makes up three excuses, each time deleting the lie after it's displayed on the screen. Only then does he compose a nuanced, equivocal answer that affirms Kathleen and gets him off the hook. Without time for reflection, Joe's shoot-from-the-hip quips would have hurt Kathleen and shot down any chance for further intimacy.

Feedback: Self-Fulfilling Prophecy

Self-fulfilling prophecy is the tendency for a person's expectation of others to evoke a response from them that confirms what he or she anticipated. Believing it's so can make it so. This process creates hyperpersonal relationships only if CMC parties first form highly favorable impressions of each other. As we've seen in the preceding sections, Walther thinks that's likely to happen. *Senders* self-select what they reveal, *receivers* create an idealized image of their partner, and the *channel* lets users express themselves the way they want, when they want. What's not to like?

Self-fulfilling prophecy
The tendency for a person's expectation of others to evoke a response from them that confirms what was originally anticipated.

Self-fulfilling prophecy is triggered when that hyperpositive image is intentionally or inadvertently *fed back* to the other, creating the CMC equivalent of the *looking-glass self* (see Chapter 5). The person perceived to be wonderful starts acting that way. Viewers of *You've Got Mail* see this type of transformation in Joe.

For most of the film, the real-life Joe glories in his take-no-prisoners, competitive approach, which forces Kathleen to close her store. On the occasions when they meet, he is spiteful and obnoxious, and these habits die hard. Even after he discovers that his Shopgirl is, in fact, Kathleen, some of his nastiness continues for a while. But not knowing NY152's true identity, Kathleen as Shopgirl continues to treat him as a wise, kind, loving friend—the sort of man she'd like to marry. Because she expects him to be this way, he becomes in real life the man she perceives online. The transformation is so complete that when Shopgirl and NY152 finally meet in person, Kathleen embraces Joe and says, "I wanted it to be you. I wanted it to be you so badly."

CRITIQUE: WALTHER'S CANDID ASSESSMENT

In 2002, Joe Walther received the Woolbert Award from the National Communication Association (NCA) for introducing social information processing theory in the 1992 journal article mentioned at the start of the chapter. This annual award honors a specific piece of scholarship that makes a lasting impact on the field of communication, so NCA waits 10 years after publication to make sure that the author's ideas have stood the test of time. Walther's SIP more than qualifies. While most scholars assumed that online communication is an inherently inferior medium for relational communication, he rejected that brand of *technological determinism*. More than a decade of experimental research and the testimonies of people who have become close through CMC validate the theory's worth. Walther appreciates the recognition of his professional colleagues, yet he openly admits that there are weaknesses and gaps in his analysis of CMC. I'll cite a couple of problems he sees with SIP and then address two deficiencies he spots in the hyperpersonal perspective.

Technological determinism
The belief that the impact of a message is determined by the medium over which it's communicated.

Walther's original breakthrough was to focus on the *rate* at which social information accrues through different media. When comparing CMC with face-to-face communication, SIP predicts normal interpersonal relationships developing at a slower tempo.[18] Yet Walther's empirical studies have shown that relationships in cyberspace often form at the same pace or even faster than they do for people who meet face-to-face.[19] Apparently the mere anticipation of future online interaction is enough to accelerate impression formation and the bonding process. While this may be good news for those who are eager to form friendships via the Internet, it causes Walther to ask if SIP's predictions fail to describe the respective progress of CMC and face-to-face relationships over time. "That indeed may be the case," he writes.[20]

Walther's second concern is with his original assumption that no matter what media people use, they are motivated by a similar desire to affiliate with others. Within a few years he had second thoughts about this assertion and wrote, "A weakness apparent in the social information processing perspective is that it has not allowed for differences in the affiliation drive."[21] He was specifically referring to the motivating effect of anticipated future interaction discussed in the previous paragraph. But Walther doesn't deal with the possibility that there could be systematic personality differences between those who pursue relationships on the Internet and those who don't. Perhaps CMC users who join online discussion groups or enter chat rooms have a higher need for affiliation than the typical person whose relationships are developed through multichannel modes of communication. If so, that stronger desire might offset the limitations of using a restricted medium.

Referring to his four-factor hyperpersonal perspective, Walther takes pains to label the sender-receiver-channel-feedback model a *perspective* rather than a *theory*. As a rigorous social scientist, he understands that a good theory should offer a central explanatory mechanism to drive a synthesis of the observed effects. Because the hyperpersonal perspective doesn't have this kind of conceptual engine, he admits that it's open to significant criticism:

> It is not clear at all whether there are any necessary theoretical linkages among and between the four major components and the more detailed processes that the

model specifies. In other words, its constructs and propositions are poorly interrelated, and its status as a robust theory is therefore tenuous.[22]

Without a theoretical glue to hold together selective self-presentation, overattribution, nonsimultaneous communication, and self-fulfilling prophecy in a unified whole, it's difficult, if not impossible, to test how these variables work together.

Walther developed the hyperpersonal perspective when it became obvious that SIP didn't account for the extraordinary closeness that some partners developed through CMC alone. The processes that he lists can help us understand how two people who have never been together can become totally wrapped up in each other. But it doesn't always happen. Sometimes online partners get turned off and log off—effectively terminating the relationship. This dark side of Internet life prompts Walther to express another reservation: "Despite its potential for understanding positive relational communication processes, the hyperpersonal perspective has been less explicit in predicting negative relational outcomes in CMC."[23] Conversely, he notes that it offers little encouragement or advice for parties who want to migrate successfully from intimacy in cyberspace to an equally intense mixed-mode relationship where they are eyeball to eyeball.[24]

Rather than being disheartened by Walther's assessment of his theoretical work, I'm encouraged by his candor. All theories have flaws and limitations. His honest evaluation gives me confidence in his upbeat summary of relational opportunities through CMC:

> The "Information Superhighway" is clearly not just a road for moving data from one place to another, but a roadside where people pass each other, occasionally meet, and decide to travel together. You can't see very much of other drivers at first, unless you do travel together for some time. There are highway bandits, to be sure, who are not as they appear to be—one must drive defensively—and there are conflicts and disagreements online as there are off-road too. While early research suggested that numerous interpersonal collisions were impending, recent research finds that interpersonal information moves at slower speeds, and in doing so, the roadway is not as dangerous as once thought. It can even offer a relational joyride.[25]

QUESTIONS TO SHARPEN YOUR FOCUS

1. *SIP* proposes that *CMC* conveys relational information just as well as *face-to-face communication,* with only one difference. What is that difference?

2. Email is a *text-based, asynchronous* message system. What other *media* fit that description? What is one text-based, *digital dyadic* message system that requires simultaneous participation?

3. The *hyperpersonal perspective* suggests that CMC effects of *sender, receiver, channel,* and *feedback* promote greater intimacy. Which factor do you think has the greatest relational impact? Which has the least?

4. Your online partner seems wonderful. However, because it's possible to create a *fictitious persona* through CMC, you want to make sure that he or she is "for real." Short of migrating offline to meet face-to-face, how would you find out?

CONVERSATIONS

View this segment online at
www.mhhe.com/griffin7 or
www.afirstlook.com.

Most of my conversation with Joe Walther centers on CMC users who have a great affinity for the Internet. Granted they can develop strong impressions of others online, but does true intimacy require face-to-face communication? Are heavy CMC users more in love with the medium than with their partners? Can those who are socially shy develop better relationships through CMC? What code of ethical online behavior would he suggest? Walther offers advice to CMC partners who want to meet in person. He also discusses the scope of SIP and the hyperpersonal perspective—whether they apply to partners who want to sustain a long-distance relationship after first meeting face-to-face.

A SECOND LOOK

Recommended resource: Joseph B. Walther, "Interpersonal Effects in Computer-Mediated Interaction: A Relational Perspective," *Communication Research*, Vol. 19, 1992, pp. 52–90.

Hyperpersonal perspective: Joseph B. Walther, "Computer-Mediated Communication: Impersonal, Interpersonal, and Hyperpersonal Interaction," *Communication Research*, Vol. 23, 1996, pp. 3–43.

State of the art: Joseph B. Walther and Malcolm R. Parks, "Cues Filtered Out, Cues Filtered In: Computer-Mediated Communication and Relationships," in *Handbook of Interpersonal Communication*, 3rd ed., Mark Knapp and J. A. Daly (eds.), Sage, Thousand Oaks, CA, 2002, pp. 529–561.

Capsule summary of SIP and hyperpersonal perspective: Joseph B. Walther and Lisa C. Tidwell, "Computer-Mediated Communication: Interpersonal Interaction On-Line," in *Making Connections: Readings in Relational Communication*, 2nd ed., Kathleen M. Galvin and Pamela J. Cooper (eds.), Roxbury, Los Angeles, 2000, pp. 322–329.

Empirical support: Lisa C. Tidwell and Joseph B. Walther, "Computer-Mediated Communication Effects on Disclosure, Impressions, and Interpersonal Evaluations: Getting to Know One Another a Bit at a Time," *Human Communication Research*, Vol. 28, 2002, pp. 317–348.

Verbal cues of affection in CMC: Joseph B. Walther, Tracy Loh, and Laura Granka, "The Interchange of Verbal and Nonverbal Cues in Computer-Mediated and Face-to-Face Affinity," *Journal of Language and Social Psychology*, Vol. 24, 2005, pp. 36–65.

Time effects in CMC: Joseph B. Walther, "Time Effects in Computer-Mediated Groups: Past, Present, and Future," in *Distributed Work*, P. Hinds and S. Kiesler (eds.), MIT Press, Cambridge, MA, 2002, pp. 235–257.

Effect of photo-realism on CMC: Joseph B. Walther, Celeste L. Slovacek, and Lisa C. Tidwell, "Is a Picture Worth a Thousand Words? Photographic Images in Long-Term and Short-Term Computer-Mediated Communication," *Communication Research*, Vol. 28, 2001, pp. 105–134.

Internet support groups: Joseph B. Walther and Shawn Boyd, "Attraction to Computer-Mediated Social Support," in *Communication Technology and Society*, C. A. Lin and D. Atkins (eds.), Hampton, Cresskill, NJ, 2002, pp. 153–188.

Online dating: Jennifer L. Gibbs, Nicole B. Ellison, and Rebecca D. Heino, "Self-Presentation in Online Personals: The Role of Anticipated Future Interaction, Self-Disclosure, and Perceived Success in Internet Dating," *Communication Research*, Vol. 33, 2006, pp. 152–177.

The term *maintenance* may call to mind an auto repair shop where workers with oil-stained coveralls and grease under their fingernails struggle to service or fix a well-worn engine. The work is hard, the conditions are messy, and the repair is best performed by mechanics who have some idea of what they're doing.

This image of rugged work is appropriate when one is thinking about the ongoing effort required to maintain a close relationship. In many ways, forming a relational bond is much easier than sustaining it. The beginning stages of intimacy are often filled with excitement at discovering another human being who sees the world as we do, with the added touch of wonder that the person we like likes us as well. As the relationship becomes more established, however, irritating habits, conflict, jealousy, and boredom can be the friction that threatens to pull the engine apart. The owner's manual of a new "Intimacy" should warn that periodic maintenance is necessary for friends, romantic partners, and even blood relatives to make it for the long haul.

Inasmuch as the image of auto upkeep and repair communicates the importance of "servicing" a relationship, the metaphor of mechanical labor is appropriate. But personal relationships aren't inanimate machines with interchangeable parts that can be adjusted with a wrench. Expanding the *maintenance* metaphor to living

"They're a perfect match—she's high-maintenance, and he can fix anything."

151

organisms underscores the importance of individualized attention in relational health. Humanist communication writer John Stewart refers to a pair's personal relationship as a "spiritual child," born as the result of their coming together.[1] His analogy stresses that a relationship requires continual care and nurture for sustained growth. Stewart thinks it's impossible to totally kill a relationship as long as one of the "parents" is still alive. Yet when people ignore or abuse the spiritual children they've created, the results are stunted or maimed relationships.

What does a healthy relationship look like? Through an extensive research program on relationship maintenance, Dan Canary (Arizona State University) and Laura Stafford (Ohio State University) conclude that long-term satisfying relationships have at least four characteristics—*liking, trust, commitment*, and *control mutuality*.[2] The first three seem like old friends and rather obvious. We may be able to work productively with a person we don't like, but it's hard to imagine a fulfilling relationship with somebody we don't enjoy. Similarly, knowing that we can trust another person to be honest and dependable is one of the main benefits of a close relationship. And a commitment to make the relationship last is probably the best way to make sure that it does, especially for a romantic couple.

Control mutuality is a less familiar concept. According to Canary and Stafford, control mutuality is "the degree to which partners agree about which of them should decide relational goals and behavioral routines."[3] They may have an egalitarian relationship, or perhaps one person regularly defers to the other, yet is genuinely happy to do so. Either way, they could each embrace the following statement: *Both of us are satisfied with the way we handle decisions.*

Stafford and Canary surveyed 662 married and single men and women involved in extended romantic relationships to find out what maintenance behaviors promoted liking, trust, commitment, and control mutuality. They consistently discovered five interpersonal actions that contribute to long-term relational satisfaction.[4]

Positivity—Cheerful, courteous talk, avoiding criticism. This upbeat form of communication is particularly linked to liking and control mutuality.

Openness—Self-disclosure and frank talk about their relationship. The effect of transparency is roughly equal across the board.

Assurances—Affirming talk about the future of their relationship. These words especially promote commitment and liking.

Networking—Spending time together with mutual friends and family. This joint social activity contributes to overall relational stability and satisfaction.

Sharing tasks—Working together on routine jobs, chores, and assignments. This cooperation seems to affect control mutuality the most.

Canary and Stafford note that not much relational maintenance research is theory driven—including their work cited above. There are, however, at least three well-known theories that speak to the issue. I've already presented Thibaut and Kelley's *social exchange* approach, which is an integral part of *social penetration theory* (see Chapter 9). These theorists regard interpersonal behavior and attitudes as the result of rewards and costs. Accordingly, when mutual benefits outweigh partners' costs, and these outcomes are well above each party's comparison level (CL), liking and relational satisfaction should be high. And when parties perceive that their option for a closer relationship with someone else is dim—each one's outcome exceeding the comparison level of alternatives (CL_{alt})—commitment will be strong and the relationship correspondingly stable. Finally, when both partners have invested a great deal of time, energy, and emotional resources in the relationship, the prospect of abandoning this investment becomes a barrier to breakup.

Leslie Baxter and Barbara Montgomery are uneasy with the concept of relational *maintenance* because the term implies that the goal is to restore the relationship to its original condition. For these communication theorists, relationship maintenance isn't as much about achieving stability as it is about coping with the stresses inherent in every intimate bond. The tug-of-war they see between connectedness and separateness means that positive words and liking are only half of the story. The pull toward openness is countered by an oppositional tug toward privacy. And the dialectical tension between predictability and spontaneity makes commitment no guarantee of a future together. Chapter 12 describes Baxter and Montgomery's *relational dialectics,* a perspective that regards these contradictions as an occasion for dialogue to *sustain* a relationship in flux rather than working to make it what it was.

Paul Watzlawick's *interactional view* of functional and dysfunctional relationships describes the family as an interconnected system. His theory claims that whether we like it or not, what one person in a family system does has an impact on every other member. He believes that either an absence or excess of metacommunication—talk about their communication with each other—is a symptom of a family in trouble. Like Canary and Stafford, Watzlawick regards relational control as a key element in a family system's equilibrium, but the relational picture he paints is more complex than the one they sketch. His emphasis on using a therapist or counselor to help reframe family communication patterns has a greater impact on the relationship than networking with friends. Chapter 13 presents the interactional view.

Relational Dialectics

of Leslie Baxter &
Barbara Montgomery

Leslie Baxter and Barbara Montgomery are central figures in a growing group of communication scholars who are interested in the communication that creates close relationships. Baxter directs an extensive program of research at the University of Iowa. Montgomery is associate vice-president for academic affairs at the University of New Hampshire.

The first time Baxter conducted a series of in-depth interviews with people about their personal relationships, she quickly gave up any hope of discovering scientific laws that neatly ordered the experiences of friends and lovers.

> I was struck by the contradictions, contingencies, non-rationalities, and multiple realities to which people gave voice in their narrative sense-making of their relational lives.[1]

She saw no law of gravitational pull to predict interpersonal attraction, no coefficient of friction that would explain human conflict. She found, instead, people struggling to respond to conflicting tugs they felt within their relationships. Although she worked independently of Baxter, Montgomery's experience was much the same.

Baxter and Montgomery each analyzed tensions inherent in romantic relationships and began to catalogue the contradictions that couples faced. They soon recognized the commonality of their work and co-authored a book on relating based on the premise that personal relationships are indeterminate processes of ongoing flux.[2]

Both scholars make it clear that the forces that strain romantic relationships are also at work among close friends and family members. They applaud the work of William Rawlins at Ohio University, who concentrates on the "communicative predicaments of friendship," and the narrative analysis of Art Bochner at the University of South Florida, who focuses on the complex contradictions within family systems. Whatever the form of intimacy, Baxter and Montgomery's basic claim is that "social life is a dynamic knot of contradictions, a ceaseless interplay between contrary or opposing tendencies."[3]

Relational dialectics
A dynamic knot of contradictions in personal relationships; an unceasing interplay between contrary or opposing tendencies.

Relational dialectics highlight the tension, struggle, and general messiness of close personal ties. The best way we can grasp Baxter and Montgomery's perspective is to examine a relational narrative similar to the ones Baxter found so gripping in her early studies. The 2002 movie *Bend It Like Beckham* is especially helpful in illustrating tensions within family, friendship, and romantic ties. Due in part to its honest portrayal of the contradictions inherent in these three types of close relationships, it became the most successful British-made and distributed film of all time. Audiences of all ages and every ethnicity could identify with the relational struggles of Jesminder Bhamra, an Indian teenager brought up in the west end of London.

Like many British teenage males, Jess is passionate about soccer, and she's better than any of the guys she plays with in pickup games at the park. A poster of England's football superstar David Beckham hangs on her bedroom wall and she often talks to his image about her game and her life. In the close-knit Indian expat community, Jess is at an age where girls are supposed to focus on marrying a well-regarded Indian boy—a union often arranged by their parents. Her mother insists that Jess quit "running around half-naked in front of men." Her dad reluctantly agrees. "Jess, your mother's right. It's not nice. You must start behaving as a proper woman. OK?"

Jules, an Anglo girl who sees Jess play, recruits her to play for an amateur women's soccer team. Jess and Jules soon become "mates," bonded together by their goal-scoring ability and joint efforts to keep Jess' participation a secret from her mom and dad. Their friendship is soon ruptured by Jules' jealousy over a romantic interest between Jess and Joe, the team's coach. Of course, that kind of relationship is out of bounds. So with her dad, best friend, and admired coach, Jess experiences the oppositional pull of contrasting forces.

THE TUG-OF-WAR DIALECTICS OF CLOSE RELATIONSHIPS

Some viewers might assume that Jess's up-again, down-again relationships with Joe, Jules, and her dad are due to her age, sex, birth order, ethnicity, or obsession with soccer. But Baxter and Montgomery caution us not to look at demographics or personal traits when we want to understand the nature of close relationships. Neither biology nor biography can account for the struggle of contradictory tendencies that Jess' and her significant others experience in this story. The tensions they face are common to all personal relationships, and those opposing pulls never quit.

Contradiction is a core concept of relational dialectics. *Contradiction* refers to "the dynamic interplay between unified oppositions."[4] A contradiction is formed "whenever two tendencies or forces are interdependent (the dialectical principle of unity) yet mutually negate one another (the dialectical principle of negation)."[5] According to Baxter, every personal relationship faces the same tension. Rather than bemoaning this relational fact of life, Baxter and Montgomery suggest that couples take advantage of the opportunity it provides: "From a relational dialectics perspective, bonding occurs in both interdependence with the other and independence from the other."[6] One without the other diminishes the relationship.

Baxter and Montgomery draw heavily on the thinking of Mikhail Bakhtin, a Russian intellectual who survived the Stalinist regime. Bakhtin saw dialectical tension as the "deep structure" of all human experience. On the one hand, a centripetal, or centralizing, force pulls us together with others. On the other hand, a centrifugal, or decentralizing, force pushes us apart.

In order to picture Bakhtin's simultaneous and conflicting forces, imagine yourself playing "crack the whip" while skating with a group of friends. You volunteer to be the outermost person on a pinwheeling chain of skaters. As you accelerate, you feel the centripetal pull from the skater beside you, who has a viselike grip on your wrist. You also feel the opposing centrifugal force that threatens to rip you from your friend's grasp and slingshot you away from the group. Skill at skating doesn't reduce the conflicting pressures. In fact, the more speed you can handle, the greater the opposing forces.

Unlike the thesis-antithesis-synthesis stages of Hegelian or Marxist dialectics, Bakhtin's fusion-fission opposites have no ultimate resolution. There is no final synthesis or end-stage of equilibrium. Relationships are always in flux; the only certainty is certain change. For Bakhtin, this wasn't bad news. He saw dialectical tension as providing an opportunity for dialogue, an occasion when partners could work out ways to mutually embrace the conflict between unity *with* and differentiation *from* each other.

Most Westerners are bothered by the idea of paradox, so Baxter and Montgomery work hard to translate the concept into familiar terms. At the start of her research interviews, Baxter introduces a dialectical perspective without ever using the phrase itself. She talks about people experiencing certain "pulls" or "tugs" in different directions. Her words call up the image of parties engaged in an ongoing *tug-of-war* created through their conversations. Within this metaphor, their communication exerts simultaneous pulls on both ends of a taut line—a relational rope under tension.

It's important to understand that when Baxter uses the term *relational dialectics,* she is not referring to *being of two minds*—the cognitive dilemma within the head of an individual who is grappling with conflicting desires. Instead, she's describing the contradictions that are "located in the relationship between parties, produced and reproduced through the parties' joint communicative activity."[7] So dialectical tension is the natural product or unavoidable result of our conversations rather than the motive force guiding what we say in them. And despite the fact that we tend to think of any kind of conflict as detrimental to our relationships, Baxter and Montgomery believe that these contradictions can be constructive. That's fortunate, because these theorists are convinced that dialectics in relationships are inevitable.

THREE DIALECTICS THAT AFFECT RELATIONSHIPS

While listening to hundreds of men and women talk about their relationships, Baxter spotted three recurring contradictions that challenge the traditional wisdom of the theories described in the relationship development section. Recall that Rogers' phenomenological approach assumes that *closeness* is the relational ideal, Berger's uncertainty reduction theory posits a quest for interpersonal *certainty,* and Altman and Taylor's social penetration theory valorizes the *transparent* or *open self.* But from the accounts she heard, Baxter concluded that these pursuits turn out to be only part of the story.

Although most of us embrace the traditional ideals of closeness, certainty, and openness in our relationships, our actual communication within family, friendship, and romance seldom follows a straight path toward these goals. Baxter and Montgomery believe this is the case because we are also drawn toward the exact opposite—autonomy, novelty, and privacy. These conflicting forces

	Internal Dialectic (within the relationship)	**External Dialectic** (between couple and community)
Integration – Separation	Connectedness - Separateness	Inclusion - Seclusion
Stability – Change	Certainty - Uncertainty	Conventionality - Uniqueness
Expression – Nonexpression	Openness - Closedness	Revelation - Concealment

FIGURE 12–1 Typical Dialectical Tensions Experienced by Relational Partners
Based on Baxter and Montgomery, *Relating: Dialogues and Dialectics*

can't be resolved by simple "either/or" decisions. The "both/and" nature of dialectical pressures guarantees that our relationships will be complex, messy, and always somewhat on edge.

Baxter and Montgomery's research has focused on three overarching relational dialectics that affect almost every close relationship: *integration-separation, stability-change,* and *expression-nonexpression*. These oppositional pairs are listed on the left side of Figure 12–1. The terms within the chart label these contrasting forces as they are experienced in two different contexts. The Internal Dialectic column describes the three dialectics as they play out *within a relationship*. The External Dialectic column lists similar pulls that cause tension *between a couple and their community*. Unlike the typical Hollywood love story, the portrayals of Jess' key relationships in *Bend It Like Beckham* are credible due to each pair's continual struggles with these contradictions. Since Baxter insists that dialectics are created through conversation, I'll quote extensively from the characters' dialogue in the film.

All researchers who explore contradictions in close relationships agree that there is no finite list of relational dialectics. Accordingly, the ragged edge at the bottom of the figure suggests that these opposing forces are just the start of a longer list of contradictions that confront partners as they live out their relationship in real time and place. For example, Rawlins finds that friends continually have to deal with the paradox of judgment and acceptance. In this section, however, I'll limit my review to the "Big Three" contradictions that Baxter and Montgomery discuss.

Integration and Separation

Baxter and Montgomery regard the contradiction between connectedness and separateness as a primary strain within all relationships. If one side wins this *me-we* tug-of-war, the relationship loses:

> No relationship can exist by definition unless the parties sacrifice some individual autonomy. However, too much connection paradoxically destroys the relationship because the individual identities become lost.[8]

Internal dialectics
Ongoing tensions played out within a relationship.

External dialectics
Ongoing tensions between a couple and their community.

Integration/separation
A class of relational dialectics that includes connectedness-separateness, inclusion-seclusion, intimacy-independence, and closeness-autonomy.

Throughout *Bend It Like Beckham,* Jess and her father portray "a stay-away close" ambivalence toward each other that illustrates the connectedness-separateness dialectic. Through much of the story she defies his "no soccer" ban, even to the extent of a stealthy overnight trip with the team to play in Germany. As for her father, his words to her suggest that he's more worried about what the Indian community thinks than he is about her well-being. Yet when an Indian friend offers to rush her away from her sister's wedding reception to play in the championship game, Jess turns to her father and says, "Dad, it doesn't matter. This is much more important. I don't want to spoil the day for you." He in turn tells her to go and "play well and make us proud." Later that night at home with the extended family he strengthens his connection with Jess by defending his decision to his irate wife: "Maybe you could handle her long face. I could not. I didn't have the heart to stop her."

Bakhtin wrote that dialectical moments are occasions for dialogue. Perhaps the best example in the film comes after Jess receives a red card in a tournament game for retaliating against an opponent who fouled her. Although the shorthanded team holds on to win, Joe reads her the riot act in the locker room: "What the hell is wrong with you, Bhamra? I don't ever want to see anything like that from you ever again. Do you hear me?" Without waiting for an answer, he turns and marches out. Jess runs after him and their dialogue reflects the ongoing tension between connection and separation in their relationship:

Jess: Why did you yell at me like that? You knew that the ref was out of order.

Joe: You could have cost us the tournament.

Jess: But it wasn't my fault! You didn't have to shout at me.

Joe: Jess, I am your coach. I have to treat you the same as everyone else. Look, Jess, I saw it. She fouled you. She tugged your shirt. You just overreacted. That's all.

Jess: That's not all. She called me a Paki, but I guess you wouldn't understand what that feels like, would you?

Joe: Jess, I'm Irish. Of course I'd understand what that feels like. [Joe then holds a sobbing Jess against his chest, a long hug witnessed by her father.]

Baxter and Montgomery maintain that even as partners struggle with the stresses of intimacy in their relationship vis-à-vis each other, as a couple they also face parallel yin-yang tensions with people in their social networks. The seclusion of private togetherness that is necessary for a relationship to gel runs counter to the inclusion of the couple with others in the community. The observed embrace certainly complicates Jess and Joe's relationship. And unless they find a way to work through the dilemma between inclusion with outsiders and seclusion for themselves, the future of their relationship is in doubt. These opposing external forces surface again when Jess runs into Joe's arms on a dimly lit soccer field to tell him that her parents will allow her to go to an American university on a soccer scholarship. But as Joe seeks their first kiss, she stops him, saying, "I'm sorry Joe. I can't." To a baffled Joe she explains, "Letting me go is a really big step for my mum and dad. I don't know how they'd survive if I told them about you."

Stability and Change

Berger's uncertainty reduction theory makes a strong case for the idea that people strive for predictability in their relationships (see Chapter 10). Baxter and Montgomery don't question our human search for interpersonal certainty, but

"Would you guys mind if I slept alone for a change?"
Reproduced by permission of Donald Orehek.

Stability/change
A class of relational dialectics that includes certainty-uncertainty, conventionality-uniqueness, predictability-surprise, and routine-novelty.

they are convinced that Berger makes a mistake by ignoring our simultaneous efforts toward its opposite, novelty. We seek the bit of mystery, the touch of spontaneity, the occasional surprise that is necessary for having fun. Without the spice of variety to season our time together, the relationship becomes bland, boring, and, ultimately, emotionally dead.

Early in their friendship, Jess asks about Jules' romantic interest in Joe. Their brief conversation can be seen as a *novel* fantasy expressed in the imagery of the *familiar*—a conventional marriage to a less-than-perfect partner:

JESS: Jules . . . you know Joe, do you like him?

JULES: Nah, he'd get sacked if he was caught shagging one of his players.

JESS: Really?

JULES: I wish I could find a bloke like him. Everyone I know is a prat. They think girls can't play as well as them, except Joe of course.

JESS: Yeah, I hope I marry an Indian boy like him, too.

The girls then laugh together—a tension release—and hug before they part. But dealing with dialectics is always tenuous. When the romantically unthinkable becomes possible for Jess, Jules lashes out: "You knew he was off-limits. Don't pretend to be so innocent. . . . You've really hurt me, Jess! . . . You've betrayed me."

It would be easy to see Jess' family relationships as a simplistic face-off between the *conventionality* of life in their culture versus the shocking *uniqueness* of an Indian girl playing British football. That's because so much of what Jesminder's sister and parents say reproduces time-honored Indian norms and practices. As her sister warns, "Look Jess, . . . do you want to be the one that everyone stares at, at every family do, 'cause you've married the English bloke?" And Jess' dream to go to college in California, play pro soccer, and have the freedom to fall in love with her Irish coach seem a unified pull in the opposite direction.

But neither Jess nor her father speak in a single voice. In conversations with friends Jess depicts herself as a dutiful daughter who gets top grades and doesn't sleep around with guys. She also describes her parents' real care for her, her desire not to hurt them, and her fear that her dad might no longer talk with her. And despite his apparently firm stance against Jess playing English football, he goes to see her play and says he doesn't want to see her disappointed. In compelling drama and in real life, the contradictory forces created through dialogue are quite complex.

Expression and Nonexpression

Expression/nonexpression
A class of relational dialectics that includes openness-closedness, revelation-concealment, candor-secrecy, and transparency-privacy.

You might recall that Irwin Altman, one of the founders of social penetration theory, ultimately came to the conclusion that self-disclosure and privacy operate in a cyclical, or wavelike, fashion over time.[9] Baxter and Montgomery pick up on Altman's recognition that relationships aren't on a straight-line path to intimacy. They see the pressures for openness and closedness waxing and waning like phases of the moon. If Jess' communication to her parents seems somewhat schizophrenic, it's because the dialectical forces for transparency and discretion are hard to juggle.

Through most of the movie, Jess is closemouthed with her parents about the extent of her soccer playing and her romantic attraction to Joe, even after her dad discovers both secrets. But on the night following the wedding (and the tournament final) she decides to come clean about one of them:

> Mum, Dad . . . I played in the final today, and we won! . . . I played the best ever. And I was happy because I wasn't sneaking off and lying to you. . . . Anyway, there was a scout from America today, and he's offered me a place at a top university with a free scholarship and a chance to play football professionally. And I really want to go. And if I can't tell you what I want now then I'll never be happy whatever I do.

Just as the openness-closedness dialectic is a source of ongoing tension within a relationship, a couple also faces the *revelation* and *concealment* dilemma of what to tell others. Baxter and Montgomery note that each possible advantage of "going public" is offset by a corresponding potential danger. For example, public disclosure is a relational rite of passage signaling partners and others that the tie that binds them together is strong. Jess seems to sense this relational fact of life when she tells Joe on the soccer field that her parents wouldn't be able to handle the news of their attraction for each other. She doesn't buy much time for their romance to develop because she's leaving for school, and Joe can't stand the uncertainty. As Jess and Jules say goodbye to their families before boarding the plane to America, Joe comes running down the concourse calling to Jess. They move a few feet away from the others and Joe implores, "Look. I can't let you go without knowin'. . . . that even with the distance—and the concerns of your family—we still might have something. Don't you think?" She gives Joe (and her parents, if they turn to look) the answer through a long first kiss. At this climactic point in the film, the viewer realizes that the force field of dialectics has irrevocably changed, but will never disappear.

SECOND GENERATION OF DIALECTICS: BAKHTIN ON DIALOGUE

Dialogue
Communication that is constitutive, always in flux, capable of achieving aesthetic moments.

Baxter says that theories are like relationships—they aren't stagnant. The good ones change and mature over time. As the chapter so far suggests, Baxter's early emphasis with Montgomery was on contradictory forces inherent in all relationships. But Baxter has recently focused on the relational implications of Mikhail Bakhtin's conception of *dialogue*. In what she calls the *second generation* of relational dialectics, Baxter highlights five dialogic strands within Bakhtin's thought.[10] Although hints of these five threads surfaced in the original theory, she now foregrounds them in order to show the centrality of dialogue in social life. The next five sections seek to unravel these strands of dialogue, for without dialogue, there is no relationship.

Dialogue as a Constitutive Process

Constitutive dialogue
Communication that creates, sustains, and alters relationships and the social world; social construction.

Baxter states that a "constitutive approach to communication asks how communication defines or constructs the social world, including our selves and our personal relationships."[11] This dialogical notion is akin to the core commitments of *symbolic interactionism* and *coordinated management of meaning* (see Chapters 5 and 6). Recall that Mead claimed that our concept of self is formed by interaction with others. Pearce and Cronen insist that persons-in-conversation co-construct their own social realities and are simultaneously shaped by the worlds they create. If Baxter and these other theorists are right, it's confusing to talk about "communication in relationships," as if communication were just one feature of a couple's relationship. A constitutive approach suggests that it works the other way around—communication creates and sustains the relationship. If a pair's communication practices change, so does their relationship.

Perhaps nowhere is the constitutive nature of dialogue more fascinating than in the study of interpersonal similarities and differences.[12] Traditional scholarship concentrates on similarities—regarding common attitudes, backgrounds, and interests as the positive glue that helps people stick together. ("My idea of an agreeable person is a person who agrees with me.") Within this framework, self-disclosure is seen as the most valuable form of communication because, through mutual revelation, people can discover similarities that already exist.

In contrast, a dialogic view considers differences to be just as important as similarities and claims that both are created and evaluated through a couple's dialogue. For example, a relative of mine married a man who is 20 years older than she is. The difference in their age is a chronological fact. But whether she and her husband regard their diverse dates of birth as a difference that makes a difference is the result of their conversations about it. So is the extent to which they see that age gap as either positive or negative.

We can see the constitutive nature of conversation when Jess tells Joe she can't wear soccer shorts because of the ghastly looking scars on her leg. "That's a stunner!" he says in awe. "I thought I had a bad one on my knee, but yours is gorgeous. Look, don't worry about it. No one's gonna care once you're out there." They then compare scars. He asks her what happened and if it affects her game. She says it doesn't and describes trying to fix beans on toast as a little girl when her trousers caught fire. She finishes the story with the wry comment, "Sure put me off beans and toast." Five minutes later she's playing in shorts with abandon. Her dialogue with coach Joe is a constitutive process that changes the meaning of things in her world.

Dialogue as Dialectical Flux

Dialectical flux
The unpredictable, unfinalizable, indeterminate nature of personal relationships.

We've already explored Bakhtin and Baxter's conviction that all social life is the product of "a contradiction-ridden, tension-filled unity of two embattled tendencies."[13] The existence of these contrasting forces means that developing and sustaining a relationship is bound to be an unpredictable, unfinalizable, indeterminate process—more like playing improvisational jazz than following the score of a familiar symphony. Since a relationship is created through dialogue that's always in flux, Baxter thinks we shouldn't be surprised that the construction project moves "by fits and starts, in what can be an erratic process of backward-forward, up-and-down motion."[14] It's messy.

Figure 12–2 is an attempt to capture the complexity of relationships as seen through the lens of dialectical flux. Note that each of the relational forces discussed in the chapter is shown in tension with every other pole. For example, *separateness* is in opposition not only with *connectedness* but also with *certainty* and all the other relational forces. Yet even that picture is too simplistic. Each line of the diagram gives the impression of a single binary contradiction. Sticking with the connectedness-separateness dialectic, the pull toward connectedness could actually take many forms—intimacy, passion, dependence, support, a meeting of minds, or any combination of these. In opposition with separateness, each of these dialectics would be experienced differently. This chaotic jumble of contradictions is far removed from such idyllic notions of communication as a one-way route to *interpersonal closeness, shared meaning,* or *increased certainty.*

Dialogue as an Aesthetic Moment

Aesthetic moment
A fleeting sense of unity through a profound respect for disparate voices in dialogue.

Taking her lead from Bakhtin's work, Baxter describes dialogue as an *aesthetic accomplishment,* "a momentary sense of unity through a profound respect for the disparate voices in dialogue."[15] That mutual sense of completion or wholeness in the midst of fragmented experience doesn't last. It's a fleeting moment that can't be sustained. Yet memories of that magic moment can support a couple through the turbulence that goes with the territory of any close relationship.

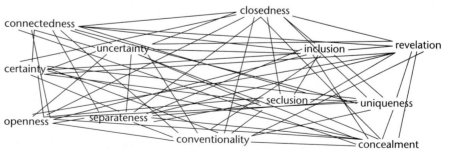

FIGURE 12–2 The Messiness of Personal Relationships

For romantic partners, turning points such as the relationship-defining talk or the first time they make love may be aesthetic moments. Baxter suggests that a meaningful ritual can be an aesthetic moment for all participants because it's "a joint performance in which competing, contradictory voices in everyday social life are brought together simultaneously."[16] For example, a marriage renewal ceremony where a couple exchanges newly crafted vows is often the occasion of an aesthetic moment for all participants.[17] So, too, the communion rail where people with diverse beliefs and practices may feel that they are one before the same God.

As for *Bend It Like Beckham*, there's a moving scene in the Bhamra home after Jess has fervently made known her dream of playing soccer in America. Hers is a desire that clearly rejects the traditional role of women in this close-knit Indian enclave—a role that her sister has enthusiastically embraced in her marriage earlier that day. As one guest whispers to another after Jess' declaration, "She's dead meat." Yet the sisters' father takes these polar-opposite visions of life and integrates them into a unified whole. He recounts a story of his own timidity and suffering when he experienced rejection, and then says:

> I don't want Jessie to suffer. I don't want her to make the same mistakes her father made of accepting life, or accepting situations. I want her to fight. I want her to win. Because I've seen her playing. She's—She's brilliant. I don't think anybody has the right stopping her. Two daughters made happy on one day. What else could a father ask for?

Dialogue as Utterance

Utterance
A portion of multivocal communication that affects and is affected by one or more other voices in the conversation.

Because Bakhtin conceived of all social life as *language in use*, he didn't use the term *utterance* to designate something said by an autonomous individual. Rather, we can picture the utterance as an expressive link that's only one of many communication links forming a dialogic chain. Therefore, a given utterance is affected by words that went before and by words that are to come.[18] This links-in-a-chain metaphor is much closer to Pearce's understanding of speech acts within his serpentine model than it is to a model of messages produced by the goal-driven cognitive plan of a single person (see Chapters 6, 8, and 10).

Baxter often cites Bakhtin's core belief that *two voices is the minimum for life, the minimum for existence,*[19] so she is particularly interested in whether an utterance gives credence to the voices of both parties in a relationship. Aesthetic moments are the prime example of dialogue reaching that multivocal standard. Other types of talk may be less elegant yet still reflect the existence of—and inherent tension between—two voices. For example, my wife, Jeanie, just called me at my office to ask when I'd be home. Mindful of Baxter's concern for multivocality, I responded, "I'm really looking forward to our time together at the Anne Lamott lecture and reception, but in order to make some progress on this chapter revision, I need to stay here until just before we go." The *but* in my answer set up the tension between the *connectedness* and *separateness* that characterize our love through 48 years of marriage.

Simultaneous expression of opposing voices is the exception rather than the rule, according to Baxter. At any given time, most relationship partners bring one voice to the foreground while pushing the other one to the background. Baxter and Montgomery have identified two typical conversational strategies for responding with relational dialectics:

Spiraling inversion
Switching back and forth between two contrasting voices, responding first to one pull, then the other.

Segmentation
A compartmentalizing tactic by which partners isolate different aspects of their relationship.

1. *Spiraling inversion* is switching back and forth between two contrasting voices, responding first to one pull, then the other. This irregular spiraling shift describes the inconsistency of Jess' communication with her family. Her lies about what she's doing are followed by incredible candor. Her open admissions precede times of silence and deception.

2. *Segmentation* is a compartmentalizing tactic by which partners isolate different aspects of their relationship. Some issues and activities resonate with one dialectical tug, while other concerns and actions resonate with the opposing pull. For example, Joe seeks to separate his roles as coach and boyfriend, a distinction that Jess tries to duplicate. His "I am your coach" statement makes a clear-cut distinction. When Jules askes Jess whether Joe is treating her too hard, her response is more mixed. "He was really nice. Just really professional."

Dialogue as a Critical Sensibility

Critical sensibility
An obligation to critique dominant voices, especially those that suppress opposing viewpoints; a responsibility to advocate for those who are muted.

The fifth sense of dialogue is an obligation to critique dominant voices, especially those that suppress opposing viewpoints. Bakhtin's analysis of a medieval carnival laid the groundwork for Baxter's understanding of this function.[20] Much like the court jester, the carnivalesque eye is characterized by "mockery of all serious, 'closed' attitudes about the world."[21]

Within the scholarly study of personal relationships, Baxter believes that a dialogue-as-carnival view offers a needed corrective to the theories of relational development presented in Chapters 9 through 11, which offer single paths to romance, friendship, or close family ties. And within relational practice, she is critical of those who regard their partners as objects of influence. This mindset often frames a relationship as one of power and domination, which then silences or ridicules any opposing point of view.[22] Consistent with Bakhtin's call for multivocality, Baxter opposes any communication practice that ignores or gags another's voice.

In this regard, the entire movie *Bend It Like Beckham* can be seen as the triumphant story of a young girl who resists traditional forces that would keep her silenced—a journey from monologue to dialogue. The director and co-writer of the film, Gurinder Chadha, admits that it's autobiographical. She notes that "Beckham's uncanny ability to 'bend' the ball around a wall of players into the goal is a great metaphor for what young girls (and film directors) go though. You see your goal, you know where you want to go, but you've got to twist and turn and bend the rules to get there."[23]

ETHICAL REFLECTION: SISSELA BOK'S PRINCIPLE OF VERACITY

Consequentialist ethics
Judging actions solely on the basis of their beneficial or harmful outcomes.

Does lying only bend the rules, or does it break and trash them as well? By looking at lies from the perspective of all who are affected by them, philosopher Sissela Bok hopes to establish when, or if, lies can be justified.

Bok rejects an absolute prohibition of lying. She believes that "there are at least some circumstances which warrant a lie . . . foremost among them, when innocent lives are at stake, and where only a lie can deflect the danger."[24] But she also rejects *consequentialist ethics*, which judge acts on the basis of whether we think they will result in harm or benefit. That approach represents a kind of bottom-line accounting that treats an act as morally neutral until we figure out if it will have positive or negative outcomes. Bok doesn't view lies as neutral. She is convinced that all lies drag around an initial negative weight that must be factored into any ethical equation. Her *principle of veracity* asserts that "truthful statements are preferable to lies in the absence of special considerations."[25]

Principle of veracity
Truthful statements are preferable to lies in the absence of special circumstances that overcome their negative weight.

Bok contends that we need the principle of veracity because liars engage in a tragic self-delusion. When they count the cost of deceit, they usually anticipate only their own short-term losses. Liars downplay the impact of their falsehood on the persons deceived and almost always ignore the long-term effects on themselves and everyone else. Bok warns, "Trust and integrity are precious resources, easily squandered, hard to regain. They can thrive only on a foundation of respect for veracity."[26] Jess isn't dead meat, but things she says to her folks in the future may be tough for them to swallow.

CRITIQUE: MEETING THE CRITERIA FOR A GOOD INTERPRETIVE THEORY

Some communication scholars question whether relational dialectics should be considered a theory at all:

> It lacks the structural intricacies of formal theories of prediction and explanation; it offers no extensive hierarchical array of axiomatic or propositional arguments. It does not represent a single unitary statement of generalizable predictions.[27]

You may be surprised that Baxter and Montgomery agree with that judgment. In fact, they are the ones who wrote those words. That's because the traditional goals of a scientific theory that they mention are not at all what these theorists are trying to do, or even think is possible when theorizing about relationships. Instead, they offer relational dialectics as a *sensitizing theory*, one that should be judged on the basis of its ability to help us see close relationships in a new light.[28] So an appropriate critique of their theory should apply the standards for evaluating an *interpretive* theory that I introduced in Chapter 3. As I briefly address these five criteria, you'll find that I think relational dialectics stacks up quite well.

1. A new understanding of people. Baxter and Montgomery offer readers a whole new way to make sense out of their close relationships. I find that many students feel a tremendous sense of relief when they read about relational dialectics. That's because the theory helps them realize that the ongoing tensions they experience with their friend, family member, or romantic partner are an inevitable part of relational life rather than a warning sign that something is terribly wrong with their partner or themselves.

2. A community of agreement. Leslie Baxter's two decades of work in relational dialectics has received high acclaim from scholars who study close personal ties. The International Association for Relationship Research designated her monograph "Relationships as Dialogues" as its 2004 Distinguished Scholar Article, an honor bestowed only once a year (see "A Second Look"). Baxter's research has changed the landscape within the field of study known as *personal relationships*.

3. Clarification of values. By encouraging a diverse group of people to talk about their relationships and taking what they say seriously, Baxter and

Montgomery model the high value that Bakhtin places on hearing multiple voices. Baxter critiques her own research as usually capturing only two distinct voices rather than multiple voices over an extended period of time.[29] As one who has tracked both partners in 45 college friendships into middle age,[30] I understand the difficulties of longitudinal relationship research and appreciate Baxter's commitment to do it.

4. Reform of society.   Not only does Baxter listen to multiple voices, but her theory seeks to carve a space where muted or ignored voices can be heard. Relational dialectics creates a *critical sensibility* that encourages dialogue rather than monologue. In this way the theory is a force for change—not only in personal relationships but in the public sphere as well.

5. Aesthetic appeal.   Figure 12–2 illustrates the difficulty of crafting an artistic representation when the objects of study—in this case, relationships—are inherently messy. Baxter's task becomes even more difficult, given her commitment to unraveling Bakhtin's multistranded conception of dialogue. Since the Russian philosopher wrote in his native language, it's difficult to translate his nuanced ideas into English in an elegant way. Accuracy has to come before artistry. Yet in describing *fleeting moments of wholeness*, Baxter holds out the promise of an aesthetic ideal to which all of us can aspire—an image that could make slogging through the morass of relational contradictions seem less frustrating. And Montgomery's imagery suggests that dealing with dialectics can actually be fun:

> I have been told that riding a unicycle becomes enjoyable when you accept that you are constantly in the process of falling. The task then becomes one of continually playing one force against another, countering one pull with an opposing motion and adapting the wheel under you so that you remain in movement by maintaining and controlling the fall. If successful, one is propelled along in a state of sustained imbalance that is sometimes awkward and sometimes elegant. From a dialectical perspective, sustaining a relationship seems to be a very similar process.[31]

QUESTIONS TO SHARPEN YOUR FOCUS

1.   How many different synonyms and equivalent phrases can you list that come close to capturing what Baxter and Montgomery mean by the word *dialectic?* What do these words have in common?

2.   Which of the eight theories discussed in previous chapters would Baxter and Montgomery consider simplistic or antidialectical?

3.   What *conflicting pulls* place the most strain on your closest personal relationship? To what extent do you and your partner use *spiraling inversion, segmentation,* and *dialogue* to deal with that *tension?*

4.   Why wouldn't typical scale items like the following reveal dialectical tension in a close relationship, even if it exists?

What characterizes your relationship?

Intimacy   :____:____:____:____:____:____:____: Independence

SELF-QUIZ    *www.mhhe.com/griffin7*

CONVERSATIONS

View this segment online at
www.mhhe.com/griffin7 or
www.afirstlook.com.

At the start of our conversation, Leslie Baxter states that all communication involves the interplay of differences, which are often competing or in opposition to each other. She explains why this dialectic tension isn't a problem to be solved, but an occasion for a relationship to change and grow. Baxter cautions that we've been seduced into thinking that relating is easy, when in fact it's hard work. Most of our discussion centers on ways to cope with the interplay of differences that we experience. She urges partners to reflect carefully on rituals that celebrate both their unity and diversity, and offers other practical suggestions as well.

A SECOND LOOK

Recommended resource: Leslie A. Baxter and Barbara M. Montgomery, *Relating: Dialogues and Dialectics*, Guilford, New York, 1996.

Second generation of theory: Leslie A. Baxter, "Relationships as Dialogues," *Personal Relationships*, Vol. 11, 2004, pp. 1–22.

Recent summary: Leslie A. Baxter and Dawn O. Braithwaite, "Social Dialectics: The Contradictions of Relating," in *Explaining Communication: Contemporary Communication Theories and Exemplars*, Bryan Whaley and Wendy Samter (eds.), Lawrence Erlbaum, Mahwah, NJ, 2007, pp. 275–292.

Personal narrative of the theory's development: Leslie A. Baxter, "A Tale of Two Voices," *Journal of Family Communication*, Vol. 4, 2004, pp. 181–192.

Relational dialectics vis-à-vis other relational approaches: Leslie A. Baxter and Barbara M. Montgomery, "Rethinking Communication in Personal Relationships from a Dialectical Perspective," in *A Handbook of Personal Relationships*, 2nd ed., Steve Duck (ed.), John Wiley & Sons, New York, 1997, pp. 325–349.

Bakhtin—primary sources: Mikhail Bakhtin, *The Dialogic Imagination*, Michael Holquist (ed.), Caryl Emerson and Holquist (trans.), University of Texas, Austin, 1981; Mikhail Bakhtin, *Art and Answerability: Early Philosophical Essays*, Michael Holquist and Vadim Liapunov (eds.), Vadim Liapunov and K. Brostrom (trans.), University of Texas, Austin, 1990.

Friendship dialectics: William Rawlins, *Friendship Matters: Communication, Dialectics, and the Life Course*, Aldine de Gruyter, New York, 1992.

Family dialectics: Arthur Bochner and E. Eisenberg, "Family Process: System Perspectives," in *Handbook of Communication Science*, Charles R. Berger and Stephen Chaffee (eds.), Sage, Beverly Hills, CA, 1987, pp. 540–563.

Comparing, contrasting, and critiquing different dialectical approaches: Barbara M. Montgomery and Leslie A. Baxter (eds.), *Dialectical Approaches to Studying Personal Relationships*, Lawrence Erlbaum, Mahwah, NJ, 1998.

Dialogue: Leslie A. Baxter, "Dialogues of Relating," in *Dialogues: Theorizing Difference in Communication Studies,* Rob Anderson, Leslie A. Baxter, and Kenneth Cissna (eds.), Sage, Thousand Oaks, CA, 2004, pp. 107–124.

Critique: Leslie A. Baxter, "Relational Dialectics Theory: Multivocal Dialogues of Family Communication," in *Engaging Theories in Family Communication: Multiple Perspectives,* Dawn O. Braithwaite and Leslie A. Baxter (eds.), Sage, Thousand Oaks, CA, 2006, pp. 130–145.

To contact Em Griffin, click on Meet and Email Em at
www.afirstlook.com.

The Interactional View
of Paul Watzlawick

The Franklin family is in trouble. A perceptive observer could spot their difficulties despite their successful facade. Sonia Franklin is an accomplished pianist who teaches advanced theory and technique to students in her own home. Her husband, Stan, will soon become a partner in a Big Four accounting firm. Their daughter, Laurie, is an honor student, an officer in her high school class, and the number two player on the tennis team. But Laurie's younger brother, Mike, has dropped all pretense of interest in studies, sports, or social life. His only passion is drinking beer and smoking pot.

Each of the Franklins reacts to Mike's substance abuse in different but less than helpful ways. Stan denies that his son has a problem. Boys will be boys, and he's sure Mike will grow out of this phase. The only time he and Mike actually talked about the problem, Stan said, "I want you to cut back on your drinking—not for me and your mother—but for your own sake."

Laurie has always felt responsible for her kid brother and is scared because Mike is getting "wasted" every few days. She makes him promise that he'll quit using and continues to introduce him to her straightlaced friends in the hope that he'll get in with a good crowd.

Sonia worries that alcohol and drugs will ruin her son's future. One weekday morning when he woke up with a hangover, she wrote a note to the school saying Mike had the flu. She also called a lawyer to help Mike when he was stopped for drunk driving. Although she promised never to tell his father about these incidents, she chides Stan for his lack of concern. The more she nags, the more he withdraws.

Mike feels caught in a vicious circle. Smoking pot helps him relax, but then his family gets more upset, which makes him want to smoke more, which. . . . During a tense dinner-table discussion he lashes out: "You want to know why I use? Go look in a mirror." Although the rest of the family sees Mike as "the problem," psychotherapist Paul Watzlawick would have described the whole family system as disturbed. He formed his theory of social interaction by looking at dysfunctional patterns within families in order to gain insight into healthy communication.

THE FAMILY AS A SYSTEM

Family system

A self-regulating, interdependent network of feedback loops guided by members' rules; the behavior of each person affects and is affected by the behavior of another.

Picture a family as a mobile suspended from the ceiling. Each figure is connected to the rest of the structure by a strong thread tied at exactly the right place to keep the system in balance. Tug on any string, and the force sends a shock wave throughout the whole network. Sever a thread, and the entire system tilts in disequilibrium.

The threads in the mobile analogy represent communication rules that hold the family together. Paul Watzlawick believed that in order to understand the movement of any single figure in the *family system,* one has to examine the communication patterns among all its members. He regarded the communication that the family members have among themselves about their relationships as especially important.

Watzlawick (pronounced VAHT-sla-vick) was a senior research fellow at the Mental Research Institute, Palo Alto, California, and clinical professor of psychiatry at Stanford University. He was one of about 20 scholars and therapists who were inspired by and worked with anthropologist Gregory Bateson. The common denominator that continues to draw the Palo Alto Group together is a commitment to study interpersonal interaction as part of an entire system. They reject the idea that individual motives and personality traits determine the nature of communication within a family. In fact, the Palo Alto researchers care little about *why* a person acts in a certain way, but they have a great interest in *how* that behavior affects everyone in the group.

A systems approach to family relationships defies simplistic explanations of why people act as they do. For example, some pop psychology books on body language claim that a listener standing in a hands-on-hips position is skeptical about what the speaker is saying. Watzlawick was certainly interested in the reaction others have to this posture, but he didn't think that a particular way of standing should be viewed as part of a cause-and-effect chain of events:

$$a \rightarrow b \rightarrow c \rightarrow d$$

Relationships are not simple, nor are they "things," as suggested by the statement "We have a good relationship." Relationships are complex functions in the same sense that mathematical functions link multiple variables:

$$x = b^2 + \frac{2c}{a} - 5d$$

Just as x will be affected by the value of a, b, c, or d, so the hands-on-hips stance can be due to a variety of attitudes, emotions, or physical conditions. Maybe the stance does show skepticism. But it also might reflect boredom, a feeling of awkwardness, aching shoulder muscles, or self-consciousness about middle-aged "hip-handles."

Watzlawick used the math metaphor throughout the book *Pragmatics of Human Communication.* Along with co-authors Janet Beavin and Don Jackson, he presented key axioms that describe the "tentative calculus of human communication." These axioms make up the *grammar of conversation,* or, to use another analogy that runs through the book, *the rules of the game.*

There is nothing particularly playful about the game the Franklins are playing. Psychologist Alan Watts says that "life is a game where rule No. 1 is: This

Games
Sequences of behavior governed by rules.

is no game, this is serious."[1] Watzlawick defined *games* as *sequences of behavior governed by rules*. Even though Sonia and Stan are involved in an unhealthy *game without end* of nag-withdrawal-nag-withdrawal, they continue to play because it serves a function for both of them. (Sonia feels superior; Stan avoids hassles with his son.) Neither party may recognize what's going on, but their rules are a something-for-something bargain. Mike's drinking and his family's distress may fit into the same category. (Getting drunk not only relieves tension temporarily, it's also a great excuse for sidestepping the pressure to excel, which is the name of the game in the Franklin family.)

Lest we be tempted to see the Franklins' relationships as typical of all families dealing with addiction, Watzlawick warned that each family plays a one-of-a-kind game with homemade rules. Just as CMM claims that persons-in-conversation co-construct their own social worlds (see Chapter 6), the Palo Alto Group insists that each family system creates its own reality. That conviction shapes its approach to family therapy:

> In the systemic approach, we try to understand as quickly as possible the functioning of this system: What kind of reality has this particular system constructed for itself? Incidentally, this rules out categorizations because one of the basic principles of systems theory is that "every system is its own best explanation."[2]

AXIOMS OF INTERPERSONAL COMMUNICATIONS

Family homeostasis
The tacit collusion of family members to maintain the status quo.

The network of communication rules that governs the Franklins' interaction makes it extremely difficult for any of them to change their behavior. Watzlawick, Beavin, and Jackson used the label *family homeostasis* to describe what many family counselors agree is the tacit collusion of family members to maintain the status quo. Interactional theorists believe that we'll fail to recognize this destructive resistance to change unless we understand the following axioms, or rules, of communication.[3]

One Cannot Not Communicate

You've undoubtedly been caught in situations where you feel obliged to talk but would rather avoid the commitment to respond that's inherent in all communication—like in high school when you come home from a date or a party, and your mother meets you inside the door and says, "Tell me all about it." Or perhaps currently you need to study but your roommate wants to chat.

In an attempt to avoid communication, you could bluntly state that your test the following morning makes studying more important than socializing. But voicing your desire for privacy can stretch the rules of good behavior and often results in an awkward silence that speaks loudly about the relationship.

Symptom strategy
Ascribing our silence to something beyond our control that renders communication justifiably impossible—sleepiness, headache, drunkenness, etc.

You could flood your mother with a torrent of meaningless words about the evening, merely say it was "fine" as you duck into your room, or plead tiredness, a headache, or a sore throat. Watzlawick called this the *symptom strategy* and said it suggests, "I wouldn't mind talking to you, but something stronger than *I*, for which I cannot be blamed, prevents me." Whatever you do, however, it would be naïve not to realize that your mother will analyze your behavior for clues about the evening's activities. His face an immobile mask, Mike Franklin may mutely encounter his parents. But he communicates in spite of himself by his facial expression and his silence. Those nonverbal messages will obviously have an impact on the rest of his family. A corollary to the first axiom is that "one cannot *not* influence."[4]

Communication = Content + Relationship

Content
The report part of a message; *what* is said verbally.

Relationship
The command part of the message; *how* it's said nonverbally.

The heading is a shorthand version of the formal axiom "Every communication has a content and relationship aspect such that the latter classifies the former and is therefore metacommunication."[5] Watzlawick chose to rename the two aspects of communication that Gregory Bateson had originally called *report* and *command*. Report, or *content*, is *what* is said. Command, or *relationship*, is *how* it's said. Edna Rogers, University of Utah communication professor and early interpreter of the interactional view, illustrates the difference with a two-word message:

> The content level provides information based on what the message is about, while the relational level "gives off" information on how the message is to be interpreted. For example, the content of the comment "You're late" refers to time, but at the relational level the comment typically implies a form of criticism of the other's lack of responsibility or concern.[6]

Figure 13–1 outlines the content-relationship distinction that is crucial to the interactional model. Yet neither the equation in the heading above nor the terms in the figure quite capture the way relationship surrounds content and provides a context, or atmosphere, for interpretation. It's the difference between data fed into a computer and the program that directs how the data should be processed. In written communication, punctuation gives direction as to how the words should be understood. Shifting a question mark to an exclamation point alters the meaning of the message. Right? Right! In spoken communication, however, tone of voice, emphasis on certain words, facial cues, and so forth direct how the message was meant to be interpreted.

Metacommunication
Communication about communication.

Watzlawick referred to the relational aspect of interaction as *metacommunication*. It is communication about communication. Metacommunication says, "This is how I see myself, this is how I see you, this is how I see you seeing me. . . ." According to Watzlawick, relationship messages are always the most important element in any communication—healthy or otherwise. But when a family is in trouble, metacommunication dominates the discussion. Mike

Content	Relationship
Report	Command
What is said	How it is said
Computer data	Computer program
Words	Punctuation
Verbal channel	Nonverbal channel
Communication	Metacommunication

FIGURE 13–1   The Content and Relationship Levels of Communication

Franklin's dinner-table outburst is an example of pathological metacommunication that shakes the entire family system. The Palo Alto Group is convinced it would be a mistake for the Franklins to ignore Mike's attack in the hope that the tension will go away. Sick family relationships get better only when family members are willing to talk with each other about their patterns of communication.

The Nature of a Relationship Depends on How Both Parties Punctuate the Communication Sequence

Consider the relational tangle described in one of the *Knots* composed by British psychotherapist R. D. Laing to describe disturbed relationships.

> He can't be happy
>> when there's so much suffering in the world
> She can't be happy
>> if he is unhappy
>> She wants to be happy
> He does not feel entitled to be happy
> She wants him to be happy
>> and he wants her to be happy
> He feels guilty if he is happy
>> and guilty if she is not happy
> She wants both to be happy
> He wants her to be happy
> So they are both unhappy[7]

The poem describes a couple tied up in knots, and their communication about unhappiness and guilt is the cord that binds them. An outsider who overheard the conversation in the following diagram would spot a reciprocal pattern of guilt and depression that has no beginning or end. But the woman enmeshed in the system *punctuates* or cleaves the sequence with point *p*, *r*, or *t* as the starting point. She's convinced that the man's guilt is the cause of her unhappiness.

Equally ensnared in the system, the man punctuates the sequence by designating the woman's need for happiness at point *q* or *s* as the initial event. He's quite sure that her depression is the reason he feels guilty. Asking either of them *Who started it?* wouldn't help because the question merely feeds into their fruitless struggle for control.

Punctuate
Interpreting an ongoing sequence of events by labeling one event as the cause and the following event as the response.

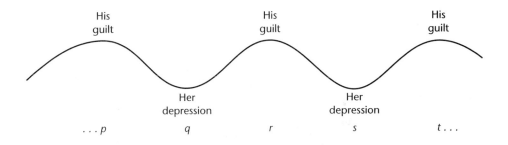

Watzlawick suggested that "what is typical about the sequence and makes it a problem of punctuation is that the individual concerned conceives of him or herself only as reacting to, but not as provoking, these attitudes."[8] This is true for both adult Franklins. Stan sees himself as withdrawing from Sonia only because of her constant nagging. Sonia feels certain that she wouldn't harp on the issue if Stan would face the problem of Mike's drinking.

All Communication Is Either Symmetrical or Complementary

This axiom continues to focus on metacommunication. While definitions of relationship include the issues of belongingness, affection, trust, and intimacy, the interactional view pays particular attention to questions of control, status, and power. Remember that Bateson's original label for relationship communication was *command*. According to Watzlawick, *symmetrical* interchange is based on equal power; *complementary* communication is based on differences in power. He makes no attempt to label one type as good and the other as bad. Healthy relationships have both kinds of communication.

Symmetrical interchange
Interaction based on equal power.

In terms of ability, the women in the Franklin family have a *symmetrical* relationship; neither one tries to control the other. Sonia has expertise on the piano; Laurie excels on the tennis court. Each of them performs without the other claiming dominance. Fortunately, their skills are in separate arenas. Too much similarity can set the stage for an anything-you-can-do-I-can-do-better competition.

Complementary interchange
Interaction based on accepted differences of power.

Sonia's relationship with Mike is *complementary*. Her type of mothering is strong on control. She hides the extent of Mike's drinking from his father, lies to school officials, and hires a lawyer on the sly to bail her son out of trouble with the police. By continuing to treat Mike as a child, she maintains their dominant–submissive relationship. Although complementary relationships aren't always destructive, the status difference between Mike and the rest of the Franklins is stressing the family system.

The interactional view holds that there is no way to label a relationship on the basis of a single verbal statement. Judgments that an interaction is either symmetrical or complementary require a sequence of at least two messages—a statement from one person and a response from the other. While at Michigan State University, communication researchers Edna Rogers and Richard Farace devised a coding scheme to categorize ongoing marital interaction on the crucial issue of who controls the relationship.

One-up communication
A conversational move to gain control of the exchange; attempted domination.

One-down communication
A conversational move to yield control of the exchange; attempted submission.

One-across communication
A conversational move to neutralize or level control within the exchange; when just one party uses it, the interchange is called *transitory*.

One-up communication (↑) is movement to *gain* control of the exchange. A bid for dominance includes messages that instruct, order, interrupt, contradict, change topics, or fail to support what the other person said. *One-down communication* (↓) is movement to *yield* control of the exchange. The bid for submission is evidenced by agreement with what the other person said. Despite Watzlawick's contention that all discourse is either symmetrical or complementary, Rogers and Farace code *one-across communication* (→) as well. They define it as *transitory* communication that moves toward *neutralizing* control.

Figure 13–2 presents the matrix of possible relational transactions. The pairs that are circled show a symmetrical interaction. The pairs in triangles indicate complementary relations. The pairs in squares reveal transitory communication. As Rogers' later research showed, bids for dominance (↑) don't necessarily result in successful control of the interaction (↑↓).[9]

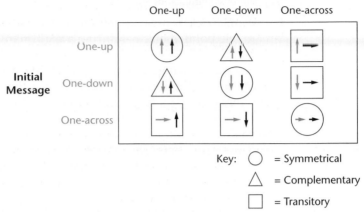

FIGURE 13–2   Matrix of Transactional Types

Adapted from Rogers and Farace, "Analysis of Relational Communication in Dyads: New Measurement Procedures"

TRAPPED IN A SYSTEM WITH NO PLACE TO GO

Enabler

Within addiction culture, a person whose nonassertive behavior allows others to continue in their substance abuse.

Family systems are highly resistant to change. This inertia is especially apparent in a home where someone has an addiction. Each family member occupies a role that serves the status quo. In the Franklin family, Mike, of course, is the one with "the problem." With the best of intentions, Sonia is the *enabler* who cushions Mike from feeling the pain caused by his chemical abuse. Stan is the "deny-er," while Laurie is the family "hero" who compensates for her brother's failure. Family therapists note that when one person in a distressed family gets better, another member often gets worse. If Mike stopped drinking and using pot, Laurie might quit the tennis team, ignore her studies, or start smoking marijuana herself. Dysfunctional families confirm the adage "the more things change, the more they stay the same."

Double bind

A person trapped under mutually exclusive expectations; specifically, the powerful party in a complementary relationship insists that the low-power party act as if it were symmetrical.

Watzlawick saw family members as often caught in the *double bind* of mutually exclusive expectations, which Bateson originally described. Parental messages such as "You ought to love me" or "Be spontaneous!" place children in an untenable position. The children are bound to violate some aspect of the injunction no matter how they respond. (Love can only be freely given; spontaneity on demand is impossible.) The paradox of the double bind is that the high-status party in a complementary relationship insists that the low-status person act as if the relationship were symmetrical—which it isn't. Stan's *demand* that his son stay sober for his *own sake* places Mike in a no-win situation. He can't obey his dad and be autonomous at the same time.

REFRAMING: CHANGING THE GAME BY CHANGING THE RULES

Reframing

The process of instituting change by stepping outside of a situation and reinterpreting what it means.

How can the members of the Franklin family break out of their never-ending game and experience real change in the way they relate to each other? According to Watzlawick, effective change for the whole family will come about only when members are helped to step outside the system and see the self-defeating nature of the rules under which they're playing. He calls this process *reframing*.

To reframe . . . means to change the conceptual and/or emotional setting or viewpoint in relation to which a situation is experienced and to place it in another frame which fits the "facts" of the same concrete situation equally well or even better, and thereby changes its entire meaning.[10]

Watzlawick compared reframing to the process of waking up from a bad dream. He pointed out that during a nightmare you may run, hide, fight, scream, jump off a cliff, or try dozens of other things to make the situation better, but nothing really changes. Relief comes only when you step outside the system by waking up. Without the intervention of a timely alarm clock or a caring roommate, relief can be a long time coming.

Reframing is the sudden "aha" of looking at things in a new light. Suppose you could talk with Watzlawick about your struggles to keep up with the assignments for your comm theory class. You've chosen to be a communication major, so you believe you ought to *like* studying the material. Since you don't, you think there's something wrong with you. You also know that your family is making a financial sacrifice for you to be in college, so you feel guilty that you aren't getting good grades or experiencing deep gratitude for their help. In fact, you resent having to be grateful.

If you described these dilemmas to Watzlawick, he would want you to reframe your attitudes as *unrealistic* and *immature*—nightmarish interpretations for most college students. Even under the best of circumstances, he'd explain, studying is an unpleasant necessity and to believe that it should be fun is ridiculous. As far as your folks are concerned, they have a right to your gratitude, but this doesn't mean you have to *enjoy* being thankful. So it's up to you. You can "continue in these immature outlooks or have the adult courage to reject them and to begin to look at life as a mixture of pleasant and unpleasant things."[11] The *facts* haven't changed, but he's given you a new way to *interpret* them. If you accept Watzlawick's frame, you'll probably cope better and feel less pain.

"Instead of 'It sucks' you could say, 'It doesn't speak to me.'"

For the Franklins, reframing means they must radically change their perspective. One way to do this is by adopting the view of Alcoholics Anonymous (AA) that Mike's addiction is a disease over which he has no control. His drinking is not a sign of moral weakness or an intentional rebuff of his family's values—he drinks because he's an alcoholic. The AA interpretation would imply that the Franklins need to abandon their fruitless search for someone to blame. Despite Mike's look-in-the-mirror accusation, the members of his family aren't responsible for his addiction. They didn't cause it, they can't cure it, and they can't control it. It's a disease. Does that mean Mike's not responsible for being chemically dependent? Right . . . but he *is* responsible for putting all of his energy into getting well.

Accepting a new frame implies rejecting the old one. The Franklins must admit that their so-called solutions are as much a problem as their son's drinking. Mike will never seek treatment for his illness as long as his family continues to shield him from the consequences of his behavior. Reframing will help Sonia see that writing excuses and hiring lawyers may be less caring than letting her son get kicked out of school or allowing his driver's license to be suspended.

Adopting a tough-love perspective or any new interpretive frame is usually accomplished only with outside help. For Watzlawick, that meant therapy. As a social constructionist, he wouldn't try to discover the "real" reason Mike drinks or worry if it's "true" that some people are genetically predisposed to addiction. In his view, the purpose of therapy is the lessening of pain. He would regard the disease model of addiction as an alternative construction—a fiction, perhaps, but for the Franklin family a useful and less painful one.[12]

Addiction model
Assumes alcoholism and other addictions are diseases to be cured rather than character disorders to be condemned.

Conversely, self-help groups called Families Anonymous (FA) are intensely committed to the *addiction model* as *the* way to realign the family network. Just as AA gives support to the recovering alcoholic, FA offers support for those who face chemical dependency within their own families. At each meeting, participants read aloud a brief selection entitled "Helping," in which they pledge to avoid manipulation, control, overprotectiveness, or any other effort to make the addicted family member fit a standard or an image. The reading closes with radical words for worried parents: "I can change myself. Others I can only love."[13] That's changing the game by changing the rules.

CRITIQUE: ADJUSTMENTS NEEDED WITHIN THE SYSTEM

Janet Beavin Bavelas co-authored *Pragmatics of Human Communication* with Watzlawick in 1967. Twenty-five years later, she reviewed the status of the axioms that are the central focus of the interactional view.[14] Based on the research program she conducted at the University of Victoria in Canada, Bavelas recommends modifying some axioms of the theory. Her proposal serves as an informed critique of the original theory.

The first axiom claims that we *cannot not communicate*. Perhaps because of the catchy way it's stated, this axiom has been both challenged and defended more than the others. Although Bavelas is fascinated by the way people avoid eye contact or physically position themselves to communicate that they don't want to communicate, she now concedes that not all nonverbal behavior is communication. Observers may draw inferences from what they see, but in the absence of a sender-receiver relationship and the intentional use of a shared code, Bavelas would describe nonverbal behavior as *informative* rather than *communicative*.

As Figure 13–1 shows, the Palo Alto Group treated the verbal and nonverbal channels as providing different kinds of information. Bavelas now thinks that the notion of functionally separate channels dedicated to different uses is wrong. She suggests a *whole-message model* that treats verbal and nonverbal acts as completely integrated and often interchangeable. In effect, she has erased the broken vertical line that divides Figure 13–1 down the middle—a major shift in thinking.

Whole-message model
Regards verbal and nonverbal components of a message as completely integrated and often interchangeable.

The content/relationship distinction of another axiom is still viable for Bavelas. As did Watzlawick, she continues to believe that the content of communication is always embedded in the relationship environment. Looking back, however, she thinks they confused readers by sometimes equating the term *metacommunication* with all communication about a relationship. She now wants to reserve the word for explicit communication about *the process of communicating.* Examples of metacommunication narrowly defined would be Laurie Franklin telling her brother, "Don't talk to me like a kid," and Mike's response, "What do you mean by that?" Laurie's raised eyebrow and Mike's angry tone of voice would also be part of their tightly integrated packages of meaning.

Equifinality
A systems-theory assumption that a given outcome could have occurred due to any or many interconnected factors rather than being a result in a cause-effect relationship.

Systems theories involving people are difficult to evaluate because of their *equifinality*—a characteristic that means a given behavioral outcome could be caused by any or many factors that are interconnected. Due to this feature, it's hard to know when the system is out of whack. However, I find Bavelas' disenchantment with a theoretical system that she helped create disquieting and a reason to question its validity.

Despite these doubts, I'm impressed with the impact that Watzlawick and his associates have had on the field of interpersonal communication. The publication of *Pragmatics of Human Communication* marked the beginning of widespread study of the way communication patterns sustain or destroy relationships. The interactional view has also encouraged communication scholars to go beyond narrow cause-and-effect assumptions. The entanglements Watzlawick described reflect the complexities of real-life relationships that most of us know. In that way, the interactional view is similar to the dialectical perspective featured in the previous chapter.

QUESTIONS TO SHARPEN YOUR FOCUS

1. *Systems theorists* compare the family system to a mobile. What part of the mobile represents *metacommunication?* If you were constructing a mobile to model your family, how would you depict *symmetrical* and *complementary* relationships?

2. For decades, the United States and the former Soviet Union were engaged in a nuclear arms race. How does Watzlawick's axiom about the *punctuation of communication sequences* explain the belligerence of both nations?

3. Can you make up something your instructor might say that would place you in a *double bind?* Under what conditions would this be merely laughable rather than frustrating?

4. Read one of the letters printed in the "Ask Amy" or "Dear Abby" column of your daily newspaper. How could you *reframe* the situation the writer describes?

A SECOND LOOK

Recommended resource: Paul Watzlawick, Janet Beavin, and Don Jackson, *Pragmatics of Human Communication,* W. W. Norton, New York, 1967.

Seminal ideas of the Palo Alto Group: Gregory Bateson, "Information and Codification," in *Communication,* Jurgen Ruesch and Gregory Bateson (eds.), W. W. Norton, New York, 1951, pp. 168–211.

System theory: B. Aubrey Fisher, "The Pragmatic Perspective of Human Communication: A View from System Theory," in *Human Communication Theory,* Frank E. X. Dance (ed.), Harper & Row, New York, 1982, pp. 192–219.

Relational control: Edna Rogers and Richard Farace, "Analysis of Relational Communication in Dyads: New Measurement Procedures," *Human Communication Research,* Vol. 1, 1975, pp. 222–239.

Relational control in families: L. Edna Rogers, "Relational Communication Theory: An Interactional Family Theory," in *Engaging Theories in Family Communication: Multiple Perspectives,* Dawn O. Braithwaite and Leslie A. Baxter (eds.), Sage, Thousand Oaks, CA, 2006, pp. 115–129.

Reframing: Paul Watzlawick, John H. Weakland, and Richard Fisch, *Change,* W. W. Norton, New York, 1974, pp. 92–160.

Pathological punctuation: R. D. Laing, *Knots,* Pantheon Books, New York, 1970.

Whether one cannot not communicate: Theodore Clevenger, Jr., "Can One Not Communicate? A Conflict of Models," *Communication Studies,* Vol. 42, 1991, pp. 340–353.

Social construction approach to therapy: Paul Watzlawick and Michael Hoyt, "Constructing Therapeutic Realities: A Conversation with Paul Watzlawick," in *Handbook of Constructive Therapies,* Michael Hoyt (ed.), Jossey-Bass, San Francisco, 1997, pp. 183–196.

Theory adjustments: Janet Beavin Bavelas, "Research into the Pragmatics of Human Communication," *Journal of Strategic and Systemic Therapies,* Vol. 11, No. 2, 1992, pp. 15–29.

Current face of the theory: L. Edna Rogers and Valentin Escudero (eds.), *Relational Communication: An Interactional Perspective to Study Process and Form,* Lawrence Erlbaum, Mahwah, NJ, 2004.

Critique: Carol Wilder, "The Palo Alto Group: Difficulties and Directions of the Interactional View for Human Communication Research," *Human Communication Research,* Vol. 5, 1979, pp. 171–186.

To access a chapter on Carl Rogers' existential theory, an alternative view of healthy relational communication that appeared in a previous edition, click on Theory Archive at *www.afirstlook.com.*

Some influence researchers focus solely on the verbal strategies people use to elicit behavioral compliance to their wishes. A study of *compliance-gaining strategies* usually asks people to imagine being in an uncomfortable social situation.[1] For example, the guy next door is hosting a wild midnight party while you're trying to sleep; your roommate's obnoxious guest has already stayed a week; or you need to borrow a car from someone you barely know. The researcher then questions you about the tactics you'd use to get the other person to do what you want.

Typically, you would rank-order a predetermined list of compliance-gaining strategies—*promises, threats, explanations, hints, compliments, warnings, accusations, direct requests,* and so forth. Advocates of compliance-gaining inquiry stress the importance of finding out what verbal strategies people actually use. Although the studies provide rich descriptive data, they aren't theory-based and have yet to generate insights with which to build new theory. There has been little explanation of why people select the tactics they do, prediction of what they will do next time, evaluation of how well the tactics work, or concern with application to other situations.

In contrast to the practice of cataloging compliance-gaining strategies, the three theories presented in this section are concerned with *attitude change*. All three come out of a socio-psychological tradition that attempts to discern how persuasive messages are processed in the minds of listeners. In that regard, they are similar to Delia's *constructivism* (see Chapter 8). To the extent that these theories capture the way people mentally react to influence attempts, each one offers practical advice on how to craft messages that will alter attitudes.

"You pay your late fines or Babar breaks your pinkie."

Attitudes are internal responses made up of what people think, feel, and intend to do. Since researchers have no way to directly observe another person's attitude, they must rely on self-reports elicited by multiple questions:

Cognitive: "What do you honestly believe?"

Affective: "Is your heart really in it?"

Behavioral: "What do you plan to do?"

For many years, social scientists seemed content to let a single point on a unidimensional seven-point scale represent a person's inner attitude. The scale below is a typical example. In Chapter 14, however, I present Muzafer Sherif's *social judgment theory*, which regards an attitude as a range of beliefs. The theory also goes beyond a simple pro-con evaluation and considers a second dimension of attitude—how important the issue is to the respondent. Sherif suggests that the amount of discrepancy between the position advocated and the stance of the listener is what makes or breaks a persuasive attempt.

Whereas social judgment theory pictures a single mental process, Richard Petty and John Cacioppo see two alternative paths to attitude change in the mind of a person who reads or hears a persuasive message. One route involves active consideration of the arguments within a message. The other route uses the credibility of the message source as well as other peripheral cues to trigger an automatic response. Chapter 15 presents these theorists' *elaboration likelihood model,* which lays out the conditions that must exist in order for listeners or readers to carefully examine the merits of a case.

Although an attitude is often regarded as a *predisposition to respond* in a certain way, the marginal relationship between people's stated opinions and their subsequent actions has proved a continual embarrassment for scholars who claim that attitudes predict behavior. In his theory of *cognitive dissonance*, Leon Festinger suggests that the influence works the other way—actions shape attitudes. Specifically, the theory makes the surprising prediction that people will change their private beliefs to match their public behaviors, but only when they have relatively little incentive to act that way. Chapter 16 fleshes out this prediction, which is based on the human drive for consistency.

The U.S. invasion of Iraq was justified.

1	2	3	4	5	6	7
Strongly Disagree	Disagree	Slightly Disagree	No Opinion	Slightly Agree	Agree	Strongly Agree

Social Judgment Theory
of Muzafer Sherif

My son Jim is an airline pilot—a job that has changed dramatically since the terrorist acts of September 11, 2001. When he walks through the airport he overhears a variety of comments about the safety of air travel. I've listed 11 statements that reflect the range of attitudes he's heard expressed. Read through these opinions and taste the diversity of viewpoints they represent.

a.   Airlines aren't willing to spend money on tight security.

b.   All life is risk. Flying is like anything else.

c.   Anyone willing to die for a cause can hijack an airplane.

d.   Air marshals with guns can deter terrorists.

e.   There are old pilots and bold pilots; there are no old, bold pilots.

f.   Pilots drink before they fly to quell their fears of skyjacking.

g.   Getting there by plane is safer than taking the train or bus.

h.   American pilots are trained to handle any in-flight emergency.

i.   It's easy to get into the cockpit of a jet airplane.

j.   Passenger screening is better since checkers were federalized.

k.   The odds of a plane crash are 1 in 10 million.

Take a few minutes to mark your reactions to these statements. If you follow each instruction before jumping ahead to the next one, you'll have a chance to experience what social judgment theory predicts.

1. To begin, read through the items again and underline the single statement that most closely represents your point of view.

2. Now look and see whether any other items seem reasonable. Circle the letters in front of those acceptable statements.

3. Reread the remaining statements and cross out the letters in front of any that are objectionable to you. If you cross out these unreasonable ideas, it's possible that all 11 statements will end up marked one way or another. It's also possible that you'll leave some items unmarked.

THREE LATITUDES: ACCEPTANCE, REJECTION, AND NONCOMMITMENT

Social judgment-involvement

Perception and evaluation of an idea by comparing it with current attitudes.

I've just taken you through on paper what social judgment theory says happens in our heads. We hear a message and immediately judge where it should be placed on the attitude scale in our minds. According to Muzafer Sherif, this subconscious sorting out of ideas occurs at the instant of perception. We weigh every new idea by comparing it with our present point of view. He called his analysis of attitudes the *social judgment-involvement approach*, but most scholars refer to it simply as *social judgment theory.*

Reference groups

Groups that members use to define their identity.

A psychologist who was associated with the University of Oklahoma, Sherif had already published two landmark studies demonstrating how individuals are influenced by reference groups—groups that members use to define their identity. His *autokinetic effect* research stimulated scores of later studies analyzing conformity pressure.[1] His *robber's cave* study explored ways to reduce intergroup conflict.[2] Both studies found that people's perceptions are altered dramatically by group membership. Social judgment theory extended his concern with perception to the field of persuasion.

Sherif believed that the three responses you made on the previous page are necessary to determine your attitude toward airline safety, or any other attitude structure. In all probability you circled a range of statements that seemed reasonable to you and crossed out a number of opinions you couldn't accept. That's why Sherif would see your attitude as a *latitude* rather than as any single statement you underlined. He wrote that an "individual's stand is not represented adequately as a point along a continuum. Different persons espousing the same position may differ considerably in their tolerance around this point."[3]

Latitude of acceptance

The range of ideas that a person sees as reasonable or worthy of consideration.

He saw an attitude as an amalgam of three zones. The first zone is called the *latitude of acceptance.* It's made up of the item you underlined and any others you circled as acceptable. A second zone is the *latitude of rejection.* It consists of the opinions you crossed out as objectionable. The leftover statements, if any, define the *latitude of noncommitment.* These were the items that you found neither objectionable nor acceptable. They're akin to marking *undecided* or *no opinion* on a traditional attitude survey. Sherif said we need to know the location and width of each of these interrelated latitudes in order to describe a person's attitude structure.

Latitude of rejection

The range of ideas that a person sees as unreasonable or objectionable.

Latitude of noncommitment

The range of ideas that a person sees as neither acceptable nor objectionable.

Suppose Jim encounters a man in the airport named Ned, who is complaining about the dangers of flight as evidenced by September 11. Assume that Jim would like to persuade Ned that flying is absolutely safe, or at least much less risky than anxious Ned believes. Social judgment theory recommends that Jim try to figure out the location and breadth of the man's three latitudes before presenting his case. Figure 14–1 shows where Ned places those 11 statements along the mental yardstick he uses to gauge safety. As you will discover in the next few pages, if my son has a good idea of this cognitive map, he'll have a much better chance to craft a message that will persuade Ned to be more optimistic about flying.

EGO-INVOLVEMENT: HOW MUCH DO YOU CARE?

There's one other thing about Ned's attitude structure that Jim needs to know—how *important* the issue of air safety is in Ned's life. Sherif called this concept *ego-involvement. Ego-involvement* refers to how crucial an issue is in our lives. Is it central to our well-being? Do we think about it a lot? Does our attitude on the

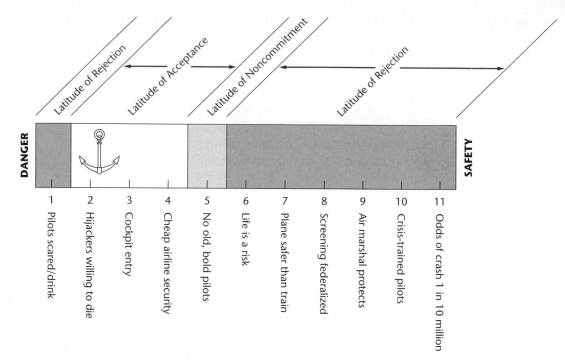

FIGURE 14–1   Ned's Cognitive Map Regarding Air Safety

matter go a long way toward defining who we are? In Figure 14–1, I've used an anchor to represent the position that most closely represents Ned's point of view—that flying is dangerous because fanatics are willing to die for their cause. Sherif said that's what our favored position does; it anchors all our other thoughts about the topic.

If air safety were only a casual concern for Ned, it would be fitting to represent his stance with a small anchor that could easily be dragged to a new position. That's probably the case for some of the nonfliers in the terminal who are simply picking up a rental car, dropping off Aunt Juanita for her flight, or perhaps retrieving a lost bag for a friend. These folks are for safe flights and against crashes, but for them air safety isn't a major personal concern.

Despite the fact that images of airplanes slamming into the twin towers of the World Trade Center are stenciled into most people's minds, not everyone who flies dwells on the topic. Those people don't argue about it, stew over it, or get sweaty palms when their jet roars down the runway. As long as everything seems normal, their ego-involvement is moderate.

But for Ned and others like him, the issue is crucial. They are frequent fliers who swap horror stories of knowing someone who died on a hijacked plane. They experience panic when three swarthy men board their flight to Chicago. Others may experience only passing anxiety about flying, but since Ned's fear is deep-seated, the hefty anchor shown in Figure 14–1 is appropriate.

People with attitude profiles similar to Ned's are highly ego-involved. Some join an airline passenger association that lobbies Congress for stricter safety regulations. One way Sherif defined high ego-involvement was *membership in a group with a known stand.* My son's pilot's license, Air Line Pilots Association union card, and employment with a major airline are indications that he's at least as ego-involved in the issue as Ned. Of course, his confidence in airline safety is at the other end of the spectrum.

Three features of Ned's attitude structure are typical of people with high ego-involvement in an issue. The first indication is that his latitude of noncommitment is almost nonexistent. People who don't care about an issue usually have a wide latitude of noncommitment, but Ned has only one statement in that category. He may not be sure about old, bold pilots, but he has definite opinions on everything else.

Second, Ned rejects all five statements that offer assurances of safety. According to social judgment theory, a wide latitude of rejection is a typical sign of high ego-involvement. Ned has intense feelings about the potential dangers of flying; he sees safety as a black-and-white issue. Persons with low ego-involvement would probably see more grays. Note that the effects of high ego-involvement on perception may be similar to those of low cognitive complexity on the perception of personal characteristics (see Chapter 8). The person with high ego-involvement may have trouble distinguishing between actual improvements in safety and empty assurances. The person with low cognitive complexity may perceive groups of people as all the same. In both cases, the observer blurs differences that could make a difference.

Finally, people who hold extreme opinions on either side of an issue almost always care deeply. While it's possible to feel passionately about middle-of-the-road positions, social judgment researchers find that massive attitude anchors are usually found toward the ends of the scale. Extreme positions and high ego-involvement go together. That's why religion, sex, and politics are traditionally taboo topics in the wardroom of a U.S. Navy ship at sea. When passions run deep, radical opinions are common, and there's little tolerance for diversity.

Everything I've presented up to this point is how social judgment theory describes the cognitive *structure* of a person's attitude. We now turn to the two-step mental *process* that Sherif said is triggered when that person hears or reads a message. Ned will first evaluate the content of the message to see where it falls vis-à-vis his own position—how far it is from his anchor. That's the *judgment* phase of social judgment theory. In the second stage of the process, Ned will adjust his anchored attitude toward or away from the message he's just encountered. The next two sections explain the way Sherif said the two stages of this influence process work.

JUDGING THE MESSAGE: CONTRAST AND ASSIMILATION ERRORS

Sherif claimed that we use our own anchored attitude as a comparison point when we hear a discrepant message. He believed there is a parallel between systematic biases in the judgments we make in the physical world and the way we determine other people's attitudes. I recently set up three pails of water in my class to illustrate this principle. Even though the contents looked the same, the water in the left bucket was just above freezing, the water in the right bucket was just below scalding, and the water in the middle bucket was lukewarm. A student volunteered to plunge her left hand into the left bucket and her right hand into the right bucket at the same time. Twenty seconds was about all she could take. I then asked her to plunge both hands into the middle bucket and judge the temperature of the water. Of course, this produced a baffling experience, because her left hand "told" her the water was hot, while her right hand sent a message that it was cold.

Contrast
A perceptual error whereby people judge messages that fall within their latitudes of rejection as further from their anchor than they really are.

Assimilation
A perceptual error whereby people judge messages that fall within their latitudes of acceptances as less discrepant from their anchor than they really are.

Sherif hypothesized a similar *contrast* effect when people who are "hot" for an idea hear a message on the topic that doesn't have the same fire. Judged by their standard, even warm messages strike them as cold. Sherif's *social judgment-involvement* label nicely captures the idea of a link between ego-involvement and perception. Highly committed people have large latitudes of rejection. Any message that falls within that range will be perceived by them as more discrepant from their anchor than it really is. The message is mentally pushed away to a position that is farther out—not within the latitude of acceptance—so the hearer doesn't have to deal with it as a viable option.

All of this is bad news for Jim. Suppose he walks up to Ned and calmly explains that a federal air marshal rode "shotgun" in the coach section of his last flight. If Ned hears this message as Jim intended, it will register at a 9 on his mental scale, where a 1 represents total danger and an 11 indicates complete safety. However, social judgment theory says Ned probably won't hear it that way. Despite Jim's well-intentioned effort, his words will strike nervous Ned as self-serving pilot propaganda. Jim's supposedly reassuring words of on-board law and order will be heard as an unsubstantiated promise of safety at 10 or 11. To Ned, these are unrealistic guarantees that he's quick to reject.

Contrast is a perceptual distortion that leads to polarization of ideas. But according to Sherif, it happens only when a message falls within the latitude of rejection. *Assimilation* is the opposite error of judgment. It's the rubberband effect that draws an idea toward the hearer's anchor so that it seems that she and the speaker share the same opinion. Assimilation takes place when a message falls within the latitude of acceptance. For example, suppose Jim tells Ned that his airline isn't willing to spend money on effective security. Although that message is at 4 on Ned's cognitive map, he will hear it as more similar to his anchoring attitude than it really is, perhaps a 3.

Sherif was unclear about how people judge a message that falls within their latitude of noncommitment. Most interpreters assume that neither perceptual bias would kick in and that the message would be heard roughly as intended.

DISCREPANCY AND ATTITUDE CHANGE

Judging how close or how far a message is from our own anchored position is the first stage of attitude change. Shifting our anchor in response is the second. Sherif thought that both stages of the influence process usually take place below the level of consciousness.

According to social judgment theory, once we've judged a new message to be within our latitude of acceptance, we will adjust our attitude somewhat to accommodate that new input. The persuasive effect will be positive but partial. We won't travel the whole distance, but there will be some measurable movement toward the speaker's perceived position. How much movement? Sherif wasn't specific, but he did claim that *the greater the discrepancy, the more hearers will adjust their attitudes.* Thus, the persuasive message that persuades the most is the one that is most discrepant from the receiver's position yet falls within his or her *latitude of acceptance.*

If we've judged a message to be within our *latitude of rejection,* we will also adjust our attitude, but in this case *away from* what we think the speaker is advocating. Since people who are highly ego-involved in a topic have broad ranges of rejection, most messages aimed to persuade them are in danger of actually driving them further away. This predicted *boomerang effect* suggests that people are often *driven* rather than *drawn* to the attitude positions they occupy.

Boomerang effect
Attitude change in the opposite direction of what the message advocated; listeners driven away from rather than drawn to an idea.

The mental processes Sherif described are automatic. He reduced interpersonal influence to the issue of the distance between the message and the hearer's position:

> Stripped to its bare essential, the problem of attitude change is the problem of the degree of discrepancy from communication and the felt necessity of coping with the discrepancy.[4]

So the only space for volition in social judgment theory is the choice of alternative messages available to the person who's trying to be persuasive.

PRACTICAL ADVICE FOR THE PERSUADER

Sherif would have advised Jim to avoid messages that claim flying is safer than taking the bus or train. Ned simply won't believe them, and they may push him deeper into his antiaviation stance. For maximum influence, Jim should select a

*"We think you could gain much wider support simply
by re-languaging your bigotry."*

message that's right on the edge of Ned's latitude of acceptance. Admit that airlines had been unwilling to spend money to achieve tight security, but stress that 9/11 terrorism has changed all that. Or perhaps use the somewhat ambiguous statement about there being no old, bold pilots, explaining how cockpit check rides have weeded out erratic pilots. According to social judgment theory, this strategy will result in a small amount of positive persuasion.

Jim wants more. But Sherif would caution Jim that it's all he can get in a one-shot attempt. If he were talking to an open-minded person with a broad latitude of acceptance, a bigger shift would be possible. But when he's dealing with a highly ego-involved traveler, he has to work within a narrow range. True conversion from one end of the scale to the other is a rare phenomenon. The only way to get large-scale change is through a series of small, successive movements. Persuasion is a gradual process.

It's also a *social* process. The lack of an interpersonal bond between Jim and Ned limits the amount of influence that's possible. If Ned heard strong reassurances of airline safety from his friends and family, it might occasion a major shift. Sherif noted that "most dramatic cases of attitude change, the most widespread and enduring, are those involving changes in reference groups with differing values."[5]

EVIDENCE THAT ARGUES FOR ACCEPTANCE

Research on the predictions of social judgment theory requires highly ego-involving issues. For example, one study that supports the theory's two-stage hypothesis presented a pro-choice message on abortion to members of a pro-life activist organization.[6] Another queried people on their attitude toward public disclosure of HIV test results.[7]

An early experiment employed a topic vitally important to all college students—sleep.[8] Before the study, most of the undergraduates had accepted the conventional wisdom that the human body functions best with eight hours of sleep at night. They then read an article written by an expert in the field that claimed young adults actually need much less. The message was the same for all with one crucial difference. Some students were told they needed eight hours, some seven, some six, and so on, right down the line. The final group actually read that humans need no sleep at all! Then each group had a chance to give their opinions.

Sherif's theory suggests that the fewer hours recommended, the more students will be swayed until they begin to regard the message as patently ridiculous. The results shown in Figure 14–2 confirm this prediction. Persuasion increased as the hours advocated were reduced to 3, a message that caused students to revise their estimate of optimum sleep down to 6.3 hours. Anything less than 3 hours apparently fell outside their latitude of acceptance and became progressively ineffective.

Three things have become clear as social judgment theory has been tested:

1.   A highly credible speaker can stretch the hearer's latitude of acceptance. When the "expert" in the sleep study was a Nobel Prize–winning physiologist rather than a YMCA director, persuasion increased.

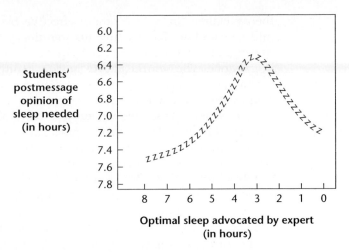

FIGURE 14–2   Sleep Study Results
Adapted from Bochner and Insko, "Communicator Discrepancy, Source Credibility and Opinion Change"

2.   **Ambiguity can often serve better than clarity.** When George W. Bush said on the campaign trail that he was a "compassionate conservative," nobody knew exactly what he meant, but it sounded good, and so the statement fell within people's latitude of acceptance. Tanya Donelly, former lead singer for Belly, takes the same approach. She says that she writes lyrics that are intentionally vague so as to appeal to a wider audience.[9]

3.   **There are some people who are dogmatic on every issue.** "Don't confuse me with the facts," they say. "My mind is made up." These cantankerous souls have a chronically wide latitude of rejection.

A striking story of social judgment theory in action comes from a university development director I know who was making a call on a rich alumnus. He anticipated that the prospective donor would give as much as $10,000. He made his pitch and asked what the wealthy businessman could do. The man protested that it had been a lean year and that times were tough—he couldn't possibly contribute more than $20,000. The fundraiser figured that he had seriously underestimated the giver's latitude of acceptance and that $20,000 was on the low end of that range. Without missing a beat he replied, "Trevor, do you really think that's enough?" The alumnus wrote a check for $25,000.

CRITIQUE: HOW WIDE IS YOUR THEORETICAL LATITUDE OF ACCEPTANCE?

How do you feel about the fundraising ploy just described? The persuasive technique obviously worked, but the application of social judgment theory raises some thorny ethical questions. Is it legitimate for fundraisers to alter their pitch based on a potential donor's latitude of acceptance? Is it all right for politicians to be intentionally vague so that their message has broad appeal? Or consider my son's genuine desire to allay the fears of the flying public. The theory claims Jim will be more effective by presenting a soft-sell message at midscale rather than stating his genuine conviction that flying is safer than driving. Is this honest?

As one who would like to have a positive influence, I appreciate Sherif's warning of the potential backlash I may create when I push a proposal that falls deep within the other's latitude of rejection. This could easily happen if I'm more concerned with *presenting my message* than I am with *understanding the other person's point of view.* The theory is practical.

Practical utility is just one of five standard criteria used to judge a social science theory. An objective theory should predict and explain, while also being testable and not overly complex. As for predictions, social judgment theory makes a number of important ones. One is that changing the opinion held by someone highly ego-involved in the issue is difficult, and sometimes impossible. Another suggests that discrepancy can be the persuader's friend. As long as the message falls within the latitude of acceptance, the more discrepant it is from the recipient's belief, the greater the amount of attitude change it will produce.

Like all cognitive explanations, the theory assumes a mental structure that goes on "behind the eyes" where no one can see it. Do people really carry a set of scales around in their heads that they use to gauge every idea they hear? And if Sherif's three latitudes are really there, how can persuasion practitioners discover where they fall? That's what audience analysis and market research are all about, but it's hard to imagine Jim handing a questionnaire to a jittery traveler in the departure lounge.

Yet Sherif's appeal to the latitudes of acceptance, rejection, and noncommitment; the perceptual distortions of assimilation and contrast; and the crucial role of ego-involvement offer a compelling explanation for why he made his specific predictions. The explanation is complex, but given Sherif's belief that attitudes can't be represented as a single point on a continuum, it's hard to imagine a simpler explanation accounting for what he claimed will happen.

As for testing the theory, there have been relatively few studies compared to empirical research on the other two theories in this section. That may be because it's hard to find a wide range of experimental subjects who have different ego-involvement and hold widely different opinions on the same topic. Once they are found, it's also tedious to measure each person's three latitudes on that issue. And comparing their highly individual responses is trickier than simply averaging numbers on the type of attitude scale shown on page 181.

Recently, however, Hee Sun Park and four other Michigan State University department of communication colleagues conducted an experiment on the effects of *involvement* on persuasion.[10] They designed the study to specifically test whether social judgment theory or the *elaboration likelihood model* presented in the next chapter better captures the way reader or listener involvement affects how they are influenced. To the researchers' surprise, they found that the quality of message arguments trumped any other factor that they measured. But in a direct comparison of the theories' treatment of persuadee involvement, Sherif's theory received more support. The theory can be tested and then validated or falsified.

Despite the questions that surround social judgment theory, it is an elegant conception of the persuasion process. There's an intuitive appeal to the idea of crafting a message that's positioned right at the edge of the listener's latitude of acceptance in order to be as effectively discrepant as possible. That would be my recommendation to Jim as he confronts a variety of air travelers. I wonder in which of his three latitudes my advice to him will fall.

QUESTIONS TO SHARPEN YOUR FOCUS

1. How does the concept of *attitudes as latitudes* help you understand your attitude toward the various requirements of this course?

2. Suppose you find out that the fellow sitting next to you is *highly ego-involved* in the issue of gun control. Based on social judgment theory, what three predictions about his attitude structure would be reasonable to make?

3. What practical advice does social judgment theory offer you if you want to ask your boss for a raise?

4. Do you have any *ethical qualms* about applying the wisdom of social judgment theory? Why or why not?

SELF-QUIZ

www.mhhe.com/griffin7

A SECOND LOOK

Recommended resource: Donald Granberg, "Social Judgment Theory," in *Communication Yearbook 6*, Michael Burgoon (ed.), Sage, Beverly Hills, CA, 1982, pp. 304–329.

Original conception: Carolyn Sherif, Muzafer Sherif, and Roger Nebergall, *Attitude and Attitude Change: The Social Judgment-Involvement Approach*, W. B. Saunders, Philadelphia, 1965.

Ego-involvement: William W. Wilmot, "Ego-Involvement: A Confusing Variable in Speech Communication Research," *Quarterly Journal of Speech*, Vol. 57, 1971, pp. 429–436.

Attitudes as latitudes: Kenneth Sereno and Edward Bodaken, "Ego-Involvement and Attitude Change: Toward a Reconceptualization of Persuasive Effect," *Speech Monographs*, Vol. 39, 1972, pp. 151–158.

Test of two-stage hypothesis: Gian Sarup, Robert Suchner, and Gitanjali Gaylord, "Contrast Effects and Attitude Change: A Test of the Two-Stage Hypothesis of Social Judgment Theory," *Social Psychology Quarterly*, Vol. 54, 1991, pp. 364–372.

Message discrepancy: Stan Kaplowitz and Edward Fink, "Message Discrepancy and Persuasion," in *Progress in Communication Sciences: Advances in Persuasion*, Vol. 13, George Barnett and Frank Boster (eds.), Ablex, Greenwich, CT, 1997, pp. 75–106.

Sleep study: S. Bochner and C. Insko, "Communicator Discrepancy, Source Credibility and Opinion Change," *Journal of Personality and Social Psychology*, Vol. 4, 1966, pp. 614–621.

Secondary source: Daniel J. O'Keefe, "Social Judgment Theory," in *Persuasion: Theory and Research*, Sage, Newbury Park, CA, 1990, pp. 29–44.

Boomerang effect: Hilobumi Sakaki, "Experimental Studies of Boomerang Effects Following Persuasive Communication," *Psychologia,* Vol. 27, No. 2, 1984, pp. 84–88.

Meaning of involvement—a meta-analysis: Blair T. Johnson and Alice H. Eagly, "Effects of Involvement on Persuasion: A Meta-Analysis," *Psychological Bulletin,* Vol. 106, 1989, pp. 290–314.

Critique: Hee Sun Park, Timothy Levine, Catherine Y. K. Waterman, Tierney Oregon, and Sarah Forager, "The Effects of Argument Quality and Involvement Type on Attitude Formation and Attitude Change," *Human Communication Research,* Vol. 33, 2007, pp. 81–102.

Elaboration Likelihood Model

of Richard Petty & John Cacioppo

Like a number of women whose children are out of the home, Rita Francisco has gone back to college. Her program isn't an aimless sampling of classes to fill empty hours—she has enrolled in every course that will help her become a more persuasive advocate. Rita is a woman with a mission.

Rita's teenage daughter was killed when the car she was riding in smashed into a stone wall. After drinking three cans of beer at a party, the girl's 18-year-old boyfriend lost control on a curve while going 80 miles per hour. Rita's son walks with a permanent limp as a result of injuries received when a high school girl plowed through the parking lot of a 7-Eleven on a Friday night. When the county prosecutor obtained a DUI (driving under the influence) conviction, it only fueled Rita's resolve to get young drinking drivers off the road. She has become active with Mothers Against Drunk Driving (MADD) and works to convince anyone who will listen that "zero tolerance" laws, which make it illegal for drivers under the age of 21 to have *any* measurable amount of alcohol in their system, should be strictly enforced. Rita also wants to persuade others that young adults caught driving with more than 0.02 percent blood alcohol content should automatically lose their driver's licenses until they are 21.

This is a tough sell on most college campuses. While her classmates can appreciate the tragic reasons underlying her fervor, few subscribe to what they believe is a drastic solution. As a nontraditional, older student, Rita realizes that her younger classmates could easily dismiss her campaign as the ranting of a hysterical parent. She's determined to develop the most effective persuasive strategy possible and wonders if she would have the most success by presenting well-reasoned arguments for enforcing zero tolerance laws. Then again, couldn't she sway students more by lining up highly credible people to endorse her proposal?

THE CENTRAL AND PERIPHERAL ROUTES TO PERSUASION

Ohio State psychologist Richard Petty thinks Rita is asking the right questions. He conducted his Ph.D. dissertation study using the topic of teenage driving to test the relative effectiveness of strong-message arguments and high source credibility. He found that the results varied depending on which of two mental routes to attitude change a *listener* happened to use. Petty labeled the two cognitive processes the *central route* and the *peripheral route*. He sees the distinction as helpful in reconciling much of the conflicting data of persuasion research. Along with his University of Chicago colleague John Cacioppo, he launched an intensive program of study to discover the best way for the persuader to activate each route.

Central route

Message elaboration; the path of cognitive processing that involves scrutiny of message content.

The central route involves message elaboration. Elaboration is "the extent to which a person carefully thinks about issue-relevant arguments contained in a persuasive communication."[1] In an attempt to process new information rationally, people using the central route carefully scrutinize the ideas, try to figure out if they have true merit, and mull over their implications. Similar to Berger's characterization of strategic message plans, elaboration requires high levels of cognitive effort (see Chapter 10).

Peripheral route

A mental shortcut process that accepts or rejects a message based on irrelevant cues as opposed to actively thinking about the issue.

The peripheral route offers a mental shortcut path to accepting or rejecting a message "without any active thinking about the attributes of the issue or the object of consideration."[2] Instead of doing extensive cognitive work, recipients rely on a variety of cues that allow them to make quick decisions. Robert Cialdini of Arizona State University lists six cues that trigger a "click, whirr" programmed response.[3] These cues allow us to fly the peripheral route on automatic pilot:

1. Reciprocation—"You owe me."
2. Consistency—"We've always done it that way."
3. Social proof—"Everybody's doing it."
4. Liking—"Love me, love my ideas."
5. Authority—"Just because I say so."
6. Scarcity—"Quick, before they're all gone."

Message elaboration

The extent to which a person carefully thinks about issue-relevant arguments contained in a persuasive communication.

Figure 15–1 shows a simplified version of Petty and Cacioppo's elaboration likelihood model (ELM) as it applies to Rita's situation. Although their model with its twin-route metaphor seems to suggest two mutually exclusive paths to persuasion, the theorists stress that the central route and the peripheral route are poles on a cognitive processing continuum that shows the degree of mental effort a person exerts when evaluating a message.[4] The elaboration scale at the top represents effortful scrutiny of arguments on the left-hand side and mindless reliance on noncontent cues on the right. Most messages receive middle ground attention between these poles, but there's always a trade-off. The more Rita's listeners work to discern the merits of strict zero tolerance enforcement, the less they'll be influenced by peripheral factors such as their friends' scoffing laughter at her suggestion. Conversely, the more her hearers are affected by content-irrelevant factors such as Rita's age, accent, or appearance, the less they will be affected by her ideas. We'll work down the model one level at a time in order to understand Petty and Cacioppo's predictions about the likelihood of Rita's message being scrutinized by students at her college.

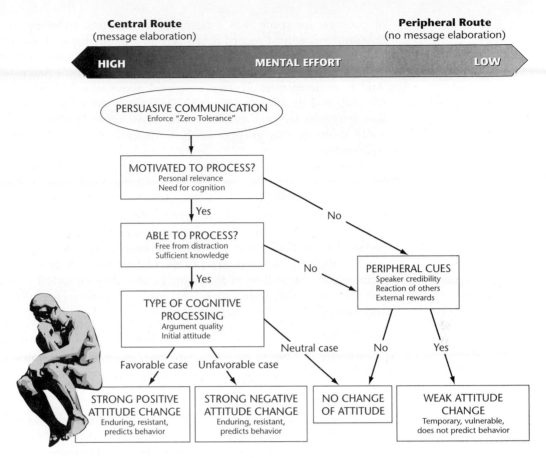

FIGURE 15-1 The Elaboration Likelihood Model

Adapted from Petty and Cacioppo, "The Elaboration Likelihood Model: Current Status and Controversies"

MOTIVATION FOR ELABORATION: IS IT WORTH THE EFFORT?

Petty and Cacioppo assume that people are motivated to hold correct attitudes. The authors admit that we aren't always logical, but they think we make a good effort not to kid ourselves in our search for truth. We want to maintain reasonable positions.

Yet a person can examine only a limited number of ideas. We are exposed to so many persuasive messages that we would experience a tremendous information overload if we tried to interact with every variant idea we heard or read about. The only way to solve this problem is by being "lazy" toward most issues in life. Petty and Cacioppo claim we have a large-mesh mental filter that allows items we regard as less important to flow through without being processed very carefully. But statements about things that are personally relevant get trapped and tested. In the terminology of social judgment theory (see Chapter 14), we're motivated to elaborate only ideas with which we are highly ego-involved.

There are few things in life more important to young Americans than the right to drive. A license is the closest thing our society has to an adolescent rite of passage; for some it is a passport to freedom. It seems unlikely, therefore, that students would regard Rita's zero tolerance proposal as trivial. Yet threatening the loss of license may have less personal relevance to students who don't drink, or to those who already make sure they don't drive when they drink. And if students over 21 aren't worried about who's driving on the road, they too may feel that Rita's proposal has little to do with them. So ELM's authors would regard teenage students who drive after drinking a few beers as especially motivated to grapple with arguments about automatic driver's license suspension.

Petty and Cacioppo maintain that as long as people have a personal stake in accepting or rejecting an idea, they will be much more influenced by what a message says than by the characteristics of the person who says it. But when a topic is no longer relevant, it gets sidetracked to the periphery of the mind, where credibility cues take on greater importance. Without the motivation of personal relevance, there probably will be little elaboration.

Need for cognition
Desire for cognitive clarity; an enjoyment of thinking through ideas even when they aren't personally relevant.

The theorists do recognize, however, that some people have a need for cognitive clarity, regardless of the issue. In fact, they've developed a *Need for Cognition Scale* to identify individuals who are most likely to carefully consider message arguments.[5] Four of the items state:

I really enjoy a task that involves coming up with new solutions to problems.

I prefer my life to be filled with puzzles that I must solve.

I like tasks that require little thought once I've learned them.

Thinking is not my idea of fun.

If you substantially agree with the first two statements and take issue with the last two, Petty and Cacioppo would anticipate that you'd be a person who works through many of the ideas and arguments you hear.

ABILITY FOR ELABORATION: CAN THEY DO IT?

Once people have shown an inclination to think about the content of a message (motivation), the next issue is whether they are *able* to do so. Since Rita's immediate audience consists of young men and women who have duly impressed a college admissions officer with their ability to think, you would imagine that the question of ability would be moot. But issue-relevant thinking (elaboration) takes more than intelligence. It also requires concentration.

Distraction disrupts elaboration. Rita's classmates will be hard-pressed to think about her point of view if it's expressed amid the din of a student union snack bar where you can't hear yourself think. Or perhaps she presents her solution for highway safety when the students are trying to concentrate on something else—an upcoming exam, a letter from home, or a mental replay of the winning shot in an intramural basketball game.

Rita may face the same challenge as television advertisers who have only the fleeting attention of viewers. Like them, Rita can use repetition to ensure that her main point comes across, but too much commotion will short-circuit a reasoned consideration of the message, no matter how much repetition is used. In that case, students will use the peripheral route and judge the message by cues that indicate whether Rita is a competent and trustworthy person.

TYPE OF ELABORATION: OBJECTIVE VERSUS BIASED THINKING

As you can see from the downward flow in the central path of their model (Figure 15–1), Petty and Cacioppo believe that motivation and ability strongly increase the likelihood that a message will be elaborated in the minds of listeners. Yet as social judgment theory suggests, they may not process the information in a fair and objective manner. Rita might have the undivided attention of students who care deeply about the right to drive, but discover that they've already built up an organized structure of knowledge concerning the issue.

When Rita claims that the alcohol-related fatal crash rate for young drivers is double that of drivers over 21, a student may counter with the fact that teenagers drive twice as many miles and are therefore just as safe as adults. Whether or not the statistics are true or the argument is valid isn't the issue. The point is that those who have already thought a lot about drinking and driving safety will probably have made up their minds and be biased in the way they process Rita's message.

Biased elaboration
Top-down thinking in which predetermined conclusions color the supporting data.

Petty and Cacioppo refer to biased elaboration as top-down thinking in which a predetermined conclusion colors the supporting data underneath. They contrast this with objective elaboration, or bottom-up thinking, which lets facts speak for themselves. Biased elaboration merely bolsters previous ideas.

Objective elaboration
Bottom-up thinking in which facts are scrutinized without bias; seeking truth wherever it might lead.

Perhaps you've seen a picture of Rodin's famous statue, *The Thinker*, a man sitting with his head propped in one hand. If the thinker already has a set of beliefs to contemplate, Petty and Cacioppo's research shows that additional thought will merely fix them in stone. Rita shouldn't assume that audience elaboration will always help her cause; it depends on whether it's biased elaboration or objective elaboration. It also depends on the quality of her arguments.

ELABORATED ARGUMENTS: STRONG, WEAK, AND NEUTRAL

If Rita manages to win an unbiased hearing from students at her school, Petty and Cacioppo say her cause will rise or fall on the perceived strength of her arguments. The two theorists have no absolute standard for what distinguishes a cogent argument from one that's specious. They simply define a strong message as one that generates favorable thoughts when it's heard and scrutinized.

Strong arguments
Claims that generate favorable thoughts when examined.

Petty and Cacioppo predict that thoughtful consideration of strong arguments will produce major shifts in attitude in the direction desired by the persuader. Suppose Rita states the following:

> National Safety Council statistics show that drivers in the 16–20 age group account for 15 percent of the miles driven in the United States, yet they are responsible for 25 percent of the highway deaths that involve alcohol.

This evidence could give students cause for pause. They may not be comfortable with the facts, but some of them might find the statistics quite compelling, and a reason to reconsider their stance. According to the ELM, the enhanced thinking of those who respond favorably will cause their change in position to *persist over time*, *resist counterpersuasion*, and *predict future behavior*—the "triple crown" of interpersonal influence.

However, persuasive attempts that are processed through the central route can have dramatically negative effects as well. Despite her strong convictions, Rita may be able to make only a weak case for changing the current law.

> When underage drinkers are arrested for violating zero tolerance rules of the road, automatic suspension of their licenses would allow the secretary of state's office to reduce its backlog of work. This would give government officials time to check driving records so that they could keep dangerous motorists off the road.

This weak argument is guaranteed to offend the sensibilities of anyone who thinks about it. Rather than compelling listeners to enlist in Rita's cause, it will only give them a reason to oppose her point of view more vigorously. The elaborated idea will cause a boomerang effect that will last over time, defy other efforts to change it, and affect subsequent behavior. These are the same significant effects that the elaborated strong argument produces, but in the opposite direction.

Rita's ideas could produce an ambivalent reaction. Listeners who carefully examine her ideas may end up feeling neither pro nor con toward her evidence. Their neutral or mixed response obviously means that they won't change their attitudes as a result of processing through the central route. For them, thinking about the pros and cons of the issue reinforces their original attitudes, whatever they may be.

PERIPHERAL CUES: AN ALTERNATIVE ROUTE OF INFLUENCE

Although the majority of this chapter has dealt with the central cognitive route to attitude change, most messages are processed on the less effortful peripheral path. Signposts along the way direct the hearer to favor or oppose the persuader's point of view without ever engaging in what Petty and Cacioppo call "issue-relevant thinking."[6] There is no inner dialogue over the merits of the proposal.

As explained earlier, the hearer who uses the peripheral route relies on a variety of cues as an aid in reaching a quick decision. The most obvious cues are tangible rewards linked to agreement with the advocate's position. Food, sex, and money are traditional inducements to change. I once overheard the conclusion of a transaction between a young man and a college senior who was trying to persuade him to donate blood in order to fulfill her class assignment. "Okay, it's agreed," she said. "You give blood for me today, and I'll have you over to my place for dinner tomorrow night." Although this type of social exchange has been going on for centuries, Petty and Cacioppo would still describe it as peripheral. Public compliance to the request for blood? Yes. Private acceptance of its importance? Not likely.

For many students of influence, speaker, or source, credibility is the most interesting cue on the peripheral route. Four decades of research confirm that people who are likable and have expertise on the issue in question can have a persuasive impact regardless of what arguments they present. Rita's appearance, manner of talking, and background credentials will speak so loudly that some students won't really hear what she says. Which students? According to Petty and Cacioppo, those students who are unmotivated or unable to scrutinize her message and therefore switch to the peripheral path.

Listeners who believe that Rita's twin tragedies have given her wisdom beyond their own will shift to a position more sympathetic to her point of view. The same holds true for those who see her as pleasant and warm. But there are students who will regard her grammatical mistakes as a sign of ignorance, or they'll be turned off by a maternal manner that reminds them of a lecture from mom. These peripheral route critics will become more skeptical of Rita's position.

"In the interest of streamlining the judicial process, we'll skip the evidence and go directly to sentencing."

Note that attitude change on this outside track can be either positive or negative, but it lacks the robust persistence, invulnerability, or link to behavior that we see in change that comes from message elaboration.

Understanding the importance of role models for persuasion, Rita scans the pages of *Rolling Stone* to see if singer Dave Matthews might have said something about teenage drivers. The music of the Dave Matthews Band is widely acclaimed by students at her college, and Matthews recently put on a live concert near the school. By somehow associating her message with credible people, she can achieve change in many students' attitudes. Yet it probably won't last long, stand up to attack, or affect their behavior. Petty and Cacioppo say that a fragile change is all that can be expected through the peripheral route.

PUSHING THE LIMITS OF PERIPHERAL POWER

What if Dave Matthews' tour bus were run off the road by a drunk teenage fan and a band member met the same fate as Rita's daughter? Would that tragic death and Matthews' avowal that "friends don't let friends drive drunk" cue students to a permanent shift in attitude and behavior? Fortunately, the band is still intact, but a high-profile tragedy in the sports world suggests that the effect of even powerful peripheral cues is short-lived at best.

In 1991, basketball superstar Magic Johnson held a candid press conference to announce that he had tested positive for HIV. The story dominated network news coverage for days. University of South Florida psychologists Louis Penner and Barbara Fritzsche had just completed a study showing that many people had little sympathy for AIDS victims who had contracted the disease through sexual transmission. When asked to volunteer a few hours to help a patient stay in school, just over half of the women and none of the men in the study volunteered. Penner and Fritzsche extended their study when they heard of Magic Johnson's illness.[7] They wondered if the tragedy that had befallen this popular star and his pledge to become an advocate for those with the disease would cause students to react more positively toward people with AIDS.

For a while it did. The week after Johnson's announcement, 80 percent of the men offered assistance. That number tapered off to 30 percent, however, within a few months. The proportion of women helping dipped below 40 percent in the same period. Penner and Fritzsche observed that people didn't grapple with the substance of Magic Johnson's message; rather, they paid attention to the man who was presenting it. Consistent with ELM's main thesis, the researchers concluded that "changes that occur because of 'peripheral cues' such as . . . being a well liked celebrity are less permanent than those that occur because of the substantive content of the persuasion attempt."[8]

Penner and Fritzsche could have added that the effects of star performer endorsements are subject to the sharp ups and downs of celebrity status. For example, the Dave Matthews Band has been so environmentally "green" that a Ben and Jerry's flavor of ice cream was named after one of the band's songs. Yet that image was besmirched when their tour bus dumped 80 gallons of human waste through a grated bridge over the Chicago River. Much of the foul-smelling sewage doused tourists having dinner on the deck of a sightseeing boat passing under the bridge. So any comment by Matthews on safe and sane driving might be treated with derision rather than help Rita's cause.[9]

Although most ELM research has measured the effects of peripheral cues by studying credibility, a speaker's competence or character could also be a stimulus to effortful message elaboration. For example, the high regard that millions of sports fans had for Magic Johnson might for the first time have made it possible to scrutinize proposals for the prevention and treatment of AIDS without a moral stigma biasing each idea. Or the fact that Johnson's magic wasn't strong enough to repel the AIDS virus might cause someone to think deeply: "If it happened to a guy like Magic, it could happen to me." Even though Figure 15–1 identifies *speaker credibility, reaction of others,* and *external rewards* as variables that promote mindless acceptance via the peripheral route, Petty and Cacioppo emphasize that it's impossible to compile a list of cues that are strictly peripheral.[10]

To illustrate this point, consider the multiple roles that the *mood* of the person listening to Rita's message might play in her attempt to persuade. Rita assumes that her classmate Sam will be a more sympathetic audience if she can present her ideas when he's in a good mood. And she's right, as long as Sam processes her message through the peripheral route without thinking too hard about what she's saying. His positive outlook prompts him to see her proposal in a favorable light.

Yet if Sam is somewhat willing and able to work through her arguments (moderate elaboration), his upbeat mood could actually turn out to be a disadvantage.

Speaker credibility
Audience perception of the message source's expertise, character, and dynamism; typically a peripheral cue.

He was feeling up, but he becomes depressed when he thinks about the death and disfigurement that Rita describes. The loss of warm feelings could bias him against Rita's arguments. Petty suggests that Sam might process her arguments more objectively if his original mood had matched the downbeat nature of Rita's experience.[11] Many variables like *perceived credibility* or the *mood of the listener* can act as peripheral cues. Yet if one of them motivates listeners to scrutinize the message or affects their evaluation of arguments, it no longer serves as a "no-brainer." There is no variable that's always a shortcut on the peripheral route.

CHOOSING A ROUTE: PRACTICAL ADVICE FOR THE PERSUADER

Petty and Cacioppo's advice for Rita (and the rest of us) is clear. She needs to determine the likelihood that her listeners will give their undivided attention to evaluating her proposal. If it appears that they have the motivation and ability to elaborate the message, she had best come armed with facts and figures to support her case. A pleasant smile, an emotional appeal, or the loss of her daughter won't make any difference.

Since it's only by thoughtful consideration that her listeners could experience a lasting change in attitude, Rita probably hopes they can go the central route. Yet if they do, it's still difficult to build a compelling persuasive case. If she fails to do her homework and presents weak arguments, the people who are ready to think will shift their attitude to a more antagonistic position.

If Rita determines that her hearers are unable or unwilling to think through the details of her plan, she'll be more successful choosing a delivery strategy that emphasizes the package rather than the contents. This could include a heartrending account of her daughter's death, a smooth presentation, and an ongoing effort to build friendships with the students. Perhaps bringing home-made cookies to class or offering rides to the mall would aid in making her an attractive source. But as we've already seen, the effects will probably be temporary.

It's not likely that Rita will get many people to elaborate her message in a way that ends up favorably for her cause. Most persuaders avoid the central route because the audience won't go with them or they find it is too difficult to generate compelling arguments. But Rita really doesn't have a choice.

Driver's licenses (and perhaps beer) are so important to most of these students that they'll be ready to dissect every part of her plan. They won't be won over by a friendly smile. Rita will have to develop thoughtful and well-reasoned arguments if she is to change their minds. Given the depth of her conviction, she thinks it's worth a try.

ETHICAL REFLECTION: NILSEN'S SIGNIFICANT CHOICE

ELM describes persuasion that's effective. University of Washington professor emeritus Thomas Nilsen is concerned with what's ethical. Consistent with the democratic values of a free society, he proposes that persuasive speech is ethical to the extent that it maximizes people's ability to exercise free choice. Since many political, religious, and commercial messages are routinely designed to bypass rather than appeal to a listener's rational faculties, Nilsen upholds the value of significant choice in unequivocal terms:

> When we communicate to influence the attitudes, beliefs, and actions of others, the ethical touchstone is the degree of free, informed, rational and critical choice—significant choice—that is fostered by our speaking.[12]

For Nilsen, truly free choice is the test of ethical influence because "only a self-determining being can be a moral being; without significant choice, there is no morality."[13] To support his claim, he cites two classic essays on the freedom of speech. John Milton's *Areopagitica*[14] argues against prior restraint of any ideas, no matter how heretical. John Stuart Mill's *On Liberty*[15] advocates a free market-place of ideas because the only way to test an argument is to hear it presented by a true believer who defends it in earnest.

Philosophers and rhetoricians have compared persuasion to a lover making fervent appeals to his beloved—wooing an audience, for example. Nilsen's ethic of significant choice is nicely captured in the courtship analogy because true love cannot be coerced; it must be freely given. Inspired by Danish philosopher Søren Kierkegaard's description of the ethical religious persuader as lover,[16] I have elsewhere presented a typology of false (unethical) lovers:[17]

> *Smother lovers* won't take no for an answer; their persistence is obnoxious.
> *Legalistic lovers* have a set image of what the other should be.
> *Flirts* are in love with love; they value response, not the other person.
> *Seducers* try deception and flattery to entice the other to submit.
> *Rapists* use force of threats, guilt, or conformity pressure to have their way.

In differing degrees, all five types of unethical persuader violate the human dignity of the persons they pursue by taking away choice that is informed and free.

Nilsen obviously would approve of persuasive appeals that encourage message elaboration through ELM's central route. Yet his standard of significant choice is not always easy to apply. Do emotional appeals seductively short-circuit our ability to make rational choices, or does heightened emotion actually free us up to consider new options? Significant choice, like beauty and credibility, may be in the eye of the beholder.

CRITIQUE: ELABORATING THE MODEL

For the last 20 years, ELM has been a leading, if not *the* leading, theory of persuasion and attitude change. Petty, Cacioppo, and their students have published more than a hundred articles on different parts of the model, and their initial dual-process conception has stimulated additional research, application, and critique. In a recent status review, the theorists state that "the term 'elaboration' is used to suggest that people add something of their own to the specific information provided in the communication."[18] Consistent with their definition, Petty and Cacioppo have elaborated their original theory by making it increasingly more complex, less predictive, and less able to offer definitive advice to the influence practitioner. This is not the direction in which a scientific theory wants to go.

I have been unable to capture all of these elaborations in a short chapter, but Miami University communication researcher Paul Mongeau and communication consultant James Stiff believe that Petty and Cacioppo face an even greater problem. They charge that "descriptions of the ELM are sufficiently imprecise and ambiguous as to prevent an adequate test of the entire model."[19] One place this stands out is in ELM's silence as to what makes a strong or weak argument.

Petty and Cacioppo define a good message as "one containing arguments such that when subjects are instructed to think about the message, the thoughts they generate are fundamentally favorable."[20] In other words, the arguments are regarded as strong if the people are persuaded but weak if folks are turned off. Like my childhood friend described in Chapter 3, ELM seems to have its own "never-miss shot." Until such time as the ELM theorists can identify what makes a case weak or strong apart from its ultimate effect on the listener, it doesn't make much sense to include strength of argument as a key variable within the model.

Yet even if Petty and Cacioppo's theory is too vague or their view of argument strength is too slippery, their elaboration likelihood model is impressive because it pulls together and makes sense out of diverse research results that have puzzled communication theorists for years. For example, why do most people pay less attention to the communication than they do to the communicator? And if speaker credibility is so important, why does its effect dissipate so quickly? ELM's explanation is that few listeners are motivated and able to do the mental work that is required for a major shift in attitude. The two-path hypothesis also helps clarify why good evidence and reasoning can sometimes have a life-changing impact but usually make no difference at all.

Attitude-change research often yields results that seem confusing or contradictory. Petty and Cacioppo's ELM takes many disjointed findings and pulls them together into a unified whole. This integrative function makes it a valuable theory of influence.

QUESTIONS TO SHARPEN YOUR FOCUS

1. Can you think of five different words or phrases that capture the idea of *message elaboration?*

2. What *peripheral cues* do you usually monitor when someone is trying to influence you?

3. Petty and Cacioppo want to persuade you that their elaboration likelihood model is a mirror of reality. Do you process their arguments for its accuracy closer to your *central route* or your *peripheral route*? Why not the other way?

4. Students of persuasion often wonder whether *high credibility* or *strong arguments* sway people more. How would ELM theorists respond to that question?

A SECOND LOOK

Recommended resource: "Richard E. Petty, John T. Cacioppo, Alan J. Strathman, and Joseph R. Priester, "To Think or Not to Think: Exploring Two Routes to Persuasion," in *Persuasion: Psychological Insights and Perspectives*, 2nd ed., Timothy Brock and Melanie Green (eds.), Sage, Thousand Oaks, CA, 2005, pp. 81–116.

Full statement: Richard E. Petty and John T. Cacioppo, *Communication and Persuasion: Central and Peripheral Routes to Attitude Change*, Springer-Verlag, New York, 1986.

Effect of involvement: Richard E. Petty and John T. Cacioppo, "Involvement and Persuasion: Tradition Versus Integration," *Psychological Bulletin*, Vol. 107, 1990, pp. 367–374.

Postulates and research: Richard E. Petty and John T. Cacioppo, "The Elaboration Likelihood Model of Persuasion," in *Advances in Experimental Social Psychology*, Vol. 19, Leonard Berkowitz (ed.), Academic Press, Orlando, FL, 1986, pp. 124–205.

Message arguments versus source credibility: Richard E. Petty, John T. Cacioppo, and R. Goldman, "Personal Involvement as a Determinant of Argument-Based Persuasion," *Journal of Personality and Social Psychology*, Vol. 41, 1981, pp. 847–855.

Effects of evidence: John Reinard, "The Empirical Study of the Persuasive Effects of Evidence: The Status After Fifty Years of Research," *Human Communication Research*, Vol. 15, 1988, pp. 3–59.

Effects of credibility: H. W. Simons, N. M. Berkowitz, and R. J. Moyer, "Similarity, Credibility and Attitude Change: A Review and a Theory," *Psychological Bulletin*, Vol. 73, 1970, pp. 1–16.

Mindless cues: Robert B. Cialdini, *Influence: Science and Practice*, 4th ed., Allyn and Bacon, Needham Heights, MA, 2001.

Cues that affect elaboration: Duane Wegener and Richard E. Petty, "Understanding Effects of Mood Through the Elaboration Likelihood and Flexible Correction Models," in *Theories of Mood and Cognition: A User's Guidebook*, L. L. Martin and G. L. Clore (eds.), Lawrence Erlbaum, Mahwah, NJ, 2001, pp. 177–210.

Current status: Richard E. Petty and Duane Wegener, "The Elaboration Likelihood Model: Current Status and Controversies," in Shelly Chaiken and Yaacov Trope (eds.), *Dual Process Theories in Social Psychology*, Guilford, New York, 1999, pp. 41–72.

Critiques of ELM: "Forum: Specifying the ELM," *Communication Theory*, Vol. 3, 1993. (Paul Mongeau and James Stiff, "Specifying Causal Relationships in the Elaboration Likelihood Model," pp. 65–72; Mike Allen and Rodney Reynolds, "The Elaboration Likelihood Model and the Sleeper Effect: An Assessment of Attitude Change over Time," pp. 73–82.)

To access titles of films that show masterful manipulation along the peripheral route, click on Chapter 15 of the Instructor's Manual at *www.afirstlook.com.*

Cognitive Dissonance Theory

of Leon Festinger

Aesop tells a story about a fox that tried in vain to reach a cluster of grapes dangling from a vine above his head. The fox leaped high to grasp the grapes, but the delicious-looking fruit remained just out of reach of his snapping jaws. After a few attempts the fox gave up and said to himself, "These grapes are sour, and if I had some I would not eat them."[1]

DISSONANCE: DISCORD BETWEEN BEHAVIOR AND BELIEF

Aesop's fable is the source of the phrase *sour grapes*. The story illustrates what former Stanford University social psychologist Leon Festinger called *cognitive dissonance*. It is the distressing mental state that people feel when they "find themselves doing things that don't fit with what they know, or having opinions that do not fit with other opinions they hold."[2]

Cognitive dissonance
The distressing mental state caused by inconsistency between a person's two beliefs or a belief and an action.

The fox's retreat from the grape arbor clashed with his knowledge that the grapes were tasty. By changing his attitude toward the grapes, he provided an acceptable explanation for abandoning his efforts to reach them.

Festinger considered the need to avoid dissonance to be just as basic as the need for safety or the need to satisfy hunger. It is an *aversive drive* that goads us to be consistent. The tension of dissonance motivates us to change either our behavior or our belief in an effort to avoid that distressing feeling. The more important the issue and the greater the discrepancy between our behavior and our belief, the higher the magnitude of dissonance we will feel. In extreme cases cognitive dissonance is like our cringing response to fingernails being scraped on a blackboard—we'll do anything to get away from the awful sound.

HEALTH-CONSCIOUS SMOKERS: DEALING WITH DISSONANCE

When Festinger first published his theory in 1957, he chose the topic of smoking to illustrate the concept of dissonance. Although authoritative medical reports on the link between smoking and lung cancer were just beginning to surface,

205

there was already a general concern across the United States that cigarette smoking might cause cancer. Ten years previously, country-and-western singer Tex Williams recorded Capitol Records' first million-seller, "Smoke! Smoke! Smoke! (That Cigarette)." The gravelly voiced vocalist expressed doubt that smoking would affect his health, but the chorus was unambiguous:

> Smoke, smoke, smoke that cigarette
> Puff, puff, puff until you smoke yourself to death
> Tell St. Peter at the Golden Gate
> That you hate to make him wait
> But you just gotta have another cigarette.[3]

At the time, many smokers and nonsmokers alike laughingly referred to cigarettes as "coffin nails." But as the number and certainty of medical reports linking smoking with lung cancer, emphysema, and heart disease increased, humorous references to cigarettes no longer seemed very funny. For the first time in their lives, a hundred million Americans had to grapple with two incompatible cognitions:

1. Smoking is dangerous to my health.
2. I smoke cigarettes.

Consider the plight of Cliff, a habitual smoker confronted by medical claims that smoking is hazardous to his health—an idea that strongly conflicts with his pack-a-day practice. Festinger said that the contradiction is so clear and uncomfortable that something has to give—either the use of cigarettes or the belief that smoking them will hurt him. "Whether the behavior or the cognition changes will be determined by which has the weakest resistance to change."[4] For Cliff it's no contest. He lights up and dismisses the health risk. In his discussion of smoking, Festinger suggested a number of mental gymnastics that Cliff might use to avoid dissonance while he smokes.[5]

Perhaps the most typical way for the smoker to avoid mental anguish is to trivialize or simply deny the link between smoking and cancer. *I think the research is sketchy, the results are mixed, and the warnings are based on junk science.* After the surgeon general's report on smoking was issued in 1964, denial became an uphill cognitive path to climb, but many smokers continue to go that route.

Smokers may counter thoughts of scary health consequences by reminding themselves of other effects they see as positive. *Smoking helps me relax, I like the taste, and it gives me a look of sophistication.* These were the motives that cigarette advertising appealed to when Festinger first published his theory. For example, Old Gold was the primary radio sponsor for Chicago Cubs baseball: "We're tobacco men, not medicine men," their ads proclaimed. "For a treat instead of a treatment, try Old Gold. . . . There's not a cough in a carload."

Although it's hard for smokers to pretend they aren't lighting up, they can elude nagging thoughts of trauma by telling themselves that the dire warnings don't apply to them since they are *moderate* smokers, or because they'll soon quit. *My boyfriend is a chain smoker, but I smoke less than a pack a day. As soon as I finish school, I'll have no problem stopping.* Conversely, other smokers manage dissonance by disclaiming any ongoing responsibility for a habit that they can't kick. *Let's face it, cigarettes are addictive. I'm hooked.* To be sure, most behaviors are not as difficult to change as the habit of smoking, but Festinger noted that almost all of our actions are more entrenched than the thoughts we have about them. Thus the focus of his theory is on the belief and attitude changes that take place because of cognitive dissonance.

REDUCING DISSONANCE BETWEEN ACTIONS AND ATTITUDES

Festinger hypothesized three mental mechanisms that people use to ensure that their actions and attitudes are in harmony. Dissonance researchers refer to them as *selective exposure, postdecision dissonance,* and *minimal justification.* I'll continue to illustrate these cognitive processes by referring to the practice of smoking, but they are equally applicable to other forms of substance abuse or addiction—alcohol, drugs, food, sex, pornography, gambling, money, shopping, workaholism. Most of us can spot at least one topic on that list where we struggle with an inconsistency between our thoughts and our actions. So if smoking isn't an issue for you, apply these ways of reducing dissonance in an area that is.

Hypothesis 1: Selective Exposure Prevents Dissonance

Festinger claimed that people avoid information that is likely to increase dissonance.[6] Not only do we tend to listen to opinions and select reading materials that are consistent with our existing beliefs, we usually choose to be with people who are like us. By taking care to "stick with our own kind," we can maintain the relative comfort of the status quo. Like-minded people buffer us from ideas that could cause discomfort. In that sense, the process of making friends is a way to select our own propaganda.

Selective exposure
The tendency people have to avoid information that would create cognitive dissonance because it's incompatible with their current beliefs.

The *selective exposure* hypothesis explains why most political conservatives only watch TV broadcasts of the Republican convention, and liberals stick to coverage of the Democratic conclave. That's why media-effects scholars who hold that the mass media have a minimal effect on their audience were quick to embrace Festinger's theory of cognitive dissonance.[7] So we should expect smokers to turn a blind eye to information about the dangers of cigarettes. But once the surgeon general's health warning was stamped on every pack of cigarettes, it was difficult for smokers to avoid dissonant information. Would that enforced exposure induce smokers to quit—or at least admit they were slowly killing themselves? Apparently not. Festinger reported an early Minnesota study that showed the more people smoked, the less they were convinced that smoking caused cancer.[8] That finding held true even after the government mandated that every cigarette ad prominently display the surgeon general's warning.

Four decades later, two communication researchers looked back over 18 experiments where people were put in dissonant situations and then had to choose what kind of information they would listen to or read. Dave D'Alessio (University of Connecticut-Stamford) and Mike Allen (University of Wisconsin-Milwaukee) discovered that the results consistently supported the selective exposure hypothesis.[9] People tended to select information that lined up with what they already believed and ignored facts or ideas that ran counter to those beliefs. But the strength of this tendency was relatively small. Selective exposure explained only about 5 percent of why they chose the information they did. That leaves 95 percent unexplained.

That modest finding hasn't deterred the sponsors of two recent media persuasion campaigns from taking the power of selective exposure quite seriously. A University of California, San Francisco, 2006 survey has documented that 75 percent of Hollywood films show attractive actors smoking, and that this modeling encourages young teens raised in smoke-free homes to adopt the practice. With some success, Harvard School of Public Health researchers are now proactively challenging directors not to introduce smoking into their films. For example, none of the fashion models nor any other characters in *The Devil Wears Prada* smoked. Audiences didn't seem to notice or mind.[10]

The "Don't Pass Gas" broadcast campaign of the American Legacy Foundation uses barnyard humor to convince the public of the intrusiveness of putrid gas. Presented in the style of a Dr. Seuss rhyme, one ad goes:

> I will not pass gas on a train. I will not pass gas on a plane.
> I will not pass gas in my house. I will not pass gas near my spouse.
> I will not pass gas in a bar. I will not pass gas in a car.
> I will not pass gas where little ones are, no matter how near or how far.
> I will not pass gas in your face, because the gas I pass is worse than mace.[11]

Only after listeners are either laughing or totally grossed out by the image of passing gas are they told that the limerick refers to secondhand smoke—too late to miss the point. It's a message most people would tune out had it not been for the use of humor with a twist.

German psychologist Dieter Frey surveyed all the pertinent research on selective exposure and concluded that even when we know we're going to hear discrepant ideas, the avoidance mechanism doesn't kick in if we don't regard the dissonant information as a threat.[12] Warm personal relationships are probably the best guarantee that we'll consider ideas that would otherwise seem threatening.

Hypothesis 2: Postdecision Dissonance Creates a Need for Reassurance

Postdecision dissonance
Strong doubts experienced after making an important, close-call decision that is difficult to reverse.

According to Festinger, close-call decisions can generate huge amounts of internal tension after the decision has been made. Three conditions heighten *postdecision dissonance:* (1) the more important the issue, (2) the longer an individual delays in choosing between two equally attractive options, and (3) the greater the difficulty involved in reversing the decision once it's been made. To the extent that these conditions are present, the person will agonize over whether he or she made the right choice.[13] Sometimes referred to as "morning-after-the-night-before" regrets, the misgivings or second thoughts that plague us after a tough choice motivate us to seek reassuring information and social support for our decision.

A classic example of postdecision dissonance is the mental turmoil a person experiences after signing a contract to buy a new car. The cost is high, there are many competing models from which to choose, and the down payment commits the customer to go through with the purchase. It's not unusual to find a customer in the library, poring over the pages of the *Consumer Reports* auto issue *after* placing an order. The buyer is seeking information that confirms the decision already made and quiets nagging doubts.

The toughest decision a smoker makes is whether or not to stop smoking—cold turkey. It's an agonizing decision, and one often delayed. Many who recover from multiple addictions testify that quitting smoking is harder than giving up booze. Just as many alcoholics turn to Alcoholics Anonymous for social support, people who try to give up tobacco often need at least one friend, family member, romantic partner, or co-worker who's also going through the pangs of withdrawal. They can remind each other that it's worth the effort.

The decision to stop smoking doesn't fulfill Festinger's third condition of a once-and-for-all, no-going-back, final choice. One can always go back to smoking. In fact, those who swear off cigarettes typically have a few lapses, and total relapses are common. Encouragement and social support are necessary to tamp down the doubts and fears that follow this tough decision.

Smokers who consciously decide *not* to quit face similar qualms and anxieties. They are bombarded with messages telling them they are putting their health at risk. People who care for them deeply are urging them to stop, and they may be surrounded by nonsmokers who look down on them because they don't. I described in Chapter 3 the camaraderie that Alan DeSantis found among regular customers at a Kentucky cigar shop. Just as smoke from cigars drives some folks away, DeSantis concludes that the friendship and collective rationalization of those who smoke cigars together hold postdecision dissonance at bay. He also sees *Cigar Aficionado* as serving the same function. He writes that although the magazine professes to simply celebrate the good life, it actually serves "to relieve the cognitive dissonance associated with the consumption of a potentially dangerous product by adding cognitions, trivializing dissonant information, selectively exposing readers to pro-smoking information, and creating a social support network of fellow cigar smokers."[14]

Hypothesis 3: Minimal Justification for Action Induces a Shift in Attitude

Suppose someone wanted to persuade an ex-smoker who is dying of lung cancer to stop publicly bashing the tobacco industry and to respect cigarette companies' right to market their product. That is one of the assignments given to Nick Naylor, the chief spokesman for tobacco companies in the movie *Thank You for Smoking*. His job is to convince "Big Tobacco's" former advertising icon—the Marlboro Man—to switch from outspoken critic to silent partner. Before cognitive dissonance theory, conventional wisdom would have suggested that Naylor work first to change the bitter man's *attitude* toward the industry. If he could convince the cowboy that the cigarette companies are well-intentioned, then the man would change his communication *behavior*. It seemed natural to think of attitude and behavior as the beginning and end of a cause-and-effect sequence.

Attitude → Behavior

Minimal justification hypothesis
A claim that the best way to stimulate an attitude change in others is to offer just enough incentive to elicit counterattitudinal behavior.

But Festinger's *minimal justification hypothesis* reversed that sequence. That hypothesis suggests that the best way for Naylor to change the Marlboro Man's attitude toward his former employers is to get him to quit speaking out against them.

Behavior → Attitude

Festinger attached one important condition, however. Instead of giving the cowboy massive incentives to abandon his public critique ($100,000 in cash, lifetime health care for his wife, or a threat to harm his kids), Naylor should offer the minimum enticement necessary to induce him to quietly step off his soap box. He concluded:

> Thus if one wanted to obtain private change in addition to mere public compliance, the best way to do this would be to offer just enough reward or punishment to elicit overt compliance.[15]

Naylor does it the old-fashioned way by throwing lots of money at him. He goes to the Marlboro Man's rundown ranch with a briefcase filled with bundles of hundred-dollar bills, which he pours out on the floor. He labels the money a gift rather than a bribe, but makes it clear that the cowboy can't keep the money if he continues to denounce the tobacco companies. As it turns out, the offer is more than enough because the dying man is worried about how his family will manage after he's gone. So the Marlboro Man takes both the money and a vow of silence, but remains antagonistic toward his former employers. *Compliance* without inner conviction. Of course for Naylor, that was enough.

There was, however, a brief moment in their discussion that suggests the potential of a minimal justification strategy. When the Marlboro Man looked longingly at the cash, he wondered out loud if he might keep half of the money and still denounce the tobacco companies. His question reveals that somewhere between 50 percent and 100 percent of the cash on the floor there's a tipping point where the cowboy becomes willing to be bought off. Festinger predicted that if Naylor were to offer that "just-enough" amount, not only would the Marlboro Man alter his communication behavior, but the dissonance he would feel would cause him to be less angry at the cigarette companies. Festinger's startling $1/$20 experiment shows how this might work.

Compliance
Public conformity to another's expectation without necessarily having a private conviction that matches the behavior.

A CLASSIC EXPERIMENT: "WOULD I LIE FOR A DOLLAR?"

There is nothing particularly radical about Festinger's first two hypotheses. His selective exposure prediction nicely explains why political rallies attract the party faithful and why the audience for religious radio and television tends to be made up of committed believers. As for postdecision dissonance, all of us have tried to convince ourselves that we've made the right choice after facing a close-call decision. But Festinger's minimal justification hypothesis is counterintuitive. Will a small incentive to act really induce a corresponding attitude change when heaping on the benefits won't? Festinger's famous $1/$20 experiment supported his claim that it will.

Festinger and James Carlsmith recruited Stanford University men to participate in a psychological study supposedly investigating industrial relations.[16] As each man arrived at the lab, he was assigned the boring and repetitive task of sorting a large batch of spools into sets of 12 and turning square pegs a quarter turn to the right. The procedure was designed to be both monotonous and tiring. At the end of an hour the experimenter approached the subject and made a request. He claimed that a student assistant had failed to show up and that he needed someone to fill in by telling a potential female subject in the waiting room how much fun the experiment was. Dissonance researchers call this *counterattitudinal advocacy*. We'd call it lying.

Counterattitudinal advocacy
Publicly urging others to believe or do something that is opposed to what the advocate actually believes.

Some of the men were promised $20 to express enthusiasm about the task; others were offered only $1. It is comforting to know that six of the men refused to take part in the deception, but most students tried to recruit the young woman. The gist of the typical conversation was similar for both payment conditions:

SHE: "I heard it was boring."

HE: "Oh no, it's really quite fun."

What differed were privately expressed attitudes after the study was over. Students who lied for $20 later confessed that they thought the task of sorting spools was dull. Those who lied for $1 maintained that it was much more enjoyable. (Festinger and Carlsmith practiced their own form of deception in the study— subjects never received the promised money.)

By now you should have a pretty good idea of how Festinger analyzed the results. He noted that $20 was a huge sum of money (worth more than $100 in today's economy). If a student felt qualms about telling a "white lie," the cash was a ready justification. Thus, the student felt little or no tension between his action and his attitude. But the men who lied for a dollar had lots of cognitive work to do. The logical inconsistency of saying a boring task was interesting had to be explained away through an internal dialogue:

> I'm a Stanford man. Am I the kind of guy who would lie for a dollar? No way. Actually, what I told the girl was true. The experiment was a lot of fun.

Festinger said that $1 was just barely enough to induce compliance to the experimenter's request, and so the students had to create another justification. They changed their attitudes toward the task to bring it into line with their behavior.

THREE STATE-OF-THE-ART REVISIONS: THE CAUSE AND EFFECT OF DISSONANCE

The $1/$20 study has been replicated and modified many times in an effort to figure out why minimal incentives for inconsistent behavior cause a change in attitude when large rewards don't. Dissonance researchers also seek to close off loopholes that would admit other explanations for the attitude change that follows induced compliance. Based on hundreds of experimental studies, most persuasion researchers today subscribe to one of three revisions of Festinger's original theory. In order to understand each of the options described in the following sections, it will help if you picture the overall dissonance arousal and reduction process as Festinger imagined it. Figure 16–1 shows that four-step sequence.

1. Self-Consistency: The Rationalizing Animal

University of California social psychologist Elliot Aronson was attracted to cognitive dissonance theory because of Festinger's startling minimal justification prediction, but he quickly determined that the theory in its original form had some "conceptual fuzziness." Specifically, it failed to state the conditions under which a person would definitely experience dissonance, the A→B link in Figure 16–1. For example, when early disciples of Festinger were uncertain what the theory predicted, their advice to each other was, "If you want to be sure, ask Leon."

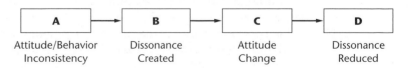

FIGURE 16–1   Festinger's Process Model of Cognitive Dissonance
Based on Festinger, *Cognitive Dissonance Theory*

Aronson concluded that the issue isn't *logical* inconsistency—as Festinger maintained—but *psychological* inconsistency. We aren't rational animals; we are rationalizing animals who want to appear reasonable to ourselves. Aronson interprets the $1/$20 experiment as a study of self-esteem maintenance. "If dissonance exists, it is because the individual's behavior is inconsistent with his self-concept."[17] The Stanford men were in a bind because they regarded themselves as decent, truthful human beings. In fact, the higher their self-esteem, the more dissonance they would feel when they told the waiting woman that the study was fun. Conversely, if they had seen themselves as liars, cheats, or jerks, they would have felt no tension. As Aronson puts it, "If a person conceives of himself as a 'schnook,' he will be expected to behave like a 'schnook.'"[18]

Following the lead of Festinger's $1/$20 experiment, most research on his minimum justification hypothesis involves public counterattitudinal advocacy. University of Nebraska social psychologist Lynn Kahle measured college students' self-esteem and then asked them to write a brief essay advocating cigarette smoking, which they thought would be read to junior high students. Similar to Festinger, she offered participants either $2 or $10 for writing the essays. If Aronson's version of dissonance theory is right, college students who received the minimal justification of $2 for fabricating a pro-smoking essay and who also possessed high self-esteem to protect should have experienced the most dissonance at point B in Figure 16–1. And when their attitude change toward smoking was measured at point C, they should have been more favorable toward the idea of kids smoking. That's what Kahle found. She concludes that "the interaction between Esteem and Pay follows directly from Aronson's refinement of dissonance theory that dissonance results from a discrepancy between cognitions about self and cognitions about behavior."[19]

According to Aronson, the amount of dissonance a person can experience is directly proportional to the effort he or she has invested in the behavior. Since boot camp in the Marines is tougher than basic training in the Army, Aronson would expect a Marine recruit to feel greater tension if he or she violated the norms of the Corps. The harder it is to get into a group, the more one values membership. Conversely, it's rare for a football player to brag that his coach sets no training rules or schedules light workouts.

Even the reactions of Aesop's fox make sense in light of the animal's low investment of energy. Aronson points out that the fox wouldn't think the grapes were sour if he had spent the whole afternoon jumping to get them. Attitudes follow behavior when the investment of effort is high.

2. Personal Responsibility for Bad Outcomes (the New Look)

Princeton psychologist Joel Cooper agrees with Aronson that logical inconsistency at point A in Figure 16–1 doesn't automatically create dissonance at point B. Yet he's not convinced that Aronson's concern for self-consistency captures the real cause of the acute mental discomfort. In his "new-look" model of cognitive dissonance, Cooper argues that it's the knowledge that one's actions have unnecessarily hurt another person that generates dissonance. For example, in the minimal justification condition of the $1/$20 experiment, the Stanford man willingly "duped a fellow student to look forward to an exciting experience" while knowing "full well that the waiting participant was in for an immense letdown."[20]

DILBERT © Scott Adams/Dist. by United Feature Syndicate, Inc.

Cooper concludes that dissonance is "a state of arousal caused by behaving in such a way as to feel personally responsible for bringing about an aversive event."[21] Note that the acceptance of personal *responsibility* requires that the person know ahead of time that his or her action will have negative consequences for someone else and yet still choose to do the dirty deed. The reactions of participants in minimal justification experiments show that they often feel bad about the potential effects of their messages.

Purdue University social psychologists Richard Heslin and Michael Amo also used a pro-smoking message prepared for junior high kids, but in this case the setup was more involving and potentially more harmful. Students in college public speaking classes were induced to deliver impromptu speeches in which they told uninformed and uncommitted seventh grade kids that smoking pot wouldn't hurt them. The speakers saw the speech after they gave it and were reminded that they'd be introduced as actually having pro-marijuana sentiments. The speakers were quite aware that their message might harm kids. One speaker blurted out, "What would my church say if they knew I was doing this?" Another pleaded, "Please don't use my speech. I don't want the course credit; just don't use my speech!"[22] Yet they changed their attitude in the direction of their advocacy. As Heslin and Amo note, their fears and attitude shift also give credence to Aronson's self-consistency interpretation of dissonance.

3. Self-Affirmation to Dissipate Dissonance

While the revisions offered by Aronson (self-consistency) and Cooper (new look) address dissonance *creation* at the front end of Festinger's model, Stanford psychologist Claude Steele's self-affirmation approach speaks to the question of dissonance *reduction* at the back end of the model—point D of Figure 16–1. Unlike those first two revisions, Steele doesn't assume that dissonance always drives people to justify their actions by changing their attitudes. He thinks that some fortunate people can call up a host of positive thoughts about themselves that will blot out a concern for restoring consistency. If he's right, high self-esteem is a resource for dissonance reduction.

According to Steele, most people are greatly motivated to maintain an overall self-image of moral and adaptive adequacy. For a participant in the $1/$20 experiment, there's no question that lying to a fellow student makes it harder to preserve that favorable self-concept. But if the guy ignores the ethical slip and focuses instead on his good grades, athletic ability, social skills, and helpfulness to friends who are hurting, the dissonance will be only a blip on the radar screen of his mind and will quickly fade away. Thus, Steele believes that denial, forgetfulness, and trivialization of the incident are alternatives to attitude change, but only for the person who already has high self-esteem.

At the start of his presidential campaign, Senator Barack Obama announced on *The Late Show with David Letterman* that he'd quit smoking. If he later relapses—as has happened before—the potential for cognitive dissonance could be great. But according to Steele's self-affirmation approach, Obama might remind himself of his esteem-raising qualities, which include "gifted orator, award winning author, and proven intellect who was the first black president of the *Harvard Law Review*."[23] In light of his charismatic personality and these accomplishments, Obama might regard relapse as a mere blip rather than a major contradiction. Voters, however, might experience dissonance.

Aronson, Cooper, and Steele each offer their respective revisions as more accurate accounts of what goes on in people's heads than Festinger's original theory provided. But we don't have to pick one and trash the others. Self-consistency, personal responsibility for bad outcomes, and self-affirmation aren't mutually exclusive explanations. As Cooper suggests, "They each describe a distinct and important piece of the overall dissonance process and, in doing so, make a unique contribution to our understanding of how cognitions about the self mediate cognitive dissonance and arousal and reduction."[24]

THEORY INTO PRACTICE: PERSUASION THROUGH DISSONANCE

I've placed this chapter in the section on interpersonal influence because Festinger and his followers focus on attitude change as an end product of dissonance. Suppose you know someone named Sam who holds an opinion that you're convinced is harmful or wrong. What practical advice does the theory offer that might help you alter Sam's conviction?

For openers, don't promise lavish benefits if Sam abandons that attitude or warn of dire consequences if he doesn't. A massive reward-punishment strategy may gain behavioral compliance, but the hard sell seldom wins the heart or mind of the person who is bribed or pressured. Instead, work to develop a friendly relationship with Sam. That way your own position will tend to bypass the *selective exposure* screen that Sam and the rest of us put up to avoid threatening ideas. And if Sam eventually adopts your viewpoint, an ongoing bond means that you'll be around to offer reassurance when *postdecision dissonance* kicks in.

To be an effective agent of change, you should offer just enough encouragement (*minimal justification*) for Sam to try out novel behavior that departs from old ways of thinking. Avoid making an offer that Sam can't refuse. As long as *counterattitudinal actions* are freely chosen and publicly taken, people are more likely to adopt beliefs that support what they've done. The greater the effort involved in acting this way, the greater the chance that their attitudes will change to match their actions.

Finally, as you seek to *induce compliance,* try to get Sam to count the cost of doing what you want and to grasp the potential downside of that behavior for others *(personal responsibility for negative outcomes).* That kind of understanding will increase the probability that Sam's attitude will shift to be consistent with his or her action. And if things turn out sour, your relationship won't.

CRITIQUE: DISSONANCE OVER DISSONANCE

When Festinger died in 1989, his obituary in *American Psychologist* testified to the impact of his work:

> Like Dostoyevski and like Picasso, Festinger set in motion a *style* of research and theory in the social sciences that is now the common property of all creative workers in the field. . . . Leon is to social psychology what Freud is to clinical psychology and Piaget to developmental psychology.[25]

I could have easily used Festinger as the exemplar of the *socio-psychological tradition* when I mapped out seven traditions in the field of communication theory (see Chapter 4). And as the *Dilbert* cartoon in this chapter suggests, cognitive dissonance is one of the few theories in this book that has achieved name recognition within popular culture. Yet despite this wide influence, Festinger's original theory and its contemporary revisions contain a serious flaw. Like my boyhood friend's never-miss shot in his driveway basketball court (see Chapter 3), there is no way the theory can be proved wrong.

Look again at the four stages of the dissonance process diagram in Figure 16–1. Almost all of the creative efforts of dissonance researchers have been aimed at inducing counterattitudinal advocacy at point A—getting people to say something in public that is inconsistent with what they believe in private. When researchers find an attitude shift at point C, they automatically *assume* that dissonance was built up at point B and is gone by point D. They don't test to see whether it's actually there.

Festinger never specified a reliable way to detect the degree of dissonance a person experiences, if any. Psychologist Patricia Devine and her University of Wisconsin–Madison colleagues refer to such an instrument as a *dissonance thermometer.* They applaud researchers' occasional attempts to gauge the *arousal* component of dissonance through physiological measures such as galvanic skin response. (When our drive state increases, we have sweaty palms.) But they are even more encouraged at the possibility of assessing the *psychological discomfort* component of dissonance by means of a self-report measure of affect. Until some kind of dissonance thermometer is a standard part of dissonance research, we will never know if the distressing mental state is for real.

Dissonance thermometer A hypothetical, reliable gauge of the dissonance a person feels as a result of inconsistency.

Cornell University psychologist Daryl Bem doesn't think it is. He agrees that attitudes change when people act counter to their beliefs with minimal justification, but he claims that *self-perception* is a much simpler explanation than cognitive dissonance. He believes we judge our internal dispositions the same way others do—by observing our behavior.

Bem ran his own $1/$20 study to test his alternative explanation.[26] People heard a recording of a Stanford man's enthusiastic account of the spool-sorting, peg-turning task. Some listeners were told he received $1 for recruiting the female subject. Since he had little obvious reason to lie, they assumed that he really liked the task. Other listeners were told that the man received $20 to

Self-perception theory
The claim that we determine our attitudes the same way that outside observers do—by observing our behavior; an alternative to cognitive dissonance theory.

recruit the woman. These folks assumed that the man was bored with the task and was lying to get the money. Bem's subjects didn't speculate about what was going on inside the Stanford man's head. They simply judged his attitude by looking at what he did under the circumstances. If people don't need an understanding of cognitive dissonance to forecast how the men would react, Bem asks, why should social scientists? Bem is convinced that cognitive dissonance theory is like the mousetrap pictured on page 31—much too convoluted. He opts for simplicity.

Advocates of cognitive dissonance in the field of communication counter that nothing about mental processes is simple. When we deal with what goes on behind the eyes, we should expect and appreciate complexity. Festinger's theory has energized scientifically oriented communication scholars for 50 years. I feel no dissonance for including cognitive dissonance theory in this text.

QUESTIONS TO SHARPEN YOUR FOCUS

1. Cognitive dissonance is a *distressing mental state.* When did you last experience this *aversive drive?* Why might you have trouble answering that question?

2. The results of Festinger's famous *$1/$20 experiment* can be explained in a number of different ways. Which explanation do you find most satisfying?

3. Suppose you want your friends to change their sexist attitudes. What advice does the *minimal justification hypothesis* offer?

4. I see cognitive dissonance theory as a "never-miss shot." What would it take to make the theory *testable?*

A SECOND LOOK

Recommended resource: Joel Cooper, Robert Mirabile, and Steven Scher, "Actions and Attitudes: The Theory of Cognitive Dissonance," in *Persuasion: Psychological Insights and Perspectives,* 2nd ed., Timothy Brock and Melanie Green (eds.), Sage, Thousand Oaks, CA, 2005, pp. 63–79.

Original statement: Leon Festinger, *A Theory of Cognitive Dissonance,* Stanford University, Stanford, CA, 1957.

State of the art: Eddie Harmon-Jones and Judson Mills (eds.), *Cognitive Dissonance: Progress on a Pivotal Theory in Social Psychology,* American Psychological Association, Washington, DC, 1999.

Selective exposure: Eva Jones, Stefan Schulz-Hardt, Dieter Frey, and Norman Thelen, "Confirmation Bias in Sequential Information Search after Preliminary Decisions: An Expansion of Dissonance Theoretical Research on Selective Exposure to Information," *Journal of Personality and Social Psychology,* Vol. 80, 2001, pp. 557–571.

Postdecision dissonance: Dave D'Alessio and Mike Allen, "Selective Exposure and Dissonance after Decisions," *Psychological Reports,* Vol. 91, 2002, pp. 527–532.

$1/$20 experiment: Leon Festinger and James Carlsmith, "Cognitive Consequences of Forced Compliance," *Journal of Abnormal and Social Psychology,* Vol. 58, 1959, pp. 203–210.

Self-consistency revision: Ruth Thibodeau and Elliot Aronson, "Taking a Closer Look: Reasserting the Role of the Self-Concept in Dissonance Theory," *Personality and Social Psychology Bulletin,* Vol. 18, 1992, pp. 591–602.

New-look revision: Joel Cooper and Russell Fazio, "A New Look at Dissonance Theory," in *Advances in Experimental Social Psychology,* Vol. 17, Leonard Berkowitz (ed.), Academic Press, Orlando, FL, 1984, pp. 229–262.

Self-affirmation revision: Claude Steele, "The Psychology of Self-Affirmation: Sustaining the Integrity of the Self," in *Advances in Experimental Social Psychology,* Vol. 21, Leonard Berkowitz (ed.), Lawrence Erlbaum, Hillsdale, NJ, 1988, pp. 261–302.

Critique: Daryl Bem, "Self-Perception: An Alternative Interpretation of Cognitive Dissonance Phenomena," *Psychological Review,* Vol. 74, 1967, pp. 183–200.

Critique: Daniel O'Keefe, "Cognitive Dissonance Theory," in *Persuasion: Theory and Research,* 2nd ed., Sage, Thousand Oaks, CA, 2002, pp. 77–100.

Experiencing cognitive dissonance may require a strong need for esteem.
To access a chapter on Abraham Maslow's hierarchy of needs that
appeared in a previous edition, click on Theory Archive at
www.afirstlook.com.

DIVISION THREE

Group and Public Communication

A cynic once said that a camel is a horse put together by a committee. Although many people share this pessimistic view, the results of research in business, education, and government show that problem-solving groups often come up with solutions that are superior to anything thought of by individual members. Referred to as *synergy*, the recurrent finding that the group product is greater than the sum of its parts has stimulated efforts to explain the typical process of group decision making.

Sixty years ago, Robert Bales of Harvard University developed a method of discussion analysis that distinguishes 12 types of verbal behavior.[1] A typical committee meeting requires the classification of 10–15 comments a minute. Figure DM–1 shows Bales' list of categories and some of the interrelationships he built into his system of observation.

The middle area of Bales' system (sections B and C) is for statements that focus on accomplishing the group task. The outer areas (sections A and D) are for comments that reflect relationships within the group. By coding everything a person says, an observer using Bales' categories is able to develop a profile of preferred interaction style for each group member. The results confirm that some people concentrate on getting the job done, while others are much more concerned with social-emotional issues. Task-oriented individuals are the pistons that drive the group machine. Relationship-oriented members are the lubricant that prevents excessive friction from destroying the group. Good groups require both kinds of people.

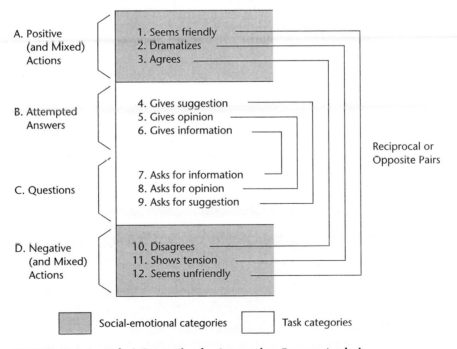

FIGURE DM–1   Bales' Categories for Interaction Process Analysis
From Bales, *Personality and Interpersonal Behavior*

You can see in Figure DM–1 that Bales' 12 categories are divided into 6 reciprocally matched pairs. *Asks for information* is balanced by *gives information*. *Seems friendly* is juxtaposed with *seems unfriendly*. The only pair that doesn't present an obvious mirror image is *dramatizes–shows tension*. As you may recall from the discussion of Bormann's symbolic convergence theory in Chapter 3, Bales originally called category 2 *relieves tension*. He found, however, that most tension-reducing comments had a storytelling or dramatic quality that served to get the group moving when it was stuck, and so he decided that the term *dramatizes* was a more accurate label.

Bales discovered that good groups maintain a rough balance among each of the six pairs. For example, a group's initial discussion is more productive when people hear answers (category 6) to their questions about the nature of their task (category 7). But the group process stalls if members seek facts that no one has, or if everyone volunteers information that nobody wants.

Contrary to those who would like to eliminate all group conflict, Bales found that a 2:1 ratio of positive to negative comments is optimum for the social-emotional category pairs shown in Figure DM–1 (1 and 12, 2 and 11, 3 and 10). Although a high proportion of cutting remarks could tear a group apart, a healthy dose of voiced skepticism is necessary to reach a quality decision. Twenty years after Bales introduced his interaction categories, Harvard psychologist Irving Janis popularized the term *groupthink*. It's a label for inferior decision making that occurs when group members have an inordinate desire for group harmony. When caught up in groupthink, members value unity so much that they refuse to voice doubts, even when they see the group headed in a dangerous direction.[2]

Bales' emphasis on group equilibrium, or balance, reflects his systems approach to group decision making. You've already had some exposure to systems thinking through Shannon and Weaver's information theory and Watzlawick's interactional view that regards the family as a system (see Chapters 4 and 13). Bales' version suggests that decision-making groups face problems posed by task requirements, social-emotional needs, and environmental factors, and he regarded the process of communication as the chief method by which groups satisfy these requirements.

"We can't come to an agreement about how to fix your car, Mr. Simons. Sometimes that's the way things happen in a democracy."

Systems theorists offer the following general model of group decision making:

Input → Process → Output

For example, we could think of *information* as input, *talk* as process, and *decisions* as output.[3] This model can help us locate the work of many communication theorists who are concerned with group decision making. Bales' interaction analysis addresses the input-process connection. So does Bormann's *symbolic interaction theory*. Yet neither Bales nor Bormann tracks the specific effects of member discussion on the quality of a group's final decision. The first theory in this section deals with the link between process and output.

Chapter 17 presents Randy Hirokawa and Dennis Gouran's *functional perspective*. Building on the task concerns of Bales, these theorists focus on the specific function communication plays in reaching a quality group judgment. Their ultimate goal is to offer practical advice on how participants can act to ensure better group decisions.

Scott Poole's *adaptive structuration theory* is concerned with the entire input-process-output group decision-making system. Adapting sociologist Anthony Giddens' concept of structuration, Poole says that group members use rules and resources (input) in interaction (process) to produce and reproduce group decisions (output). The intriguing feature of structuration is that the decision not only is *affected by* the input of the group but also bounces back and *affects* those same rules and resources. Chapter 18 explains these concepts in detail.

Psychologists who study group process often focus on member composition. These analysts tend to assume that the personality and opinion of participants will automatically determine the ultimate outcome. The communication theorists featured in this section disagree. They believe that communication is neither a waste of time nor a corrosive agent that disfigures an elegant solution. Both theories carve a space for the quiet, powerless, or marginalized members of groups to speak out in order that the group might produce better decisions. If we suspect that a camel is a horse put together by a committee, we should remember that the ungainly looking beast turns out to be an ideal solution for a group of desert nomads.

To access chapters on two group decision theories that
appeared in previous editions—Irving Janis' groupthink and B. Aubrey Fisher's
interact system model of decision emergence—click on theory Archive at
www.afirstlook.com.

Functional Perspective on Group Decision Making

of Randy Hirokawa & Dennis Gouran

Have you ever wondered how your communication professors got their jobs? Over a 15-month period, I served on four separate departmental search committees appointed to select final candidates for positions in rhetoric, theater, journalism, and broadcast production. Of course, the whole department expected each group to come up with top-notch candidates, and consistent with a discipline that values rational discourse, they likely assumed that we'd make our high-quality decisions after systematic and reasoned discussion.

As the committee meetings piled up, however, I wondered if the time and energy we put into discussing the applicants might not be wasted effort. Given the mix of communication interests, academic knowledge, and personal prejudices that committee members brought to the table, weren't our final choices likely to be made on political rather than rational grounds? Even if we could be objective, I feared that our free-for-all debate over candidates would so cloud our judgment that we'd end up making second-rate choices.

Nagging doubts about the role of group discussion are reflected and magnified in oft-heard criticisms that cynical committee members voice when they talk in the corridor after a meeting:[1]

"If you want something done, do it yourself."

"Too many cooks spoil the broth."

"A committee is a group that keeps minutes and wastes hours."

"Committees lure fresh ideas down a cul-de-sac and quietly strangle them."

Randy Hirokawa (dean of liberal arts, University of Hawaii at Hilo) and Dennis Gouran (professor of communication, Pennsylvania State University) believe that these pessimistic views are unwarranted. Assuming that group members care about the issue, are reasonably intelligent, and face a challenging task that calls for more facts, new ideas, or clear thinking, Hirokawa and Gouran are convinced that group interaction has a positive effect on the final decision. Hirokawa speaks of *quality* solutions.[2] Gouran refers to decisions that are *appropriate*.[3] Both scholars regard talk as the social tool that helps groups reach better conclusions than they otherwise might. As the Hebrew proverb suggests, "Without counsel plans go wrong, but with many advisers they succeed."[4]

Functional perspective
A prescriptive approach that describes and predicts task-group performance when four communication functions are fulfilled.

The *functional perspective* described in this chapter illustrates the wisdom of joint interaction. Gouran laid the groundwork for the theory with his early writing on group decision making. Hirokawa developed the core principles of the theory during his graduate studies, and today his research tests and refines this theory. On the chance that you might be intrigued by a behind-the-scenes look at the faculty hiring process, I'll draw on my search committee experience to illustrate Hirokawa and Gouran's functional perspective.

FOUR FUNCTIONS OF EFFECTIVE DECISION MAKING

Consistent with Bales and other pioneer researchers, Hirokawa and Gouran draw an analogy between small groups and biological systems. Complex living organisms must satisfy a number of functions, such as respiration, circulation, digestion, and elimination of bodily waste, if they are to survive and thrive in an ever-changing environment. In like manner, Hirokawa and Gouran see the group decision-making process as needing to fulfill four task requirements if members are to reach a high-quality solution. Hirokawa and Gouran refer to these conditions as *requisite functions* of effective decision making—thus the "functional perspective" label.[5] The four functions are (1) problem analysis, (2) goal setting, (3) identification of alternatives, and (4) evaluation of positive and negative consequences.

Requisite functions
Requirements for positive group outcome; problem analysis, goal setting, identification of alternatives, and evaluation of pluses and minuses for each.

1. Analysis of the Problem

Is something going on that requires improvement or change? To answer that question, group members must take a realistic look at current conditions. Defenders of the status quo are fond of saying, "If it ain't broke, don't fix it." But as Hirokawa warns, any misunderstanding of the situation tends to be compounded when the members make their final decision. He also notes that the clearest example of faulty analysis is a failure to recognize a potential threat when one really exists.[6] After people acknowledge a need to be addressed, they still must figure out the nature, extent, and probable cause(s) of the problem that confronts the group.

Problem analysis
Determining the nature, extent, and cause(s) of the problem facing the group.

Most communication departments have little difficulty analyzing the situation when a faculty member resigns or retires—departments move quickly to initiate a search for a new hire. To the extent that an opening provides the opportunity to shore up a weak area or enhance the reputation of an already recognized concentration, a vacancy is a nice problem to have. My department's searches for a rhetorician, a theater director, and a broadcast production person presented no apparent difficulties. In each case, we formed a search committee, drafted a position description, published it throughout the profession, and checked with friends on other campuses to see who might be interested.

The journalism search was another matter. This newly created position had been on the books for two years, but none of us seemed in a hurry to fill it. We were holding out for one of two nationally recognized reporters who had expressed interest in coming to Wheaton. But the timing wasn't right. We did, however, have confidence that the students were well served by a part-time instructor. Although he had few academic credentials, he was a marvelous teacher and mentor. No problem, right? Then, for the first time, someone on our rather dormant committee asked whether we'd be able to keep the full-time faculty line if we didn't fill it for another year. She was addressing the function of problem analysis, and her question forced us to take a realistic look at the situation. When we consulted the dean, he said, in effect, "Use it or lose it." We quickly switched into an active search mode.

2. Goal Setting

Goal setting
Establishing criteria by which to judge proposed solutions.

Because group members need to be clear on what they are trying to accomplish, Hirokawa and Gouran regard discussion of goals and objectives as the second requisite function of decision making. A group needs to establish criteria by which to judge proposed solutions. If the group fails to satisfy this task requirement, it's likely that the decision will be driven by politics rather than reason.[7]

Faculty members involved in our search for a rhetorician agreed unanimously that a successful candidate should possess an earned doctorate, have taught at the college level for at least five years, and be a scholar publishing actively in communication journals. Because our school is first and foremost a teaching institution, we also insisted that finalists demonstrate their ability to engage our students in a live classroom situation. Finally, consistent with Wheaton's worldview that all truth is God's truth, we informed applicants that we were looking for a scholar with a faith commitment who was unafraid to pursue knowledge from a liberal arts perspective. This rather exacting set of standards reduced our pool of applicants, but the criteria gave us increased confidence in our final decision.

3. Identification of Alternatives

Identification of alternatives
Generation of options to sufficiently solve the problem.

Hirokawa and Gouran stress the importance of marshaling a number of alternative solutions from which group members can choose:

> If no one calls attention to the need for generating as many alternatives as is realistically possible, then relatively few may be introduced, and the corresponding possibility of finding the acceptable answer will be low.[8]

Limited choice was never an issue in our search for a drama coach. More than 150 candidates applied for the opening. In the initial stage, all we had to do was open the envelopes. The broadcast production search was a different story, however. We wanted a person with industry experience, a doctorate or a master of fine arts degree, and equal abilities to teach radio *and* television production. Numerous audio technicians with radio experience applied for the post, but only a few had the advanced degree we required. And none of these applicants had a background in video production. After three months we had no viable alternatives.

At that point, one of our members reminded us that we were a *search* committee and suggested that we get off our butts and start beating the bushes for candidates who met our criteria. So we held a brainstorming session, where everyone kicked in ideas on ways to extend the search. As a result, phone, fax,

"Gentlemen, the fact that all my horses and all my men couldn't put Humpty together again simply proves to me that I must have <u>more</u> horses and <u>more</u> men."

and email messages tapped into a network of production houses, station managers, deans, and college presidents. By fulfilling the functional requirement of generating relevant alternatives, the group discovered two candidates who not only met our basic criteria, but also brought desired ethnic diversity to our department.

4. Evaluation of Positive and Negative Characteristics

After a group has identified alternative solutions, the participants must take care to test the relative merits of each option against the criteria they believe are important. This point-by-point comparison doesn't take place automatically. Hirokawa and Gouran warn that groups get sloppy and often need one member to remind the others to consider both the positive and negative features of each alternative.

As a case in point, the search committee was tremendously impressed with the credentials, talent, and personality of Mark, the leading candidate for the position of theater director. He brought extensive professional experience on the

Evaluation of positive and negative characteristics
Testing the relative merits of each option against the criteria selected; weighing the benefits and costs.

stage, had directed a well-received play on campus as guest director the year before, and showed an interpersonal warmth that connected with students and faculty alike. All of our drama majors signed a petition urging that we select him for the position. It took our committee "realist" to point out that Mark had never worked in an academic setting. If he came, we shouldn't underestimate the difficulty this creative artist would have adapting to the routine chores of grading, academic advising, attending committee meetings, and filling out reports.

We almost made the opposite error in another search. An otherwise strong applicant had not received tenure at his current school, and the circumstances surrounding that denial seemed to dominate our discussion to the exclusion of his many strengths. The same pragmatic committee member urged us to spend time examining the applicant's positive characteristics, which far outweighed the negative.

Hirokawa notes that some group tasks have a *positive bias* in that spotting the favorable characteristics of alternative choices is more important than identifying negative qualities.[9] For example, the recommendation forms for "Teacher of the Year" at my school accentuate the positive. A rating of "good enough" is not good enough to get the award. Hirokawa says that other group tasks have a *negative bias*—the unattractive characteristics of candidates carry more weight than do the positive attributes. Tenure committee deliberations at colleges where there's a premium on teaching rather than research tend to be more influenced by instructors' shortcomings. That's because committee members are loath to condemn future generations of students to mediocre teachers who've been granted job security for life.

PRIORITIZING THE FUNCTIONS

The word *prioritizing* could mean addressing the four requisite functions in a logical progression. Or it could refer to deciding which one is most important. In much of their writing, Hirokawa and Gouran maintain that both are nonissues. The theorists repeatedly state that all four functions need to be accomplished to maximize the probability of a high-quality decision, but that no single function is inherently more central than the others.[10] Likewise, no one group agenda or plan of attack seems to get the job done better. As long as the group ends up dealing with all four functions, the route its members take doesn't appear to make much difference. Hirokawa does add, however, that groups that successfully resolve particularly tough problems often take a common decision-making path.[11]

Figure 17–1 portrays the path that seems to offer a natural problem-solving progression. Groups start with problem analysis, then deal with goal setting and identifying alternatives, and end by evaluating the positive and negative characteristics of each alternative before making the final choice. This decision-making flow parallels the advice I heard on National Public Radio's *Car Talk*. Asked how car owners should handle close-call decisions on auto repair, mechanics Tom and Ray Magliozzi ("Click and Clack, the Tappet Brothers") gave a street-smart answer that ran something like this:

> First, figure out what's broke. Then, make up your mind how good you want to fix it. Or before that ask your mechanic to list the choices you've got. Either way, you gotta do both. Finally, weigh the bang-for-the-buck that each job gives. Then decide.

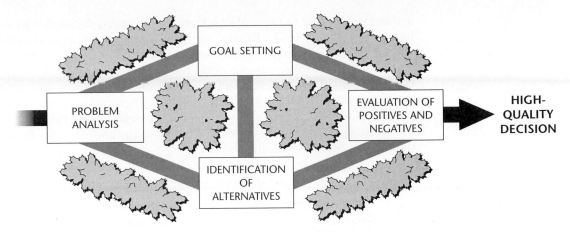

FIGURE 17–1   An Effective Decision-Making Path from a Functional Perspective

Earlier this decade, Hirokawa and University of Redlands business professor Marc Orlitzky conducted a meta-analysis of 60 empirical research studies on the functional perspective. They published the results under this intriguing title: "To Err Is Human, to Correct for It Divine." One of the errors referred to was Hirokawa and Gouran's assumption that each of the requisite functions was equally important. The study showed that *evaluation of negative consequences of alternative solutions* was by far the most crucial to ensure a quality decision.[12] Perhaps to stress its importance, Hirokawa now splits up the overall evaluation function into a positive one and a negative one, and speaks of five requisite functions rather than four. He also now refers to the *functional theory* when he wants to distinguish his work from Janis' groupthink, Bales' interaction categories, or other work that takes a functional perspective toward group communication.[13]

THE ROLE OF COMMUNICATION IN FULFILLING THE FUNCTIONS

Most communication scholars believe that discussion among members has a significant effect on the quality of group decisions. Traditional wisdom suggests that talk is the medium, or conduit, through which information travels between participants.[14] Verbal interaction makes it possible for members to (1) distribute and pool information, (2) catch and remedy errors, and (3) influence each other. Similar to Shannon and Weaver's concept of channel noise causing a loss of information (see Chapter 3), group researcher Ivan Steiner claimed that[15]

$$\begin{matrix} \text{Actual Group} \\ \text{Productivity} \end{matrix} = \begin{matrix} \text{Potential} \\ \text{Productivity} \end{matrix} - \begin{matrix} \text{Losses Due} \\ \text{to Processes} \end{matrix}$$

It follows that communication is best when it doesn't obstruct or distort the free flow of ideas.

While not rejecting this traditional view, Hirokawa believes that communication plays a more active role in crafting quality decisions. Like social constructionists (see Chapters 6, 12, and 13), he regards group discussion as a tool or instrument that group members use to create the social reality in which decisions are made.[16] Discussion exerts its own impact on the end product of the group.

How does this work in practice? Think of the dark, wide lines in Figure 17–1 as safe trails through a dense thicket—paths that connect the four key task functions and lead ultimately to the goal of a high-quality group decision. Members can easily wander off that goal path and get caught up in a tangle of prickerbushes that thwart the group's progress. The bushes in this analogy represent distractions or barriers that retard movement toward the goal. Hirokawa and Gouran list a number of thorny obstacles—ignorance of the issue, faulty facts, misguided assumptions, sloppy evaluation of options, illogical inferences, disregard of procedural norms, and undue influence by powerful members. They believe that people go astray through talk, but they also believe that communication has the power to pull them back onto the goal-directed path.

Consistent with these convictions, Hirokawa and Gouran outline three types of communication in decision-making groups:

1. Promotive—interaction that moves the group along the goal path by calling attention to one of the four requisite decision-making functions.

2. Disruptive—interaction that diverts, retards, or frustrates group members' ability to achieve the four task functions.

3. Counteractive—interaction that members use to get the group back on track.

Hirokawa and Gouran suggest that most comments from group members disrupt rather than promote progress toward the goal. They conclude, therefore, that "effective group decision-making is perhaps best understood as a consequence of the exercise of counteractive influence."[17] In other words, someone has to say something that will get the group back on track.

Hirokawa has made repeated efforts to develop a conversational coding system that classifies the function of specific statements. Much like Bales' interaction categories outlined in the introduction to group decision making, Hirokawa's Function-Oriented Interaction Coding System (FOICS) requires researchers to categorize each *functional utterance,* which is "an uninterrupted statement of a single member that appears to perform a specified function within the group interaction process."[18]

Figure 17–2 shows a FOICS checklist that researchers might use to analyze communication within a group. As you can see, raters are asked to make two judgments: (1) Which of the four requisite functions, if any, does an utterance address? (2) Does the remark facilitate (*promote*), inhibit (*disrupt*), or redirect (*counteract*) the group's focus on that function? Ideally, this 4 × 3 classification scheme provides 12 discrete categories of group discussion. With that information, researchers could determine the effect of communication on the quality of the decision the group makes.

In practice, however, analyzing the content of group discussion is fraught with difficulty. In the first place, independent raters find it difficult to agree on how a statement should be coded. Extensive training boosts the reliability of their judg-

Functional utterance
An uninterrupted statement of a single member that appears to perform a specific function.

FOICS
Function Oriented Interaction Coding System; a tool to record and classify the function of utterances during a group's discussion.

	Problem Analysis	Goal Setting	Identification of Alternatives	Evaluation of Positives/Negatives
Promote				
Disrupt				
Counteract				

FIGURE 17–2 Function-Oriented Interaction Coding System (FOICS) Checklist

ments, but Hirokawa is keenly aware that a single comment may serve multiple functions. In addition, words that appear helpful on the surface may have hidden power to disrupt, or vice versa. The process of coding comments has turned out to be an ongoing problem for all researchers who want to study the nature and effects of group communication. Hirokawa continues to work on refining his methodology, but he ruefully cites the tongue-in-cheek words of Tom Scheidel, former communication department chair at the University of Washington:

> All group communication researchers should employ the method of interaction analysis once in his/her career . . . to learn never to use it again.[19]

FROM THE TINY POND TO THE BIG OCEAN

The heading of this section was Hirokawa's title for the 1999 B. Aubrey Fisher Memorial Lecture—an end-of-the-century review of the functional perspective's status.[20] His pond-ocean metaphor refers to the risks and challenges of taking results from tightly controlled laboratory studies and finding out whether they are robust enough to hold their own in the turbulent "real world" where multiple forces come into play.

In a typical laboratory study of the functional perspective, Hirokawa presents a problem to 30 or more newly formed 3-person groups.[21] For example, he might ask them to develop specific recommendations for fair and reasonable discipline of a student caught cheating on a term-paper assignment. In order to determine how well each group meets the four requisite functions, he has trained FOICS raters to watch videotapes of the discussions. As a way to determine the quality of each group's decision, he submits their final recommendations to teacher-administrators who have lots of experience dealing with plagiarism. Finally, he compares each group's FOICS rating with the quality of its decision.

Summing over a dozen empirical studies of the functional perspective, Hirokawa has found that it's quite good at predicting which groups will make high-quality decisions. Specifically, his theory is able to account for over 60 percent of the total variance in group performance.[22] To explain what this means, Hirokawa asks us to imagine entering a Las Vegas casino and discovering that it has a game called *Predict how well the group will do*. The game is simple. We watch a videotape of a group discussing a decision, and just before the members decide, we must bet on whether their decision will turn out to be good or bad. To say that the functional perspective accounts for 60 percent of the variance means that if we were to place our bets based on our knowledge of how well the group fulfilled the four functional requisites identified by the theory, we would win roughly 60 percent of the time. If we bet the same amount of money every time, we'd be among the few who leave Las Vegas as winners.[23]

As impressive as these results might be, Hirokawa doesn't believe the functional perspective will forge a stronger connection between communication and good group decisions until he can isolate specific comments that move a group along its goal path. Using the FOICS matrix, his raters can approximate the quantity of statements that "speak" to each task function, but they have a tough time gauging the quality of those contributions. Yet Hirokawa is convinced that group decision-making performance is dependent more on the *quality*, than on the *quantity*, of functional utterances.[24]

In 1995, Hirokawa moved the functional perspective out of the laboratory and into the field—literally. He joined a four-person medical team that served rural Iowa communities that had no physician. Members of the team were *student* health care professionals—a future doctor, dentist, pharmacist, and nurse. Consistent with the four requisite functions specified by the functional perspective, team members jointly discussed the symptoms, diagnosis, potential quality of life, and treatment options for each patient. The results were gratifying. Hirokawa discovered that the quality of medical service they offered was more satisfying to the patients and less expensive to the state than was the case when an established physician visited the community on an individual basis.

Hirokawa's health care experience strengthened his faith in the vitality of the functional perspective in a real-world context where life-and-death decisions are made. But he also saw some cases where the group thoroughly addressed all four requisite functions yet the patient got worse. Hirokawa believes that the crucial challenge now facing group researchers is "to discover precisely when a group's performance of functional requisites yields effective group decisions and when it does not."[25]

PRACTICAL ADVICE FOR AMATEURS AND PROFESSIONALS

How can you and I use the functional perspective to facilitate better group decisions? We can start with a healthy dose of humility concerning the wisdom of our own opinions. Hirokawa and Gouran report that groups often abandon the rational path due to the persuasive efforts of members who are convinced that they alone have the right answer. Their discussion style proclaims, "Don't confuse me with the facts; my mind's made up," and they wear down the opposition. We can make sure that we don't come to the table with the sort of closed-minded attitude that contributes to the problem rather than the solution. Additionally, we should be wary of pushing any "intuitive hunch" or "gut feeling" that we can't back up with reasonable evidence. These are errors to avoid.

We can also take proactive measures to promote clear thinking within the group. In almost every article they write, Hirokawa and Gouran acknowledge their intellectual debt to early-twentieth-century American pragmatist philosopher John Dewey.[26] Dewey's pragmatism was based on the hopeful assumption that practical decisions can be brought under more intelligent control through the process of rational inquiry.[27] He advocated a six-step process of *reflective thinking* that parallels a doctor's approach to treating a patient:[28]

Reflective thinking
Thinking that favors rational consideration over intuitive hunches or pressure from those with clout.

1. Recognize symptoms of illness.
2. Diagnose the cause of the ailment.
3. Establish criteria for wellness.
4. Consider possible remedies.
5. Test to determine which solutions will work.
6. Implement or prescribe the best solution.

Note that Hirokawa and Gouran's four requisite functions are almost exact replicas of steps 2, 3, 4, and 5 in Dewey's reflective-thinking process. Both lists recommend that group members discuss issues in a way that promotes problem analysis, goal setting, discovery of alternatives, and evaluation of these options.

When we're tempted to make remarks that will detract from the process, Hirokawa and Gouran suggest that we bite our tongues. And when others say things that sidetrack the group from fulfilling the four functional requisites, the theorists urge us to counter with a comment aimed at getting the group back on a rational path.

You may be hesitant to counteract the dubious logic of a powerful leader or a high-status member of the group, but Hirokawa and Gouran don't advocate direct criticism. Instead, they recommend a strategy of insisting on a careful process. By raising questions, calling for more alternatives, and urging a thorough evaluation of evidence, a low-status member can have a high-power impact on the quality of the final decision.

ETHICAL REFLECTION: HABERMAS' DISCOURSE ETHICS

German philosopher Jürgen Habermas suggests a rational group process through which people can determine right from wrong—a different kind of decision than Hirokawa and Gouran usually study. In order to develop guidelines for ethical action, the Frankfurt School critical theorist pictures a diverse group of people engaged in public discourse. Habermas' ethical approach seeks an after-the-fact discussion about what we did in a particular situation and why we decided to do it. Being ethical means being accountable.[29]

Habermas assumes that people within a given culture or community can pretty much agree on the good they want to accomplish, and over time they've built up practical wisdom on how to achieve it. For example, your campus newspaper reporters assume that it's good for students to know more about what's going on within the school's administration ("the people's right to know") and that guaranteeing confidentiality to insiders is the best way to find out ("protecting their sources"). This newsroom common sense is a good place to start doing journalistic ethics, but reporters' justification of the practice typically lacks reflective rigor. It often doesn't take into account the interests of everyone affected by their stories.

Discourse ethics
Jürgen Habermas' vision of the ideal speech situation in which diverse participants could rationally reach a consensus on universal ethical standards.

Habermas' *discourse ethics* sets up a discursive test for the validity of any moral claim. The person who performed an act must be prepared to discuss what he or she did and why he or she did it in an open forum. This deliberative process is a two-stage process of justification and application. The actor must reveal the general ethical principle that he or she used to justify the action and then show why it was the appropriate thing to do in those particular circumstances. Habermas imagines an *ideal speech situation* where participants are free to listen to reason and speak their minds without fear of constraint or control.[30] He's convinced that a validity of any ethical consensus can be reached only to the extent that three requirements are met:[31]

Ideal speech situation
A discourse on ethical accountability in which discussants represent all who will be affected by the decision, pursue discourse in a spirit of seeking the common good, and are committed to finding universal standards.

1. *Requirement for access.* All people affected by the ethical norm being debated can attend and be heard, regardless of their status. That means that donors, administrators, professors, students, and minimum-wage staff at the school are welcome at the table without prejudice.

2. *Requirement for argument.* All participants are expected to exchange their points of view in the spirit of genuine reciprocity and mutual understanding. They aren't merely trying to advance their own interests but are trying to figure out whether an action serves the common good.

3. *Requirement for justification.* Everyone is committed to a standard of universalization. What makes ethical claims legitimate is their "acceptance not only among those who agree to live with and by them but by anyone *affected* by them."[32]

Habermas understands that thoroughly noncoercive dialogue is a utopian dream, yet he finds his conception of the ideal speech situation helpful in gauging the degree to which a discussion is rational. This, of course, is a major goal of Hirokawa, Gouran, and Dewey. The trick is getting group members to do it.

CRITIQUE: IS RATIONALITY OVERRATED?

In their review of the small-group communication literature, John Cragan and David Wright conclude that there are three leading theories.[33] One is Bormann's *symbolic convergence theory*, discussed in Chapter 4. The second is Scott Poole's *adaptive structuration theory*, which I introduce in Chapter 18. The third is Hirokawa and Gouran's functional perspective. In their critique of the functional perspective, Purdue University communication researchers Cynthia Stohl and Michael Holmes explain why it is so highly regarded:

> The basic premise of the perspective, that communication serves task functions and the accomplishment of those functions should be associated with effective group decisions, is intuitively appealing and sensible. It also meets the standards of an objective theory in that it explains, is testable, simple, and practical.[34]

As a result, many communication scholars endorse the theory as a model for group discussion and decision making. One of my students is so convinced that he wrote, "A list of the four functions should be woven into the carpet of every committee room."

Yet Hirokawa's exclusive focus on rational talk may be the reason researchers get mixed results when they test his theory's predictions.[35] Note that the FOICS method of coding conversation all but ignores comments about relationships inside or outside the group. By treating relational statements as a distraction, Hirokawa commits the same mistake that the late Aubrey Fisher admitted he made in his own task-focused research:[36]

> The original purpose of the investigation . . . was to observe verbal task behavior free from the confounding variables of the socioemotional dimension. That purpose, of course, was doomed to failure. The two dimensions are interdependent.[37]

Stohl and Holmes' critique frames the same issue in a slightly different way. They contend that most real-life groups have a prior decision-making history and are embedded within a larger organization. They advocate adding a *historical function* that requires the group to talk about how past decisions were made. They also recommend an *institutional function* that is satisfied when members discuss the reality of power brokers and stakeholders who aren't at the table, but whose views clearly affect and are affected by the group decision.

Dennis Gouran has recently raised doubts about how useful the functional perspective may be for many small-group discussions.[38] He notes that almost all group dynamics research has dealt with decision making and problem solving—a focus reflected in the title I've given this section of the text. Although he and Hirokawa attempted to craft a one-size-fits-all model for group communication, he now believes that it's beneficial for members to fulfill the four requisite functions only when they are addressing *questions of policy*. That's not always the case.

Investigative panels and juries deal with *questions of fact* such as "What happened?" or "Who's responsible?" College admission boards and product design teams face *questions of conjecture*, trying to figure out what's likely to happen in an uncertain future without any current way of knowing if their predictions are right. Religious and addiction recovery support groups face emotionally loaded *questions of value*, members sharing or debating what they believe is acceptable, appropriate, ethical, or morally right. None of these questions has a discernable "right" or "high-quality" answer. Gouran doesn't believe that these alternative group goals invalidate the functional perspective, but he does suggest their existence shows that the theory isn't relevant in every situation. The scope of the functional perspective is more limited than first thought.

QUESTIONS TO SHARPEN YOUR FOCUS

1. Hirokawa and Gouran claim that small groups are like living *systems*. Do you see parallels between the four *functional requisites* of task groups and the body's need for respiration, circulation, digestion, and elimination?

2. Given that the functional theory focuses on *decision-making* and *problem-solving* groups, why is its silence on *relationship* issues a problem?

3. Think of a time when you've been part of a task group that strayed from the *goal path*. What *counteractive statement* could you have made that might have brought it back on track?

4. Why might you find it frustrating to use Hirokawa's *Function-Oriented Interaction Coding System (FOICS)* to analyze a group discussion?

SELF-QUIZ For chapter self-quizzes go to the book's Online Learning Center at *www.mhhe.com/griffin7*

CONVERSATIONS

View this segment online at www.mhhe.com/griffin7 or www.afirstlook.com

As you might expect from an objective theorist discussing a rational theory, Randy Hirokawa gives clear, concise responses to my opening questions about group decision making. Is the order in which functions are addressed important? Is one function more important than the others? Is it possible he will find a yet undiscovered fifth function? But as the conversation continues, Hirokawa voices ideas not usually heard from thoroughgoing empiricists. He refers to the irony of questionable motives producing beneficial actions, a subjective standard to determine whether a decision is good, and his belief that there are no guarantees in life. Many students consider this segment the best one on the web.

A SECOND LOOK

Recommended resource: Dennis Gouran, Randy Hirokawa, Kelly Julian, and Geoff Leatham, "The Evolution and Current Status of the Functional Perspective on Communication in Decision-Making and Problem-Solving Groups," in *Communication Yearbook 16,* Stanley Deetz (ed.), Sage, Newbury Park, CA, 1993, pp. 573–600.

Original statement: Dennis Gouran and Randy Hirokawa, "The Role of Communication in Decision-Making Groups: A Functional Perspective," in *Communications in Transition,* Mary Mander (ed.), Praeger, New York, 1983, pp. 168–185.

State-of-the-art review: Randy Hirokawa, "From the Tiny Pond to the Big Ocean: Studying Communication and Group Decision-Making Effectiveness from a Functional Perspective," 1999 B. Aubrey Fisher Memorial Lecture, Department of Communication, University of Utah, Salt Lake City.

Role of communication: Randy Hirokawa and Dirk Scheerhorn, "Communication in Faulty Group Decision-Making," in *Communication and Group Decision-Making,* Randy Hirokawa and M. Scott Poole (eds.), Sage, Beverly Hills, CA, 1986, pp. 63–80.

Coding group interaction: Randy Hirokawa, "Functional Approaches to the Study of Group Discussion," *Small Group Research,* Vol. 25, 1994, pp. 542–550.

Additional propositions: Dennis Gouran and Randy Hirokawa, "Effective Decision Making and Problem Solving in Groups: A Functional Perspective," in *Small Group Communication: Theory and Practice,* 8th ed., Randy Hirokawa, Robert Cathcart, et al. (eds.), Roxbury, Los Angeles, 2003, pp. 27–38.

Survey of group theories taking a functional perspective: Andrea B. Hollinshead, Gwen Wittenbaum, et al., "A Look at Groups from the Functional Perspective," in *Theories of Small Groups: Interdisciplinary Perspectives,* M. Scott Poole and Andrea B. Hollingshead (eds.), Sage, London, 2005, pp. 21–62.

Critique: Cynthia Stohl and Michael Holmes, "A Functional Perspective for Bona Fide Groups," *Communication Yearbook 16,* 1993, pp. 601–614.

Theorist's assessment of limited scope: Dennis Gouran, "Reflections on the Type of Question as a Determinant of the Form of Interaction in Decision-Making and Problem-Solving Discussions," *Communication Quarterly,* Vol. 53, 2003, pp. 111–125.

CHAPTER 18

Adaptive Structuration Theory

of Marshall Scott Poole

Imagine that you are a third-year communication major who signed up late for a required course in communication theory. Since you missed the first class and haven't seen the syllabus, you aren't sure what to expect. When you walk into the room, you're surprised to find out that there are only 12 students in the class, no course syllabus, and no instructor present. When the other students start to talk about tests and papers, the scope of assignments, and the breadth and depth of coverage, the guy sitting next to you fills you in. The prof has made this an experimental section and has given students the responsibility to structure the course before he returns to class.

In the discussion that follows it becomes apparent that there are at least a few parameters or rules. The class will meet from noon till 2 P.M. every Tuesday and Thursday for the entire term. The instructor has adopted a text that introduces over 30 communication theories, and he will be there from the third week on to serve as a resource. No matter how final grades are assigned, they should reflect what individuals have really learned—nobody gets an automatic A. Other than those givens, class members have two weeks to decide which theories to cover, how to use the scheduled class time, what course projects to assign, and how students should be evaluated. Essentially, the group is free to shape the course any way it wants.

After an hour, you seriously consider dropping the course. Josh, the prof's teaching assistant, and Paige, a sophomore transfer student, are totally monopolizing the discussion. Everything Josh is for, Paige is against, and vice versa. Michelle's only contribution is to insist that she doesn't want to take part in a group project. Mike, a varsity linebacker, and Karla, a campus beauty, chat about plans for Saturday night while ignoring the rest of the discussion. A few other students offer tentative suggestions, but Megan looks confused and Pete puts his head on the desk and snoozes.

You decide to stick it out but ask yourself, *Will the group stay this way for the entire semester, or will it change?* You worry that this specific mix of individual motivations and personalities makes more of the same a foregone conclusion.

235

And even though the prof has labeled the class format "experimental," you also wonder, *Are we really free to create whatever we want or are the results inevitable, given the academic setting?*

The first question raises the issue of group stability versus group change. The second question revisits the dilemma presented in Chapter 1—members' freely chosen actions versus their behavior determined by existing social structures. These are the two group-related questions that University of Illinois communication professor Scott Poole seeks to answer with adaptive structuration theory. When asked to state the core idea of his theory, Poole offers this synopsis:

> Members in groups are creating the group as they act within it. . . . A lot of times people in groups build up structures or arrangements that are very uncomfortable for them, but they don't realize that they're doing it. The point of structuration theory is to make them aware of the rules and resources that they're using so that they can have more control over what they do in groups.[1]

The implication of Poole's claim is that you and other class members are just as responsible for Josh and Paige's domination of class discussion as they are. Will things change? Only if you and the others make it happen. Are all of you free to change the way you're reacting? Only to the extent that you are aware of what you're doing.

At first glance these answers may seem simplistic. But they are derived from an understanding of *structuration*, a concept that is quite sophisticated. Poole adopted the idea only after a decade of empirical research convinced him that no single model of group development adequately explains what takes place in decision-making groups. Let's see what he found.

PHASING OUT THE PHASE MODEL

For much of the twentieth century, small-group researchers thought they had spotted a universal pattern of communication that all groups use when they make a decision. These scholars generally agreed that there was a good fit between the following single-sequence model and the actual phases that groups go through as the members reach agreement:[2]

> *Orientation*—efforts are unfocused because group goals are unclear; relationships are uncertain; members need more information.
>
> *Conflict*—factions disagree on how to approach the problem and argue against other viewpoints; members justify their own positions.
>
> *Coalescence*—tensions are reduced through peaceful negotiation; members allow others to "save face" by adopting solutions acceptable to all.
>
> *Development*—the group concentrates on ways to implement a single solution; members are involved and excited.
>
> *Integration*—the group focuses on tension-free solidarity rather than the task; members reward each other for cohesive efforts.

If the phase model is right, your communication theory group is now in the conflict stage, but it will sooner or later shift to a more cooperative pattern.

Despite widespread acceptance of this one-size-fits-all phase model of group decision making, Poole wasn't convinced. Beginning with his dissertation research in 1980 and extending throughout that decade, he sought to find out *if* and *when* ongoing groups actually conform to the single-sequence model when making tough decisions on important issues. Poole tracked 47 specific decisions made by 29 different groups in natural settings—real people making real decisions.[3]

Early in his research, Poole discovered that only a quarter of the groups actually followed the discussion pattern laid out in the single-sequence model. But just as Hirokawa and Gouran offer their functional perspective as a preferred procedure for task groups to adopt (see Chapter 17), Poole was still hopeful that the five phases offered a blueprint for reaching high-quality decisions. He wrote that "the unitary sequence provides a logically ideal format for decision making and it may well be the simplest effective path a decision-making group could follow."[4]

Yet the longer Poole examined the complexity of group decision making, the less optimistic he became that any theory or model would be able to predict a specific sequence of action. By the end of the decade, he was disenchanted with the scientific quest to discover a fixed pattern of group behavior. He became convinced that group dynamics are far too complicated to be reduced to a few propositions or a predictable chain of events. He also grew uncomfortable with the phase model's objectivist assumption that group and task structures dictate the way a decision is made. In effect, the model claims that communication has no significant impact on the process or the outcome; group members are just along for a five-stage ride.

Social structures
Rules and resources of a group; characteristics such as composition, norms, communication networks, status hierarchies, task requirements, and peer pressure.

Poole continued to think that group members are affected by *social structures* such as group composition, communication networks, status hierarchies, task requirements, group norms, and peer pressure. But he no longer saw these structures as *determining* how the group reached a decision or what that decision might be. He was convinced that what people say and do makes a difference.

Given this commitment, Poole and two other communication scholars, Robert McPhee (Arizona State University) and David Seibold (University of California, Santa Barbara), became intrigued by the work of British sociologist Anthony Giddens. Giddens suggests that people in society are *active agents* in the sense that they are "able to act otherwise" and have the capacity "to make a difference."[5] McPhee went on to apply Giddens' core ideas in an organizational context, while Seibold used them to analyze the structure of arguments. But in Giddens' macrotheory of societal structuration, Poole saw insights that could be adapted and applied to the microlevel of small-group activity.

STRUCTURATION ACCORDING TO GIDDENS

Currently the director of the London School of Economics, Anthony Giddens was the chief intellectual adviser to former British prime minister Tony Blair. Colleagues call him "the most important English social philosopher of our time."[6] Giddens openly admits that *structuration* "is an unlovely term at best,"[7] yet he believes that no other word adequately captures the process of social structures shaping people's actions while at the same time being shaped by their actions. Specifically, *structuration* refers to "the production and reproduction of the social systems through members' use of rules and resources in interaction."[8]

Structuration
The production and reproduction of social systems through group members' use of rules and resources in interaction.

By using the word *interaction*, as opposed to the more passive term *behavior*, Giddens signals his belief that people are relatively free to act as they will. They aren't merely pawns in the game of life or unsuspecting dupes controlled by unseen forces they can't resist. He says that every social actor knows a lot about the way society works, and when asked, these competent social agents can explain most of what they do.[9]

Giddens uses the phrase *rules and resources* interchangeably with the term *structures*. *Rules* are implicit formulas for action, recipes for how to "get on" in life.[10] They are guides for participants on how to play the game. *Resources* refers to all the relevant personal traits, abilities, knowledge, and possessions people bring to an interaction. Resources are almost always in short supply and tend to be unequally distributed within a society. Because rules and resources (structures) are constantly changing, structuration is a fluid process.

Production of social systems is a process akin to the "creation of social realities" in CMM (see Chapter 6), although Giddens refers to sweeping changes across an entire society, not just among persons-in-conversation. Production happens when people use rules and resources in interaction. So does reproduction. *Reproduction* occurs whenever actions reinforce features of systems already in place, and thus maintain the status quo.

Poole applies and extends these key concepts of structuration within small groups, but a brief example of societal structuration may help you picture the kind of large-scale process that Giddens imagines. The sexual revolution that began in the 1960s illustrates how the widespread adoption of new rules and resources dramatically transformed patterns of physical intimacy. Through faithful use (a rule) of "the Pill" (a resource) prior to sexual intercourse (an interaction), women increased their control over their own bodies (production). The change in contraception meant that men worried less about unwanted pregnancy, thus reinforcing (nonbiological reproduction) the sexual double standard that it is men's role to push for greater sexual intimacy and women's responsibility to say when to stop (a rule).

Giddens' concept of structuration is the core idea that spawned adaptive structuration theory. Poole calls his theory *adaptive structuration* because he observes members of task groups intentionally adapting rules and resources in order to accomplish their decision-making goals. His "adaptive" label also seems appropriate because, along with his then University of Minnesota colleague Gerry DeSanctis, he's tailored Giddens' macrosociological principles to the microworld of small groups. When applied to group interaction, structuration obviously describes a process more intricate than the five-phase model presented earlier in the chapter. That's fine with Poole. He believes that the "value of a theory of group decision making hinges on how well it addresses the complexities of interaction."[11]

In the rest of the chapter I'll continue to use the example of an experimental communication theory course to illustrate key elements of adaptive structuration theory. Although this example is hypothetical, every part of the case study is drawn from actual class experience. Since Poole recommends *ethnography* as one of the ways to explore structuration, I'll write you into the picture and ask you to think of yourself as a participant observer in the events that I describe.[12] I'll follow the same *interaction, rules and resources, production and reproduction* order that I used to parse Giddens' concept of structuration.

INTERACTION: CONCERNS OF MORALITY, COMMUNICATION, AND POWER

Group structuration is the result of action, and so whenever members interact, they have an impact on the group. If the rules and resources of the group change, it's because members do something that changes them. But Poole makes it clear that action doesn't always *alter* rules and resources. "If the structure of the group stays the same, it is because members are acting in such a way that the same structure is created and maintained with every act."[13] That seems to describe the entire two hours of the first class you attended.

The next class is different. Right from the start, class members interact with each other on how to design the course. Even Pete wakes up to the realization that he has a stake in what's decided and voices a depth-over-breadth rationale for concentrating on fewer theories—perhaps only a dozen. Michelle piggybacks on his idea, suggesting that each student become an expert on a different theory. Andrew welcomes the chance to specialize in one area—on the condition that he can pick a theory of new media that will intersect with his double major of communication and computer science. This surge of *interaction* supports Poole's optimistic assumption that group members are "skilled and knowledgeable actors who reflexively monitor their activities as they navigate a continuous flow of intentionality."[14]

Interaction
Intentional acts of group members who are aware of what they are doing.

Skilled and knowledgeable actors don't always agree, however. Paige expresses concern that people will select only theories that are familiar or within their comfort zone. She thinks everyone should discuss theories that question unjust corporate control of the media and propose ways in which poor people could have a voice. Mike wants Pete to explain what he means by studying theory *in depth*. If he's referring to practical application, fine. If he means wading through primary sources, no way. Reminding the class of his special status as the professor's TA, Josh claims that the prof won't let the group concentrate on only a dozen theories while ignoring the other 20 that are in the book. Note that these class members raised issues of *morality, communication,* and *power*—issues that Poole and Giddens agree are fundamental in any social interaction. Poole writes that these three elements are mixed together in every group action. He says that it's "hard to use moral norms without considering their interpretation—a matter of meaning—and how they are 'made to count'—a matter of power."[15]

Megan, always a sensitive observer of the human scene, notices that Lauren seems hesitant to speak. By specifically asking for her opinion, Megan tries to create a space for Lauren to be heard. In a soft voice, Lauren wishes there could be a midrange compromise on the breadth/depth issue. After class you overhear her thanking Megan for caring what she thinks. No doubt Megan's intentions were good, but in subsequent classes you observe that Lauren is even quieter. This confirms Poole's structuration research, which suggests that advocacy can sometimes hurt rather than help a reticent member of the group.[16] Megan's encouragement may simply reinforce Lauren's tendency to wait for an invitation before speaking up. Even actions that are well-thought-out have unanticipated consequences.

The class experience I've described so far highlights two key points of adaptive structuration theory. First, communication in small task-groups makes a difference. We might know the structure of a group, the nature of its task, and even the history and personality of each member. But it is impossible to predict what decisions the group will make without hearing what's been said. Communication matters.

Second, adaptive structuration theory has a "critical edge."[17] Recall that critical theories strive to reveal unfair social practices and free people from oppressive systems (see Chapter 4). By highlighting the way in which undemocratic group processes can be altered, Poole hopes to empower people who are now treated as second-class citizens.

THE USE AND ABUSE OF RULES AND RESOURCES

Rules
Propositions that indicate how things ought to be done or what is good or bad; recipes for actions.

Resources
Materials, possessions, or attributes that can be used to influence or control the actions of the group or its members.

Poole refers to small-group *rules* as "propositions that indicate how something ought to be done or what is good or bad."[18] Although rarely put into words, these rules contain the collective practical wisdom that members have gleaned on how best to reach the group goal. The *resources* that individuals bring to the task are "materials, possessions, or attributes that can be used to influence or control the actions of the group or its members."[19] As a research strategy, Poole selects a few structures that appear to be pivotal and then examines them in greater depth.

Personal relationships quickly emerge as a resource for the class discussion. Megan and Lauren's growing friendship and Mike and Karla's romantic closeness seem to add impact to their words. You find that when any of them say something in class, you tend to assume that they speak for their partner as well. But it is Andrew who possesses the most effective relational resource. In contrast to the computer geek stereotype, he's a genuinely warm guy whom everyone likes. When the two of you took the same interpersonal course, he turned out to be the most competent face-to-face communicator in the class. When Andrew speaks, others listen, and vice versa.

Topic expertise is often another key resource in group decision making. Although none of you have any training in education methods or curriculum development, some students start the course with more knowledge about communication theories than others do. Because he's performed months of library and Internet research for the instructor you've yet to meet, Josh has inside knowledge of the type of theory that this prof would value. Josh presents these insights in a self-confident manner; thus, his insights carry more weight in the discussion. Status structures are almost always important in group structuration.

Some of you know that Michelle carries a 4.0 GPA and is a member of Lambda Pi Eta, the national communication honor society. She's a loner who doesn't say much in class, so you imagine that she must be impatient with the value the group places on relationships rather than intellectual resources. *After all*, she might reason, *I'm in this class to learn communication theory, not to join a social club*. Her likely frustration highlights Poole's claim that group structures can constrain members from acting freely. And if Michelle doesn't bring her knowledge and intelligence to bear on designing the course, it ceases to be a resource for the group. Conversely, one who makes the effort to understand and use these structures—as Josh does—can become an effective player.

Appropriation
Adopting a rule or resource from another group or the larger culture.

A group's rules and resources are often borrowed from parent organizations or from the larger culture. Poole calls this process *appropriation*. Given that students in your class come from a variety of backgrounds and have experienced different leadership styles, Poole wouldn't be surprised if the rules you appropriate for making decisions don't square with standard parliamentary procedure. As it turns out, he anticipates how your class reaches a decision on the depth/breadth issue when he writes, "Different groups may appropriate the political norm of majority rule in a variety of ways. One group may regard the rule as a last resort, to be used only if consensus cannot be attained. . . ."[20]

Consensus is the only decision path acceptable to most students in your group. You personally feel that way because it's a seminar type of course and you don't want to ride roughshod over one or two people and then see them be bitter for the rest of the term. But Pete and Megan want a formal vote so that everyone is on record as supporting the decision. The group ends up appropriating both structures! When Josh, Paige, and Andrew coalesce around a compromise plan of reading the entire book yet concentrating class time on just 12 theories, no vote is taken until all doubts and hesitations are worked through. With some fine-tuning, the class crafts a plan that all 12 of you can embrace, and then Josh calls for a unanimous vote—a ritual to seal your mutual commitment.

RESEARCHING THE USE OF RULES AND RESOURCES

Group decision support systems (GDSS)
Media technology designed to promote democratic decision making by displaying all ideas anonymously.

Working with DeSanctis, Poole has spent the bulk of his structuration research exploring how groups use computerized *group decision support systems (GDSS)*—high-tech media that have the potential to improve meetings and help make better decisions. Since new media scholars find adaptive structuration theory helpful in understanding the interface between computers and users, perhaps this is the theory that Andrew is looking for. I won't attempt to explain the hardware and software of computer-assisted meetings, but structures built into the system are designed to promote democratic decision making. These structures include features such as equal opportunity to participate, one vote per person, and anonymous idea generation and balloting so that every member feels safe to participate.

Just as we refer to the "spirit of the law," Poole and DeSanctis call the values behind the system the "spirit of the technology." They explain that "*spirit* is the principle of coherence that holds a set of rules and resources together."[21] In Poole's terms, a *faithful appropriation* of the technology is one that is consistent with the spirit of the resource. For example, suppose your experimental communication theory class met in a GDSS-equipped lab on campus to make final decisions about the course. A faithful appropriation of these rules and resources would be to use the system in a way that gives Lauren a real voice in the discussion while making it hard for Josh to dominate it.

Faithful appropriation
Using a rule or resource as it was originally intended.

Although your classroom isn't GDSS-equipped, it has a built-in computer with video projection capacity, so most of you use PowerPoint technology when you present the results of your research. Pete's report on constructivism turns out to be a real media event (see Chapter 8). Backgrounds change, words tumble into place, text dissolves, clip art scrolls. The sight and sound of exploding fireworks punctuate Pete's announcement that he found a journal article by Delia that the textbook doesn't mention. And when he suggests that his high RCQ score certifies him as cognitively complex, a picture of the Mona Lisa smiles. The class laughs throughout and applauds wildly when it's over.

Ironic appropriation
Using a rule or resource in a way that thwarts its original purpose.

Poole notes that group members sometimes appropriate rules or resources in ways that thwart their intended use. He calls this an *ironic appropriation* because it goes against the spirit of the structure. This seems to be the case with Pete's use of PowerPoint. By projecting over a hundred slides in a 10-minute presentation, he uses it to dazzle rather than clarify. His most vivid slides underscore his reactions to the theory rather than creating a deeper understanding of cognitive complexity, goal-based message plans, or person-centered messages. In the discussion that follows, Pete admits with a wry smile, "The developers of PowerPoint would probably be shocked at how I used the system."[22] Poole doesn't think all adaptations of technology or other rules and resources *ought* to be faithful. Ironic appropriation can be an impetus to creativity that doesn't necessarily take away from task accomplishment. But he's a strong believer in being able to identify when and how this type of structuration takes place.

PRODUCTION OF CHANGE, REPRODUCTION OF STABILITY

So far my description of adaptive structuration theory has focused on group *process*—members' use of rules and resources in interaction. Poole is also interested in group *product*—that which is produced and reproduced through the interaction.

Crafting the Decision

Decision-making groups produce decisions. After everyone in your group agrees that you'll focus on 12 theories, you also decide that the student who selects a given theory should be the one to write a quiz that probes whether class members understand it. The instructor will grade the quizzes, but students write the questions. As for the other 20 theories, the prof can assess how well you understand them by reading your application logs—ongoing journals of ways you might use these theoretical principles in everyday life. Group members quickly reach these decisions after Mike reminds them that the instructor has a reputation for writing nitpicky tests.

Production
The use of rules and resources to create a new structure; change.

If Poole was aware of what you decided and how you reached that decision, he would point out that the end product was both *produced* and *reproduced*. By deciding to focus on a dozen self-selected theories and empowering students to write the quizzes, you produced *change*—a break from normal class procedure. Since the prof can no longer ask specific questions about minor details, you can now focus your study on learning the basic thrust of each theory. On the other hand, by adopting the familiar educational structures of tests and student journals, you reproduce *stability*. When it comes to grading, your course will resemble other classes on campus.

Reproduction
The use of rules and resources to reinforce structures already in place.

Duality of Structure

Duality of structure
The idea that rules and resources are both the means and the ends of group interaction.

Poole would be even more curious to know the effect of the structuration process on the rules and resources of the group. Poole believes that Giddens' *duality of structure* concept is the key to discovering that impact. Duality of structure refers to the idea that rules and resources are both the *medium* and the *outcome* of interaction.[23] In terms of group decision making, this means that the decision not only is *affected by* the structures of the group but at the same time has an *effect upon* the same rules and resources. This is crucial to Poole because it helps explain why groups are sometimes stable and predictable—as the single-sequence model of group development suggests—yet why they are often changing and unpredictable. According to Poole, it depends on how group members appropriate rules and resources:

> Both stability and change are products of the same process. Structures are stable if actors appropriate them in a consistent way, reproducing them in similar form over time. Structures may also change, either incrementally or radically through structuration.[24]

DILBERT: © Scott Adams/Dist. by United Feature Syndicate, Inc.

Stability. You can't know from a few class meetings whether the rules and resources you've used so far will be employed the same way in the future. My guess is that consensus seeking among students and a relative independence vis-à-vis the instructor will continue to be enacted and be group norms even after he rejoins the class. You've already developed a sense of camaraderie, but it will survive only if spokespeople like Josh and Megan confidently instruct your instructor on the decisions you've made, and the rest of you back them up. Because structures exist only when they are put into practice—a use-it-or-lose-it structurational principle—a united front can reproduce the group's rules and resources. Members' continual use of the same rules and resources can form layers of solidified group structures much like sedimented rock.

Change. Reproduction does not necessarily mean replication. Even when a group appears stable, the rules and resources that members use can change gradually over time through the process Poole calls *interpenetration of structures.* Since any group action draws upon multiple rules and resources, Poole's phrase helps us picture how one structure might affect (or infect) the other. Think again of the way your class incorporates voting into a consensus structure. If no one ever casts a negative vote because agreement has already been reached, the consensus structure has mediated the meaning of the voting structure.

Interpenetration of structures
Unnoticed change over time as reproduced structures affect each other.

Although your class was able to create a way for voting and consensus to coexist, Poole notes that there are times when group structures are in direct contradiction, each undermining the other. This may be the case with the professor's knowledge of communication theory and the students' sense of autonomy. In his brief appearance on the first day of class, the prof relinquished his authority to structure the course but expressed his desire to serve as a resource for the group. Yet when he returns, you may find yourselves hesitant to ask questions. You want to tap his wealth of knowledge but fear falling back into the dependency of the traditional teacher-student relationship. If you don't draw on his knowledge, he will cease to be a resource for the group. Rules and resources survive and thrive only as group members actively put them in play.

HOW SHOULD WE THEN LIVE—IN A GROUP?

Browsing through a bookstore recently, I spotted the intriguing title *How Should We Then Live?* The question goes way beyond the scope of this chapter, but a scaled-down version seems appropriate. The core claim of adaptive structuration theory is that groups create themselves, yet members don't always realize they are crafting and reinforcing the tools that do the work.[25] If Poole is right, how should we then live our lives with others in a task group that makes decisions? The answer is implicit in the hierarchy below:

Some people make things happen.
Some people watch things happen.
Some people have things happen to them.
Some people don't even know things are happening.

Step up from a passive role to having an active voice within your group!

Poole is hopeful that a knowledge of how rules and resources work will equip low-power members to become agents of change within their groups: "If actors are unaware of a factor or do not understand how it operates, then it is likely to be a strong influence. To the extent that members are aware of a factor, they can use it or even change it."[26] Are you a group member with little or no say in the decisions made by others? Poole would encourage you to alter what you do and say in little ways. Small moves won't threaten high-power members who tend to resist change. Yet if you are consistent and persistent, these small changes can shift the direction of the group and your role in it.[27] How shall we live our lives in groups? Aware, free, as active agents of change who make things happen. That's the critical edge of adaptive structuration theory.

CRITIQUE: TIED TO GIDDENS—FOR BETTER OR WORSE

Along with symbolic convergence theory and the functional perspective (see Chapters 3 and 17), adaptive structuration theory is one of the three leading theories of group communication.[28] That's because Poole makes a serious attempt to deal with the dilemmas of change versus stability, and free will versus determinism in the context of group decision making. In essence, he asks, *What happens when an irresistible force (freely chosen human action) meets an immovable object (group structures that are no respecters of persons)?* Structuration is his answer—a resolution that privileges human choice and accounts for both stability and change. Poole's assessment of his theory's strength is similar:

> The advantage of this theory is that it mediates the seeming dichotomy between action and structure that is inherent in much group research. It gives an account of how group members produce and maintain social structures, which acknowledges creativity and self-reflexivity.[29]

The high standing of Poole's theory within the communication discipline is also enhanced by its grounding in Giddens' concept of structuration. For the academic community, this close tie provides the kind of scholarly clout that other theorists get by claiming Aristotle, Darwin, Freud, or Marx as an intellectual ancestor.

Surprisingly, Poole's indebtedness to Giddens has not resulted in a group theory that's blatantly critical of oppressive structures. Poole does try to raise consciousness of unseen power dynamics that affect group discussion, and he encourages members to act assertively. But this soft critical edge seems tame for a theory so deeply rooted in the ideas of Giddens, a leading figure in the critical tradition.

Ken Chase, a colleague at Wheaton, puts much of the responsibility on Giddens. Chase claims that the mark of a good critical theorist is that he or she "avoids separating ethical responsibility from theory construction and, accordingly, provides theory with an internal standard for moral argument."[30] Although structuration theory takes communication seriously and claims that morality is an issue in all interactions, Giddens doesn't provide a moral compass that indicates a clear ethical direction. Other critical theorists featured later in the book offer critiques grounded in the ethical assumptions of their theories (see Chapters 20, 26, 34, 35). They leave no doubt about what kinds of communication they are for, and what they're against.

Poole's faithful adaptation of Giddens' ideas and terminology has another drawback. The complexity of Giddens' thinking overwhelms most readers, and his ideas are couched in a prose style that even his admirers describe as *dense, thick, unforgiving,* and *impenetrable.* Poole's writing is much more accessible, yet Giddens' heaviness still comes through. Ironically, Poole reports that Giddens doesn't recognize his ideas when they're applied in a microanalysis of small-group structuration. Apparently, the British sociologist pictures sedimented structures being built across an entire society over decades, rather than layers of rules and resources forming within a group after a few meetings.

Poole acknowledges that structuration is a tough concept to grasp and apply. He critiques all group communication theories—his own included—for often failing to capture the imagination of students and practitioners:

> We have not intrigued, puzzled, or spoken to most people's condition. I fear we have overemphasized technique and propositional soundness at the expense of creativity. Creativity and a certain element of playfulness are just as important as sound theory construction.[31]

Adaptive structuration theory may not be playful, but it holds out the satisfying promise that every group member can be a player in the process of what the group creates. Some readers might wish that Poole had never abandoned the simple five-step path of group decision making. That route is certainly less complex than the sedimented, rock-strewn landscape of structuration that Poole describes. Yet it makes no sense to stick with a simplistic theory when the actual dynamics of group life have proved to be quite complicated and rather unpredictable, probably because people are that way. Poole has therefore chosen to craft a theory of commensurate complexity. I for one would prefer he tell it like it is rather than try to dumb it down.

QUESTIONS TO SHARPEN YOUR FOCUS

1. Poole refers to group communication as *action* rather than *behavior.* How does his choice of words reflect a rejection of the *phase* or *single-sequence model* of group decision making?

2. Poole and Giddens regard *duality of structure* as the key to understanding structuration. How does the Dilbert cartoon on page 243 illustrate this crucial concept?

3. Suppose you've been elected by communication majors to represent student opinion to department faculty. In what way is your role both a *rule* and a *resource*? How could you *produce* and/or *reproduce* student influence?

4. Why do you or don't you consider *adaptive structuration theory* to be a separate theory from Giddens' *structuration theory*? Should both names appear in the chapter heading? (Poole and Giddens?) (Giddens and Poole?)

CONVERSATIONS

View this segment online at www.mhhe.com.griffin7 or www.afirstlook.com.

In my conversation with Scott Poole, the author of adaptive structuration theory admits that it's a hard theory to grasp. Yet in this seven-minute segment, Poole makes the difficult notion of structuration come alive. He is clear, concise, and vivid as he gently corrects my naïve imagery of the duality of structure. He also illustrates rules and resources by referring to status hierarchies and the process of voting, which are typical group structures. Poole then clarifies the way in which his theory has a critical edge. If you got bogged down in the jargon of structuration, you'll be grateful for this interview.

A SECOND LOOK

Recommended resource: Marshall Scott Poole, "Group Communication and the Structuring Process," in *Small Group Communication: Theory & Practice,* 8th ed., Robert Cathcart, Randy Hirokawa, Larry Samovar, and Linda Henman (eds.), Roxbury, Los Angeles, 2003, pp. 48–56.

Expanded treatment: Marshall Scott Poole, David Seibold, and Robert McPhee, "The Structuration of Group Decisions," in *Communication and Group Decision Making,* 2nd ed., Randy Hirokawa and Marshall Scott Poole (eds.), Sage, Thousand Oaks, CA, 1996, pp. 114–146.

Initial statement: Marshall Scott Poole, David Seibold, and Robert McPhee, "Group Decision-Making as a Structurational Process," *Quarterly Journal of Speech,* Vol. 71, 1985, pp. 74–102.

Giddens' theory of structuration: Anthony Giddens, *The Constitution of Society: Outline of the Theory of Structuration,* University of California, Berkeley, 1984, pp. 281–284, 373–377.

Profile of Giddens: Robert Boynton, "The Two Tonys," *The New Yorker,* October 6, 1997, pp. 66–74.

GDSS research: Marshall Scott Poole and Gerardine DeSanctis, "Microlevel Structuration in Computer-Supported Group Decision Making," *Human Communication Research,* Vol. 19, 1992, pp. 5–49.

Faithful appropriation of GDSS: Moez Limayem, Probir Banerjee, and Louis Ma, "Impact of GDSS: Opening the Black Box," *Decision Support Systems,* Vol. 42, 2006, pp. 945–957.

Structuration in organizations: Robert McPhee, "Formal Structure and Organizational Communication," in *Organizational Communication: Traditional Themes and New Directions,* Robert McPhee and Phillip Tompkins (eds.), Sage, Beverly Hills, CA, 1985, pp. 149–178.

Rules for decision making: Sunwolf and David Seibold, "Jurors' Intuitive Rules for Deliberation: A Structurational Approach to Communication in Jury Decision Making," *Communication Monographs,* Vol. 65, 1998, pp. 282–307.

Self-critique: Marshall Scott Poole, "Do We Have Any Theories of Group Communication?" *Communication Studies,* Vol. 41, 1990, pp. 237–247.

State-of-the-art critique: Bryan Seyfarth, "Structuration Theory in Small Group Communication: A Review and Agenda for Future Research," in *Communication Yearbook 23,* Michael Roloff (ed.), Sage, Thousand Oaks, CA, 2000, pp. 341–380.

What do the following organizations have in common—the *United States Navy, McDonald's, General Motors,* and the *Green Bay Packers*? The first three are gigantic organizations, the middle two sell a tangible product, and the last three are publicly owned corporations that try to make a profit. But in terms of organizational communication, their most important common feature is that each is a prime example of *classical management theory* in action. Figure OC–1 lists some of the principles of this traditional approach to management.

The Mechanistic Approach.   Classical management theory places a premium on productivity, precision, and efficiency. As York University management professor Gareth Morgan notes, these are the very qualities that you expect from a well-designed, smoothly running machine. Morgan uses the machine metaphor because he finds significant parallels between mechanical devices and the way managers traditionally think about their organizations.[1] In classical management theory, workers are seen as cogs in vast machines that function smoothly as long as their range of motion is clearly defined and their actions are lubricated with an adequate hourly wage.

Machines repeat straightforward, repetitive tasks, just as McDonald's workers have cooked more than 100 billion hamburgers, each one in exactly the same way. Machines have interchangeable parts that can be replaced when broken or worn out, just as a National Football League coach can insert a new player into the tight end slot when the current starter is injured or begins to slow down. A new Chevrolet comes with a thick operator's manual that specifies how the car should be driven, but the General Motors employees' handbook is thicker and contains even more detailed instructions on how things are done within the company. As for the U.S. Navy, the fleet is an integral part of the country's war machine, and officers at every level are most comfortable when it runs like one.

Unity of command—an employee should receive orders from only one superior.

Scalar chain—the line of authority from superior to subordinate, which runs from top to bottom of the organization; this chain, which results from the unity of command principle, should be used as a channel for communication and decision making.

Division of work—management should aim to achieve a degree of specialization designed to achieve the goal of the organization in an efficient manner.

Authority and responsibility—attention should be paid to the right to give orders and to exact obedience; an appropriate balance between authority and responsibility should be achieved.

Discipline—obedience, application, energy, behavior, and outward marks of respect in accordance with agreed rules and customs.

Subordination of individual interest to general interest—through firmness, example, fair agreements, and constant supervision.

FIGURE OC–1   Selected Principles of Classical Management Theory
(Excerpted from Gareth Morgan, "Organizations as Machines" in *Images of Organizations*)

THE FAR SIDE®   By GARY LARSON

"And so you just threw everything together? ... Matthews, a posse is something you have to *organize*."

At least three theories view classical management theory as outmoded and reject the mechanistic analogies on which bureaucratic organizations are based. The theorists offer alternative ways of thinking about organizing people and the tasks they do. Each approach is based on a different image of the organization that counters the dominant machine model.

The Living Systems Approach.   Karl Weick regards hierarchical structures, chain-of-command lines of communication, and standard operating procedures as enemies of innovation. This University of Michigan professor of organizational behavior and psychology sees organizations as living organisms that must constantly adapt to a changing environment in order to stay alive. They do this by sorting through vast amounts of information and trying to figure out what it all means. Weick believes that organizations survive and thrive only when their members engage in free-flowing, interactive communication.[2]

The Cultural Approach. Symbolic interactionists assume that human beings act toward things on the basis of the meanings those things have for them (see Chapter 5). Given impetus by the theoretical and ethnographic insights of anthropologist Clifford Geertz, cultural researchers look for shared meanings that are unique to a given organization. Chapter 19 describes the interpretive frame that Michael Pacanowsky uses to decipher corporate culture. For Pacanowsky and other interpretive theorists, culture is not something that an organization *has*; culture is something an organization *is*. Even in two mechanistic organizations where the task is routine, repetitive, and boring, employees may interpret their work differently. Workers under the golden arches often cope with tedium by referring derisively to their "McJobs." On the other hand, civil servants sorting mail eight hours a day may go "postal." The cultural approach takes language seriously by listening carefully for clues to the unique shared meaning that is at the heart of any organization.

The Critical Approach. In his critical theory of communication, Stan Deetz criticizes the traditional manager's overwhelming concern for control as the preferred means of cost cutting and efficiency. To experience managerial control firsthand you need only make a phone call to customer service at a large corporation. After wending your way through a series of phone-tree options (which serve the company but not the customer), you reach the department and hear one final recording: "This call may be monitored to ensure quality control." Deetz agrees with CMM's premise that persons-in-conversation create their own social realities (see Chapter 6). Yet in most corporations, the manager controls the meaningful conversation, and so he or she creates a world in which many live, yet few have a say in the design of the company or the decisions it makes. Chapter 20 introduces Deetz' democratic approach to corporate decision making. He suggests that all people who are significantly affected by company policy are legitimate stakeholders and should be invited to participate in decisions that affect them.

To access a chapter on Weick's information systems approach to organizations that appeared in a previous edition, click on Theory Archive at *www.afirstlook.com*.

Cultural Approach to Organizations

of Clifford Geertz & Michael Pacanowsky

Princeton anthropologist Clifford Geertz writes that "man is an animal suspended in webs of significance that he himself has spun."[1] He pictures culture as those webs. In order to travel across the strands toward the center of the web, an outsider must discover the common interpretations that hold the web together. Culture is shared meaning, shared understanding, shared sensemaking.

Geertz has conducted field research in the islands of Indonesia and on the Moroccan highlands, rural settings remote from industrial activity. His best-known monograph is an in-depth symbolic analysis of the Balinese cockfight. Geertz has never written a treatise on the bottom line, never tried to decipher the significance of the office Christmas party, and never met a payroll—a disqualifying sin in the eyes of many business professionals. Despite his silence on the topic of big business, Geertz' interpretive approach has proved useful in making sense of organizational activity.

In the field of communication, former University of Colorado professor Michael Pacanowsky has applied Geertz' cultural insights to organizational life. He says that if culture consists of webs of meaning that people have spun, and if spun webs imply the act of spinning, "then we need to concern ourselves not only with the structures of cultural webs, but with the process of their spinning as well."[2] That process is communication. It is communication that "creates and constitutes the taken-for-granted reality of the world."[3]

CULTURE AS A METAPHOR OF ORGANIZATIONAL LIFE

The use of culture as a root metaphor was undoubtedly stimulated by Western fascination with the economic success of Japanese corporations in the 1970s and 1980s. Back then, when American business leaders traveled to the Far East to study methods of production, they discovered that the superior quantity and quality of Japan's industrial output had less to do with technology than with workers' shared cultural value of loyalty to each other and to their corporation. Organizations look radically different depending on how people in the host culture structure meaning. Communal face-saving in Japan is foreign to the class antagonism of Great Britain or the we're-number-one competitive mindset of the United States.

Today the term *corporate culture* means different things to different people. Some observers use the phrase to describe the surrounding environment that constrains a company's freedom of action. (U.S. workers would scoff at singing a corporate anthem at the start of their working day.) Others use the term to refer to a quality or property of the organization. (Acme Gizmo is a friendly place to work.) They speak of *culture* as synonymous with *image, character,* or *climate.* But Pacanowsky is committed to Geertz' symbolic approach and thus considers culture as more than a single variable in organizational research:

> Organizational culture is not just another piece of the puzzle; it is the puzzle. From our point of view, culture is not something an organization has; a culture is something an organization is.[4]

WHAT CULTURE IS; WHAT CULTURE IS NOT

Geertz admits that the concept of culture as *systems of shared meaning* is somewhat vague and difficult to grasp. Unlike popular usage, which equates culture with concerts and art museums, he refuses to use the word to signify *less primitive.* No modern anthropologist would fall into the trap of classifying people as high- or low-culture.

Culture
Webs of significance; systems of shared meaning.

Culture is not whole or undivided. Geertz points out that even close-knit societies have subcultures and countercultures within their boundaries. For example, employees in the sales and accounting departments of the same company may eye each other warily—the first group calling the accountants *number crunchers* and *bean counters,* the accountants in turn labeling members of the sales force *fast talkers* and *glad-handers.* Despite their differences, both groups may regard the blue-collar bowling night of the production workers as a strange ritual compared with their own weekend ritual of a round of golf.

For Pacanowsky, the web of organizational culture is the residue of employees' performances—"those very actions by which members constitute and reveal their culture to themselves and to others."[5] He notes that job performance may play only a minor role in the enactment of corporate culture.

Cultural performance
Actions by which members constitute and reveal their culture to themselves and others; an ensemble of texts.

> People do get the job done, true (though probably not with the singleminded task-orientation communication texts would have us believe); but people in organizations also gossip, joke, knife one another, initiate romantic involvements, cue new employees to ways of doing the least amount of work that still avoids hassles from a supervisor, talk sports, arrange picnics.[6]

Geertz calls these cultural performances "an ensemble of texts . . . which the anthropologist strains to read over the shoulder of those to whom they properly belong."[7] The elusive nature of culture prompts Geertz to label its study a *soft science.* It is "not an experimental science in search of law, but an interpretive one in search of meaning."[8] The corporate observer is one part scientist, one part drama critic.

The fact that symbolic expression requires interpretation is nicely captured in a story about Pablo Picasso recorded by York University (Toronto) writer Gareth Morgan.[9] A man commissioned Picasso to paint a portrait of his wife. Startled by the nonrepresentational image on the canvas, the woman's husband complained, "It isn't how she really looks." When asked by the painter how she really looked, the man produced a photograph from his wallet. Picasso's comment: "Small, isn't she?"

THICK DESCRIPTION—WHAT ETHNOGRAPHERS DO

Ethnography
Mapping out social discourse; discovering who people within a culture think they are, what they think they are doing, and to what end they think they are doing it.

Geertz refers to himself as an *ethnographer*. You'll recall that I first introduced his name when I presented ethnography as one of the four main communication research methodologies (see Chapter 2). Just as geographers chart the physical territory, ethnographers map out social discourse. They do this "to discover who people think they are, what they think they are doing, and to what end they think they are doing it."[10] There's no shortcut for the months of participant observation required to collect an exhaustive account of interaction. Without that raw material, there would be nothing to interpret.

Geertz spent years in Indonesia and Morocco, developing his deep description of separate cultures. Pacanowsky initially invested nine months with W. L. Gore & Associates, best known for its Gore-Tex line of sports clothing and equipment. Like Geertz, he was completely open about his research goals, and during the last five months of his research he participated fully in problem-solving conferences at the company. Later, Pacanowsky spent additional time at the W. L. Gore plants in Delaware as a consultant. In order to become intimately familiar with an organization *as members experience it*, ethnographers must commit to the long haul. More recently, Pacanowsky has committed to the long haul of working full time at Gore, this despite his earlier caution against "going native." At that time he warned that the researcher must

> maintain a posture of radical naïveté and allow himself or herself to experience organizational life as "strange," so that he or she will be sure to prompt organizational members for the resources (or knowledge) they are drawing upon which allow them to take for granted those very same organizational experiences.[11]

Thick description
A record of the intertwined layers of common meaning that underlie what a particular people say and do.

The daily written accounts of intensive observation invariably fill the pages of many ethnographic notebooks. The visual image of these journals stacked on top of each other would be sufficient justification for Geertz to refer to ethnography as *thick description*. The term, however, describes the intertwined layers of common meaning that underlie what a particular people say and do. Analysis of corporate culture requires interpretation as well as observation. It's not enough to preserve copies of office memos or to make transcripts of meetings. Thick description is tracing the many strands of a cultural web and tracking evolving meaning.

Thick description starts with a state of bewilderment. *What the devil's going on?* Geertz asks himself as he wades into a new culture. The only way to reduce the puzzlement is to observe as if one were a stranger in a foreign land. This can be difficult for a manager who is already enmeshed in a specific corporate culture. He or she might overlook many of the signs that point to common interpretation. Worse yet, the manager might assume that office humor or the company grapevine has the same significance for people in this culture as it does for those in a previous place of employment. Geertz says it will always be different.

Behaviorists would probably consider employee trips to the office water-cooler of little interest. If they did regard water breaks worth studying, they would tend to note the number of trips and length of stay for each worker. Ethnographers would be more interested in the significance this seemingly mundane activity had for these particular employees. Instead of a neat statistical summary, they'd record pages of dialogue at the watercooler. Pacanowsky fears that a frequency count would only bleach human behavior of the very properties that interest him. Classifying performances across organizations would yield superficial generalizations at the cost of localized insight. He'd rather find out what makes a particular tribal culture unique.

Although Pacanowsky would pay attention to all cultural performances, he would be particularly sensitive to the imaginative language members used, the stories they told, and the nonverbal rites and rituals they practiced. Taken together, these three forms of communication provide helpful access to the unique shared meanings within an organization.

METAPHORS: TAKING LANGUAGE SERIOUSLY

Metaphor
Clarifies what is unknown or confusing by equating it with an image that's more familiar or vivid.

When used by members throughout an organization (and not just management), *metaphors* can offer the ethnographer a starting place for accessing the shared meaning of a corporate culture. Pacanowsky records a number of prominent metaphors used at W. L. Gore & Associates, none more significant than the oft-heard reference within the company to Gore as a *lattice organization*.[12] If one tried to graph the lines of communication at Gore, the map would look like a lattice rather than the traditional pyramid-shaped organizational chart. The crosshatched lines would show the importance of one-on-one communication and reflect the fact that no person within the company needs permission to talk to anyone else. Easy access to others is facilitated by an average plant size of 150 employees, with voice mail and paging systems that encourage quick responses.

This lack of hierarchical authority within the lattice organization is captured in the egalitarian title of *associate* given to every worker. People do have differential status at Gore, but it comes from technical expertise, a track record of good judgment, and evidence of follow-through that leads to accomplishment.

The company's stated objective (singular) is "to make money and have fun."[13] The founder, Bill Gore, was famous for popping into associates' offices and asking, "Did you make any money today? Did you have any fun today?" But work at Gore is not frivolous. The *waterline* operating principle makes it clear that associates should check with others before making significant decisions:

> Each of us will consult with appropriate Associates who will share the responsibility of taking any action that has the potential of serious harm to the reputation, success, or survival of the Enterprise. The analogy is that our Enterprise is like a ship that we are all in together. Boring holes above the waterline is not serious, but below the waterline, holes could sink us.[14]

After nine months of studying communication performances at W. L. Gore & Associates, Pacanowsky floated three different metaphors of his own to describe crucial features of that unique culture.[15] He thought of Gore as a *cluster of peasant villages* in its passion for decentralization and its extraordinary orality. He saw Gore like a *large improvisational jazz group* because of its attraction for people who love to create something new but want to fit in with other like-minded players. And he compared the people at Gore to *factions in Colonial America* inasmuch as the majority of associates thought that the company's innovative charter was the best thing since the invention of the wheel, yet a significant minority were cynical about the idealistic goals. For both the discovery and the communication of corporate culture, ethnographers find metaphor a valuable tool.

THE SYMBOLIC INTERPRETATION OF STORY

Stories that are told over and over provide a convenient window through which to view corporate webs of significance. Pacanowsky asks, "Has a good story been told that takes you to the heart of the matter?"[16] He focuses on the scriptlike qualities of narratives that portray an employee's part in the company play. Although workers have room to improvise, the anecdotes provide clues as to what it means to perform a task in this particular theater. Stories capture memorable performances and pass on the passion the actor felt at the time.

Pacanowsky suggests three types of narrative that dramatize organizational life. *Corporate stories* carry the ideology of management and reinforce company policy. Every McDonald's franchisee hears about the late Ray Kroc, who, when he was chairman of the board, picked up trash from the parking lot when he'd visit a store. *Personal stories* are those that company personnel tell about themselves, often defining how they would like to be seen within the organization. If you've seen NBC's hit television comedy *The Office*, you've witnessed Dwight Schrute's interviews with the camera crew. During these interviews, he talks about his excellence as an employee and how he deserves the respect of others in the Dunder Mifflin paper company. These are Dwight's personal accounts. *Collegial stories* are positive or negative anecdotes told about others in the organization. When the camera crew interviews Dwight's colleagues Jim and Pam, we hear stories of Dwight's eccentricity and lack of basic social awareness. These collegial stories describe Dwight as someone who is not to be taken seriously. Since these tales aren't usually sanctioned by management, collegial accounts pass on how the organization "really works."

Stories at Dixie

Throughout most of my life, I've had access to some of the cultural lore of Dixie Communications, a medium-size corporation that operates a newspaper and a television station in a Southern city. Like so many other regional companies, Dixie has been taken over by an out-of-state corporation that has no local ties. The following three narratives are shorthand versions of stories heard again and again throughout the company.

> Although the original publisher has been dead for 30 years, old-timers fondly recall how he would spend Christmas Eve with the workers in the press room. Their account is invariably linked with reminders that he initiated health benefits and profit sharing prior to any union demand. (Corporate)

> The current comptroller is the highest-ranking "local boy" in the corporation. He often tells the story about the first annual audit he performed long before computers were installed. Puzzled when he ran across a bill for 50 pounds of pigeon feed, he discovered that the company used homing pigeons to send in news copy and circulation orders from a town across the bay. The story usually concludes with an editorial

Corporate stories
Tales that carry management ideology and reinforce company policy.

Personal stories
Tales told by employees that put them in a favorable light.

Collegial stores
Positive or negative anecdotes about others in the organization; descriptions of how things really work.

comment about pigeons being more reliable than the new machines. His self-presentation reminds listeners that he has always been cost-conscious, yet it also aligns him with the human side of the "warm people versus cold machines" issue. (Personal)

Shortly after the takeover, a department head encouraged the new publisher to meet with his people for a few minutes at the end of the day. The new boss declined the invitation on the grounds of efficiency: "To be quite candid, I don't want to know about a woman's sick child or a man's vacation plans. That kind of information makes it harder to fire a person." Spoken in a cold, superior tone, the words *quite candid* are always part of the story. (Collegial)

Both Geertz and Pacanowsky caution against any analysis that says, "This story means. . . ." Narratives contain a mosaic of significance and defy a simplistic, one-on-one translation of symbols. Yet taken as a whole, the three stories reveal an uneasiness with the new management. This interpretation is consistent with repeated metaphorical references to the old Dixie as *family* and the new Dixie as *a faceless computer.*

Fiction as a Form of Scholarly Discourse

Not only has Pacanowsky shown that narratives are a prime source of cultural wisdom for the ethnographer, but he has also demonstrated that scholars can use a fictional format to convey the results of their research. In the *Quarterly Journal of Speech*, Pacanowsky published an imaginative account that captures the angst felt within a subculture of academics. In the introduction he claims that "fictional descriptions, by the very nature of their implicitness and impressionism can fully capture (can I be so strong?) both the bold outlines and the crucial nuances of cultural ethos."[17] Figure 19–1 shows an excerpt of a conversation between two communication professors during an annual convention. Nick Trujillo, a co-author with Pacanowsky on other organizational culture articles, refers to the piece as a *confessional tale.*[18]

RITUAL: THIS IS THE WAY IT'S ALWAYS BEEN AND ALWAYS WILL BE

Geertz wrote about the Balinese rite of cockfighting because the contest represented more than a game. "It is only apparently cocks that are fighting there. Actually it is men." The cockfight is a dramatization of status. "Its function is interpretive: It is a Balinese reading of Balinese experience, a story they tell themselves about themselves."[19]

Ritual
Texts that articulate multiple aspects of cultural life, often marking rites of passage or life transitions

Pacanowsky agrees with Geertz that some rituals (like the Balinese cockfight) are "texts" that articulate *multiple* aspects of cultural life.[20] These rituals are nearly sacred, and any attempt to change them meets with strong resistance. Although the emphasis on improvisation and novelty reduces the importance of ritual at Gore, organizational rites at more traditional companies weave together many threads of corporate culture.

Over a generation ago, workers in the classified advertising department at Dixie created an integrative rite that survives to the present. The department is staffed by over 50 telephone sales representatives who work out of a large common room. At Dixie, these representatives not only take the "two lines/two days/two dollars" personal ads over the phone, but they also initiate callbacks to find out if customers were successful and might want to sell other items. Compared with similar operations at other papers, classified advertising at Dixie is a major

Slouching Towards Chicago

He and Radner were such different people, and they were not really close friends. But at every convention, they would get together over dinner and appraise their professional careers and personal lives in a surpisingly intimate manner. One year, Radner had side-splitting tales to tell of his affair with the wife of his department chairman. The next year, he cried as he worked his way through the details of his divorce. For his part, Jack was inclined to reflect on the transitions of his life—how strangely happy he was to have gotten married in a church, how being a father brought him to heights of joy and depths of anger he'd never before felt capable of experiencing, how he would become seized by intense physical cold on those occasions when he really thought about his father's death. "Our lives in review" was the way Jack thought about those dinners with Radner.

"You know," said Radner, "in seven years, I have authored or co-authored 48 convention papers, and published 14 articles in refereed journals, and had 10 chapters invited for various textbooks and readers. . . But you're a known item in the field. People read your work. They talk about it. They get worked up about it. I mean, I hate to admit it, but it's true. Nobody really gets worked up about my stuff. But your stuff—"

"Hype. I get calls in the night from 24-year-old groundbreakers-to-be who can't add. 'I have to put together my prospectus and I don't want to do a traditional, quantitative study, and I read your article in *QJ*, and I wondered if you could send me anything else you've written that I can use to, you know, develop my position, I mean, everybody here is so traditional, I don't know if they'll let me do an interpretive study . . .' on and on."

"But that's what I mean. People get excited."

"I don't. You know what I want? What I want more than 70 articles or people getting excited or calling me up? What I want is to write one good solid book-length piece of interpretive research. No more diddly articles. No more 'this is what we should be doing.' Just one solid book. And then I'd get excited."

"Why don't you then?"

"I can't!" Jack pounded the table with his fist. "I gotta worry about tenure. I gotta worry about building my vita. So I piss away my time on these damned convention papers, on these 'take-a-potshot-at-the-other-guy' articles instead of—"

"Oh, come on. You're going to get tenure. Why don't you stop doing this other shit and work on a book?"

It was not a question that Jack had never heard before, not with the frequency with which he would launch into his 'pissing my life away' refrain. But maybe it was because it was during "life in review" that the question suddenly hit him with a force and an eeriness that he hadn't felt before. He was silent for a moment. "Because," he said finally, shaken with the realization, "I don't know if I really have it in me to write a book. And it scares me to think I might find that out."

FIGURE 19–1   Excerpt from "Slouching Towards Chicago" by Michael Pacanowsky

profit center with low employee turnover. The department continues to have the *family atmosphere* of premerger Dixie. Most of the phone representatives are women under the age of 40. They regard Max, the male manager who has held his position for over 30 years, as a *father confessor*—a warm, nonjudgmental person with a genuine concern for their lives. Whenever a female employee has a baby, Max visits her in the hospital and offers help to those at home preparing for her return. Women announce their pregnancy by taping a dime within a large picture frame on the outer wall of Max' office, inscribing their name and anticipated day of delivery. This rite of integration serves multiple functions for the women:

> At a time of potential anxiety, it is an occasion for public affirmation from the larger community.

> The rite is a point of contact between work and those outside of Dixie. Employees often take pride in describing the ritual to customers and friends.

Although the dime-on-the-wall practice originated with the workers, the authorized chronicle of decades of expected births proclaims a sense of permanence. It says in effect: "The company doesn't consider motherhood a liability; your job will be here when you get back."

From the management's standpoint, the rite ensures that there will be no surprises. Max has plenty of time to schedule the employee's maternity leave, arrange for another salesperson to cover her accounts, and anticipate stresses that she might be encountering.

It is tempting to read economic significance into the fact that employees use dimes to symbolize this major change in their lives. But the women involved refer to the small size of the token rather than its monetary value. Geertz and Pacanowsky would caution that this is *their* story; we should listen to *their* interpretation.

CAN THE MANAGER BE AN AGENT OF CULTURAL CHANGE?

The popularity of the cultural metaphor when it was first introduced to the corporate world in the 1980s was undoubtedly due to business leaders' desire to shape interpretation within the organization. Symbols are the tools of management. Executives don't operate forklifts or produce widgets; they create a vision, state goals, process information, send memos, and engage in other symbolic behavior. If they believe that culture is the key to worker commitment, productivity, and sales, the possibility of changing culture becomes a seductive idea. Creating favorable metaphors, planting organizational stories, and establishing rites would seem an ideal way to create a corporate myth that would serve managerial interests.

But can culture be created? Geertz regards shared interpretations as naturally emerging from all members of a group rather than consciously engineered by leaders. In *The Office*, Jim, Pam, Stanley, and Phyllis all play a part in developing their corporate culture. And you'll notice that despite his best efforts, manager Michael Scott can't alter it single-handedly. Managers may articulate a new vision in a fresh vocabulary, but it is the workers who smile, sigh, snicker, or scoff. For example, Martin Luther King's "I Have a Dream" speech, which will be discussed in Chapter 21, was powerful because he touched a chord that was already vibrating within millions of listeners.

DILBERT: © Scott Adams / Dist. by United Feature Syndicate, Inc.

Shared meanings are hard to dispel. Symbol watchers within a company quickly discount the words of management if they don't square with performance. Yet even if culture *could* be changed, there still remains the question of whether it *should* be. Symbolic anthropologists have traditionally adopted a non-intrusive style appropriate to examining fine crystal—look, admire, but don't touch. So managers who regard themselves as agents of cultural change create bull-in-a-china-shop fears for ethnographers who have ethical concerns about how their corporate analyses might be used. University of Massachusetts management professor Linda Smircich notes that ethnographers would draw back in horror at the idea of using their data to extend a tribal priest's control over the population, yet most communication consultants are hired by top management to do just that.[21]

CRITIQUE: IS THE CULTURAL APPROACH USEFUL?

By now you understand that Geertz would regard the quest to alter culture as both inappropriate and virtually impossible. This purist position exposes him and his admirers within our discipline to criticism from corporate consultants who not only desire to understand organizational communication but also want to influence it.

A different kind of objection comes from critical theorists who fault the cultural approach because interpretive scholars like Geertz and Pacanowsky refuse to evaluate the customs that they portray. For example, if Pacanowsky were to discover that women associates at Gore hit a glass ceiling when they try to advance, these advocates insist that he should *expose* and *deplore* this injustice rather than merely *describe* and *interpret* it for readers.[22]

For researchers who take a cultural approach to organizational life, both of these objections miss the point of their work. Contrary to the traditional aims of consultants funded by the organizations they study, the purpose of ethnography is not to change the organization or help managers exert more control. Nor is it to pass moral judgment. The goal of symbolic analysis is to create a better understanding of what it takes to function effectively within the culture. In most organizations, members are free to decide whether they want to belong. A sensitive cultural analysis could help them make an intelligent choice. Perhaps managers and social justice advocates fail to appreciate the value of thick description because they have yet to make an effort to sort out the webs of significance within their own organizations.

There might be another reason that interest in the cultural approach has waned in the last decade. In Chapter 3, I cited *aesthetic appeal* as one of the criteria for a good interpretive theory. The force of an ethnographic analysis depends in large measure on the prose in which it's couched. In the *Times Literary Supplement* (U.K.), T. M. Luhrmann gives testimony to the compelling power of Geertz' writing: "Rarely has there been a social scientist who has also been so acute a writer; perhaps there has never been one so quotable."[23] Indeed, Geertz' interpretation of a Balinese cockfight reads like an engrossing novel that the reader can't put down. Though Pacanowsky writes well, it may not be until a perceptive ethnographer with Geertz' compelling way with words focuses on organizational life that the cultural approach will spark renewed interest.

QUESTIONS TO SHARPEN YOUR FOCUS

1. Based on the concept of organizational culture as systems of *shared meaning*, how would you describe the culture at your school to a prospective student?

2. Consider Pacanowsky's "Slouching Towards Chicago" as an *ethnographer's thick description*. What can you deduce about Jack and Radner's subculture from the fragment of narrative in Figure 19–1?

3. Think of your extended family as an *organizational culture*. What family *ritual* might you analyze to *interpret* the webs of significance you share to someone visiting your home?

4. What favorite *story* do you tell to others about your most recent place of employment? Is it as a *corporate, personal,* or *collegial* narrative?

SELF-QUIZ

www.mhhe.com/griffin7

A SECOND LOOK

Recommended resource: Clifford Geertz, *The Interpretation of Cultures*, Basic Books, New York, 1973. (See especially "Thick Description: Toward an Interpretive Theory of Culture," pp. 3–30; and "Deep Play: Notes on the Balinese Cockfight," pp. 412–453.)

Culture as performance: Michael Pacanowsky and Nick O'Donnell-Trujillo, "Organizational Communication as Cultural Performance," *Communication Monographs 50,* 1983, pp. 127–147.

Nonmanagerial orientation: Michael Pacanowsky and Nick O'Donnell-Trujillo, "Communication and Organizational Cultures," *Western Journal of Speech Communication*, Vol. 46, 1982, pp. 115–130.

Cultural metaphor: Gareth Morgan, "Creating Social Reality: Organizations as Cultures," in *Images of Organization*, Sage, Newbury Park, CA, 1986, pp. 111–140.

Corporate ethnography: Michael Pacanowsky, "Communication in the Empowering Organization," in *Communication Yearbook 11,* James Anderson (ed.), Sage, Newbury Park, CA, 1988, pp. 356–379.

Corporate stories: Joanne Martin, Martha Feldman, Mary Jo Hatch, and Sim Sitkin, "The Uniqueness Paradox in Organizational Stories," *Administrative Science Quarterly*, Vol. 28, 1983, pp. 438–453.

Rites: Harrison Trice and Janice Beyer, "Studying Organizational Cultures Through Rites and Ceremonials," *Academy of Management Review*, Vol. 9, 1984, pp. 653–669.

Interpretive vs. functional approach: Linda L. Putnam, "The Interpretive Perspective: An Alternative to Functionalism," in *Communication and Organizations: An Interpretive Approach*, Linda L. Putnam and Michael Pacanowsky (eds.), Sage, Newbury Park, CA, 1982, pp. 31–54.

Brief autobiography: Clifford Geertz, *A Life of Learning* (ACLS Occasional Paper No. 45), American Council of Learned Societies, New York, 1999.

Webs of shared meaning at the ballpark: Nick Trujillo, "Interpreting (the Work and the Talk of) Baseball: Perspectives on Ballpark Culture," *Western Journal of Communication*, Vol. 56, 1992, pp. 350–371.

Current scholarship: Anat Fafaeli and Monica Worline, "Symbols in Organizational Culture," in *Handbook of Organizational Culture & Climate,* Neal Ashkanasy, Celeste P. M. Wilderom, and Mark Peterson (eds.), Sage, Thousand Oaks, CA, 2000, pp. 71–84.

Interpretive research: Bryan Taylor and Nick Trujillo, "Qualitative Research Methods," in *The New Handbook of Organizational Communication,* Fredric Jablin and Linda L. Putnam (eds.), Sage, Thousand Oaks, CA, 2001, pp. 161–194.

Rationale for corporate ethnography: Brigitte Jordan and Brinda Dalal, "Persuasive Encounters: Ethnography in the Corporation," *Field Methods,* Vol. 18, No. 4, 2006, pp. 1–24.

To find out which communication theory textbooks
discuss a cultural approach to organizations,
click on Compare Texts at
www.afirstlook.com.

Critical Theory of Communication in Organizations

of Stanley Deetz

Based on a true story, the 1999 film *Erin Brockovich* dramatizes the four-year quest of a novice legal researcher to win compensation and damages for victims of corporate irresponsibility.[1] Played by Julia Roberts, who received the year's Best Actress Academy Award for her performance, Brockovich becomes an advocate for over 600 people poisoned by water contaminated by Pacific Gas & Electric (PG&E). As the story unfolds, Brockovich uncovers a series of managerial decisions that eventually cost the company $333 million—the largest judgment awarded in a direct-action lawsuit in U.S. history. Aimed at cutting corporate costs, these managerial moves also resulted in catastrophic health problems for the residents of Hinkley, California, and cost some of them their lives.

Like most producers of electricity, PG&E used water to cool the turbine blades of its generators. But it added a rust inhibitor containing hexavalent chromium to prolong the life of the blades. Unlike other chromium compounds that are benign or even beneficial, scientists have long known that chrome 6 is harmful to humans and animals. Highly toxic water was piped into unlined outdoor ponds, where it seeped into the ground and contaminated the well water in the nearby town. Long-term residents experienced chronic headaches and nosebleeds, bone deterioration, liver failure, lung failure, reproductive failure, heart failure, and many forms of lethal cancer.

Using the chrome 6 additive was a bad decision to begin with. Internal company documents showed that decades before the danger became public, managers in the San Francisco headquarters knew about the well water contamination. Deciding not to fix the problem was the second tragic decision. Directing Hinkley branch officials to say nothing about the contaminated water was the third. Company-paid doctors treated those who became ill but told patients that there was no connection between the generating plant and their illnesses. And when a regulatory board mandated an environmental cleanup, plant managers assured a

261

meeting of 200 concerned citizens that the chromium additive was harmless and even sent out a pamphlet saying that it was good for them. Actually, the water contained 10 times the allowable level of hexavalent chromium.

PG&E managers showed continual bad judgment when Ed Masry, the lawyer who employed Erin, tried to negotiate for a family in which the father had Hodgkin's disease and the mother faced a hysterectomy and a double mastectomy. They sent a low-level flunky who offered to buy their home for $250,000 but had no authority to negotiate or discuss health claims. Yet he apparently had been instructed to warn Ed and Erin that they were dealing with a $28 billion company. Big mistake. PG&E later had to pay that family $5 million.

Erin Brockovich is just one of many feature films about corporate managers who make decisions without regard for the negative consequences to their employees, consumers, or the general public—others include *The Insider, Roger and Me, Silkwood,* and *The China Syndrome.* These movies tap a growing concern among Americans that something is wrong with the way decisions are reached at the highest levels of business. The modern corporation is protected from direct public control, yet it's the place where the crucial decisions that affect the everyday lives of citizens are made.

University of Colorado communication professor Stanley Deetz has developed a critical communication theory to explore ways to ensure the financial health of corporations while increasing the representation of diverse—and often noneconomic—human interests. He does this by first showing that corporations have become political institutions, as well as economic ones. He then employs advances in communication theory to point out how communication practices within corporations can distort decision making. Finally, he outlines how workplaces can become more productive and democratic through communication reforms.

CORPORATE COLONIZATION OF EVERYDAY LIFE

Deetz views multinational corporations such as GM, AT&T, IBM, Time Warner, Disney, and Microsoft as the dominant force in society—more powerful than the church, state, or family in their ability to influence the lives of individuals. For example, over 90 percent of the mass media outlets—newspapers, broadcast, cable, telephone lines, and satellites—are owned by just a handful of corporations.[2] Deetz notes that continual reporting of the Dow-Jones Industrial Average underscores the absence of an equivalent index of the arts, health care, or environmental quality. Media preoccupation with corporate well-being makes President George W. Bush's post–9/11 equation of consumer spending with patriotism seem almost logical.

The corporate executive suite is the place where most decisions are made regarding the use of natural resources, development of new technologies, product availability, and working relations among people. Deetz says that corporations "control and colonize" modern life in ways that no government or public body since the feudal era ever thought possible.[3] Yet the fallout of corporate control is a sharp decrease in the human quality of life for the vast majority of citizens.

Corporate colonization
Encroachment of modern corporations into every area of life outside the workplace.

Within the lifetime of most of today's college students, the average American workweek has increased from 40 to 50 hours, and leisure time has declined by a corresponding 10 hours. Despite the fact that 85 percent of families with children now have mothers working outside the home, their real standard of living has *decreased* over the last two decades. The number of full-time workers whose income has fallen below the poverty line has increased by half, yet compensation for chief executive officers (CEOs) has risen from 24 times to over 175 times that of the average worker.[4] Deetz suggests that "we need to consider in depth what type of 'business' this is, who the moral claimants are, how privilege is organized, and what the possible democratic responses are."[5]

Deetz' theory of communication is *critical* in that he wants to critique the easy assumption that "what's good for General Motors is good for the country." More specifically, he wants to examine communication practices in organizations that undermine fully representative decision making and thus reduce the quality, innovation, and fairness of company policy.

INFORMATION OR COMMUNICATION: A DIFFERENCE THAT MAKES A DIFFERENCE

Deetz begins his analysis by challenging the view that communication is the transmission of information. Even though a majority of human communication scholars now dismiss Shannon and Weaver's information theory (see Chapter 4), the conduit model is still taken for granted in organizations and in everyday life. There's an intuitive appeal in the idea that words refer to real things—that by using the right words we can express state-of-the-art knowledge. As Deetz notes, "Clearly, the public really wants to believe in an independent reality."[6] He warns, however, that as long as we accept the notion that communication is merely the transmission of information, we will continue to perpetuate corporate dominance over every aspect of our lives.

Information model
A view that communication is merely a conduit for the transmission of information about the real world.

Consider PG&E's annual report. The sanitized numbers present themselves as facts compiled and categorized according to "standard accounting procedures." Yet Deetz contends that each line item is *constitutive*—created by corporate decision makers who had the power to make their decisions stick. What seems to be value-free information is really meaning *in formation*. The end-of-the-year audit is not fact—it's artifact. All corporate information is an outcome of political processes that are usually undemocratic and have consequences that usually hurt democracy.

In place of the *information model* of messages, Deetz presents a *communication model* that regards language as the principal medium through which social reality is created and sustained. He states that "language does not represent things that already exist. In fact, language is a part of the production of the thing that we treat as being self-evident and natural within the society."[7] Humanists like I. A. Richards have long pointed out that meanings are in people, not in words (see Chapter 4). But Deetz moves even further away from a representational view of language when he raises the question, *Whose meanings are in people?* Once we accept that organizational forms are continually produced and reproduced through language, we'll understand that PG&E produces not only electricity, but also meaning.

Communication model
A view that language is the principal medium through which social reality is created and sustained.

People who adopt the lingo of big business may not be aware that they are putting corporate values into play. For example, the bottom line on a profit-and-loss statement is only that—the last line on the financial report. Yet a CEO's continual use of the term *bottom line* to justify all managerial decisions produces a perceived reality that shuts out nonfinancial considerations. When ordinary citizens begin to use this economic idiom to characterize the deciding or crucial factor in their own family decisions, they reinforce and

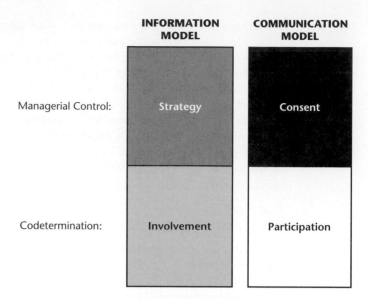

**INFORMATION
MODEL**

**COMMUNICATION
MODEL**

Managerial Control: Strategy   Consent

Codetermination: Involvement   Participation

FIGURE 20–1   Two Approaches to Organizational Practice

Based on Deetz, *Transforming Communication, Transforming Business,* Chapter 7

expand the influence of corporate thinking in life without even realizing they
are doing so.

Figure 20–1 contrasts Deetz' communication approach to organizational
practices with an information approach that regards language as neutral and
neutered. Like Pearce and Cronen (see Chapter 6), Deetz considers communication to be the ongoing social construction of meaning. But his critical
theory differs from CMM in that he thinks that the issue of power runs
through all language and communication. Deetz would not be surprised that
PG&E workers or residents of Hinkley had no say in the plant's environmental policies. He believes that managerial control often takes precedence over
representation of conflicting interests and long-term company and community health.

> The fundamental issue in my analysis is control and how different groups are rep-
> resented in decision making. . . . Since industrialization, managers in American
> corporations have primarily operated from a philosophy of control.[8]

The upper level of Figure 20–1 represents corporate decision processes that
systematically exclude the voices of people who are directly affected by the decisions. Deetz labels this practice *managerial control.* The bottom half of the figure
pictures decision processes that invite open dialogue among all stakeholders.
Deetz calls the practice *codetermination.* When coupled with the constitutive view
of communication, codetermination represents the "collaborative collective constructions of self, other, and the world"[9] that Deetz believes are the product of
participatory democracy.

Codetermination
Collaborative decision
making; participatory de-
mocracy in the work-
place.

The 2 × 2 nature of Figure 20–1 yields four different ways in which public
decisions—including corporate ones—can be made: *strategy, consent, involvement,*
and *participation.* Deetz' analysis of these four corporate practices provides the
core of his critique of managerialism.

STRATEGY: OVERT MANAGERIAL MOVES TO EXTEND CONTROL

Managerialism
A systematic logic, set of routine practices, and ideology that values control over all other concerns.

Consistent with Deetz' view of corporate control, *Erin Brockovich* never portrays a PG&E manager whom the viewer can despise. Deetz makes it clear that individual managers are not the problem. The real culprit is *managerialism*. Deetz describes managerialism as discourse based on "a kind of systematic logic, a set of routine practices, and ideology" that values control above all else.[10] Stockholders want profits and workers desire freedom, but management craves control.

The film gives the viewer a glimpse of managerial control when lawyer Ed teams up with a large corporate firm to pursue the legal actions against the power company. Although Erin is the one who did extensive research at the county water board and later spent months garnering signed complaints from all 634 adult residents of Hinkley, the "suits" at the large firm regard her as unprofessional and try to shut her out from their deliberations. Many workers experience that same dictatorial style in the expressed and implied messages that come down from the top:

"Because I'm the boss."
"Because I say so."
"If you don't like it, quit."
"It's my way or the highway."

Some employees do object by saying, in effect, "Take this job and shove it," but this doesn't increase representation. Choice is often limited to loyalty or exit—"love it or leave it." Without a voice, workers have no say in the decisions that affect them during the majority of their waking hours. Deetz argues that while control of this sort is disappearing in most enlightened corporations, new forms of control based in communication systems impede any real worker voice in structuring work.

Stockholders face the same either/or dilemma. They can choose to hold their shares or sell them, but neither option offers a way to influence corporate policy. Although management presents itself as making decisions on behalf of stockholders (the owners), Deetz says that the interests of the two groups are often not the same. Because of stock options and "golden parachutes," top management has benefited more than any other group from the merger mania of the last two decades. Whereas long-term growth would help the average investor, quick profits and tight control of costs are the manager's ticket up the corporate ladder. Regardless of a company's product line or service, "control is the management product and is most clearly the one on which individual advancement rests."[11]

Initially, managers may regard efficiency as a means to the end of higher profits. Deetz is convinced, however, that the desire for control soon becomes a valued end in itself. The desire for control can exceed the desire for corporate performance. Talking in terms of money is often more for control than respect for efficiency or profits.

> The control drive of managerialism seeks the medium of its extension, and money is it. . . . Everything that cannot be adequately translated into money is implicitly suppressed, and all competing rights of decisions regarding one's life are made marginal.[12]

Nowhere is this quest for control more apparent than in the corporate aversion to public conflict. The managerial rule of thumb seems to be that conflict is to be "dealt with" rather than openly discussed. Managers are rewarded for "putting out fires," "running a tight ship," or "making things run smoothly." The impersonal nature of these metaphors suggests that executives should place responsibility to the company ahead of personal feelings or ethical concerns. In the corporate context, claims of "company policy" and "just doing my job" provide sufficient moral justification for suppressing almost any act of employee resistance or dissent.

Other than accelerating advancement on the managerial career path, there is little evidence that strategic control has beneficial effects. Deetz claims that most corporate successes (or failures) are the result of factors beyond managerial control.[13] Control does have distinct disadvantages, however. The cost is high, and workers resent the constant surveillance. Frequent references to "clearing out the deadwood" or "trimming the fat" create an understandable jumpiness among employees, and sometimes their fear is acted out in covert rebellion, as illustrated in *Erin Brockovich*.

When the suit against PG&E appears to be dead in the water because there is no proof that the parent company knew what was going on, a man approaches Erin in a bar. He asks her what she would do if he told her he'd been ordered to shred documents about the toxic water when he worked at the local plant. The papers included a letter from corporate headquarters that said, in effect, *the water is poisonous, but it would be better for all involved if this weren't discussed with the community.* Erin asks him if he destroyed the papers as he was told to do. With a conspiratorial smile, he admits that he wasn't a very good employee. Because dominance creates this kind of resistance, most modern managers prefer to maintain control through the voluntary consent of the worker rather than by relying on the strategic use of raw power.

CONSENT: WILLING ALLEGIANCE TO COVERT CONTROL

Deetz is for capitalism, but he's convinced that corporations are unreasonable. "They expect more than a fair day's work for a fair day's pay; they want love, respect, and above all loyalty."[14] Even though the company gets the workers' most rested, alert, and chemical-free portion of the day, apparently that's not enough. Management insists that allegiance to the company should come before family, friends, church, and community. Through the process Deetz calls *consent*, most employees willingly give that loyalty without getting much in return. "Consent is the term I use to designate the variety of situations and processes in which someone actively, though unknowingly, accomplishes the interests of others in the faulty attempt to fulfill his or her own interests. The person is complicit in her or his own victimization."[15]

Consent
The process by which employees actively, though unknowingly, accomplish managerial interests in a faulty attempt to fulfill their own.

Lynn, a former student of mine, wrote an application log entry for Deetz' critical theory that poignantly captures the human cost of consent:

> My father was very loyal to his company in the interest of moving up the ladder for pay increases. When my brother and I were babies and toddlers, my family lived in four different places in three years because the company required that we move. Later on, my father spent much of his time traveling and lived in New York for over six months while the rest of us lived in Baltimore. During my high school years, he worked until about eight or nine o'clock in the evening even though it wasn't demanded of him. His entire department was often there because it was common practice to spend that much time getting the job done.

DILBERT: © Scott Adams/Dist. by United Feature Syndicate, Inc.

I would love to see the ideal world where employees have a lot more power in their communication within a large company. I think that it would possibly save families like mine from growing up without a full-time father.

I can see further implications. If employees, especially men, feel like they have more power in the workplace, they will be less likely to come home and feel the need to prove their power at home by demeaning their wives in many different ways. I think that if Deetz' proposals ever worked on a wide scale, our country would see a decrease in domestic violence.[16]

How do companies manage to strike such an unfair bargain with their employees? It's tempting to point to the workaholism of Lynn's father as the core of the problem, but Deetz lays more of the blame on managerial control of workplace language, information, forms, symbols, rituals, and stories. Although these are the practices that Pacanowsky and other interpretive scholars treat as indicators of a given organizational culture (see Chapter 19), Deetz views them as attempts to produce and reproduce a culture that is sympathetic to managerial interests. All corporations have their own sets of constitutive practices. The question he asks is not *What do these mean?* Rather, it is *Whose meanings are these?*

Managerialism promotes worker consent through a process Deetz calls *systematically distorted communication.* Unlike strategic control, which is open and deliberate, systematically distorted communication operates without employees' overt awareness. When this happens, expectations and norms within a group setting restrict what can be openly expressed or even thought. Deetz emphasizes that the workers deceive themselves because they believe they are interacting freely, while in reality only certain options are available. As an example, Deetz notes that arbitrary authority relations within an organization may be disguised as legitimate divisions of labor. That way any talk about power relations must assume the validity of the status quo, thus reproducing the organizational hierarchy rather than challenging it. Real interactive decisions can't be made in such a context.

Systematically distorted communication requires suppression of potential conflict. This process, which Deetz calls *discursive closure,* occurs in a variety of ways. For example, certain groups of people within the organization may be classified as

Systematically distorted communication
Operating outside of employees' awareness, a form of discourse that restricts what can be said or even considered.

Discursive closure
Suppression of conflict without employees realizing that they are complicit in their own censorship.

"disqualified" to speak on important issues. Arbitrary definitions can be labeled as "natural" to avoid further discussion. The values that guided a manager's judgment call may be kept hidden so that it appears to be an objective decision. A group may discourage members from talking about certain subjects. Or the organization may allow the discussion of a topic such as gender-linked job classification or pay differences but discount its importance or quickly divert attention to other issues.

Deetz suggests that the force of an organizational practice is strongest when no one even thinks about it. If someone were to question such a routine, employees would be hard-pressed to explain why it is standard operating procedure. The best response they could muster would be a nonanswer: "That's the way it's done around here." Practices that have this taken-for-granted quality are often equated with common sense. Without a clear understanding that communication produces rather than reflects reality (the right side of Figure 20–1), employees will unknowingly consent to the managerial mentality that wants to expand corporate control.

INVOLVEMENT: FREE EXPRESSION OF IDEAS, BUT NO VOICE

For anyone who has a stake in corporate decisions (all of us?), shifting from the top to the bottom of Figure 20–1 is a crucial move. In political terms, it represents a switch from autocracy to liberal democracy—from managerial decisions made behind closed doors to open discussions where all have the opportunity to express their opinions.

Involvement
Stakeholders' free expression of ideas that may, or may not, affect managerial decisions.

Employee *involvement* in corporate choices began with a suggestion box mounted on a wall. In some companies, this invitation for expression evolved over decades into open forums that look like early-American town meetings. At their best, these attempts at corporate democracy are based on a commitment to free speech and the value of an open marketplace of ideas (see Nilsen's ethic of significant choice, pp. 201–202). Deetz notes, however, that this liberal democracy model works only in companies where everyone shares a common set of values.[17] In today's heterogeneous, postmodern society, that's seldom the case.

Both in national politics and in corporate governance, meaningful democracy requires that people affected by decisions have *forums* at which they can discuss the issues, and a *voice* in the final result. Forums provide the opportunity for involvement—the free expression of ideas. But according to Deetz, voice is not just having a say. It means expressing interests that are freely and openly formed, as well as having those interests represented in joint decisions.[18] People won't have a voice if they regard communication as the transmission of information—the left side of Figure 20–1.

As Deetz surveys corporate communication practices, he concludes that "the right of expression appears more central than the right to be informed or to have an effect."[19] Through involvement in discussions of company policy, employees have a chance to air their grievances, state their desires, and recommend alternative ways of working. Many managers use these sessions as a way to give employees a chance to let off steam. But advocacy is not negotiation. When workers find out that their ideas aren't represented in the final decision, they quickly become cynical about the process. Deetz thinks this is tragic:

> The combination of belief in a "reality" *and* cynicism is disastrous for a democracy. The belief that all claims are merely opinions is used to stop discussions rather than start them.[20]

PARTICIPATION: STAKEHOLDER DEMOCRACY IN ACTION

Deetz' theory of communication is critical, but not just negative. While he strongly criticizes the managerial strategy of ever-increasing control over workers, engineering their consent, and granting them free expression without giving them a voice in decisions, he also believes that joint, open decisions in the workplace are possible. Deetz is convinced that "meaningful democratic participation creates better citizens and better social choices, and provides important economic

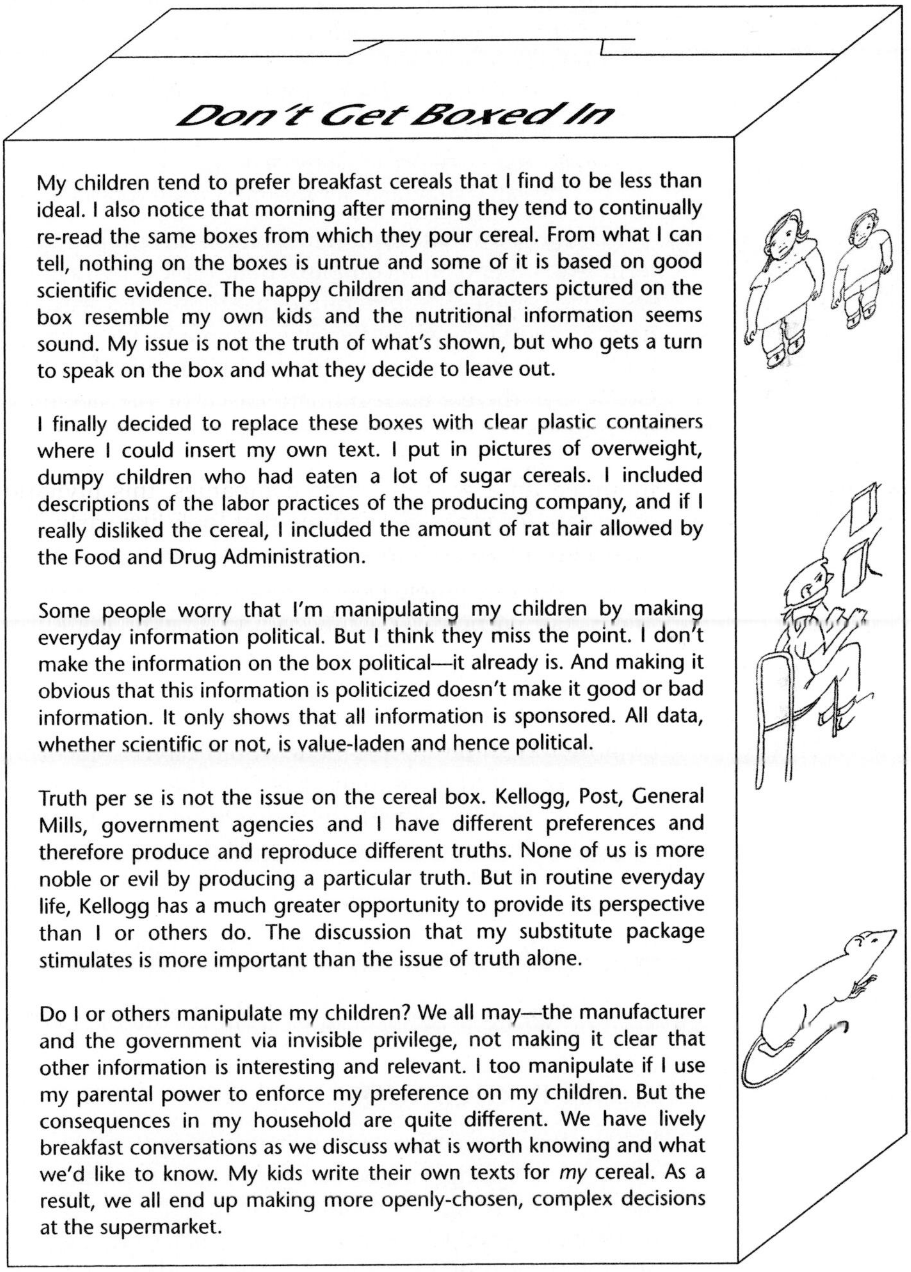

Don't Get Boxed In

My children tend to prefer breakfast cereals that I find to be less than ideal. I also notice that morning after morning they tend to continually re-read the same boxes from which they pour cereal. From what I can tell, nothing on the boxes is untrue and some of it is based on good scientific evidence. The happy children and characters pictured on the box resemble my own kids and the nutritional information seems sound. My issue is not the truth of what's shown, but who gets a turn to speak on the box and what they decide to leave out.

I finally decided to replace these boxes with clear plastic containers where I could insert my own text. I put in pictures of overweight, dumpy children who had eaten a lot of sugar cereals. I included descriptions of the labor practices of the producing company, and if I really disliked the cereal, I included the amount of rat hair allowed by the Food and Drug Administration.

Some people worry that I'm manipulating my children by making everyday information political. But I think they miss the point. I don't make the information on the box political—it already is. And making it obvious that this information is politicized doesn't make it good or bad information. It only shows that all information is sponsored. All data, whether scientific or not, is value-laden and hence political.

Truth per se is not the issue on the cereal box. Kellogg, Post, General Mills, government agencies and I have different preferences and therefore produce and reproduce different truths. None of us is more noble or evil by producing a particular truth. But in routine everyday life, Kellogg has a much greater opportunity to provide its perspective than I or others do. The discussion that my substitute package stimulates is more important than the issue of truth alone.

Do I or others manipulate my children? We all may—the manufacturer and the government via invisible privilege, not making it clear that other information is interesting and relevant. I too manipulate if I use my parental power to enforce my preference on my children. But the consequences in my household are quite different. We have lively breakfast conversations as we discuss what is worth knowing and what we'd like to know. My kids write their own texts for *my* cereal. As a result, we all end up making more openly-chosen, complex decisions at the supermarket.

FIGURE 20–2   A Morning Exercise Created by Stan Deetz

benefits."[21] One of the goals of his theory is to reclaim the possibility of open negotiations of power. He calls it *stakeholder democracy.*

The first move Deetz makes is to expand the list of people who should have a say in how a corporation is run. He sees at least six groups of stakeholders with multiple needs and desires.[22]

Participation
Stakeholder democracy; the process by which all stakeholders in an organization negotiate power and openly reach collaborative decisions.

Investors want security of principal and a decent return on their investment.

Workers want a reasonable wage, safe working conditions, a chance to take pride in their labor, security of employment, and time for their families.

Consumers want quality goods and services at a fair price.

Suppliers want a stable demand for their resource with timely payment upon delivery.

Host communities want payment for services provided, stable employment, environmental care, and the quality of family and public life enhanced rather than diminished.

Greater society and the world community want environmental care, economic stability, overall civility, and fair treatment of all constituent groups (racial, ethnic, gender).

Deetz notes that some stakeholders have taken greater risks and made longer-term investments in a company than typical owners of stock or top-level managers.[23] He believes it's imperative that those who are affected by corporate decisions have a say in how such decisions are made. Of course, this stance runs counter to traditional notions of exclusive stockholder rights or managerial prerogatives, but Deetz says there's no legitimate basis for privileging one group of stakeholders over another. He reminds us that nature did not make corporations—we did.

The rights and responsibilities of people are not given in advance by nature or by a privileged, universal value structure, but are negotiated through interaction.[24]

Once PG&E discovered that contaminated wastewater was leaching into the underground aquifer, Deetz would envision a negotiation that would include more than corporate executives and stockholders. Consumers, employees who came in contact with the water, Hinkley residents developing tumors, and perhaps Erin Brockovich herself would also be at the table. Certainly the discussions would be heated. From Deetz' perspective, that would be fine. The final decision on how to handle the problem would have to incorporate all of their interests.

Deetz would have managers take the role of mediators rather than persuaders. They would coordinate the conflicting interests of all parties affected by corporate decisions. He understands that even those who are committed to open dialogue would feel insecure as they relinquished control. He suggests a good way to start is to "complicate" their perceptions of subordinates by being around them, talking with them, and learning their hopes, dreams, fears, values, and needs. Managers could take notes on how to do this from Erin Brockovich. That's how she communicated with people in Hinkley.

MODELS OF STAKEHOLDER PARTICIPATION

In *Transforming Communication, Transforming Business*, Deetz cited the Saturn Corporation as an example of the benefits to be had when discussion and negotiation take the place of managerial control.[25] He described a workplace where every employee thought and acted like an owner. When managers suggested a short-term relaxation of quality to catch up on dealer demand, workers protested and ultimately convinced them that it was in the company's long-term interest to build a car that consumers would trust. He noted that at Saturn all information, including financial, was shared openly among all employees. Workers could find out what they needed to know to make informed decisions; they were also involved in the production of knowledge.

In a previous edition of this text, I chose AES Corp. as the antithesis of PG&E, the power company that Erin Brockovich exposed as disdainful toward the environment and cavalier with the health of its neighbors. Two of the company's core values are social responsibility and fairness. In an industry that's a prime contributor to acid rain and global warming, AES plants emit less than two-thirds of the sulfur dioxide allowed by law and only 35 percent of the industry standard for nitrogen oxide. For AES, fairness means that all employees have equal access to information. Even details of potential acquisitions aren't kept secret. Salaries and bonuses are confidential, but all other financial and market information is widely circulated. These stakeholder values are so important to the company that the Securities and Exchange Commission insists that AES provide fair warning to potential investors: "If the Company perceives a conflict between these values and profits, the Company will try to adhere to its values—even though doing so might result in diminished profits of foregone opportunities.[26]

Unfortunately, neither Saturn nor AES today is an exemplar of stakeholder participation. Wall Street analysts who treat quarterly profits as the sole sign of corporate health, plus changes in top management at each company, have created a business climate less friendly for workers to have a voice in the decisions that affect them. In assessing the corporate conditions and best practices for workplace democracy, University of Utah communication professor George Cheney concludes that "the possibilities for the survival of 'post bureaucratic,' relatively egalitarian organizations remain debatable."[27] He adds that "evidence weighs heavily against the long-term maintenance of the 'integrity' of highly democratic organizations," but he, like Deetz, is hopeful that small, highly adaptable, process-oriented companies can lead the way in sustaining participatory democracy among stakeholders. In that regard, the ongoing story of Springfield ReManufacturing Corporation (SRC) offers hope.

In 1982, SRC was an International Harvester, Missouri, operation employing just over a hundred workers to retrofit diesel engines for trucks. The plant lost $2 million that year, employee morale was low, and the parent company was ready to close it down. Headed by Jack Stack, a college dropout in his 20s, a dozen managers pooled their funds and negotiated a leveraged buyout. Stock in the low-tech repair business was worth 10¢ per share.

Stack was a firm believer in closing the gap between blue-collar workers and managers. He concluded that "the best, most efficient, most profitable way to operate a business is to give everybody in the company a voice in saying how the company is run and a stake in the financial outcome, good or bad."[28] Stack quickly moved to establish open-book management. Impressed by workers' memory and mastery of baseball statistics, he figured that with some training they could understand the company's detailed income statement and balance sheet. He sparked their interest by calling this the "Great Game of Business" and organized seminars to teach workers the rules of the game, how to read the scorecard, the way to win the game, and how to play as a team. Armed with that knowledge, employees could be effective players rather than passive spectators in determining the company's future. But to take part in the decision-making process, they had to know everything that the managers knew. Information would be a resource for everyone, not an instrument of managerial control.

The effectiveness of employee participation was underlined when a janitor confronted him: "Have you looked at your balance sheet? Do you know 76% of your receivables are in the truck market? You have all your eggs in one basket. They have a recession every six years. You're going to lay us all off."[29] Stack discovered the janitor was right and the whole workforce began looking for ways to diversify. They figured out that the need for auto parts would increase when the truck market was weak, so the company was able to survive and thrive during the downturn.

Stack made the game more fun by transferring ownership in the business to everyone who worked at the plant. He also established a bonus system based on corporate earnings and reaching targets that all employees helped set. Since then, SRC has made a profit every year and has never laid off any workers. The company now has 900 workers, and a share of SRC stock at the end of 2004 was worth $100—a thousand times its value two decades before. Stakeholder participation can be a long-term success.

ETHICAL REFLECTION: WEST'S PROPHETIC PRAGMATISM

Cornel West is a pragmatist philosopher who is now a professor of religion at Princeton University. Along with the best-known American pragmatist, John Dewey (see Chapter 17), West regards pragmatism as "a mode of cultural critical action that focuses on the ways and means by which human beings have, do, and can overcome obstacles, dispose predicaments, and settle problematic situations."[30] The moral obstacle West wants to overcome is the institutional oppression of "the disadvantaged, degraded, and dejected" people who struggle on the margins of society.[31] They face racism, sexual discrimination, and economic injustice. West agrees with the analysis of Christian realist Reinhold Niebuhr, who deplored the inhuman treatment of workers in Henry Ford's auto factory.[32] Both men say that these evils exist not just because of ignorance or apathy—they are the result of pervasive human sin.

West is also sympathetic to a Marxist critique of capitalism,[33] but his own brand of pragmatism is deeply rooted in the narratives of the Scriptures:

> I have dubbed it "prophetic" in that it harks back to the Jewish and Christian tradition of prophets who brought urgent and compassionate critique to bear on the evils of their day. The mark of the prophet is to speak the truth in love with courage—come what may.[34]

For example, Hebrew prophets like Amos demanded social justice for the powerless; Jesus' parable of the Good Samaritan reminds believers that they are responsible to help those who are hurting, whoever and wherever they are.[35]

As a prophetic pragmatist, Cornel West applauds an action-oriented approach to empower rather than exploit the disadvantaged, degraded, and dejected who are excluded from decision-making processes. Deetz' call for all stakeholders to have an effective say in corporate decisions that affect their lives aligns well with West's commitments. Yet the specific ethical implications of West's prophetic pragmatism aren't always clear-cut. In 1995 he took flak from most whites and many blacks for supporting Nation of Islam minister Louis Farrakhan's Million Man March on Washington.

West acknowledged that he faced a tragic moral choice: "After all, I am a radical democrat devoted to a downward redistribution of wealth and a Christian freedom-fighter in the King legacy—which condemns any xenophobia, including patriarchy, homophobia, and anti-semitism."[36] These commitments put him at odds with Farrakhan's rhetoric. But West said that he and Farrakhan agreed on the importance of highlighting black suffering, and he was convinced by Dr. Martin Luther King's example of forming alliances and coalitions across racial, gender, class, and religious lines. And so he marched.

CRITIQUE: IS WORKPLACE DEMOCRACY JUST A DREAM?

Deetz' approach to corporate decision making is inherently attractive because it is built on values that many of us in the field of communication share. By reserving a seat at the decision-making table for every class of stakeholder, Deetz affirms the importance of democratic participation, fairness, equality, diversity, and cooperation.

Without question, Deetz' insistence on the constitutive nature of all communication can help us understand consent practices in the workplace. Yet his advocacy of stakeholder rights and participatory democracy isn't necessarily furthered by his constructionist view of communication. In fact, his reform agenda could be hindered. If, contrary to the U.S. Declaration of Independence, there are no self-evident truths on which to stand, everything is in play and it doesn't make much sense to assume that we have a right to participate in decisions that affect us.

Political realism may be another problem. As applied to corporate life, Deetz' theory is a critique of managerialism. Arizona State University communication professor Robert McPhee offers a somewhat tongue-in-cheek summary: "If we just didn't find it natural and right and unavoidable to hand power over to managers, everything would be very different and our problems would be solved."[37] Although a caricature, this capsule statement underscores the problematic nature of the stakeholder negotiations that Deetz pictures and the incredible difficulty of getting all parties to sit at the table as equals.

Deetz admits that a positive alternative to managerialism is difficult to work out in conception and in practice.[38] He'd like to do better, but democracy has never been neat and tidy. Perhaps it's asking too much of one theory that it reform both commonsense conceptions of communication *and* corporate business practices at the same time. Moving from the dark quadrant of *consent* to the clear quadrant of *participation* in Figure 20–1 is a quantum leap. Deetz is encouraged, however, by the number of companies that have begun to implement at least modified stakeholder models of decision making. He hopes that his theory will further the dialogue and hasten that trend.

Moving from the theory to the theorist, Deetz suggests that critical scholars should be "filled with care, thought, and good humor."[39] That third quality may surprise you, for like prophets, critical theorists have the reputation of being a rather grim bunch. But Deetz suggests that with good humor we can smile at our inconsistencies, contradictions, and bruised pride. We are to take the plight of the oppressed—not ourselves—seriously. "The righteousness and pretense is gone, we must act without knowing for sure. The grand narratives are dead, but there is meaning and pleasure in the little ones. The pleasure embarrasses us but also gives us energy and a smile at ourselves."[40] To sample a mix of Deetz' care, thought, and humor, read through his morning exercise printed on the cereal box in Figure 20–2. I find the contents a compelling reason not to dismiss his theory.

QUESTIONS TO SHARPEN YOUR FOCUS

1. Deetz contrasts *information* models that assume language *reflects* reality with *communication* models that assume reality emerges out of a relationship among self, others, language, and the world. What other theories already covered fit the communication model?

2. Managers use *strategy* and *consent* to maintain *control* over subordinates. According to Deetz, which practice is more effective? Why?

3. The *stakeholder model* requires *participation*, not just *involvement*. What is the difference between the two practices?

4. To what extent do you agree with the following statement: "Autocracy at work is the price we pay for *democracy* after hours."? Does it apply equally to work in the classroom?

CONVERSATIONS

View this segment online at www.mhhe.com.griffin7 or www.afirstlook.com.

In this eight-minute segment, critical theorist Stan Deetz offers a host of pithy opinions. Here's a sample. *On communication:* "The field for a long time argued that meanings were in people. I raise the opposite kind of question: Whose meanings are in people?" *On management:* "A lot of managers talk about thinking out of the box, but they don't understand . . . that you do not think out of the box by commanding the box." *On corporate assets:* "Their primary assets are not what investors gave them, but what employees gave them. . . . Their primary assets go down the elevator every night." And there are lots more. Watch and discover your favorites.

A SECOND LOOK

Recommended resource: Stanley Deetz, *Transforming Communication, Transforming Business: Building Responsive and Responsible Workplaces,* Hampton, Cresskill, NJ, 1995.

Critical foundation: Stanley Deetz, *Democracy in an Age of Corporate Colonization: Developments in Communication and the Politics of Everyday Life,* State University of New York, Albany, 1992.

Critique of communication theory and practice: Stanley Deetz, "Critical Theory," in *Engaging Organizational Communication Theory: Multiple Perspectives,* S. May and Dennis Mumby (eds.), Sage, Thousand Oaks, CA, 2004, pp. 85–111.

Overview of organizational communication: Stanley Deetz, "Conceptual Foundations," in *The New Handbook of Organizational Communication,* 2nd ed., Fred Jablin and Linda Putnam (eds.), Sage, Thousand Oaks, CA, 2000, pp. 3–46.

State-of-the-art review: George Cheney et al., "Democracy, Participation, and Communication at Work: A Multidisciplinary Review," in *Communication Yearbook 21,* Michael Roloff (ed.), Sage, Thousand Oaks, CA, 1998, pp. 35–91.

Organizational politics: "Interests, Conflict, and Power: Organizations as Political Systems," Gareth Morgan, *Images of Organizations,* 2nd ed., Sage, Thousand Oaks, CA, 1997, pp. 153–213.

Ethical foundations of stakeholder theory: Tanni Hass and Stanley Deetz, "Between the Generalized and the Concrete Other," in *Rethinking Organizational & Managerial Communication from Feminist Perspectives,* Patrice M. Buzzanell (ed.), Sage, Thousand Oaks, CA, 2000, pp. 24–46.

International Communication Association 1997 presidential address: Stanley Deetz, "Communication in the Age of Negotiation," *Journal of Communication*, Vol. 47, No. 4, 1997, pp. 118–135.

Employee participation and cultural change: Stanley Deetz, Sarah J. Tracy, and Jennifer Lyn Simpson, *Leading Organizations Through Transition*, Sage, Thousand Oaks, CA, 2000, pp. 92–115.

Stakeholder participation at SRC: Jack Stack, *The Great Game of Business*, Bantam, New York, 1994.

Confidence in worker collaboration: Rosabeth Moss Kanter, *Confidence: How Winning Streaks and Losing Streaks Begin and End*, Three Rivers, New York, 2006, pp. 216–255.

Review and critique: Branislav Kovačić, "The Democracy and Organizational Communication Theories of Deetz, Mumby, and Associates," in *Watershed Research Traditions in Communication Theory*, Donald Cushman and Branislav Kovačić (eds.), State University of New York, Albany, 1995, pp. 211–238.

To access titles and cue times of scenes from other feature films that
illustrate managerial control, click on Movie Clips at
www.afirstlook.com.

Aristotle defined rhetoric as "an ability, in each particular case, to see the available means of persuasion."[1] That designation centers attention on the intentional act of using words to have an effect. I use the term *public rhetoric* in this section to refer to a speaking context in which the speaker has an opportunity to monitor and adjust to the response of his or her immediate audience.

Rhetoricians have always had a special interest in judicial argument, legislative debate, political rallies, religious sermons, and speeches given at special celebrations.

For citizens in ancient Greece, knowing how to speak in public was part of their democratic responsibility. Later on, when Rome ruled the world, rhetorical ability was a survival skill in the rough-and-tumble politics of the forum.

In each setting, teachers and practitioners championed the art of rhetoric as a means of ensuring that speakers of truth would not be at a disadvantage when trying to win the hearts and minds of an audience.

The Greeks and Romans distinguished five parts, or divisions, of the study of rhetoric:

1. *Invention*—discovery of convincing arguments
2. *Arrangement*—organization of material for best impact
3. *Style*—selection of appropriate language
4. *Delivery*—coordination of voice and gestures
5. *Memory*—mastery and rehearsal of content

I'll say more about these *five canons of rhetoric* in Chapter 21, Aristotle's rhetoric. For now, note that with the possible exception of memory, they all require that a speaker first analyze and then adapt to a specific group of listeners. We can, of course, react to the idea of audience adaptation in two different ways. If we view speakers who adjust their message to fit a specific audience in a positive light, we'll praise their rhetorical sensitivity and flexibility. If we view them negatively, we'll condemn them for their cynical pandering and lack of commitment to the truth. Rhetorical thought across history swings back and forth between these two conflicting poles. The words of most rhetoricians reflect the tension they feel between "telling it like it is" and telling it in a way such that the audience will listen.

Greek philosopher Plato regarded rhetoric as mostly flattery. Far from seeing it as an art, he described rhetoric as a *knack*—similar to cooking or the clever use of cosmetics. Both are attempts to make things seem better than they really are.[2] In spite of his scorn, Plato imagined an ideal rhetoric based on a speaker's understanding of listeners with different natures and dispositions.

Plato's ideal discourse was an elite form of dialogue meant for private, rather than public, consumption. This philosophic, one-on-one mode of communication is known as *dialectic* (a different meaning for the term than its use in Baxter and Montgomery's relational dialectics). Unlike typical oratory in Athens, where speakers addressed large audiences on civic issues, Plato's dialectic focused on exploring eternal Truths in an intimate setting.

Although Plato hoped that philosophic dialectic would supplant public rhetoric, his best student, Aristotle, rejuvenated public rhetoric as a serious academic subject.

"I found the old format much more exciting."

More than 2,000 years ago, Aristotle's *Rhetoric* systematically explored the topics of speaker, message, and audience. Chapter 21 presents his theory of rhetoric, the majority of which has stood the test of time. His ideas form a large proportion of the advice presented in contemporary public speaking texts. Yet even though Aristotle defined rhetoric as the art of discovering all available means of persuasion, this conception doesn't solve the problem of how to get audiences to listen to hard truths.

Religious rhetors face the same paradox. In many ways the apostle Paul seemed to personify the lover of diverse souls that Plato had earlier described. In his first letter to the Corinthians, Paul reminds the people of Corinth that he made a conscious decision to let his message speak for itself ("My speech and my proclamation were not with plausible words of wisdom"[3]). Yet further on in the letter he outlines a conscious rhetorical strategy ("I have become all things to all people, that I might by all means save some"[4]). Four centuries later, Augustine continued to justify the conscious use of rhetoric by the church. Why, he asked, should defenders of truth be long-winded, confusing, and boring, when the speech of liars was brief, clear, and persuasive?

The tension between the logic of a message and the appeal it has for an audience wasn't easily resolved when the university became the seat of rhetoric. British philosopher Francis Bacon sought to integrate the two concerns when he wrote that "the duty of rhetoric is to apply Reason to Imagination for the better moving of the will."[5] French scholar Peter Ramus offered a more radical solution to the problem. He split the five canons of rhetoric into two parts. Invention, arrangement, and memory became the province of logic. That left only style and delivery for rhetoricians to explore, and for centuries rhetoric was more concerned with form than with substance.

American teachers of rhetoric rediscovered Aristotle in the early 1900s; neo-Aristotelianism became *the* standard for rhetorical research and practice. But not all scholars are content to analyze speeches using Aristotle's categories of logical, emotional, and ethical proof. At least two twentieth-century rhetoricians have offered conscious alternatives to Aristotle's way of thinking.

Kenneth Burke's *dramatism* proposes a *new rhetoric*. He claims that speaker identification with an audience is a better way to understand the human drama than Aristotle's *old rhetoric* of persuasion. Walter Fisher argues that the rational world paradigm of Aristotle is too limited. He regards all communication as story and offers his *narrative paradigm* as a new way to understand both private and public rhetoric. I present Burke's dramatism in Chapter 22 and Fisher's narrative paradigm in Chapter 23.

Despite the claims of newness by Burke and Fisher, each theorist has to deal with the old question that Aristotle faced: "How do you move an audience without changing your message or losing your integrity?" As you read, see which theorist comes up with an answer that is most satisfying for you.

To find out what other communication theory texts discuss theories
of public rhetoric, or any other theory referred to in this
book, click on Compare Texts at
www.afirstlook.com.

The Rhetoric

of Aristotle

Aristotle was a student of Plato in the golden age of Greek civilization, four centuries before the birth of Christ. He became a respected instructor at Plato's Academy but disagreed with his mentor over the place of public speaking in Athenian life.

Ancient Greece was known for its traveling speech teachers called Sophists. Particularly in Athens, those teachers trained aspiring lawyers and politicians to participate effectively in the courts and deliberative councils. In hindsight, they appear to have been innovative educators who offered a needed and wanted service.[1] Yet since their advice was underdeveloped theoretically, Plato scoffed at the Sophists' oratorical devices. His skepticism is mirrored today in the negative way people use the term *mere rhetoric* to label the speech of *tricky* lawyers, *mealy-mouthed* politicians, *spellbinding* preachers, and *fast-talking* salespeople.

Aristotle, like Plato, deplored the demagoguery of speakers using their skill to move an audience while showing a casual indifference to the truth. Yet unlike Plato, he saw the tools of rhetoric as a neutral means by which the orator could either accomplish noble ends or further fraud: " . . . by using these justly one would do the greatest good, and unjustly, the greatest harm."[2] Aristotle believed that truth has a moral superiority that makes it more acceptable than falsehood. But unscrupulous opponents of the truth may fool a dull audience unless an ethical speaker uses all possible means of persuasion to counter the error. Speakers who neglect the art of rhetoric have only themselves to blame when their hearers choose falsehood. Success requires wisdom *and* eloquence.

Both the *Politics* and the *Ethics* of Aristotle are polished and well-organized books compared with the rough prose and arrangement of his text on rhetoric. The *Rhetoric* apparently consists of Aristotle's reworked lecture notes for his course at the academy. Despite the uneven nature of the writing, the *Rhetoric* is a searching study of audience psychology. Aristotle raised rhetoric to a science by systematically exploring the effects of the speaker, the speech, and the audience. He regarded the speaker's use of this knowledge as an art. Quite likely, the text your communication department uses for its public speaking classes is basically a contemporary recasting of the audience analysis provided by Aristotle 2,300 years ago.

RHETORIC: MAKING PERSUASION PROBABLE

Rhetoric
Discovering all possible means of persuasion.

Aristotle saw the function of *rhetoric* as the discovery in each case of "the available means of persuasion." He never spelled out what he meant by persuasion, but his concern with noncoercive methods makes it clear that he ruled out force of law, torture, and war. His threefold classification of speech situations according to the nature of the audience shows that he had affairs of state in mind.

The first in Aristotle's classification is courtroom (forensic) speaking, which addresses judges who are trying to decide the facts of a person's guilt or innocence. Prosecutor Marcia Clark and the late attorney Johnnie Cochran's closing arguments at the O. J. Simpson trial are examples of judicial rhetoric centering on accusation and defense. The second, political (deliberative) speaking, attempts to influence legislators or voters who decide future policy. The 2004 presidential debates gave John Kerry and George W. Bush a chance to sway undecided voters. The third, ceremonial (epideictic) speaking, heaps praise or blame on another for the benefit of spectators. Lincoln gave his Gettysburg Address in order to honor "the brave men, living and dead, who struggled here."

Because his students were familiar with the question-and-answer style of Socratic dialogue, Aristotle classified rhetoric as a counterpart or an offshoot of dialectic. Dialectic is one-on-one discussion; rhetoric is one person addressing many. Dialectic is a search for truth; rhetoric tries to demonstrate truth that's already been found. Dialectic answers general philosophical questions; rhetoric addresses specific, practical ones. Dialectic deals with certainty; rhetoric deals with probability. Aristotle saw this last distinction as particularly important: Rhetoric is the art of discovering ways to make truth seem more probable to an audience that isn't completely convinced.

RHETORICAL PROOF: *LOGOS, ETHOS, PATHOS*

According to Aristotle, the available means of persuasion are based on three kinds of proof: logical (*logos*), ethical (*ethos*), and emotional (*pathos*). Logical proof comes from the line of argument in the speech, ethical proof is the way the speaker's character is revealed through the message, and emotional proof is the feeling the speech draws out of the hearers. Some form of *logos, ethos,* and *pathos* is present in every public presentation, but perhaps no other modern-day speech has brought all three appeals together as effectively as Martin Luther King, Jr.'s "I Have a Dream," delivered in 1963 to civil rights marchers in Washington, D.C. In the year 2000, American public address scholars selected King's "I Have a Dream" as the greatest speech of the twentieth century. We'll look at this speech throughout the rest of the chapter to illustrate Aristotle's rhetorical theory.

Case Study: "I Have a Dream"

At the end of August 1963, a quarter of a million people assembled at the Lincoln Memorial in a united march on Washington. The rally capped a long, hot summer of sit-ins protesting racial discrimination in the South. (The film *Mississippi Burning* portrayed one of the tragic racial conflicts of that year.) Two months before the march, President John F. Kennedy submitted a civil rights bill to Congress that would begin to rectify the racial injustices, but its passage was seriously in doubt. The organizers of the march hoped that it would put pressure on Congress to outlaw segregation in the South, but they also wanted the demonstration to raise the national consciousness about economic exploitation of blacks around the country.

Martin Luther King shared the platform with a dozen other civil rights leaders, each limited to a five minute presentation. King's successful Montgomery, Alabama, bus boycott, freedom rides across the South, and solitary confinement in a Birmingham jail set him apart in the eyes of demonstrators and TV viewers. The last of the group to speak, King had a dual purpose. In the face of a Black Muslim call for violence, he urged blacks to continue their nonviolent struggle without hatred. He also implored white people to get involved in the quest for freedom and equality, to be part of a dream fulfilled rather than contribute to an unjust nightmare.

A few years after King's assassination, I experienced the impact his speech continued to have upon the African-American community. Teaching public address in a volunteer street academy, I read the speech out loud to illustrate matters of style. The students needed no written text. As I came to the last third of the speech, they recited the eloquent "I have a dream" portion word for word with great passion. When we finished, all of us were teary-eyed.

David Garrow, author of the Pulitzer Prize–winning biography of King, called the speech the "rhetorical achievement of a lifetime, the clarion call that conveyed the moral power of the movement's cause to the millions who watched the live national network coverage."[3] King shifted the burden of proof onto those who opposed racial equality. Aristotle's three rhetorical proofs can help us understand how he made the status quo of segregation an ugly option for the moral listener.

Logical Proof: Lines of Argument That Make Sense

Aristotle focused on two forms of *logos*—the *enthymeme* and the *example*. He regarded the enthymeme as "the strongest of the proofs."[4] An enthymeme is merely an incomplete version of a formal deductive syllogism. To illustrate, logicians might create the following syllogism out of one of King's lines of reasoning.

> Major or general premise: *All people are created equal.*
> Minor or specific premise: *I am a person.*
> Conclusion: *I am equal to other people.*

Logos
Logical proof, which comes from the line of argument in a speech.

Typical enthymemes, however, leave out a premise that is already accepted by the audience: *All people are created equal. . . . I am equal to other people.* In terms of style, the enthymeme is more artistic than a stilted syllogistic argument. But as emeritus University of Wisconsin rhetorician Lloyd Bitzer notes, Aristotle had a greater reason for advising the speaker to suppress the statement of a premise that the listeners already believe.

> Because they are jointly produced by the audience, enthymemes intuitively unite speaker and audience and provide the strongest possible proof. . . . The audience itself helps construct the proof by which it is persuaded.[5]

Enthymeme
An incomplete version of a formal deductive syllogism that is created by leaving out a premise already accepted by the audience or by leaving an obvious conclusion unstated.

Most rhetorical analysis looks for enthymemes embedded in one or two lines of text. In the case of "I Have a Dream," the whole speech is one giant enthymeme. If the logic of the speech were to be expressed as a syllogism, the reasoning would be as follows:

> Major premise: *God will reward nonviolence.*
> Minor premise: *We are pursuing our dream nonviolently.*
> Conclusion: *God will grant us our dream.*

King used the first-two thirds of the speech to establish the validity of the minor premise. White listeners are reminded that blacks have been "battered by the storms of persecution and staggered by winds of police brutality." They have "come fresh from narrow jail cells" and are "veterans of creative suffering." Blacks are urged to meet "physical force with soul force," not to allow "creative protest to degenerate into physical violence," and never to "satisfy our thirst for freedom by drinking from the cup of bitterness and hatred." The movement is to continue to be nonviolent.

King used the last third of the speech to establish his conclusion; he painted the dream in vivid color. It included King's hope that his four children would not be "judged by the color of their skin, but by the content of their character." He pictured an Alabama where "little black boys and black girls will be able to join hands with little white boys and white girls as sisters and brothers." And in a swirling climax, he shared a vision of all God's children singing, "Free at last, free at last. Thank God Almighty we are free at last." But he never articulated the major premise. He didn't need to.

King and his audience were already committed to the truth of the major premise—that God would reward their commitment to nonviolence. Aristotle stresses that audience analysis is crucial to the effective use of the enthymeme. The centrality of the church in American black history, the religious roots of civil rights protest, and the crowd's frequent response of "My Lord" suggest that King knew his audience well. He never stated what to them was obvious, and this strengthened rather than weakened his logical appeal.

The enthymeme uses deductive logic—moving from global principle to specific truth. Arguing by example uses inductive reasoning—drawing a final conclusion from specific cases. Since King mentioned few examples of discrimination, it might appear that he failed to use all possible means of logical persuasion. But pictures of snarling police dogs, electric cattle prods used on peaceful demonstrators, and signs over drinking fountains stating "Whites only" appeared nightly on TV news. As with the missing major premise of the enthymeme, King's audience supplied its own vivid images.

Ethical Proof: Perceived Source Credibility

According to Aristotle, it's not enough for a speech to contain plausible argument. The speaker must *seem* credible as well. Many audience impressions are formed before the speaker ever begins. As poet Ralph Waldo Emerson cautioned over a century ago, "Use what language you will, you can never say anything but what you are."[6] Some who watched Martin Luther King on television undoubtedly tuned him out because he was black. But surprisingly, Aristotle said little about a speaker's background or reputation. He was more interested in audience perceptions that are shaped by what the speaker does or doesn't say. In the *Rhetoric* he identified three qualities that build high source credibility—*intelligence*, *character*, and *goodwill*.

1. Perceived Intelligence. The quality of intelligence has more to do with practical wisdom and shared values than it does with training at Plato's Academy. Audiences judge intelligence by the overlap between their beliefs and the speaker's ideas. ("My idea of an agreeable speaker is one who agrees with me.") King quoted the Bible, the United States Constitution, the patriotic hymn "My Country, 'Tis of Thee," Shakespeare's *King Lear*, and the Negro spiritual

"I see our next speaker needs no introduction. . . ."

© 2008, Reprinted Courtesy of Bunny Hoest.

"We Shall Overcome." With the exception of violent terrorists and racial bigots, it's hard to imagine anyone with whom he didn't establish a strong value identification.

2. Virtuous Character. Character has to do with the speaker's image as a good and honest person. Even though he and other blacks were victims of "unspeakable horrors of police brutality," King warned against a "distrust of all white people" and against "drinking from the cup of bitterness and hatred." It would be difficult to maintain an image of the speaker as an evil racist while he was being charitable toward his enemies and optimistic about the future.

3. Goodwill. Goodwill is a positive judgment of the speaker's intention toward the audience. Aristotle thought it possible for an orator to possess extraordinary intelligence and sterling character yet still not have the listeners' best interest at heart. King was obviously not trying to reach "the vicious racists" of Alabama, but no one was given a reason to think that King bore them ill will. His dream included "black men and white men, Jews and Gentiles, Protestants and Catholics."

Ethos
Ethical proof, which comes from the speaker's intelligence, character, and goodwill toward the audience, as these personal characteristics are revealed through the message.

Although Aristotle's comments on *ethos* were stated in a few brief sentences, no other portion of his *Rhetoric* has received such close scientific scrutiny. The results of sophisticated testing of audience attitudes show that his three-factor theory of source credibility stands up remarkably well.[7] Listeners definitely think in terms of competence (intelligence), trustworthiness (character), and care (goodwill). As Martin Luther King spoke in front of the Lincoln Memorial, most listeners perceived him as strong in all three.

Emotional Proof: Striking a Responsive Chord

Recent scholarship suggests that Aristotle was quite skeptical about the emotion-laden public oratory typical of his era.[8] He preferred the reason-based discussion more characteristic of relatively small councils and executive deliberative bodies. Yet he understood that public rhetoric, if practiced ethically, benefits society. Thus, Aristotle set forth a theory of *pathos*. He offered it not to take advantage of an audience's destructive emotions but as a corrective measure that could help a speaker craft emotional appeals that inspire reasoned civic decision making. To this end, he catalogued a series of opposite feelings, then explained the conditions under which each mood is experienced, and finally described how the speaker can get an audience to feel that way. Aristotle scholar and translator George Kennedy claims that this analysis of pathos is "the earliest systematic discussion of human psychology."[9] If Aristotle's advice sounds familiar, it may be a sign that human nature hasn't changed much in 2,300 years.

Pathos
Emotional proof, which comes from the feelings the speech draws out of those who hear it.

Anger versus Mildness.   Aristotle's discussion of anger was an early version of Freud's frustration-aggression hypothesis. People feel angry when they are thwarted in their attempt to fulfill a need. Remind them of interpersonal slights, and they'll become irate. Show them that the offender is sorry, deserves praise, or has great power, and the audience will calm down.

Love or Friendship versus Hatred.   Consistent with present-day research on attraction, Aristotle considered similarity the key to mutual warmth. The speaker should point out common goals, experiences, attitudes, and desires. In the absence of these positive forces, a common enemy can be used to create solidarity.

Fear versus Confidence.   Fear comes from a mental image of potential disaster. The speaker should paint a vivid word picture of the tragedy, showing that its occurrence is probable. Confidence can be built up by describing the danger as remote.

Shame versus Shamelessness.   We feel embarrassed or guilty when loss is due to our own weakness or vice. The emotion is especially acute when a speaker recites our failings in the presence of family, friends, or those we admire.

Indignation versus Pity.   We all have a built-in sense of fairness. As the producers of *60 Minutes* prove weekly, it's easy to arouse a sense of injustice by describing an arbitrary use of power upon those who are helpless.

Admiration versus Envy.   People admire moral virtue, power, wealth, and beauty. By demonstrating that an individual has acquired life's goods through hard work rather than mere luck, admiration will increase.

THE FIVE CANONS OF RHETORIC

Canons of rhetoric
The principle divisions of the art of persuasion, established by ancient rhetoricians—invention, arrangement, style, delivery, and memory.

Although the organization of Aristotle's *Rhetoric* is somewhat puzzling, scholars and practitioners synthesize his words into four distinct standards for measuring the quality of a speaker: the construction of an argument (invention), ordering of material (arrangement), selection of language (style), and techniques of delivery. Later writers add memory to the list of skills the accomplished speaker must master. As previewed in the introduction to this section on public rhetoric, the five canons of rhetoric have set the agenda of public address instruction for more than 2,000 years. Aristotle's advice strikes most students of public speaking as refreshingly up-to-date.

Invention. To generate effective enthymemes and examples, the speaker draws on both specialized knowledge about the subject and general lines of reasoning common to all kinds of speeches. Imagining the mind as a storehouse of wisdom or an informational landscape, Aristotle called these stock arguments *topoi*, a Greek term that can be translated as "topics" or "places." As Cornell University literature professor Lane Cooper explains, "In these special regions the orator hunts for arguments as a hunter hunts for game."[10] When King argues, "We refuse to believe that there are insufficient funds in the great vaults of opportunity of this nation," he marshals the specific American topic or premise that the United States is the land of opportunity. When he contends that "many of our white brothers, as evidenced by their presence here today, have come to realize that their destiny is tied up with our destiny," he establishes a causal connection that draws from Aristotle's general topics of cause/effect and motive.

Arrangement. According to Aristotle, you should avoid complicated schemes of organization. "There are two parts to a speech; for it is necessary first to state the subject and then to demonstrate it."[11] The introduction should capture attention, establish your credibility, and make clear the purpose of the speech. The conclusion should remind your listeners what you've said and leave them feeling good about you and your ideas. Like speech teachers today, Aristotle decried starting with jokes that have nothing to do with the topic, insisting on three-point outlines, and waiting until the end of the speech to reveal the main point.

Style. Aristotle's treatment of style in the *Rhetoric* focuses on metaphor. He believed that "to learn easily is naturally pleasant to all people" and that "metaphor most brings about learning."[12] Furthermore, he taught that "metaphor especially has clarity and sweetness and strangeness."[13] But for Aristotle, metaphors are more than aids for comprehension or aesthetic appreciation. Metaphors help an audience visualize—a "bringing-before-the-eyes" process that energizes listeners and moves them to action.[14] King was a master of metaphor:

> The Negro lives on a *lonely island* of poverty in the midst of a *vast ocean* of material prosperity.
> To rise from the *dark and desolate valleys* of segregation to the *sunlit path* of racial justice.

King's use of metaphor was not restricted to images drawn from nature. Perhaps his most convincing imagery was an extended analogy picturing the march on Washington as people of color going to the federal bank to cash a check written by the Founding Fathers. America had defaulted on the promissory note and had sent back the check marked "insufficient funds." But the marchers refused to believe that the bank of justice was bankrupt, that the vaults of opportunity were empty. These persuasive images gathered listeners' knowledge of racial discrimination into a powerful flood of reason:

> Let justice roll down like waters
> and righteousness like a mighty stream.[15]

Memory. Aristotle's students needed no reminder that good speakers are able to draw upon a collection of ideas and phrases stored in the mind. But Roman teachers of rhetoric found it necessary to stress the importance of

Invention
A speaker's "hunt" for arguments that will be effective in a particular speech.

memory. In our present age of word processing and teleprompters, memory seems to be a lost art. Yet the stirring I-have-a-dream litany at the end of King's speech departed from his prepared text and effectively pulled together lines he had used before. Unlike King and many Athenian orators, most of us aren't speaking in public every day. For us, the modern equivalent of memory is rehearsal.

Delivery.   Audiences reject delivery that seems planned or staged. Naturalness is persuasive; artifice just the opposite. Any form of presentation that calls attention to itself takes away from the speaker's proofs.

ETHICAL REFLECTION: ARISTOTLE'S GOLDEN MEAN

Aristotle's *Rhetoric* is the first known systematic treatise on audience analysis and adaptation. His work therefore begs the same question discussed in the introduction to this section on public rhetoric: *Is it ethical to alter a message to make it more acceptable for a particular audience?*

The way I've phrased the question reflects a Western bias for linking morality with behavior. Does an act produce benefit or harm? Is it right or wrong to do a certain deed? Aristotle, however, spoke of ethics in terms of character rather than conduct, inward disposition instead of outward behavior. He took the Greek admiration for moderation and elevated it to a theory of virtue.

When Barry Goldwater was selected as the Republican party's nominee for president in 1964, he boldly stated: "Extremism in the defense of liberty is no vice . . . moderation in the pursuit of justice is not virtue."[16] Aristotle would have strongly disagreed. He assumed virtue stands between the two vices.[17] Aristotle saw wisdom in the person who avoids excess on either side. Moderation is best; virtue develops habits that seek to walk an intermediate path. This middle way is known as the *golden mean*. That's because out of the four cardinal virtues—courage, justice, temperance, and practical wisdom—temperance is the one that explains the three others.

Golden mean
The virtue of moderation; the virtuous person develops habits that avoid extremes.

As for audience adaptation, Aristotle would counsel against the practice of telling people only what they want to hear, pandering to the crowd, or "wimping out" by not stating what we really think. He would be equally against a disregard of audience sensitivities, riding roughshod over listeners' beliefs, or adopting a take-no-prisoners, lay-waste-the-town rhetorical belligerence. The golden mean would lie in winsome straight talk, gentle assertiveness, and appropriate adaptation.

Whether the issue is truth-telling, self-disclosure, or risk-taking when making decisions, Aristotle's golden mean suggests other middle-way communication practices:

Extreme	Golden Mean	Extreme
Lies	Truthful statements	Brutal honesty
Secrecy	Self-disclosure	Soul-baring
Cowardice	Courage	Recklessness

The golden mean will often prove to be the best way to persuade others. But for Aristotle, that's not the ethical issue. Aristotle advocates the middle way because it is the well-worn path taken by virtuous people.

CRITIQUE: STANDING THE TEST OF TIME

For many teachers of public speaking, criticizing Aristotle's *Rhetoric* is like doubting Einstein's theory of relativity or belittling Shakespeare's *King Lear*. Yet the Greek philosopher often seems less clear than he urged his students to be. Scholars are puzzled by Aristotle's failure to define the exact meaning of *enthymeme*, his confusing system of classifying metaphor according to type, and the blurred distinctions he makes between deliberative (political) and epideictic (ceremonial) speaking. At the beginning of the *Rhetoric*, Aristotle promised a systematic study of *logos, ethos,* and *pathos,* but he failed to follow that three-part plan. Instead, it appears that he grouped the material in a speech-audience-speaker order. Even those who claim that there's a conceptual unity to Aristotle's theory admit that the book is "an editorial jumble."[18] We must remember, however, that Aristotle's *Rhetoric* consists of lecture notes rather than a treatise prepared for the public. To reconstruct Aristotle's meaning, scholars must consult his other writings on philosophy, politics, ethics, drama, and biology. Such detective work is inherently imprecise.

Some present-day critics are bothered by the *Rhetoric's* view of the audience as passive. Speakers in Aristotle's world seem to be able to accomplish any goal as long as they prepare their speeches with careful thought and an accurate audience analysis. Other critics wish Aristotle had considered a fourth component of rhetoric—the situation. Any analysis of King's address apart from the context of the march on Washington would certainly be incomplete.

Referring to Aristotle's manuscript in a rare moment of sincere appreciation, French skeptic Voltaire declared what many communication teachers would echo today: "I do not believe there is a single refinement of the art that escapes him."[19] Despite the shortcomings and perplexities of this work, it remains a foundational text of our discipline—a starting point for social scientists and rhetoricians alike.

QUESTIONS TO SHARPEN YOUR FOCUS

1. For most people today, the term *rhetoric* has unfavorable associations. What synonym or phrase captures what Aristotle meant yet doesn't carry a negative connotation?

2. What *enthymemes* have advocates on each side of the abortion issue employed in their public *deliberative rhetoric?*

3. Aristotle divided *ethos* into issues of *intelligence, character,* and *goodwill.* Which quality is most important to you when you hear a campaign address, sermon, or other public speech?

4. Most scholars who define themselves as rhetoricians identify with the humanities rather than the sciences. Can you support the claim that Aristotle took a *scientific approach to rhetoric?*

 **SELF-QUIZ**

www.mhhe.com/griffin7

A SECOND LOOK

Recommended resource: Aristotle, *On Rhetoric: A Theory of Civil Discourse*, George A. Kennedy (ed. and trans.), Oxford University, New York, 1991.

Key scholarship: Richard Leo Enos and Lois Peters Agnew (eds.), *Landmark Essays on Aristotelian Rhetoric*, Lawrence Erlbaum, Mahwah, NJ, 1998.

Rhetoric as art: George A. Kennedy, "Philosophical Rhetoric," in *Classical Rhetoric*, University of North Carolina, Chapel Hill, 1980, pp. 41–85.

Rhetoric as science: James L. Golden, Goodwin F. Berquist, and William E. Coleman, *The Rhetoric of Western Thought*, Kendall/Hunt, Dubuque, IA, 1976, pp. 25–39.

Recent scholarship: Alan Gross and Arthur Walzer (eds.), *Rereading Aristotle's Rhetoric*, Southern Illinois University, Carbondale, 2000.

Enthymeme: Lloyd F. Bitzer, "Aristotle's Enthymeme Revisited," *Quarterly Journal of Speech*, Vol. 45, 1959, pp. 399–409; also in Enos and Agnew, pp. 179–191.

Metaphor: Sara Newman, "Aristotle's Notion of 'Bringing-Before-the-Eyes': Its Contributions to Aristotelian and Contemporary Conceptualizations of Metaphor, Style, and Audience," *Rhetorica*, Vol. 20, 2002, pp. 1–23.

Measuring ethos: James McCroskey and Jason Teven, "Goodwill: A Reexamination of the Construct and Its Measurement," *Communication Monographs*, Vol. 66, 1999, pp. 90–103.

Ethos and oral morality: Charles Marsh, "Aristotelian Ethos and the New Orality: Implications for Media Literacy and Media Ethics," *Journal of Mass Media Ethics*, Vol. 21, 2006, pp. 338–352.

Rhetoric and ethics: Eugene Garver, *Aristotle's Rhetoric: An Art of Character*, University of Chicago, Chicago, 1994.

History of rhetoric: Thomas Conley, *Rhetoric in the European Tradition*, Longman, New York, 1990.

Analysis of King's speech: Alexandra Alvarez, "Martin Luther King's 'I Have a Dream,'" *Journal of Black Studies*, Vol. 18, 1988, pp. 337–357.

March on Washington: David J. Garrow, *Bearing the Cross*, William Morrow, New York, 1986, pp. 231–286.

To access thought-provoking discussion questions on Aristotle's
rhetoric or any other theory, click on Instructor's Manual
and then on the chapter of your choice at
www.afirstlook.com.

Dramatism

of Kenneth Burke

American audiences want straightforward advice from their film critics. Roger Ebert and the late Gene Siskel created the successful television show *Sneak Previews* by describing a movie's plot, showing a brief clip, commenting on the quality of acting, and recommending whether people should see the film or skip it. The thumbs-up–thumbs-down nature of their judgment left little room for trying to discern the writer's purpose or the director's motivation. In this sense, Siskel and Ebert were *reviewers* of cinema rather than *critics*.

Kenneth Burke, on the other hand, was a critic. Along with the symbolic theorists we've already discussed (Bormann, Mead, Pearce and Cronen, Geertz and Pacanowsky), Burke believed that language is a strategic human response to a specific situation. "Verbal symbols are meaningful acts from which motives can be derived." He considered clusters of words as dances of attitudes. According to Burke, the critic's job is to figure out why a writer or speaker selected the words that were choreographed into the message. The task is ultimately one of assessing motives.

Until his death in 1993 at the age of 96, Burke picked his way through the human "motivational jungle" by using the tools of philosophy, literature, psychology, economics, linguistics, sociology, and communication. He spent his young adult years in Greenwich Village, a New York bohemian community that included E.E. Cummings and Edna St. Vincent Millay. Like many intellectuals during the depression of the 1930s, Burke flirted with communism but was disillusioned by Stalin's intolerance and brutality. Although he never earned a college degree, he taught for 15 years at Bennington College in Vermont and filled visiting lectureships at Harvard, Princeton, Northwestern, and the University of Chicago.

Burke's writing shows an intellectual breadth and depth that leads admirers to refer to him as a Renaissance man. He called himself a "gypsy scholar" and responded to questions about his field of interest by asking, "What am I but a word man?" *Dramatism* was Burke's favorite word to describe what he saw going on when people open their mouths to communicate.

As Burke viewed it, life is not *like* a drama; life *is* drama. The late Harry Chapin (who happened to be Burke's grandson) captured some of the tragedy and comedy of everyday life by putting words to music in *story songs*. My personal favorite is "Cat's in the Cradle," the timeless tale of a father too busy to spend time with his son. Any male who hears the song realizes that he has a part in the drama rather than the role of a passive listener.

The latest somebody-done-somebody-wrong country-and-western song makes it clear that a critic's skills could be helpful in understanding human motivation. But it wasn't until 1952 that University of Illinois rhetorician Marie Hochmuth Nichols alerted the field of communication to the promises of Burke's dramatistic methodology.[1] Since that time, thousands of communication scholars have used his perspectives of *identification, dramatistic pentad*, and *guilt-redemption cycle* as ways to analyze public address.

IDENTIFICATION: WITHOUT IT, THERE IS NO PERSUASION

Although he was a great admirer of Aristotle's *Rhetoric*, Burke was less concerned with enthymeme and example than he was with a speaker's overall ability to identify with an audience.

> The key term for the "old rhetoric" was *persuasion* and its stress upon deliberative design. The key term for the "new rhetoric" is *identification* and this may include partially unconscious factors in its appeal.[2]

Identification
The recognized common ground between speaker and audience such as physical characteristics, talents, occupation, experiences, personality, beliefs, and attitudes; consubstantiation.

Identification is the common ground that exists between speaker and audience. Burke used the word *substance* as an umbrella term to describe a person's physical characteristics, talents, occupation, experiences, personality, beliefs, and attitudes. The more overlap between the substance of the speaker and the substance of the listener, the greater the identification. Behavioral scientists have used the term *homophily* to describe perceived similarity between speaker and listener,[3] but Burke preferred religious language to scientific jargon. Borrowing from Martin Luther's description of what takes place at the communion table, Burke said identification is *consubstantiation*. The theological reference calls to mind the oft-quoted Old Testament passage where Ruth pledges solidarity with her mother-in-law, Naomi: "For where you go I will go, and where you lodge I will lodge; your people shall be my people, and your God my God."[4] That's identification. It's also a part of Ruth and Naomi's story. We'll revisit Ruth's pledge of loyalty in Chapter 23, Walter Fisher's narrative paradigm.

Audiences sense a joining of interests through style as much as through content. Burke said that the effective communicator can show consubstantiality by giving signs in language and delivery that his or her properties are the same as theirs. The style of a typical tent evangelist probably turns off cosmopolitan New Yorkers more than does the content of the message. The mood and manner of revival-style preaching signal a deep division between the evangelist and urbane listeners. To the extent that the speaker could alter the linguistic strategy to match the hearers' sophisticated style, they'd think the speaker was "talking sense."

Burke said that identification works both ways. Audience adaptation not only gives the evangelist a chance to sway the audience, it also helps the preacher fit into the cultural mainstream. But identification in either direction will never be complete. If nothing else, our tennis elbow or clogged sinuses constantly remind us that each of us is separate from the rest of the human race. But without some kind of division in the first place, there would be no need for identification. And without identification, there is no persuasion.

THE DRAMATISTIC PENTAD

Dramatistic pentad
A tool to analyze how a speaker attempts to get an audience to accept his or her view of reality by using five key elements of the human drama—act, scene, agent, agency, and purpose.

Burke regarded persuasion as the communicator's attempt to get the audience to accept his or her view of reality as true. The *dramatistic pentad* is a tool to analyze how the speaker tries to do it. The five-pronged method is a shorthand way to "talk about their talk about." Burke's pentad directs the critic's attention to five crucial elements of the human drama—*act, scene, agent, agency,* and *purpose.*

> In a well-rounded statement about motives, you must have some word that names the act (names what took place in thought or deed), and another that names the scene (the background of the act, the situation in which it occurred); also you must indicate what person or kind of person (agent) performed the act, what means or instruments he used (agency), and the purpose.[5]

Although Burke was an advocate of creativity, he believed the critic's choice of labels should be constrained by the language that the speaker actually selects. Burke recommended a content analysis that identifies key terms on the basis of frequency and intensity of use. The speaker's *god term* is the word to which all other positive words are subservient. When critics discover the god term, they should avoid dictionary definitions as a way of determining its exact meaning. A speaker's god term is best understood by the other words that cluster around it, known by the company it keeps. In like fashion, a *devil term* sums up all that a speaker regards as bad, wrong, or evil. Consistent with the Sapir-Whorf hypothesis described in the socio-cultural tradition (see Chapter 4), Burke's analysis sees words as *terministic screens* that dictate interpretations of life's drama.[6]

God term
The word a speaker uses to which all other positive words are subservient.

Devil term
The word a speaker uses that sums up all that is regarded as bad, wrong, or evil.

Burke illustrated the importance of taking language seriously by having the reader imagine a parallel pentad with substitute terms:

act	scene	agent	agency	purpose
response	situation	subject	stimulus	target

He said that the dramatistic pentad on the top assumes a world of intentional action, whereas the scientific terms on the bottom describe motion without intention or purpose.

The dramatistic pentad is deceptively similar to the standard journalistic practice of answering *who, what, where, when, why,* and *how* in the opening paragraph of a story. Because Burke regarded himself as an interpreter rather than a reporter, he was not content merely to label the five categories. By evaluating the ratio of importance between individual pairs (scene-agency, agent-act), the critic can determine which element provides the best clue to the speaker's motivation.

The pentad offers a way to determine why the speaker selected a given rhetorical strategy to identify with the audience. When a message stresses one element over the other four, it reveals a speaker's philosophy or worldview.

Act. A critic's label for the act illustrates what was done. A speech that features dramatic verbs demonstrates a commitment to realism.

Scene. The description of the scene gives a context for where and when the act was performed. Public speaking that emphasizes setting and circumstance downplays free will and reflects an attitude of situational determinism ("I had no choice").

Agent.   The agent is the person or people who performed the act. Some messages are filled with references to self, mind, spirit, and personal responsibility. This focus on character and the agent as instigator is consistent with philosophical idealism.

Agency.   Agency is the means the agent used to do the deed. A long description of methods or technique reflects a "get-the-job-done" approach that springs from the speaker's mindset of pragmatism.

Purpose.   The speaker's purpose is the stated or implied goal of the address. An extended discussion of purpose within the message shows a strong desire on the part of the speaker for unity or ultimate meaning in life, common concerns of mysticism.

Burke was somewhat confusing in his use of the terms *purpose* and *motivation*. Is the concern for purpose (as one of the five terms of the pentad) separate from the quest for underlying motivation, which the entire dramatistic metaphor is designed to uncover? Perhaps it's the distinction between an immediate localized goal and the ultimate direction of all human activity. According to this view, the pentad can be seen as offering a static photograph of a single scene in the human drama. The guilt-redemption cycle, the third perspective, would be the plot of the whole play.

GUILT-REDEMPTION CYCLE: THE ROOT OF ALL RHETORIC

The immediate purpose of a speech may vary according to the scene or agent, but Burke was convinced that the ultimate motivation of all public speaking is to purge ourselves of an ever-present, all-inclusive sense of guilt. Guilt is his catchall term to cover every form of tension, anxiety, embarrassment, shame, disgust, and other noxious feelings that he believed intrinsic to the human condition. His *Definition of Man* is a discouraging counterpoint to the optimism of Carl Rogers. (Like most writers of an earlier generation, Burke used the word *man* to designate human beings of both genders. Given his record of using words to startle and stretch his readers, if he were writing today, one wonders if he might suddenly recast his definition in exclusively feminine symbols. But in order to remain faithful to what he wrote, I won't alter his gender-loaded references.)

Guilt
Burke's catchall term for tension, anxiety, embarrassment, shame, disgust, and other noxious feelings intrinsic to the human condition.

> Man is
> the symbol-using inventor of the negative
> separated from his natural condition by instruments
> of his own making
> goaded by the spirit of hierarchy
> and rotten with perfection.[7]

Burke started out by acknowledging our animal nature, but like Mead (see Chapter 5) he emphasized the uniquely human ability to create, use, and abuse language. The rest of his definition makes it clear that the capacity to manipulate symbols is not an unmixed blessing. The remaining lines suggest three linguistic causes for the sense of inner *pollution*.

By writing "inventor of the negative," Burke claimed that it's only through man-made language that the possibility of choice comes into being. There is no "Don't" or "Thou shalt not" in nature. Symbolic interaction is a precondition of "no-ing."

The phrase "separated from his natural condition by instruments of his own making" bounces off the traditional description of a human as a *tool-using animal*.

Here again, Burke suggested that our technological inventions get us into trouble (see Chapter 24). Murphy's Law states that anything that can go wrong will.[8] When it comes to interpersonal relations, Burke would say Murphy was an optimist.

Burke wrote extensively about hierarchies, bureaucracies, and other ordered systems that rank how well people observe society's negative rules. He was convinced that no matter how high you climb on the performance ladder, you'll always feel a strong sense of embarrassment for not having done better. The guilt-inducing high priests of the hierarchy are the professional symbol users of society—teachers, lawyers, journalists, artists, and advertising copy writers.

The final phrase, "rotten with perfection," is an example of what Burke called *perspective by incongruity*.[9] The device calls attention to a truth by linking two incongruous words. Burke uses this technique to suggest that our seemingly admirable drive to do things perfectly can hurt us and others in the process. Our greatest strength is also our greatest weakness. Both our successes and our failures heighten our desire to find someone on whom we can dump our load of guilt. Burke believed that getting rid of guilt is the basic plot of the human drama. At its root, rhetoric is the public search for a perfect scapegoat.

Redemption Through Victimage

Those who have rejected or never had a religious commitment may be impatient with Burke's continual use of theological terms. Surprisingly, he made no claim to be a man of faith, nor did he ask his readers to believe in God. Regardless of whether you accept the Christian doctrine of human sin and divine redemption, Burke claimed that the "purely social terminology of human relations can not do better than to hover about that accurate and succinct theological formula."[10] He regarded theology as a field that has fine-tuned its use of language, and he urged the social critic to look for secular equivalents of the major religious themes of guilt and purification. This quest brought him to view rhetoric as a continual pattern of redemption through victimage.

Mortification
Confession of guilt and request for forgiveness.

Burke said that the speaker has two choices. The first option is to purge guilt through self-blame. Described theologically as *mortification*, this route requires confession of sin and a request for forgiveness. Yet even obvious candidates (Richard Nixon, O. J. Simpson, Bill Clinton) find it excruciatingly difficult to admit publicly that they are the cause of their own grief. Since it's much easier for people to blame their problems on someone else—the second option—Burke suggested that we should look for signs of *victimage* in every rhetorical act. He was sure that we would find them.

Victimage
Scapegoating; the process of naming an external enemy as the source of all personal or public ills.

Victimage is the process of designating an external enemy as the source of all our ills. The list of candidates is limited only by our imagination—Eastern liberals, Al Qaeda, the Colombian drug cartel, the military-industrial complex, blacks, Communists, Jews, chauvinistic males, homosexuals, religious fundamentalists, the police, rich capitalists, and so forth. Since the terrorism of 9/11, Americans would probably nominate Osama bin Laden, whose massively callous acts make him seem the personification of evil. Perfect guilt requires a perfect victim. God terms are only as powerful as the devil terms they oppose.

Burke was not an advocate of redemption through victimization, but he said he couldn't ignore the historical pattern of people uniting against a common

The world was going down the tubes. They needed a scapegoat. They found Wayne.

enemy ("congregation through segregation"). We've already discussed his claim that identification is the central strategy of the new rhetoric. The easiest way for an orator to identify with an audience is to lash out at whatever or whomever the people fear ("My friend is one who hates what I hate").

A RHETORICAL CRITIQUE USING DRAMATISTIC INSIGHT

Many rhetorical critics in communication have adopted Burke's techniques of literary criticism to inform their understanding of specific public address events. I asked Ken Chase, a colleague at Wheaton, and Glen McClish at San Diego State University to perform a Burkean analysis of Malcolm X's famous speech "The Ballot or the Bullet."[11] The critique that follows is the result of their combined insight.

Malcolm X, "The Ballot or the Bullet"

Often paired with Martin Luther King, Jr., Malcolm X was one of the most influential civil rights speakers of the 1960s. Malcolm's rhetoric, though, was more militant, angry, and for many African Americans, more realistic than the idealism of King's "I Have a Dream." Malcolm delivered his famous speech, "The Ballot or the Bullet," in April 1964, only 11 months before his assassination.

By viewing public rhetoric as an attempt to build a particular social order, Kenneth Burke helps reveal the power of "The Ballot or the Bullet." Malcolm's address portrays America as a nation that promises full equality, dignity, and freedom for all its citizens, yet African Americans have never received their birthright. Epitomizing his commitment to Black Nationalism, Malcolm urges his brothers and sisters to start their own businesses and elect their own leaders. At the same time he attacks white politicians who impede civil rights. The audience at the Corey Methodist Church in Cleveland, Ohio, interrupted Malcolm X with applause and laughter over 150 times during the lengthy oration.

Malcolm asserts that the struggle for civil rights is not only the work of his fellow Black Muslims but is shared by all concerned African Americans. By strategically aligning himself with Christian ministers like King and Adam Clayton Powell, he minimizes the alienation his Islamic faith could potentially create. He emphasizes the shared heritage of all African Americans: "Our mothers and fathers invested sweat and blood. Three hundred and ten years we worked in this country without a dime in return. . . ." In this way, Malcolm creates a strong sense of *identification* as he coaxes his audience to share his social purpose and his means for achieving it.

The title of the speech, "The Ballot or the Bullet," refers to the means, or *agency*, by which the *agents*—African Americans—can *act* as citizens to accomplish the *purpose* of equality, dignity, and freedom. Malcolm strategically places his audience within the larger context of American history and the international struggle for human rights. It is this *scene* that motivates the militant message that African Americans will proclaim—"We've got to fight until we overcome."

Malcolm's emphasis on the means to achieve his purpose ("by whatever means necessary") results in a high agency–purpose ratio—an indicator of his pragmatic motivation. The ballot enforces civil rights legislation; the bullet defends blacks from white violence. The bullet also warns white society that equality must not be delayed: "Give it to us now. Don't wait for next year. Give it to us yesterday, and that's not fast enough."

Malcolm criticizes his brothers and sisters for failing to show the courage, knowledge, and maturity that are necessary to reap the full benefits of citizenship. It is the white man, however, who has enslaved, lynched, and oppressed the Africans living on American soil, and it is he who must bear the brunt of collective *guilt*. Through *victimage*, the white man and his society become the *scapegoat* that must be sacrificed for the *redemption* of blacks. Within the drama of African-American life, "Black Nationalism" serves as the *god term* that embodies the spirit of the movement. Conversely, "white man" is the *devil term* that epitomizes all who oppose equality, dignity, and freedom for all.

CRITIQUE: EVALUATING THE CRITIC'S ANALYSIS

Kenneth Burke was perhaps the foremost rhetorician of the twentieth century. Burke wrote about rhetoric; other rhetoricians write about Burke. Universities offer entire courses on Burkean analysis. On two occasions the National Communication Association featured the man and his ideas at its national convention. The Kenneth Burke Society holds conferences and competitions that give his followers the opportunity to discuss and delight over his wide-ranging thoughts.

KB Journal exists solely to explain, clarify, and critique Burke's ideas. He obviously had something to say.

The problem for the beginning student is that he said it in such a roundabout way. Burke was closely tied to symbolic interactionism (see Chapter 5), and complexity seems to be characteristic of much of the writing within that tradition. Even advocates like Nichols feel compelled to explain why Burke was frequently confusing and sometimes obscure: "In part the difficulty arises from the numerous vocabularies he employs. His words in isolation are usually simple enough, but he often uses them in new contexts."[12] Clarity is compromised further by Burke's tendency to flood his text with literary allusions. Unless a student is prepared to grapple with Coleridge's "The Rime of the Ancient Mariner," Augustine's *Confessions*, and Freud's *The Psychopathology of Everyday Life*—all on the same page—Burke's mental leaps and breadth of scholarship will prove more frustrating than informative.

Yet Burke enthusiasts insist that the process of discovery is half the fun. Like a choice enthymeme, Burke's writing invites active reader participation as he surrounds an idea. And no matter what aspect of rhetoric that idea addresses, the reader will never again be able to dismiss words as "mere rhetoric." Burke has done us all a favor by celebrating the life-giving quality of language.

Without question, the dramatistic pentad is the feature of Burke's writing that has gained the most approval. The integrated procedure offers five artistic "cookie cutters" for the critic to use in slicing human interaction into digestible, bite-sized morsels. Many have found it helpful in pinpointing a speaker's motivation and the way the speech serves that need or desire.

Burke's concept of rhetoric as identification is a major advance in a field of knowledge that many scholars had thought complete. Rather than opposing Aristotle's definition, he gave it a contemporary luster by showing that common ground is the foundation of emotional appeal. Communication scientists can't test Burke's claim that unconscious identification produces behavior and attitude change, but they can confirm that perceived similarity facilitates persuasion.

Of all Burke's motivational principles, his strategies of redemption are the most controversial. Perhaps that's because his "secular religion" takes God too seriously for those who don't believe, yet not seriously enough for those who do. Both camps have trouble with Burke's unsubstantiated assumption that guilt is the primary human emotion that underlies all public address. There's no doubt that Malcolm X's "The Ballot or the Bullet" exploited a guilt-scapegoat linkage, but whether the same religious drama is played out in every important public event is another matter.

I appreciate Burke's commitment to an ethical stance that refuses to let desirable ends justify unfair means. He urged speakers not to make a victim out of someone else in order to become unified with the audience. True believers in the dramatistic gospel maintain that it's unwise to talk about communication without some understanding of Burke. The inclusion of this chapter is my response to their claim.

QUESTIONS TO SHARPEN YOUR FOCUS

1. Burke says that without *identification*, there is no persuasion. A number of the theories already covered deal with ideas or principles akin to identification. Can you name five?

2. Burke encourages the *rhetorical critic* to discover communicators' *motives* by analyzing the *god terms* and *devil terms* they use. As presented in this chapter, what are Burke's god terms and devil terms?

3. Apply the *dramatistic pentad* to the nonverbal rhetoric of a Friday night party on campus. Which of the five elements of the pentad would you stress to capture the meaning of that human drama?

4. Burke claims that all rhetoric ultimately *expiates guilt through victimage*. If he's right, is it the guilt of the speaker, the listener, or the victim that is being purged?

A SECOND LOOK

Recommended resource: Sonja Foss, Karen Foss, and Robert Trapp, *Contemporary Perspectives on Rhetoric*, 3rd ed., Waveland, Prospect Heights, IL, 2002, pp. 187–232.

Dramatism: Kenneth Burke, "Dramatism," in *The International Encyclopedia of the Social Sciences*, Vol. 7, David L. Sills (ed.), Macmillan, New York, 1968, pp. 445–451.

Key scholarship: Barry Brummet (ed.), *Landmark Essays on Kenneth Burke*, Hermagoras, Davis, CA, 1993.

Identification: Kenneth Burke, *A Rhetoric of Motives*, Prentice-Hall, Englewood Cliffs, NJ, 1950, pp. 20–46.

Dramatistic pentad: Kenneth Burke, *A Grammar of Motives*, Prentice-Hall, Englewood Cliffs, NJ, 1945, pp. xvii–xxv.

Guilt-redemption cycle: Kenneth Burke, "On Human Behavior Considered 'Dramatistically,'" in *Permanence and Change*, Bobbs-Merrill, Indianapolis, 1965, pp. 274–294.

Human nature: Kenneth Burke, "Definition of Man," in *Language as Symbolic Action*, University of California, Berkeley, 1966, pp. 3–24.

Contemporary analysis: Ross Wolin, *The Rhetorical Imagination of Kenneth Burke*, University of South Carolina, Columbia, 2001.

Contemporary Burkean analysis: Robert L. Ivie, "The Rhetoric of Bush's 'War' on Evil," *KB Journal*, Vol. 1, No. 1, 2004, www.kbjournal.org/modules.php?name=News&file=artic e&sid=2.

Burkean analysis of King's rhetoric: Edward C. Appel, "The Rhetoric of Dr. Martin Luther King, Jr.: Comedy and Context in Tragic Collision," *Western Journal of Communication*, Vol. 61, 1997, pp. 376–402.

Limits of dramatism: James W. Chesebro, "Extensions of the Burkean System," *Quarterly Journal of Speech*, Vol. 78, 1992, pp. 356–368.

Explication and critique of guilt-redemption cycle: Kristy Maddux, "Finding Comedy in Theology: A Hopeful Supplement to Kenneth Burke's Logology," *Philosophy and Rhetoric*, Vol. 39, 2006, pp. 208–232.

Feminist critique: Celeste Michelle Condit, "Post-Burke: Transcending the Substance of Dramatism," *Quarterly Journal of Speech*, Vol. 78, 1992, pp. 349–355; also in Brummet, pp. 3–18.

To access links to numerous Web sites on Kenneth Burke, click on Links at *www.afirstlook.com*.

Narrative Paradigm

of Walter Fisher

People are storytelling animals. This simple assertion is Walter Fisher's answer to the philosophical question *What is the essence of human nature?*

Many of the theorists discussed in earlier chapters offer different answers to this key question of human existence. For example, Thibaut and Kelley's social exchange theory operates on the premise that humans are rational creatures. Berger's uncertainty reduction theory assumes that people are basically curious. More pertinent for students of communication, Mead's symbolic interactionism insists that our ability to use symbols is what makes us uniquely human. (See Chapters 9, 10, and 5.)

Fisher doesn't argue against any of these ideas, but he thinks that human communication reveals something more basic than rationality, curiosity, or even symbol-using capacity. He is convinced that we are narrative beings who "experience and comprehend life as a series of ongoing narratives, as conflicts, characters, beginnings, middles, and ends."[1] If this is true, then all forms of human communication that appeal to our reason need to be seen fundamentally as stories.[2]

Walter Fisher is a professor at the University of Southern California's Annenberg School of Communication. Throughout his professional life he has been uncomfortable with the prevailing view that rhetoric is only a matter of evidence, facts, arguments, reason, and logic that has its highest expression in courts of law, legislatures, and other deliberative bodies. In 1978, he introduced the concept of *good reasons*, which led to his proposal of the narrative paradigm in 1984.[3] There he proposed that offering good reasons has more to do with telling a compelling story than it does with piling up evidence or constructing a tight argument.

Fisher soon became convinced that all forms of communication that appeal to our reason are best viewed as stories shaped by history, culture, and character. When we hear the word *story*, most of us tend to think of novels, plays, movies, TV sitcoms, and yarns told at night sitting around a campfire. Some of us also call to mind accounts of our past—tales we tell to others in which we are the central character. But with the exception of jokes, *Hi, How are you?* greetings, and other forms of *phatic communication*, Fisher regards almost *all* types of communication as story. Obviously, he sees differences in form between a Robert Frost poem, an Anne Tyler novel, or a performance of *King Lear* on the one hand, and a philosophical essay, historical report, political debate, theological discussion,

Phatic communication
Communication aimed at maintaining relationships rather than passing information or saying something new.

or scientific treatise on the other. Yet if we want to know whether we should believe the "truth" each of these genres proclaims, Fisher maintains that all of them could and should be viewed as narrative. He uses the term *narrative paradigm* to highlight his belief that there is no communication of ideas that is purely descriptive or didactic.

TELLING A COMPELLING STORY

Most religious traditions are passed on from generation to generation through the retelling of stories. The faithful are urged to "tell the old, old story" to encourage believers and convince those in doubt. American writer Frederick Buechner takes a fresh approach to passing on religious story. His book *Peculiar Treasures* retells the twelfth-century B.C. biblical story of Ruth's devotion to Naomi, her mother-in-law, in a twenty-first-century style.[4] Buechner's account of true friendship provides a vehicle for examining Fisher's narrative paradigm in the rest of this chapter. The story begins after the death of Naomi's husband and two sons:

> Ruth was a Moabite girl who married into a family of Israelite transplants living in Moab because there was a famine going on at home. When her young husband died, her mother-in-law, Naomi, decided to pull up stakes and head back for Israel where she belonged. The famine was over by then, and there was no longer anything to hold her where she was, her own husband having died about the same time that Ruth's had. She advised Ruth to stay put right there in Moab and to try to snag herself another man from among her own people.
>
> She was a strong-willed old party, and when Ruth said she wanted to go to Israel with her, she tried to talk her out of it. Even if by some gynecological fluke she managed to produce another son for Ruth to marry, she said, by the time he was old enough, Ruth would be ready for the geriatric ward. But Ruth had a mind of her own too, besides which they'd been through a lot together what with one thing and another, and home to her was wherever Naomi was. "Where you go, I go, and where you live, I live," Ruth told her, "and if your God is Yahweh, then my God is Yahweh too" (*Ruth 2:10–17*). So Naomi gave in, and when the two of them pulled in to Bethlehem, Naomi's home town, there was a brass band to meet them at the station.
>
> Ruth had a spring in her step and a fascinating Moabite accent, and it wasn't long before she caught the eye of a well-heeled farmer named Boaz. He was a little long in the tooth, but he still knew a pretty girl when he saw one, and before long, in a fatherly kind of way, he took her under his wing. He told the hired hands not to give her any trouble. He helped her in the fields. He had her over for a meal. And when she asked him one day in her disarming Moabite way why he was being so nice to her, he said he'd heard how good she'd been to Naomi, who happened to be a distant cousin of his, and as far as he was concerned, she deserved nothing but the best.
>
> Naomi was nobody's fool and saw which way the wind was blowing long before Ruth did. She was dead-set on Ruth's making a good catch for herself, and since it was obvious she'd already hooked old Boaz whether she realized it or not, all she had to do was find the right way to reel him in. Naomi gave her instructions. As soon as Boaz had a good supper under his belt and had polished off a nightcap or two, he'd go to the barn and hit the sack. Around midnight, she said, Ruth should slip out to the barn and hit the sack too. If Boaz's feet just happened

to be uncovered somehow, and if she just happened to be close enough to keep them warm, that probably wouldn't be the worst thing in the world either (*Ruth 3:1–5*). But she wasn't to go too far. Back in Jericho, Boaz's mother, Rahab, had had a rather seamy reputation for going too far professionally, and anything that reminded him of that might scare him off permanently.

Ruth followed her mother-in-law's advice to the letter, and it worked like a charm. Boaz was so overwhelmed that she'd pay attention to an old crock like him when there were so many young bucks running around in tight-fitting jeans that he fell for her hook, line and sinker, and after a few legal matters were taken care of, made her his lawful wedded wife.

They had a son named Obed after a while, and Naomi came to take care of him and stayed on for the rest of her life. Then in time Obed had a son of his own named Jesse, and Jesse in turn had seven sons, the seventh of whom was named David and ended up as the greatest king Israel ever had. With Ruth for his great-grandmother and Naomi for his grandfather's nurse, it was hardly a wonder.[5]

NARRATION AND PARADIGM: DEFINING THE TERMS

Narration
Symbolic actions—words and/or deeds—that have sequence and meaning for those who live, create, or interpret them.

Fisher defines *narration* as "symbolic actions—words and/or deeds—that have sequence and meaning for those who live, create, or interpret them."[6] Ruth's life and Buechner's account of it clearly qualify as narrative. But Fisher's definition is broad and is especially notable for what it doesn't exclude. On the basis of his further elaboration,[7] I offer this expanded paraphrase of his definition:

> Narration is communication rooted in time and space. It covers every aspect of our lives and the lives of others in regard to character, motive, and action. The term also refers to every verbal or nonverbal bid for a person to believe or act in a certain way. Even when a message seems abstract—is devoid of imagery—it is narration because it is embedded in the speaker's ongoing story that has a beginning, middle, and end, and it invites listeners to interpret its meaning and assess its value for their own lives.

Under this expanded definition, Ruth's *my god is Yahweh* statement is as much a story of love and trust as it is a declaration of belief. Yet framed in the context of King David's genealogy, it is also an early episode in the *Greatest Story Ever Told*. Those who identify with the human love, trust, loyalty, and commitment described in the narrative can't help but feel the solidarity of an extended family of faith.

Paradigm
A conceptual framework; a universal model that calls for people to view events through a common interpretive lens.

Fisher uses the term *paradigm* to refer to a *conceptual framework*. You'll remember from Delia's constructivism that the perception of people is not so much a matter of the physics of sight and sound as it is one of interpretation (see Chapter 8). Meaning isn't inherent in events; it's attached at the workbench of the mind. A paradigm is a universal model that calls for people to view events through a common interpretive lens.

In *The Structure of Scientific Revolutions*, Thomas Kuhn argues that an accepted paradigm is the mark of a mature science.[8] Responding to this challenge, communication scientists in the 1970s sought to discover a universal model that would explain communication behavior. Fisher's narrative paradigm is an interpretive counterpart to their efforts. Fisher offers a way to understand all communication and to direct rhetorical inquiry. He doesn't regard the narrative paradigm as a specific rhetoric. Rather, he sees it as "the foundation on which a complete rhetoric needs to be built. This structure would provide a comprehensive explanation of the creation, composition, adaptation, presentation, and reception of symbolic messages."[9]

PARADIGM SHIFT: FROM A RATIONAL WORLD PARADIGM TO A NARRATIVE ONE

Fisher begins his book *Human Communication as Narration* with a reference to the opening line of the Gospel of John: "In the beginning was the word (*logos*)." He notes that the Greek word *logos* originally included story, reason, rationale, conception, discourse, thought—all forms of human communication. Imagination and thought were not yet distinct. So the story of Naomi and Ruth was *logos*.

According to Fisher, the writings of Plato and Aristotle reflect the early evolution from a generic to a specific use of *logos*—from story to statement. *Logos* had already begun to refer only to philosophical discourse, a lofty enterprise that relegated imagination, poetry, and other aesthetic concerns to a second-class status. Rhetoric fell somewhere between *logos* and *mythos*. As opposed to the abstract discourse of philosophy, it was practical speech—the secular combination of pure logic on the one hand and emotional stories that stir up passions on the other. The Greek citizen concerned with truth alone should steer clear of rhetoric and consult an expert on wisdom—the philosopher.

Fisher says that 2,000 years later the scientific revolution dethroned the philosopher-king. For the last few centuries, the only knowledge that seems to be worth knowing in academia is that which can be spotted in the physical world. The person who wants to understand the way things are needs to check with a doctor, a scientist, an engineer, or another technical expert. Despite the elevation of technology and the demotion of philosophy, both modes of decision making are similar in their elitist tendencies to "place that which is not *formally* logical or which is not characterized by *expertise* within a somehow subhuman framework of behavior."[10] Fisher sees philosophical and technical discussion as scholars' standard approach to knowledge. He calls this mindset the *rational-world paradigm*. Hirokawa and Gouran's functional perspective on group decision making is a perfect example (see Chapter 17).

Rational-world paradigm
A scientific or philosophical approach to knowledge that assumes people are logical, making decisions on the basis of evidence and lines of argument.

Fisher lists five assumptions of the prevailing rational-world paradigm. See if they match what you've been taught all along in school.[11]

1. People are essentially rational.

2. We make decisions on the basis of arguments.

3. The type of speaking situation (legal, scientific, legislative) determines the course of our argument.

4. Rationality is determined by how much we know and how well we argue.

5. The world is a set of logical puzzles that we can solve through rational analysis.

Viewed through the rational-world paradigm, the story of Ruth is suspect. Ruth ignores Naomi's argument, which is based on uncontestable biological facts of life. Nor does Ruth offer any compelling rationale for leaving Moab or for worshiping Yahweh. Once they are back in Israel, Naomi's scheme for Ruth to "reel in" Boaz has nothing to do with logic and everything to do with emotional bonds. Other than the Old Testament passage, the author offers no evidence that Naomi and Ruth are historical characters, that any kind of god exists, or that a book about friendship, kinship, and romance deserves a place in the Old Testament canon. Thus, from a rational-world perspective, the story makes little sense.

Fisher is convinced that the assumptions of the rational-world paradigm are too limited. He calls for a new conceptual framework (a paradigm shift) in order to better understand human communication. His *narrative paradigm* is built on five assumptions similar in form to the rational-world paradigm, but quite different in content.[12]

Narrative paradigm
A theoretical framework that views narrative as the basis of all human communication.

1. People are essentially storytellers.
2. We make decisions on the basis of good reasons, which vary depending on the communication situation, media, and genre (philosophical, technical, rhetorical, or artistic).
3. History, biography, culture, and character determine what we consider good reasons.
4. Narrative rationality is determined by the coherence and fidelity of our stories.
5. The world is a set of stories from which we choose, and thus constantly re-create, our lives.

Viewing human beings as storytellers who reason in various ways is a major conceptual shift. For example, in a logical system, values are emotional nonsense. From the narrative perspective, however, values are the "stuff" of stories. Working from a strictly logical standpoint, aesthetic proof is irrelevant, yet within a narrative framework, style and beauty play a pivotal role in determining whether we get into a story. Perhaps the biggest shift in thinking has to do with who is qualified to assess the quality of communication. Whereas the rational-world model holds that only experts are capable of presenting or discerning sound arguments, the narrative paradigm maintains that, armed with a bit of common sense, almost any of us can see the point of a good story and judge its merits as the basis for belief and action. Fisher would say that each of us will make his or her judgment about Buechner's account of Ruth (or any story) based upon *narrative rationality*.

NARRATIVE RATIONALITY: COHERENCE AND FIDELITY

According to Fisher, not all stories are equally good. Even though there's no guarantee that people won't adopt a bad story, he thinks that everybody applies the same standards of *narrative rationality* to whatever stories he or she hears. Will we accept a cross-cultural tale of a young widow's total commitment to her mother-in-law and of Naomi's enthusiastic efforts to help Ruth remarry and have children by another man? Fisher believes that our answer depends on whether Buechner's account meets the twin tests of *narrative coherence* and *narrative fidelity*. Together they are measures of a story's truthfulness and humanity.

Narrative rationality
A way to evaluate the worth of stories based on the twin standards of narrative coherence and narrative fidelity.

Narrative Coherence: Does the Story Hang Together?

Narrative coherence
Internal consistency with characters acting in a reliable fashion; the story hangs together.

Narrative coherence has to do with how probable the story sounds to the hearer. Does the narrative *hang together*? Do the people and events it portrays seem to be of one piece? Are they part of an organic whole? Do the characters act consistently?

Buechner's version of Ruth and Naomi's relationship translates this ancient tale of interpersonal commitment into a contemporary setting. To the extent that

"I know what you're thinking, but let me offer a competing narrative."

his modern-day references to a brass band at the station, polishing off a night-cap, and young bucks running around in tight-fitting jeans consistently portray the present, the story has structural integrity. Fisher regards the internal consistency of a narrative as similar to lines of argument in a rational-world paradigm. In that sense, his *narrative paradigm doesn't discount or replace logic.* Instead, Fisher lists the test of reason as one, but only one, of the factors that affect narrative coherence.

Stories hang together when we're convinced that the narrator hasn't left out important details, fudged the facts, or ignored other plausible interpretations. We often judge the coherence of a narrative by comparing it with other stories we've heard that deal with the same theme. How does Buechner's account of feminine wiles used to move an older man toward marriage without going "too far" stack up against the seduction scenes in the film *Heartbreakers?* To the extent that Ruth's ploy seems more believable than the blatant tactics of Jennifer Love Hewitt and Sigourney Weaver's characters, we'll credit Buechner's biblical update with coherence.

For Fisher, the ultimate test of narrative coherence is whether we can count on the characters to act in a reliable manner. We are suspicious of accounts where characters behave "uncharacteristically." We tend to trust stories of people who show continuity of thought, motive, and action. Whether you regard Buechner's Naomi as a wise matchmaker or an overcontrolling mother-in-law, her consistent concern that Ruth find a man to marry is a thread that gives the fabric of the story a tight weave.

Narrative Fidelity: Does the Story Ring True and Humane?

Narrative fidelity is the quality of a story that causes the words to strike a responsive chord in the life of the listener. A story has fidelity when it rings true

Narrative fidelity
Congruence between values embedded in a message and what listeners regard as truthful and humane; the story strikes a responsive chord.

with the hearers' experiences; it squares with the stories they might tell about themselves.[13]

Have we, like Boaz, done special favors for a person we found especially attractive? Like Naomi, have we stretched the rules of decorum to help make a match? Or like Ruth, have we ever experienced a bond with a relative that goes beyond obligation to family? To the extent that the details of this 3,000-year-old story portray the world we live in, the narrative has fidelity.

Fisher's book *Human Communication as Narration* has the subtitle *Toward a Philosophy of Reason, Value, and Action.* He believes a story has fidelity when it provides good reasons to guide our future actions. When we buy into a story, we buy into the type of character we should be. Thus, values are what set the narrative paradigm's logic of good reasons apart from the rational-world paradigm's mere logic of reasons.

The *logic of good reasons* centers on five value-related issues. Fisher says we are concerned with (1) the values embedded in the message, (2) the relevance of those values to decisions made, (3) the consequence of adhering to those values, (4) the overlap with the worldview of the audience, and (5) conformity with what the audience members believe is "an ideal basis for conduct."[14] The last two concerns—congruity with the listeners' values and the actions they think best—form the basis for Fisher's contention that people tend to prefer accounts that fit with what they view as truthful and humane. But what specific values guide audiences as they gauge a story's truth or fidelity? Fisher suggests that there is an *ideal audience* or permanent public that identifies the humane values that a good story embodies:

Ideal audience
An actual community existing over time that believes in the values of truth, the good, beauty, health, wisdom, courage, temperance, justice, harmony, order, communion, friendship, and oneness with the cosmos.

> It appears that there is a permanent public, an actual community existing over time, that believes in the values of truth, the good, beauty, health, wisdom, courage, temperance, justice, harmony, order, communion, friendship, and oneness with the Cosmos—as variously as those values may be defined or practiced in "real" life.[15]

Fisher admits that other communities are possible—ones based on greed or power, for example. Yet he maintains that when people are confronted by "the better part of themselves," these less idealistic value systems wouldn't be "entirely coherent or true to their whole lives, or to the life that they would most like to live."[16] Fisher believes, then, that the humane virtues of the ideal audience shape our logic of good reasons. If we are convinced that this audience of good people would scoff at Boaz' protection of Ruth or squirm in discomfort at her midnight visit to the barn, Buechner's version of the biblical narrative will lack fidelity. But inasmuch as we think that these ideal auditors would applaud Ruth's rarified devotion to Naomi—while appreciating the older woman's down-to-earth approach to courtship—Buechner's words will have the ring of truthfulness and humanity.

According to Fisher, when we judge a story to have fidelity, we are not merely affirming shared values. We are ultimately opening ourselves to the possibility that those values will influence our beliefs and actions. For example, many engaged couples for whom the love of Ruth rings true have adopted her words to Naomi as a model for their wedding vows:

> I will go wherever you go and live wherever you live.
> Your people will be my people, and your God will be my God.[17]

A good story is a powerful means of persuasion.

CRITIQUE: DOES FISHER'S STORY HAVE COHERENCE AND FIDELITY?

Fisher's narrative paradigm offers a fresh reworking of Aristotelian analysis, which has dominated rhetorical thinking in the field of communication. His approach is strongly democratic. When communication is viewed as narrative, people usually don't need specialized training or expertise to figure out if a story holds together or offers good reasons for believing it true. There's still a place for experts to provide information and explanation in specialized fields, but when it comes to evaluating coherence and fidelity, people with ordinary common sense are competent rhetorical critics.

In *Human Communication as Narration*, Fisher applies the principles of narrative coherence and narrative fidelity to analyze various types of communication. He explains why a sometimes illogical President Ronald Reagan was aptly known as "The Great Communicator." He examines the false values of Willy Loman that lead to his downfall in *Death of a Salesman*. And he explores the consequences of adopting the rival philosophies embedded in the stories of two Greek thinkers—Socrates and Callicles. According to Fisher, the very fact that the narrative paradigm can be applied to this wide range of communication genres provides strong evidence of its validity.

Of course, Fisher's theory is itself a story, and as you might expect, not everyone accepts his tale. For example, many critics charge that he is overly optimistic when, similar to Aristotle, Fisher argues that people have a natural tendency to prefer the true and the just. Challenging Fisher's upbeat view of human nature, rhetorical critic Barbara Warnick at the University of Washington calls attention to the great communicative power of evil or wrongheaded stories such as Hitler's *Mein Kampf*. Fisher declares that Hitler's opus "must be judged a bad story,"[18] but as Warnick notes, it "struck a chord in an alienated, disunited, and despairing people."[19] Hitler's success in scapegoating the Jews ranks as one of history's most notorious acts of rhetoric, yet in its time and place it achieved both coherence and fidelity. Fisher thinks Warnick is confusing Hitler's *effective* discourse with the *good* discourse that people tend to prefer. But he grants that evil can overwhelm that tendency and thinks that's all the more reason for identifying and promoting the humane values described by the narrative paradigm.

An unsettling extension of Warnick's concern is the inherent power of the stories told by those who control the mass media. The influence of privileged stories is dramatically magnified when their continual repetition drowns out or demonizes alternative versions. This problem doesn't negate Fisher's narrative paradigm, but it suggests that he—and we—should pay more attention to the potentially oppressive power of stories that promote the status quo. This issue is at the heart of *cultural studies*, which will be discussed in the Media and Culture section (see Chapter 26).

In a somewhat wry fashion, Fisher credits his detractors for bolstering the validity of the narrative paradigm:

> I want to thank my critics, for they cannot but substantiate the soundness of my position. They do this in two ways: whatever line of attack they may take, they end up criticizing either the coherence or fidelity of my position, or both. And whatever objections they may make, the foundation for their objections will be a rival story, which, of course, they assume to be coherent and which has fidelity.[20]

Is most communication story, and do we judge every message we hear on the basis of whether it hangs together and rings true with our values? If you take Fisher's ideas seriously, you won't need me or a trained rhetorician to give you the final word. Like everyone else, you can spot the difference between a good story and a bad story.

QUESTIONS TO SHARPEN YOUR FOCUS

1. Using Fisher's definition of *narration*, can you think of any types of communication other than jokes or phatic communication that don't fit within the *narrative paradigm?*

2. Fisher claims that the *rational-world paradigm* dominates Western education. Can you list courses you've had at college that adopt the assumptions of this conceptual framework?

3. What is the difference between *narrative coherence* and *narrative fidelity?*

4. You apply a *logic of good reasons* to the stories you hear. What are the *values* undergirding Buechner's story of Ruth? Which one do you most admire? What *values* do you hold that cause you to ultimately accept or reject his narrative?

A SECOND LOOK

Recommended resource: Walter R. Fisher, *Human Communication as Narration: Toward a Philosophy of Reason, Value, and Action,* University of South Carolina, Columbia, 1987.

Original statement: Walter R. Fisher, "Narration as a Human Communication Paradigm: The Case of Public Moral Argument," *Communication Monographs,* Vol. 51, 1984, pp. 1–22.

Storytelling and narrativity in communication research: Journal of Communication, Vol. 35, No. 4, 1985, entire issue.

Scientific communication as story: Walter R. Fisher, "Narration, Knowledge, and the Possibility of Wisdom," in *Rethinking Knowledge: Reflections Across the Disciplines,* Robert F. Goodman and Walter R. Fisher (eds.), State University of New York, Albany, 1995, pp. 169–197.

Narration and community: Walter R. Fisher, "Narration, Reason, and Community," in *Memory, Identity, Community: The Idea of Narrative in the Human Sciences,* Lewis Hinchman and Sandra Hinchman (eds.), State University of New York, Albany, 1997, pp. 307–327.

Narrative ethics: Walter R. Fisher, "The Ethic(s) of Argument and Practical Wisdom," in *Argument at Century's End,* Thomas Hollihan (ed.), National Communication Association, Annandale, VA, 1999, pp. 1–15.

Telling the old story in a new way: Frederick Buechner, *Peculiar Treasures,* Harper & Row, New York, 1979.

Coherent life stories: Dan McAdams, "The Problem of Narrative Coherence," *Journal of Constructivist Psychology,"* Vol. 19, 2006, pp. 109–125.

Ethics as story: Richard Johannesen, "A Rational World Ethic Versus a Narrative Ethic for Political Communication," in *Ethics in Human Communication,* 5th ed., Waveland, Prospect Heights, IL, 2002, pp. 269–277.

Narrative insight from folklore: Kathleen G. Roberts, "Texturing the Narrative Paradigm: Folklore and Communication," *Communication Quarterly,* Vol. 52, 2004, pp. 129–142.

Critique: Barbara Warnick, "The Narrative Paradigm: Another Story," *Quarterly Journal of Speech,* Vol. 73, 1987, pp. 172–182.

DIVISION FOUR

Mass Communication

Students who begin to study the relationship between media and culture quickly run across multiple references to *postmodernism*. While most of us understand that this term refers to many elements of contemporary Western society, we may be hard-pressed to explain the specific values or practices that distinguish a postmodern culture from others. Since media expression is at the heart of postmodernism, I'll illustrate six of its defining features by referring to *Blade Runner*, a film that Canadian sociologist David Lyon refers to as the "acme of postmodern movies."[1]

> Los Angeles, AD 2019, provides the setting for *Blade Runner*. A group of "replicants," bio-engineered near-people who normally reside "off world," have returned to confront their makers, the high-tech Tyrell corporation. Their complaint is simple; understandably they object to their four-year lifespan and seek an extension to full human status. Deckard, the "blade runner," has the unenviable task of tracking these escaped replicants and eliminating or "retiring" them.[2]

1. *Postmodern describes a period of time when the promise of modernism no longer seems justified.* In *Blade Runner*, Los Angeles is a discouraging site of urban decay and pollution. Average citizens seem to have little hope or meaning in their daily existence. Deckard has no enthusiasm for his assignment as a blade runner; he sets out to eliminate replicants only to save his own skin.

The modernistic ideologies that postmodernism rejects include the industrial revolution, nationalistic imperialism, the rationality of the Enlightenment, faith in science, and any sense that the world is on an upward trajectory. Although European intellectuals began to offer a critique of Western culture shortly after World War II, it wasn't until the 1980s that those social ideas began to gain traction in America.

In his essay "On Nihilism," Jean Baudrillard, a leading French postmodernist, claims that he and his colleagues are neither optimistic nor pessimistic. Yet the absence of meaning he describes strikes most readers as devoid of hope.

> I have the impression with postmodernism that there is an attempt to rediscover a certain pleasure in the irony of things. Right now one can tumble into total hopelessness—all the definitions, everything, it's all been done. What can one do? What can one become? And postmodernity is the attempt . . . to reach a point where one can live with what is left. It is more a survival amongst the remnants than anything else.[3]

Unlike Merrill Lynch, Baudrillard is not "bullish on America."

2. *We have become tools of our tools.* In the futuristic world of *Blade Runner*, a biotech company has created human replicants that are superior to the "real thing" so that they can perform the dangerous, dirty work of space colonization. To ensure mastery over these androids, their creators build into them a short life span and then limit their activity to off-Earth locations. But in a Frankensteinian move, one of the six out-of-control replicants confronts his creator and kills him.

Twenty years before *Blade Runner* was filmed, Canadian Marshall McLuhan surveyed the history of media technology and observed that *we shape our tools and they in turn shape us*. He claimed that all media are extensions of some human faculty—psychic or physical. For example, the wheel is an extension of the foot, the book is an extension of the eye, clothing is an extension of the skin, and electronic circuitry is an extension of the central nervous system.[4] Although moviegoers saw the high-tech replicants in *Blade Runner* turn on their inventors, McLuhan didn't picture computers plotting to spread a virus and take over the world. He thought that the influence of media upon us is much more subtle.

According to McLuhan, when we continually use a communication technology it alters our symbolic environment—the socially constructed, sensory world of meanings that shapes our perceptions, experiences, attitudes, and behavior. We concentrate on analyzing or resisting the content of media messages, yet we miss the fact that the medium itself is actually the message. He suggested that the media are best understood ecologically. Chapter 24 presents McLuhan's theory of *media ecology.*

3. *In a postmodern world, any claim of truth or moral certainty is suspect.* Nowhere in *Blade Runner* does a human seek to justify an action on the basis of a universal principle of justice or commitment to the greater good. After replicant Rachael saves Deckard's life, she asks him if he will still try to kill her. Based on his own personal code, he answers, "No. Because I owe you." Yet he continues to hunt down and "retire" the others. As for truth, replicants desperately cling to the hope that they are human, but photographs of families and implanted memories offer no certainty. By the end of this *film noir,* the viewer wonders if there is any difference between those who are labeled *human* and those who are not.

In his book *The Postmodern Condition,* Baudrillard's countryman Jean-Francois Lyotard was the first to popularize the use of the term *postmodern* to describe our culture. "Simplifying to the extreme," wrote Lyotard, "I define *postmodern* as incredulity towards metanarratives."[5] He was referring specifically to any systems of thought that claimed to be true for all people, such as Marxism, Freudianism, or Christianity. But the relativity of knowledge applies to any assertion of truth. In postmodern thinking, we can't know anything for certain. There are no facts, only interpretations.

Under postmodern skepticism, anything that appears solid melts into thin air. This is a major reason film critics label *The Matrix* and *Memento* as postmodern art. The success of the television show *Seinfeld* suggests that even light-hearted comedy can have the same ephemeral quality. As its creator often claimed, "It's a show about nothing."

4. *Images become more important than what they represent.* At the beginning of *Blade Runner* the distinction between humans and replicants is clear. Humans are real; replicants are mere simulation—perfect "skin jobs." But as the story unfolds, the line between them becomes blurred. Replicants are smarter, stronger, and faster than humans, and despite denials by their inventor, they experience human emotions. By the end of the film, the line no longer exists. Indeed, Rachael may live indefinitely, while Deckard may, in fact, be a replicant. One can never be sure.

Postmodernists are convinced that recurrent media images take on a *hyperreality*—they are more real than real. Our mental pictures of the perfect body, house, meal, vacation, and sexual relationship have been created through exposure to constantly recycled media depictions that have no basis in fact—but it is these images that create our expectations. As Baudrillard suggests, "It's not TV

as a mirror of society but just the reverse: *it's society as the mirror of television.*"[6] For postmodernists, the issue is not whether media distort reality. In today's world the media have become reality—the only one we have.

The study of the relationship between images and what they signify is called *semiotics*. Chapter 25 presents French literary critic Roland Barthes' theory of semiotics, which analyzes media images and the way that they are co-opted to serve alternative ends.

5. *With a media assist, we can mix and match diverse styles and tastes to create a unique identity.* The movie *Blade Runner* exemplifies a mixture of film genres—it's a science fiction, romantic, action, mystery thriller. The film presents a Los Angeles that is a pastiche of mean streets, gothic architecture, an apartment decorated like a Mayan palace, and a 700-story office building in the shape of an Egyptian pyramid with a modern interior. The main characters are just as diverse, yet all are seeking to craft satisfying answers to three questions: *Where do I come from? Where am I going? How long have I got?*

Lyotard regards this kind of eclecticism as the norm for postmodern culture. "One listens to reggae, watches a Western, eats McDonald's food for lunch and local cuisine for dinner, wears Paris perfume in Tokyo and 'retro' clothes in Hong Kong; knowledge is a matter for TV games."[7] The possibilities of identity construction are endless in an urban setting with hundreds of cable channels and a high-speed Internet connection to provide infinite variety. Postmodernism is an age of individualism rather than one of community.

6. *Postmodernism can also be seen as a new kind of economic order—a consumer society based on multinational capitalism.* The world of *Blade Runner* isn't run by a nation or political alliance but by a high-tech conglomerate—the Tyrell Corporation. In such a world, information rather than production is the key to profits. Money is especially important in a consumer society because *people are what they consume.*

Operating from a neo-Marxist perspective, Duke University literature professor Frederic Jameson is a high-profile postmodernist who takes this economic view. He sees in our current era "the emergence of a new type of social life and a new economic order,"[8] specifically a late stage of capitalism. He is not surprised to see the erosion of the old distinction between high culture and so-called popular culture. In the absence of aesthetic standards, profits become the measure of whether art is good or bad. Thus, media conglomerates such as Disney and Time Warner cannot help but work in the interest of those who already have financial control.

Stuart Hall's *cultural studies*, presented in Chapter 26, takes a similar neo-Marxist approach. Hall's objective is to unmask the role of the media in maintaining the status quo of power relationships in society. Thus, Hall is an advocate for people who are systematically relegated to the margins of society.

McLuhan, Barthes, and Hall do not specifically refer to themselves as postmodern theorists. Yet the insights they offer have contributed to the postmodern analysis of the relationship between media and culture. And as with avowed postmodernist scholars, their methodological approach is highly interpretive rather than empirical. Media theorists who take a scientific approach focus more on measurable effects and will be featured in the section following this one (see Chapters 27–29).

CHAPTER 24

Media Ecology

of Marshall McLuhan

The critical and popular success of the film *An Inconvenient Truth* caught nearly everyone by surprise. Not even dedicated environmentalists expected former Vice President Al Gore's slide-show lecture on global warming to create the buzz it did, nor did they anticipate that Gore would be honored with the 2007 Nobel Peace Prize for his effort. Yet *An Inconvenient Truth* became one of the highest-grossing documentaries of all time, won the 2006 Academy Award for best picture in that category, and appears to have been the tipping point in Americans' concern about the effects of global warming.

Of course, not everyone liked the film. Some people stayed away, because they knew what they'd see and hear (see Chapter 16). Others argued strongly against Gore's claims. Science may prove that the climate is heating up for now, but climates are dynamic, they suggested, and the current rise in temperature may just be an uptick in a cycle that will later go down. These skeptics also asked how it's possible to know if human beings are directly responsible for the ongoing climate changes.[1]

The debate on global warming turns on our attitude toward the relationship between modern civilization and the environment. Do human inventions and actions really matter when it comes to the stability of global temperatures? Are we affecting our atmosphere and, if so, does it affect us in return?

Media
Generic term for all human-invented technology that extends the range, speed, or channels of communication.

In the 1960s, University of Toronto English professor Marshall McLuhan burst onto the public scene by asking similar questions about the relationship between *media* and culture. Like *An Inconvenient Truth*, McLuhan's *Understanding Media* was a surprise hit that generated both admiration and dissension. His theory suggests that media should be understood ecologically. Changes in technology alter the *symbolic environment*—the socially constructed, sensory world of meanings that in turn shapes our perceptions, experiences, attitudes, and behavior.

Symbolic environment
The socially constructed, sensory world of meanings.

THE MEDIUM IS THE MESSAGE

McLuhan's theory of media ecology is best captured in his famous aphorism: "The medium is the message." This pithy statement is meant to upset our expectations. We're accustomed to thinking of the message as separate from the medium itself. The *medium* delivers the message. McLuhan, however, collapsed the distinction between the message and the medium. He saw them as one and the same.

When considering the cultural influence of *media*, however, we are usually misled by the illusion of *content*. McLuhan wrote, "For the 'content' of a medium is like the juicy piece of meat carried by the burglar to distract the watchdog of the mind."[2] We focus on the content and overlook the *medium*—even though content doesn't exist outside of the way it's mediated. *Moby Dick* is a book. *Moby Dick* is a movie. *Moby Dick* is an oral tale. These are different stories. For this reason, we shouldn't complain that a movie is not like the book, because a movie can never be like a book. A movie can only be a movie.

Whether a TV show is about killer whales, current events, crime scene investigations, or discovering the next American pop star, the message is always television. It is the distinct experience of TV that alters the symbolic environment. From the perspective of media ecology, the Diehard Peyton MasterCard ad discussed in Chapter 2 is important not for its content but for its televisual characteristics, such as its reliance on humor and 10 cuts in a 30-second commercial. Media ecologists might point out that neither Glenn nor Marty even mentioned these features in their analysis.

Medium
A specific type of media; for example, a book, newspaper, radio, television, telephone, film, Web Site. or email.

THE CHALLENGE OF MEDIA ECOLOGY

Media ecology
The study of different personal and social environments created by the use of different communication technologies.

Any understanding of social and cultural change is impossible without a knowledge of the way media work as environments.[3] Yet evaluating the *ecology of media* is a difficult enterprise because all environments are inherently intangible and interrelated. An environment is not a thing to identify; rather, it is the intricate association of many things. By definition, these things are part of the background. They are everything and no thing. McLuhan noted that "their ground rules, pervasive structure, and overall patterns elude easy perception."[4]

Invisibility of Environments

McLuhan was fond of quoting the mantra of anthropologists: "We don't know who discovered water, but we're pretty sure it wasn't the fish." In the same way, we have trouble recognizing "the way media work as environments" because we are so immersed in them.

McLuhan's theory of media differs from the traditional warnings against technological advances. The tales of *Frankenstein*, *Jurassic Park*, and *The Matrix* posit technology gone awry and turning on its maker. These fantastical threats prove to be horribly obvious. As long as our technologies are not chasing after us, we are supposedly safe from the consequences of our creations.

Technology
According to McLuhan, human inventions that enhance communication.

According to McLuhan, it's not technological abnormality that demands our attention, since it's hard *not* to notice the new and different. Instead, we need to focus on our everyday experience of *technology*. A medium shapes us because we partake of it over and over until it becomes an extension of ourselves. Because every medium emphasizes different senses and encourages different habits, engaging a medium day after day conditions the senses to take in some stimuli and not register other things. A medium that emphasizes the ear over the eye alters the ratios of sense perception. Like a blind man who begins to develop a heightened sense of hearing, society is shaped in accordance with the dominant medium of the day.

It's the ordinariness of media that makes them invisible. When a new medium enters society, there's a period of time in which we're aware of its novelty. It's only when it fades into the background of our lives that we're truly subjected to its patterns—that is, its environmental influence. In the same way that a girl growing up in California may unconsciously absorb a West Coast attitude, a boy growing up in our electronic age may unconsciously absorb a digital attitude.

Complexity of Environments

In *An Inconvenient Truth*, Gore offers scientific evidence that the planet is experiencing a critical change in climate. Even when global warming skeptics grudgingly admit a rise in average temperature, they suggest that there's no direct relationship between this change in climate and the emissions of carbon dioxide and other greenhouse gases from human activities. Because environments are incredibly intricate, there are always a number of other factors and conditions that opponents can claim are contributing to the climate. As we saw in Chapter 13, systems theorists call this *overdetermination*. When it comes to the environment, there is no easy formula for a cause and effect relationship such as *global warming increases 0.0001 degrees for every million of gallons of gas burned*.

Overdetermination
Equifinality; a systems theory assumption that a given outcome could be effectively caused by any or many interconnected factors.

This lack of a one-to-one relationship is also why it's so easy to ignore our contributions to global warming. If the sun got brighter and hotter every time we filled our tank with gas, we'd probably look for an alternative energy source. In like manner, if our ears grew and our eyes dimmed every time we used the cell phone, we'd surely take notice. Understanding the influential relationship between the media environment and society is a subtle yet crucial endeavor that demands a complex sense of both incremental and sudden change. For this reason, McLuhan traced the major ecological shifts in media throughout human history.

A MEDIA ANALYSIS OF HUMAN HISTORY

McLuhan was critical of social observers who analyzed the Western world but bypassed the effects of symbolic environments—be they oral, print, or electronic. He specifically accused modern scholars of being "ostrichlike" in refusing to acknowledge the revolutionary impact of electronic media on the sensory experience of contemporary society.

As Figure 24–1 shows, McLuhan divided all human history into four periods, or epochs—a tribal age, a literate age, a print age, and an electronic age. According to McLuhan, the crucial inventions that changed life on this planet were the phonetic alphabet, the printing press, and the telegraph. In each case the world was wrenched from one era into the next because of new developments in media technology. Those of us born in the twentieth century are living through one of those turbulent transitions—at the tail end of the *print* age and near the beginning of the *electronic* age.

1. The Tribal Age: An Acoustic Place in History

Tribal age
An acoustic era; a time of community because the ear is the dominant sense organ.

According to McLuhan, the tribal village was an acoustic place where the senses of hearing, touch, taste, and smell were developed far beyond the ability to visualize. In untamed settings, hearing is more valuable than seeing because it allows you to be more immediately aware of your surroundings. With sight, we

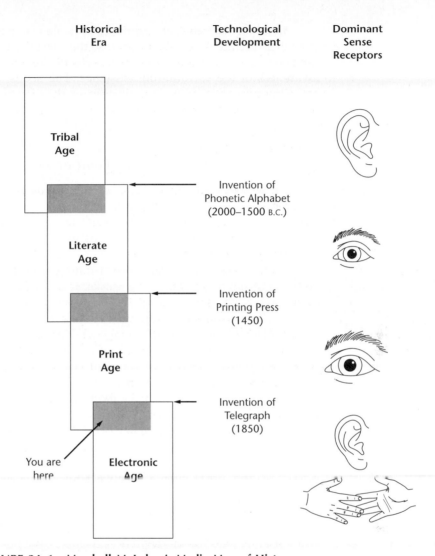

Historical Era	Technological Development	Dominant Sense Receptors

FIGURE 24–1   Marshall McLuhan's Media Map of History

are limited to direction and distance. We can only sense what is clearly in front of us. If a preying animal is behind us or hidden behind a tree, we are hopelessly unaware without a sensitivity to sound or smell. Hearing and smelling provide a sense of that which we cannot see, a crucial ability in the tribal age.

The omnidirectional quality of sound also enhances community. The spoken word is primarily a communal experience. To tell a secret, we must whisper or speak directly in someone's ear or make sure that no one else is listening. The sense of sound works against privatization. Listening to someone speak in a group is a unifying act. Everyone hears at the same time.

The spoken word is also immediate and alive. It exists only at the moment it is heard. There is no sense of the word as something that is fixed or objectified. Spoken words lack materiality. In order to keep an idea or an event alive, it must constantly be shared and reiterated and passed down. The ethereal quality of speech doesn't allow for detached analysis. In a tribal age, hearing is believing.

McLuhan claimed that "primitive" people led richer and more complex lives than their literate descendants because the ear, unlike the eye, encourages a more holistic sense of the world. There is a deeper feeling of community and greater awareness of the surrounding existence. The acoustic environment also fosters more passion and spontaneity. In this world of surround sound, everything is more immediate, more present, and more actual.

Then someone invented the alphabet.

2. The Age of Literacy: A Visual Point of View

Turning sounds into visible objects radically altered the symbolic environment. Suddenly, the eye became the heir apparent. Hearing diminished in value and quality. To disagree with this assessment merely illustrates McLuhan's belief that a private, left-brain "point of view" becomes possible in a world that encourages the visual practice of reading texts.

Literary age
A visual era; a time of private detachment because the eye is the dominant sense organ.

Words fixed on a page detach meaning from the immediacy of context. In an acoustic environment, taking something out of context is nearly impossible. In the age of literacy, it's a reality. Both writer and reader are always separate from the text. Words are no longer alive and immediate. They can be read and reread. They can be thoroughly analyzed. Hearing no longer becomes trustworthy. "Seeing it in writing" becomes proof that it's true.

Literacy also jarred people out of collective tribal involvement into "civilized" private detachment. Reading words, instead of hearing them, transforms group members into individuals. Even though the words may be the same, the act of reading a text is an individual one. It requires singular focus. A tribe no longer needs to come together to get information. Proximity becomes less important.

McLuhan also claimed that the phonetic alphabet established the line as the organizing principle in life. In writing, letter follows letter in a connected, orderly line. Logic is modeled on that step-by-step linear progression. According to McLuhan, when literate people say, "I don't follow you," they mean, "I don't think you are logical." He alleged that the invention of the alphabet fostered the sudden emergence of mathematics, science, and philosophy in ancient Greece. He cited the political upheaval in colonial Africa as twentieth-century evidence that literacy triggers an ear-to-eye switch that isolates the reader. When oppressed people learned to read, they became independent thinkers.

3. The Print Age: Prototype of the Industrial Revolution

If the phonetic alphabet made visual dependence possible, the printing press made it widespread. In *The Gutenberg Galaxy*, McLuhan argued that the most important aspect of movable type was its ability to reproduce the same text over and over again, and a press run of 100,000 copies of *Understanding Media* suggests that he was right. Because the print revolution demonstrated mass production of identical products, McLuhan called it the forerunner of the industrial revolution.

Print age
A visual era; mass-produced books usher in the industrial revolution and nationalism, yet individuals are isolated.

He saw other unintended side effects of Gutenberg's invention. The homogenization of fluid regional tongues into a fixed national language was followed closely by the rise of nationalism. Concurring with this new sense of unification was a countering sense of separation and aloneness.

Printing, a ditto device, confirmed and extended the new visual stress. It created the portable book, which men could read in privacy and in isolation from others.[5]

Many libraries have the words "The truth will set you free" carved in stone above the main entrance.[6] From McLuhan's perspective, libraries provide readers with the freedom to be alienated from others and from the immediacy of their surroundings.

4. The Electronic Age: The Rise of the Global Village

With the tap-tap-tap of the telegraph, the power of the printed word lost its bearings. Of course, Samuel Morse's invention was only the first of the new electronic media devices that would make the corner Radio Shack seem, to previous generations, like a magic shop.

Electronic age
An era of instant communication; a return to the global village with all-at-once sound and touch.

Telegraph   Telephone   Radio
Film projector   Phonograph   Television
Photocopier   Answering machine
Computer   VCR   Compact disc
Cellular phone   Fax   Video game
Internet   DVD   PDA   MP3 player

McLuhan insisted that electronic media are retribalizing the human race. Instant communication has returned us to a pre-alphabetic oral tradition where sound and touch are more important than sight. We've gone "back to the future" to become a village unlike any other previous village. We're now a *global village*.

Global village
A worldwide electronic community where everyone knows everyone's business and all are somewhat testy.

Electronic media bring us in touch with everyone, everywhere, instantaneously. Whereas the book extended the eye, electronic circuitry extends the central nervous system.[7] Constant contact with the world becomes a daily reality. All-at-once-ness is our state of being. Closed human systems no longer exist. The rumble of empty stomachs in Bombay and of roadside bombs in Baghdad vibrate in the living rooms of Boston. For us, the first postliterate generation, privacy is either a luxury or a curse of the past. The planet is like a general store where nosy people keep track of everyone else's business—a 12-way party line or a "Dear Abby" column writ large. "The new tribalism is one where everyone's buiness is everyone else's and where we all are somewhat testy."[8] Citizens of the world are back in acoustic space.

Linear logic is useless in the electronic society that McLuhan described. Acoustic people no longer inquire, "Do you see my point?" Instead we ask, "How does that grab you?" What we feel is more important than what we think.

5. The Digital Age? Rewiring the Global Village

When *Wired*, a magazine on digital culture, was launched in 1992, the editors declared Marshall McLuhan the magazine's "patron saint." There was a sense that another revolution was looming, and many returned to the words of McLuhan for guidance. However, digital technology doesn't pull the plug on the electronic age, because, quite frankly, it still needs its power source. The *digital age* is wholly electronic.

Digital age
A possible fifth era of specialized electronic tribes contentious over diverse beliefs and values.

With that said, there's no doubt that the introduction of digital technology is altering the electronic environment. The mass age of electronic media is

"You see, Dad, Professor McLuhan says the environment that man createsbecomes his medium for defining his role in it. The invention of type created linear, or sequential, thought, separating thought from action. Now, with TV and folk singing, thought and action are closer and social involvement is greater. We again live in a village. Get it?"

becoming increasingly personalized. Instead of one unified electronic tribe, we have a growing number of digital tribes forming around the most specialized ideas, beliefs, values, interests, and fetishes. Instead of mass consciousness, which McLuhan viewed rather favorably, we have the emergence of a tribal warfare mentality. Despite the contentious nature of this tribalization of differences, many see a benefit in the resulting decentralization of power and control.

Were he alive today, McLuhan undoubtedly would have spotted other ways that digital media are altering our present environment. And he would probably speculate on whether the electronic environment is the destiny of humankind, or if there's another media force waiting to upset the ecology of the previous century.

ETHICAL REFLECTION: POSTMAN'S FAUSTIAN BARGAIN

McLuhan's probes stimulated others to ponder whether specific media environments were beneficial or destructive for those immersed within them. Neil Postman founded the media ecology program at New York University and was regarded by many as McLuhan's heir apparent. Like McLuhan, Postman believed that the forms of media regulate and even dictate what kind of content the form of a given medium can carry.[9] For example, smoke signals implicitly discourage philosophical argument.

> Puffs of smoke are insufficiently complex to express ideas on the nature of existence and even if they were not, a Cherokee philosopher would run short of either wood or blankets long before he reached his second axiom. You cannot use smoke to do philosophy. Its form excludes the content.[10]

Yet unlike McLuhan, Postman believed that the primary task of media ecology is to make moral judgments. "To be quite honest about it," he once proclaimed, "I don't see any point in studying media unless one does so within a moral or ethical context."[11]

Faustian bargain
A deal with the devil; selling your soul for temporary earthly gain.

According to Postman, a new technology always presents us with a *Faustian bargain*—a potential deal with the devil. As Postman was fond of saying, "Technology giveth and technology taketh away. . . . A new technology sometimes creates more than it destroys. Sometimes, it destroys more than it creates. But it is never one-sided."[12] His media ecology approach asks, *What are the moral implications of this bargain? Are the consequences more humanistic or antihumanistic? Do we, as a society, gain more than we lose, or do we lose more than we gain?*

Postman argued that television is detrimental to society because it has led to the loss of serious public discourse. Television changes the form of information "from discursive to nondiscursive, from propositional to presentational, from rationalistic to emotive."[13] *Sesame Street, 60 Minutes,* and *Survivor* all share the same ethos—amusement. The environment of television turns everything into entertainment and everyone into juvenile adults. Triviality trumps seriousness.

Shortly before the 2004 U.S. presidential election, *Daily Show* comedian Jon Stewart shocked TV audiences by confronting the hosts of *Crossfire* for hurting public discourse in America. He suggested that their program turned debate into theater and "partisan hackery." Some compared Stewart's criticism to Neil Postman's sentiments in his book *Amusing Ourselves to Death*. Stewart's criticism seemed warranted, yet it was significantly different than Postman's critique of television news shows. Whereas Stewart argued that shows like *Crossfire* should be more responsible, Postman believed that, on television, panelists are unable to respond in a serious manner. *Crossfire*, which is no longer on the air, was bad at public discourse because, for a while, it was good at being television—silly and shallow.

Like McLuhan, Postman preferred questions to answers, so it is fitting that his legacy be defined by three questions he urged us to ask about any new technology:

1. What is the problem to which this technology is a solution?
2. Whose problem is it, actually?
3. If there is a legitimate problem here to be solved, what other problems will be created by my using this technology?

To this end, Postman expressed concerns about the coming age of computer technology. He questioned if we were yielding too easily to the "authority" of computation and the values of efficiency and quantification. He pondered whether the quest for technological progress was becoming increasingly more important than being humane. He wondered if information was an acceptable substitute for wisdom. While Postman was primarily concerned with the ecology of television, his work set a precedent for considering the moral consequences of all symbolic environments.

CRITIQUE: HOW COULD HE BE RIGHT? BUT WHAT IF HE WAS?

McLuhan likened himself to "Louis Pasteur telling doctors that their greatest enemy is quite invisible, and quite unrecognized by them."[14] Of course, the major difference is that Pasteur was a scientist, who ultimately gave tangible evidence for his germ theory. The problem with McLuhan's theory is that it suggests objectivity without scientific evidence. In other words, he used the subjective approach to make objective claims.

McLuhan faced harsh criticism from the scholarly community. He was one of the first academic superstars of the TV era, so perhaps his enormous popularity gave added impetus to critics' scorn for his methods and message. The pages of *McLuhan: Hot & Cold* and *McLuhan: Pro & Con*, collections of essays that critique his ideas, are filled with denunciation:

> [McLuhan] prefers to rape our attention rather than seduce our understanding.[15]

> He has looted all culture from cave painting to *Mad* magazine for fragments to shore up his system against ruin.[16]

> The style . . . is a viscous fog through which loom stumbling metaphors.[17]

George Gordon, then chairman of the department of communication at Fordham University, labeled McLuhan's work "McLuhanacy" and dismissed it as worthless. Gordon stated, "Not one bit of sustained and replicated scientific evidence, inductive or deductive, has to date justified any one of McLuhan's most famous slogans, metaphors, or dicta."[18] Indeed, it is hard to know how one could prove that the phonetic alphabet created Greek philosophy, that the printing press fostered nationalism, or that television is a tactile medium.

It is also hard to say that he was wrong, because it's difficult to be certain what he said. As a writer, McLuhan often abandoned the linearity and order that he claimed were the legacy of print technology. As a speaker, he was superb at crafting memorable phrases and 10-second sound bites, but his truths were enigmatic and seldom woven into a comprehensive system. He preferred to offer theoretical punch lines for people to accept or reject at face value.

For those who regard falsifiability as a mark of a good theory, McLuhan's leaps of faith make it difficult to take his ideas seriously. However, history is littered with theories that were ahead of their time and couldn't immediately be tested. Tom Wolfe reverses the question: "What if he's right? Suppose he is what he sounds like, the most important thinker since Newton, Darwin, Freud, Einstein and Pavlov?"[19]

McLuhan's historical analysis has heightened awareness of the possible cultural effects of new media technologies. Other scholars have been more tempered in their statements and more rigorous in their documentation, but none has raised media consciousness to the level achieved by McLuhan with his catchy statements and dramatic metaphors.

If there is criticism of McLuhan to be made within his own system, it may be regarding the actual "effect" of his work. Do his pithy ideas produce shallow consciousness like a good advertising campaign? Has McLuhan merely McDonaldized an important idea? Can a slogan or punch line really make a significant difference?

The late economist Kenneth Boulding, who headed the Institute of Behavioral Sciences at the University of Colorado, captured both the pro and con reactions to McLuhan by using a metaphor of his own: "It is perhaps typical of very creative minds that they hit very large nails not quite on the head."[20]

QUESTIONS TO SHARPEN YOUR FOCUS

1. What would McLuhan say about the impact of the Internet on the *global village?* Consider the fact that civic, political, and religious participation are declining in America.[21] Has *electronic technology* increased social connectedness?

2. How are portable media devices such as PDAs, cell phones, MP3 players, and handheld video games altering the *media environment?* How are these devices shaping sensibilities?

3. Beyond changes in content, what are the differences in experiencing a book and its translations into film or television?

4. Can you conceive of any way that McLuhan's idea of *media ecology* could be proven false?

SELF-QUIZ *www.mhhe.com/griffin7*

A SECOND LOOK

Recommended resource: Marshall McLuhan, *"Playboy* Interview: A Candid Conversation with the High Priest of Popcult and Metaphysician of Media," March 1969, p. 53ff. Reprinted in *Essential McLuhan*, Eric McLuhan and Frank Zingrone (eds.), BasicBooks, New York, 1995, pp. 233–269.

McLuhan primer: Marshall McLuhan and Quentin Fiore, *The Medium Is the Massage,* Gingko, Corte Madera, CA, 2005.

Impact of print media: Marshall McLuhan, *The Gutenberg Galaxy,* University of Toronto, Toronto, 1962.

Impact of electronic media: Marshall McLuhan, *Understanding Media,* McGraw-Hill, New York, 1964.

Impact of digital media à la McLuhan: Paul Levinson, *Digital McLuhan: A Guide to the Information Millennium,* Routledge, London, 1999.

Early vs. late McLuhan: Bruce E. Gronbeck, "McLuhan as Rhetorical Theorist," *Journal of Communication,* Vol. 31, 1981, pp. 117–128.

Intellectual roots: Harold Innis, *The Bias of Communication,* University of Toronto, Toronto, 1964.

Methodology: Paul Levinson, "McLuhan and Rationality," *Journal of Communication,* Vol. 31, 1981, pp. 179–188.

Further developments in media ecology: Walter Ong, *Orality and Literacy: The Technologizing of the Word*, Methuen, London, 1982.

Neil Postman's ethical view of new media: Neil Postman, *Amusing Ourselves to Death: Public Discourse in the Age of Show Business*, Viking, NY, 1985; Neil Postman, *Technopoly: The Surrender of Culture to Technology*, Knopf, New York, 1992.

Rethinking McLuhan through critical theory: Paul Grosswiler, *Method Is the Message*, Black Rose, Montreal, 1998.

Postmodern connections: Gary Genosko, "McLuhan's Legacy of Indiscipline," in *Undisciplined Theory*, Sage, London, 1998, pp. 154-182.

Critique: Gerald Stearn (ed.), *McLuhan: Hot & Cool*, Dial, New York, 1967.

CHAPTER 25

Semiotics

of Roland Barthes

During the 1991 Persian Gulf War, when the United States launched Operation Desert Storm against Saddam Hussein's Iraq, students at a Texas liberal arts college competed in a strange outdoor decorating contest. It began when members of a service organization tied large yellow ribbons on virtually every tree on campus. Shortly before the cease-fire, another student group responded by placing black ribbons on many of the same trees. The combined symbolic activity of the students stirred up feelings of bewilderment, frustration, and amusement within the campus community.

How should a communication scholar view these carefully placed, dueling strips of cloth? According to French literary critic and semiologist Roland Barthes (rhymes with "smart"), these public objects are sophisticated, multifaceted signs waiting to be read. Interpreting signs is the goal of semiology; Barthes held the chair of literary semiology at the College of France when he was struck and killed by a laundry truck in 1980. In his highly regarded book *Mythologies*, Barthes sought to decipher the cultural meaning of a wide variety of visual signs—from sweat on the faces of actors in the film *Julius Caesar* to a magazine photograph of a young African soldier saluting the French flag.

Unlike most intellectuals, Barthes frequently wrote for the popular press and occasionally appeared on television to comment on the foibles of the French middle class. His academic colleagues found his statements witty, disturbing, flashy, overstated, or profound—but never dull. He obviously made them think. With the exception of Aristotle, the four-volume *International Encyclopedia of Communication* refers to Barthes more than to any other theorist in this book.[1]

Semiology (or semiotics, as it is better known in America) is concerned with *anything that can stand for something else.* Italian semiologist and novelist Umberto Eco has a clever way of expressing that focus. Semiotics, he says, is "the discipline studying everything which can be used in order to lie, because if something cannot be used to tell a lie, conversely it cannot be used to tell the truth; it cannot, in fact, be used to tell at all."[2] Barthes was interested in signs that are seemingly straightforward but that subtly communicate ideological or connotative meaning and perpetuate the dominant values of society. As such, they are deceptive.

Barthes was a mercurial thinker who changed his mind about the way signs work more than once over the course of his career. Yet most current practitioners

Semiotics (semiology)
The study of the social production of meaning from sign systems; the analysis of anything that can stand for something else.

of semiotics follow the basic analytical concepts of his original theory. His approach provides great insight into the use of signs, particularly those channeled through the mass media.

WRESTLING WITH SIGNS

Myth
The connotative meaning that signs carry wherever they go; myth makes what is cultural seem natural.

Barthes initially described his semiotic theory as an explanation of *myth*. He later substituted the term *connotation* to label the ideological baggage that signs carry wherever they go, and most students of Barthes' work regard connotation as a better word choice to convey his true concern.

Barthes' theory of connotative meaning won't make sense to us, however, unless we first understand the way he views the structure of signs. His thinking was strongly influenced by the work of Swiss linguist Ferdinand de Saussure, who coined the term *semiology* and advocated its study.[3] To illustrate Barthes' core principles I'll feature portions of his essay on pro wrestling à la Hulk Hogan. We'll then have the semiotic resources to interpret the provocative power of ribbons on trees during Desert Storm.

1. A Sign Is the Combination of Its Signifier and Signified

The distinction between signifier and signified can be seen in Barthes' graphic description of the body of a wrestler who was selected by the promoter because he typified the repulsive slob:

> As soon as the adversaries are in the ring, the public is overwhelmed with the obviousness of the roles. As in the theatre, each physical type expresses to excess the part which has been assigned to the contestant. Thauvin, a fifty-year-old with an obese and sagging body . . . displays in his flesh the characters of baseness. . . . I know from the start that all of Thauvin's actions, his treacheries, cruelties and acts of cowardice, will not fail to measure up to the first image of ignobility he gave me. . . . The physique of the wrestlers therefore constitutes a basic sign, which like a seed contains the whole fight.[4]

Sign
The inseparable combination of the signifier and the signified.

According to Barthes, the image of the wrestler's physique is the *signifier*. The concept of ignobility or injustice is the *signified*. The combination of the two—the villainous body—is the *sign*.

This way of defining a sign differs from our customary use of the word. We would probably say that the wrestler's body *is a sign* of his baseness—or whatever else comes to mind. But Barthes considered the wrestler's body to be just *part* of the overall sign; it's the signifier. The other part is the concept of hideous baseness. The signifier isn't a sign of the signified. Rather, they work together in an inseparable bond to form a unified sign.

Signifier
The physical form of the sign as we perceive it through our senses; an image.

Barthes' description of a sign as the correlation between the signifier and the signified came directly from Saussure. The Swiss linguist visualized a sign as a piece of paper with writing on both sides—the signifier on one side, the signified on the other. If you cut off part of one side, an equal amount of the other side automatically goes with it.

Signified
The meaning we associate with the sign.

Is there any logical connection between the image of the signifier and the content of the signified? Saussure insisted that the relationship is arbitrary—one of correlation rather than of cause and effect. Barthes wasn't so sure. He was willing to grant the claim of Saussure (and I. A. Richards) that words have no inherent meaning. For example, there is nothing about the word *referee* that makes it stand for the third party in the ring who is inept at making Thauvin follow the rules. But nonverbal signifiers seem to have a natural affinity with their signifieds. Barthes noted that Thauvin's body was so repugnant that it provoked nausea. He classified the relationship between signifiers and signifieds as "quasi-arbitrary." After all, Thauvin really did strike the crowd as vileness personified.

2. A Sign Does Not Stand on Its Own: It Is Part of a System

Barthes entitled his essay "The World of Wrestling," for like all other semiotic systems, wrestling creates its own separate world of interrelated signs:

> Each moment in wrestling is therefore like an algebra which instantaneously unveils the relationship between a cause and its represented effect. Wrestling fans certainly experience a kind of intellectual pleasure in *seeing* the moral mechanism function so perfectly. . . . Wrestlers, who are very experienced, know perfectly how to direct the spontaneous episodes of the fight so as to make them conform to the image which the public has of the great legendary themes of its mythology. A wrestler can irritate or disgust, he never disappoints, for he always accomplishes completely, by a progressive solidification of signs, what the public expects of him.[5]

Barthes noted that the grapplers' roles are tightly drawn. There is little room for innovation; the men in the ring work within a closed system of signs. By responding to the unwavering expectation of the crowd, the wrestlers are as much spectators as the fans who cheer or jeer on cue.

Wrestling is just one of many semiotic systems. Barthes also explored the cultural meaning of designer clothes, French cooking, automobiles, Japanese gift giving, household furniture, urban layout, and public displays of sexuality. He attempted to define and classify the features common to all semiotic systems. This kind of structural analysis is called *taxonomy*, and Barthes' book *Elements of Semiology* is a "veritable frenzy of classifications."[6] Barthes later admitted that his taxonomy "risked being tedious," but the project strengthened his conviction that all semiotic systems function the same way despite their apparent diversity.

Barthes believed that the significant semiotic systems of a culture lock in the status quo. The mythology that surrounds a society's crucial signs displays the world as it is today—however chaotic and unjust—as *natural, inevitable,* and *eternal.* The function of myth is to bless the mess. We now turn to Barthes' theory of connotation, or myth, which suggests how a seemingly neutral or inanimate sign can accomplish so much.

THE YELLOW RIBBON TRANSFORMATION: FROM FORGIVENESS TO PRIDE

According to Barthes, not all semiological systems are mythic. Not every sign carries ideological baggage. How is it that one sign can remain emotionally neutral while other signs acquire powerful inflections or connotations that suck people into a specific worldview? Barthes contended that a mythic or connotative system is a *second-order semiological system*—built off a preexisting sign system. The sign of the first system becomes the signifier of the second. A concrete example will help us understand Barthes' explanation.

In an *American Journal of Semiotics* article, Donald and Virginia Fry of Emerson College examined the widespread American practice of displaying yellow ribbons during the 1980 Iranian hostage crisis.[7] They traced the transformation of this straightforward yellow symbol into an ideological sign. Americans' lavish display of yellow ribbons during Operation Desert Storm a decade later adds a new twist to the Frys' analysis. I'll update their yellow ribbon example to illustrate Barthes' semiotic theory.

"Tie a Yellow Ribbon Round the Ole Oak Tree" was the best-selling pop song of 1972 in the United States.[8] Sung by Tony Orlando and Dawn, the lyrics express the thoughts of a convict in prison who is writing to the woman he loves. After three years in jail, the man is about to be released and will travel home by bus. Fearing her possible rejection, he devises a plan that will give her a way to signal her intentions without the potential embarrassment of a face-to-face confrontation.

Since he'll be able to see the huge oak planted in front of her house when the bus passes through town, he asks her to use the tree as a message board. If she still loves him, wants him back, and can overlook the past, she should tie a yellow ribbon around the trunk of the tree. He will know that all is forgiven and join her in rebuilding a life together. But if this bright sign of reconciliation isn't there, he'll stay on the bus, accept the blame for a failed relationship, and try to get on with his life without her.

The yellow ribbon is obviously a sign of acceptance, but one not casually offered. There's a taint on the relationship, hurts to be healed. Donald and Virginia Fry labeled the original meaning of the yellow ribbon in the song as "forgiveness of a stigma."

Yellow ribbons in 1991 continued to carry a "we want you back" message when U.S. armed forces fought in Operation Desert Storm. Whether tied to trees, worn in hair, or pinned to lapels, yellow ribbons still proclaimed, "Welcome home." But there was no longer any sense of shameful acts to be forgiven or disgrace to be overcome. Vietnam was ancient history and America was the leader of the "new world order." Hail the conquering heroes.

The mood surrounding the yellow ribbon had become one of triumph, pride, and even arrogance. After all, hadn't we intercepted Scud missiles in the air, guided "smart bombs" into air-conditioning shafts, and "kicked Saddam Hussein's butt across the desert"? People were swept up in a tide of "yellow fever." More than 90 percent of U.S. citizens approved of America's actions in the Persian Gulf. The simple yellow ribbon of personal reconciliation now served as a blatant sign of nationalism. What had originally signified forgiveness of a stigma now symbolized pride in victory.

THE MAKING OF MYTH: STRIPPING THE SIGN OF ITS HISTORY

According to Barthes' theory, the shift from "forgiveness of stigma" to "pride in victory" followed a typical semiotic pattern. Figure 25–1 shows how it's done.

Barthes claimed that every ideological sign is the result of two interconnected sign systems. The first system is strictly descriptive—the signifier image and the signified concept combining to produce a denotative sign. The three elements of the sign system based on the "Tie a Yellow Ribbon . . ." lyrics are marked with Arabic numerals at the top left portion of the diagram. The three segments of the connotative system are marked with Roman numerals. Note that the sign of the first system does double duty as the signifier of the

Denotative sign system
A descriptive sign without ideological content.

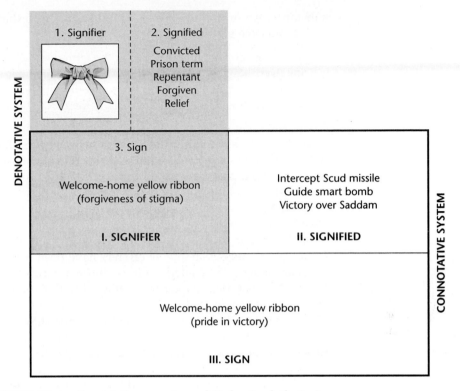

FIGURE 25–1   Connotation as a Second-Order Semiotic System
Adapted from Barthes, "Myth Today"

Gulf War connotative system. According to Barthes, this lateral shift, or connotative sidestep, is the key to transforming a neutral sign into an ideological tool. Follow his thinking step-by-step through the diagram.

The signifier (1) of the *denotative sign system* is the image of a yellow ribbon that forms in the mind of the person who hears the 1972 song. The content of the signified (2) includes the stigma that comes from the conviction of a crime and a term in jail, the prisoner's willingness to take responsibility for the three-year separation, and the explosive release of tension when the Greyhound passengers cheer at the sight of the oak tree awash in yellow ribbons. The corresponding denotative sign (3) is "forgiveness of a stigma." For those who heard the song on the radio, the yellow ribbon sign spoke for itself. It was a sign rich in regret and relief.

Current usage takes over the sign of the denotative system and makes it the signifier (I) of a secondary (connotative) system. The "welcome-home" yellow ribbon is paired with the mythic content of a signified (II) that shouts to the world, "Our technology can beat up your technology." But as the symbol of the yellow ribbon is expropriated to support the myth of American nationalism, the sign loses its historical grounding.

As a mere signifier of the *connotative sign system*, the yellow ribbon is no longer rooted in the details of the song. It ceases to stand for three years of hard time in prison, repentance, wrongdoing, or forgiveness that gains meaning because there is so much to be forgiven. Now in the service of the mythic semiotic system, the yellow ribbon becomes empty and timeless, a form without

Connotative sign system
A mythic sign that has lost its historical referent; form without substance.

substance. According to Barthes, that doesn't mean that the meaning of the original denotative sign is lost:

> The essential point in all this is that the form does not suppress the meaning, it only impoverishes it, it puts it at a distance, it holds it at one's disposal. One believes that the meaning is going to die, but it is a death with reprieve; the meaning loses its value, but keeps its life, from which . . . the myth will draw its nourishment.[9]

In the connotative system, the generalized image of a yellow ribbon is now paired with the signified content of victory in the Persian Gulf War as seen on CNN. But since the signifier can't call up a historical or cultural past, the mythic sign (III) of which it is a part carries the "crust of falsity."[10] For example, there's no sense of American culpability in supplying arms to Saddam Hussein until the time he invaded Kuwait. And since mythic communication is unable to imagine anything alien, novel, or other, the sign sweeps away second thoughts about civilian deaths in Baghdad. The transformed yellow ribbon is now a lofty sign that allows no room for nagging doubts that love of oil may have been our country's prime motivation for championing the United Nations' "humanitarian" intervention.

As I review this chapter for a new edition, America continues to be engaged in a second war in Iraq, a prolonged and bloody encounter. Millions of yellow ribbon magnets declaring "Support Our Troops" have been displayed on the backs of cars and trucks. Does the fact of Al Qaeda's 9/11 attack or the words on the ribbon change how Barthes would analyze this mythic sign system? Probably not. Were he alive, Barthes would certainly point out that the sign still conceals any

history of wrongdoing or sense of shame—this despite a history of abuse of prisoners at Abu Ghraib and Guantanamo Bay, the lack of armor for humvee carriers, and the absence of a plan to secure the peace after Saddam Hussein was driven from power.

As a semiologist who relished uncovering the ideological subtext in apparently straightforward signs, Barthes might also note that the support-our-troops yellow ribbon is not merely an appeal to write encouraging letters, pray for their safety, and praise them for their service when they come home. In effect, the exhortation makes it unpatriotic to openly criticize President George W. Bush's decision to invade Iraq. The juxtaposition of yellow ribbons with Bush-Cheney bumper stickers prior to the 2004 election, as well as the conservative stance of Web sites selling the magnets, makes it clear that these are not neutral denotative signs.

UNMASKING THE MYTH OF A HOMOGENEOUS SOCIETY

Barthes was convinced that only those with semiotic savvy can spot the hollowness of connotative signs. For most Americans, the yellow ribbon will continue to elicit an unreflective "we're number one" feeling of national pride. Of course, it goes without saying that people will love their country. But that's precisely the problem with mythic signs. They *go without saying*. They don't explain, they don't defend, and they certainly don't raise questions. So it's up to the semiologist to expose or deconstruct the mythic system.

Deconstruction
The process of unmasking contradictions within a text; debunking.

This same deconstructive urge inspired the left-leaning students of the antiwar student group to tie black ribbons on campus trees. In their view, the yellow ribbon signs placed by the student patriots merely perpetuated the destructive nationalism that gripped the country. Acting as fledgling semiologists, these social activists presented a competing sign to expose what they believed to be the jingoistic connotative system supported by the trees adorned with yellow ribbons.

Throughout his life, Roland Barthes deciphered and labeled the *ideologies* foisted upon naïve consumers of images. Although the starting-point signifiers varied, Barthes concluded that society's connotative spin always ends up the same. *Mythic signs reinforce the dominant values of their culture.* For example, the wrestling match we examined earlier seems at first glance to be no more than a harmless Saturday night diversion. Under Barthes' watchful eye, however, it was the site of dangerous mythmaking. He explained that the honorable wrestler's eventual triumph over the rule-breaking villain signifies a make-believe ideology of pure "justice." The "good guys win" simplicity of the spectacle provides false comfort for an audience that lives in a world of dubious morality and inherent inequality:

> What is portrayed in wrestling therefore is an ideal understanding of things; it is the euphoria of men raised for a while above the constitutive ambiguity of everyday situations and placed before the panoramic view of a univocal Nature, in which signs at last correspond to causes, without obstacle, without evasion, without contradiction.[11]

Ideology
Knowledge presented as common sense or natural, especially when its social construction is ignored or suppressed.

According to Barthes, ideological signs enlist support for the status quo by transforming history into nature—pretending that current conditions are the natural order of things. As with the ribbons and the wrestling match, everything that is personal, conditional, cultural, and temporal disappears. We are left with a sign that makes the world seem inevitable and eternal. Barthes' analysis calls to mind the final words of the "Gloria Patri," a choral response that many Christians sing in worship:

> As it was in the beginning,
> Is now and ever shall be,
> World without end. Amen. Amen.

For believers, singing these words about anything or anyone but God would be unthinkable. Barthes wouldn't grant even that exception. All his semiotic efforts were directed at unmasking what he considered the heresy of those who controlled the images of society—the naturalizing of history.

THE SEMIOTICS OF MASS COMMUNICATION: "I'D LIKE TO BE LIKE MIKE"

Like wrestlers and ribbons, most semiotic signs gain cultural prominence when broadcast through the electronic and print media. Because signs—as well as issues of power and dominance—are integral to mass communication, Barthes' semiotic analysis has become a seminal media theory. As Kyong Kim, author of a book on semiotics, concludes:

> Information delivered by mass media is no longer information. It is a commodity saturated by fantasized themes. Mass audiences are nothing more than consumers of such commodities. One should not forget that, unlike nature, the media's reality is always political. The mass signification arising in response to signs pouring from the mass media is not a natural process. Rather it is an artificial effect calculated and induced by the mass media to achieve something else.[12]

The advertisements that make commercial television so profitable also create layers of connotation that reaffirm the status quo. During the 1998 NBA playoffs, one of the most frequently aired spots featured Chicago Bulls' superstar Michael Jordan slam-dunking the basketball over a variety of helpless defenders. He then gulps down Gatorade while a host of celebrity and everyday admirers croon his praises. The most memorable of these adoring fans is a preschool African-American boy, who stares up in awe at the towering Jordan. "Sometimes I dream," we hear him sing, "that he is me." He *really* wants to be like Mike!

Obviously, the commercial is designed to sell Gatorade by linking it to the virtually unlimited achievement of basketball's greatest player. To partake of this liquid is to reach for the stars. In that sense, the little boy, rather than MJ himself, becomes the spot's crucial sign. Within this denotative system, the youngster's rapt gaze is the signifier, and his dream of becoming a famous athlete is the signified. The resultant denotative sign—a look of yearning—has the potential to move cartons of Gatorade off the shelf. But as the signifier of a secondary connotative system, it has greater cultural impact.

At the connotative level, the original "look of yearning" suggests a new second-order signified—a more general kind of dreaming about one's future in which the ad's audience is invited to participate. Viewers are encouraged to wish for careers and goals that are virtually unobtainable, even in the best of circumstances. The CEO of Microsoft, the conductor of the New York Philharmonic, Hollywood's most glamorous talent, the President of the United States, and the world's leading AIDS researcher constitute the lofty heights surveyed by the gaze that the connotative shift implies. With its attractive visuals, uplifting soundtrack, and good-natured humor, the commercial functions as a glorification of *unfulfilled desire*, the very essence of its second-order sign. This is America, after all, so think big, aim high, and don't be satisfied with anything but the top. Do what it takes—and purchase what is required—to be the very best. Ideologically speaking, it is this kind of naturalized longing that enslaves the average citizen and fuels the capitalist system. Although the commercial evokes a warm, fuzzy reaction from the viewer, it surreptitiously enforces our fundamental cultural myths about unlimited possibilities for success, myths that—according to Barthes—maintain the dominance of those who hold the reins of commerce and power.

Furthermore, Barthes would no doubt seek to expose the semiotic sleight of hand that subtly drains the second-order connotative system of the historical reality implicit in the original sign. At this denotative level, the African-American boy's fixation with MJ is necessarily embedded in a long history of racial injustice and economic hardship. Michael Jordan's accomplishments, as well as the dream of his pint-sized fan, exist in a world in which African Americans must strive particularly hard to succeed. As the documentary *Hoop Dreams* brilliantly portrays, the desire-filled faces of the youngsters who populate the rough basketball courts of urban America also reflect the poverty, substance abuse, shattered families, and harsh, big-city surroundings that constantly threaten to engulf them. Nonetheless, the yearning connoted by the second-order system generated by the commercial is utterly stripped of this rather grim social reality. The boy, his life, and his dream are deftly co-opted by the system. Or so Barthes would argue.

CRITIQUE: DO MYTHIC SIGNS ALWAYS REAFFIRM THE STATUS QUO?

Barthes' interpretations of cultural signs are usually fascinating and frequently compelling. But are connotative systems always ideological, and do they inevitably uphold the values of the dominant class? Perhaps there are significant semiotic systems that suggest divergent perspectives or support alternative voices. To some students of signification, Barthes' monolithic Marxist approach to mythmaking borders on a conspiracy theory. These interpreters are unwilling to accept the idea that all representation is a capitalistic plot, or that visual signs can't be used to promote resistance to dominant cultural values, like the black ribbons.

University of Pennsylvania political scientist Anne Norton expands Barthes' semiotic approach to account for other possibilities. For example, she argues that Madonna's MTV persona signifies an autonomous, independent sexuality that inspires young girls to control—rather than to be controlled by—their environments. In effect, Madonna's "construction of herself as a 'material girl' subverts the hierarchies and practices evolved by its dense tissue of references."[13]

In much the same vein, University of Texas media scholar Douglas Kellner writes that through Madonna's deliberate manipulation of stereotypes and imagery, female "wannabes" are "empowered in their struggles for *individual* identity." Although her provocative outfits and unabashed eroticism may seem at first glance to reinforce traditionally patriarchal views of women, her onstage character refigures her body as "the means to her wealth" and recasts her sexuality as "a form of feminine power."[14] In the same way, those black ribbons exemplified a counterculture connotative system that challenged the status quo. By hanging black crepe on trees, the protesters reminded a campus heavily supportive of Operation Desert Storm that war always means ghastly death for human beings on both sides. Stephen Spielberg's *Saving Private Ryan* offers the same gritty, connotative feel.

Perhaps the truth is somewhere in between. In his book-length analysis of British working-class youth, sociologist Dick Hebdige studied the personal appearance and style of mods, punks, hipsters, teddy boys, and other counterculture groups. He argues that although their semiotic activity is eventually co-opted by mainline society, their deviant style often enjoys a brief time of subversive signification. For a while, the clothing, haircuts, and guitar riffs of the Sex Pistols signified that punk-rock group's stylistic challenge to the symbolic order of mainline society, but those signs of refusal soon became status quo clichés.[15]

Whether or not we accept Barthes' claim that all connotative signs reinforce dominant values, his semiotic approach to imagery remains a core theoretical perspective for a wide variety of communication scholars, particularly those who emphasize media and culture. For example, cultural studies guru Stuart Hall builds directly on Barthes' analysis of myth to establish his critique of the "hegemonic" effects of mass communication.[16] Hall's innovative analysis, though, deserves a chapter all its own.

QUESTIONS TO SHARPEN YOUR FOCUS

1. What are the *signifier* and *signified* of a favorite item of clothing or jewelry? Can you think of a way that this sign has already *been stripped of history?*

2. Why did Barthes think it was crucial to *unmask* or *deconstruct* the original *denotation* of a sign?

3. Identify two or more distinct *nonverbal signifiers* from different television reality shows that have basically the same *signified*—"You're out of here."

4. "It's not over 'til the fat lady sings": what are the *denotative signifier, signified,* and *sign* to which this statement originally refers? When spoken about a baseball game, what *connotative shift* has altered the meaning of the original sign?

A SECOND LOOK

Recommended resource: Roland Barthes, *Mythologies*, Annette Lavers (trans.), Hill and Wang, New York, 1972, especially "The World of Wrestling" and "Myth Today," pp. 15–25, 109–159.

Barthes' structuralism: Annette Lavers, *Roland Barthes: Structuralism and After*, Harvard University, Cambridge, MA, 1982.

Essays on semiotics: Roland Barthes, *The Semiotic Challenge*, Richard Howard (trans.), Hill and Wang, New York, 1988.

Saussure on signs: Ferdinand de Saussure, *A Course in General Linguistics*, McGraw-Hill, New York, 1966.

Introduction to semiotics: Daniel Chandler, *Semiotics: The Basics*, Routledge, London, 2002.

Intermediate semiotics: Kyong Kim, *Caged in Our Own Signs: A Book About Semiotics*, Ablex, Norwood, NJ, 1996.

Applied semiotics: Wendy Leeds-Hurwitz, *Semiotics and Communication: Signs, Codes, Cultures,* Lawrence Erlbaum, Hillsdale, NJ, 1993.

Yellow ribbon in a second-order semiotic system: Donald Fry and Virginia Fry, "Continuing the Conversation Regarding Myth and Culture: An Alternative Reading of Barthes," *American Journal of Semiotics,* Vol. 6, No. 2/3, 1989, pp. 183–197.

Interpreting media signs: John Fiske and John Hartley, *Reading Television,* Methuen, London, 1978.

Relationship between semiotics and rhetoric: Don Paul Abbott, "Splendor and Misery: Semiotics and the End of Rhetoric," *Rhetorica,* Vol. 24, 2006, pp. 303–323.

Autobiography: Roland Barthes, *Roland Barthes,* Richard Howard (trans)., Hill and Wang, New York, 1977.

Barthes' critique of his own theory: Roland Barthes, "Inaugural Lecture, College de France," in *A Barthes Reader,* Susan Sontag (ed.), Hill and Wang, New York, 1982, pp. 457–478.

To access a chapter on Charles Osgood's mediational theory of meaning, a theory
of language that focuses on denotation, click on Theory Archive at
www.afirstlook.com.

CHAPTER 26

Cultural Studies
of Stuart Hall

Cultural studies picks up where semiotics leaves off. For that reason, I'll continue to use the 1991 Gulf War to illustrate Stuart Hall's media theory. At the time when amateur semiologists were battling it out around tree trunks with yellow and black ribbons, a similar yet much larger conflict was being waged on television, through print, and in the minds of American media consumers. This media war was ideological, fought on both sides with formidable weapons of propaganda, live coverage, nationalism, and censorship. Yet Hall would argue that the semiotic skirmish on the college campus was a microcosm of what was taking place in the mass media. The yellow ribbons vastly outnumbered the black ones. The mass media supported the status quo in that they subtly drew people toward the ideological position of the majority who favored the invasion of Iraq.

Stuart Hall is a Jamaican-born emeritus professor of sociology at Open University, Milton Keynes, England. In previous pages you read about the ideas of the Frankfurt School sociologists, Stanley Deetz, and Roland Barthes (see Chapters 4, 20, and 25). Hall joins this group of critical scholars who attack "mainstream" communication research that is empirical, quantitative, and narrowly focused on discovering cause-and-effect relationships. In particular, Hall doubts the social scientists' ability to find useful answers to important questions about media influence. He rejects the "body counts" of survey research, which are "consistently translating matters that have to do with signification, meaning, language, and symbolization into crude behavioral indicators." For Hall, the question is not what percentage of Americans supported U.S. participation and leadership in the 1991 fight against Saddam Hussein. Rather, the crucial issue is how the media created unified support for the invasion of Iraq among a public that had previously been split on the issue.

Although cultural studies theorists select different communication topics to study, they are similar in that all are heavily influenced by a *Marxist interpretation* of society, which is suspicious of any analysis that ignores power relationships. Theorists like Hall take Marx' epitaph as a mission statement for their work: "The philosophers have only *interpreted* the world in various ways; the point, however, is to *change* it." The change that Hall and most critical theorists want to accomplish is to empower people who are on the margins of society,

Cultural studies
A neo-Marxist critique that sets forth the position that mass media manufacture consent for dominant ideologies.

people who have little say in the direction of their lives and who are scrambling just to survive.

THE MEDIA AS POWERFUL IDEOLOGICAL TOOLS

Ideology
Frameworks through which we interpret, understand, and make sense of social existence.

Hall believes the mass media maintain the dominance of those already in positions of power. Broadcast and print outlets serve the Bill Gateses, Steve Forbeses, and Ted Turners of the world. Conversely, the media exploit the poor and powerless. Hall charges that the field of communication continues to be "stubbornly sociologically innocent." He is "deeply suspicious of and hostile to empirical work that has no ideas because that simply means that it does not know the ideas it has."[1] Noncritical researchers represent their work as pure science with no presuppositions, but every media theory by its very nature has ideological content. Hall defines *ideology* as "those images, concepts and premises which provide the frameworks through which we represent, interpret, understand and 'make sense' of some aspect of social existence."[2]

Democratic pluralism
The myth that society is held together by common norms such as equal opportunity, respect for diversity, one person–one vote, individual rights, and rule of law.

As for mainstream mass communication research in the United States, Hall believes that it serves the myth of *democratic pluralism*—the pretense that society is held together by common norms, including equal opportunity, respect for diversity, one person–one vote, individual rights, and rule of law. The usual finding that media messages have little effect celebrates the political claim that democracy works. Such research claims that the American dream has been empirically verified, and science beckons developing countries to become "fully paid-up members of the consensus club."

Hall claims that typical research on individual voting behavior, brand loyalty, or response to dramatic violence fails to uncover the struggle for power that the media mask. He thinks it's a mistake to treat communication as a separate academic discipline (a view that may or may not endear him to your instructor). Academic isolation tends to separate messages from the culture they inhabit:

> All the repetition and incantation of the sanitized term *information*, with its cleansing cybernetic properties, cannot wash away or obliterate the fundamentally dirty, semiotic, semantic, discursive character of the media in their cultural dimensions.[3]

Articulate
The process of speaking out on oppression and linking that subjugation with media representations; the work of cultural studies.

Therefore, Hall refers to his work as *cultural studies* rather than *media studies*, and in the decade of the 1970s he directed the Center for Contemporary Cultural Studies (CCCS) at the University of Birmingham. Under Hall, the staff and graduate students at CCCS sought to articulate their perception of the cultural struggle between the haves and the have-nots. Hall uses the term *articulate* in the dual sense of *speaking out* on oppression and *linking* that subjugation with the communication media because they provide the terrain where meaning is shaped. He says he doesn't seek to be a "ventriloquist" for the masses but does desire to "win some space" where their voices can be heard. The effort to jar people loose from their entrenched power positions often requires harsh words, but a "cozy chat among consenting scholars" won't dissolve the ideology that is the glue binding together most communication study.

The language Hall uses reflects his commitment to a broad Marxist interpretation of history. Since one of Hall's stated aims is to unmask the power imbalances within society, he says the cultural studies approach is valid if it "deconstructs" the current structure of a media research establishment that fails to deal with ideology. Just as Deetz wants to give a meaningful voice to stakeholders affected by corporate decisions (see Chapter 20), Hall wants to liberate people from an unknowing acquiescence to the dominant ideology of the culture. Obviously, *critical theory* and *cultural studies* are close relatives. However, Hall places less emphasis on rationality and more emphasis on resistance. As far as he's concerned, the truth of cultural studies is established by its ability to raise our consciousness of the media's role in preserving the status quo.

EARLY CULTURAL CRITICS

Cultural studies is a complex movement. In order to grasp Hall's theory, we must first understand its roots. Hall has tapped into the economic determinism of Marxist scholars from the Frankfurt School (see Chapter 4), the deep textual analysis of semiotics (see Chapter 25), and the philosophical/linguistic critique of a French theorist I haven't mentioned before, Michel Foucault. All of these European scholars knew of and were influenced by each other's work.

Proletariat
The laboring class who lack capital or the means of production and so must sell their labor to live.

By the end of World War II, it was clear that the revolt of the *proletariat* that Marx had predicted wasn't producing egalitarian societies free of oppression, nor were the dominant capitalist economies of the world deteriorating. The question was simply *Why not?*

Frankfurt School theorists were the first to take up the question. What Marx failed to predict, they concluded, was the modern era takeover of public discourse by private industry. They argued that the working classes had not yet revolted because corporate-owned media were effective in tailoring messages that supported the capitalist system.[4] Both news and entertainment media present a picture of the world in which capitalism is natural, eternal, and unalterable.

Economic determinism
The belief that human behavior and relationships are ultimately caused by differences in financial resources and the disparity in power that those gaps create.

As rather orthodox Marxists, the Frankfurt School theorists adhered to a hard-line *economic determinism*. Where Marx speaks of "the means of production" whose owners dominate society, the Frankfurt School theorists write of "the means of production of culture" whose owners have an undue influence over ideology and political power. The idea of *culture industries* is more heavy-handed than Hall's analysis 30 years later, but he agrees that the corporate control of public communication tends to maintain the status quo by constraining free expression. He also thinks that the average citizen is blissfully unaware of that fact.

Culture industries
The producers of culture; television, radio, music, film, fashion, magazines, newspapers, etc.

Hegemony
The subtle sway of society's haves over its have-nots.

Hall adopts the term *hegemony* when he speaks of the cultural role of the media.[5] On the international scene, *hegemony* usually refers to the preponderant influence or domination of one nation over another. The word is little used by Americans, perhaps because it describes how many countries see the United States. In a specific cultural context, Hall employs the term to describe the subtle sway of society's *haves* over its *have-nots*. He emphasizes that media hegemony is not a conscious plot, it's not overtly coercive, and its effects are not total. The broadcast and print media present a variety of ideas, but then they tend to prop up the status quo by privileging the already accepted interpretation of reality. The result is that the role of mass media turns out to be *production of consent* rather than a *reflection of consensus* that already exists.

Recall that Stan Deetz used the term *consent* to describe how workers unwittingly accomplish the desires of management in the faulty attempt to fulfill their own interests. They are complicit in their own victimization (see Chapter 20). In the same way, Hall believes that the consent-making function of the mass media is to convince readers and viewers that they share the same interests as those who hold the reins of power. Note also that I haven't given any specific examples of culture industries or hegemony. That was the Frankfurt School's problem. They were strong on abstract analysis but offered few case studies that would validate their claims. That's where Barthes' *semiotics* proved valuable.

Roland Barthes provided a way to start with concrete media images and systematically deconstruct their shift in meaning. Recall that one of Barthes' recurrent themes was that mythic signs reinforce the dominant values of culture. Through semiotic analysis in Chapter 25, we saw how the "all-is-forgiven" yellow ribbon was co-opted to become a mythic sign that validated American power and all-out victory. So we can appreciate that semiotics became the source of tangible illustrations of how societal power is preserved and communicated through everyday objects and symbols.

One of the problems semiotics has, however, is its inability to separate ideological or mythic signs from nonideological or oppositional signs. For example, at what point does wearing a Sex Pistols T-shirt change from being an antiestablishment sign of rebellion to being a sign of middle-age nostalgia and corporate sellout? Semiotics lacked an adequate explanation of why certain meanings get attached to certain symbols at certain historical times. Since Barthes had no answer, Hall turned to the ideas of radical and eccentric French philosopher Foucault.

Michel Foucault claimed that both Marxists and semiologists are missing the point about the relationship between societal power and communication. He thought it wrong to view signs and symbols as somehow separate from mass media messages. The microlevel semiotics of yellow ribbons and the macrolevel CNN reports broadcast live from Baghdad are unified through their common *discursive* nature. What Foucault meant is that they both require *frameworks of interpretation* in order to make sense. He believed that the framework people use is provided through the dominant discourse of the day.[6]

Discourse
Frameworks of interpretation.

Foucault's concept of *discourse* established a bridge between semiotics and economic determinism. His construction can account for the changing nature of meaning over time, while keeping a steady eye on power relations. Hall describes the contribution of Foucault's work to the study of communication with revolutionary fervor: "The 'discursive turn' in the social and cultural sciences is one of the most significant shifts of direction in our knowledge of society which has occurred in recent years."[7] As I now turn to central tenets of Hall's cultural studies, remember that you are constantly hearing Foucault's voice in the background.

MAKING MEANING THROUGH DISCOURSE

In his book *Representation*, Hall states that the primary function of discourse is to *make meaning*. Many students of communication would agree that words and other signs contain no intrinsic meaning. That's why in I. A. Richards' semantic triangle, the line along the base that connects the word and its referent is dotted rather than solid (see Figure 4–2, Chapter 4). A catchy way of stating this reality is "Words don't mean; people mean." But Hall asks us to push further and ask, *Where do people get their meanings?* After all, humans don't come equipped with ready-made meanings, either. Hall's answer is that they learn what signs mean through discourse—through communication and culture:

> Primarily, culture is concerned with the production and exchange of meanings—
> "the giving and taking of meaning"—between the members of a society or group.
> To say that two people belong to the same culture is to say that they interpret the

world in roughly the same ways and can express themselves, their thoughts and feelings about the world in ways that will be understood by each other.[8]

To illustrate that meaning comes through discourse, Hall asks his readers how they know that a red light means *stop* and a green light means *go*. The answer is that someone, many years ago, told them so. The process is the same when we consider signs such as a picture of Osama bin Laden, the golden arches, or the word *welfare*. But it is not enough that we simply recognize that meaning is created in discourse. We must also examine the *sources* of that discourse, especially the originators or "speakers" of it.

Hall was struck by Foucault's extensive study of mental illness, sexuality, and criminality in different historical eras. Foucault concentrated on what people were saying, what people were *not* saying, and *who* got to say it. As you might suspect, he discovered that throughout history, not everyone in society had an equal voice or power. That's certainly true in America today. Undoubtedly, CNN founder Ted Turner has more discursive power than I have. Yet due to the fact that I've authored a college textbook, I'm aware that I have more power to frame meaning than do many of the students who read it.

Discursive formation
The process by which unquestioned and seemingly natural ways of interpreting the world become ideologies.

In terms of mental illness, Foucault found that the definition of what constitutes insanity and what to do about it have changed dramatically over time.[9] People with power drew arbitrary lines between the normal and the abnormal, and these distinctions became *discursive formations* that had real, physical effects on those deemed to belong to each group.[10] Over time, these unquestioned and seemingly natural ways of interpreting the world became ideologies, which then perpetuated themselves through further discourse. The right to make meaning can literally be the power to make others crazy.

CORPORATE CONTROL OF MASS COMMUNICATION

Hall has worked to move the study of communication away from the compartmentalized areas reflected in the organization of this text: relationship development, influence, media effects, gender and communication, and so on. He believes we should be studying the unifying *atmosphere* in which they all occur and from which they emanate—human culture. Yet consistent with Marxist theory, he also insists that communication scholarship should examine power relations and social structures. For Hall, stripping the study of communication away from the cultural context in which it is found and ignoring the realities of unequal power distribution in society have weakened our field and made it less theoretically relevant.

Hall and other cultural studies advocates wish to place the academic spotlight directly on the ways media representations of culture reproduce social inequalities and keep the average person more or less powerless to do anything but operate within a corporatized, commodified world. At least within the United States, the vast majority of information we receive is produced and distributed by corporations. If your family room television is tuned to CNN, and the table beneath it holds a copy of *Sports Illustrated* (*SI*), your home is a virtual advertisement for a media conglomerate. Time Warner owns *SI*, CNN, and most likely the cable company that brings the signal to your house. And if you switch channels to HBO to watch a flick produced by the largest Hollywood studio, you'll get a double dose of meanings produced and sponsored by Time Warner.

As long as subscription rates don't go up, what difference does monopoly ownership make? Hall would answer that corporate control of such influential information sources prevents many stories from being told. Consider the plight of people in East Timor. A few years ago that would have been hard to do if you'd never heard about the "ethnic cleansing" of that Pacific island colony; somehow accounts of Indonesian-sanctioned brutality never made the evening news or became the subject of a television drama. But even if the story had been widely told, Hall is sure it would have been with a spin quite sympathetic to Western multinational corporations. The ultimate issue for cultural studies is not *what* information is presented but *whose* information it is.

THE MEDIA ROLE IN THE 1991 GULF WAR: WAR AS THEATER

The yellow ribbons that garnished trees all over the country during 1991 were an important symbolic activity for semiologists and those involved in cultural studies. Yet they were only one piece of an elaborate mosaic of cultural activity that worked toward a unified ideological end, whether intentional or not. Douglas Kellner (UCLA), an early cultural studies pioneer, describes some of the significant but frequently overlooked ways in which an array of cultural products can be deployed to generate popular support for the dominant ideology.[11] If we were scripting the effort, the plan would be to regulate and mold the discourse so that some messages are first encoded by mass media, then decoded, internalized, and acted upon by the audience—all while other ideas remain unvoiced. Hall calls this *hegemonic encoding*. Kellner says that the term describes actual media practice during the 1991 Gulf War.

According to Kellner, the major television networks were effective in disguising the war as theater. The media portrayal of the war erased the horrors of conflict, such as the loss of Iraqi civilian lives, by treating the war as a major TV event filled with drama, heroism, and special effects:

> The media framed the war as an exciting narrative, as a nightly miniseries with dramatic conflict, action and adventure, danger to allied troops and civilians, evil perpetuated by villainous Iraqis, and heroics performed by American military planners, technology, and troops. Both CBS and ABC used the logo "Showdown in the Gulf" during the opening hours of the war . . . coding the event as a battle between good and evil. Indeed, the Gulf War was presented as a war movie with beginning, middle, and end.[12]

Perhaps no single image is more associated with that Gulf War than the on-board camera shots of "smart bombs" being delivered through ventilation shafts of Iraqi buildings. As this footage was replayed throughout the 100-day battle, the visual sequence emphasized the superiority of U.S. military technology and the surgical precision of modern warfare. Kellner points out that such images have multiple benefits for dominant ideological coding. Primarily, watching such gee-whiz weaponry at work impresses the viewer with its pinpoint accuracy and stealth, while suppressing the real purpose of the weapon—to destroy things and people.

The image of the bomb reducing the building to rubble is encoded to communicate the inherent superiority of the American military and the laughable folly of an Iraqi army trying to oppose it. Frequent replays of sophisticated weapons in action distract attention from the *morality* of the war, focusing instead on the tactical aesthetics. Kellner says that it is much easier to cheer for an effective weapons system than it is to engage the complex question of whether these weapons should be used at all. When they explode, they look really cool. And they are ours.

By avoiding the intrinsic ethical issues of using a military option, the media frame for the story could be designed for the *making* of war. Kellner says that instead of offering objective description from the battlefront, U.S. media took sides and became "active propagandists" for the coalition forces. The appropriate narrative form was a simplistic "good guys versus bad guys" showdown. Of course, this frame required the creation of heroes and villains, and the culture industries were more than willing to do their part.

Hall talks about the media's tendency to *commodify* whatever they present, and the Gulf War was no exception. Kellner notes that war itself was a lucrative commodity. High ratings produced increased advertising revenue, and T-shirts, buttons, bumper stickers, toys, videos, and yellow ribbons went on sale within a couple of weeks. Much of the merchandise contained a not-so-subtle racial slur. One T-shirt depicted an Arab man on a camel with military planes flying overhead. The caption stated: "I'd fly 10,000 miles to smoke a Camel."[13]

Taken together, these texts, images, and behaviors created a discourse that framed opposition to the war as a nonoption. To be a "good American" was to support the troops. Hall refers to this media process as *ideological discourses of constraint*. The practical effect is to limit the range of alternatives and then make those restricted choices seem like that's all there ever could be.[14]

POST–9/11 MEDIA COVERAGE: THE CHILL OF CONSTRAINT

On the night of September 11, a decade after the 1991 Gulf War, ABC broadcasters Peter Jennings and Ted Koppel discussed the question that was on many Americans' minds: *Why do some people hate America so much that they respond with glee at the carnage caused by terrorists?* Both commentators spoke of extended assignments in Asia, Africa, and the Middle East among people in abject poverty who had only seen America's wealth, power, and arrogance. For 15 minutes, two of the country's top news analysts spoke in a personal and soul-searching way about seething frustrations among the poor in two-thirds of the world. They avoided the good-guy/bad-guy stereotyping that I had heard on other channels. This was surely not Hall's ideological discourse of constraint that took place during the 1991 Gulf War.

It turned out to be a one-night stand. That was the only time these broadcasters suggested that American political and corporate policy might be a contributing cause of enmity. A week later CBS anchor Dan Rather appeared on the *Late Show with David Letterman* and declared something like unconditional fealty to President George W. Bush and the "War on Terrorism."

> But I couldn't feel stronger, David, that this is a time for us—and I'm not preaching about it—George Bush is the President. He makes the decisions, and—you know as just one American—wherever he wants me to line up, just tell me where.[15]

Two lesser-known journalists criticized Bush shortly after the attack for matters of style. One said he appeared "stiff and boyish," while the other took issue with the president's characterization of America's response to terrorism as a "crusade." But both commentators quickly apologized for their outspokenness. For the next month, *never was heard a discouraging word.*

Perhaps the most unusual patriotic appeal after the 9/11 terrorism was President Bush's equation of love of country with spending money. He suggested that this was an especially good time to buy a new car, a statement that he permitted to be used in numerous car commercials.[16] Whether it was patriotism or zero percent financing, new car sales increased 31 percent in the first two months after the tragedy. Here again, no network news show questioned the administration's linkage of consumer purchasing and patriotism. But comedian George Carlin drew a laugh of derision from a *Tonight Show* audience when he deadpanned: "Go out and buy some jewelry and a new car. Otherwise the terrorists win."

Hall believes the mass media provide the guiding myths that shape our perception of the world and serve as important instruments of social control.[17] This seems to describe U.S. media treatment of weapons of mass destruction (WMD) as justification for invading Iraq in 2003. Although the broadcast and print media faithfully reported chief U.N. weapons inspector Hans Blix' failure to discover WMD prior to the invasion, like the Bush administration, they never questioned the existence of a chemical or nuclear threat. News stories instead dwelled on when and where WMD would be found. The media's creation of a popular consensus was so thorough that even after the 9/11 Commission concluded that Saddam Hussein had no such weapons, large segments of the population continued to believe in their existence. Only in late 2004 did media outlets begin to examine why they never questioned the government's position.

How do multiple media outlets end up speaking on a major issue with what seems to be a single voice? Given the country's shared images of airliners impaling the twin towers of the World Trade Center, the buildings' subsequent collapse, and the 95 percent approval rating of the president's response, each news editor's decision may seem an easy one. But Hall suggests that hegemonic encoding occurs all the time, though it's not a conscious plot. A story in an op-ed piece in the *Los Angeles Times,* written by Alexander Cockburn, is suggestive:

> When he was joining the London Times in the 1920s, my father asked his uncle, who was on the Times' board, who really formulated Times' policy. "My boy," his uncle said, "the policy of the London Times is set by a committee that never meets."[18]

AN OBSTINATE AUDIENCE

The fact that the media present a preferred interpretation of human events is no reason to assume that the audience will correctly "take in" the offered ideology. I once heard Robert Frost recite his famous poem "Stopping by Woods on a Snowy Evening." After completing the last stanza—

> These woods are lovely, dark and deep,
> But I have promises to keep,
> And miles to go before I sleep,
> And miles to go before I sleep.[19]

—the New England poet said in a crusty voice, "Some people think I'm talking about death here, but I'm not." Yet poems, like media depictions, have a life of their own. Despite his words, I have continued to interpret the verse as referring to obligations to be met before we die.

Hall holds out the possibility that the powerless may be equally obstinate by resisting the dominant ideology and translating the message in a way more congenial to their own interests. He outlines three decoding options:

1. *Operating inside the dominant code.* The media produce the message; the masses consume it. The *audience reading* coincides with the *preferred reading.*

2. *Applying a negotiable code.* The audience assimilates the leading ideology in general but opposes its application in specific cases.

3. *Substituting an oppositional code.* The audience sees through the establishment bias in the media presentation and mounts an organized effort to demythologize the news.

With all the channels of mass communication in the unwitting service of the dominant ideology, Hall has trouble believing that the powerless can change the system ("pessimism of the intellect"). Yet he is determined to do everything he can to expose and alter the media's structuring of reality ("optimism of the will"). Hall has a genuine respect for the ability of people to resist the dominant code. He doesn't regard the masses as cultural dupes who are easily manipulated by those who control the media, but he is unable to predict when and where the resistance will spring up.

Hall cites one small victory by activists in the organized struggle to establish that black is beautiful. By insisting on the term *black* rather than *Negro* or *colored,* people of African heritage began to give dignity in the 1970s to what was once a racial slur. Jesse Jackson's call for an African-American identity is a continuing effort to control the use of symbols. This is not a matter of mere semantics, as some would charge. Although there is nothing inherently positive or negative in any of these racial designations, the connotative difference is important because the effects are real. The ideological fight is a struggle to capture language. Hall sees those on the margins of society doing semantic battle on a media playing field that will never be quite level.

CRITIQUE: YOUR JUDGMENT WILL DEPEND ON YOUR IDEOLOGY

In his early work, Marshall McLuhan was highly critical of television. Hall accuses McLuhan of being coopted by the media establishment in his later years. He characterizes McLuhan's final position as one of "lying back and letting the media roll over him; he celebrated the very things he had most bitterly attacked." No one has ever accused Stuart Hall of selling out to the dominant ideology of Western society. Many communication scholars, however, question the wisdom of performing scholarship under an ideological banner.

Do such explicit value commitments inevitably compromise the integrity of research? Former surgeon general C. Everett Koop lamented that pro-choice researchers always conclude that abortion does no psychological harm to the mother, whereas pro-life psychologists invariably discover that abortion leaves long-term emotional scars. In like manner, the findings of the economically conservative American Enterprise Institute in Washington D.C., differ greatly from the conclusions reached at the Center for Contemporary Cultural Studies under the direction of Hall. Ever since Copernicus thought the unthinkable, that the earth is not the center of the universe, truth has prospered by investigating what *is*, separately from what we think it *ought* to be. Hall seems to blur that distinction.

Although Hall is recognized as a founding figure of cultural studies, there are those who work within this fast-growing field who are critical of his leadership. While appreciating his advocacy for ethnic minorities and the poor, many women decried his relative silence on their plight as equal victims of the hegemony he railed against. Hall belatedly became an advocate for women and acquiesced to their demand for shared power at the Birmingham Center. Yet his now famous description of the feminist entry into British cultural studies shows that for him the necessary change was painful and messy: "As the thief in the night, it broke in; interrupted, made an unseemly noise, seized the time, crapped on the table of cultural studies."[20]

The most often heard criticism of Hall's work is that he doesn't offer specific remedies for the problems he identifies. While it's true that he has no grand action agenda for defusing the media's influence on behalf of the powerful elite, he has worked hard to expose racism that's reinforced by press reporting. For example, Hall served as a key member of a commission that issued an influential report in 2000 on the future of a multiethnic Britain. The following excerpt is a sample of Hall's impact on the commission's call for a change in the way ethnic groups are represented in the media.

> A study by the *Guardian* of its own coverage of Islam in a particular period in 1999 found that the adjective "Islamic" was joined with "militants" 16 times, "extremists" 15 times, "fundamentalism" eight times and "terrorism" six times; in the same period the adjective "Christian" was joined, in so far as it appeared at all, to positive words and notions or to neutral ones such as tradition or belief.[21]

Hall's most positive contribution to mass communication study is his constant reminder that it's futile to talk about meaning without considering power at the same time. Cliff Christians, director of the Institute for Communication Research at the University of Illinois and a leading writer in the field of media ethics, agrees with Hall that the existence of an idealistic communication situation where no power circulates is a myth. Christians is lavish in his praise of Hall's essay "Ideology and Communication Theory," which I've listed as a Second Look resource: "His essay, like the Taj Mahal, is an artistic masterpiece inviting a pilgrimage."[22]

Stuart Hall has attracted tremendous interest and a large following. Samuel Becker, former chair of the communication studies department at the University of Iowa, describes himself as a besieged empiricist and notes the irony of Hall's attack. Hall knocks the dominant ideology of communication studies, yet he "may himself be the most dominant or influential figure in communication studies today."[23]

QUESTIONS TO SHARPEN YOUR FOCUS

1. *Hegemony* is not a household word in the United States. How would you explain what the term means to your roommate? Can you think of a metaphor or an analogy that would clarify this critical concept?

2. What is the nature of Hall's complaint about *American media scholarship*?

3. Hall says that the *media encode the dominant ideology of our culture*. If you don't agree with his thesis, what *evidence* could he muster that would convince you that he's right? What evidence would you provide to counter his argument?

4. In what way is Roland Barthes' *semiotic* perspective (see Chapter 25) similar to Hall's cultural studies? How do they differ?

A SECOND LOOK

Recommended resource: Stuart Hall, "Introduction" and "The Work of Representation," in *Representation: Cultural Representations and Signifying Practices*, Stuart Hall (ed.), Sage, London, 1997, pp. 1–64.

Intellectual biography: Helen Davis, *Understanding Stuart Hall*, Sage, Thousand Oaks, CA, 2004.

Hall's critique of the dominant communication paradigm: Stuart Hall, "Ideology and Communication Theory," in *Rethinking Communication Theory*, Vol. 1, Brenda Dervin, Lawrence Grossberg, Barbara O'Keefe, and Ellen Wartella (eds.), Sage, Newbury Park, CA, 1989, pp. 40–52. (See also multiple reactions following.)

Commentary: David Morley and Kuan-Hsing Chen (eds.), *Stuart Hall: Critical Dialogues in Cultural Studies*, Routledge, New York, 1996.

Marxist interpretations: Samuel Becker, "Marxist Approaches to Media Studies: The British Experience," *Critical Studies in Mass Communication*, Vol. 1, 1984, pp. 66–80.

Articulation of black: Stuart Hall, "Signification, Representation, Ideology: Althusser and the Post-Structuralist Debates," *Critical Studies in Mass Communication*, Vol. 2, 1985, pp. 91–114.

American cultural studies: Lawrence Grossberg, *Bringing It All Back Home: Essays on Cultural Studies*, Duke University Press, Durham, NC, 1997.

Historical perspective: Stuart Hall, "Cultural Studies and Its Theoretical Legacies," in *Cultural Studies,* Lawrence Grossberg, Cary Nelson, and Paula Treichler (eds.), Routledge, New York, 1992, pp. 277–294.

Focused research: Paul du Gay et al., *Doing Cultural Studies: The Story of the Sony Walkman,* Sage, London, 1997.

Media coverage of the ongoing Iraq war: Deepa Kumar, "Media, War, and Propaganda: Strategies of Information Management During the 2003 Iraq War," *Communication and Critical/Cultural Studies,* Vol. 3, 2006, pp. 48–69.

Appreciative retrospective: Paul Gilroy, Lawrence Grossberg, and Angela McRobbie (eds.), *Without Guarantees: In Honour of Stuart Hall,* Verso, London, 2000.

Critical retrospective: Chris Rojek, *Stuart Hall,* Polity, Cambridge, 2003.

Critique from quantitative perspective: Justin Lewis, "What Counts in Cultural Studies?" *Media, Culture & Society,* Vol. 19, 1997, pp. 83–97.

Critique from qualitative perspective: Patrick Murphy, "Media Cultural Studies' Uncomfortable Embrace of Ethnography," *Journal of Communication Inquiry,* Vol. 23, 1999, pp. 205–221.

To access links to Web sites devoted to theorists or theories
discussed in this book, click on Links at
www.afirstlook.com.

In 1940, before the era of television, a team of researchers from Columbia University headed by Paul Lazarsfeld descended on Erie County, Ohio, an area that had reflected national voting patterns in every twentieth-century presidential election. By surveying people once a month from June to November, the interviewers sought to determine how the press and radio affected the people's choice for the upcoming presidential election.[1]

Contrary to the then-accepted *hypodermic needle* model of direct media influence, the researchers found little evidence that voters were swayed by what they read or heard. Political conversions were rare. The media seemed merely to reinforce the decisions of those who had already made up their minds.

Lazarsfeld attributed the lack of media effect to *selective exposure* (see Chapter 16). Republicans avoided articles and programs that were favorable to President Franklin Roosevelt; Democrats bypassed news stories and features sympathetic to the Republican Wendell Willkie. The principle of selective exposure didn't always test out in the laboratory, where people's attention was virtually guaranteed, but in a free marketplace of ideas it accounted for the limited, short-term effects of mass communication.

The Erie County results forced media analysts to recognize that friends and family affect the impact of media messages. They concluded that print and electronic media influence masses of people only through an indirect *two-step flow of communication.* The first stage is the direct transmission of information to a small group of people who stay well-informed. In the second stage, those opinion leaders pass on and interpret the messages to others in face-to-face discussion.

The two-step flow theory surfaced at a time of rapid scientific advancement in the fields of medicine and agriculture. The model accurately described the diffusion of innovation among American doctors and farmers in the 1950s, but the present era of saturation television and Internet news has made alterations necessary. The first step of the *revised two-stage theory* of media influence is the transmission of information to a mass audience. The second step is validation of the message by people the viewer respects.[2]

In 1953, Fredric Wertham's *Seduction of the Innocent* documented the glorification of violence in comic books.[3] Since then, mass communication researchers have sought to establish a relationship between media usage and aggression. Ad hoc studies have produced conflicting results, but two theory-based programs of research have established causal links between television and violent behavior.

University of Alabama media researcher Dolf Zillmann's *excitation transfer theory* recognizes that TV has the power to stir up strong feelings.[4] Although we use labels like *fear, anger, humor, love,* and *lust* to describe these emotional states, the heightened physiological arousal is similar no matter what kind of TV program elicited the response. It's easy to get our emotional wires crossed when the show is over. Zillmann says that the heightened state of arousal takes a while to dissipate, and the leftover excitation can amplify any mood we happen to be feeling. If a man is mad at his wife, the emotional stimulation he gets from televised aggression can escalate into domestic violence. But Zillmann says that the arousal that comes from an erotic bedroom scene or a hilarious comedy often has the same effect.

Excitation transfer can account for violent acts performed immediately after TV viewing. But Stanford psychologist Albert Bandura's *social learning theory* takes it a step further and predicts that the use of force modeled on television today may erupt in antisocial behavior years later.[5] Although Bandura's theory can explain imitation in many contexts, most students of his work apply it specifically to the vicarious learning of aggression through television.

Social learning theory postulates three necessary stages in the causal link between television and the actual physical harm that we might inflict on another some time in the future. The three-step process is attention, retention, and motivation. Video violence grabs our *attention* because it's simple, distinctive, prevalent, useful, and depicted positively. If you doubt that last quality, remember that television draws in viewers by placing attractive people in front of the camera. There are very few overweight bodies or pimply faces on TV. When the winsome star roughs up a few hoods to rescue the lovely young woman, aggression is given a positive cast.

Without any risk to ourselves, watching media violence can expand our repertoire of behavioral options far beyond what we'd discover on our own through trial-and-error learning. For example, we see a knife fighter holding a switchblade at an inclined angle of 45 degrees and that he jabs up rather than lunging down. This kind of street smarts is mentally filed away as a visual image. But Bandura says that *retention* is strongest when we also encode vicarious learning into words: *Hold the pistol with both hands. Don't jerk the trigger; squeeze it. Aim six inches low to compensate for recoil.*

Without sufficient *motivation*, we may never imitate the violence that we saw and remember. But years later we may be convinced that we won't go to jail for shooting a prowler lurking in our backyard or that we might gain status by punching out a jerk who is hassling a friend. If so, what we learned earlier and stored in our memory bank is now at our disposal.

Communication scholars have shown surprisingly little interest in studying the dynamics of television advertising. However, practitioner Tony Schwartz theorizes that commercials are effective when they strike a *responsive chord* within the viewer.[6] Schwartz claims that media persuasion is not so much a matter of trying to put an idea into consumers' heads as it is seeking to draw an emotional response out of them. The best commercials use sight and sound to resonate with an audience's past experience.

CALVIN AND HOBBES © 1995 Watterson. Reprinted with permission of Universal Press Syndicate.

The three theories in this section were instrumental in reestablishing a powerful-effects view of mass communication. Chapter 27 presents George Gerbner's *cultivation theory*, which postulates a relationship between heavy television viewing and people's worldview. Specifically, Gerbner suggests that exposure to vast amounts of symbolic violence on the screen conditions viewers to view the world as a mean and scary place. He's not concerned that TV viewers will *commit* violence, but he's convinced that heavy viewers will come to have an unrealistic fear that they will be *victims* of it—an anxiety that will affect how they think and act.

Chapter 28 outlines Maxwell McCombs and Donald Shaw's theory of the *agenda-setting* function of the media. Their theory originally claimed that the news media don't try to tell people what to think, but the selection of news in the broadcast and print media has a powerful effect on what the public will think about.

Chapter 29 presents Elisabeth Noelle-Neumann's *spiral of silence.* Her theory describes the chilling effect of public opinion on the expression of unpopular views. She believes the process is accelerated when most media outlets echo the same idea over and over.

Although the three theories in this section offer different explanations for the media's impact, all of them hold that these effects can be measured objectively. Cultivation theory, agenda-setting theory, and the spiral of silence are exactly the kind of behavioral theories that Stuart Hall rails against because he's convinced that they ignore questions of meaning, power, and ideology. But if you want to be able to explain, predict, and even alter the effect of media messages, these theories are a good place to start. Each one is stated in a way that makes it possible to prove it false if it's really wrong. All three have garnered an impressive amount of empirical evidence to support their claims.

Cultivation Theory

of George Gerbner

What are the odds that you'll be involved in some kind of violent act within the next seven days? 1 out of 10? 1 out of 100? 1 out of 1,000? 1 out of 10,000?

According to Hungarian-born George Gerbner, the answer you give may have more to do with how much TV you watch than with the actual risk you face in the week to come. Gerbner, who died in 2005, was dean emeritus of the Annenberg School for Communication at the University of Pennsylvania and founder of the Cultural Environment Movement. He claimed that heavy television users develop an exaggerated belief in *a mean and scary world*. The violence they see on the screen can cultivate a social paranoia that counters notions of trustworthy people or safe surroundings.

Like Marshall McLuhan, Gerbner regarded television as the dominant force in shaping modern society. But unlike McLuhan, who viewed the medium as the message, Gerbner was convinced that TV's power comes from the symbolic content of the real-life drama shown hour after hour, week after week. At its root, television is society's institutional storyteller, and a society's stories give "a coherent picture of what exists, what is important, what is related to what, and what is right."[1]

Until the advent of broadcast media, the only acceptable storytellers outside the home were those passing down religious tradition. Today, the TV set is a key member of the household, with virtually unlimited access to every person in the family. Television dominates the environment of symbols, telling most of the stories, most of the time. Gerbner claimed that people now watch television as they might attend church, "except that most people watch television more religiously."[2]

What do they see in their daily devotions? According to Gerbner—violence. During the turmoil of the late 1960s, the National Commission on the Causes and Prevention of Violence suggested that violence is as American as cherry pie.[3] Instead of being a deviant route to power, physical force and its threat are traditionally ways people gain a larger slice of the American dream. Gerbner wrote that violence "is the simplest and cheapest dramatic means to demonstrate who wins in the game of life and the rules by which the game is played."[4] Those who are immersed in the world of TV drama learn these "facts of life" better than occasional viewers do.

Most people who decry violence on television are worried that all-too-receptive young viewers will imitate aggression on the screen. As noted in

349

the introduction to this section, Stanford psychologist Albert Bandura's research suggests that this fear has some basis in fact, at least for a small minority of the audience.[5] Gerbner, however, was concerned with a much broader and potentially more harmful emotional effect—that television violence convinces viewers it is indeed "a jungle out there."

Gerbner's voice was only one of many that proclaim a link between communication media and violence. Critics have publicly warned against the chaotic effects of comic books, gangsta rap, and computer games, as well as television. But the man who for many years was the editor of the *Journal of Communication* thought that TV is a special case. For almost two decades he spearheaded an extensive research program that monitored the level of violence on television, classified people according to how much TV they watch, and compiled viewer perceptions of potential risk and other socio-cultural attitudes. His cultivation explanation of the findings is one of the most talked about and argued over theories of mass communication.

AN INDEX OF VIOLENCE

Alarmed parents, teachers, and critics of television assume that the portrayal of violence has been escalating. But is the level of dramatic aggression really on the rise? As director of the *Cultural Indicators research project*, Gerbner sought to develop an objective measure that would allow TV's friends and foes to discuss the trend on the basis of fact rather than feeling. He defined *dramatic violence* as "the overt expression of physical force (with or without a weapon, against self or others) compelling action against one's will on pain of being hurt and/or killed or threatened to be so victimized as part of the plot."[6]

Dramatic violence
The overt expression or threat of physical force as part of the plot.

The definition rules out verbal abuse, idle threats, and pie-in-the-face slapstick. But it includes the physical abuse presented in a cartoon format. When the coyote pursuing the roadrunner is flattened by a steamroller or the Mighty Morphing Power Rangers crush their enemies, Gerbner labeled the scene violent. He also counted auto crashes and natural disasters. From an artistic point of view, these events are no accident. The screenwriter inserted the trauma for dramatic effect. Characters die or are maimed just as effectively as if they'd taken a bullet in the chest.

Cultural Indicators project
The systematic tracking of changes in television content and how those changes affect viewers' perceptions of the world.

For over two decades, Cultural Indicators researchers randomly selected a week during the fall season and videotaped every prime-time (8 to 11 P.M.) network show. They also recorded programming for children on Saturday and Sunday (8 A.M. to 2 P.M.). After counting up the incidents that fit their description, they gauged the overall level of violence with a formula that included the ratio of programs that scripted violence, the rate of violence in the programs that did, and the percentage of characters involved in physical harm and killing. They found that the annual index was remarkably stable and remarkably high.

EQUAL VIOLENCE, UNEQUAL RISK

Gerbner reported that regardless of whether the dramas are *Las Vegas*, *The Sopranos*, *Lost*, *CSI*, or dozens of forgettable shows canceled after a 13-week run, the cumulative portrayal of violence varies little from year to year. Over half of prime-time programs contain actual bodily harm or threatened violence. *The Office* and *Everybody Loves Raymond* are not typical. Dramas that include violence average 5 traumatic incidents per viewing hour. Almost all the weekend children's shows major in mayhem. They average 20 cases an hour. By the time the typical TV viewer graduates from high school, he or she has observed 13,000 violent deaths.

On any given week, two-thirds of the major characters are caught up in some kind of violence. Heroes are just as involved as villains, yet there is great inequality as to the age, race, and gender of those on the receiving end of physical force. Old people and children are harmed at a much greater rate than are young or middle-aged adults. In the pecking order of "victimage," African Americans and Hispanics are killed or beaten more than their Caucasian counterparts. Gerbner noted that it's risky to be "other than clearly white." It's also dangerous to be female. The opening lady-in-distress scene is a favorite dramatic device to galvanize the hero into action. And finally, blue-collar workers "get it in the neck" more often than do white-collar executives.

The symbolic vulnerability of minority-group members is quite striking, given their gross underrepresentation in TV drama. Gerbner's analysis of the world of television recorded that 50 percent of the people are white, middle-class males, and women are outnumbered by men 3 to 1. Although one-third of our society is made up of children and teenagers, they appear as only 10 percent of the characters on prime-time shows. Two-thirds of the United States labor force have blue-collar or service jobs, yet that group constitutes a mere 10 percent of the players on television. African Americans and Hispanics are only occasional figures, but the elderly are by far the most excluded minority. Less than 3 percent of the dramatic roles are filled by actors over the age of 65. If insurance companies kept actuarial tables on the life expectancy of television characters, they'd discover that the chance of a poor, elderly black woman's avoiding harm for the entire hour is almost nil.

"You do lovely needlepoint, grandma, but . . ."
Reproduced by permission of Punch Limited.

In sum, Gerbner's Cultural Indicators project revealed that people on the margins of American society are put into a symbolic double jeopardy. Their existence is understated, but at the same time their vulnerability to violence is overplayed. When written into the script, they are often made visible in order to be a victim. Not surprisingly, these are the very people who exhibit the most fear of violence when the TV set is turned off.

ESTABLISHING A VIEWER PROFILE

Equipped with the sure knowledge of TV drama's violent content, Gerbner and his associates gathered surveys of viewer behavior and attitudes. Although some later researchers have tried to create saturation exposure in an experimental setting, Gerbner said the nature of his cultivation hypothesis makes testing in the laboratory impossible. He believed that the effects of heavy TV viewing can be seen only after years of slow buildup. The pervasive presence of television also rules out a control group. Gerbner regarded everyone as a consumer. His questions merely aimed to distinguish between "light" and "heavy" users.

Heavy viewers
TV viewers who report that they watch at least four hours per day; television types.

Most of Gerbner's work established a self-report of two hours a day as the upper limit of light viewing. He labeled *heavy viewers* as those who admit an intake of four hours or more. He also referred to the heavy viewer as *the television type*, a more benign term than *couch potato* with its allusion to either a steady diet of television and potato chips or a vegetable with many eyes. There are more heavy viewers than light viewers, but each group makes up about one-fourth of the general population. People whose viewing habits are in the two- to four-hour midrange make up the other half, but Gerbner wanted to compare people with distinctly different patterns of television exposure.

Gerbner claimed that television types don't turn on the set in order to watch *ER* or *Friday Night Lights*. They simply want to watch television per se. Light viewers are more selective, turning the set off when a favorite program is over. Gerbner's reason for segmenting the audience was to test whether those with heavy viewing habits regard the world as more dangerous than do those with occasional or light viewing habits. Cultivation theory predicts that they do.

MINDS PLOWED BY TELEVISION GROW FEARFUL THOUGHTS

Believing that violence is the backbone of TV drama and knowing that people differ in how much TV they see, Gerbner sought to discover the *cultivation differential*. That's his term for "the difference in the percent giving the 'television answer' within comparable groups of light and heavy viewers."[7] He referred to *cultivation differential* rather than to *media effects* because the latter term implies a comparison between *before*-TV exposure and *after*-TV exposure. But Gerbner believed there is no before-television condition. Television enters people's lives in infancy. His survey targeted four attitudes.

Cultivation differential
The difference in the percentage giving the television answer within comparable groups of light and heavy TV viewers.

1. *Chances of involvement with violence.* The question at the start of the chapter addresses this issue. Those with light viewing habits predict that their weekly odds of being a victim are 1 out of 100; those with heavy viewing habits fear the risk to be 1 out of 10. Actual crime statistics indicate that 1 out of 10,000 is more realistic. Of course, the prediction of those with heavy viewing habits may be due to their greater willingness to justify physical aggression. Children who are

habitual TV watchers agree that it's "almost always all right [to hit someone] if you are mad at them for a good reason."

2. *Fear of walking alone at night.* Not surprisingly, more women than men are afraid of dark streets. But for both sexes, the fear of victimization correlates with time spent in front of the tube. People with heavy viewing habits tend to over-estimate criminal activity, believing it to be 10 times worse than it really is. In actuality, muggers on the street pose less bodily threat than does injury from cars.

3. *Perceived activity of police.* People with heavy viewing habits believe that 5 percent of society is involved in law enforcement. Their video world is peopled with police, judges, and government agents. People with light viewing habits estimate a more realistic 1 percent. Gerbner's television type assumes that police officers draw their guns almost every day, which isn't true.

4. *General mistrust of people.* Those with heavy viewing habits are suspicious of other people's motives. They subscribe to statements that warn people to expect the worst:

"Most people are just looking out for themselves."
"In dealing with others, you can't be too careful."
"Do unto others before they do unto you."

Gerbner called this cynical mindset the *mean world syndrome.*

Mean world syndrome
The cynical mindset of general mistrust of others subscribed to by heavy TV viewers.

The Cultural Indicators evidence suggests that the minds of heavy TV viewers become fertile ground for sowing thoughts of danger. Yet Gerbner spotted two separate mechanisms that plow deeper furrows in two subsets of heavy viewers than in others. *Mainstreaming* is the process that shapes groups of viewers whose socioeconomic and educational backgrounds would other-wise align them with distinctly liberal or conservative political positions. *Resonance* is the mechanism that affects heavy viewers who have already been victims of violence.

MAINSTREAMING: BLURRING, BLENDING, AND BENDING OF VIEWER ATTITUDES

Mainstreaming is Gerbner's word to describe the process of "blurring, blending and bending" that those with heavy viewing habits undergo. He thought that through constant exposure to the same images and labels, television types develop a commonality of outlook that doesn't happen with radio. Radio stations segment the audience to the point where programming for left-handed truck drivers who bowl on Friday nights is a distinct possibility. But instead of *nar-rowcasting* their programs, TV producers *broadcast* in that they seek to "attract the largest possible audience by celebrating the moderation of the mainstream."[8]

Mainstreaming
The blurring, blending, and bending process by which heavy TV viewers develop a common so-cially conservative out-look through constant exposure to the same im-ages and labels.

Television homogenizes its audience so that those with heavy viewing habits share the same orientations, perspectives, and meanings with each other. We shouldn't ask how close this collective interpretation of how the world works is to the mainstream of culture. According to Gerbner, the television answer is the mainstream.

He illustrated the mainstream effect by showing how television types blur economic and political distinctions. TV glorifies the middle class, and those with heavy viewing habits assume that label, no matter what their income. But those with light viewing habits who have blue-collar jobs accurately describe themselves as working-class people.

In like fashion, those with heavy viewing habits label themselves as political *moderates*. Most characters in TV dramas frown on political extremism—right or left. This nonextremist ethic is apparently picked up by the constant viewer. It's only from the ranks of sporadic TV users that Gerbner found people who actually label themselves *liberal* or *conservative*.

Social scientists have come to expect political differences between rich and poor, blacks and whites, Catholics and Protestants, city dwellers and farmers. Those distinctions still emerge when sporadic television viewers respond to the survey. But Gerbner reported that traditional differences diminish among those with heavy viewing habits. It's as if the light from the TV set washes out any sharp features that would set them apart.

Even though those with heavy viewing habits call themselves moderates, the Cultural Indicators team noted that their positions on social issues are decidedly conservative. Heavy viewers consistently voice opinions in favor of lower taxes, more police protection, and stronger national defense. They are against big government, free speech, homosexual marriage or gays in the military, the Equal Rights Amendment, abortion, interracial marriage, open-housing legislation, and affirmative action. The *mainstream* is not *middle of the road*.

Saturation viewing seems to bend television types toward the political right, although such viewers do support greater funding of Social Security, health services, and education. Gerbner labeled the mix of attitudes and desires the *new populism* and saw its rise as evidence that those with heavy viewing habits have been sucked into the mainstream. The almost complete overlap between the new populism and the policies of Ronald Reagan could explain the former president's reputation as being the *great communicator* when he went directly to the people on television. His message was like an old friend they'd grown up with on prime-time TV. In like manner, when President George W. Bush presented himself as a "compassionate conservative," he was carried along by the same mainstream current.

RESONANCE: RELIVING EXPERIENCE OF REAL-LIFE VIOLENCE

Gerbner claimed that other heavy viewers grow more apprehensive through the process of *resonance*. These viewers have had at least one firsthand experience with physical violence—armed robbery, rape, bar fight, mugging, auto crash, military combat, or lover's quarrel that became vicious. The actual trauma was bad enough. But Gerbner thought that a repeated symbolic portrayal on the TV screen could cause the viewer to replay the real-life experience over and over in his or her mind: "The congruence of the television world and real-life circumstances may 'resonate' and lead to markedly amplified cultivation patterns."[9] Heavy viewers who have experienced physical violence get a double dose.

Resonance
The process by which congruence of symbolic violence on television and real-life experiences of violence amplifies the fear of a mean and scary world.

For three years I was a volunteer advocate in a low-income housing project. Although I felt relatively safe walking through the project, police and social workers told stories of shootings and stabbings. Even peace-loving residents were no strangers to violence. I can't recall ever entering an apartment where the TV was silent. Gerbner would expect that the daily diet of symbolic savagery would reinforce people's experience of doorstep violence, making life even more frightening. The hesitation of most tenants to venture outside their apartments would seem to confirm his resonance assumption.

The resonance hypothesis is an after-the-fact explanation of why a large group of people who watch lots of television find the world an extra-scary place. In contrast, he noted that most media effects research focuses on only the few people who imitate the violence they see on TV.

> But it is just as important to look at the large majority of people who become more fearful, insecure, and dependent on authority; and who may grow up demanding protection and even welcoming repression in the name of security.[10]

DOES DRAMATIC VIOLENCE STILL CULTIVATE FEAR?

Gerbner began his cultivation analysis more than 30 years ago. The media landscape has changed radically during those three decades. Whereas viewers had a choice of 4 channels back then, today most households have access to 40 or more stations and can use a clicker to constantly channel surf for specialized shows. Reality TV shows have replaced shoot-'em-up Westerns, and time at the computer keyboard or using a multipurpose cell phone has cut into time in front of the tube. Does the dramatic portrayal continue to cultivate the fear of a mean and scary world, or is the media consumer's world more benign?

Until his death a few years ago, Gerbner continued to monitor the amount of violence shown on TV, establish a demographic profile of the victims, and measure viewers' social perceptions and attitudes. He found that the more things changed, the more they stayed the same. The graphic violence in computer games and pictures of the aftermath of violence shown on the local news have more than made up for any decline in violence on network television. And there's evidence that not long after the scenes have been seen, viewers can't remember which were real and which were fictionalized.[11]

Were he alive today, Gerbner would emphasize the implication of heightened personal anxiety for the public policy. In the midst of his Cultural Indicators research program he testified before a congressional subcommittee on communication about the social cost of fear:

> Fearful people are more dependent, more easily manipulated and controlled, more susceptible to deceptively simple, strong, tough measures and hard-line postures. . . . They may accept and even welcome repression if it promises to relieve their insecurities. That is the deeper problem of violence-laden television.[12]

CRITIQUE: IS THE CULTIVATION DIFFERENTIAL REAL, LARGE, CRUCIAL?

For most observers, Gerbner's claim that the dramatic content of television creates a fearful climate makes sense. How could the habitual viewer watch so much violence without it having a lasting effect? Yet over the last 30 years communication journals have been filled with the sometimes bitter charges and countercharges of critics and supporters. Opponents have challenged Gerbner's definition of violence, the programs he selected for content analysis, his decision to lump together all types of dramatic programs (action, soap operas, sitcoms, and so on), his assumption that there is always a consistent television answer, his nonrandom methods for selecting respondents, his simple hours-per-day standard for categorizing viewers as *light* or *heavy*, his multiple-choice technique to measure their perceived risk of being mugged, his statistical method of analyzing the data, and his interpretation of correlational data.

Communication researchers Michael Morgan (University of Massachusetts) and James Shanahan (Cornell University) catalogue the various criticisms of Gerbner's theory and systematically respond to their charges.[13] In a few cases these cultivation theory advocates grant the substance of a specific critique, yet they insist that by focusing on *methodological minutiae*, critics divert attention from the powerful social role of television as society's storyteller. They contrast Gerbner's *big picture* perspective with what they believe is the *methodological exercise* approach of his critics:

> Efforts to provide greater specificity and precision have helped sharpen the analysis but often seem to result in losing track of the real social significance of it all. We suggest that, after 20 years, researchers put aside the quibbles to focus critically on the social role of television.[14]

Morgan and Shanahan also suggest that at least a portion of the strident attack on cultivation theory is politically motivated. If so, we shouldn't be surprised. After all, cultivation theory refutes the television industry's easy assurance that the violence it depicts does no harm. In addition, Gerbner's words contain a thinly veiled criticism of a Rush Limbaugh–type of conservative populism that the theorist believes is nightly supported by the narrative images of prime-time programming. Be that as it may, the main issue for us to decide is how to interpret the consistent yet small relationship that Gerbner and others have established between heavy TV viewing and belief in a mean and scary world.

In order to provide a map that will allow students of cultivation theory to maneuver through the minefield of confusing and sometimes conflicting findings, Morgan and Shanahan performed a *meta-analysis* on 82 separate cultivation studies.[15] Meta-analysis is a technique of statistically blending independent studies that explore the same connection—in this case the link between hours in front of a TV set and the subsequent tendency to give *television answers* to questions about the likelihood of violence, gender role attitudes, political viewpoints, and so forth. They discovered a consistent positive relationship ($r = .091$).

Meta-analysis
A statistical procedure that blends the results of multiple empirical and independent research studies exploring the same relationship between two variables (e.g., TV viewing and fear of violence).

What does this numerical index mean? There are three different ways to answer that question. In the first place, given the large and multiple samples used in cultivation research, a correlation of $+.091$ is *statistically significant*. That means it would almost never occur by chance if there weren't an actual relationship between viewing and viewpoint. In short, Gerbner predicted that exposure to television and social attitudes are linked; Morgan and Shanahan's analysis confirms that they are.

A second way to interpret the meta-analysis is to note that there are many reasons people view their world as mean and scary. Televised violence is just one factor among many. The study shows that the amount of time spent in front of a TV is a consistent but *small portion of the total picture*. To illustrate the little part that viewing symbolic violence seems to play, think of putting everyone's fear of victimization into a pie—sour apple or bitter lemon might be appropriate. Suppose the pie were sliced into pieces and you ate one small bite of one piece. That single taste would represent the amount of fear that can be explained by heavy television viewing. What's left over—almost the entire pie—is the fear people feel for reasons other than their exposure to televised violence.[16] Does the small portion that Gerbner has identified represent a difference that makes a difference?

In response to this criticism, Shanahan and Morgan ask us to imagine a cherry pie, of which only 1 percent is bourbon or, for that matter, anthrax. The taste and potential effect would surely be quite different. And, of course, a 1 percent swing in voting patterns for president this decade would have twice changed the U.S. political landscape. This leads to a third possible interpretation of the study.

A final answer to the question of what the data might mean has to do with the crucial *importance* of the issue at hand. Fear of violence is a paralyzing emotion. As Gerbner repeatedly pointed out, worry can make people prisoners in their own homes, change the way they vote, affect how they feel about themselves, and dramatically lower their quality of life. With consistent evidence that heavy television viewing produces some effect on a person's worldview, Morgan and Shanahan call on media scholars to move beyond methodological arguments and begin to develop theoretical perspectives that speak to the issue of who controls the production and distribution of cultural stories. Of course, Stuart Hall's *cultural studies* attempts to do precisely that (see Chapter 26).

As for Gerbner, in 1996 he founded the Cultural Environment Movement, a coalition of organizations and social activists who believe that it's vitally important who gets to tell the stories within a culture, and whose stories don't get told. They are committed to changing the stories that American television tells and are convinced that this will happen only when the public wrests back control of the airwaves from media conglomerates. Gerbner underscored the movement's agenda with repeated references to a line from Scottish patriot Andrew Fletcher:

> If a man were permitted to make all the ballads, he need not care who should make the laws of a nation.[17]

QUESTIONS TO SHARPEN YOUR FOCUS

1. How would you change Gerbner's *definition of dramatic violence* so that his index of TV violence would measure what you think is important?

2. What types of people are underrepresented in television drama? What types of people are overrepresented? Who are the victims of symbolic violence on the screen?

3. How do your *political* and *social values* differ from, or coincide with, the *mainstream* attitudes of Gerbner's *television type*?

4. The *meta-analysis* finding of a +.091 relationship between TV exposure and worldview can be seen as *significant, small,* and/or *crucial.* How do these interpretations differ? Which do you regard as most important?

SELF-QUIZ *www.mhhe.com/griffin7*

A SECOND LOOK   *Recommended resource:* George Gerbner, Larry Gross, Michael Morgan, Nancy Signorielli, and James Shanahan, "Growing Up with Television: Cultivation Processes," in *Media Effects: Advances in Theory and Research,* 2nd ed., Jennings Bryant and Dolf Zillmann (eds.), Lawrence Erlbaum, Mahwah, NJ, 2002, pp. 43–67.

Primary sources: Michael Morgan (ed.), *Against the Mainstream: The Selected Works of George Gerbner,* Peter Lang, New York, 2002.

Violence index: George Gerbner, Larry Gross, Marilyn Jackson-Beeck, Suzanne Jeffries-Fox, and Nancy Signorielli, "Cultural Indicators: Violence Profile No. 9," *Journal of Communication,* Vol. 28, No. 3, 1978, pp. 176–207.

Violence update: Stacy L. Smith, Amy I. Nathenson, and Barbara J. Wilson, "Prime-Time Television: Assessing Violence During the Most Popular Hours," *Journal of Communication,* Vol. 52, No. 1, 2002, pp. 84–111.

Introduction to key concepts: George Gerbner, "Cultivation Analysis: An Overview," *Mass Communication & Society,* Vol. 1, 1998, pp. 175–194.

Profile of Gerbner: Scott Stossel, "The Man Who Counts the Killings," *Atlantic,* May 1997, pp. 86–104.

Mainstreaming and resonance: George Gerbner, Larry Gross, Michael Morgan, and Nancy Signorielli, "The 'Mainstreaming' of America: Violence Profile No. 11," *Journal of Communication,* Vol. 30, No. 3, 1980, pp. 10–29.

Mainstreaming and resonance research: L. J. Shrum and Valerie D. Bischak, "Mainstreaming, Resonance, and Impersonal Impact: Testing Moderators of the Cultivation Effect for Estimates of Crime Risk," *Human Communication Research,* Vol. 27, 2001, pp. 187–215.

Research review and meta-analysis: Michael Morgan and James Shanahan, "Two Decades of Cultivation Research: An Appraisal and a Meta-Analysis," in *Communication Yearbook 20,* Brant Burleson (ed.), Sage, Thousand Oaks, CA, 1997, pp. 1–45.

Television news violence: Daniel Romer, Kathleen Hall Jamieson, and Sean Aday, "Television News and the Cultivation of Fear of Crime," *Journal of Communication,* Vol. 53, 2003, pp. 88–104.

Computer game violence: Dmitri Williams, "Virtual Cultivation: Online Worlds, Offline Perceptions," *Journal of Communication,* Vol. 56, 2006, pp. 69–87.

Causality with correlation data: Constanze Rossmann and Hans-Bernd Brosius, "The Problem of Causality in Cultivation Research," *Communications,* Vol. 29, 2004, pp. 379–397.

Critique: Dolf Zillmann and Jacob Wakshlag, "Fear of Victimization and the Appeal of Crime Drama," in *Selective Exposure to Communication,* Dolf Zillmann and Jennings Bryant (eds.), Lawrence Erlbaum, Hillsdale, NJ, 1985, pp. 141–156.

To access a chapter on Albert Bandura's social learning theory, a theory that predicts viewers will imitate violence they see on TV, click on Theory Archive at *www.afirstlook.com.*

CHAPTER 28

Agenda-Setting Theory
of Maxwell McCombs & Donald Shaw

For some unexplained reason, in June 1972, five unknown men broke into the Democratic National Committee headquarters looking for undetermined information. It was the sort of local crime story that rated two paragraphs on page 17 of the *Washington Post*. Yet editor Ben Bradlee and reporters Bob Woodward and Carl Bernstein gave the story repeatedly high visibility even though the public initially seemed to regard the incident as trivial.

President Nixon dismissed the break-in as a "third-rate burglary," but over the following year Americans showed an increasing public awareness of Watergate's significance. Half the country became familiar with the word Watergate over the summer of 1972. By April 1973, that figure had risen to 90 percent. When television began gavel-to-gavel coverage of the Senate hearings on the matter a year after the break-in, virtually every adult in the United States knew what *Watergate* was about. Six months after the hearings President Nixon still protested, "I am not a crook." But by the spring of 1974, he was forced from office because the majority of citizens and their representatives had decided that he was.

THE ORIGINAL AGENDA: NOT WHAT TO *THINK*, BUT WHAT TO THINK *ABOUT*

Agenda-setting hypothesis
The mass media have the ability to transfer the salience of issues on their news agenda to the public agenda.

Journalism professors Maxwell McCombs and Donald Shaw regard Watergate as a perfect example of the agenda-setting function of the mass media. They were not surprised that the Watergate issue caught fire after months on the front page of the *Washington Post*. McCombs and Shaw believe that the "mass media have the ability to transfer the salience of items on their news agendas to the public agenda."[1] They aren't suggesting that broadcast and print personnel make a deliberate attempt to influence listener, viewer, or reader opinion on the issues. Reporters in the free world have a deserved reputation for independence and fairness. But McCombs and Shaw say that we look to news professionals for cues on where to focus our attention. "*We* judge as important what the *media* judge as important."[2]

Although McCombs and Shaw first referred to the agenda-setting function of the media in 1972, the idea that people desire media assistance in determining political reality had already been voiced by a number of current events analysts. In an attempt to explain how the United States had been drawn into World War I, Pulitzer Prize–winning author Walter Lippmann claimed that the media act as a mediator between "the world outside and the pictures in our heads."[3] McCombs

359

and Shaw also quote University of Wisconsin political scientist Bernard Cohen's observation concerning the specific function the media serve: "The press may not be successful much of the time in telling people what to think, but it is stunningly successful in telling its readers what to think about."[4]

Starting with the Kennedy-Nixon contest in 1960, political analyst Theodore White wrote the definitive account of four presidential elections. Independently of McCombs and Shaw, and in opposition to then-current wisdom that mass communication had limited effects upon its audience, White came to the conclusion that the media shaped those election campaigns:

> The power of the press in America is a primordial one. It sets the agenda of public discussion; and this sweeping political power is unrestrained by any law. It determines what people will talk and think about—an authority that in other nations is reserved for tyrants, priests, parties and mandarins.[5]

A THEORY WHOSE TIME HAD COME

McCombs and Shaw's agenda-setting theory found an appreciative audience among mass communication researchers. The prevailing selective exposure hypothesis claimed that people would attend only to news and views that didn't threaten their established beliefs. The media were seen as merely stroking pre-existent attitudes. After two decades of downplaying the influence of newspapers, magazines, radio, and television, the field was disenchanted with this limited-effects approach. Agenda-setting theory boasted two attractive features: it reaffirmed the power of the press while still maintaining that individuals were free to choose.

McCombs and Shaw's agenda-setting theory represents a back-to-the-basics approach to mass communication research. Like the initial Erie County voting studies,[6] the focus is on election campaigns. The hypothesis predicts a cause-and-effect relationship between media content and voter perception. Although later work explores the conditions under which the media priorities are most influential, the theory rises or falls on its ability to show a match between the media's agenda and the public's agenda later on. McCombs and Shaw supported their main hypothesis with results from surveys they took while working together at the University of North Carolina at Chapel Hill.[7] (McCombs is now at the University of Texas.) Their analysis of the 1968 race for president between Richard Nixon and Hubert Humphrey set the pattern for later agenda-setting research. The study provides an opportunity to examine in detail the type of quantitative survey research that Stuart Hall and other critical theorists so strongly oppose.

MEDIA AGENDA AND PUBLIC AGENDA: A CLOSE MATCH

Media agenda
The pattern of news coverage across major print and broadcast media as measured by the prominence and length of stories.

McCombs and Shaw's first task was to measure the *media agenda*. They determined that Chapel Hill residents relied on a mix of nine print and broadcast sources for political news—two Raleigh papers, two Durham papers, *Time, Newsweek,* the out-of-state edition of the *New York Times,* and the CBS and NBC evening news.

They established *position* and *length* of story as the two main criteria of prominence. For newspapers, the front-page headline story, a three-column story on an inside page, and the lead editorial were all counted as evidence of significant focus on an issue. For news magazines, the requirement was an opening story in the news section or any political issue to which the editors devoted a full column. Prominence in the television news format was defined by placement as one of the first three news items or any discussion that lasted over 45 seconds.

Because the agenda-setting hypothesis refers to substantive issues, the researchers discarded news items about campaign strategy, position in the polls, and the personalities of the candidates. The remaining stories were then sorted into 15 subject categories, which were later boiled down into 5 major issues. A composite index of media prominence revealed the following order of importance: foreign policy, law and order, fiscal policy, public welfare, and civil rights.

Public agenda
The most important public issues as measured by public opinion surveys.

In order to measure the *public's agenda*, McCombs and Shaw asked Chapel Hill voters to outline what each one considered the key issue of the campaign, regardless of what the candidates might be saying. People who were already committed to a candidate were dropped from the pool of respondents. The researchers assigned the specific answers to the same broad categories used for media analysis. They then compared the aggregate data from undecided voters with the composite description of media content. The rank of the five issues on both lists was nearly identical.

WHAT CAUSES WHAT?

McCombs and Shaw believe that the hypothesized agenda-setting function of the media is responsible for the almost perfect correlation they found between the media and public ordering of priorities:

Media Agenda → Voters' Agenda

But as critics of cultivation theory remind us, correlation is not causation. It's possible that newspaper and television coverage simply reflects public concerns that already exist:

Voters' Agenda → Media Agenda

The results of the Chapel Hill study could be interpreted as providing support for the notion that the media are just as market-driven in their news coverage as they are in programming entertainment. By themselves, McCombs and Shaw's findings were impressive, but equivocal. A true test of the agenda-setting hypothesis must be able to show that public priorities lag behind the media agenda. I'll briefly describe three research studies that provide evidence that the media agenda is, in fact, the *cause*, while the public agenda is its somewhat delayed *effect*.

During the 1976 presidential campaign that led to Jimmy Carter's election, McCombs and three other researchers systematically *surveyed* public opinion at three locations across the country. Between February and December, they interviewed voters in Lebanon, New Hampshire; Indianapolis, Indiana; and Evanston, Illinois, on nine occasions. During the same period, they also monitored election coverage over the three major TV networks and in the local newspapers. A correlational time-lag analysis showed that the public agenda reliably trailed the media agenda by about four to six weeks. The correlation was highest during the primary season, but media priorities were later reflected in voters' priorities throughout the campaign.[8]

Is it possible that *both* the media agenda and the public agenda merely reflect current events as they unfold, but that news professionals become aware of what's happening sooner than most of us do? To examine that possibility, communication researcher Ray Funkhouser, now retired from Pennsylvania State University, undertook an extensive *historical* review of stories in news magazines from 1960 to 1970.[9]

He charted the rise and fall of media attention on issues and compared these trends with annual Gallup poll responses to a question about "the most important problem facing America." Funkhouser's results make it clear that the twin agendas aren't mere reflections of reality. For example, the number of American troops in Vietnam increased until 1968, but news coverage peaked two years before that. The same was true of urban violence and campus unrest. Press interest cooled down while cities and colleges were still heating up. It appears that Walter Lippmann was right—the actual environment and the pictures in our mind are two different worlds.

These survey and historical studies provided strong support for McCombs and Shaw's basic agenda-setting hypothesis. But it took a tightly controlled *experiment* run by Yale researchers to establish a cause-and-effect chain of influence from the media agenda to the public agenda.[10] Political scientists Shanto Iyengar, Mark Peters, and Donald Kinder spliced previously aired news features into tapes of current network newscasts. For four days straight, three groups of New Haven residents came together to watch the evening news and fill out a questionnaire about their own concerns. Each group saw a different version—one version contained a daily story on environmental pollution, another had a daily feature on national defense, and a third offered a daily dose of news about economic inflation. Viewers who saw the media agendas that focused on pollution and defense elevated those issues on their own lists of concerns—definite confirmation of a cause-and-effect relationship between the media agenda and the public agenda. (As it turned out, inflation was already an important topic for most participants, so there wasn't any room for that issue to move up on the third group's agenda.)

WHO SETS THE AGENDA FOR THE AGENDA SETTERS?

In their experiment, Iyengar, Peters, and Kinder gave increased visibility to the issues of economic inflation, national defense, and environmental pollution. Although they could have selected other news topics, they were limited to the extent that they could only pick among stories that actually had been aired. In fact, 75 percent of the stories that come across a news desk are never printed or broadcast. News doesn't select itself. Who sets the agenda for the agenda setters?

One view regards a handful of news editors as the guardians, or "gatekeepers," of political dialogue. Nothing gets put on the political agenda without the concurrence of a few select people—the operation chiefs of the Associated Press, the *New York Times*, the *Washington Post, Time, Newsweek*, ABC, NBC, CBS, CNN, Fox, and MSNBC. Although there is no evidence to support right-wing conservative charges that the editors are part of a liberal, eastern-establishment conspiracy, these key decision makers are undeniably part of a media elite that doesn't represent a cross section of U.S. citizens. The media elite consists of middle-aged Caucasian males who attend the same conferences, banquets, and parties. As Watergate demonstrated, when one of them features an issue, the rest of the nation's media tend to pick up the story. This intermedia effect is especially strong when the *New York Times* takes the lead.

An alternative view regards the candidates themselves as the ultimate source of issue salience. During the 1988 presidential election, George Bush successfully focused media attention on Willie Horton, a convict who raped and murdered a woman while he was on furlough from a prison in Massachusetts. Bush's media handlers (sometimes referred to as "spin doctors") turned the tragedy into a commentary on the Democratic governor's liberalism, and not a day went by without some effort to smear his opponent with Horton's crime. By winning the election, Bush inherited the power that a president has to raise any issue to national prominence with a few remarks. He was able to put the tax issue on the table with his famous statement "Read my lips—no new taxes!" But he was unable to get the issue off the table when he broke that pledge. He also tried to dismiss the economic recession as a "mild technical adjustment." The press and the populace decided it was major.

Current thinking on news selection focuses on the crucial role of public relations professionals working for government agencies, corporations, and interest groups. Even prestigious newspapers with large investigative staffs such as the *Washington Post* and the *New York Times* get more than half of what they print straight from press releases and press conferences.[11]

Interest aggregations are becoming increasingly adept at creating news that must be reported. Columbia University sociologist Robert Merton coined this term to refer to clusters of people who demand center stage for their one, overriding concern, whatever it might be—antiabortion, antiwar, anticommunism, antipollution, anti-free trade, anti-immigration, anti-gay marriage. As the examples indicate, these groups usually rally around a specific action that they oppose. They stage demonstrations, marches, and other media events so that television and the press will be forced to cover their issue. The net effect is that various power centers are vying for the right to be heard. The media seem to pay attention to those who grab it.

On rare occasions, news events are so compelling that editors have no choice but to feature them for extended periods of time. The monthlong Florida recount in 2000 to determine whether George W. Bush or Al Gore would be president was one such case. And, of course, the 9/11 terrorist attack totally dominated U.S. print and broadcast news, pushing almost every other story off the front page and television screen for the rest of the year. More recently, the 2004 Indian Ocean tsunami that swept over 200,000 people to death also swept everything else off the media agenda. So did the flood waters that engulfed New Orleans when Hurricane Katrina struck in 2005.

Interest aggregations
Clusters of people who demand center stage for their one, overriding concern; pressure groups.

WHO IS MOST AFFECTED BY THE MEDIA AGENDA?

Even in their original Chapel Hill study, McCombs and Shaw understood that "people are not automatons waiting to be programmed by the news media."[12] They suspected that some viewers might be more resistant to the media's political priorities than others—that's why they filtered out the responses of voters who were already committed to a candidate. In follow-up studies, McCombs and Shaw turned to the *uses and gratifications* approach, which suggests that viewers are selective in the kinds of TV programs they watch. The theorists sought to discover exactly what kind of person is most susceptible to the media agenda. They concluded that people who have a willingness to let the media shape their thinking have a high *need for orientation*. Others refer to it as an *index of curiosity*.

Index of curiosity
A measure of the extent to which individuals' need for orientation motivates them to let the media shape their views.

Need for orientation arises from high *relevance* and *uncertainty*. For example, because I'm a dog and cat owner, any story about cruelty to animals always catches my attention (high relevance). However, I don't really know the extent to which medical advances require experimentation on live animals (high uncertainty). According to McCombs and Shaw, this combination would make me a likely candidate to be influenced by media stories about vivisection. If the news editors of *Time* and ABC think it's important, I probably will too.

It's hard for me to imagine broadcast and print media providing saturation coverage on the issue of animal welfare. Yet even if they did and I had a high need for orientation on the issue, my response to the coverage would depend on what *aspects* of the story they featured. They might stress dogs in pain, medical breakthroughs, coldhearted scientists, or vivisection as the alternative to human guinea pigs. As discussed in the next two sections of this chapter, that selection process has a powerful effect on readers and viewers.

FRAMING: TRANSFERRING THE SALIENCE OF ATTRIBUTES

Until the 1990s, almost every article about the theory included a reiteration of the agenda-setting mantra—*the media aren't very successful in telling us what to think, but they are stunningly successful in telling us what to think about.* In other words, the media make some issues more *salient.* We pay greater attention to those issues and regard them as more important. By the mid-1990s, however, McCombs was saying that the media do more than that. They do, in fact, influence the way we think. The specific process he cites is one that many media scholars discuss—*framing.*

James Tankard, one of the leading writers on mass communication theory, defines a media frame as "the central organizing idea for news content that supplies a context and suggests what the issue is through the use of *selection, emphasis, exclusion,* and *elaboration.*"[13] The final four nouns in that sentence suggest that the media not only set the agenda for what issues, events, or candidates are most important but also transfer the salience of specific attributes belonging to those potential objects of interest. My own "final four" experience may help explain the distinction.

Framing
The selection of a restricted number of thematically related attributes for inclusion on the media agenda when a particular object or issue is discussed.

I'm writing this section while visiting relatives in St. Petersburg, Florida. The *St. Petersburg Times* is filled with stories about the finals of the NCAA men's basketball tournament that starts here tomorrow. The field of 64 teams has now been narrowed to 4, and it's hard to imagine anything the newspaper or television stations could do to make this Final Four event more prominent for local residents. No one seems to talk about anything else.

What is it about the Final Four extravaganza that captures people's attention? For some it's the high quality of basketball play they expect to see. For others it's a rooting interest for a particular team. But beyond these inherent characteristics of a basketball tournament, there are many other potential features of the event that might come to mind:

Gambling—there's more money bet on this game than on the Super Bowl.

Party scene—a guy leans out the window and yells, "This is where it's at."

Local economy—this is the weekend that could keep Florida green.

Exploitation of players—how many of these guys will ever graduate?

Beach forecast—it will be sunny and warm both today and tomorrow.

The morning paper carried separate stories on all these features, but coverage on benefits to the local economy and the gambling angle were front-page features that ran five times as long as the brief article on player exploitation buried inside.

We see, therefore, that there are two levels of agenda setting. The first level, according to McCombs, is the transfer of salience of an *attitude object* in the mass media's pictures of the world to a prominent place among the pictures in our head. The Final Four becomes important to us. This is the agenda-setting function that survey researchers have traditionally studied.

"Your royal command has been obeyed, Highness. Every town crier in the land is crying: 'Old King Cole is a merry ole soul.' Before nightfall we'll have them all believing it."

Cartoon by Ed Frascino. Reprinted by permission.

The second level of agenda setting is the transfer of salience of a dominant set of *attributes* that the media associate with an attitude object to the specific features of the image projected on the walls of our minds.[14] When I now think of the Final Four, I imagine money changing hands for a variety of reasons. I don't think about GPAs or diplomas. According to McCombs, the agenda setting of attributes mirrors the process of framing that Robert Entman describes in his article clarifying the concept:

> To frame is to select some aspects of a perceived reality and make them more salient in a communication text, in such a way as to promote a particular problem definition, causal interpretation, moral evaluation and/or treatment recommendation for the item described.[15]

NOT JUST WHAT TO THINK ABOUT, BUT HOW TO THINK ABOUT IT

Is there evidence that the process of framing as defined by agenda-setting theorists actually alters the pictures in the minds of people when they read the newspaper or tune in to broadcast news? Does the media's construction of an agenda with a cluster of related attributes create a coherent image in the minds of subscribers, listeners, and viewers? McCombs cites two national election studies in other countries that show this is how framing works. One was conducted in

Japan,[16] the other in Spain.[17] I find compelling evidence in a third study conducted by Salma Ghanem for her doctoral dissertation under McCombs' supervision at the University of Texas.[18]

Ghanem analyzed the changing percentage of Texans who ranked crime as the most important problem facing the country between 1992 and 1995. The figure rose steadily from 2 percent in 1992 to 37 percent of the respondents in 1994 and then dipped back to a still high 21 percent a year later. Ironically, even as public concern about crime was on the rise the first two years, the actual frequency and severity of unlawful acts were actually going down. On the basis of many first-level agenda-setting studies like the Chapel Hill research, Ghanem assumed that the increased salience of crime was driven by media that featured crime stories prominently and often. She found a high correlation (+.70) between the amount of media coverage and the depth of public concern.

Ghanem was more interested in tracking the transfer of salience of specific crime attributes—the second level of agenda setting. Of the dozen or so media frames for stories about crime, two bundles of attributes were strongly linked to the public's increasing alarm. The most powerful frame was one that cast crime as something that could happen to anyone. The stories noted that the robbery took place in broad daylight, or the shooting was random and without provocation.

The second frame was where the crime took place. Out-of-state problems were of casual interest, but when a reported felony occurred locally or in the state of Texas, concern rose quickly. Note that both frames were features of news stories that shrank the psychological distance between the crimes they described and the average citizens who read or heard about them. Many concluded, "I could be next." The high correlations (+.78, +.73) between these media frames and the subsequent public concern suggest that attribute frames make compelling arguments for the choices people make after exposure to the news.

Framing is not an option. Reporters inevitably frame a story by the personal attributes of public figures they select to describe. For example, the media continually reported on the "youthful vigor" of John F. Kennedy while he was alive but made no mention of his extramarital affairs, which were well-known to the White House press corps. The 1988 presidential race was all but over after *Time* framed the contest between George Bush, Sr., and Michael Dukakis as "The Nice Man vs. the Ice Man." And in 1996 Republican spin doctors fought an uphill battle positioning their candidate once media stories focused on Bob Dole's lack of passion—"Dead Man Walking" was the quip of commentator Mark Shields. Media depictions in the 2004 campaign for president focused on conflicting candidate attributes. Senator John Kerry was repeatedly described as "flip-flopping" on the issues. George W. Bush was labeled as "stubborn." Media outlets are constantly searching for material that they regard as *newsworthy.* When they find it, they do more than tell their audiences *what to think about.*

McCombs and Shaw no longer subscribe to Cohen's classic remark about the media's limited agenda-setting role. They now headline their work with a revised and expanded version that describes agenda setting as a much more powerful media function:

> The media may not only tell us what to think about,
> they also may tell us how and what to think about it,
> and perhaps even what to do about it.[19]

BEYOND OPINION: THE BEHAVIORAL EFFECT OF THE MEDIA'S AGENDA

Most of the 400 empirical studies on agenda setting have measured the effect of media agendas on public *opinion*. But some intriguing findings suggest that media priorities also affect people's *behavior*. For example, Alexander Bloj, a graduate student of McCombs, had access to the sales records of a major airline in a large northeastern city.[20] He was also able to find out about the purchase pattern of flight insurance sold at the airport. Bloj predicted that prominent stories of airplane crashes and hijackings in the *New York Times* would both lower ticket sales and increase the purchases of trip insurance the following week. He defined media salience of flight safety as any story running for two days that reported a crash with double-digit fatalities or a skyjacker gaining control of a plane in the air.

Fortunately, disaster-salient weeks over a five-year period in the early 1970s were much less common than were weeks when air safety wasn't an issue. But when the stories appeared, fewer people bought tickets, while more bought flight insurance. Of course, 30 years later no one doubts that saturation media coverage affects travel behavior. Most of us have a televised image of an airliner crashing into the World Trade Center etched in our minds, with the result that the number of people flying plummeted and didn't recover for over two years.

In a similar but more sophisticated study, communication scholar Deborah Blood (University of Connecticut) and economist Peter Phillips (Yale University) also used the *New York Times* to gauge a fluctuating media agenda related to financial news. They sampled headlines every month from 1980 to 1993 to discover whether the newspaper was bullish or bearish on the U.S. economy. They found little relationship between the media agenda and the prevailing economic conditions as measured by the Index of Leading Economic Indicators, a measure tied to business and consumer behavior. They did, however, discover a strong *media malady effect.*

Media malady effect
Negative economic headlines and stories that depress consumer sentiment and leading economic indicators.

> Negative economic headlines were found to have a significant and negative impact on subsequent consumer sentiment [and] an adverse effect on subsequent leading economic indicators up to a five-month time lag. . . . Clearly news organizations hold the power to effect change.[21]

Nowhere is the behavioral effect of the media agenda more apparent than in the business of professional sports. In his book *The Ultimate Assist,* John Fortunato explores the commercial partnership between network television's agenda and the National Basketball Association (NBA).[22] Television dramatically raised the salience of the game (the first level of agenda setting) by consistently scheduling the best teams in prime-time viewing slots. It also grabbed viewer attention by focusing the camera on these teams' premier players. During the peak years of Michael Jordan's playing career, it was "all Michael, all the time."

Television shaped an attractive picture of the NBA in viewers' minds (the second level of agenda setting) through a series of off-court frames. Interviews with select players and coaches, color commentary, graphics, and instant replays of players' spectacular moves all created a positive image of the NBA. As for the rape accusation against L.A. Lakers superstar Kobe Bryant, and later his feud with teammate Shaq O'Neal that split the team, the media cooperated in downplaying those attributes that tarnish the NBA's image.

This 30-year effort to shape the public agenda has not only had a spectacular effect on fan behavior but has also altered the face of popular culture. From 1970 to 2000, the number of NBA teams and the number of games basically doubled. The number of fans going to games quadrupled. But the astronomical difference is in the money. In 1970, television provided $10 million in revenue to the NBA. In 2000, the payout was $20 billion—no small change. McCombs' comment: "Agenda setting the theory, can also be agenda setting the business plan."[23]

Will New Media Continue to Guide Focus, Opinions, and Behavior?

Ironically, the power of agenda setting that McCombs and Shaw describe may be on the wane. In a creative experiment, University of Illinois researchers Scott Althaus and David Tewksbury predicted that traditional print media would be more effective than new electronic media in setting a reader's agenda.[24] They reasoned that people who are reading a newspaper know that editors consider a long, front-page article under a banner headline as more important than a short story buried on an inside page. Not only are these comparative cues absent on the computer screen, but online readers can click on links to similar stories and never see accounts of events that paper readers would see as they thumbed through the pages.

Althaus and Tewksbury recruited students to spend 30–60 minutes a day for 5 days reading either a print version or an online version of the *New York Times* under controlled conditions. For both groups it was their only exposure to news that week. On the sixth day, the researchers tested recognition and recall of the week's stories and assessed which problems facing the country students personally regarded as most important. Not only did those who read the traditional paper remember more content but they also selected a higher percentage of international issues as more important to them, thus aligning them closer to the prioritized agenda of the *Times'* editors. The researchers conclude that "by providing users with more content choices and control over exposure, new technologies may allow people to create personalized information environments that shut them off from larger flows of public information in a society."[25] They might also add that traditional news media may not have as much power to transfer the salience of issues or attributes as they have in the past.

ETHICAL REFLECTION: CHRISTIANS' COMMUNITARIAN ETHICS

Clifford Christians is a professor at the Institute of Communications Research at the University of Illinois at Urbana-Champaign and is lead author of *Good News: Social Ethics and the Press*.[26] Although he values free speech, he doesn't share the near-absolute devotion to the First Amendment that seems to be the sole ethical commitment of many journalists. Christians rejects reporters and editors' insistence on an absolute right of free expression that is based on the individualistic rationalism of John Locke and other Enlightenment thinkers. In our age of ethical relativism where *continue the conversation* is the best that philosophy has to offer,[27] Christians believes that discovering the truth is still possible if we are willing to examine the nature of our humanity. The human nature he perceives is, at root, personhood in community.[28]

Christians agrees with Martin Buber that the relation is the cradle of life. ("In the beginning is the relation."[29]) He is convinced, therefore, that mutuality is the essence of humanness. People are most fully human as "persons-in-relation" who live simultaneously for others and for themselves.

Communitarian ethics
A moral responsibility to promote community, mutuality, and persons-in-relation who live simultaneously for others and for themselves.

A moral community demonstrates more than mere interdependence; it is characterized by mutuality, a will-to-community, a genuine concern for the other apart from immediate self-interest. . . . An act is morally right when compelled by the intention to maintain the community of persons; it is wrong if driven by self-centeredness.[30]

Christians understands that a commitment to mutuality would significantly alter media culture and mission. His *communitarian ethics* establish civic transformation rather than objective information as the primary goal of the press. Reporters' aim would thus become a revitalized citizenship shaped by community norms—morally literate and active participants, not just readers and audiences provided with data.[31] Editors, publishers, and owners—the gatekeepers of the media agenda—would be held to the same standard. Christians insists that media criticism must be willing to reestablish the idea of moral right and wrong. Selfish practices aimed at splintering community are not merely misguided; they are evil.[32]

Agape love
An unconditional love for others because they are created in the image of God.

Christians' communitarian ethics are based on the Christian tradition of *agape love*—an unconditional love for others because they are created in the image of God. He believes journalists have a social responsibility to promote the sacredness of life by respecting human dignity, truthtelling, and doing no harm to innocents.[33] With an emphasis on establishing communal bonds, alienated people on the margins of society receive special attention from communitarians. Christians ultimately judges journalists on the basis of how well they use the media's power to champion the goal of social justice. For example, Christians asks:

> Is the press a voice for the unemployed, food-stamp recipients, Appalachian miners, the urban poor, Hispanics in rural shacks, the elderly, women discriminated against in hiring and promotion, ethnic minorities with no future in North America's downsizing economy?[34]

If the media sets that kind of agenda and features attributes that promote community, he believes they are fulfilling their communitarian responsibility.

CRITIQUE: ARE THE EFFECTS TOO LIMITED, THE SCOPE TOO WIDE?

When McCombs and Shaw first proposed the agenda-setting hypothesis, they saw it as a sharp break from the limited-effects model that had held sway in media research since Lazarsfeld introduced the concept of *selective exposure* (see the introduction to Media Effects). Although not reverting to the old hypodermic needle model or magic bullet conception of media influence, McCombs and Shaw ascribed to broadcast and print journalism the significant power to set the public's political priorities. As years of careful research have shown, however, it doesn't always work. Perhaps the best that could be said until the mid 1990s was that the media agenda affects the salience of some issues for some people some of the time. So in 1994, McCombs suggested that "agenda setting is a theory of limited media effects."[35] That would be quite a comedown from its original promise.

The new dimension of framing reasserts a powerful media effects model. As Ohio State University journalism professor Gerald Kosicki states,

> Media "gatekeepers" do not merely keep watch over information, shuffling it here and there. Instead, they engage in active construction of the messages, emphasizing certain aspects of an issue and not others.[36]

But Kosicki questions whether framing is even a legitimate topic of study under an agenda-setting banner. He sees nothing in McCombs and Shaw's original model that anticipates the importance of interpretive frames.

As McCombs is fond of pointing out, the evidence is there. In the lead article of a 1977 book that he and Shaw edited, they clearly previewed the current "New Frontiers" of agendas of attributes and framing:

> Agenda setting as a concept is not limited to the correspondence between salience of topics for the media and the audience. We can also consider the saliency of various attributes of these objects (topics, issues, persons or whatever) reported in the media. To what extent is our view of an object shaped or influenced by the picture sketched in the media, especially by those attributes which the media deem newsworthy?[37]

McCombs' definition of framing appears to be quite specific: "Framing is the selection of a restricted number of thematically related attributes for inclusion on the media agenda when a particular object is discussed."[38] It doesn't seem to include the emotional connotation of key terms used in ongoing public debate of issues such as abortion. For example, the effect on the audience may be quite different if a story is labeled as *antiabortion forces* versus *freedom of choice* rather than *right-to-life advocates* versus *proabortion advocates*. The definition also seems to exclude presentational factors such as a broadcaster's raised eyebrow while saying one of these phrases.

In contrast, the popularity of framing as an *interpretive* construct in media studies has resulted in diverse and ambiguous meanings. The way that Stuart Hall and other critical theorists use the term is so elastic that the word seems to refer to anything they don't like. Thus, I regard a narrow view of framing as a distinct advantage for empirically based media effects research.

Whether or not we accept a restricted definition of framing, the agenda-setting function of the mass media has earned a firm place in media effects literature. McCombs and Shaw have established a plausible case that some people look to print and broadcast news for guidance on which issues are really important. Agenda-setting theory also provides a needed reminder that news stories are just that—stories. The message always requires interpretation. For these reasons, McCombs and Shaw have accomplished the function they ascribe to the media. Agenda-setting theory has a priority place on the agenda of mass communication theory and research.

QUESTIONS TO SHARPEN YOUR FOCUS

1. If the media aren't telling you what to think, why is their ability to tell you *what to think about* so important?

2. What *type of person* under what *type of circumstances* is most susceptible to the media's *agenda-setting function?*

3. Hillary Clinton continues to be one of the most controversial public figures in America. What *dominant set of attributes* could you use to *frame* her visit to a children's hospital to make her look good? How could you make her look bad?

4. Is there a recent issue that *news reporters and commentators* are now talking about daily that you and the people you know don't care about? Do you think you'll still be unconcerned two months from now?

CONVERSATIONS

View this segment online at
www.mhhe.com/griffin7 or
www.afirstlook.com.

In our conversation, Max McCombs discusses the process of framing and how this concept has changed the scope of his theory. He also answers questions posed by my students. How many issues can a person focus on at one time? If he ran the classic Chapel Hill study today, would he use CNN as a media outlet that sets the public agenda? Do TV entertainment shows have an agenda-setting function? I wanted to know how he saw potential media bias. Are all news stories delivered with a spin? Does he see anything sinister about intentionally framing a story? Is there a liberal bias in the national media? I think you'll be surprised by his direct responses.

A SECOND LOOK

Recommended resource: Maxwell McCombs and Amy Reynolds, "News Influence on Our Pictures of the World," in *Media Effects: Advances in Theory and Research,* Jennings Bryant and Dolf Zillmann (eds.), Lawrence Erlbaum, Mahwah, NJ, 2002, pp. 1–18.

Comprehensive summary of theory and research: Maxwell McCombs, *Setting the Agenda,* Polity, Cambridge, UK, 2004.

Historical development: Maxwell McCombs and Tamara Bell, "The Agenda-Setting Role of Mass Communication," in *An Integrated Approach to Communication Theory and Research,* Michael Salwen and Donald Stacks (eds.), Lawrence Erlbaum, Hillsdale, NJ, 1996, pp. 93–110.

Five stages of agenda-setting research and development: Maxwell McCombs, "A Look at Agenda-Setting: Past, Present and Future," *Journalism Studies,* Vol. 6, 2005, pp. 543–557.

Prototype election study: Maxwell McCombs and Donald Shaw, "The Agenda-Setting Function of the Mass Media," *Public Opinion Quarterly,* Vol. 36, 1972, pp. 176–187.

Framing. Maxwell McCombs and Salma Ghanem, "The Convergence of Agenda Setting and Framing," in *Framing Public Life,* Stephen Reese, Oscar Gandy, Jr., and August Grant (eds.), Lawrence Erlbaum, Mahwah, NJ, 2001, pp. 67–81.

Relationship of agenda setting, framing, and priming: Dietram Scheufele and David Tewksbury, "Framing, Agenda Setting, and Priming. The Evolution of Three Media Effects Models," *Journal of Communication,* Vol. 57, 2007, pp. 9–20.

Bundles of attributes: Maxwell McCombs, "New Frontiers in Agenda Setting: Agendas of Attributes and Frames," *Mass Comm Review 24,* 1997, pp. 4–24.

Sophisticated election study: Maxwell McCombs, Esteban Lopez-Escobar, and Juan Pablo Llamas, "Setting the Agenda of Attributes in the 1996 Spanish General Election," *Journal of Communication,* Vol. 50, No. 2, 2000, pp. 77–92.

Anthology of earlier agenda-setting research: David Protess and Maxwell McCombs, *Agenda Setting: Readings on Media, Public Opinion, and Policymaking,* Lawrence Erlbaum, Hillsdale, NJ, 1991.

Later scholarship: Maxwell McCombs, Donald Shaw, and David Weaver, *Communication and Democracy: Exploring the Intellectual Frontiers in Agenda-Setting Theory,* Lawrence Erlbaum, Mahwah, NJ, 1997.

Focus on the theorist: William Davie and T. Michael Maher, "Maxwell McCombs: Agenda-Setting Explorer," *Journal of Broadcasting and Electronic Media,* Vol. 50, 2006, pp. 358–364.

Critique: Gerald Kosicki, "Problems and Opportunities in Agenda-Setting Research," *Journal of Communication,* Vol. 43, No. 2, 1993, pp. 100–127.

Spiral of Silence

of Elisabeth Noelle-Neumann

The 1980 U.S. presidential election seemed too close to call. Polls reported that President Jimmy Carter and challenger Ronald Reagan were in a virtual dead heat during the final two months of the campaign. But according to Elisabeth Noelle-Neumann, professor of communication research at the University of Mainz in Germany, most pollsters asked the wrong question. Instead of asking, *Who do you plan to vote for?* they should have asked, *Who do you think will win the election?*

They would have discovered that even while voter preference was holding equal, the expectation that Reagan would win was growing from week to week. Noelle-Neumann claims that people's assessment of the political climate, and especially their forecast of future trends, are early and reliable indicators of what will happen in an election. In Carter's case they were. The night before the vote, Democratic pollster Pat Caddell went to the president and sadly announced that the contest was over. Millions of voters were taking part in a last-minute swing for Reagan. The actual vote the next day buried Carter in a Republican landslide.

Public opinion
Attitudes one can express without running the danger of isolating oneself; a tangible force that keeps people in line.

Noelle-Neumann's spiral of silence is a theory that explains the growth and spread of *public opinion*. As founder and director of the Public Opinion Research Center in Allensbach (the German counterpart of America's Gallup poll organization), she has come to recognize the power of public opinion. Like seventeenth-century philosopher John Locke, she regards public opinion as a *tangible force* that keeps people in line. Locke outlined three forms of law—*divine, civil*, and *opinion*. He claimed that the law of opinion is the only law by which people really abide.[1] For any morally loaded topics that are strongly controversial, Noelle-Neumann defines public opinion as "attitudes one can express without running the danger of isolating oneself."[2]

Spiral of silence
The increasing pressure people feel to conceal their views when they think they are in the minority.

The term *spiral of silence* refers to the increasing pressure people feel to conceal their views when they think they are in the minority. Noelle-Neumann believes that television accelerates the spiral, but to grasp the role of the mass media in the process we first must understand people's extraordinary sensitivity to the ever-changing standard of what society will tolerate.

A QUASI-STATISTICAL ORGAN SENSING THE CLIMATE OF OPINION

Noelle-Neumann is constantly amazed at the human ability to discern the climate of public opinion. Science has fixed on five bodily receptors through which people sense their environment: eye (sight), ear (sound), tongue (taste), nose (smell), skin (touch). Only half facetiously, the veteran pollster suggests that humans have a *quasi-statistical organ*—a sixth sense that tallies up information about what society in general is thinking and feeling. It's as if people come equipped with antennae that quiver to every shift in the social breeze. How else, she says, can we account for the fact that "when a swing in the climate occurs for or against a party, a person, or a particular idea, it seems to be sensed everywhere at almost exactly the same time, by [everybody?]"[3] Without benefit of random samples, interview schedules, or frequency distributions, average people can tell which way the wind is blowing before the scientific polls capture the climate of public opinion.

Quasi-statistical organ
A sixth sense that tallies up information about what society in general is thinking and feeling.

Noelle-Neumann recommends two questions to get at the barometric readings inside people's heads:

1. Present climate: *Regardless of your personal opinion, do you think most people . . . ?*

2. Future forecast: *Will more or fewer people think this way a year from now?*

People rarely respond, "How should I know?" or "I'm no prophet."[4] She believes that assessing the public mood, present or future, is the most natural thing in the world for people to do. More than 30 years of survey experience has convinced her that people usually get it right. Even when they misread the present, they still can spot future trends. For example, near the end of every year, poll-takers from her research center ask a representative sample of German men and women, "Do you look forward to the coming year with hopes or with fears?" The level of optimism expressed shows no relationship to economic growth in the year the question is asked, but it gives an uncanny forecast of the actual rise or fall in the growth rate of the nation's GNP for *the following year.*

The human ability to spot momentum in public opinions is not used frivolously. Noelle-Neumann says it requires an unbelievable expenditure of energy to figure out which ideas are on the increase and which are on the decline. The tremendous concentration required to monitor social trends makes sense only when compared with a greater strain—the danger of isolating oneself with an opinion that has gone out of style. "The effort spent in observing the environment is apparently a smaller price to pay than the risk of losing the goodwill of one's fellow human beings—of becoming rejected, despised, alone."[5]

FEAR OF ISOLATION: THE ENGINE THAT DRIVES THE SPIRAL OF SILENCE

According to Noelle-Neumann, the fear of isolation is the centrifugal force that accelerates the spiral of silence. She draws heavily on the famous conformity research of Swarthmore psychologist Solomon Asch to support her claim. Asch demonstrated that people will ignore the plain evidence of their senses and yield to perceived group pressure.[6]

A _____
B _____
C _____
X _____

Look at the lines above. Which line—A, B, or C—is the same length as line X? The answer seems obvious, and left alone, everyone picks line A. But put an individual in a group of experimental confederates who unanimously state that line B is the right answer, and the unsuspecting subject will feel great anxiety. Thoughts of isolation are very real to the person who considers standing firm: *Will these folks frown, argue, or curse my stubbornness? Worse yet, will they snicker or laugh at me? If I say what I really think, will they turn away in contempt or kick me out of the group?* Asch found that most people placed in this stressful situation would conform to the group's judgment at least some, if not all, of the time.

Is fear of isolation a trait peculiar to Americans? Noelle-Neumann rejects that possibility on the basis of Yale psychologist Stanley Milgram's follow-up study conducted in Europe. Milgram selected France and Norway as nations with strikingly diverse cultures—the first one highly individualistic, the other with a strong sense of cohesiveness. As he anticipated, Norwegians conformed more than the French. But like their American counterparts, the majority of people from both countries were unable to stand firm in the face of group pressure.[7]

Noelle-Neumann also considers the possibility that people conform more out of a desire to identify with a winner than to avoid isolation. For example, after an important election is over, a greater percentage of people report voting for the victor than the ballot totals would indicate. But she doesn't consider false reports as attempts to climb belatedly on the bandwagon and bask in reflected glory. Rather, she interprets the petty lies as a defensive strategy to avoid the social stigma that comes from being a deviant on value-laden issues. Even though a go-along-to-get-along approach might brand a person as a conformist or a hanger-on, the people responding to her surveys indicate that rejection is even worse.

Banishment from the group, long-term solitary confinement, and sanctioned public ridicule are regarded as cruel punishments in most parts of the world. Noelle-Neumann says that only the criminal or moral hero doesn't care what society thinks. The rest of us want the peace and contentment that come from belonging. Nobel Prize–winner Mother Teresa affirmed Noelle-Neumann's analysis: "The worst sickness is not leprosy or tuberculosis, but the feeling of being respected by no one, of being unloved, deserted by everyone."[8] That's why individuals are constantly trying to assess the climate of public opinion.

THE POWERFUL ROLE OF THE MASS MEDIA

Noelle-Neumann believes that the media accelerate the muting of the minority in the spiral of silence. Although every human being comes equipped with a quasi-statistical organ with which to analyze the climate of public opinion, that early warning system requires data to process. Direct observation gives us only a small proportion of the information we use; the print and electronic media provide most of our knowledge about the world around us. Marshall McLuhan claimed that different media are extensions of specific physical senses. Noelle-Neumann regards *all* types of media as agents of that hypothetical sixth sense, but she isn't convinced that they always serve us well. That's because opinions supported by the influential media are often overestimated. She suspects that anytime people have a mistaken idea of what the public's opinion really is—a condition called *pluralistic ignorance*—it's probably due to the media not presenting a mix of viewpoints proportionate to their strength in society.[9]

Pluralistic ignorance
People's mistaken idea that everyone thinks like they do.

For decades after the 1940 Erie County voter study, American media sociologists insisted that selective exposure on the part of the reader or viewer neutralized any persuasive effect that the print and broadcast media might have. Like other European scholars, Noelle-Neumann rejects the view that the media only reinforce preexisting beliefs. She admits that the written word's power to change attitudes may be limited by selective exposure. Given the existing variety of newspapers, magazines, and current events literature, it's quite possible for a reader to avoid contrary opinions. But she thinks television is a different matter: "The effects of mass media increase in proportion to the degree in which selective perception is made difficult."[10] A fabled account of a crooked poker game in a small rural town illustrates her claim.

A farm worker regularly received his wages at the end of the day on Friday. Each week he then walked to the local tavern and lost all his money gambling in a backroom poker game of five-card draw. After a few months a friend took him aside and advised, "Don't play with those guys any more—they're cheating you blind." "Oh I know the game is rigged," the farmhand replied, "but it's the only game in town."

Television is often the only game in town, yet Noelle-Neumann says that media researchers usually fail to recognize that fact. They try to test for media effects in the laboratory, but they can't re-create the "ubiquity, consonance, and cumulation" that give TV its power. She's referring to television's all-surrounding presence, its single point of view, and the constant repetition of its message. These factors override selective exposure, therefore biasing a whole nation's judgment of the prevailing opinion. How powerful does Noelle-Neumann think the broadcast media are?

> I have never found a spiral of silence that goes against the tenor of the media, for the willingness to speak out depends in part upon sensing that there is support and legitimation from the media.[11]

Thus, Noelle-Neumann agrees with Stuart Hall's pessimistic assessment concerning the media's intrusive role in democratic decision making (see Chapter 26). She ascribes a function to the media that goes one step beyond agenda setting (see Chapter 28). The media in general and television in particular not only tell us what to think about but also provide the sanctioned view of what everyone else is thinking.

Given the media's role in crystallizing public opinion, media access becomes crucial for those who desire to shape the public mood. It's no longer enough for potential opinion leaders to have well-thought-out positions and the courage of their convictions. They must be ready, willing, and *able* to command media attention. This gives anybody with an assault rifle, friends in high places, or inherited wealth an advantage over the average citizen in programming the quasi-statistical organ that readers and viewers possess.

As an example of a false consensus promoted by the media, Noelle-Neumann cites the negative attitude of her country's journalists toward the overall German character. In the 1950s and 1960s, commentators consistently bad-mouthed German materialism, rudeness, and love for authority. These and other negative stereotypes permeated the media. Data from her research center show that the continual pounding took its toll. The center's annual survey included an item about the German character: "Generally speaking, what do you consider to be the best qualities of the German?" In 1952 only 4 percent of the people answered, "Don't know of any." That figure rose to 14 percent in 1962. By 1972, 20 percent of the people were unable to voice a single positive trait. Noelle-Neumann concludes that the mass media can make a majority look like a minority. Television transmits public opinion; television also creates it.

A TIME TO SPEAK AND A TIME TO KEEP SILENT

Since people can tell when they are out of sync with public opinion and they fear being isolated for holding views that aren't in favor, we might expect those who see themselves in the minority to keep silent. This is precisely what Noelle-Neumann predicts:

> Individuals who . . . notice that their own personal opinion is spreading and is taken over by others, will voice this opinion self-confidently in public. On the other hand, individuals who notice that their own opinions are losing ground, will be inclined to adopt a more reserved attitude.[12]

She is not suggesting that the latter group will easily abandon an unpopular conviction and change their minds. People aren't weather vanes. But men and women who realize they are fighting a headwind may duck their heads and keep their own counsel. Their silence will probably pass unnoticed or be taken as tacit agreement, so they won't be hassled. When President George W. Bush declared war on terrorism after 9/11, citizens of the United States who spoke out against the military action in Afghanistan had to be either very brave or very foolish. The situation was different when President Clinton sent American troops into Bosnia. Sensing that public opinion was not in favor of intervention, and that the media would play up the dangers of the mission, people felt free to voice their dissent.

In the first 1988 presidential debate, George Bush, Sr. invoked the "L word." He called Michael Dukakis a liberal—"a card-carrying member of the ACLU," an organization, he noted, that defends atheists, criminals, and child pornographers. Millions of liberals around the country winced at this verbal body blow to their position. Conservatism had been on the rise for over a decade; liberalism had been in retreat. Liberals could have protested that the American Civil Liberties Union also defended conservative patriot Ollie North, or that Bush's positions on social security, Medicare, and relations with China were originally advocated by liberals. But consistent with Noelle-Neumann's prediction, they found it safer to suffer in silence.

The German Public Opinion Research Center has developed a way to find out whether people are willing to speak out in favor of their viewpoint. Suppose, for example, that the topic is abortion. They ask:

> Assume that you have five hours of train or plane travel ahead of you, and somebody [next to you] begins to talk about abortion. Would you like to talk with this person or would you rather not talk?[13]

Train/plane test
A question about conversation with a stranger while traveling, used to determine whether people are willing to speak out in support of their viewpoint.

The *train/plane test* reveals a series of factors that determine the likelihood that people will voice their opinions. The first factor is by far the most important.

1. Those who favor the majority position are more willing to express their views than those who belong to the minority faction. Feeling in harmony with the spirit of the age loosens the tongue.[14]

2. If perception of the present opinion climate doesn't match a person's forecast for the future, willingness to speak out depends more on the future trend.

"One final question: Do you now own or have you ever owned a fur coat?"

3. People are more willing to speak to those who share their thoughts than to those who disagree. When you fear isolation, friends are safer than foes.

4. Low self-esteem will cause a person to remain mute. Noelle-Neumann's research team identifies these individuals by their agreement with a survey statement about relationships: *I know very few people.*

5. Males, young adults, and people of the middle and upper classes find it easier to speak out.

6. Existing law encourages people to express their opinion when they feel outnumbered. The U.S. Supreme Court's *Roe v. Wade* decision emboldened "closet pro-choice" women who had been fearing public reprisal.

THE ACCELERATING SPIRAL OF SILENCE

You now have the building blocks that Noelle-Neumann uses to construct her model of public opinion:

Human ability to gauge trends of public sentiment.

Individuals' justifiable fear of isolation.

People's hesitancy to express minority views.

She integrates these factors in the following description of the plight of those who sense minority status. Her summary of the theory reveals that they are indeed caught in a spiral of silence.

People . . . live in perpetual fear of isolating themselves and carefully observe their environment to see which opinions increase and which ones decrease. If they find that their views predominate or increase, then they express themselves freely in public; if they find that their views are losing supporters, then they become fearful, conceal their convictions in public and fall silent. Because the one group express themselves with self-confidence whereas the others remain silent, the former appear to be strong in public, the latter weaker than their numbers suggest. This encourages others to express themselves or to fall silent, and a spiral process comes into play.[15]

Figure 29–1 pictures the journey of minority factions down the spiral of silence. The ball represents people who sense a slight discrepancy between their position and the prevailing public opinion, much like President Jimmy Carter's supporters in the early fall of 1980. Up to this point they feel comfortable expressing their views in public, perhaps even displaying campaign buttons or bumper stickers. But then the nagging fear of isolation—insistent as the pull of gravity—convinces them to be more circumspect in what they say. Bumper stickers disappear, and they avoid arguments with Reaganites. Carter hasn't lost any voting strength; only the outward fervor has tapered off. However, the Republican clamor for Reagan is undiminished, so Carter backers get the impression of a dip in support for their man.

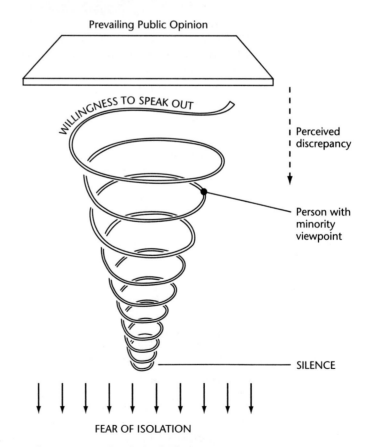

FIGURE 29–1 The Downward Spiral of Silence

Carter's people have now come full circle. Their political antennae register a relative shift in public sentiment even before it shows up in the polls. Reagan's apparent strength becomes a self-fulfilling prophecy because it causes Democrats to see a widening gap between themselves and the majority opinion. To an even greater degree, they draw back from public scrutiny and, thus, begin a tighter circuit on the accelerating downward spiral toward silence. The greater the perceived discrepancy between the prevailing public opinion and their own viewpoint, the more they feel the force of society's demand that they give in. Finally, the pressure to conform becomes so great that uncommitted voters and wavering Democrats who are most fearful of isolation switch sides. The result is a surprising (but predictable) landslide for Ronald Reagan.

THE HARD CORE AND AVANT-GARDE: HOLDOUTS WHO CAN CHANGE THE WORLD

Early critics of the spiral of silence pointed out that there are people who will never be silenced. Even though their cause appears hopeless, they continue to voice their opinions. Noelle-Neumann now describes two types of individuals who form this vocal minority that remains at the top of the spiral in defiance of threats of isolation. She calls them the *hard core* and the *avant-garde*.

Hard-core nonconformists
People who have already been rejected for their beliefs and have nothing to lose by speaking out.

Hard-core nonconformists are those who "have been overpowered and relegated to a completely defensive position in public."[16] Already beaten down, they have nothing to lose by speaking out. Noelle-Neumann cites Cervantes' Don Quixote as an example. The man from La Mancha tilts at windmills and "finds himself isolated, laughed at, defeated, and yet he remains true to the ideals of chivalry" that belong to a world that hasn't existed for 200 years.[17] People in the hard core cling to the past and regard isolation as the price they have to pay.

The avant-garde are the intellectuals, artists, and reformers who form the vanguard of new ideas. Unlike the hard core, they seek public response, even though it's usually negative. "Those who belong to the avant-garde are committed to the future and thus by necessity, are also isolated; but their conviction that they are ahead of their time enables them to endure."[18] Although Noelle-Neumann acknowledges the reality of hard core and avant-garde minorities, they are not predicted by her spiral of silence. In that sense they represent boundary conditions that stake out when the theory applies and when it doesn't.

Avant-garde
Intellectuals, artists, and reformers in the isolated minority who speak out because they are convinced they are ahead of the times.

Noelle-Neumann regards the hard-core and avant-garde minorities as the only hope for future swings in public sentiment.

> The chance to change or mold public opinion is reserved to those who are not afraid of being isolated. By saying and doing the unpopular, by shocking, they . . . can carry their ideas to supremacy.[19]

French social psychologist Serge Moscovici agrees with Noelle-Neumann's assessment, but he doesn't believe she does justice to the pervasive impact of committed deviants upon public opinion. Moscovici has spent his professional life explaining how opinions and attitudes of the majority are susceptible to change by the influence of a minority that stands firm. He considers Noelle-Neumann's discussion of the hard core and the avant-garde as an afterthought, or "finagle factor," to cover the times when the main features of her theory fail to account for shifts in the public mood.[20]

CRITIQUE: FATAL FLAWS IN MAPPING THE SPIRAL?

University of Chicago sociologist Mihaly Csikszentmihal regards Elisabeth Noelle-Neumann's spiral of silence as "the most original, comprehensive, and useful" theory of public opinion yet proposed.[21] Despite this praise, he and other scholars raise serious questions about three specific research practices that they consider overly simplistic, or simply wrong.

1.   Assuming that fear of isolation is the cause of people's silence. Noelle-Neumann bases her spiral of silence on people's fear of isolation, yet her extensive survey work seldom questions whether individuals who remain silent feel it more than those who speak out. This is similar to the practice of Leon Festinger and his followers, who assume that people change their attitudes in order to reduce cognitive dissonance but never check to see if they are actually experiencing that noxious feeling (see Chapter 16). Noelle-Neumann's reliance on the Asch conformity experiment to prove her point also seems questionable. When participants in that study had just one "true partner" who shared their judgment, they were able to withstand group pressure. Undoubtedly some people tend to remain mute more than others, but that reticence might be due to shyness, disinterest, or a desire not to embarrass a person with an opposing viewpoint.

2.   Relying on the hypothetical train/plane test to measure willingness to speak out. Although Noelle-Neumann's train/plane test seems to be a clever way to assess people's enthusiasm or reluctance to share their opinions with others, the artificial nature of the question may trigger answers that don't reflect what people do or don't do in typical conversations. Cornell University communication professor Carroll Glynn and two colleagues performed a meta-analysis of 17 studies that correlated people's perception of support for their opinion with their stated willingness to speak out in a train-test type of situation. The minuscule correlation ($r = .05$) gave scant confidence of any meaningful connection. Although the researchers aren't ready to dismiss the theory, they conclude that "future research on the spiral of silence should concentrate on observations of actual willingness to speak out as opposed to hypothetical willingness."[22]

3.   Focusing on national climate rather than reference group opinion. Noelle-Neumann insists that public opinion is what we perceive to be the judgment of *strangers in an anonymous public;* that's the force that constrains what we say.[23] Critics counter that the apparent mood of the nation exerts less pressure than do the attitudes of family, friends, and other reference groups. For example, consider the ostracizing force that a few devout evangelicals or Roman Catholics in the United States might fear within their church fellowship if they took a public pro-choice stance on abortion. The fact that legalized abortion is the law of the land and that a majority of Americans support *Roe v. Wade* wouldn't temper the threat. A recent study of attitudes toward affirmative action suggests that it's "perceptions of opinion in the 'micro-climate' of one's family and friends that are most closely linked to one's willingness to speak out."[24]

Do these flaws isolate Noelle-Neumann within the field of communication or render her theory invalid? Definitely not, but the criticisms do suggest the wisdom of changing the research paradigm for testing its predictions. A recent study conducted by Dietram Scheufele, a communication professor at Cornell University, addressed these three major flaws in spiral of silence inquiry. While sampling perceptions of public opinion toward biotechnology, his research team measured fear of isolation—treating it as a variable to be tested rather than assuming it was present. They also determined willingness to speak out through participants' responses to a real-life invitation to join a focus group discussing the pros and cons of biotech gene manipulation. And finally, the researchers questioned participants about prior conversations they might have had about the topic with people in their reference groups. With these corrective procedures in place, perception of public opinion proved to be a much better predictor of willingness to speak out than had been seen in the 17 survey studies referred to earlier.[25] The spiral of silence is alive and well in the twenty-first century.

Noelle-Neumann is not surprised when her theory pans out. In addition to her own survey research, she has culled the writings of philosophers and social historians to assemble evidence to support her theory. She draws upon the insights of Enlightenment thinkers Locke, Hume, Rousseau, Goethe, and James Madison in the *Federalist Papers* to illustrate the force and consolidation of public opinion. She found that Alexis de Tocqueville, in his nineteenth-century analysis of the decline of religion before the French Revolution, was probably the first to describe the entire spiraling process:

> People still clinging to the old faith were afraid of being the only ones who did so, and as they were more frightened of isolation than of committing an error, they joined the masses even though they did not agree with them. In this way, the opinion of only part of the population seemed to be the opinion of all and everybody, and exactly for this reason seemed irresistible to those who were responsible for this deceptive appearance.[26]

But just as compelling are the words that nonconformist Henry David Thoreau wrote about his own civil disobedience: "It is always easy to break the law, but even the Bedouins in the desert find it impossible to resist public opinion."[27]

QUESTIONS TO SHARPEN YOUR FOCUS

1. Noelle-Neumann writes that *public opinions are attitudes or behaviors one must express in public if one is not to isolate oneself.* What basic assumptions of her theory are embedded in this description?

2. According to Noelle-Neumann, under what conditions is our *quasi-statistical sixth sense* uncannily correct? When is it prone to lead us into *pluralistic ignorance?*

3. Based on Noelle-Neumann's *train/plane test,* under what circumstances would you expect it likely that a person would remain silent about a controversial issue?

4. On a *controversial moral issue,* have you ever been part of a small vocal minority that didn't *spiral into silence?* Which term best describes you as you spoke out? (a) hard core (b) avant-garde (c) shameless (d) clueless

A SECOND LOOK

Recommended resource: Elisabeth Noelle-Neumann, "The Theory of Public Opinion: The Concept of the Spiral of Silence," in *Communication Yearbook 14*, James A. Anderson (ed.), Sage, Newbury Park, CA, 1991, pp. 256–287.

Full statement: Elisabeth Noelle-Neumann, *The Spiral of Silence: Public Opinion—Our Social Skin*, 2nd ed., University of Chicago, Chicago, 1993.

Conformity pressure: Solomon E. Asch, "Effects of Group Pressure upon the Modification and Distortion of Judgments," in *Group Dynamics: Research and Theory*, Dorwin Cartwright and Alvin Zander (eds.), Row, Peterson, Evanston, IL, 1953, pp. 151–162.

Fear of isolation: Kurt Neuwirth, Edward Frederick, and Charles Mayo, "The Spiral of Silence and Fear of Isolation," *Journal of Communication*, Vol. 57, 2007, pp. 450–468.

Role of mass media: Elisabeth Noelle-Neumann, "Mass Media and Social Change in Developed Societies," in *Mass Media and Social Change*, Elihu Katz and Tamas Szecsko (eds.), Sage, London, 1981, pp. 137–166.

Hard-core minorities: Serge Moscovici, "Silent Majorities and Loud Minorities," in *Communication Yearbook 14*, James A. Anderson (ed.), Sage, Newbury Park, CA, 1991, pp. 298–308.

Empirical support: Dietram Scheufele, James Shanahan, and Eunjung Lee, "Real Talk: Manipulating the Dependent Variable in Spiral of Silence Research," *Communication Research*, Vol. 28, 2001, pp. 304–324.

Classical testimony: Elisabeth Noelle-Neumann, "Public Opinion and the Classical Tradition: A Reevaluation," *Public Opinion Quarterly*, Vol. 43, 1979, pp. 143–156.

Carter-Reagan election study: Carroll Glynn and Jack McLeod, "Public Opinion du Jour: An Examination of the Spiral of Silence," *Public Opinion Quarterly*, Vol. 48, 1984, pp. 731–740.

Powerful effects–minimal effects: Elisabeth Noelle-Neumann, "The Effect of Media on Media Effects Research," *Journal of Communication*, Vol. 33, No. 3, 1983, pp. 157–165.

Comparative cross-culture study: Huiping Huang, "A Cross-Cultural Test of the Spiral of Silence," *International Journal of Public Opinion Research*, Vol. 12, 2005, pp. 324–345.

Backdrop of theory's development: Christopher Simpson, "Elisabeth Noelle-Neumann's 'Spiral of Silence' and the Historical Context of Communication Theory," *Journal of Communication*, Vol. 46, No. 3, 1996, pp. 149–173.

Critique: Dietram Scheufele and Patricia Moy, "Twenty-Five Years of the Spiral of Silence: A Conceptual Review and Empirical Outlook," *International Journal of Public Opinion Research*, Vol. 12, 2000, pp. 3–28.

To access a list of key names in each chapter,
click on Instructor's Manual at
www.afirstlook.com.

DIVISION FIVE

Cultural Context

When we think of *culture,* most of us picture a place—the South American culture of Brazil, the Middle Eastern culture of Saudi Arabia, or the Far Eastern culture of Japan. But Gerry Philipsen, a professor of communication at the University of Washington who specializes in intercultural communication, says that culture is not basically geographical. Nor is it essentially political or a matter of race. Philipsen describes *culture* as "a socially constructed and historically transmitted pattern of symbols, meanings, premises, and rules."[1] At root, culture is a code.

Ethnographers study the speech and nonverbal communication of people in order to crack that code. We've already looked at Mead's reliance on participant observation (see Chapter 5) and Geertz' use of thick description (see Chapter 19) to unravel the complex web of meanings that people share within a society or culture. In like manner, Philipsen spent three years in a multiethnic, blue-collar Chicago neighborhood studying what it means to speak like a man in "Teamsterville," home of the late mayor Richard J. Daley and a place where the "Grabowski fans" of Mike Ditka's football world feel at home. Communication there is used to show solidarity with friends who are part of the neighborhood.[2]

After completing his ethnographic research in Teamsterville, Philipsen spent more than a year studying the communication patterns of a dispersed group he called the "Nacirema" (*American* spelled backward). He found a ritualized form of their metacommunication—talk about talk—on display five times a week in the daytime television talk show *Donahue,* a forerunner to *Oprah.* Together with University of Massachusetts communication professor Donal Carbaugh, Philipsen discovered that any appeal to a universal standard of ethical conduct was considered by persons in the audience to be an infringement of their right to be unique individuals. The ultimate issue of every conversation on *Donahue* was the presentation of *self.*[3]

For many years the *Donahue* show was filmed in a Chicago television studio located within 5 miles of Teamsterville, yet the two cultures these communities reflect seem to be worlds apart. Philipsen was not content to merely describe the contrasting cultures he studied; he wanted to develop a general theory that would explore the relationship between communication and culture. Chapter 32 presents his *speech codes theory,* which seeks to explain—and even predict—the discourse within a language community.

Is there a way to measure the relative discrepancy between any two patterns of communication or systems of meanings—between two cultures? From a study of multinational corporations in more than 50 countries, Dutch researcher Geert Hofstede concluded that there are four crucial dimensions on which to compare cultures.[4]

1. *Power distance*—the extent to which the less powerful members of society accept that power is distributed unequally (Americans—small; Japanese—medium)

2. *Masculinity*—clearly defined sex roles with male values of success, money, and things dominant in society (Americans—high; Japanese—extremely high)

3. *Uncertainty avoidance*—the extent to which people feel threatened by ambiguity and create beliefs and institutions to try to avoid it (Americans—low; Japanese—extremely high)

4. *Individualism*—people look out for themselves and their immediate families as opposed to identifying with a larger group that is responsible for taking care of them in exchange for group loyalty (Americans—extremely high; Japanese—low)

Many researchers agree that Hofstede's distinction between individualism and collectivism is the crucial dimension of cultural variability. The *we-centered* focus of Teamsterville sets it apart from individualistic American society in general, and from the extremely *I-centered* preoccupation of its Nacirema subculture in particular. Cultural anthropologist Edward Hall was the first to label the communication style of collectivistic cultures *high-context* and the style of individualistic cultures *low-context*. The designation divides groups of people on the basis of how they interpret messages.

> A high-context communication or message is one in which most of the information is either in the physical context or internalized in the person, while very little is in the coded, explicit part of the message. A low-context communication is just the opposite, i.e., the mass of information is vested in the explicit code.[5]

Hall contrasts American and Japanese cultures to illustrate the difference between collectivistic societies that have a message-*context* orientation and individualistic societies that rely more on message *content*.[6]

Americans believe in straight talk. Assertiveness is saying what you mean; honesty is meaning what you say. Both are highly prized. Perhaps the highest art form of explicit communication is the legal contract. A U.S. lawyer's dream is to prepare a verbal document that allows no room for interpretation. Hall says that Japanese communication is more subtle. Bluntness is regarded as rude; patience and indirection are the marks of a civilized person. What is said is less important than how it is said and who did the saying. Meaning is embedded in the setting and the nonverbal code. In Japan, the highest form of communication competency is empathy—the ability to sense what others are thinking and feeling without their having to spell it out for you.

The term *cross-cultural communication* is usually reserved for theory and research that compare specific interpersonal variables such as conversational distance, self-disclosure, and styles of conflict resolution across two or more different cultures. Chapter 31 presents Stella Ting-Toomey's *face-negotiation theory,*

© Zits Partnership. King Features Syndicate.

which distinguishes people's approach to conflict based on the individualistic or collectivistic orientation of their culture. Although her original theory reflects a cross-cultural approach to communication, subsequent versions also suggest ways of bridging cultural differences.

Howard Giles' *communication accommodation theory* is also concerned with intercultural encounters where parties think in terms of either their personal identity or their social identity. Giles suggests that people who see themselves as unique individuals will adjust their speech style and content to mesh with the other in order to gain their approval. Conversely, when people who have a strong group identification interact with folks outside the group, the theory predicts that they'll speak in a way that accentuates their differences. Chapter 30 outlines when each of these intercultural approaches will be employed and predicts whether the response will be positive or negative.

CHAPTER 30

Communication Accommodation Theory

of Howard Giles

I was born, raised, and educated in the Great Lakes region of the United States. During my sophomore year of college, my folks moved from the south side of Chicago to the Deep South, a region where the style of speech was foreign to my ear. When speaking with other college students I met there over summer vacation, I noticed that I started to talk slower, pause longer, maintain less eye contact, and drop the final *g* off of words ending with *ing* ("Nice *talkin'* with you"). Although I didn't adopt a southern drawl, I definitely adjusted my style of speaking to better match that of those I met. As an outsider, I wanted to fit in.

Although I couldn't lose my Chicago twang, one of the guys I met commented on my go-along-to-get-along effort. "You're beginning to talk just like us," he said. His smile suggested appreciation rather than scorn. Not so my older sister when I drove her from San Antonio, Texas, to Anniston, Alabama, the following Christmas. "You sound ridiculous," was her disdainful reaction when she heard me talk to people in restaurants and motels along the way.

In 1973, Welsh social psychologist Howard Giles suggested that my experience was typical. Now a professor of communication at the University of California, Santa Barbara, Giles claimed that when two people from different ethnic or cultural groups interact, they tend to accommodate each other in the way they speak in order to gain the other's approval.[1] He specifically focused on the nonverbal adjustments of speech rate, accent, and pauses. Based on the principle that we tend to like others who strike us as similar, Giles claimed that speech accommodation is a frequently used strategy to gain the appreciation of people who are from different groups or cultures. This process of seeking approval by meshing with another's style of speaking is at the core of what he then labeled *speech accommodation theory.*

387

A SIMPLE NOTION BECOMES A COMPREHENSIVE COMMUNICATION THEORY

Giles and his colleagues launched an extensive program of lab and field research to answer the questions that the practice of speech accommodation raises. For example:

Are there times we don't adjust our speech style to match that of others?

If so, what is our motive for not accommodating?

How do groups with which we identify affect our accommodation choices?

Is accommodation always conscious?

Do others accurately perceive our intent when we shift our speech style?

To what extent do we adjust *what* we say as well as the *way* we say it?

What are the social consequences if we overaccommodate?

Because the answers to these questions led Giles to communication issues that go far beyond the narrow issue of accent mobility, pauses, and pronunciation, the scope of the theory expanded dramatically. In 1987 Giles changed the name of the theory to *communication accommodation theory (CAT)* and offered it as "a theory of intercultural communication that actually attends to communication."[2]

Accommodation
The constant movement toward or away from others by changing your communicative behavior.

The early research of Giles and his colleagues centered on interethnic communication, often between two bilingual groups in the same country. For example, psychologist Richard Bourhis at the University of Quebec in Montreal studied which language French-Canadian and English-Canadian pedestrians in that city used when responding to a request for directions.[3] In the last two decades, however, CAT researchers have also shown a consistent interest in exploring *communication accommodation* in an intergenerational context. They broadly define *young* communicators as those who are teenagers up to adults in their 40s or even 50s. They define *old* or *elderly* communicators as those who are 65 and over.[4] To what extent do members of these two groups adjust their communication when talking to someone of the other generation?

Since the vast majority of this book's readers fall within that younger classification, I'll use intergenerational communication to illustrate the main predictions of the theory. That way you'll have a personal stake in understanding the theory's claims. So will I. In the spirit of full disclosure, you should know that for the past five years I've qualified as a member of the elder group. Of course this means that every communication theory class I teach is a potential laboratory to explore intergenerational communication. I also have ongoing experience in the other direction. My wife's 99-year-old mother has lived with us for the past four years.

COMMUNICATION ACCOMMODATION STRATEGIES

Throughout the theory's extensive development, Giles has consistently contrasted two strategic forms of communication that diverse people use when they interact—*convergence* and *divergence*. He sees both types of behavior as accommodation because they each involve a constant movement toward or away from others through a change in communicative behavior.

Convergence

Convergence is a strategy by which you adapt your communication behavior in such a way as to become more similar to another person. As we've already seen, one

Convergence
A strategy of adapting your communication behavior in such a way as to become more similar to another person.

way to do this is to adjust your speaking style to approximate that of your conversational partner. If you're talking with an octogenarian man who speaks in short phrases delivered in a gravelly voice, you could abandon smoothly flowing sentences in favor of brief, raspy responses. You wouldn't try to mimic his voice, but you'd try to get closer to its sound and cadence. Note how similar this idea is to constructivism's ideal of person-centered messages (see Chapter 8). In this case, however, it would be audience adaptation to reduce nonverbal differences. If the elderly man desires to converge toward your speaking style, he might need to speak with more energy, display greater facial expression, and increase vocal variety.

Another way you could converge toward the elderly gentleman would be to talk in a way that would make it easier for him to grasp what you're saying. If you notice that he's hard of hearing, convergence would involve speaking one notch louder, while clearly enunciating consonants. Or if he seems to have trouble tracking with abstract ideas, you could aid his comprehension by using examples to illustrate what you're saying. For his part, he might help you interpret what he's saying by not assuming you know the political background of the Korean War or Snooky Lanson's style of singing on *Your Hit Parade*.

An additional way to bridge the generation gap can be through *discourse management*—the sensitive selection of topics to discuss. Giles and Angie Williams (Cardiff University, Wales) elicited college students' retrospective accounts of both satisfying and frustrating intergenerational conversations. They found that young people greatly appreciated the elderly when they discerned what stories the students wanted to hear. For example, one girl wrote, "She just talked about the history of the team and all that she knew. . . . I stayed and listened to her stories, which were fascinating."[5] They also appreciated elders who sensed when not to pry: "I'm glad she didn't ask anything about Bekki and my relationship. . . . I would have felt awkward."[6]

Although not part of the original theory, CAT researchers now regard communication that meets the emotional needs of another as a clear case of convergence. For most young people who spend time with a senior citizen, that means the elderly person being "supportive, listening, and attentive to the younger person, giving compliments, and telling interesting stories."[7] In the absence of CAT research surveying the emotional needs of those over 65, one has to assume that many of these communication behaviors would also strike the elderly as accommodating.

Divergence

Divergence
A communication strategy of accentuating the differences between yourself and another person.

Divergence is a communication strategy of accentuating the differences between yourself and another person. In interethnic encounters, you might insist on using a language or dialect with which the other is uncomfortable. In terms of speech style, you could diverge by employing a thicker accent, adopting a rate of speaking distinct from that used by the other person, or speaking in either a monotone or with exaggerated animation. Linguistically, divergence could be signaled by a deliberate substitution of words. Giles offers an example where a young speaker flippantly says to an elderly man, "Okay, mate, let's get it together at my place around 3:30 tomorrow." The disdainful elder might reply, "Fine, young man, we'll meet again at 15:30, at your house tomorrow."[8] All of these communication moves are examples of counter-accommodation—direct ways of maximizing the difference between two speakers.

"Hey, Gramps, is 'deathbed' one word or two?"

Self-handicapping
For the elderly, a face-saving strategy that invokes age as a reason for not performing well.

Maintenance
Persisting in your original communication style regardless of the communication behavior of the other; similar to divergence; underaccommodation.

During intergenerational encounters, CAT researchers have found that divergence is the norm and convergence the exception, especially when the two aren't members of the same family. Young people typically characterize the elderly as *closed-minded, out of touch, angry, complaining,* and *negatively stereotyping youth.*[9] The elderly often increase the social distance through the process of *self-handicapping*—a defensive, face-saving strategy that uses age as a reason for not performing well. Coupland et al. cite multiple comments from a frail elderly woman that may not only justify her low level of competence, but also increase her social distance from the younger woman who's visiting her: *I can't do that anymore; these old bones won't . . . ; over the last few years, I just can't remember as well as . . . ;* and so on.[10]

Giles and his colleagues describe two other forms of divergence that are a bit more subtle. *Maintenance* (or *underaccommodation*) is the strategy of persisting in your original communication style regardless of the communication behavior of the other. Although the original speech accommodation theory defined maintenance as a strategy distinct from convergence or divergence, subsequent research has shown that it has roughly the same effect as divergence, so I list it here. Giles offers a college student's recollections of a dissatisfying conversation with a senior citizen as a description of underaccommodation: "He did most of the talking and did not really seem to care about what I said. . . . He appeared to be so closed minded and unreceptive to new ideas."[11] Conversely, an older person is likely to feel woefully underaccommodated if she shares a fear or frustration and then only hears a quick, "I know exactly how you feel," before the younger person changes the topic.[12]

The other form of divergence is *overaccommodation*, which may be well-intended, but has the effect of making the recipient feel worse. Giles describes overaccommodation as "demeaning or patronizing talk . . . when excessive concern is paid to vocal clarity or amplitude, message simplification, or repetition"[13] Often characterized as "baby talk," this way of talking can frustrate the elderly, thus leading to a perception that they are irritable or grumpy. Alternatively, frequent overaccommodation from caregivers can not only make the recipient feel less competent, but actually talk them into becoming less so (see Chapter 5).

Overaccommodation
Demeaning or patronizing talk; excessive concern paid to vocal clarity or amplitude, message simplification, or repetition.

If overaccommodating communication is often counterproductive and sometimes harmful, why do younger folks talk that way? For that matter, other than sheer obstinacy, why would old or young people opt for any kind of divergent strategy rather than one that's convergent? The next section shows that the motivation for these contrasting behaviors is tied to people's concern for their identity.

DIFFERENT MOTIVATIONS FOR CONVERGENCE AND DIVERGENCE

As the first page of this chapter indicates, CAT theorists have always regarded *desire for social approval* as the main motivation for convergence. You meet a person different than you and you'd like him or her to think well of you, respect you, or find you attractive. As one of the theorems of *uncertainty reduction theory* states, there's a positive relationship between similarity and attraction (see Chapter 10). So you identify with the other person by adjusting what you say and the way you say it in order to appear more similar. As long as you're both acting as unique individuals who are shaping their own personal identities and relationships, representing convergence as a two-step, cause-and-effect relationship seems justified:

Desire for approval (personal identity) → Convergence → Positive response

There are two problems, however. First, this motivational sequence can't explain why we frequently communicate in a divergent way, and second, the causal chain doesn't take into account the fact that we often act as a representative of a group. Giles and other CAT theorists draw upon *social identity theory*, the work of Henri Tajfel (University of Bristol, UK) and John Turner (Macquarie University, Australia) to solve that problem.[14]

Social Identity Theory

Social identity
Group memberships and social categories that we use to define who we are.

Tajfel and Turner suggest that we often communicate not as individual actors, but as representatives of groups that help define who we are. Our *social identity* is based upon our intergroup behavior. As University of Arizona communication professor Jake Harwood puts it, "We are not random individuals wandering the planet with no connections to others, and our connections to others cannot be understood purely as a function of individual phenomena."[15] Our group memberships—whether formal associations or allegiances only in our minds—can greatly affect our communication.

As a case in point, if you click on "Meet and Email Em" at *www.afirstlook. com*, you'll find that I identify with groups of communication professors, conflict mediators, people of faith, pilots, an extended Griffin family, and those who work for economic justice in the developing world. By accident of birth, I also have at least four other group identifications; I'm an older, white, American male. According to Tajfel and Turner, whenever any of these associations comes to mind when I talk with others, my motivation will be to reinforce and defend my ties to those groups. After all, they make up my social identity. And when these groups are salient at the start of an interaction with someone different, CAT claims that my communication will diverge away from my partner's speech rather than converge toward it.

Tajfel and Turner picture a motivational continuum with *personal identity* on one end of the scale and *social identity* at the other pole. As long as both parties consider themselves and their conversational partner as unencumbered, autonomous individuals acting for themselves, the theorists believe the *desire for approval → convergence → positive response* sequence is what takes place. But if one (or both) of the interactants regards self or other as a representative of a group of people, then Tajfel and Turner say that their communication will likely become divergent because of their need to emphasize their distinctiveness. So when group identity is salient, the two-step, cause-and-effect sequence is quite different:

Need for distinctiveness (social identity) → Divergence → Negative response

Giles and his colleagues believe that this alternative sequence occurs quite frequently. They hold out the possibility that a person could seek approval and distinctiveness within the same conversation when their personal and social identities are both salient. For example, consider an interracial friendship where buddies never lose sight of their ethnicity. Or think of a loving marriage where both husband and wife are keenly aware of their sex roles. But your first look at communication accommodation theory will come into focus more easily if we stick with Tajfel and Turner's either/or conception of one of the two motivations holding sway in a given interaction. To the extent that this is so, how can we predict whether concerns for personal identity or social identity will kick in? According to Giles there's no hard-and-fast rule. But a person's *initial orientation* is a somewhat reliable predictor.

Initial orientation
Communicators' predisposition to focus on either their individual identity or group identity during a conversation.

Initial Orientation

Initial orientation is the predisposition a person has toward focusing on either individual identity or group identity. Predicting which route a person will take is difficult, but the additive presence of five factors increases the odds that a communicator will see the conversation as an intergroup encounter. I'll continue to illustrate these factors by referring to intergenerational encounters.

1. Collectivistic cultural context. As noted in the introduction to this intercultural communication section, the distinction between collectivistic and individualistic cultures is probably the crucial dimension of cultural variability. The *we-centered* focus of collectivism emphasizes similarity and mutual concern within the culture—definitely oriented toward social identity. Their communication toward outgroup members is often divergent. The *I-centered* focus of individualistic cultures valorizes the individual actor— definitely oriented toward individual identity. So all things being equal, people raised in Pacific Rim countries such as Japan, Korea, China, and the Philippines will regard a stranger from another land as a member of a homogeneous outgroup and will assume that these outsiders will respond the same way. People from individualistic cultures such as the United States, Canada, Australia, and Germany are less likely to see the foreign visitor as a tiny replica of his or her culture. As for intergenerational relationships, despite the cultural value of respect for elders shared among East Asian cultures, there's strong evidence that Pacific Rim young people and their Western counterparts both regard the elderly as a group apart.[16] Age transcends ethnic culture.

2.   **Distressing history of interaction.** If previous interactions were uncomfortable, competitive, or hostile, both interactants will tend to ascribe that outcome to the other person's social identity. *(Men are like that. The poor are lazy. Presbyterians are God's frozen people.)* If the previous time together was positive, the result is often ascribed to the individual rather than to a group or class to which he or she belongs. *(By the end I felt good knowing that not all older people hate the younger generation. The fact that he was content and that old satisfied me. Every other elder I've talked to has made me fear or want to avoid getting old.)*[17]

3.   **Stereotypes.** The more specific and negative the images that people have of an outgroup, the more likely they are to think of the other in terms of social identity and then resort to divergent communication. This is a big factor in intergenerational communication. The young tend to stereotype the elderly as *irritable, nagging, grouchy, verbose,* and *addled.*[18] Conversely, the elderly stereotype "youth today" as *spoiled,* an accusation often introduced with the phrase, *Why, when I was your age. . . .* These rigid group stereotypes make convergent communication across generations a rare and difficult achievement.

Norms

Expectations about behavior that members of a community feel should (or should not) occur in particular situations.

4.   **Norms for treatment of groups.** Norms can be defined as "expectations about behavior that members of a community feel should (or should not) occur in particular situations."[19] These expectations can affect whether a member of one group regards a person from another group as an individual or as "one of them." The oft-stated rule to "respect your elders" suggests that the elderly are a group of people who deserve high regard because they've stayed alive, rather than because they have individual worth. The result of that group norm may be young adults showing deference to an elderly person, but *biting their tongue* and *not talking back.* That would be convergence without satisfaction. In the process the young could build up resentment toward a group that they may join someday.

5.   **High group solidarity / high group dependence.** Picture Lucile, a 70-year-old widow living in a small retirement village where residents rely on each other for social, emotional, and even physical well-being. As the organizer of a successful food co-op, she's at the nexus of communication and has a higher status among her neighbors than she's ever had before. When a young county health department official questions the co-op's food handling practices, Lucile goes to talk with him in what she regards as an us-against-them encounter. Giles would predict that she would have an initial intergroup orientation because of her strong identification with the group and her high dependence on it for relational warmth and a sense of worth.[20]

No single factor determines a person's initial orientation, yet if all five factors line up in the direction of public identity, they make it almost certain that a communicator will approach a conversation with an intergroup mindset. That seems to be the case in most intergenerational interactions. Giles would note, however, that a person may change orientations during a conversation.

RECIPIENT EVALUATION OF CONVERGENCE AND DIVERGENCE

Let's start with the bottom line. After 35 years of multiple revisions, restatements, and research studies, Giles and his colleagues continue to believe what he wrote about accommodation in his first monograph—that listeners regard convergence as positive and divergence as negative. Specifically, converging speakers are viewed as more competent, attractive, warm, and cooperative.[21] On the other hand, "divergence is often seen by its recipients as insulting, impolite, or downright hostile."[22] Yet CAT researchers are quick to remind us that accommodation is in the eyes and ears of the beholder. What's ultimately important is not how the communicator converged or diverged, but how the other *perceived* the communicator's behavior.

Objective Versus Subjective Accommodation

Early in his research, Giles realized that there was a disconnect between the communication behavior that he and other neutral researchers observed and what participants heard and saw. He described the gap as the difference between *objective* and *subjective* accommodation. For example, a speaker's accent, rate, pitch, and length of pauses could actually be shifting toward a conversational partner's style of speaking, but the partner might regard it as divergent. In light of this discrepancy, Giles says that it's recipients' subjective evaluation that really matters, because that's what will shape their response.

Speakers who desire to seek approval by converging with the other's way of speaking may also misperceive what that style really is. From an objective point of view, what strikes them as the other group's preferred style of communication may woefully miss the mark. For example, a granddad might try to identify with his grandkids by using phrases like *right on, really hep,* or *that's square*, not realizing that these phrases were more typical of teenagers in the late 1960s than of teens today. Giles notes that "one does not converge toward (or diverge from) the *actual* speech of the recipient, but toward (from) one's *stereotype* about the recipient's speech."[23]

Attribution Theory

Our response to others' communication hinges not only on the behavior we perceive, but also on the intention or motive we ascribe to them for speaking that way. Giles draws from *attribution theory* to cast light on how we'll interpret our conversational partners' convergent or divergent behavior. In two different versions of attribution theory, social psychologists Fritz Heider (University of Kansas) and Harold Kelley (UCLA) suggest that we attribute an internal disposition to the behavior we see another enact.[24] As amateur psychologists, our default assumption is that *people who do things like that are like that*. Yet three mitigating factors may come into play: (1) the other's ability, (2) external constraints, and (3) the effort expended.

Attribution
The perceptual process by which we observe what people do and then try to figure out their intent or disposition.

Suppose you're talking with an elderly man who continually asks you to repeat what you've said. If you know that his hearing is good (high ability) and the room is quiet (no external constraints), yet he's not paying much attention (low effort), you'll attribute his divergent behavior to his lack of respect for you. You'll be more understanding if you know he's hard of hearing (low ability). But as one research study shows, you'll still be irritated by his lack of consideration if he freely chooses not to wear a hearing aid (low effort).[25] What if you know he's almost deaf (low ability), the room is noisy (environmental constraint), and he's wearing a hearing aid and still struggling to catch your words (high effort)? You'll probably appreciate the fact that he cares about what you're saying and wants to understand, even if you find the conversation tiring or uncomfortable.

Overall, listeners who interpret convergence as a speaker's desire to break down cultural barriers react quite favorably.[26] That response is at the core of CAT. But because there's a societal constraint or norm that those with less power (workers, patients, students, immigrants) ought to accommodate to the communication practices of those with higher status (bosses, doctors, professors, citizens), upward convergers don't get as much credit as when status is relatively equal. Still, this moderate reaction is much more favorable than the response toward a low-power person who adopts a divergent strategy. As a case in point, consider the anger of many Anglo-Americans toward Latin-American immigrants who "refuse" to become bilingual.

There are benefits and costs to both convergent and divergent strategies. CAT research continues to document the positive interpersonal relationship development that can result from appropriate convergence. The practice also facilitates better comprehension and understanding. But these gains come at the potential risk of offending other in-group members, just as my sister was disgusted by my attempt to talk as a "down-home" southerner. They may feel that converging toward an out-group is diverging from them. And of course, the one who accommodates may also feel a sense of inauthenticity.

The interpersonal tension that is created by divergence or maintenance can certainly block the formation of intergroup or intercultural relationships and understanding. But the upside for the communicator is the reaffirmed social identity and solidarity that comes from enacting a divergent strategy. In that sense, divergence is an accommodation strategy just as much as convergence, but it's accommodation to the in-group rather than members of the out-group.

CAT'S VIEW OF AGE-OLD STEREOTYPES

Giles' CAT provides a theoretical basis for pursuing intergenerational communication research and practice. The theory claims that when people are constantly aware of each other's discrepant group ties, the style and content of their talk will diverge and inhibit the growth of interpersonal closeness. Based on the findings of multiple studies inspired by CAT, that's indeed what happens when young and old interact. For example, University of Arizona communication professor Jake Harwood and two colleagues discovered that many of the ways that the elderly talk continually remind younger listeners that their grandparents are old.[27]

1. Talk about age: *You're so young. I turn 70 next December.*
2. Talk about health: *They warned of blood clots with my hip replacement surgery.*

3. **Don't understand the world today:** *When you say IM, do you mean intramural?*
4. **Patronizing:** *You kids today don't know the meaning of hard work.*
5. **Painful self-disclosure:** *I cried when she said that to me. It still hurts.*
6. **Difficulty hearing:** *Please speak up and try not to mumble.*
7. **Mental confusion:** *I can't think of the word. What were we talking about?*

These features consistently make the speakers' age salient for the listener, and all seven leave a negative impression. They might just as well tattoo GZR on their foreheads. In fact, many young people are hard-pressed to recall an instance when an elderly person tried to adapt their style to reach out to them. Consistent with CAT's claim, when young listeners do experience an instance of accommodative speech, they usually ascribe it to an unusual senior who didn't "talk old."

In their communication with the elderly, those who are younger typically feel a sense of obligation to adapt to the old person's interests and capabilities. They may do so, but often reluctantly. This leaves a residue of boredom, frustration, or anger. Yet since they see their conversational partner as stereotypically old, their attempts to converge often result in overaccommodation, where they treat the mature senior as a child. Giles reports a study of 33 women ages 65–94 in which 40 percent of them reported being talked down to or patronized.[28] According to Giles, this kind of demeaning talk is not merely irritating.

> The danger of overaccommodating the elderly is that it may act as a sort of self-fulfilling prophecy. By treating an older person in a way that denigrates his or her capacities, it may cause the person to view themselves in the same way.[29] If an older person is subject to being overaccommodated and condescended to in a variety of situations, it will take a very resilient person indeed not to accept this categorization of themselves as "old" and "past it."[30]

How can young and old break this discouraging cycle? In addition to Giles' aforementioned advice to *listen, be supportive,* and *offer compliments,* Harwood discovered three types of conversational approaches that don't signal "old" and that are appreciated by grandkids. They are telling entertaining stories from the past (without rambling), offering tidbits of wisdom from their experience without moralizing, and talking about one of their grandkids' parents when he or she was young.[31] As for those who aren't elderly, Giles suggests that a realistic, doable, and important practical goal "should be to treat older people as individuals rather than as positive or negative representations of a social group."[32] If they can adopt that approach, they may end up experiencing what one of Giles' informants reported: "Our dramatic age difference did not matter."[33]

A final note of encouragement and/or caution. I've used intergenerational communication to illustrate communication accommodation theory because senior citizenship is the one minority group that hopefully all of us will have a chance to experience. As the punch line of the longstanding joke about old age goes, "It sure beats the alternative." I'm finding it a delightful time of life. But the principles that CAT puts forth apply equally to any type of intercultural encounter between people from different countries, races, sexes, economic classes, religions, ethnicities, or educational backgrounds. If communication with the elderly is a rare experience for you, I encourage you to apply the theory to your communication in one of these other intercultural arenas.

CRITIQUE: ENORMOUS SCOPE AT THE COST OF CLARITY

From a modest beginning as a narrowly conceived theory of social psychology, communication accommodation theory has morphed into a communication theory of enormous scope. Giles' adoption of *social identity theory of group behavior and attribution theory,* which are essential to CAT's explanation of accommodation, demonstrates that Giles' theory has never abandoned its social psych roots. It's appropriate, therefore, to use the five criteria for good social science theories presented at the start of the book to evaluate CAT.

1. Explanation of data. CAT not only describes communication behavior, it explains why it happens. The dual theoretical engines of *desire for approval* and *need to maintain a distinctive social identity* are compelling reasons for two very different communication strategies. Further, Giles and his colleagues offer multiple factors to clarify which motivation will kick in at any given time. You should know, however, that I've greatly oversimplified 35 years of theorizing and research so that the uninitiated can make sense of it on a first look. Glancing at the recurring names of multiple scholars in the Second Look and Endnotes sections will also convince you that the theory has been a hugely cooperative effort—not just the work of Giles.

2. Prediction of the future. Giles doesn't shy away from forecasting what will happen in specific situations. As the scope of the theory has expanded, he's found it necessary to alter or qualify many of these predictions, but CAT places its bets ahead of time. As a communication scholar who was first trained in experimental methodology, I find this put-up-or-shut-up approach appealing. I also appreciate Giles' movement toward qualitative methods as he attempts to predict how recipients will interpret accommodating behavior.

3. Relative simplicity. CAT is an extraordinarily complex theory presented in multiple versions that are sometimes offered simultaneously. The fact that Giles is a co-author on almost every article or chapter published about the theory gives the illusion of unity—as well as justification for attributing almost every new idea to him. But as Cindy Gallois (University of Queensland, Australia), Tania Ogay (University of Geneva, Switzerland), and Giles admit in a summary chapter, CAT's "structure and the underlying terminology are not always represented consistently in texts and propositions."[34] Even the meaning of *accommodation* within the theory is slippery. Sometimes the term seems to be synonymous with convergence (as opposed to divergence), while other times it's used to refer to any adjustment of communication behavior. In the same chapter, Gallois, Ogay, and Giles take on the challenge of "explaining the increased propositional complexity in terms of a parsimonious and unique set of integrative principles."[35] The end result of this attempt to simplify is not for the faint of heart. In fairness, the authors could respond, "Intercultural communication is devilishly complicated. Let's not pretend it isn't."

4. Testable hypotheses. The complexity problem just raised spills over into the possibility of being able to demonstrate that the theory is false. In 1998, Gallois and Giles wrote:

> CAT has become very complex, so that the theory as a whole probably cannot be tested at one time. This means that researchers using CAT must develop mini-

theories to suit the contexts in which they work, while at the same time keeping the whole of the theory in mind.[36]

In their recent summary chapter they look back and admit that it's not clear what "the whole of the theory" actually is.[37] If they aren't sure, it's hard for others to know. *Falsifiable* it isn't.

5. Practical utility. Giles' application of the theory to intergenerational communication demonstrates CAT's usefulness in an important arena of human life. In choosing that issue to illustrate the theory, I opted for depth rather than breadth. But if you thought my focus on that topic was due to the theory's limited applicability, let me assure you that it's not. CAT can be beneficially applied to any situation where people from different groups or cultures come in contact.

QUESTIONS TO SHARPEN YOUR FOCUS

1. Can you think of a time when you found another's *divergence* in *speech style* delightful or another's *convergence* distressing?

2. To what extent is it possible to interact with another person and not have *age, sex, race, nationality, sexual orientation, religious commitment,* or *political ideology* be *salient* when you know that one or more of these differs from your own?

3. In what way might you *overaccommodate* to the *stereotypical image* you hold of opposite-sex communication behavior?

4. As you read about the actions and reactions of young people cited from *intergenerational research*, with which strategies and responses do you identify? Which do you believe are uncharacteristic of you?

SELF-QUIZ   *www.mhhe.com/griffin7*

A SECOND LOOK
Recommended resource: Howard Giles and Tania Ogay, "Communication Accommodation Theory," in *Explaining Communication: Contemporary Theories and Exemplars,* Bryan Whaley and Wendy Samter (eds.), Lawrence Erlbaum, Mahwah, NJ, 2007, pp. 293–310.

Original statement of speech accommodation theory: Howard Giles, "Accent Mobility: A Model and Some Data," *Anthropological Linguistics,* Vol. 15, 1973, pp. 87–109.

SAT expanded and renamed CAT: Howard Giles, Anthony Mulac, James Bradac, and Patricia Johnson, "Speech Accommodation Theory: The First Decade and Beyond," in *Communication Yearbook 10,* Margaret L. McLaughlin (ed.), Sage, Newbury Park, CA, 1987, pp. 13–48.

Propositional synthesis: Cindy Gallois, Tania Ogay, and Howard Giles, "Communication Accommodation Theory: A Look Back and a Look Ahead," in *Theorizing About Intercultural Communication,* William Gudykunst (ed.), Sage, Thousand Oaks, CA, 2005, pp. 121–148.

Social identity theory: Henri Tajfel and John C. Turner, "The Social Identity Theory of Intergroup Behavior," in *The Psychology of Intergroup Relations,* L. Worchel and W. Austin (eds.), Nelson Hall, Chicago, 1986, pp. 7–24.

Importance of social identity: Jake Harwood, "Communication as Social Identity," in *Communication as . . . Perspectives on Theory,* Gregory Shepherd, Jeffrey St. John, and Ted Striphas (eds.), Sage, Thousand Oaks, CA, 2006, pp. 84–90.

Intergenerational communication: Nikalos Coupland, Justine Coupland, Howard Giles, and Karen Henwood, "Accommodating the Elderly, Invoking and Extending a Theory," *Language and Society,* Vol. 17, 1988, pp. 1–41.

Intergenerational communication research: Angie Williams and Howard Giles, "Intergenerational Conversations: Young Adults' Retrospective Accounts," *Human Communication Research,* Vol. 23, 1996, pp. 220–250.

Accommodation within families: Jake Harwood, Jordan Soliz, and Mei-Chen Lin, "Communication Accommodation Theory: An Intergroup Approach to Family Relationships," in *Engaging Theories in Family Communication,* Dawn O. Braithwaite and Leslie A. Baxter (eds.), Sage, Thousand Oaks, CA, 2006, pp. 19–34.

Recent research and revised propositions: Howard Giles, Michael Willemyns, Cindy Gallois, and M.C. Anderson, "Accommodating a New Frontier: The Context of Law Inforcement," in *Social Communication,* Klaus Fiedler (ed.), Psychology Press, New York, 2007, pp. 129–162.

Face-Negotiation Theory

of Stella Ting-Toomey

For the past decade I've served as a volunteer mediator at a metropolitan center for conflict resolution. My role as a mediator is to help people in conflict reach a voluntary agreement that satisfies both sides. I'm neither a judge nor a counselor, and I work hard not to make moral judgments about who's right and who's wrong. As a mediator, I'm a neutral third party whose sole job is to facilitate the process of negotiation. That doesn't mean it's easy.

Most disputants come to the center in a last-ditch effort to avoid the cost and intimidation of a day in court. The service is free, and we do everything possible to take the threat out of the proceedings. But after failing or refusing to work out their differences on their own, people walk in the door feeling various degrees of anger, hurt, fear, confusion, and shame. On the one hand, they hope that the negotiation will help resolve their dispute. On the other hand, they doubt that talk around a table will soften hard feelings and change responses that seem to be set in stone.

The professional staff at the center instructs volunteers in a model of negotiation that maximizes the chance of people's reaching a mutually acceptable agreement. From the first day of training, the staff insists that "the mediator controls the process, not the outcome." Figure 31–1 lists some of the techniques that mediators use to ensure progress without suggesting the shape of the solution. Used artfully, the techniques work well. The majority of the negotiations end in freely signed and mutually kept agreements.

The model of negotiation doesn't work equally well for everyone, however. Although the center serves a multiethnic urban area, my colleagues and I have noticed that the number of people of Asian origin seeking conflict mediation is disproportionately small. On rare occasions when Japanese, Vietnamese, Chinese, or Koreans come to the office, they're more embarrassed than angry. If they do reach agreement, they seem more relieved that the conversation is over than pleased with the solution.

Stella Ting-Toomey's face-negotiation theory helps explain cultural differences in responses to conflict. A communication professor at California State University, Fullerton, Ting-Toomey assumes that people of every culture are always negotiating *face*. The term is a metaphor for our public self-image, the way we want others to see us and treat us. *Facework* refers to "specific verbal and non-verbal messages that help to maintain and restore face loss, and to uphold and

Face
The projected image of one's self in a relational situation.

Assure impartiality: "Since neither of you have met me before, I have no stake in what you decide."

Guarantee confidentiality: "What you say today is strictly between us. I'll rip up my notes before you go."

Display disputant equality: "Nate, thanks for not interrupting while Beth was telling her story. Now it's your turn. What do you want to tell me?"

Avoid 'why' questions: Harmful—"Why did you do that?" Helpful—"What would you like to see happen?"

Acknowledge emotions while defusing their force: "I can understand that you were bothered when you found the bike was broken."

Summarize frequently : "I'd like to tell you what I've heard you say. If I don't get it right, fill me in."

Hold individual private conferences: "I wanted to meet privately with you to see if there's anything you want to tell me in confidence that you didn't feel you could say with Beth in the room."

Reframe issues of "right" and "wrong" into interests: "Beth, I'm not sure I understand. Tell me, how will Nate's going to jail give you what you need?"

Brainstorm: "Let's see how many different solutions you can think of that might solve the problem. Just throw out any ideas you have and we'll sort through them later."

Perform a reality check: "Have you checked to see if the bike can be put back in mint condition?"

Consider the alternative: "What are you going to do if you don't reach an agreement today?"

Move toward agreement: "You've already agreed on a number of important issues. I'm going to begin to write them down."

FIGURE 31–1   Selected Techniques of Third-Party Mediation

Facework
Specific verbal and non-verbal messages that help to maintain and restore face loss, and to uphold and honor face gain.

honor face gain."[1] Our identity can always be called into question, and the anxiety and uncertainty churned up by conflict make us especially vulnerable. Face-negotiation theory postulates that the facework of people from individualistic cultures like the United States or Germany will be strikingly different from the facework of people from collectivistic cultures like Japan or China. Ting-Toomey's face-negotiation theory suggests that face maintenance is the crucial intervening variable that ties culture to people's ways of handling conflict. In the following sections of this chapter, I'll unpack the meaning of the four concepts that are linked together in the causal chain:

$$\text{Type of Culture} \rightarrow \text{Type of Self-Construal} \rightarrow \text{Type of Face Maintenance} \rightarrow \text{Type of Conflict Management}$$

COLLECTIVISTIC AND INDIVIDUALISTIC CULTURES

Ting-Toomey bases her face-negotiation theory on the distinction between *collectivism* and *individualism*. The most extensive differentiation between the two types of cultures has been made by University of Illinois psychologist Harry Triandis. He says that the three important distinctions between collectivistic and individualistic cultures are the different ways members perceive *self, goals,* and *duty*.[2]

Consider a man named Em. Collectivistic Em might think of himself as a father, Christian, and teacher. Individualistic Em would probably define himself simply as Em, independent of any group affiliation. Collectivistic Em wouldn't go against group goals, but his individualistic counterpart would naturally pursue personal interests. Collectivistic Em would have been socialized to enjoy duty that requires sacrifice in the service of others; individualistic Em would employ the minimax principle to determine a course of action that he would see as enjoyable and personally rewarding (see Chapter 9).

Collectivistic culture
Wherein people identify with a larger group that is responsible for providing care in exchange for group loyalty; *we*-identity; a high-context culture.

Individualistic culture
Wherein people look out for themselves and their immediate families; *I*-identity; a low-context culture.

More than two-thirds of the world's people are born into collectivistic cultures, while less than one-third of the population lives in individualistic cultures.[3] To help you draw a clearer mental picture of the distinctions, I'll follow the lead of cross-cultural researchers who cite Japan and the United States as classic examples of collectivistic and individualistic cultures, respectively. Note that it would be equally appropriate to use most countries in Asia, Africa, the Middle East, or Latin America to represent a collectivistic perspective. I could also insert Australia, Germany, Switzerland, or one of the Scandinavian societies as the model of an individualistic approach. It is Ting-Toomey's grouping of national cultures within the collectivistic and individualistic categories that separates her theory of conflict management from a mere listing of national characteristics, so feel free to make mental substitutions.

Triandis says that the Japanese value collective needs and goals over individual needs and goals. They assume that in the long run, each individual decision affects everyone in the group. Therefore, a person's behavior is controlled by the norms of the group. This *we*-identity of the Japanese is quite foreign to the *I*-identity of the American who values individualistic needs and goals over group needs and goals. The American's behavior is governed by the personal rules of a freewheeling self that is concerned with individual rights rather than group responsibilities. Marching to a different drummer is the rule in the United States, not the exception.

Triandis claims that the strong in-group identity of the Japanese people leads them to perceive others in us-them categories. It is more important for the Japanese to identify an outsider's background and group affiliation than the person's attitudes or feelings—not because they don't care about their guest, but because unique individual differences seem less important than group-based information. People raised in the United States show a different curiosity. They are filled with questions about the interior life of visitors from other cultures. What do they think? What do they feel? What do they plan to do? Americans assume that every person is unique, and they reduce uncertainty by asking questions to the point of cross-examination.

With this understanding of the differences between collectivistic and individualistic cultures in mind, read through the description of mediation techniques in Figure 31–1. Taken as a whole, the list provides a reliable window to the values that guide this type of conflict resolution. Participants who come to the conflict center are treated as responsible individuals who can make up their own minds about what they want. The mediator encourages antagonists to deal directly with their differences and keeps the conversation focused on the possibility of a final agreement. While the mediator is careful never to pressure clients to reach an accord, the climate of immediacy suggests this is their best chance to put the whole mess behind them in an acceptable way and get on with their lives. The mediator works hard to make sure that the individual rights of both parties are respected.

Whether or not disputants reach an agreement, the mediation approach outlined in Figure 31–1 offers a safe place where no one need feel embarrassed—at least no one from an individualistic American culture! As it turns out, the open discussion of conflict, encouragement to voice specific needs and interests, and the explicit language used to document any agreement all make the process quite uncomfortable for people raised in a high-context culture. No wonder potential clients from collectivistic cultures stay away or leave dissatisfied.

SELF-CONSTRUAL: VARIED SELF-IMAGES WITHIN A CULTURE

Self-construal
Self-image; the degree to which people conceive of themselves as relatively autonomous from, or connected to, others.

People aren't cultural clones. Just as cultures vary along a scale anchored by individualistic or collectivistic orientations, so, too, do their members. Ting-Toomey emphasizes that people *within* a culture differ on the relative emphasis they place on individual self-sufficiency or group solidarity. She uses the terms *independent* and *interdependent self* to refer to "the degree to which people conceive of themselves as relatively autonomous from, or connected to, others."[4] Psychologists Hazel Markus and Shinobu Kitayama call this dimension *self-construal*, or the more familiar term *self-image*.[5]

The independent self values *I*-identity and is more self-face oriented, so this concept of self is prevalent within individualistic cultures like the United States. Yet due to the ethnic diversity of American society, there are people raised in the United States who are highly interdependent. The interdependent self values *we*-identity, emphasizes relational connectedness, and is therefore closely aligned with collectivism. Yet again, it would be dangerous to stereotype all members of a collectivist society as having the same self-construal. Culture is an overall framework for faceconcern, but individuals within a culture have different images of self as well as varied views on the degree to which they give others face or restore their own face in conflict situations.

The relational reality of self-image differences within two cultures is represented in the following diagram. Each circle (●) stands for the self-construal of a person raised in a collectivistic society that socializes its members to be interdependent and includes everyone in face concerns. Each triangle (▲) stands for the self-construal of a person raised in an individualistic culture that stresses independence and self-reliance. The cultures are obviously different. But the overlap shows that an American might have a self-image more interdependent than a person raised in Japan with a relatively high independent self-construal.

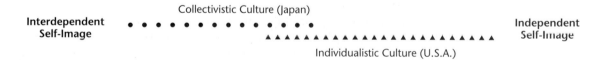

| Interdependent Self-Image | Collectivistic Culture (Japan) ●●●●●●●●●●●●●● ▲▲▲▲▲▲▲▲▲▲▲▲▲▲▲▲▲▲▲▲▲▲▲ Individualistic Culture (U.S.A.) | Independent Self-Image |

As you will see in the following sections, Ting-Toomey built her theory on the foundational idea that people from collectivistic/high-context cultures are noticeably different in the way they manage face and conflict situations than people from individualistic/low-context cultures. In a dozen scholarly articles she has defended that basic conviction. Yet more recently, Ting-Toomey and colleague John Oetzel from the University of New Mexico have discovered that "self-construal is a better predictor of conflict styles than ethnic/cultural background."[6] You can now see why face-negotiation theory is "in progress," and Ting-Toomey writes that "more theorizing effort is needed to 'decategorize' the colossal concepts of 'individualism' and 'collectivism' . . . into finer *culture-level, explanatory-categories*."[7]

Ting-Toomey and Oetzel identify people's self-construal by asking them to respond to surveys about real or imagined conflict situations. Strong agreement with the first two of the following four statements indicates an *independent* self-image. Endorsing the last two shows an *interdependent* self-image.[8]

"It was important for me to be able to act as a free and independent person."

"I tried not to depend on others."

"I sacrificed my self-interest for the benefits of our relationship."

"I was sensitive to the wishes of the other person."

The distinction between collectivistic and individualistic cultures is still important because culture has a strong effect on an individual's self-construal. But that sense of individual identity is one step closer to the person's preferred style of dealing with conflict, so it predicts dispute behavior better than generalized culture.

THE MULTIPLE FACES OF FACE

Although popular Western wisdom regards *face* as an Asian preoccupation, Ting-Toomey and other relational researchers find it to be a universal concern. That's because face is an extension of self-concept, a vulnerable, identity-based resource. As Ting-Toomey notes, most of us blush. It's a telltale sign that we feel awkward, embarrassed, ashamed, or proud—all face-related issues.[9] In their well-developed theory of politeness, University of Cambridge linguists Penelope Brown and Stephen Levinson define face as "the public self-image that every member of society wants to claim for himself/herself."[10] Many Western writers regard face as an almost tangible good that can rise or fall like soybean futures on the commodity exchange at the Board of Trade. Taiwanese writer Lin Yutang calls face "a psychological image that can be granted and lost and fought for and presented as a gift."[11] The term includes the patrician concern for dignity, honor, and status. Yet it also covers the effect of arrogant trash talk after a slam dunk on the basketball court—"in your face!" Ting-Toomey simply refers to face as "the projected image of one's self in a relational situation."[12]

Although an overall view of face as public self-image is straightforward and consistent with Mead's concept of the *generalized other* (see Chapter 5), Ting-Toomey highlights several issues that turn face into a multifaceted object of study. Face means different things to different people depending first on their culture, and second on how they construe their personal identities.

The question *Whose face are you trying to save?* may seem ridiculous to most Americans or members of other individualistic cultures. The answer is obvious: *mine!* Yet Ting-Toomey reminds us that in over two-thirds of the world, face concerns focus on the other person. Even in the midst of conflict, people in these collectivistic cultures pay more attention to maintaining the face of the other party than they do to preserving their own. Their answer to the *face-concern* question would honestly be an altruistic *yours.*

Face concern
Regard for self-face, other-face, or mutual-face.

But self-face and other-face concerns don't exhaust the possibilities. Ting-Toomey describes a third orientation, where there's an equal concern for both parties' images, as well as the public image of their relationship. She calls this a *mutual-face* concern, and people who have it would answer the *Whose face . . . ?* question with *ours.*

Self-concerned *face-restoration* is the facework strategy used to stake out a unique place in life, preserve autonomy, and defend against loss of personal freedom. Not surprisingly, face-restoration is the typical face strategy across individualistic cultures. *Face-giving* out of concern for others is the facework strategy used to defend and support another person's need for inclusion. It means taking care not to embarrass or humiliate the other in public. Face-giving is the characteristic face strategy across collectivistic cultures.

Threats to our own image can be like slaps or punches to the face. When that happens, do we feel the sting and try to fix the damage by justifying our actions or blaming the situation? Or perhaps we counterpunch and fight back? People from individualistic societies tend to retroactively regain lost face by using these self-face restoration strategies.[13] Conversely, are we more inclined to duck or ward off the blow before it hits? According to Ting-Toomey, people from collectivistic cultures are likely to use self-effacing strategies to proactively deflect face threats for the other party, and perhaps for themselves as well. These are other-face and mutual-face maintenance moves.

Of course, collectivism and individualism aren't all-or-nothing categories. The difference between other-face and self-face concerns is not absolute. Just as relational dialectics insists that everyone wants connectedness *and* separateness in a close relationship (see Chapter 12), so, too, all people desire affiliation and autonomy within their particular society. People raised in Japan or other Asian countries do have personal wants and needs; Americans and northern Europeans still desire to be part of a larger group. The cultural difference is always a matter of degree.

Yet when push comes to shove, most people from a collectivistic culture tend to privilege other-face or mutual-face over self-face. In like manner, people raised in an individualistic culture are normally more concerned with self-face than they are with other-face.

PREDICTABLE STYLES OF CONFLICT MANAGEMENT

Based on the work of M. Afzalur Rahim, professor of management and marketing at Western Kentucky University, Ting-Toomey initially identified five distinct responses to situations where there is an incompatibility of needs, interests, or goals. The five styles are *avoiding (withdrawal), obliging (giving in), compromising (negotiation), integrating (problem solving),* and *dominating (competing).*[14] Most Western writers refer to the same five styles of conflict, although they often use the labels in parentheses.[15]

Suppose, for example, that you are the leader of a group of students working together on a class research project. Your instructor will assign the same grade to all of you based on the quality of the group's work, and that project evaluation will count for two-thirds of your final grade in the course. As often happens in such cases, one member of the group has just brought in a shoddy piece of work and you have only three days to go until the project is due. You don't know this group member well, but you do know that it will take 72 hours of round-the-clock effort to fix this part of the project. What mode of conflict management will you adopt?

Face-restoration
The self-concerned facework strategy used to preserve autonomy and defend against loss of personal freedom.

Face-giving
The other-concerned facework strategy used to defend and support another person's need for inclusion.

Avoiding
Responding to conflict by withdrawing from open discussion.

Obliging
Accommodating or giving in to the wishes of another in a conflict situation.

Compromising
Conflict management by negotiation or bargaining; seeking a middle way.

"My first choice, of course, is to solve things amicably."

© The New Yorker Collection 2004 Mike Twohy from cartoonbank.com. All Rights Reserved.

Dominating
Competing to win when people's interests conflict.

Integrating
Problem solving through open discussion; collaborating for a win-win resolution of conflict.

Avoiding: "I would avoid discussing my differences with the group member."

Obliging: "I would give in to the wishes of the group member."

Compromising: "I would use give-and-take so that a compromise could be made."

Dominating: "I would be firm in pursuing my side of the issue."

Integrating: "I would exchange accurate information with the group member to solve the problem together."

These five styles of conflict management have been discussed and researched so often that they almost seem to be chiseled in stone. Yet Ting-Toomey and Oetzel remind us that these styles have surfaced in work situations in Western countries. Using an ethnically diverse sample, they have identified three additional styles of conflict management that American individualistic-based scholarship has missed. The styles are *emotional expression, passive aggression*, and *third-party help.*[16] In the student project example described earlier, these styles might be expressed the following way:

Emotional expression
Managing conflict by disclosure or venting of feelings.

Passive aggression
Making indirect accusations, showing resentment, procrastination, and other behaviors aimed at thwarting another's resolution of conflict.

Emotional expression: "Whatever my 'gut' and my 'heart' tell me, I would let these feelings show."

Passive aggression: "Without actually accusing anyone of being lazy, I'd try to make him or her feel guilty."

Third-party help: "I would enlist the professor to aid us in solving the conflict."

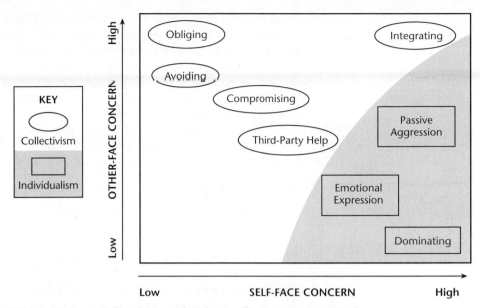

FIGURE 31–2   A Cultural Map of Eight Conflict Management Styles
Adapted from Stella Ting-Toomey and John Oetzel, *Managing Intercultural Conflict Effectively*

Figure 31–2 charts Ting-Toomey and Oetzel's map of conflict styles, arranged according to their culture-related face concern. The chart plots self-face concern on the horizontal axis and other-face concern on the vertical axis. For example, obliging is the behavior of choice for people who are concerned for another's public image, but not their own. Conversely, dominating is the act of someone who is concerned with his or her own face repair but doesn't care about promoting or honoring another's reputation. The smaller, shaded area on the right side depicts individualistic cultures that usually spawn conflict styles of emotional expression, passive aggression, and attempts to dominate. The larger, clear area on the left side reflects collectivistic cultures where obliging, avoiding, compromising, third-party help, and integrating are more the norm. Several explanations are in order.

You may be surprised to see *avoiding* rating almost as high as *obliging* on concern for the other person's face. Isn't withdrawing showing a casual disregard for the issue or your conversational partner? Ting-Toomey would disagree:

> It should be noted that in U.S. conflict management literature, obliging and avoiding conflict styles often take on a Western slant of being negatively disengaged (i.e., "placating" or "flight") from the conflict scene. However, collectivists do not perceive obliging and avoiding conflict styles as negative. These two styles are typically employed to maintain mutual-face interests and relational network interests.[17]

Third-party help
A method of conflict management in which disputing parties seek the aid of a mediator, arbitrator, or respected neutral party to help them resolve their differences.

Ting-Toomey would also point out that *third-party help* as practiced in a collectivistic culture is quite different from the interest-based mediation that I described at the start of the chapter. In these societies, parties in conflict voluntarily go to someone they greatly admire who has a good relationship with both of them. In order to "give face" to this wise elder or high-status person, they may be willing to follow his or her advice and in the process honor each other's image as well.[18] Perhaps that's why third-party help is sought out by conflicting parties in collectivistic cultures, but the vast majority of Western-style mediations are court-ordered. Most people with an independent self-construal think first of getting a lawyer.

Of course, the entire figure assumes that people from a given culture construe their self-image consistent with the collectivistic or individualistic nature of their society. In one multiethnic study, Ting-Toomey and Oetzel identified some people whose self-image embraced both interdependence and independence. The researchers now believe that these "biconstrual" individuals possess a wider repertoire of behavioral options to use in different conflict situations.[19] Face-negotiation theory predicts that regardless of his or her culture of origin, "the biconstrual type is associated positively with compromising/integrating conflict style."[20]

Given that an integrating, or win-win, style of conflict resolution is extolled among theorists and practitioners in the West, why does the cultural map place it across the border in the land of collectivists?[21] Ting-Toomey suggests that collectivists who adopt this interpersonal style focus on relational-level collaboration, whereas individualists concentrate on solving the task in a way that brings closure.[22] "Problem solving," the alternative label, has a distinctly impersonal tone.

Figure 31–2 is a freeze-frame snapshot of what people in different cultures report they do, and according to face-negotiation theory, why they do it. Yet as summarized near the start of the chapter, the theory lays out a multiple-stage *process* that captures the dynamics of response to conflict, and shows where the crucial matter of face concern fits in that flow. Using basically the same information that informed the map just discussed, Figure 31–3 depicts the comparative flow of the

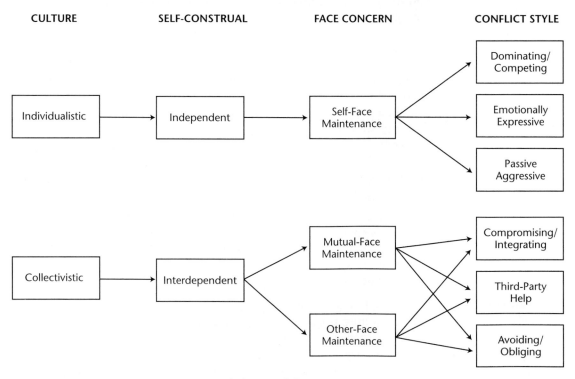

FIGURE 31–3   Face-Negotiation Model
Based on Ting-Toomey's hypotheses in "The Matrix of Face: An Updated Face-Negotiation Theory"

parallel processes for people with different face concerns. It incorporates most of the 24 propositions that form the backbone of Stella Ting-Toomey's theory.

APPLICATION: COMPETENT INTERCULTURAL FACEWORK

Ting-Toomey's ultimate goal for her theory goes beyond merely identifying the ways people in different cultures negotiate face or handle conflict. She believes that cultural *knowledge, mindfulness,* and facework *interaction skill* are the three require-ments for effectively communicating across cultures. Imagine that you are a Japanese student in a U.S. college. As the appointed leader of the class research proj-ect, you feel it is your uncomfortable duty to talk with the nonproductive American member of the group. How might you achieve competent intercultural facework?

Knowledge is the most important dimension of facework competence. It's hard to be culturally sensitive unless you have some idea of the ways you might differ from your classmate. Ting-Toomey's theory offers basic insights into col-lectivistic and individualistic cultures, self-construals, face concerns, and conflict styles, all of which could help you understand the American student's perspec-tive, and vice versa. If you've read this chapter carefully, this knowledge will stand you in good stead.

Mindfulness shows a recognition that things are not always what they seem. It's a conscious choice to seek multiple perspectives on the same event. Perhaps the other's inferior work is not due to laziness but is the best he or she can do in this situation. The student might have a learning disability, an emotional prob-lem, a lack of clarity about the assignment, or a desire to merely pass the course. Of course, your initiation of a conversation to discuss the project is also open to multiple interpretations. Ting-Toomey writes:

> Mindfulness means being particularly aware of our own assumptions, viewpoints, and ethnocentric tendencies in entering any unfamiliar situation. *Simultaneously,* mindfulness means paying attention to the perspectives and interpretive lenses of dissimilar others in viewing an intercultural episode.[23]

When you are mindful, you mentally switch off automatic pilot and process the situation and conversation through the central route of the mind as ELM suggests (see Chapter 15). But you are also freed up to empathize with the other student and approach the discussion with a fresh or creative mindset. The result might be a novel solution that takes advantage of your different ways of thinking.

Interaction skill is your ability to communicate appropriately, effectively, and adaptively in a given situation. Perhaps you are studying communication to gain that type of competence. Hopefully your department offers a course in interper-sonal or intercultural communication that includes structured exercises, role plays, or simulations. Without hands-on learning and feedback from others on how you're doing, it's hard to improve. Volunteers at the center for conflict resolution practice their mediation skills through this kind of experiential learning. A number of the techniques listed in Figure 31–1 parallel skills that Ting-Toomey regards as crucial in cross-cultural communication. For example, *displaying disputant equality* and *acknowledging emotions* are designed to preserve or give face to parties rather than threaten their public self-image. That would be a helpful skill to have when talking to the student in your research group. So would American-type straight talk that individualistic/low-context people understand. By using the two skills together, you might increase mutual face and get the research project back on track.

Mindfulness
Recognizing that things are not always what they seem, and therefore seek-ing multiple perspectives in conflict situations.

CRITIQUE: PASSING THE TEST WITH A GOOD GRADE

Like Clifford Geertz, most cross-cultural researchers analyze different cultures from a highly interpretive perspective (see Chapter 19). Ting-Toomey and her coresearcher, John Oetzel, are different because they are committed to an objective social science research agenda that looks for measurable commonalities across cultures. They then link these transcultural similarities (individualism or collectivism) to subsequent behavioral outcomes—in this case, response to others in conflict situations. In the course of this chapter you've seen that face-negotiation theory uses the concept of face concern to explain, predict, and ultimately advise. The theory's value therefore rests on the extent to which it can be tested, and whether it can withstand that close scrutiny. Like all objective social science theories, it ultimately has to meet the "put-up-or-shut-up" test.

In 2003, Oetzel and Ting-Toomey conducted a four-nation survey to test the core of the theory.[24] Over 700 students from collectivistic cultures (China and Japan) and individualistic cultures (United States and Germany) responded to scales that reliably measure self-construal. The students then recounted a specific case of conflict with someone from their country and filled out scales that tapped into the face concern they felt and the way they acted in that situation. The test was simplified in that mutual-face wasn't factored in and the researchers measured only the three primary conflict styles—*dominating, integrating,* and *avoiding.*

Figure 31–4 shows the links that were examined. All of the solid lines represent significant relationships among variables that were validated by the data. The results were sufficiently strong that they couldn't be explained away as mere chance findings. The two dotted lines represent predicted relationships that didn't materialize. Despite these two failures, I regard the overwhelming positive results as clear support for the theory.

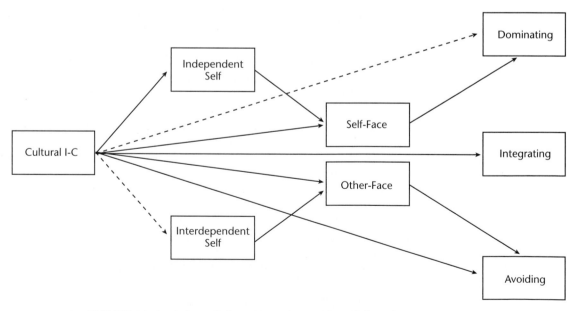

FIGURE 31–4   A Four-Culture Test of Face-Negotiation Theory

Based on Oetzel and Ting-Toomey, "Face Concerns in Interpersonal Conflict: A Cross-Cultural Empirical Test of Face-Negotiation Theory"

The findings regarding face concern were especially impressive. In earlier critiques of the theory I had questioned whether knowing a person's face concern would actually improve the model's prediction of conflict behavior. Note that the lines running directly from the individualistic-collectivistic (I-C) cultures at the beginning of the process to the three conflict styles at the end represent a way to find out if cutting out face concern would create a model that fits the data better. It did not. The results showed the *culture → self-construal → face concern → conflict style* paths provided a better prediction of what people reported than did the *culture → conflict style* direct route. In fact, when people scored high in *self-face* ("I was concerned with protecting my self-image"), they always took a *dominating* stance ("I insisted my position be accepted during the conflict").

Oetzel and Ting-Toomey's procedures and findings still provide some cause for pause. First, we must remember that their analysis is based solely on self-report data. That's certainly an appropriate way to identify the internal attitudes of self-construal and face concern, but self-reports of behavior are often self-serving. Respondents might be trying to save their face, give public face to a person they care about, or even try to give face to the researchers by giving them what they want. But even with this potential problem, asking what people did in a specific instance of conflict is a definite improvement on querying what they think they might do in a hypothetical situation.

As a mediator who highly values the goal of integrating, collaborating, and a win-win outcome, I'm bothered by the questions that supposedly assessed this conflict-resolution behavior. The survey items used referred to "meeting the other person halfway," proposing a "middle ground," and "'give and take' so that a compromise could be made." These items would seem to be a great way to assess *compromising,* but they don't measure what I and other mediators mean by *integration.* Nor do I believe they do justice to what Ting-Toomey describes as behavior springing from high other-face *and* high self-face concerns.

Finally, the researchers report that "both individualistic and collectivistic samples had more independence and self-face tendencies than interdependence and other face tendencies."[25] They suggest that college students in a collectivistic culture may be more competitive (or selfish?) than the rest of the population. But until this unexpected finding is explored further, we could be forgiven for wondering if citizens of collectivistic nations are quite as other-oriented as the theory suggests.

I'm impressed by the ambitious research program that Ting-Toomey has headed, and I also admire her willingness to adjust face-negotiation theory when confronted by unanticipated results. To create and test a theory that's later supported by empirical evidence obviously creates face within the research community. So does revising the theory when parts of it are disconfirmed. Stella Ting-Toomey has done both well. I look forward to the next edition of her theory.

QUESTIONS TO SHARPEN YOUR FOCUS

1. Based upon what you've learned about Afghanistan, is that culture *individualistic* or *collectivistic?* Does that society have a large or small *power distance?* What clues do you have?

2. Do you see yourself as having more of an *independent* or an *interdependent self?* Does this go with the flow of your culture, or are you swimming upstream?

3. What *face concern* (*self-face, other-face, mutual-face*) does your religious faith, political ideology, or personal set of values embrace? To what extent is the *facework* you do in your relationships with others consistent with that face concern?

4. What *style of conflict management* would you use with the group member who did poor work? Do you think that your response is based on your culture, self-construal, gender, or status? What other factors affect your decision?

CONVERSATIONS

View this segment online at www.mhhe.com/griffin7 or www.afirstlook.com.

While talking with Stella Ting-Toomey, I raise the embarrassing possibility that our students may be bored while watching this discussion. If so, both she and I have some serious facework to do. Ting-Toomey shows how she, a child of a collectivistic culture, might give face to students. She then role-plays how I, the product of an individualistic culture, might save face. Later in the conversation I ask if she's bothered that self-construal has turned out to be a better predictor of conflict style than cultural origin—a potentially face-threatening question. You then get to see Ting-Toomey's real-life facework.

A SECOND LOOK

Recommended resource: Stella Ting-Toomey, "The Matrix of Face: An Updated Face-Negotiation Theory," in *Theorizing About Intercultural Communication*, William Gudykunst (ed.), Sage, Thousand Oaks, CA, 2004, pp. 71–92.

Progression of the theory: Stella Ting-Toomey and Atsuko Kurogi, "Facework Competence in Intercultural Conflict: An Updated Face-Negotiation Theory," *International Journal of Intercultural Relations*, Vol. 22, 1998, pp. 187–225.

Original theory: Stella Ting-Toomey, "Intercultural Conflict Styles: A Face-Negotiation Theory," in *Theories in Intercultural Communication*, Young Yun Kim and William Gudykunst (eds.), Sage, Newbury Park, CA, 1988, pp. 213–235.

Literature review: Stella Ting-Toomey and John Oetzel, "Cross-Cultural Face Concerns and Conflict Styles," in *Handbook of International and Intercultural Communication*, 2nd ed., William Gudykunst and Bella Mody (eds.), Sage, Thousand Oaks, CA, 2002, pp. 143–163.

Comprehensive treatment of face: Stella Ting-Toomey (ed.), *The Challenge of Facework*, State University of New York, Albany, 1994.

Collectivistic/individualistic culture: Harry C. Triandis, *Individualism & Collectivism*, Westview, Boulder, CO, 1995.

Theory into practice: Stella Ting-Toomey, "Translating Conflict Face-Negotiation Theory into Practice," in *Handbook of Intercultural Training*, 3rd ed., Dan Landis, Jane Bennett, and Milton Bennett (eds.), Sage, Thousand Oaks, CA, 2004, pp. 217–248.

Conflict in intercultural communication: Stella Ting-Toomey and John Oetzel, *Managing Intercultural Conflict Effectively*, Sage, Thousand Oaks, CA, 2001.

Face-negotiation in the workplace: Frances Brew and David Cairns, "Styles of Managing Interpersonal Workplace Conflict in Relation to Status and Face Concern: A Study with Anglos and Chinese," *International Journal of Conflict Management*, Vol. 15, 2004, pp. 27–56.

Introduction to the concept of face: William Cupach and Sandra Metts, *Facework,* Sage, Thousand Oaks, CA, 1994.

A personal account of face: Stella Ting-Toomey, "An Intercultural Journey: The Four Seasons," in *Working at the Interface of Cultures: Eighteen Lives in Social Science,* Michael Bond (ed.), Routledge, New York, 1997, pp. 202–215.

Test and critique of the theory: John Oetzel and Stella Ting-Toomey, "Face Concerns in Interpersonal Conflict: A Cross-Cultural Empirical Test of the Face-Negotiation Theory," *Communication Research,* Vol. 36, 2003, pp. 599–624.

To access a chapter on John Thibaut and Harold Kelley's social exchange theory, a different theoretical approach to conflict, click on Theory Archive at *www.afirstlook.com.*

CHAPTER 32

Speech Codes Theory
of Gerry Philipsen

After three years on the staff of a youth organization, I resigned to pursue full-time graduate work in communication at Northwestern University. Gerry Philipsen was one of my classmates. When I finished my Ph.D. course work, the labor market was tight; I felt fortunate to receive an offer to teach at Wheaton College. A while later I heard Gerry was doing youth work on the south side of Chicago. I remember thinking that while my career was progressing, Gerry's was going backward. How wrong I was. As articles in the *Quarterly Journal of Speech* soon made evident, Gerry Philipsen was doing ethnography.[1]

In Chapter 1, I introduced ethnography as a research method that places a premium on discovering the meanings that people share within a given culture. It is, for example, the approach of the symbolic interactionist who is a participant observer in the life of the community (see Chapter 4). We've already seen results of ethnographic research conducted in an organizational setting (see Chapter 19). Pacanowsky's analysis of the unique corporate culture of W. L. Gore & Associates illustrates anthropologist Clifford Geertz' claim that ethnography is "not an experimental science in search of law, but an interpretive science in search of meaning."[2]

While at Northwestern, Philipsen read an article by University of Virginia anthropologist and linguist Dell Hymes, "The Ethnography of Speaking." Hymes called for a "close to the ground" study of the great variety of communication practices around the world.[3] Philipsen decided to start in the Chicago community where he worked, a place he dubbed "Teamsterville," since driving a truck was the typical job for men in the community. For three years Philipsen talked to kids on street corners, women on front porches, men in corner bars, and everyone at the settlement house where he worked so that he would be able to describe the speech code of Teamsterville residents. By *speech code*, Philipsen "refers to a historically enacted, socially constructed system of terms, meanings, premises, and rules, pertaining to communicative conduct."[4]

Even though the people of Teamsterville spoke English, Philipsen noted that their whole pattern of speaking was radically different from the speech code he knew and heard practiced within his own family of origin, by his friends at school, and across many talk shows on radio and TV. The stark contrast motivated him to conduct a second, multiyear ethnographic study, which began while he was teaching communication at the University of California, Santa Barbara, and

Ethnography
The work of a naturalist who watches, listens, and records communicative conduct in its natural setting in order to understand a culture's concept web of meanings.

Speech code
A historically enacted, socially constructed system of terms, meanings, premises, and rules, pertaining to communicative conduct.

414

continued when he went to the University of Washington. Although most of his "cultural informants" were from Santa Barbara or Seattle, the speech code community from which they were drawn was not confined to the West Coast of the United States. He labeled them the "Nacirema" (*American* spelled backward), because their way of using language was intelligible to, and practiced by, a majority of Americans. Typical Nacirema speech is a "generalized U.S. conversation that is carried out at the public level (on televised talk shows) and at the interpersonal level in face-to-face interaction."[5] For Philipsen, me, and many reading this text, "Nacirema are us."

Philipsen defines the Nacirema culture by speech practices rather than geographical boundaries or ethnic background. As mentioned in the introduction to Intercultural Communication, Nacirema talk was epitomized by the speech of TV host Phil Donahue, his guests, and his audience on *Donahue*.[6] It's a style of speaking about self, relationships, and communication itself that emerged for Philipsen as he spent hundreds of hours listening to tapes of dinner-table conversations, life stories, and ethnographic interviews.

Just as cultural markers emerge gradually for the ethnographer, so the defining features of the Nacirema code will become more clear as you read the rest of the chapter. But for starters, one characteristic feature of that speech code is a preoccupation with metacommunication—their talk about talk.[7]

As Philipsen intended, the Teamsterville and Nacirema ethnographic studies provided rich comparative data on two distinct cultures. But he also wanted to go beyond mere description of interesting local practices. His ultimate goal was to develop a general theory that would capture the relationship between communication and culture. Such a theory would guide cultural researchers and practitioners in knowing what to look for and would offer clues on how to interpret the way people speak.

Based on the suggestion of Dell Hymes, Philipsen first referred to his emerging theory as the *ethnography of communication*. He has found, however, that many people can't get past the idea of ethnography as simply a research method, so now that his theory has moved from description to explanation, Philipsen labels his work *speech codes theory*. Specifically, the theory seeks to answer questions about the existence of speech codes, their substance, the way they can be discovered, and their force upon people within a culture.

Philipsen outlines the core of speech codes theory in the following six general propositions. He is hopeful, however, that their presentation can be intertwined with the story of his fieldwork and the contributions of other scholars that stimulated the conceptual development of the theory. I've tried to capture that narrative mix within the limited space of this chapter.

THE DISTINCTIVENESS OF SPEECH CODES

Proposition 1: Wherever there is a distinctive culture, there is to be found a distinctive speech code.

Philipsen describes an ethnographer of speaking as "a naturalist who watches, listens, and records communicative conduct in its natural setting."[8] When he entered the working-class, ethnic world of Teamsterville, Philipsen found patterns of speech that were strange to his ears. After many months in the community, he was less struck by the pronunciation and grammar that was characteristic of then Chicago mayor Richard J. Daley than he was by the practice of "infusing a concern with place into every conversation."[9] He realized that Teamsterville residents say little until they've confirmed the nationality, ethnicity, social status, and place of residence of the person with whom they're speaking. Most conversations start (and end) with the question *Where are you from and what's your nationality?*

Philipsen gradually discovered that discussion of "place" is related to the issue of whether a person is from "the neighborhood." This concern isn't merely a matter of physical location. Whether or not a person turns out to be from "around here" is a matter of cultural solidarity. Unlike *Mister Rogers' Neighborhood*, Teamsterville does not welcome diversity. As Philipsen heard when he first entered a corner tavern, "We don't want no yahoos around here."

While Philipsen discovered that Teamsterville conversation is laced with assurances of common place among those in the neighborhood, he found that speech among the Nacirema is a way to express and celebrate psychological uniqueness. Dinnertime is a speech event where all family members are encouraged to have their say. Everyone has "something to contribute," and each person's ideas are treated as "uniquely valuable."

In Teamsterville, children are "to be seen, not heard." Among the Nacirema, however, it would be wrong to try to keep a child quiet at the dinner table. Communication is the route by which kids develop "a positive self-image," a way to "feel good about themselves." Through speech, family members "can manifest their equality and demonstrate that they pay little heed to differences in status—practices and beliefs that would puzzle and offend a proper Teamsterviller."[10]

Philipsen was raised in a largely Nacirema speech community, but until his research in Teamsterville, he hadn't thought of his family's communication as a particular cultural practice. Its taken-for-granted quality illustrates the saying that's common among ethnographers: "We don't know who discovered water, but we're pretty sure it wasn't the fish."

THE MULTIPLICITY OF SPEECH CODES

> *Proposition 2:* In any given speech community, multiple speech codes are deployed.

Philipsen recently added this proposition to the other five that he first stated in 1997.[11] He did so because he and his students now observe times when people are affected by other codes or employ dual codes at the same time. In his Teamsterville ethnography, Philipsen stressed the unified nature of their neighborhood speech patterns. Yet he noticed that the men gauge their relative worth by comparing their style of talk with that of residents in other city neighborhoods. They respect, yet resent, middle-class northside residents who speak Standard English. On the other hand, they are reassured by their perceived ability to speak better than those whom they refer to as lower-class "Hillbillies, Mexicans, and Africans." Just as Giles described the risk of communication convergence outside a minority group for in-group members, any attempt a man makes to "improve" his speech is regarded as an act of disloyalty that alienates him from his friends (see Chapter 30). Thus, the men define their way of speaking by contrasting it with other codes.

The awareness of another speech code is equally strong among the Nacirema. Their repeated references to the importance of "a good talk" or "meaningful dialogue" distinguish speech that they value from "mere talk," or what today is parodied as "blah, blah, blah." As Philipsen notes, the Nacirema characterized "their present way of speaking ('really communicating') by reference to another way of speaking and another communicative conduct that they had now discarded."[12]

Dell Hymes suggested that there may be more than one code operating within a speech community.[13] Philipsen's Washington colleague, Lisa Coutu, performed an in-depth analysis of language used in Robert McNamara's book *In Retrospect: The Tragedy and Lessons of Vietnam*.[14] McNamara was the architect of U.S. policy in Vietnam and his detractors referred to it as "McNamara's War." He wrote the book "to put before the American people why their government and its leaders behaved as they did and what we may learn from the experience."[15]

According to Coutu, McNamara's account reflects a *code of rationality*. He deeply regrets that he didn't force a knock-down, drag-out debate over the merits of fighting in Vietnam. In retrospect, he believes that had he insisted on a frank and probing discussion, America wouldn't have gone to war.

Coutu's analysis of press and public reaction to the book shows a competing code at work. Reviewers across the political spectrum wrote and spoke in a way that reflects a *code of spirituality*. Regardless of their evaluation, commentators used morally laden terms such as *evil, sin, shame, confession, contrition, forgiveness, atonement, absolution,* and *faith.* Therefore, Coutu concludes there are multiple codes within a speech community. Writing from his code of rationality, McNamara questioned whether the war could be won. Working from their ethical/spiritual code, the book's reviewers were concerned with whether the war was moral.

THE SUBSTANCE OF SPEECH CODES

> *Proposition 3:* A speech code involves a culturally distinctive psychology, sociology, and rhetoric.

With this proposition, Philipsen takes a step back from the cultural relativism that characterizes most ethnographers. He continues to maintain that every culture has its own unique speech code; there's no danger we'll mistake a Nacirema discussion of personal worth with Teamsterville talk of neighborhood solidarity. But this third proposition asserts that whatever the culture, the speech code reveals structures of self, society, and strategic action. The Teamsterville code of when to speak and when to remain silent illustrates the following three functions of social life.

Psychology. According to Philipsen, every speech code "thematizes" the nature of individuals in a particular way. The Teamsterville code defines people as a bundle of social roles. In the Nacirema code, however, the individual is conceptualized as unique—someone whose essence is defined from the inside out. This again squares with communication accommodation theory's distinction between people who emphasize their *social identity* and those who focus on their *personal identity* (see Chapter 30).

Sociology. Philipsen writes that "a speech code provides a system of answers about what linkages between self and others can properly be sought, and what symbolic resources can properly and efficaciously be employed in seeking those linkages."[16] According to the unwritten code of Teamsterville, speech is not a valued resource for dealing with people of lower status—wives, children, or persons from outside the neighborhood who are lower on the social hierarchy. Nor is speech a resource for encounters with bosses, city officials, or other higher-status outsiders. In cases where the latter kind of contact is necessary, a man draws on his personal connections with a highly placed intermediary who will state his case. Speech is reserved for symmetrical relationships with people matched on age, gender, ethnicity, occupational status, and neighborhood location. Words flow freely with friends.

Rhetoric
Both the discovery of truth and a persuasive appeal.

Honor
A code that grants worth to an individual on the basis of adherence to community values.

Dignity
The worth an individual has by virtue of being a human being.

Rhetoric. Philipsen uses the term *rhetoric* in the double sense of *discovery of truth* and *persuasive appeal*. Both concepts come together in the way Teamsterville young and adult men talk about women. To raise doubts about the personal hygiene or sexual purity of a man's wife, mother, or sister is to attack his honor. *Honor* is a code that grants worth to an individual on the basis of adherence to community values. The language of the streets in Teamsterville makes it clear that a man's social identity is strongly affected by the women he's related to by blood or marriage. "If she is sexually permissive, talks too much, or lacks in personal appearance, any of these directly reflects on the man and thus, in turn, directly affects his honor."[17] In contrast, Philipsen discovered that a verbalized code of dignity holds sway among the Nacirema. *Dignity* refers to the worth that an individual has by virtue of being a human being. "Discourse spoken in a code of dignity prejudices the talk—and the hearing of the talk—in favor of treating individuals in terms of their 'intrinsic humanity divested of all socially imposed roles or norms.'"[18] Within a code of dignity, personal experience is given a moral weight greater than logical argument or appeal to authority. Communication is a resource to establish an individual's uniqueness.

THE INTERPRETATION OF SPEECH CODES

Proposition 4: The significance of speaking depends on the speech codes used by speakers and listeners to create and interpret their communication.

Proposition 4 can be seen as Philipsen's speech code extension of I. A. Richards' maxim that words don't mean; people mean (see Chapter 4). If we want to understand the significance of a prominent speech practice within a culture, we must listen to the way people talk about it and respond to it. It's their practice; they decide what it means.

No speech practice is more important among the Nacirema than the way they use the term *communication*. Philipsen and Tamar Katriel have shown that the Nacirema use this key word as a shorthand way of referring to *close, open, supportive speech*.[19] These three dimensions set communication apart from speech that their informants dismissed as *mere communication, small talk,* or *normal chitchat*.

Close relationships contrast with *distant* affiliations, where others are "kept at arm's length."

Open relationships, in which parties listen and demonstrate a willingness to change, are distinct from routine associations, where people are stagnant.

Supportive relationships, in which people are totally "for" the other person, stand in opposition to *neutral* interactions, where positive response is conditional.

You may have noticed my not-so-subtle switch from a description of *communication* to a discussion of *relationships*. Philipsen and Katriel say that Nacirema speakers use the two words almost interchangeably. In Burkean terms (see Chapter 22), when not qualified by the adjective *casual, communication* and *relationship* are "god terms" of the Nacirema. References to *self* have the same sacred status.

Although the people of Teamsterville know and occasionally use the word *communication,* it holds none of the potency that it has for the Nacirema. To the contrary, for a Teamsterville male involved in a relationship with someone of higher or lower status, communicating is considered an unmanly thing to do. Philipsen first discovered this part of the Teamsterville speech code through his work with youth at the community center. He ruefully recalls, "When I spoke to unruly Teamsterville boys in order to discipline them I was judged by them to be unmanly because, in such circumstances, I spoke."[20] The guys "naturally" expected this older male to use power or physical force to bring them in line. They were confused when Philipsen, consistent with his Nacirema speech code, sat down with them to "talk things out." The only explanation that made sense to them was that their youth leader was a homosexual. Not until much later did their conclusion get back to him.

THE SITE OF SPEECH CODES

> *Proposition 5:* The terms, rules, and premises of a speech code are inextricably woven into speaking itself.

How can we spot the speech code of a given culture—our own or anyone else's? The answer is to analyze the speech of native speakers. Philipsen is convinced that speech codes are on public display as people speak; they are open to scrutiny by anyone who cares enough to take a long look. Proposition 5 suggests that it couldn't be otherwise.

Dell Hymes recommends that we start by looking for patterns in who talks to whom, in what settings, toward what ends, and about what topics. It was this framework of inquiry that first helped Philipsen notice the importance of a man's *place* when men talked together in Teamsterville bars. Hymes also suggests that a good way to get at the meaning of speech events is by examining the words that people use to label them. For example, Tamar Katriel used this ethnographic technique when she returned to her native Israel and analyzed a distinctive style of speaking that Israeli Jews call *dugri*.[21] It's a blunt form of straight talk based on the assumption that the other person wants what's best for the community and is able to handle criticism ("I tell you *dugri,* I don't like what you're doing").

Philipsen focuses on highly structured cultural forms that often display the cultural significance of symbols and meanings, premises, and rules that might not be accessible through normal conversation. For example, *social dramas* are public confrontations in which one party invokes a moral rule to challenge the conduct of another. The response from the person criticized offers a way of testing and validating the legitimacy of the "rules of life" that are embedded in a particular speech code.

Philipsen analyzed the late Mayor Daley's reply in the city council to charges of nepotism—in this case the appointment of his best friend's son to a political position.[22] By all accounts, Daley went ballistic. Most reporters regarded the speech as an irrational diatribe, yet his appeal to place, honor, and traditional gender roles resonated with the values of Teamsterville. When Philipsen asked people in the neighborhood if it was right for Daley to favor his friends, they responded, "Who should he appoint, his enemies?"

Totemizing ritual
A careful performance of a structured sequence of actions that pays homage to a sacred object.

Totemizing rituals offer another window to a culture's speech code. They involve a careful performance of a structured sequence of actions that pays homage to a sacred object. Philipsen and Katriel spotted a *communication ritual* among the Nacirema that honors the sacred trinity of self, communication, and relationships.[23] Known as "a good talk," the topic is often a variation on the theme of how to be a unique, independent *self* yet still receive validation from close others. The purpose of the ritual is not problem solving per se. Instead, people come together to express their individuality, affirm each other's identity, and experience intimacy.

The communication ritual follows a typical sequence:

1. Initiation—a friend voices a need to work through an interpersonal problem.

2. Acknowledgment—the confidant validates the importance of the issue by a willingness to "sit down and talk."

3. Negotiation—the friend self-discloses, the confidant listens in an empathic and nonjudgmental way, the friend in turn shows openness to feedback and change.

4. Reaffirmation—both the friend and the confidant try to minimize different views, and they reiterate appreciation and commitment to each other.

By performing the communication ritual correctly, both parties celebrate the central tenet of the Nacirema code: "Whatever the problem, communication is the answer."

THE FORCE OF SPEECH CODES IN DISCUSSIONS

> *Proposition 6:* The artful use of a shared speech code is a sufficient condition for predicting, explaining, and controlling the form of discourse about the intelligibility, prudence, and morality of communication conduct.

Does the knowledge of people's speech codes in a given situation help an observer or a participant *predict* or *control* what others will say and how they'll interpret what is said? Philipsen thinks it does. It's important, however, to understand clearly what Philipsen is *not* saying.

Let's assume that Philipsen is again working with youth and now knows the code of when a man should speak in Teamsterville. Proposition 6 does not claim he should or could keep an unruly kid in line with a smack on the head. Speech codes theory deals with only one type of human behavior—speech acts. Nor does it claim that fathers in Nacirema homes will always encourage their kids to talk at the dinner table. As we saw under Proposition 3, even when people give voice to a speech code, they still have the power, and sometimes the desire, to resist it. Perhaps the father had a bad day and wants some peace and quiet. Proposition 6 does suggest, however, that by a thoughtful use of shared speech codes, participants can guide metacommunication—the talk about talk. This is no small matter.

The dad-at-the-dinner-table example can help us see how prediction and control might work. Suppose a Nacirema father growls at his kids to finish their dinner without saying another word. Inasmuch as we understand the speech code of the family, we can confidently predict that his children will say that his demand is unfair, and his wife will object to his verbal behavior. As for artful control, she could choose to pursue the matter in private so that her husband wouldn't lose face in front of the children. She might also tie her objection to shared values ("If you don't communicate with our kids, they're going to grow up bitter and end up not liking you"). In this way she would tap into issues that her husband would recognize as legitimate and would set the moral agenda for the rest of the discussion about the way he talks with the kids.

The dinner-table example I've sketched is based on an actual incident discussed by Philipsen.[24] He uses it to demonstrate the rhetorical force of appealing to shared speech codes. While the scope of Proposition 6 is limited to metacommunication, talk about the clarity, appropriateness, and ethics of a person's communication is an important feature of everyday life. In the vernacular of the Nacirema, "It's a big deal." For people who study communication, it's even bigger.

PERFORMANCE ETHNOGRAPHY

In an extension and critique of the style of ethnography that Philipsen conducts, some researchers have stopped talking about *doing* ethnography in favor of *performing* ethnography. Much like Philipsen, the late Dwight Conquergood, a Northwestern University performance ethnographer, spent several years with teenagers in the "Little Beirut" district of Chicago. Conquergood was living in a multiethnic tenement and performing participant observation among local street gangs. *Performance ethnography* is more than a research tool; it is grounded in several theoretical principles.

Performance ethnography
A research methodology committed to performance as both the subject and method of research, to researchers' work being performance, and to reports of fieldwork being actable.

The first principle is that performance is both the *subject* and the *method* of performance ethnography. All social interactions are performance because, as Philipsen notes, speech not only reflects but also alters the world. Thus, Conquergood viewed the daily conversations of gang members who were hangin' on the street corner as performances. Of particular interest to Conquergood were rituals, festivals, spectacles, dramas, games, and other metaperformances. The ritualistic handshakes and elaborate graffiti enacted by the gangs are examples of metaperformance because the gang members themselves recognized the actions to be symbolic. Neither fiction nor farce, metaperformances are reminders that life consists of "performances about performances about performances."[25]

These researchers also consider their work performative. Fieldwork is performance because it involves suspension of disbelief on the part of both the participant observer and the host culture. In the act of embodied learning, researchers recognize that they are doing ethnography *with* rather than *of* a people group—they are co-performers. Conquergood didn't merely observe the greetings of gang members on the street; he greeted them.

In reporting their fieldwork, performance ethnographers are no less concerned about performance. They consider the thick descriptions traditionally produced to be a bit thin. By taking speech acts out of dialogues and dialogues out of context, published ethnographies smooth all the voices of the field "into the expository prose of more or less interchangeable 'informants.'"[26] Thus, the goal of performance ethnographies is to produce actable ethnographies. As Conquergood wrote, "What makes good theatre makes more sensitive and politically committed anthropological writing."[27]

Conquergood performed his ethnographies through public reading and even acting the part of a gang member. This kind of performance enables the ethnographer to recognize the limitations of, and uncover the cultural bias in, his or her written work. For those participating as audience members, performance presents complex characters and situations eliciting understanding that's actively responsive rather than passive.

Performance ethnography almost always takes place among marginalized groups. The theoretical rationale underlying this fact is that oppressed people are not passive but create and sustain their culture and dignity. In the face of daily humiliations, they create "subtle, complex, and amazingly nuanced performances that subversively key the events and critique the hierarchy of power."[28] Consistent with the belief of critical theorists that communication theory shouldn't be neutral toward power structures and politics, Conquergood was committed to chronicling the performances of the oppressed in order to give them a voice in the larger society. He said of his own research among Chicago gangs, "What I have to do is create a space for an alternate hearing."[29]

CRITIQUE: DIFFERENT SPEECH CODES IN COMMUNICATION THEORY

A favorite grad school professor of mine was fond of saying, "You know you're in the wrong place on an issue if you aren't getting well-roasted from all sides." By this "golden mean" standard, Gerry Philipsen is on the right academic path.

Most interpretive scholars applaud Philipsen's commitment to long-term participant observation and his perceptive interpretations, but they are critical of his efforts to generalize across cultures. Granted, he doesn't reduce cultural variation to a single issue such as an individualistic-collectivistic dichotomy. Philipsen's critics recoil, however, when he talks about explanation, prediction, and control—the traditional goals of science. Any theory that adopts these aims, no matter how limited its scope, strikes them as reductionist.

Theorists who operate from a feminist, critical, or cultural studies perspective (see Chapters 34–35, 20, and 26, respectively) charge that Philipsen is silent and perhaps naive about power relationships. His description of the Nacirema speech code fails to unmask patterns of domination, and he doesn't speak out against male hegemony in Teamsterville. In response, Philipsen says that the practice of ethnography that he recommends gives voice to the people who are observed.

> For most speech codes researchers, their open eyes and listening ears are directed to what the people being studied, in a given inquiry, insert into the discourse they produce and find in the discourse they experience.[30]

If power is an issue—as it was in Mayor Daley's city council speech—he believes it will be evident in the way people speak. If it's not an issue, the ethnographer shouldn't make it one.

As one trained in the empirical tradition, I could wish for a bit more scientific rigor before generalizations are made. Philipsen's grounded research in Teamsterville is impressive, but his study of the Nacirema raises a number of questions. What are the boundaries of this speech community? Isn't it circular to first identify a dispersed speech community on the basis of common discursive practices and then do ethnographic research to determine their speech code? Has the language of this speech community so infused academic departments of communication that we as scholars are unable to analyze the code objectively?

Most of all, I could wish for a few more data sets than the two Philipsen presents. The Teamsterville and Nacirema codes are so diametrically opposed, it's tempting to divide the world into two cultural clusters:

Teamsterville	Nacirema
Collectivistic	Individualistic
Hierarchical	Egalitarian
Code of honor	Code of dignity
A man's world	A woman's world

This certainly isn't Philipsen's intention, but without an example of a culture that draws from both columns, there's no evidence to the contrary.

My concerns are minor compared with what I believe Philipsen has accomplished. He accepted Dell Hymes' challenge and became the first ethnographer of communication in our discipline. He has trained an increasing number of cultural scholars, who have all performed their own ethnographic studies. Of the most significance for this text, he has elevated ethnography from its former status as a rarely used research method in the field of communication to its present position as an intriguing theoretical perspective.

QUESTIONS TO SHARPEN YOUR FOCUS

1. Most of *speech codes theory* is concerned with *cross-cultural* rather than *intercultural* communication. What is the difference? Which incidents described in the chapter are examples of intercultural encounters?

2. Which three *propositions* of the theory suggest a *scientific* approach to the study of speech codes?

3. Many scholars still think of Philipsen's work as the *ethnography of communication*. Why do you (or don't you) think *speech codes theory* is a better name?

4. Philipsen says that the *Nacirema* way of talking is the prevailing *speech code* in the United States. What *research* cited in this chapter supports his claim?

CONVERSATIONS

View this segment online at www.mhhe.com/griffin7 or www.afirstlook.com.

My conversation with Gerry Philipsen is an exploration of contrasts. Philipsen highlights differences in cultures by listing topics that a Sioux interpersonal communication textbook would cover as opposed to the typical Nacirema text, which emphasizes self-disclosure. He then distinguishes between the ethnography of communication and his theory of speech codes. Philipsen goes on to suggest why the potential of using a culture's speech code to explain, predict, and even control people's behavior isn't at odds with the interpretive approach of ethnography. Finally, he discusses the fine line that he draws between learning to understand and appreciate how other people see the world and still embracing his own ethical standards.

A SECOND LOOK

Recommended resource: Gerry Philipsen, "A Theory of Speech Codes," in *Developing Communication Theory*, Gerry Philipsen and Terrance Albrecht (eds.), State University of New York, Albany, 1997, pp. 119–156.

Revision and update: Gerry Philipsen, Lisa M. Coutu, and Patricia Covarrubias, "Speech Codes Theory: Restatement, Revisions, and Response to Criticisms," in *Theorizing About Intercultural Communication,* William Gudykunst (ed.), Sage, Thousand Oaks, CA, 2005, pp. 55–68.

Extended treatment: Gerry Philipsen, *Speaking Culturally: Explorations in Social Communication,* State University of New York, Albany, 1992.

Review of scholarship on culture and communication: Gerry Philipsen, "Cultural Communication," in *Handbook of International and Intercultural Communication,* 2nd ed., William Gudykunst and Bella Mody (eds.), Sage, Thousand Oaks, CA, 2002, pp. 51–67.

Fieldwork in Teamsterville: Gerry Philipsen, "Speaking 'Like a Man' in Teamsterville: Culture Patterns of Role Enactment in an Urban Neighborhood," *Quarterly Journal of Speech,* Vol. 61, 1975, pp. 13–22; Gerry Philipsen, "Places for Speaking in Teamsterville," *Quarterly Journal of Speech,* Vol. 62, 1976, pp. 15–25.

Fieldwork with Nacirema: Tamar Katriel and Gerry Philipsen, "'What We Need Is Communication': Communication as a Cultural Category in Some American Speech," *Communication Monographs,* Vol. 48, 1981, pp. 302–317.

Speech codes theory applied to discursive force in racism dispute: Gerry Philipsen, "Permission to Speak the Discourse of Difference: A Case Study," *Research on Language and Social Interaction,* Vol. 33, 2000, pp. 213–234.

Oppositional codes within a speech community: Lisa M. Coutu, "Communication Codes of Rationality and Spirituality in the Discourse of and About Robert S. McNamara's *In Retrospect,*" *Research on Language and Social Interaction,* Vol. 33, 2000, pp. 179–211.

Original call for ethnography of communication: Dell Hymes, "The Ethnography of Speaking," in *Anthropology and Human Behavior,* T. Gladwin and W. C. Sturtevant (eds.), Anthropological Society of Washington, Washington, DC, 1962, pp. 13–53.

Ethnography of speaking: Gerry Philipsen and Lisa M. Coutu, "The Ethnography of Speaking," in *Handbook of Language and Social Interaction,* Kristine L. Fitch and Robert Sanders (eds.), Lawrence Erlbaum, Mahwah, NJ, 2005, pp. 355–379.

Review essay: Donal Carbaugh, "The Ethnographic Communication Theory of Philipsen and Associates," in *Watershed Research Traditions in Communication Theory,* Donald Cushman and Branislav Kovačić (eds.), State University of New York, Albany, 1995, pp. 241–265.

Performance ethnography: Dwight Conquergood, "Homeboys and Hoods: Gang Communication and Cultural Space," in *Group Communication in Context,* Lawrence Frey (ed.), Lawrence Erlbaum, Hillsdale, NJ, 1994, pp. 23–55.

Critique: John Stewart, "Developing Communication Theories," in *Developing Communication Theories,* Gerry Philipsen and Terrance Albrecht (eds.), State University of New York, Albany, 1997, pp. 183–186.

To discover what other communication theory texts discuss speech codes theory, or any other theory covered in this book, click on Compare Texts at *www.afirstlook.com.*

Most of us believe that women and men interact differently. When we think about the differences (and most of us think about them a lot), we usually draw on the rich data of our lives to construct our own minitheories of masculine-feminine communication.

For example, I recently sat from 9 A.M. to 4 P.M. in a large room at the federal courthouse with a hundred other prospective jurors. We entered as strangers, but by midmorning the women were sitting in clusters of three to seven, engrossed in lively discussions. All the men sat by themselves. I thought about that stark difference as I went to my interpersonal communication class. Reviewing the class list, I realized that 70 percent of the students who took the course as an elective were female. Conversely, two-thirds of those who opted for my persuasion course were male. On the basis of this limited personal experience, I jumped to the conclusion that women talk more than men and that their communication goal is connection rather than influence.

Yet stereotyping is a risky business. The distinction between women's focus on intimacy and men's concern for power has held up well under scrutiny by communication researchers. But most studies of gender differences show that women actually talk *less* than men in mixed groups.

Linguist Robin Lakoff of the University of California, Berkeley, was one of the first scholars who attempted to classify regularities of women's speech that differentiate "women-talk" from "men-talk."[1] Lakoff claimed that women's conversation is marked by tentativeness and submission. Unfortunately, this conclusion and others were based mainly on her personal reflection and anecdotal evidence—much like my courthouse and classroom theorizing. Three decades of systematic research offers at least three cautions.

1. There are more similarities among men and women than there are differences. After conducting a meta-analysis of hundreds of research studies that reported gender differences on topics such as talk time, self-disclosure, and styles of conflict management, University of Wisconsin–Milwaukee communication professor Kathryn Dindia found that the differences were actually quite small. She parodies the popular belief that men and women come from two different worlds in the way she summarizes her findings: "Men are from North Dakota, Women are from South Dakota."[2] Can you really spot a difference? If I tell you that Pat talks fast, uses big words, and holds eye contact—your chances of guessing whether Pat is male or female are just slightly better than 50/50.[3]

2. Greater variability of communication style exists among women and among men than between the two groups. Scores on the *Sex-Role Inventory*, developed by Stanford University psychologist Sandra Lipsitz Bem, illustrate this within-group diversity.[4] Bem asks people to rate themselves on a series of gender-related descriptions—many related to speech. A person who marks *soft-spoken, eager to soothe hurt feelings*, and *does not use harsh language* ranks high in femininity. A person who marks *assertive, defends own beliefs*, and *willing to take a stand* ranks high in masculinity. As you might expect, males tend to fit masculine sex roles and females tend to fit feminine sex roles, but the scores from a group of people of the same sex are typically all over the map. Sometimes individuals—male or

"How is it gendered?"

female—score high on both scales. Bem regards this combination as the best of both worlds and refers to these people with blended identities as *androgynous*. Obviously, gender-related speech isn't an either/or proposition.

3. Sex is a fact; gender is an idea.[5] Within the literature of the field, the sex-related terms *male* and *female* are typically used to categorize people biologically, as they do at the Olympics—by chromosomes and genitalia. On the other hand, the terms *men* and *women* or *masculine* and *feminine* are usually employed to describe an idea that's been learned from and reinforced by others. When we forget that our concept of gender is a human construction, we fall into the trap of thinking that there is a real-in-nature category called *man*—an early Clint Eastwood archetype who smokes Marlboros, doesn't eat quiche, won't cry, and lives by the code that *a man's got to do what a man's got to do*. Sex is a given, but we negotiate, or work out, our concept of gender with others throughout our lives.

The three theories discussed in this section attempt to identify crucial differences between masculine and feminine styles of communication and explain why the differences persist. Chapter 33 presents Deborah Tannen's theory of genderlect styles, which attributes misunderstanding between men and women to the fact that women's talk focuses on connection, while men communicate to achieve status and maintain independence. The *genderlect* label reflects Tannen's belief that male-female conversation is cross-cultural communication. When inevitable mistakes occur, no one is particularly to blame. Although Dindia says Tannen ignores the striking similarities between men's and women's communication, she regards Tannen's best-selling *You Just Don't Understand* as the most responsible statement of the two-culture hypothesis.

Sandra Harding and Julia Wood agree that men and women have separate perspectives, but they don't regard them as equally valid. Because different locations within the social hierarchy affect what is seen, they think that women and other oppressed groups perceive a different world than do those who view it from a position of privilege and power. Chapter 34 describes Harding and Wood's version of *standpoint theory.* It suggests that research starting from the lives of women, gays and lesbians, racial minorities, and the poor provides a less false view of the world than does typical academic research that comes from an advantaged perspective.

Rooted in feminist analysis, Cheris Kramarae's version of *muted group theory* regards talk between men and women as an unequal interchange between those who have power in society and those who do not. As discussed in Chapter 35, Kramarae's belief is that women are less articulate than men in public because the words of our language and the norms for their use have been devised by men. As long as women's conversation is regarded as tentative and trivial, men's dominant position is secure. But just as men have a vested interest in accentuating the differences between men's and women's speech, muted group theory has a reformist agenda of contesting the masculine bias in language. Kramarae is convinced that as women become less muted, their control over their own lives will increase.

CHAPTER 33

Genderlect Styles

of Deborah Tannen

"Male-female conversation is cross-cultural communication."[1] This simple statement is the basic premise of Deborah Tannen's *You Just Don't Understand*, a book that seeks to explain why men and women often talk past each other.

Tannen is a linguistics professor at Georgetown University, and her research specialty is conversational style—not what people say but the way they say it. In her first book on conversational style she offers a microanalysis of six friends talking together during a two-and-a-half-hour Thanksgiving dinner.[2]

Tannen introduces this sociolinguistic study with a quote from E. M. Forster's novel *A Passage to India:* "A pause in the wrong place, an intonation misunderstood, and a whole conversation went awry."[3] Forster's novel illustrates how people of goodwill from different cultures can grossly misunderstand each other's intentions. Tannen is convinced that similar miscommunication occurs all the time between women and men. The effect may be more insidious, however, because the parties usually don't realize that they are in a cross-cultural encounter. At least when we cross a geographical border we anticipate the need to overcome a communication gap. In conversing with members of the opposite sex, Tannen notes, our failure to acknowledge different conversational styles can get us into big trouble. Most men and women don't grasp that "talking through their problems" with each other will only make things worse if it's their divergent ways of talking that are causing the trouble in the first place.

Tannen's writing is filled with imagery that underscores the mutually alien nature of male and female conversation styles. When she compared the style of boys and girls who were in second grade, she felt she was looking at the discourse of "two different species." For example, two girls could sit comfortably face to face and carry on a serious conversation about people they knew. But when boys were asked to talk about "something serious," they were restless, never looked at each other, jumped from topic to topic, and talked about games and competition. These stylistic differences showed up in older kids as well. Tannen notes that "moving from the sixth-grade boys to the girls of the same age is like moving to another planet."[4] There is no evidence that we grow out of these differences as we grow up. She describes adult men and women as speaking "different words from different worlds," and even when they use the same terms, they are "tuned to different frequencies."

Tannen's cross-cultural approach to gender differences departs from much of feminist scholarship that claims that conversations between men and women reflect men's efforts to dominate women. She assumes that male and female conversational styles are equally valid: "We try to talk to each other honestly, but it seems at times that we are speaking different languages—or at least different genderlects."[5] Although the word *genderlect* is not original with Tannen, the term nicely captures her belief that masculine and feminine styles of discourse are best viewed as two distinct cultural dialects rather than as inferior or superior ways of speaking.

Genderlect

A term suggesting that masculine and feminine styles of discourse are best viewed as two distinct cultural dialects.

Tannen realizes that categorizing people and their communication according to gender is offensive to many women and men. None of us like to be told, "Oh, you're talking just like a (wo)man." Each of us regards himself or herself as a unique individual. But at the risk of reinforcing a simplistic reductionism that claims that biology is destiny, Tannen insists that there *are* gender differences in the ways we speak.

> Despite these dangers, I am joining the growing dialogue on gender and language because the risk of ignoring differences is greater than the danger of naming them.[6]

WHEN HARRY MET SALLY: THE CLASH OF TWO CULTURES

Do men and women really live in different worlds? Tannen cites dialogue from Anne Tyler's *The Accidental Tourist*, Ingmar Bergman's *Scenes from a Marriage*, Alice Walker's *The Temple of My Familiar*, Erica Jong's *Fear of Flying*, and Jules Feiffer's *Grown Ups* to support her claim that the different ways women and men talk reflect their separate cultures.

Whenever I discuss Tannen's theory in class, students are quick to bring up conversations between Billy Crystal and Meg Ryan in the 1989 Rob Reiner film *When Harry Met Sally*. I'll use the words of Harry and Sally in the film written by Nora Ephron to illustrate the gender differences that Tannen proposes.

The movie begins as two University of Chicago students who have never met before share an 18-hour ride to New York City. Harry is dating Sally's good friend Amanda. Their different perspectives become obvious when Harry makes a verbal pass at his traveling companion just a few hours into the drive:

SALLY: Amanda is my friend!

HARRY: So?

SALLY: So, you're going with her.

HARRY: So?

SALLY: So you're coming on to me.

HARRY: No I wasn't. . . .

SALLY: We are just going to be friends, OK?

HARRY: Great, friends, best thing. [Pause] You realize of course we could never be friends.

SALLY: Why not?

HARRY: What I'm saying is . . . , and this is not a come-on in any way, shape or form . . . , is that men and women can't be friends because the sex part always gets in the way.

SALLY: That's not true, I have a number of men friends and there is no sex involved.

HARRY: No you don't. . . .

SALLY: Yes I do.

HARRY: No you don't.

SALLY: Yes I do.

HARRY: You only think you do.

SALLY: You're saying I've had sex with these men without my knowledge?

HARRY: No, what I'm saying is that they all want to have sex with you.

SALLY: They do not.

HARRY: Do too.

SALLY: They do not.

HARRY: Do too.

SALLY: How do you know?

HARRY: Because no man can be friends with a woman that he finds attractive. He always wants to have sex with her.

SALLY: So you're saying that a man can be friends with a woman he finds unattractive?

HARRY: No, you pretty much want to nail them too.

Harry next meets Sally five years later on an airplane. He surprises her when he announces that he's getting married. Sally obviously approves, but the ensuing conversation shows that they are still worlds apart in their thinking:

SALLY: Well it's wonderful. It's nice to see you embracing life in this manner.

HARRY: Yeah, plus, you know, you just get to a certain point where you get tired of the whole thing.

SALLY: What whole thing?

HARRY: The whole life of a single guy thing. You meet someone, you have the safe lunch, you decide you like each other enough to move on to dinner. You go dancing, . . . go back to her place, you have sex, and the minute you're finished you know what goes through your mind? How long do I have to lie here and hold her before I can get up and go home? Is thirty seconds enough?

SALLY: [Incredulous tone] That's what you're thinking? Is that true?

HARRY: Sure. All men think that. How long do you like to be held afterward? All night, right? See that's the problem. Somewhere between thirty seconds and all night is your problem.

SALLY: I don't have a problem.

HARRY: Yeah you do.

The casual viewer of these scenes will hear little more than two individuals quarreling about sex. Yet neither conversation is about the desirability of sex per se, but about what sex means to the parties involved. Tannen's theory of genderlect styles suggests that Harry's and Sally's words and the way they are said reflect the separate worlds of men and women. Harry would probably regard Sally as a resident of *Mister Rogers' Neighborhood*, while Sally might see Harry as coming from the *Planet of the Apes* or *Animal House*. But each person obviously finds the other's view alien and threatening. Sally, as a woman, wants intimacy. Harry, as a man, wants independence.

WOMEN'S DESIRE FOR CONNECTION VERSUS MEN'S DESIRE FOR STATUS

Tannen says that more than anything else women seek human *connection*. Harry's initial come-on irritates Sally because he is urging her to ignore her friendship with Amanda. She is further saddened at Harry's conviction that women and men can't be friends. But she is especially shocked at Harry's later revelation that for him the act of sex marks the end of intimacy rather than its beginning. Both times Harry insists that he is speaking for all men. If what Harry says is true, Sally does indeed have a problem. Harry's words imply that true solidarity with a man would be difficult to achieve, if not impossible.

According to Tannen, men are concerned mainly with *status*. They are working hard to preserve their independence as they jockey for position on a hierarchy of competitive accomplishment. In both conversations, Harry is the one who introduces the topic, starts to argue, talks the most, and enjoys the last word. In other words, he wins. For Harry, sexual intercourse represents achievement rather than communion. "Nailing" a woman is a way to score in a never-ending game of who's on top. A woman's desire for *intimacy* threatens his freedom and sidetracks him from his quest to be *one up* in all his relationships.

Harry's opinion that *all* men think like he does may strike you as extreme. Tannen agrees. She believes that some men are open to intimacy, just as some women have a concern for power. You'll recall that Baxter and Montgomery's relational dialectics assumes that all people feel a tension between connectedness and separation in their relationships (see Chapter 11). Tannen agrees that many men and women would like to have intimacy *and* independence in every situation if they could, but she doesn't think it's possible. As a result, these differences in priority tend to give men and women differing views of the same situation.

> Girls and women feel it is crucial that they be liked by their peers, a form of involvement that focuses on symmetrical connection. Boys and men feel it is crucial that they be respected by their peers, a form of involvement that focuses on asymmetrical status.[7]

RAPPORT TALK VERSUS REPORT TALK

Why is Tannen so certain that women focus on connection while men focus on status? Her answer is that she listens to men and women talk. Just as an ethnographer pores over the words of native informants to discover what has meaning within their society, so Tannen scrutinizes the conversation of representative speakers from the feminine culture and the masculine culture to determine their core values. She offers numerous examples of the divergent styles she observes in everyday communication. These linguistic differences give her confidence that the connection-status distinction structures every verbal contact between women and men.

Consider the following types of talk, most of which are evident in the film *When Harry Met Sally*. At root, each of these speech forms shows that women value *rapport* talk, while men value *report* talk.

Rapport talk
The typical conversational style of women, which seeks to establish connection with others.

1. Private Speaking Versus Public Speaking

Folk wisdom suggests that women talk more than men. Tannen cites a version of an old joke that has a wife complaining to her husband, "For the past 10 years you've never told me what you're thinking." Her husband caustically replies, "I didn't want to interrupt you." Tannen grants the validity of the wordy-woman–mute-male stereotype as it applies to a couple alone. She finds that women talk more than men in private conversations, and she endorses Alice Walker's notion that a woman falls in love with a man because she sees in him "a giant ear."[8] Sally continually tries to connect with Harry through words. She also shares the details of her life over coffee with her close friends Alice and Marie. But according to Tannen, Sally's rapport style of relating doesn't transfer well to the public arena, where men vie for ascendancy and speak much more than women do.

Report talk
The typical monologic style of men, which seeks to command attention, convey information, and win arguments.

Harry's lecture style is typical of the way men seek to establish a *one-up* position. Tannen finds that men use talk as a weapon. The function of the long explanations they use is to command attention, convey information, and insist on agreement. Even Harry's rare self-disclosure to his buddy Jess is delivered within the competitive contexts of jogging, hitting a baseball in a batting cage, and watching a football game. When men retreat from the battle to the safety of their own homes, they no longer feel compelled to talk to protect their status. They lay their weapons down and retreat into a peaceful silence.

Harry is unusual in that he's willing to talk about the nuances of his life with Sally. Most men avoid this kind of small talk. Yet in private conversation with Sally, Harry still speaks as though he were defending a case in court. He codifies rules for relationships, and when Sally raises a question, he announces an "amendment to the earlier rule." Men's monologic style of communication is appropriate for report, but not for rapport.

2. Telling a Story

Along with theorists Clifford Geertz, Michael Pacanowsky, and Walter Fisher (see Chapters 19 and 23), Tannen recognizes that the stories people tell reveal a great deal about their hopes, needs, and values. Consistent with men's focus on status and Billy Crystal's portrayal of Harry, Tannen notes that men tell more stories than women—especially jokes. Telling jokes is a masculine way to negotiate status. Men's humorous stories have a *can-you-top-this?* flavor that holds attention and elevates the storyteller above his audience.

When men aren't trying to be funny, they tell stories in which they are heroes, often acting alone to overcome great obstacles. On the other hand, women tend to express their desire for community by telling stories about others. On rarer occasions when a woman is a character in her own narrative, she usually describes herself as doing something foolish rather than acting in a clever manner. This downplaying of self puts her on the same level with her hearers, thus strengthening her network of support.

3. Listening

A woman listening to a story or an explanation tends to hold eye contact, offer head nods, and react with *yeah, uh-huh, mmmn, right,* or other responses that indicate *I'm listening* or *I'm with you.* For a man concerned with status, that overt style of active listening means *I agree with you,* and so he avoids putting himself in a submissive, or *one-down,* stance. Women, of course, conclude that men aren't listening, which is not necessarily true.

When a woman who is listening starts to speak before the other person is finished, she usually does so to add a word of agreement, to show support, or to finish a sentence with what she thinks the speaker will say. Tannen labels this *cooperative overlap*. She says that from a woman's perspective, cooperative overlap is a sign of rapport rather than a competitive ploy to control the conversation. She also recognizes that men don't see it that way. Men regard any interruption as a power move to take control of the conversation, because in their world that's how it's done. Those who win the conversational game can take a don't-talk-while-I'm-interrupting-you stance and make it stick. Tannen concludes that these different styles of conversation management are the source of continuing irritation in cross-gender talk. "Whereas women's cooperative overlaps frequently annoy men by seeming to co-opt their topic, men frequently annoy women by usurping or switching the topic."[9]

Cooperative overlap
A supportive interruption often meant to show agreement and solidarity with the speaker.

4. Asking Questions

When Sally and Harry started out on their trip to New York, Sally produced a map and a detailed set of directions. It's safe to assume that Harry never used them. According to Tannen, men don't ask for that kind of help. Every admission of ignorance whittles away at the image of self-sufficiency that is so important for a man. "If self-respect is bought at the cost of a few extra minutes of travel time, it is well worth the price," she explains.[10]

Women ask questions to establish a connection with others. Even a five-minute stop at a gas station to check the best route to New York can create a sense of community, however brief. Tannen notes that when women state their opinions, they often tag them with a question at the end of the sentence ("That was a good movie, *don't you think*?"). *Tag questions* soften the sting of potential disagreement that might drive people apart. They are also invitations to participate in open, friendly dialogue. But to men, they make the speaker seem wishy-washy.

Tag question
A short question at the end of a declarative statement, often used by women to soften the sting of potential disagreement or invite open, friendly dialogue.

Ever since *You Just Don't Understand* was published, Tannen has entertained questions during television interviews, radio call-in shows, and discussions following lectures. Women almost always seek more information or offer their own experiences that validate her insights. That's now true for men as well. But when the book was riding high on best-seller lists, men would often pose questions that seemed designed to bring her down from her high horse or establish their own expertise. Even though she understands that public face is crucially important to men, she identifies with the words of a wife in a short story: "I'd have been upset about making the mistake—but not about people *knowing*. That part's not a big deal to me." Her husband replied, "Oh, is it ever a big deal to me."[11]

5. Conflict

In the second half of *When Harry Met Sally*, Harry blows up at their friends Jess and Marie and then storms out of the room. After making an excuse for his behavior, Sally goes to him to try to calm him down.

HARRY: I know, I know, I shouldn't have done it.

SALLY: Harry, you're going to have to try and find a way of not expressing every feeling that you have every moment that you have them.

HARRY: Oh, really?

SALLY: Yes, there are times and places for things.

HARRY: Well the next time you're giving a lecture series on social graces, would you let me know, 'cause I'll sign up.

SALLY: Hey. You don't have to take your anger out on me.

HARRY: Oh, I think I'm entitled to throw a little anger your way. Especially when I'm being told how to live my life by Miss Hospital Corners.

SALLY: What's that supposed to mean?

HARRY: I mean, nothing bothers you. You never get upset about anything.

This scene illustrates Tannen's description of much male-female strife. Since they see life as a contest, many men are more comfortable with conflict and are therefore less likely to hold themselves in check. By trying to placate Harry and excuse his anger toward their friends, Sally responds in what Tannen believes is an equally typical fashion. "To most women, conflict is a threat to connection—to be avoided at all costs."[12]

The dialogue illustrates another feature of conflict between men and women. As often happens, Sally's attempt to avert a similar outburst in the future sparks new conflict with Harry. Tannen says that men have an early warning system that's geared to detect signs that they are being told what to do. Harry bristles at the thought that Sally is trying to limit his autonomy, so her efforts backfire.

"NOW YOU'RE BEGINNING TO UNDERSTAND"

What if Tannen is right and all conversation between men and women is best understood as cross-cultural communication? Does this mean that genderlect can be taught like French, Swahili, or any other foreign language? Tannen offers a qualified "yes." She regards sensitivity training as an effort to teach men how to speak in a feminine voice, while assertiveness training is an effort to teach women how to speak in a masculine voice. But she's aware of our ethnocentric tendency to think that it's the other person who needs fixing, so she expresses only guarded hope that men and women will alter their linguistic styles.

Tannen has much more confidence in the benefits of multicultural understanding. She believes that understanding each other's style, and the motives behind it, is a first move in overcoming destructive responses.

> The answer is for both men and women to try to take each other on their own terms rather than applying the standards of one group to the behavior of the other. . . . Understanding style differences for what they are takes the sting out of them.[13]

Tannen suggests that one way to measure whether we are gaining cross-gender insight is a drop in the frequency of the oft-heard lament *You just don't understand*. Sally basically says that in so many words when Harry declares his love for her at a New Year's Eve party after months of estrangement. "It just doesn't work that way," she cries. Yet Harry shows that he *does* understand what's important to Sally and that he can cross the cultural border of gender to connect through rapport talk.

"And do you, Deborah Tannen, think they know what they're talking about?"

Then how 'bout this way. I love that you get cold when it's seventy-one degrees out. I love that it takes you an hour and a half to order a sandwich. I love that you get a little crinkle above your nose when you're looking at me like I'm nuts. I love that after I spend a day with you I can still smell your perfume on my clothes. And I love that you are the last person I want to talk to before I go to sleep at night.

Dumbfounded, Sally realizes that Harry understands a lot more than she thought he did, and he used her linguistic style to prove it. The viewer hopes that Sally has an equal understanding of report talk, which is the native tongue of Harry and other men who live in the land of the status hierarchy.

ETHICAL REFLECTION: GILLIGAN'S DIFFERENT VOICE

For more than 30 years, Carol Gilligan was a professor of education in the Harvard Graduate School of Education. Her book *In a Different Voice* presents a theory of moral development claiming that women tend to think and speak in an ethical voice different from that of men.[14] Gilligan's view of gender differences parallels Deborah Tannen's analysis of men as wanting independence and women as desiring human connection. Gilligan is convinced that most men seek autonomy and think of moral maturity in terms of *justice*. She's equally certain that women desire to be linked with others and that they regard their ultimate ethical responsibility as one of *care*.

On the basis of the quantity and quality of feminine relationships, Gilligan contrasts *women who care* with *men who are fair*. Individual rights, equality before the law, fair play, a square deal—all these masculine ethical goals can be pursued without personal ties to others. Justice is impersonal. But women's moral judgment is more contextual, more immersed in the details of relationships and narratives.[15] Sensitivity to others, loyalty, self-sacrifice, and peacemaking all reflect interpersonal involvement.

Gilligan's work arose in response to the theory of moral development of her Harvard colleague Lawrence Kohlberg, who identified increasing levels of ethical maturity by analyzing responses to hypothetical moral dilemmas.[16] According to his justice-based scoring system, the average young adult female was a full stage behind her male counterpart. Women were rated as less morally mature than men because they were less concerned about abstract concepts like justice, truth, and freedom. Instead, they based their ethical decisions on considerations of compassion, loyalty, and a strong sense of responsibility to prevent pain and alleviate suffering. Their moral reasoning was more likely to reflect Buber's call for genuine I-Thou relationships than Kant's categorical imperative.

Gilligan is comfortable with the idea that men and women speak in different ethical voices. Yet she's disturbed that when women don't follow the normative path laid out by men, "the conclusion has generally been that something is wrong with women."[17] She points out "the unfair paradox that the very traits that have traditionally defined the 'goodness' of women are those that mark them as deficient in moral development."[18]

Although Gilligan's theory is more descriptive than prescriptive, the underlying assumption is that the way things *are* reflects the way things *ought to be*. Most ethical theorists are bothered by the idea of a double standard—justice from some, care from others. Traditional moral philosophy has never suggested different ethics for different groups, yet readers of both sexes report that Gilligan's theory resonates with their personal experience.

CRITIQUE: IS TANNEN SOFT ON RESEARCH AND MEN?

Is male-female conversation really cross-cultural communication? Tannen suggests that we should use the *aha factor* to test the validity of her two-culture hypothesis:

Aha factor
A subjective standard ascribing validity to an idea when it resonates with one's personal experience.

> If my interpretation is correct, then readers, on hearing my explanation, will exclaim within their heads, "Aha!" Something they have intuitively sensed will be made explicit. . . . When the subject of analysis is human interaction—a process that we engage in, all our lives—each reader can measure interpretation against her/his own experience.[19]

If we agree to this subjective standard of validity, Tannen easily makes her case. For example, in the book *You Just Don't Understand*, she describes how women who verbally share problems with men are often frustrated by the masculine response tendency to offer solutions. According to Tannen, women don't want advice; they're looking for the gift of understanding. When I first read this section I had the kind of *aha* reaction that Tannen says validates her theory. I suddenly realized that her words described me. Anytime my wife, Jean, tells me about a problem she's facing, I either turn coldly analytic or dive in and try to fix things for the woman I love. I now know that Jean would rather have me just listen or voice some version of *I feel your pain.*

Apparently Tannen's analysis of common misunderstandings between men and women has struck a responsive chord in a million other readers. *You Just Don't Understand* was on the best-seller list for most of the 1990s. And in that decade it was rated the best of 1,000 self-help books by hundreds of mental health professionals.[20] But does a chorus of *ahas* mean that she is right? The late astrologer and psychic Jeane Dixon might have made 10 predictions, and if only one came true, that's the prophecy people remembered and lauded her for. They forgot that the other nine turned out to be wrong. According to many social scientists, Tannen's "proof" may be like that.

Perhaps using selective data is the only way to support a reductionist claim that women are one way and men are another. Tannen's theme of intimacy versus independence echoes one of the dialectics Leslie Baxter and Barbara Montgomery observe in Chapter 12. However, Tannen suggests none of the flux, internal contradiction, or ongoing complexity of human existence that relational dialectics describes. Tannen's women are programmed within their gendered culture to embrace connection and deny any desire for autonomy. Her men seek autonomy but avoid connection. Neither group feels any sense of internal contradiction. Saying it's so may eventually make it so—self-fulfilling prophecy is a powerful force. But as I stated in the introduction to this section, most gender researchers spot more diversity *within* each gender than *between* them.

Communication scholars Ken Burke (not the Burke of Chapter 22), Nancy Burroughs-Denhart, and Glen McClish offer a rhetorical critique of Tannen's work.[21] They say that although Tannen claims both female and male styles are equally valid, many of her comments and examples tend to put down masculine values. Certainly Tannen is not alone in this practice. In a widely discussed article that appeared in the *Journal of Applied Communication Research,* Julia Wood and Christopher Inman (University of North Carolina) observe that the prevailing ideology of intimacy discounts the ways that men draw close to each other.[22] They suggest rapport talk is only one route to connection.

Adrianne Kunkel (University of Kansas) and Brant Burleson directly challenge the different-cultures perspective that is at the heart of Tannen's genderlect theory. Recall that Burleson has headed an ongoing research program on comforting communication as a skill of cognitively complex people who are able to craft person-centered messages (see Chapter 8). According to Tannen's two-culture worldview, this kind of verbal support should be highly desired in the world of women, but a skill of little value in the competitive world of men. Kunkel and Burleson's empirical research doesn't bear out Tannen's claim. They say that while it's true that women often *do* it better, both sexes place an equally high value on comforting communication:

Both men and women view highly person-centered comforting messages as most sensitive and effective; both see messages low in person-centeredness as relatively insensitive and ineffective. . . . Both sexes view comforting skills as important in the context of various personal relationships and as substantially more important than instrumentally focused communication skills.[23]

On the basis of this shared meaning, Kunkel and Burleson reject the different-cultures perspective. They believe it's a myth that has lost its narrative force. Men and women do understand.

A very different critique comes from feminist scholars. For example, German linguist Senta Troemel-Ploetz accuses Tannen of having written a dishonest book that ignores issues of male dominance, control, power, sexism, discrimination, sexual harassment, and verbal insults. "If you leave out power," she says, "you do not understand talk."[24] The two genderlects are anything but equal. "Men are used to dominating women; they do it especially in conversations. . . . Women are trained to please; they have to please also in conversations."[25]

Contrary to Tannen's thesis that mutual understanding will bridge the culture gap between the sexes, Troemel-Ploetz believes that "men understand quite well what women want but they give only when it suits them. In many situations they refuse to give and *women cannot make them give*."[26] She thinks it's ridiculous to assume that men will give up power voluntarily. To prove her point, she suggests doing a follow-up study on men who read Tannen's best seller. Noting that many women readers of *You Just Don't Understand* give the book to their husbands to read, Troemel-Ploetz states that if Tannen's theory is true, a follow-up study should show that these men are now putting down their papers at the breakfast table and talking empathetically with their wives. She doesn't think it will happen.

The discussion of gender and power will continue in the next two chapters.

QUESTIONS TO SHARPEN YOUR FOCUS

1. Based on Tannen's *genderlect analysis*, do you agree with Harry that men and women can't be friends? Why or why not?

2. Apart from the topics of conflict, questions, listening, storytelling, and public versus private speaking, can you come up with your own examples of how *rapport talk* is different from *report talk*?

3. What are the practical implications for you if talk with members of the opposite sex is, indeed, *cross-cultural communication?*

4. Tannen's *aha factor* is similar to Carl Rogers' standard of basing our knowledge on personal experience (see Chapter 4). What are the dangers of relying solely on the aha factor?

SELF-QUIZ   *www.mhhe.com/griffin7*

A SECOND LOOK   *Recommended resource:* Deborah Tannen, *You Just Don't Understand*, Ballantine, New York, 1990.

Conversational style: Deborah Tannen, *That's Not What I Meant!* William Morrow, New York, 1986.

Linguistic microanalysis of conversation: Deborah Tannen, *Conversational Style: Analyzing Talk Among Friends,* Ablex, Norwood, NJ, 1984.

Gender differences in children's talk: Deborah Tannen, "Gender Differences in Topical Coherence: Creating Involvement in Best Friends' Talk," *Discourse Processes,* Vol. 13, 1990, pp. 73–90.

Defense of multiple methodologies: Deborah Tannen, "Discourse Analysis: The Excitement of Diversity," *Text,* Vol. 10, 1990, pp. 109–111.

Discourse analysis: Deborah Tannen, *Gender and Discourse,* Oxford University, Oxford, UK, 1994/96.

Gendered language in the workplace: Deborah Tannen, *Talking from 9 to 5: Women and Men at Work—Language, Sex, and Power,* Avon, New York, 1994.

Gendered language in the family: Deborah Tannen, *I Only Say This Because I Love You: Talking in Families,* Ballantine, New York, 2002.

Support of two-culture hypothesis: Anthony Mulac, James Bradac, and Pamela Gibbons, "Empirical Support for the Gender-as-Culture Hypothesis: An Intercultural Analysis of Male/Female Language Differences," *Human Communication Research,* Vol. 27, 2001, pp. 121–152.

Critique of two-culture hypothesis: Adrianne Kunkel and Brant Burleson, "Social Support and the Emotional Lives of Men and Women: An Assessment of the Different Cultures Perspective," in *Sex Differences and Similarities in Communication,* Daniel Canary and Kathryn Dindia (eds.), Lawrence Erlbaum, Mahwah, NJ, 1998, pp. 101–125.

Communication scholars' dialogue on two-culture hypothesis: "Reflections on the Different Cultures Hypothesis: A Scholars' Symposium," Sandra Metts (ed.), *Personal Relationships,* Vol. 4, 1997, pp. 201–253.

Appeal for reform of academic discourse: Deborah Tannen, "Agonism in Academic Discourse," *Journal of Pragmatics,* Vol. 34, 2002, pp. 1651–1669.

Critique centering on power discrepancy: Senta Troemel-Ploetz, "Review Essay: Selling the Apolitical," *Discourse and Society,* Vol. 2, 1991, pp. 489–502.

To read how other students apply gender theories to
their lives, click on Application Logs at
www.afirstlook.com.

Standpoint Theory

of Sandra Harding & Julia T. Wood

As you've seen throughout the book, many communication theories raise questions about knowledge—for example,

> Can cognitive complexity help us craft person-centered messages?
>
> What's the best way to reduce uncertainty about someone you've just met?
>
> Does the "bottom line" in an annual report reflect corporate reality?
>
> How can we find out whether television has a powerful effect?
>
> Are men and women from different cultures?

If you're interested in communication, you'll want to find the answers. ("Inquiring minds want to know.") Standpoint theorists Sandra Harding and Julia Wood claim that one of the best ways to discover how the world works is to start the inquiry from the standpoint of women and other groups on the margins of society.

Standpoint

A place from which to critically view the world around us.

A *standpoint* is a place from which to view the world around us. Whatever our vantage point, its location tends to focus our attention on some features of the natural and social landscape while obscuring others. Synonyms for *standpoint* include *viewpoint, perspective, outlook,* and *position.* Note that each of these words suggests a specific location in time and space where observation takes place, while referring to values or attitudes. Sandra Harding and Julia Wood think the connection is no accident. As standpoint theorists, they claim that "the social groups within which we are located powerfully shape what we experience and know as well as how we understand and communicate with ourselves, others, and the world."[1] Our standpoint affects our worldview.

Harding is a philosopher of science who holds joint appointments in women's studies, education, and philosophy at the University of California, Los Angeles. To illustrate the effect of standpoint, she asks us to imagine looking into a pond and seeing a stick that appears to be bent.[2] But is it really? If we walk around to a different location, the stick seems to be straight—which it actually is. Of course, physicists have developed a theory of light refraction that explains why this visual distortion occurs. In like manner, standpoint theorists suggest that we can use the inequalities of gender, race, class, and sexual orientation to observe how different locations within the social hierarchy tend to generate distinctive accounts of nature and social relationships. Specifically, Harding claims

441

that "when people speak from the opposite sides of power relations, the perspective from the lives of the less powerful can provide a more objective view than the perspective from the lives of the more powerful."[3] Her main focus is the standpoint of women who are marginalized.

Just as Harding is recognized as the philosopher who has most advanced the standpoint theory of knowledge among feminist scholars,[4] Julia Wood, a professor of communication at the University of North Carolina at Chapel Hill, has championed and consistently applied standpoint logic within the field of communication. She regards all perspectives as partial, but she insists that some standpoints are "more partial than others since different locations within social hierarchies affect what is likely to be seen."[5] Although Wood believes that social location definitely shapes women's lives as distinct from men's, she emphasizes that a woman's location on the margin of society doesn't necessarily confer a feminist standpoint. It is only through critical reflection on unjust power relations and working to resist this oppression that a feminist standpoint is formed. In that sense a feminist standpoint is *achievement* rather than a piece of territory automatically inherited by being a woman.[6]

For communication researchers, taking women's location seriously means heeding Wood's call to choose research topics that are responsive to women's concerns:

> Abiding concern with oppression leads many feminist scholars to criticize some of the topics that dominate research on relationships. When four women are battered to death by intimate partners every day in North America, study of how abusive relationships are created and sustained seems more compelling than research on heterosexual college students' romances. Is it more significant to study friendships among economically comfortable adolescents or social practices that normalize sexual harassment and rape?[7]

As a male researcher who has already studied romance and friendship on a private college campus, I am compelled to explore the logic of Harding and Wood's standpoint agenda. But their standpoint epistemology raises other questions. Do all women share a common standpoint? Why do Harding and Wood believe a feminist standpoint is more objective or less partial than other starting points for inquiry? Would grounding future research in the lives of women compel me to regard every report of feminine experience as equally true? Should we disregard what men have to say? The rest of this chapter will explore these issues and other questions raised by standpoint theory. The answers to these questions will make more sense if we understand the varied intellectual resources standpoint theorists have drawn upon to inform their analyses.

A FEMINIST STANDPOINT ROOTED IN PHILOSOPHY AND LITERATURE

In 1807, German philosopher Georg Hegel analyzed the master-slave relationship to show that what people "know" about themselves, others, and society depends on which group they are in.[8] For example, those in captivity have a decidedly different perspective on the meaning of chains, laws, childbirth, and punishment than do their captors who participate in the same "reality." But since masters are backed by the established structure of their society, it is they who have the power to make their view of the world stick. They are the ones who write the history books.

Following Hegel's lead, Karl Marx and Friedrich Engels referred to the *proletarian standpoint*. They suggested that the impoverished poor who provide sweat equity are society's *ideal knowers*, as long as they understand the class struggle in which they are involved.[9] Harding notes that standpoint theory "was a project 'straining at the bit' to emerge from feminist social theorists who were familiar with Marxian epistemology."[10] By substituting *women* for *proletariat*, and *gender discrimination* for *class struggle,* early feminist standpoint theorists had a ready-made framework for advocating women's way of knowing.

As opposed to the economic determinism of Marx, George Herbert Mead claims that culture "gets into individuals" through communication (see Chapter 5). Drawing on this key principle of symbolic interactionism, Wood maintains that gender is a cultural construction rather than a biological characteristic. "More than a variable, gender is a system of meanings that sculpts individuals' standpoints by positioning most males and females in disparate material, social and symbolic circumstances."[11]

Strains of postmodernism also weave throughout standpoint theory. When Jean-Francois Lyotard announced an "incredulity toward metanarratives," he included Enlightenment rationality and Western science.[12] Since many feminists regard these two enterprises as dominated by men who refuse to acknowledge their male-centered bias, they embrace a postmodern critique. In reciprocal fashion, postmodernists applaud the standpoint emphasis on knowledge as locally situated, though they push the idea to the point where there is no basis for favoring one perspective over another. As we shall see, Harding and Wood reject that kind of absolute relativism.

Harding and Wood have drawn upon these somewhat conflicting intellectual traditions without letting any one of them dictate the shape or substance of their standpoint approach. The resulting theory might seem a bewildering crosshatch of ideas were it not for their repeated emphasis on starting all scholarly inquiry from the lives of women and others who are marginalized. In order to honor this central tenet of standpoint theory and to illustrate the way of knowing that Harding and Wood propose, I've excerpted events and dialogue from Toni Morrison's novel *Beloved*. Morrison won the Nobel Prize in Literature in 1993 and won the Pulitzer Prize for Fiction for this book about Sethe, an African-American woman who escaped from slavery.

Sethe was raised and married on a Kentucky farm belonging to a comparatively benign man who owned six slaves. When the owner died, an in-law known as "schoolteacher" arrived to "put things in order." Besides overseeing the farm, he worked on a book about the lives of slaves. In a grim caricature of ethnographic analysis, schoolteacher asked slaves many questions and wrote down what they said in the notebook he always carried. He also tutored his two teenage nephews on the way to whip Sethe without breaking her spirit, instructed them to keep a detailed record of her animal characteristics, and referred to Sethe's value in terms of breeding potential—property that reproduces itself without cost.

The pivotal event in the novel occurs a month after Sethe and her children have escaped to her mother-in-law's home in Ohio. While working in the garden she sees four men in the distance riding toward the house—schoolteacher, a nephew, a slave catcher, and the sheriff. Sethe frantically scoops up her kids and runs to the woodshed behind the house. When schoolteacher opens the door a minute later, he sees a grizzly scene of death—two boys lying open-eyed in sawdust, a girl pumping the last of her blood from a throat slit by a crosscut saw, and Sethe trying to bash in the head of her baby girl. Speaking for the four men, the nephew asks in bewilderment, "What she want to go and do that for?" Much of the book is an answer to that question as Toni Morrison describes the oppositional standpoints of a male slaveowner (schoolteacher) and a female slave (Sethe).

WOMEN AS A MARGINALIZED GROUP

Standpoint theorists see important differences between men and women. Wood uses the relational dialectic of autonomy-connectedness as a case in point (see Chapter 12): "While all humans seem to seek both autonomy and connectedness, the relative amount of each that is preferred appears to differ rather consistently between genders."[13] Men tend to want more autonomy; women tend to want more connectedness. This difference is evident in each group's communication. The masculine community uses speech to accomplish tasks, assert self, and gain power. The feminine community uses speech to build relationships, include others, and show responsiveness.[14]

Wood does not attribute gender differences to biology, maternal instinct, or women's intuition. To the extent that women are distinct from men, she sees the difference largely as a result of cultural expectations and the treatment that each group receives from the other. For example, Sethe would get "blood in her eye" whenever she heard a slur against any woman of color. When Paul D, the only living black male from her slave past, tells Sethe that he has a "bad feeling" about a homeless young woman she's taken in, Sethe retorts:

> "Well feel this, why don't you? Feel how it feels to have a bed to sleep in and somebody there not worrying you to death about what you got to do each day to deserve it. Feel how that feels. And if you don't get it, feel how it feels to be a coloredwoman roaming the roads with anything God made liable to jump on you. Feel that."[15]

Paul D protests that he never mistreated a woman in his whole life. Sethe snaps back, "That makes one in the world."

Sethe's words illustrate how otherness is *engendered* in women by the way men respond to them. The reality she describes also reflects the power discrepancies that Harding and Wood say are found in all societies: "A culture is not experienced identically by all members. Cultures are hierarchically ordered so that different groups within them have positions that offer dissimilar power, opportunities, and experiences to members."[16] Along these lines, feminist standpoint theorists suggest that women are underadvantaged, and thus men are overadvantaged—a gender difference that makes a huge difference.

Harding and Wood are quick to warn against thinking of women as a monolithic group. They point out that not all women share the same standpoint, nor for that matter do all men. Besides the issue of gender, Harding stresses economic condition, race, and sexual orientation as additional cultural identities that can either draw people to the center of society or push them out to the fringes. Thus, an intersection of minority positions creates a highly looked-down-upon location in the social hierarchy. Impoverished African-American lesbian women are almost always marginalized. On the other hand,

"Actually, Lou, I think it was more than just my being in the right place at the right time. I think it was my being the right race, the right religion, the right sex, the right socioeconomic group, having the right accent, the right clothes, going to the right schools . . ."

positions of high status and power are overwhelmingly "manned" by wealthy, white, heterosexual males.

Even more than Harding, Wood is troubled by the tendency of some feminists to talk as if there were an "essence of women," then to "valorize" that quality. She believes that Carol Gilligan made this mistake by claiming that women, as opposed to men, speak in an ethical voice of care (see Chapter 33). For Wood, biology is not destiny. She fears that "championing any singular model of womanhood creates a mold into which not all women may comfortably fit."[17] Yet as an unapologetic feminist committed to the equal value of all human life, Wood understands that a sense of solidarity is politically necessary if women are to effectively critique an androcentric world.

Standpoint theorists emphasize the importance of social location because they are convinced that people at the top of the societal hierarchy are the ones privileged to define what it means to be female, male, or anything else in a given culture. We can see this power when Sethe recalls a time when schoolteacher accuses a slave named Sixo of stealing a young pig. When Sixo denies stealing the animal, schoolteacher takes on the role of Grand Interpreter:

> "You telling me you didn't steal it, and I'm looking right at you?"
> "No, sir."
> Schoolteacher smiled. "Did you kill it?"
> "Yes, sir."
> "Did you butcher it?"

"Yes, sir."

"Did you cook it?"

"Yes, sir."

"Well, then. Did you eat it?"

"Yes, sir. I sure did."

"And you telling me that's not stealing?"

"No, sir. It ain't."

"What is it then?"

"Improving your property, sir."

"What?"

" . . . Sixo take and feed the soil, give you more crop. Sixo take and feed Sixo give you more work."

Clever, but schoolteacher beat him anyway to show him that definitions belonged to the definers—not the defined.[18]

KNOWLEDGE FROM NOWHERE VERSUS LOCAL KNOWLEDGE

Why is standpoint so important? Because, Harding argues, "the social group that gets the chance to define the important problematics, concepts, assumptions, and hypotheses in a field will end up leaving its social fingerprints on the picture of the world that emerges from the results of that field's research process."[19] Imagine how different a book by schoolteacher entitled *Slaves* would be from one of the same title written by Sethe (as told to Toni Morrison). The texts would surely differ in starting point, method, and conclusion.

Harding's insistence on *local knowledge* contrasts sharply with the claim of traditional Western science that it discovers "Truth" that is value-free and accessible to any objective observer. In her book *Whose Science? Whose Knowledge?* Harding refers to empiricism's claims of disembodied truths as "views from nowhere," or in the words of feminist writer Donna Haraway, "the God trick."[20] As for the notion of value-free science, Harding characterizes the claim as promoting "a fast gun for hire" and chides detached scientists that "it cannot be value-free to describe such social events as poverty, misery, torture, or cruelty in a value-free way."[21] Even Galileo's democratic ideal of interchangeable knowers is open to question. His statement *Anyone can see through my telescope* has been interpreted by empirical scientists as dismissing concern for any relationship between the knower and the known.

Harding and other standpoint theorists insist that there is no possibility of an unbiased perspective that is disinterested, impartial, value-free, or detached from a particular historical situation. Both the physical and the social sciences are always situated in time and place. She writes that "each person can achieve only a partial view of reality from the perspective of his or her own position in the social hierarchy."[22] Unlike postmodernists, however, she is unwilling to abandon the search for reality. She simply thinks that the search for it should begin from the lives of those in the underclass.

Suppose you were to do research on the topic of *family values*. Rather than analyzing current political rhetoric or exploring the genesis of the growing home-school movement, Harding would suggest that you frame your research questions and hypotheses starting with the family values of people like Baby Suggs, Sethe's mother-in-law. For example, Morrison explains why this freed slave values a son more than a man:

Local knowledge
Knowledge situated in time, place, experience, and relative power, as opposed to knowledge from nowhere that's supposedly value-free.

It made sense for a lot of reasons because in all of Baby's life, as well as Sethe's own, men and women were moved around like checkers. Anybody Baby Suggs knew, let alone loved, who hadn't run off or been hanged, got rented out, loaned out, bought up, brought back, stored up, mortgaged, won, stolen or seized. So Baby's eight children had six fathers. What she called the nastiness of life was the shock she received upon learning that nobody stopped playing checkers just because the pieces included her children.[23]

Neither Harding nor Wood claims that the standpoint of women or any other marginalized group gives them a clear view of the way things are. *Situated knowledge*—the only kind there is—will always be partial. Standpoint theorists do maintain, however, that "the perspectives of subordinate groups are more complete and thus, better than those of privileged groups in a society."[24]

STRONG OBJECTIVITY: LESS PARTIAL VIEWS FROM THE STANDPOINT OF WOMEN

Strong objectivity
The strategy of starting research from the lives of women and other marginalized groups, thus providing a less false view of reality.

Harding uses the term *strong objectivity* to refer to the strategy of starting research from the lives of women and other marginalized groups whose concerns and experience are usually ignored.[25] Her choice of label not only suggests the wisdom of taking all perspectives into account but also suggests that knowledge generated from the standpoint of dominant groups offers, by contrast, only a *weak* objectivity. To illustrate this claim, she speaks directly of the oppositional standpoints of the kind described in Toni Morrison's *Beloved:* "It is absurd to imagine that U.S. slaveowners' views of Africans' and African Americans' lives could outweigh in impartiality, disinterestedness, impersonality, and objectivity their slaves' view of their own and slaveowners' lives."[26]

Why should the standpoints of women and other marginalized groups be less partial, less distorted, or less false than the perspectives of men who are in dominant positions? Wood offers two explanations: "First, people with subordinate status have greater motivation to understand the perspective of more powerful groups than vice versa."[27] Even if the meek don't inherit the earth, they have a special interest in figuring out what makes it turn, and so taking the role of the other is a survival skill for those who have little control over their own lives. Lacking this motivation, those who wield power seem to have less reason to wonder how the "other half" views the world.

Wood's second reason for favoring the standpoint of groups that are constantly put down is that they have little reason to defend the status quo. Not so for those who have power. She asserts that "groups that are advantaged by the prevailing system have a vested interest in not perceiving social inequities that benefit them at the expense of others."[28] For the overprivileged, ignorance of the other's perspective is bliss, so it's folly to be wise. Certainly the men who come to take Sethe and her children back into slavery could be assigned to that clueless category. "What she want to go and do that for?" they ask in real bewilderment. If they or anyone else really wanted to know why a runaway slave would slit her daughter's throat, they'd need to begin their inquiry from the standpoint of slaves—women slaves—not from the perspective of masters, or even that of black men. They would discover Sethe's utter desperation:

She saw them coming and recognized schoolteacher's hat. . . . And if she thought anything, it was No. No. Nonono. Simple. She just flew. Collected every bit of life she had made, all the parts of her that were precious and fine and beautiful and carried, pushed dragged them through the veil, out, away, over there where no one could hurt them. Over there. Outside this place, where they would be safe. . . .

When she got back from the jail house, she was glad the fence was gone. That's where they had hitched their horses—where she saw, floating above the railing as she squatted in the garden, schoolteacher's hat. By the time she faced him, looked him dead in the eye, she had something in her arms that stopped him in his tracks. He took a backward step with each jump of the baby heart until finally there were none.

"I stopped him," she said, staring at the place where the fence used to be. "I took and put my babies where they'd be safe."[29]

As gripping as these words are, Harding would not ask us to automatically accept Sethe's explanation or approve her drastic response just because they are the words and actions of a marginalized woman. After all, many of the free African-American women in Morrison's novel condemn Sethe's drastic way of keeping her daughter Beloved safe from schoolteacher's hands. But Sethe's wrenching fear for her children's welfare is the stark reality of enslaved women everywhere (see the book/film *Sophie's Choice*). Harding emphasizes that it's the "objective perspective *from women's lives*" that provides a preferred standpoint from which to generate research projects, hypotheses, and interpretations.[30] Perhaps such research could seriously explore perceptions of "a fate worse than death."

THEORY TO PRACTICE: COMMUNICATION RESEARCH BASED ON WOMEN'S LIVES

If we want to see a model of communication research that starts from the lives of women, a good place to begin is Julia Wood's in-depth study of caregiving in the United States. Consistent with standpoint theory's insistence that all knowledge is situated in a time and place, the first chapter of Wood's *Who Cares? Women, Care, and Culture* describes her own situation as a white, heterosexual, professional woman who for nine years took on the consuming responsibility of caring for her infirm parents until they died. Her experience squared with her subsequent research findings:

> First, it seems that caring can be healthy and enriching when it is informed, freely chosen, and practiced within a context that recognizes and values caring and those who do it. On the other hand, existing studies also suggest that caring can be quite damaging to caregivers if they are unaware of dangers to their identities, if they have unrealistic expectations of themselves, and/or if caring occurs within contexts that fail to recognize its importance and value.[31]

Wood discovered that gendered communication practices reflect and reinforce our societal expectation that caregiving is women's work. After rejecting his daughter's proposal to hire a part-time nurse, her father mused, "It's funny, Julia. I used to wish I had sons, but now I'm glad I have daughters, because I couldn't ask a son to take this kind of time away from his own work just to take care of me."[32] She heard similar messages that devalued caregiving from male colleagues at her university. While praising Wood for her sacrifice, they reassured a fellow professor that he had taken the proper action by placing his mother in a nursing home: "Well, she surely understood that as busy as you are with your work you couldn't be expected to take on that responsibility."[33] Wood says these comments reveal the opposing, gender-based privileges and restraints in our society. As illustrated in the book/film *One True Thing*, women are given the freedom to make caregiving a priority but are denied the right to put their work first and still be a "good woman." Men are given the freedom to make their work a priority but are deprived of the right to focus on caregiving and still be a "good man."

Wood suggests that a standpoint approach is practical to the extent that it generates an effective critique of unjust practices. She believes that "our culture itself must be reformed in ways that dissociate caring from its historical affiliations with women and private relationships and redefine it as a centrally important and integral part of our collective public life."[34] Perhaps a proposal in President Clinton's 1999 State of the Union address was a first step. He endorsed a $1,000 tax write-off for families taking care of an incapacitated relative in their homes. A male network news commentator dismissed the idea as "more symbolic than significant." The female cohost chided that the symbolic recognition of worth was *quite* significant. She shared Wood's standpoint.

THE STANDPOINT OF BLACK FEMINIST THOUGHT

Patricia Hill Collins, an African-American sociologist at Brandeis University, claims that the patterns of "intersecting oppressions" that black women in the United States have experienced puts them in a different marginalized place in society than either white women or black men. In her book *Black Feminist Thought*, Collins says that "the heavy concentration of U.S. black women in domestic work coupled with racial segregation in housing and schools" enabled them to construct a common body of wisdom about how to survive in the world.[35] She agrees with other black feminists that "we have to see clearly that we are a unique group set undeniably apart because of race and sex with a unique set of challenges."[36] That different social location means that black women's way of knowing is different from Harding and Wood's standpoint epistemology.

I'll use Collins' words to describe the four ways that she says black women validate knowledge claims:[37]

1. *Lived experience as a criterion of meaning.* For most African-American women, those individuals who have lived through the experience about which they claim to be experts are more believable and credible than those who have merely read or thought about such experiences.

2. *The use of dialogue in assessing knowledge claims.* For ideas to be tested and validated, everyone in the group must participate. To refuse to join in, especially if one really disagrees with what has been said, is seen as "cheating."

3. *The ethic of caring.* Emotion indicates that a speaker believes in the validity of an argument. The sound of what is being said is as important as the words themselves, in what is, in a sense, a dialogue of reason and emotion.

4. *The ethic of personal accountability.* Assessments of an individual's knowledge claims simultaneously evaluate an individual's character, values, and ethics.

Collins doesn't claim that a black feminist standpoint epistemology provides African-American women with the best view of how the social world works. She rejects an additive model of oppression that would claim that poor, black, lesbian women are more oppressed than any other marginalized group. But when the same ideas are validated as true through black feminist thought, and from the standpoints of other oppressed groups as well, then those ideas become the least partial, most "objective" truths available.

ETHICAL REFLECTION: BENHABIB'S INTERACTIVE UNIVERSALISM

Seyla Benhabib has undertaken a formidable task. Recall that Enlightenment thinkers such as Kant, Locke, and Habermas have always believed "that reason is a natural disposition of the human mind, which when governed by proper education can discover certain truths."[38] Benhabib, who is a professor of government at Harvard University, wants to maintain that a universal ethical standard is a viable possibility. But she also feels the force of three major attacks on Enlightenment rationality in general, and Habermas' discourse ethics in particular (see pages 231–232). Thus, she sets out to "defend the tradition of universalism in the face of this triple-pronged critique by engaging the claims of feminism, communitarianism, and postmodernism."[39] At the same time, she wants to learn from them and incorporate their insights into her interactive universalism. I'll discuss them in reverse order.

Postmodern critique.   Recall that in his widely discussed 1984 treatise *The Postmodern Condition*, Jean-Francois Lyotard declares that there are no longer any *grand narratives* on which to base a universal version of truth.[40] Postmodernists dismiss any *a priori* assumptions, or givens, that attempt to legitimate the moral ideals of the Enlightenment and Western liberal democracy. They are suspicious of consensus and Habermas' attempt to legislate rationality. Benhabib sums up the postmodern critique: "transcendental guarantees of truth are dead; . . . there is only the endless struggle of local narratives vying with one another for legitimization."[41] She appreciates the postmodern insistence that a moral point of view is an accomplishment rather than a discovery, but she is not "content with singing the swan-song of normative thinking in general."[42] Benhabib holds out the possibility that instead of reaching a consensus on how everyone *should act*, interacting individuals can align themselves with a *common good*.

Communitarian critique.   If there is one commitment that draws communitarians and postmodernists together, it is the "critique of Western rationality as seen from the perspective of the margins, from the standpoint of what and whom it excludes, suppresses, delegitimatizes, renders mad, imbecilic or childish."[43] Benhabib realizes the danger of pressing a global moral template onto a local situation. If we regard people as disembodied moral agents who are devoid of history, relationships, or obligations, we'll be unable to deal with the messiness of real-life contexts. To avoid this error, Benhabib insists that any panhuman ethic be achieved through interaction with collective concrete others—ordinary people who live in community—rather than imposed on them by a rational elite.

Feminist critique.   Carol Gilligan, Deborah Tannen, Sandra Harding, Julia Wood, and Cheris Kramarae (see Chapter 35) all agree that women's experiences and the way they talk about them are different from men's. Yet typical of rationalistic approaches, Habermas virtually ignores gender distinctions. His conception of discourse ethics speaks to issues of political and economic justice in the masculine-dominated public sphere. But he relegates the activities to which women have historically been confined—rearing children, housekeeping, satisfying the emotional and sexual needs of the male, tending to the sick and the elderly—to a private sphere where norms of freedom, equality, and reciprocity don't seem to apply.[44] Because of its emphasis on open dialogue in which no topics are regarded as trivial, interactive universalism would avoid privatizing women's experiences.

Despite these three critiques, Benhabib believes that a new breed of universal ethic is still possible. "Such a universalism would be interactive not legislative, cognizant of gender differences, not gender blind, contextually sensitive and not situation indifferent."[45] It would be a moral framework that values the diversity of human beliefs without thinking that every difference is ethically significant.[46] Perhaps it would include a commitment to help all people survive and thrive.

CRITIQUE: DO STANDPOINTS ON THE MARGINS GIVE A LESS FALSE VIEW?

Patricia Collins warns that "if African-American women's experiences are more different than similar, then Black feminist thought does not exist."[47] As stated in a previous section, she claims the similarities are greater than the differences. Can the same be said for all women? Julia Wood says that the concept of women as a single social group is politically useful to bring about needed reforms, but is this reality or just needed fiction? As proponents become more and more specific about the standpoints from which particular women communicate, the concept of group solidarity that is at the heart of standpoint theory becomes questionable.

Feminist scholars such as Susan Hekman and Nancy Hirschmann are concerned that Harding's version of standpoint theory underestimates the role that language plays in expressing one's sense of self and view of the world.[48] As theorists throughout this book have maintained, people's communication choices are never neutral or value-free, so people can't separate their standpoint from the language they use to describe it. The words they choose inevitably are influenced by their cultural and societal filters. This critique of standpoint theory doesn't negate the importance of situated knowledge, but it complicates our reception of anyone's take on reality, whether it comes from the center or the margins of the social fabric. In fact, voices from the edge may be particularly difficult to express, since linguistic conventions traditionally are controlled by the privileged. This point is developed in the context of *muted group theory* in the next chapter.

Other critics of Harding and Wood's position regard the concept of *strong objectivity* as inherently contradictory.[49] In postmodern fashion, standpoint theorists argue that standpoints are relative and can't be evaluated by any absolute criteria. Yet they propose that the oppressed are less biased or more impartial than the privileged. This appears to bring universal standards of judgment back into play. Thus, on the matter of transcendental truths, the theory seems to want to have it both ways.

Despite these difficulties, I find the logic of standpoint theory appealing. If all knowledge is tainted by the social location of the knower, then we would do well to start our search for truth from the perspective of people who are most sensitive to inequities of power. They will have the least to lose if findings challenge the status quo. Wood acknowledges that we may have trouble figuring out which social groups are more marginalized than others. As a white, professional woman, is Wood lower on the social hierarchy than her African-American male colleague who has attained the same faculty rank at the university? Standpoint theory doesn't say, but it clearly suggests that we should question much of the received wisdom that comes from a male-dominated, Western European research establishment and replace it when a *strong objectivity* provides a more complete picture of the world. The idea energizes University of Wisconsin–Milwaukee sociologist Lynn Worsham and others who believe that minority standpoints can be a partial corrective to the biased knowledge that now passes for truth:

> In what I consider, in all sincerity, to be a heroic and marvelous conception, Harding turns the tables on philosophy and the sciences and constructs a sort of feminist alchemy in which the idea of standpoint, revamped by postmodern philosophy, becomes the philosophers' stone capable of transforming the West's base materials into resources for producing a more "generally useful account of the world."[50]

QUESTIONS TO SHARPEN YOUR FOCUS

1. What is common to the standpoints of *women, African Americans, the poor,* and *homosexuals* that may provide them with a *less false view* of the way society works?

2. How could we test the claim that *strong objectivity from women's lives* provides a more accurate view of the world than knowledge generated by a predominantly male research establishment?

3. I am a privileged white male who decided which theories would be covered in this book. Suppose I were a disadvantaged African-American woman. What theories might I drop and which might I keep? Why might this be a ridiculous question?

4. *Standpoint epistemology* draws on insights from *Marxism, symbolic interactionism,* and *postmodernism.* Based on what you've read in this chapter, which of these intellectual influences do you see as strongest? Why?

A SECOND LOOK

Recommended resource: Julia T. Wood, *Communication Theories in Action,* 3rd ed., Wadsworth, Belmont, CA, 2004, pp. 212–220.

Comprehensive statement: Sandra Harding, *Whose Science? Whose Knowledge? Thinking from Women's Lives,* Cornell University Press, Ithaca, NY, 1991.

Reconstruction of scientific objectivity: Sandra Harding, *Is Science Multicultural? Postcolonialisms, Feminisms and Epistemologies,* Indiana University, Bloomington, 1998.

Standpoint critique of science: Sandra Harding, *Science and Social Inequality: Feminist and Postcolonial Issues,* University of Illinois, Urbana, 2006, pp. 80–97.

Avoiding essentialism: Julia T. Wood, "Gender and Moral Voice: Moving from Woman's Nature to Standpoint Epistemology," *Women's Studies in Communication,* Vol. 15, 1993, pp. 1–24.

Women and care: Julia T. Wood, *Who Cares? Women, Care, and Culture,* Southern Illinois University Press, Carbondale, 1994.

Standpoint of women in communication discipline: Lynn O'Brien Hallstein (ed.), *Women's Studies in Communication*, Vol. 23, Spring 2000, special issue on standpoint theories.

Diverse forms of standpoint theory: Sandra Harding (ed.), *The Feminist Standpoint Theory Reader: Intellectual and Political Controversies*, Routledge, New York, 2004.

Black feminist thought: Patricia Hill Collins, *Black Feminist Thought: Knowledge, Consciousness, and the Politics of Empowerment*, 2nd ed., Routledge, New York, 2000.

Collins' stand on standpoint theory: Patricia Hill Collins, *Fighting Words: Black Women and the Search for Justice*, University of Minnesota, Minneapolis, 1998, pp. 201–228.

Comparing two feminist theories: Julia T. Wood, "Feminist Standpoint Theory and Muted Group Theory: Commonalities and Divergences," *Women and Language*, Vol. 28, 2005, pp. 61–64.

Interactive universalism: Seyla Benhabib, *Situating the Self: Gender, Community and Postmodernism in Contemporary Ethics*, Routledge, New York, 1992.

Feminist critique: Lynn Worsham, "Romancing the Stones: My Movie Date with Sandra Harding," *Journal of Advanced Composition*, Vol. 15, 1995, pp. 565–571.

To access Web sites linked to specific theories or theorists, click on Links at
www.afirstlook.com.

CHAPTER 35

Muted Group Theory

of Cheris Kramarae

Cheris Kramarae maintains that language is literally a *man*-made construction.

> The language of a particular culture does not serve all its speakers equally, for not all speakers contribute in an equal fashion to its formulation. Women (and members of other subordinate groups) are not as free or as able as men are to say what they wish, when and where they wish, because the words and the norms for their use have been formulated by the dominant group, men.[1]

According to Kramarae and other feminist theorists, women's words are discounted in our society; women's thoughts are devalued. When women try to overcome this inequity, the masculine control of communication places them at a tremendous disadvantage. Man-made language "aids in defining, depreciating and excluding women."[2] Women are thus a muted group.

For many years Kramarae was a professor of speech communication and sociology at the University of Illinois. She is now a visiting professor at the Center for the Study of Women at the University of Oregon and recently served as a dean for the International Woman's University in Germany. She began her research career in 1974 when she conducted a systematic study of the way women were portrayed in cartoons.[3] She found that women were notable mostly by their absence. A quick survey of the cartoon art I've used in this book will show that little has changed since Kramarae's study. Only 20 of the 52 cartoons contain female characters, and only 11 of these women speak. All but two of the cartoonists are men.

Kramarae discovered that women in cartoons were usually depicted as emotional, apologetic, or just plain wishy-washy. Compared with the simple, forceful statements voiced by cartoon males, the words assigned to female characters were vague, flowery, and peppered with adjectives like *nice* and *pretty*. Kramarae noted at the time that women who don't appreciate this form of comic put-down are often accused by men of having no sense of humor or simply told to "lighten up." According to Kramarae, this type of male dominance is just one of the many ways that women are rendered inarticulate in our society. For the last 25 years Kramarae has been a leader in the effort to explain and alter the muted status of women and other marginalized groups.

MUTED GROUPS: BLACK HOLES IN SOMEONE ELSE'S UNIVERSE

The idea of women as a *muted group* was first proposed by Oxford University social anthropologist Edwin Ardener. In his monograph "Belief and the Problem of Women," Ardener noted the strange tendency of many ethnographers to claim to have "cracked the code" of a culture without ever making any direct reference to the half of society made up of women. Field researchers often justify this omission by reporting the difficulty of using women as cultural informants. Females "giggle when young, snort when old, reject the question, laugh at the topic," and generally make life difficult for scholars trained in the scientific (masculine) method of inquiry.[4] Ardener acknowledged the problem, but he also reminded his colleagues how suspicious they'd be of an anthropologist who wrote about the men of a tribe on the sole basis of talking only to the women.

Ardener initially assumed that inattention to women's experience was a problem of gender unique to social anthropology. But along with his Oxford co-worker Shirley Ardener, he began to realize that mutedness is due to the lack of power that besets any group occupying the low-end of the totem pole. People with little clout have trouble giving voice to their perceptions. Edwin Ardener says that their "muted structures are 'there' but cannot be 'realized' in the language of the dominant structure."[5] As a result, they are overlooked, muffled, and rendered invisible—"mere black holes in someone else's universe."[6]

Muted group

People with little power who have trouble giving voice to their perceptions because they must re-encode their thoughts to make them understood in the public sphere; e.g., women.

Shirley Ardener cautions that a theory of mutedness doesn't necessarily imply that the *muted group* is always silent. The issue is whether people can say what they want to say when and where they want to say it, or must they "re-encode their thoughts to make them understood in the public domain?"[7] Cheris Kramarae is certain that men's dominant power position in society guarantees that the public mode of expression won't be directly available to women. Her extension of the Ardeners' initial concept offers insight into why women are muted and what can be done to loosen men's lock on public modes of communication.

Kramarae argues that the ever-prevalent *public-private* distinction in language is a convenient way to exaggerate gender differences and pose separate sexual spheres of activity. This is, of course, a pitfall into which Deborah Tannen virtually leaps (see Chapter 33). Within the logic of a two-sphere assumption, the words of women usually are considered appropriate in the home—a "small world" of interpersonal communication. This private world is somehow less important than the "large world" of significant public debate—a place where the words of men resonate. Kramarae wonders what it would be like if there were a word that pointed to the *connection* of public and private communication. If there were such a word in everyone's speaking vocabulary, its use would establish the idea that both spheres have equal worth and that similarities between women and men are more important than their differences.

Since there is no such word in our lexicon, I think of this textbook as a *public* mode of communication. I am a male. I realize that in the process of trying to present muted group theory with integrity, I may unconsciously put a masculine spin on Kramarae's ideas and the perceptions of women. In an effort to minimize this bias, I will quote extensively from Kramarae and other feminist scholars. Kramarae is just one of many communication professionals who seek to unmask the systematic silencing of a feminine *voice*. I'll also draw freely on the words and experiences of other women to illustrate the communication double bind that Kramarae says is a feminine fact of life. This reliance on personal narrative is consistent with a feminist research agenda that takes women's experiences seriously.

THE MASCULINE POWER TO NAME EXPERIENCE

Kramarae starts with the assumption that "women perceive the world differently from men because of women's and men's different experience and activities rooted in the division of labor."[8] Kramarae rejects Freud's simplistic notion that "anatomy is destiny." She is certain, however, that power discrepancies between the sexes ensure that women will view the world in a way different from men. While women vary in many ways, in most cultures, if not all, women's talk is subject to male control and censorship. French existentialist Simone de Beauvoir underscored this common feminine experience when she declared, "'I am woman': on this truth must be based all further discussion."[9]

The problem facing women, according to Kramarae, is that further discussions about how the world works never take place on a level playing field. "Because of their political dominance, the men's system of perception is dominant, impeding the free expression of the women's alternative models of the world."[10]

Note that my phrase *level playing field* is a metaphor drawn from competitive team sports—an experience familiar to more men than women. This is precisely Kramarae's point. As possessors of the public mode of expression, men frame the discussion. If a man wants to contest the point about a tilted playing field, he can argue in the familiar idiom of sports. But a woman who takes issue with the metaphor of competition has to contest it with stereotypical masculine linguistic terms.

Mead's symbolic interactionist perspective asserts that the extent of knowing is the extent of naming (see Chapter 5). If this is true, whoever has the ability to make names stick possesses an awesome power. Kramarae notes that men's control of the dominant mode of expression has produced a vast stock of derogatory, gender-specific terms to refer to women's talking—*catty, bitchy, shrill, cackling, gossipy, chitchat, sharp-tongued,* and so forth. There is no corresponding vocabulary to disparage men's conversation.

In case you think this lexical bias is limited to descriptions of speech, consider the variety of terms in the English language to describe sexually promiscuous individuals. By one count, there are 22 gender-related words to label men who are sexually loose—*playboy, stud, rake, gigolo, player, Don Juan, lothario, womanizer,* and so on. There are more than 200 words that label sexually loose women—*slut, whore, hooker, prostitute, trollop, mistress, harlot, Jezebel, hussy, concubine, streetwalker, strumpet, easy lay,* and the like.[11] Since most surveys of sexual activity show that more men than women have multiple sexual partners, there's no doubt that the inordinate number of terms describing women serves the interests of men.

Under the socio-cultural tradition in Chapter 4, I introduced the Sapir-Whorf hypothesis, which claims that language shapes our perception of reality. Kramarae suggests that women are often silenced by not having a publicly recognized vocabulary through which to express their experience. She says that "words constantly ignored may eventually come to be unspoken and perhaps even unthought."[12] After a while, muted women may even come to doubt the validity of their experience and the legitimacy of their feelings.

MEN AS THE GATEKEEPERS OF COMMUNICATION

Even if the public mode of expression contained a rich vocabulary to describe feminine experience, women would still be muted if *their* modes of expression were ignored or ridiculed. Indeed, Kramarae describes a "good ole boys" cultural establishment that virtually excludes women's art, poetry, plays, film scripts, public address, and scholarly essays from society's mass media. She notes that women were locked out of the publishing business for 500 years. It wasn't until the 1970s and the establishment of women's presses in the Western world that women could exercise ongoing influence through the print medium. For that reason, Kramarae sees traditional mainstream communication as *malestream expression.*

Gatekeepers
Editors and other arbiters of culture who determine which books, essays, poetry, plays, film scripts, etc. will appear in the mass media.

Long before Edwin Ardener noted women's absence in anthropological research, Virginia Woolf protested women's nonplace in recorded history. The British novelist detected an incongruity between the way men characterize women in fiction and how women concurrently appear in history books. "Imaginatively she is of the highest importance; practically she is completely insignificant. She pervades poetry from cover to cover; she is all but absent from history."[13]

Feminist writer Dorothy Smith claims that women's absence from history is a result of closed-circuit masculine scholarship.

> Men attend to and treat as significant only what men say. The circle of men whose writing and talk was significant to each other extends backwards in time as far as our records reach. What men were doing was relevant to men, was written by men about men for men. Men listened and listen to what one another said.[14]

As an example of men's control of the public record, Cheris Kramarae cites the facts surrounding her change of name. When she was married in Ohio, the law required her to take the name of her husband. So at the direction of the state, she became *Cheris Rae Kramer.* Later, when it became legal for her to be her own person, she reordered the sounds and spelling to Cheris Kramarae. Many people questioned Kramarae about whether her name change was either loving or wise. Yet no one asked her husband why he kept *his* name. Kramarae points out that both the law and the conventions of proper etiquette have served men well.

THE UNFULFILLED PROMISE OF THE INTERNET

We might assume that the advent of the Internet has put an end to men's gatekeeping role—at least as far as access to the World Wide Web is concerned. Kramarae's ongoing research suggests that it isn't so. She says that "just as we are developing the tools needed to study them, traditional power relations between women and men are being quickly established in cyberspace."[15] Almost all the early designers and users of the Internet in the 1970s and 1980s were male. By the year 2000, half of Internet users were female, but "if we consider the amount of time spent on computers, the type of equipment, and the influence of programming, everywhere the technological elite overwhelmingly are men. . . ."[16] For example, although abuse of women is a well-researched topic, many databases have no separate heading for the term *battered.* You can tell that women aren't designing the Internet search categories when the first listing under "Women of the Internet" shows *Playboy* nudes.[17] Kramarae concludes that the Internet still has the potential to facilitate interaction among women across time and space, but it seems to be emerging as a men's forum and playground.

Since Kramarae believes that gender is accomplished in discourse, she would have us pay close attention to the imagery that's used to describe the Internet. Four common metaphors show why women continue to be muted and the promise of gender equality has yet to be fulfilled. Metaphors matter; each shapes a certain way of thinking.

Information superhighway.   This early utopian analogy ignored the established social and economic structures. The start-up cost of access to the Internet makes it a toll road that only a small percentage of women around the world can afford. The digital divide is growing. Those who can pay the price of entry often find "the basic terminology, category system, and content of the World Wide Web is not basically designed to welcome actual women or their interests."[18] Some women suggest that they are "roadkill" as men race down the highway.

New frontier.   Kramarae suggests that this metaphor calls to mind an unsettled space where courageous individuals are free to do what they wish. Studies in schools show that little boys quickly learn that they *can* and *may* push girls off classroom computers. The anarchy of the rough-and-tumble atmosphere doesn't appeal to many women, especially when they are flamed in response to their posting on a listserv or bulletin board. To avoid online harassment, many women who participate present themselves as men.

Democracy.   As in the privacy of a voting booth, an individual can state his or her opinion on the Web with anonymity. That seclusion can be an advantage for women. Unlike "the loud, pompous, ego-driven discourse of talk radio, the Quiet of the Internet gives women the space to express themselves sincerely and intimately."[19] But one must be both computer-literate and conversant in the English language, the lingua franca of the Internet. Kramarae also notes that the downside of a democratic Net is that anyone can post anything, even if it has no basis in reality. Then she adds,

> Of course for women trying to figure out what is real has been a lifelong project. We haven't been the knowledge makers. We have learned to be skeptical of the "truths" we've been told. Now we have to be even more careful perhaps, but this is not a new problem for us.[20]

Global community.   For Kramarae, the Internet holds the possibility of being a user-friendly place of connection with other like-minded women around the world. Women can share their concerns and information about global topics such as breast cancer, eating disorders, child rearing, sex tourism, ecology, peace, spirituality, and the jerks they have for bosses in a way that may not be available to them face-to-face. Yet the Internet seems to offer community to those already online rather than encouraging those who aren't present to participate. And there's always the threat of male imposters shattering the integrity of "women-only" sites that attempt to develop a sense of trust.

Although male-oriented Internet norms have already been established, Kramarae continues to see great potential for cyberspace to be a humane place for women because the technology is interactive. She imagines "computer terminals connected to community systems in Laundromats, homeless shelters, daycare centers, etc.—with sufficient support so that most people have access to the Internet."[21] Until then, many women will continue to be muted.

WOMEN'S TRUTH INTO MEN'S TALK: THE PROBLEM OF TRANSLATION

Assuming masculine dominance of public communication to be a current reality, Kramarae concludes that "in order to participate in society women must transform their own models in terms of the received male system of expression."[22] Like speaking in a second language, this translation process requires constant effort and usually leaves a woman wondering whether she's said it "just right." One woman writer says men can "tell it straight." Women have to "tell it slant."[23]

Think back again to Mead's symbolic interactionism (see Chapter 5). His theory describes *minding* as an automatic momentary pause before we speak in order to mentally consider how those who are listening might respond. These periods of hesitation grow longer when we feel linguistically impoverished. According to Kramarae, women have to choose their words carefully in a public forum. "What women want to say and can say best cannot be said easily because the language template is not of their own making."[24]

I have gained a new appreciation of the difficulty women face in translating their experiences into man-made language by discussing Kramarae's ideas with three women friends. Marsha, Kathy, and Susan have consciously sought and achieved positions of leadership in professions where women are rarely seen and almost never heard.

Marsha is a litigation attorney who was the first woman president of the Hillsborough County Bar Association (Florida) and was chair of a branch of the Federal Reserve Board that advised Alan Greenspan. A local magazine article spotlighted five "power players of Tampa Bay." The hero of the 1991 Gulf War, General Norman Schwarzkopf, was one; Marsha was another. Marsha attributes her success to a conscious shifting of gears when she addresses the law.

> I've learned to talk like a man. I consciously lower my voice, speak more slowly, think bigger, and use sports analogies. I care about my appearance, but a woman who is too attractive or too homely has a problem. A man can be drop-dead gorgeous or ugly as sin and get along OK. I've been told that I'm the most feared and respected attorney in the firm, but that's not the person I live with day by day. After work I go home and make reindeer pins out of dog biscuits with my daughters.

Kathy is an ordained minister who works with high school students and young adults. She is the best speaker I've ever heard in a public address class. Working in an organization that traditionally excludes women from up-front speaking roles, Kathy is recognized as a star communicator. Like Marsha, she feels women have little margin for error when they speak in public.

> Women have to work both sides to pull it off. I let my appearance and delivery say feminine—jewelry, lipstick, warm soft voice. But I plan my content to appeal to men as well. I can't get away with just winging it. I prepare carefully, know my script, use lots of imagery from the world of guys. Girls learn to be inter-

"The committee on women's rights will now come to order."

Reproduced by permission of Punch Limited

ested in whatever men want to talk about, but men aren't used to listening to the things that interest women. I rarely refer to cooking or movies like *Thelma and Louise*.

Susan is the academic dean of a professional school within a university. When her former college closed, Susan orchestrated the transfer of her entire program and faculty to another university. She recently received the Professional of the Year award in her field. When she first attended her national deans' association, only 8 out of 50 members were women.

> I was very silent. I hated being there. If you didn't communicate by the men's rules you were invisible. The star performers were male and they came on strong. But no one was listening; everyone was preparing their own response. The meeting oozed one-upmanship. At the reception it was all "Hail fellow well met." You wouldn't dare say, "Look, I'm having this rough situation I'm dealing with. Have you ever faced this problem?" It was only when some of the women got together for coffee or went shopping that I could be open about my experiences.

Although their status and abilities clearly show that Marsha, Kathy, and Susan are remarkable individuals, their experience as women in male hierarchical structures supports muted group theory. Kramarae says that "men have structured a value system and a language that reflects that value system. Women have had to work through the system organized by men."[25] For women with less skill and self-confidence than Marsha, Kathy, or Susan, that prospect can be daunting.

SPEAKING OUT IN PRIVATE: NETWORKING WITH WOMEN

Susan's relief at the chance to talk freely with other female deans illustrates a central tenet of muted group theory. Kramarae states that "females are likely to find ways to express themselves outside the dominant public modes of expression used by males in both their verbal conventions and their nonverbal behavior."[26]

Kramarae lists a variety of back-channel routes that women use to discuss their experiences—diaries, journals, letters, oral histories, folklore, gossip, chants, art, graffiti, poetry, songs, nonverbal parodies, gynecological handbooks passed between women for centuries, and a "mass of 'noncanonized' writers whose richness and diversity we are only just beginning to comprehend."[27] She labels these outlets the female "sub-version" that runs beneath the surface of male orthodoxy.

The runaway success of Anita Diamant's novel *The Red Tent* is a case in point. Not only is Dinah's story told in a voice that empowers women, it was three years of word-of-mouth recommendation among women that first put the unadvertised book on the *New York Times* best-seller list.[28]

Men are often oblivious to the shared meanings women communicate through alternative channels. In fact, Kramarae is convinced that "males have more difficulty than females in understanding what members of the other gender mean."[29] She doesn't ascribe men's bewilderment to biological differences between the sexes or to women's attempts to conceal their experience. Rather, she suggests that when men don't have a clue about what women want, think, or feel, it's because they haven't made the effort to find out. When British author Dale Spender was editor of *Woman's Studies International Quarterly,* she offered a further interpretation of men's ignorance. She proposed that many men realize that a commitment to listen to women would necessarily involve a renunciation of their privileged position. "The crucial issue here is that if women cease to be muted, men cease to be so dominant and to some males this may seem unfair because it represents a loss of rights."[30] A man can dodge that equalizing bullet by innocently declaring, "I'll never understand women."

SPEAKING OUT IN PUBLIC: A FEMINIST DICTIONARY

Like other forms of critical theory, feminist theory is not content to merely point out asymmetries in power. The ultimate goal of muted group theory is to change the man-made linguistic system that keeps women "in their place." According to Kramarae, reform includes challenging dictionaries that "ignore the words and definitions created by women and which also include many sexist definitions and examples."[31] Traditional dictionaries pose as authoritative guides to proper language use, yet because of their reliance on male literary sources, lexicographers systematically exclude words coined by women.

In 1985, Kramarae and Paula Treichler compiled a feminist dictionary that offers definitions for women's words that don't appear in *Webster's New International* and presents alternative feminine readings of words that do. Reissued in 1992, the dictionary "places *women* at the center and rethinks language from that crucially different perspective."[32] Kramarae and Treichler don't claim that all women use words the same way, nor do they believe women constitute a single, unified group. But they include women's definitions of approximately 2,500 words in order to illustrate women's linguistic creativity and to help empower women to change their muted status. Figure 35–1 provides a sample of brief entries and acknowledges their origin.

Appearance: A woman's appearance is her work uniform. . . . A woman's concern with her appearance is not a result of brainwashing; it is a reaction to necessity. (A Redstockings Sister)

Cuckold: The husband of an unfaithful wife. The wife of an unfaithful husband is just called a wife. (Cheris Kramarae)

Depression: A psychiatric label that . . . hides the social fact of the housewife's loneliness, low self-esteem, and work dissatisfaction. (Ann Oakley)

Doll: A toy playmate given to, or made by children. Some adult males continue their childhood by labeling adult female companions "dolls." (Cheris Kramarae)

Family man: Refers to a man who shows more concern with members of the family than is normal. There is no label *family woman,* since that would be heard as redundancy. (Cheris Kramarae)

Feminist: "I myself have never been able to find out precisely what feminism is: I only know that people call me a feminist whenever I express sentiments that differentiate me from a doormat." (Rebecca West)

Gossip: A way of talking between women in their roles as women, intimate in style, personal and domestic in topic and setting; a female cultural event which springs from and perpetuates the restrictions of the female role, but also gives the comfort of validation. (Deborah Jones)

Guilt: The emotion that stops women from doing what they may need to do to take care of themselves as opposed to everyone else. (Mary Ellen Shanesey)

Herstory: The human story as told by women and about women. . . . (Anne Forfreedom)

Ms.: A form of address being adopted by women who want to be recognized as individuals rather than being identified by their relationship with a man. (Midge Lennert and Norma Wilson)

One of the boys: Means NOT one of the girls. (Cheris Kramarae)

Parenthood: A condition which often brings dramatic changes to new mothers — "loss of job, income, and status; severing of networks and social contacts; and adjustments to being a 'housewife.' Most new fathers do not report similar social dislocations." (Lorna McKee and Margaret O'Brien)

Pornography: Pornography is the theory and rape is the practice. (Andrea Dworkin)

Sexual harassment: Refers to the unwanted imposition of sexual requirements in the context of a relationship of unequal power. (Catharine Mackinnon)

Silence: Is not golden. "There is no agony like bearing an untold story inside you." (Zora Neale Hurston) "In a world where language and naming are power, silence is oppressive, is violence." (Adrienne Rich)

FIGURE 35–1   Excerpts from Kramarae and Treichler's Feminist Dictionary

Kramarae and Treichler, *A Feminist Dictionary: Amazons, Bluestockings and Crones*

SEXUAL HARASSMENT: COINING A TERM TO LABEL EXPERIENCE

Perhaps more than any other single entry in the Kramarae and Treichler dictionary, the inclusion of *sexual harassment* illustrates a major achievement of feminist communication scholarship—encoding women's experience into the received language of society. Although stories of unwanted sexual attention on the job are legion, until recently women haven't had a common term to label what has been an ongoing fact of feminine life.

Sexual harassment
An unwanted imposition of sexual requirements in the context of a relationship of unequal power.

In 1992, the *Journal of Applied Communication Research* published 30 stories of communication students and professionals who had been sexually embarrassed, humiliated, or traumatized by a person who was in a position of academic power. All but 2 of the 30 accounts came from women. As Kramarae notes, "Sexual harassment is rampant but not random."[33] The following anonymous story is typical.

He was fifty; I was twenty-one. He was the major professor in my area; I was a first year M.A. student. His position was secure; mine was nebulous and contingent on his support of me. He felt entitled; I felt dependent. He probably hasn't thought much about what happened; I've never forgotten.

Like most beginning students, I was unsure of myself and my abilities, so I was hungry for praise and indicators of my intellectual merit. . . . Then, one November morning I found a note in my mailbox from Professor X, the senior faculty member in my area and, thus, a person very important to me. In the note Professor X asked me to come by his office late that afternoon to discuss a paper I'd written for him.

The conversation closed with his telling me that we should plan on getting to know each other and working together closely. I wanted to work with him and agreed. We stood and he embraced me and pressed a kiss on me. I recall backing up in surprise. I really didn't know what was happening. He smiled and told me that being "friends" could do nothing but enhance our working relationship. I said nothing, but felt badly confused. . . . This man was a respectable faculty member and surely he knew more about norms for student-faculty relationships than I did. So I figured I must be wrong to feel his behavior was inappropriate, must be mis-construing his motives, exaggerating the significance of "being friendly." . . . So I planned to have an "open talk" with him.

I was at a disadvantage in our "open talk," because I approached it as a chance to clarify feelings while he used it as an occasion to reinterpret and redefine what was happening in ways that suited his purposes. I told him I didn't feel right "being so friendly" with him. He replied that I was over-reacting and, further, that my small-town southern upbringing was showing. . . . I told him I was concerned that he wasn't being objective about my work, but was praising it because he wanted to be "friends" with me; he twisted this, explaining he was judging my work fairly, BUT that being "friends" did increase his interest in helping me professionally. No matter what I said, he had a response that defined my feelings as inappropriate.[34]

Muted group theory can explain this woman's sense of confusion and lack of power. Her story is as much about a struggle for language as it is a struggle over sexual conduct. As long as the professor can define his actions as "being friendly," the female student's feelings are discounted—even by herself. Had she been equipped with the linguistic tool of "sexual harassment," she could have validated her feelings and labeled the professor's advances as inappropriate and illegal.

According to Kramarae, when *sexual harassment* was first used in a court case in the late 1970s, it was the only legal term defined by women. Senatorial response to Anita Hill's testimony at the 1991 Clarence Thomas Supreme Court confirmation hearings showed that there is more work to be done before women can make their definition stick. For muted group theory, the struggle to contest man-made language continues.

CRITIQUE: DO MEN MEAN TO MUTE?

Feminist scholars insist that "the key communication activities of women's experiences—their rituals, vocabularies, metaphors, and stories—are an important part of the data for study."[35] In this chapter I've presented the words of 30 women who give voice to the muteness they've experienced because they aren't men. I could have easily cited hundreds more. It strikes me that ignoring or discounting their testimony would be the ultimate confirmation of Kramarae's muted group thesis.

Unlike Deborah Tannen in her approach to gender differences, presented in Chapter 33, Cheris Kramarae claims that questions of power are central to all human relationships. Both theories covered in the section on relationship maintenance support her contention (see Chapters 12 and 13). Baxter and Montgomery's relational dialectics regards the willingness to relinquish a portion of personal power as central to the tug-of-war between separateness and connectedness. Watzlawick's interactional view states that all communication is either symmetrical or complementary. These theorists don't speak to Kramarae's assertion that we live in a patriarchal society, but their scholarship does validate her focus on *control* issues between men and women.

The question of men's motives is more problematic. Tannen criticizes feminist scholars like Kramarae for assuming that men are trying to control women. Tannen acknowledges that differences in male and female communication styles sometimes lead to imbalances of power, but unlike Kramarae, she is willing to assume that the problems are caused primarily by men's and women's "different styles." Tannen cautions that "bad feelings and imputation of bad motives or bad character can come about when there was no intention to dominate, to wield power."[36]

Kramarae thinks that Tannen's apology for men's abuse of power is naïve at best. She notes that men often ignore or ridicule women's statements about the problems of being heard in a male-dominated society. Rather than blaming *style differences,* Kramarae points to the many ways that our political, educational, religious, legal, and media systems support gender, race, and class hierarchies. Your response to muted group theory may well depend on whether you are a beneficiary or a victim of these systems.

For men and women who are willing to hear what Kramarae has to say, the consciousness-raising fostered by muted group theory can prod them to quit using words in a way that preserves inequities of power. The term *sexual harassment* is just one example of how women's words can be levered into the public lexicon and give voice to women's collective experience. Phrases like *date rape, glass ceiling,* and *second shift* weren't even around when Kramarae and Treichler compiled their feminist dictionary in 1985, yet now these terms are available to label social and professional injustices that women face. Cheris Kramarae's insights and declarations of women as a group muted by men have helped shake up traditional patterns of communication between men and women.

QUESTIONS TO SHARPEN YOUR FOCUS

1. What words do you use with your same-sex friends that you don't use with members of the opposite sex? Does this usage support Kramarae's hypothesis of *male control of the public mode of expression?*

2. In a journal article about *dictionary bias,* Kramarae wrote the sentence "I *vaginated* on that for a while."[37] Can you explain her wordplay in light of the principles of muted group theory? How does the meaning of the sentence change when you replace her provocative term with alternative verbs?

3. Given a definition of *sexual harassment* as "unwanted imposition of sexual requirements in the context of a relationship of unequal power," can you think of a time you harassed, or were harassed by, someone else?

4. Do you tend to agree more with Tannen's genderlect perspective or Kramarae's muted group theory? To what extent is your choice influenced by the fact that you are a *male* or a *female?*

CONVERSATIONS

View this segment online at www.mhhe.com/griffin7 or www.afirstlook.com.

In my conversation with Cheris Kramarae, she suggests that the creation of university departments of women's studies is an encouraging sign that women aren't doomed to remain muted. When I asked if there should also be a "men's studies" program, her unexpected response not only made me laugh but also underscored the rationale for her theory. Describing her *Encyclopedia of Women's Experience* entry on *witches*, she gives a fascinating account of how the meaning of that word has changed to women's disadvantage. I conclude the interview by asking Kramarae to look back on our conversation to see if I had said or done something that constrained what she said. See if you agree with her assessment.

A SECOND LOOK

Recommended resource: "Cheris Kramarae," in *Feminist Rhetorical Theories*, Karen A. Foss, Sonja K. Foss, and Cindy L. Griffin, Sage, Thousand Oaks, CA, 1999, pp. 38–68.

Comprehensive statement: Cheris Kramarae, *Women and Men Speaking*, Newbury House, Rowley, MA, 1981, pp. v–ix, 1–63.

Original concept of mutedness: Edwin Ardener, "Belief and the Problem of Women" and "The 'Problem' Revisited," in *Perceiving Women*, Shirley Ardener (ed.), Malaby, London, 1975, pp. 1–27.

Kramarae's reflection on her theory: Cheris Kramarae, "Muted Group Theory and Communication: Asking Dangerous Questions," *Women and Language*, Vol. 22, 2005, pp. 55–61.

Dictionary of women's words: Cheris Kramarae and Paula Treichler, *A Feminist Dictionary: Amazons, Bluestockings and Crones*, 2nd ed., Pandora, London, 1992.

Worldwide feminist scholarship: Cheris Kramarae and Dale Spender (eds.), *Routledge International Encyclopedia of Women: Global Women's Issues and Knowledge* (4 vol.), Routledge, New York, 2000.

Unfulfilled promise of the Internet: Jana Kramer and Cheris Kramarae, "Women's Political Webs: Global Electronic Networks," in *Gender, Politics and Communication*, Annabele Sreberny and Liesbet van Zoonen (eds.), Hampton, Cresskill, NJ, 2000, pp. 205–222.

Reviewing books on women in CMC vocations: Cheris Kramarae, "Women, Work and Computing/Unlocking the Clubhouse," *NWSA Journal*, Vol. 15, No. 2, Summer 2003, pp. 207–210.

Sexual harassment: Julia T. Wood (ed.), "Special Section—'Telling Our Stories': Sexual Harassment in the Communication Discipline," *Journal of Applied Communication Research*, Vol. 20, 1992, pp. 349–418.

Giving voice to women through online learning: Cheris Kramarae, *The Third Shift: Women Learning Online*, American Association of University Women Educational Foundation, Washington, DC, 2001.

Alternative interpretations of gender differences in discourse: Candace West, Michelle M. Lazar, and Cheris Kramarae, "Gender in Discourse," in *Discourse as Social Interaction*, Vol. 2, Teun van Dijk (ed.), Sage, Thousand Oaks, CA, 1997, pp. 119–143.

Further theoretical construction based on muted group and standpoint theories: Mark Orbe, "From the Standpoint(s) of Traditionally Muted Groups: Explicating a Co-Cultural Communication Theoretical Model," *Communication Theory*, Vol. 8, 1998, pp. 1–26.

Critique: Celia J. Wall and Pat Gannon-Leary, "A Sentence Made by Men: Muted Group Theory Revisited," *European Journal of Women's Studies*, Vol. 6, 1999, pp. 21–29.

DIVISION SIX

Integration

Friends who know that I've written a book about communication theory often ask which theory is the best. Although I have my personal favorites, I find myself unable to come up with a satisfying answer. I take comfort in the words of Karl Weick, professor of organizational behavior and psychology at the University of Michigan, who assures us that there are inevitable trade-offs in any theory.[1] I am also convinced that his idea of categorizing theories according to the compromises their authors make keeps us from becoming too impatient if we spot a flaw in their construction. Creating theory isn't easy.

Weick introduces the dilemma that empirically oriented theorists face by citing University of Alberta psychologist Warren Thorngate's Postulate of Commensurate Complexity: "It is impossible for a theory of social behavior to be simultaneously general, simple or parsimonious, and accurate."[2] The term *commensurate complexity* refers to the necessity of tacking on qualifications so that a theory can account for special circumstances. Thorngate expands on his postulate:

> The more general a simple theory, the less accurate it will be in predicting specifics. . . . The more accurate a simple theory . . . the less able it will be to account for something more than the most simple or contrived situation. . . . General and accurate theories cannot be [simple].[3]

The clock face in Figure CT–1 shows how Weick portrays the relationship of the three ideals. The hours of twelve, four, and eight align with Weick's three criteria—*generalizability, accuracy,* and *simplicity,* respectively. The remaining hour positions represent various combinations of the two criteria they fall between.

As you can see, no one position can combine the three ideals, and to move closer to one is to move farther away from at least one other.

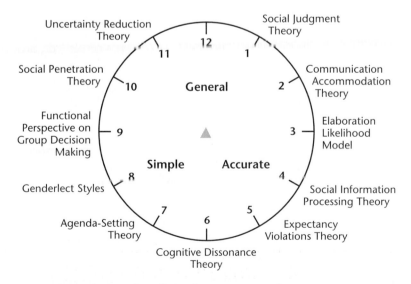

FIGURE CT–1 Theoretical Trade-Offs in Theory Construction
Based on Karl Weick's Clock-Face Model

In order to appreciate Weick's point about the trade-offs that confront a communication theorist, you have to be able to tell theoretical time. I'll make one circuit of the clock so that you can be clear about what the numbers represent. The placement of specific theories on the clock face reflects my evaluation of the difficult priority decisions their authors have made.

I stated in Chapter 3 that a good objective theory is useful. Since a theory placed at twelve o'clock could be applied in every situation, it would more than fulfill that requirement. But Weick suggests that there are no completely context-free approaches to social behavior. David Mortensen, a University of Wisconsin communication professor, agrees: "Communication never takes place in a vacuum; it is not a 'pure' process devoid of background or situational overtones."[4]

By giving up the fiction that their theories apply across the board, theorists at a two-o'clock position gain accuracy. A two-o'clock approach enlarges questions, adds conditions, and recognizes multiple causes for the same behavior. But a theory that holds true under most conditions will naturally be very complicated. Because of its intricate predictions of when strategic convergence or divergence produce positive or negative outcomes, Giles' communication accommodation theory comes to mind.

The theorist at four o'clock is pure scientist—stating, testing, and rejecting null hypotheses. Chapter 3 claimed that a good objective theory is testable. The four-o'clock emphasis on accuracy looks for explanations that pass the test, like social information processing theory. The public often responds with "So what?"

Description at the bottom of the dial is *context specific*. When asked to predict future trends, a six-o'clock theorist responds, "It depends. . . ." Quantitative research that originates here is usually run in the lab under highly contrived conditions. Studies of cognitive dissonance are a good example. Qualitative research at the six-o'clock position is an interpretive collage of case study, grounded theory, participant observation, and ethnography. The data are rich, but application in other situations is limited. The speech code of one culture doesn't tell us much about other cultures.

Eight-o'clock theories collapse data into a single conclusion or a short list of principles that are easy to grasp. Deborah Tannen says that men's genderlect reveals that they inhabit a culture of status, while women live in a culture of connection. Like other theorists who operate from this stance, Tannen is open to the charge of reductionism.

I find that students are often attracted to social penetration theory, which is at the ten-o'clock location on Weick's theoretical clock. That spot combines simplicity with relevance. Knowledge is distilled into easy-to-remember aphorisms or vivid metaphors. Intuitive hunches and inner feelings gain dignity when cast as speculative theory, which is portable across situations. Of course, ten-o'clock inquiry may elevate intriguing error to a position of truth, but Weick doesn't regard the danger as necessarily fatal:

> All explanations, no matter how bizarre, are likely to be valid part of the time. It's simply up to the originator of the idea to be smart enough or lucky enough to find those sites where the theory is accurately supported.[5]

Weick's clock-face representation of Thorngate's postulate explains why no approach in this book can avoid criticism. Each theory has at least one "soft spot," or Achilles' heel. It's not surprising that many question the validity of the information-seeking axiom of uncertainty reduction theory—the theory is five hours away

FIGURE CT–2 Anne Elk (John Cleese) Describes Her Brontosaurus Theory to Interviewer Graham Chapman on *Monty Python's Flying Circus*

from *accurate* on the clock. In like manner, the intricate description of attitudes as multiple latitudes makes Sherif's social judgment theory anything but simple. The pursuit of two virtues is always at the expense of the third, but as Weick maintains, two out of three isn't bad. He says that theorists who try to do everything usually end up accomplishing nothing. The results are trivial, bland, and boring—easy targets for those who want to poke fun at academic pretention.

The Monty Python parody of theorizing is a case in point. The comedy troupe's brontosaurus sketch is a satire of theorists who are overly impressed with their ideas (see Figure CT–2). Appearing on a television talk show, Anne Elk proudly presents her theory, which tries to do it all:

> My theory that belongs to me . . . goes as follows and begins now. All brontosauruses are thin at one end, much thicker in the middle and then thin again at the far end. That is my theory, it is mine, and belongs to me and I own it.[6]

The theory is certainly *accurate,* undeniably *simple,* and *general* to the extent that it applies to every beast of that type. It is also trivial. To avoid this trap, Weick recommends that theorists intentionally select their preferred position on the face of the clock and then "relax gracefully" with the problems that go with the territory.

Although Thorndike's postulate describes the compromises inherent in theories that aim to be objective, it's not hard to imagine interpretive theorists facing similar trade-offs. Recall from Chapter 3 that good interpretive theories (1) create an understanding of people, (2) clarify values, (3) elicit aesthetic appreciation, (4) stimulate a community of agreement, and (5) change society. Consider two theories in this book that investigate gender and communication within a society. Neither Clifford Geertz' cultural approach to gender roles in Bali nor Cheris Kramarae's version of muted group theory is able to fulfill all of these functions.

Geertz' thick description of men's struggle for status at a Balinese cockfight strikes a responsive chord in males around the world. And the imagery he uses as he tells the story of their risky wagers has great aesthetic appeal for readers of both sexes. But the inviting prose Geertz uses and the community of agreement that he generates preclude any attempt to change Indonesian society. A reformer he is not.

Geertz' weakness is Kramarae's strength. Feminist theory is meant to challenge the unequal distribution of power perpetuated by male control of the dominant modes of expression. Although Kramarae is high on intent to reform, she doesn't expect a broad spectrum of men who hold power to agree with her analysis. As for aesthetics, criticism of power abuse never looks elegant.

Along with Weick, I'm convinced that all theorists can't help but make trade-offs that inevitably prevent their constructions from being everything we might want. A certain forbearance on our part is appropriate. We should, however, try to understand the choices they've made.

As a way to help you pull together much of what you've learned, the final chapter identifies 10 principles that are central to multiple theories you've studied this term. I refer to these principles as *threads* because they tie together theories that come out of different traditions and address problems faced in different communication contexts. If you should find this attempt at synthesis not entirely satisfying, I ask for the same tolerance that Weick extends to the theorists. Confusion doesn't yield easily to clarity.

"For heaven's sake, Harry! Can't you just relax and enjoy art, music, religion, literature, drama and history, without trying to tie it all together?"

Reproduced by permission of Punch Limited.

CHAPTER 36

Common Threads in Comm Theories

The first four chapters in the book laid the groundwork for understanding the relationship among the wide range of theories you would study. Chapter 1 presented a working definition of both *theory* and *communication* so you could see what all of these communication theories have in common. Chapter 2 introduced the objective-interpretive distinction that is the basis for placing theories along a scale according to their authors' basic intellectual commitments. Chapter 3 laid out separate lists of five criteria for evaluating these two types of theories—another way of spotting similarities and differences. And Chapter 4 mapped out seven distinct scholarly traditions that spawned different types of theories, the offspring within a tradition bearing a marked family resemblance. Hopefully these integrative tools have helped you compare and contrast the theories you've studied throughout the course.

In this final chapter, I present another approach to identifying similarities and differences among the theories; I couldn't do this earlier because it wouldn't have made sense until you were familiar with them. I'll now identify 10 recurring principles that in one form or another appear in multiple theories. I refer to these as *threads* because each strand weaves in and out of theories that might otherwise seem unrelated.

Threads

Explicit or implicit principles of communication that are integral to multiple and varied communication theories.

In order to qualify as a thread in the tapestry that is communication theory, I've decided that the principle or concept must be a significant feature of at least five different theories covered in the text. It could be the engine that drives a theory, a common characteristic of messages, a variable that's related to the process of communication, or the outcome of symbolic interaction. To avoid merely repackaging comparisons made previously, I limit my selection of theoretical threads to ideas that span at least two of the traditions presented in Chapter 4, and also apply to a minimum of two communication contexts—interpersonal, group and public, mass, and cultural.

This final chapter is slightly longer than the others, but unraveling the threads isn't intended to exhaust all possibilities—nor to be exhausting. So with two exceptions, I'll limit the number of theories a thread ties together to no more than seven. Some of you may enjoy thinking of additional theories that I've either skipped over or missed by mistake.

Each thread is introduced with a *shorthand label* followed by a summary statement set in boldface. I then illustrate the principle with an *exemplar* theory that's clearly entwined with that thread. The rest of the section recounts how

471

other theorists employ this key idea, often with a twist, and sometimes at odds with how it's used in the exemplar. That's the *contrast* of this compare-and-contrast integration.

A review of how different theorists employ an idea can produce some *aha moments* of realization that deepen your understanding of the matrix of ideas you've studied this term. Consistent with the critique sections that close each theory chapter of the text, I end each thread discussion with a *cause for pause* reservation that those who warmly embrace the thread might ponder. Since almost all of the ideas I recap are referenced in Chapters 5–35, with a few exceptions, I limit citations to chapter numbers in parentheses. This will give you an easy way to revisit how each theorist uses the core concept.

One final note. When I present these threads in my comm theory class, students tell me that the principles serve a dual purpose: the threads not only help make new connections between the theories, but also serve as a comprehensive review. I hope they do both of these for you.

1. MOTIVATION

Communication is motivated by our basic social need for affiliation, achievement, and control, as well as our strong desire to reduce our uncertainty and anxiety.

Social exchange theory holds that relationships develop based upon the perceived benefits and costs of interaction. Recall that in *social penetration theory*, Altman and Taylor adopt the principles of *social exchange theory* in order to predict when people will become more vulnerable in their depth and breadth of self-disclosure (Ch. 9). The greater the probable outcome (benefits minus costs), the more transparent a person will be. Of course, potential rewards and costs are in the eye of the beholder. We each have a different comparison level (CL)—an outcome threshold above which relationships are satisfying. We also may reach a personal point of relationship instability when we figure we can get better outcomes being with someone else—our comparison level of alternatives (CL_{alt}). As the statement of the motivation thread suggests, perceived rewards and costs may also vary from person to person because they experience different preeminent needs. Yet almost every theory you've read about invokes at least one of the motives named in this principle. I'll select two theories to illustrate the strong pull that each of these five needs exerts.

Motivation
Needs and desires that drive or draw us to think, feel, and act as we do.

Need for affiliation. Since *social penetration theory* describes the development of close relationships, it assumes a human need for affiliation and concentrates on how that desire is satisfied through mutual self-disclosure (Ch. 9). Noelle-Neumann's *spiral of silence* defines public opinion as attitudes one can express without running the danger of isolating oneself (Ch. 29). This fear of isolation—the loss of affiliation—is what causes those in the minority to remain silent, thus giving the impression of unanimity. Both theories assume that affiliation with others is a strong panhuman need.

Need for achievement. Hirokawa and Gouran's *functional perspective on group decision making* claims that problem-solving groups must analyze the problem, set goals, identify alternatives, and evaluate the relative merits of each option in order to achieve a high-quality solution (Ch. 17). Any member comment that

"On the one hand, eliminating the middleman would result in lower costs, increased sales, and greater consumer satisfaction; on the other hand, we're the middleman."

doesn't directly address one of these four requisite functions is considered a distraction that disrupts the group's effort to achieve their goal. Delia's *constructivism* describes the process of creating message plans to achieve a communication goal (Ch. 8). Delia regards cognitive complexity as a necessary condition for crafting person-centered messages that have a high probability of success. It's a skill that won't be activated unless the speaker first sets specific goals.

Need for control.   The excessive need for control exhibited by powerful group and organizational leaders is what makes critical theories necessary. Deetz' *critical theory of communication in organizations* unmasks what he refers to as "corporate colonization." According to Deetz, managerialism insists on an unnecessary and unjust corporate control that reduces the quality of life for employees and other stakeholders (Ch. 20). Kramarae's *muted group theory* claims that men mute women in the public sphere by controlling language and the rules for its use (Ch. 35). In terms of motivation, both theories suggest that members of marginalized groups need to have a greater voice. Those who have the power are resistant to empowering others; the status quo looks good to them.

Need to reduce uncertainty.   Berger's *uncertainty reduction theory* suggests that the motive for most communication is to gain knowledge and create understanding. When we first meet another person, we want to discover information that will increase our ability to predict how future interaction will go (Ch. 10). Our desire to reduce uncertainty is especially high when we know we'll see someone in the future, the other person has something we want, or the person is acting in a weird way. This need to know is stronger in some people than in others. According to McCombs and Shaw's *agenda-setting theory*, the broadcast and print media have their strongest impact on people who have the most curiosity—what the theorists refer to as a high need for orientation (Ch. 28).

Need to reduce anxiety.   Burke's "Definition of Man" suggests that the language of perfection makes us all feel guilty that we aren't better than we are. Guilt is his catchall term to cover every form of anxiety, tension, embarrassment, shame, and disgust that's intrinsic to the human condition. His *dramatism* offers two ways to get rid of this noxious feeling. The first option is confessing our sin and inadequacy and then asking forgiveness. The second option is to blame someone else—redemption through victimage (Ch. 22). Festinger claimed that *cognitive dissonance* is an aversive drive. In order to avoid anxiety-producing dissonance, we'll selectively expose ourselves to information that reinforces our existing beliefs, seek social support after making a close-call decision, and change our opinions to keep them consistent with counterattitudinal behavior (Ch. 16).

Cause for pause: If it's true that all of my communication—including this book—is undertaken solely to meet my own personal needs and interests, then it strikes me that I am a totally selfish person. I don't doubt that my desire for affiliation, achievement, and control shape much of my conversation, as does my desire to reduce my levels of doubt and fear. But I prefer to think that I'm drawn by these desires rather than driven to them by an irresistible force. If so, there are times when I could (and should) say "no" to the pull of these needs out of a care for others or a sense of ethical responsibility. As the two lexical roots of the word suggest, *responsibility* implies being *able* to *respond*. To the extent that social exchange theory or any other theory of motivation suggests that I really have no choice, I choose to be skeptical.

2. SELF-IMAGE

Communication affects and is affected by our sense of identity, which is strongly shaped within the context of our culture.

Self-image
Identity; a mental picture of who I see myself to be—greatly influenced by the way others respond to me.

Mead's **symbolic interactionism** claims that our concept of self is formed through communication (Ch. 5). By taking the role of the other and seeing how we look to them, we develop our sense of identity. In turn, this looking-glass self shapes how we think and act within the community. In their *coordinated management of meaning*, Pearce and Cronen see us as less passive in the creation process than does Mead (Ch. 6). Their hierarchical model of meaning shows how our jointly created image of self becomes a crucial factor in how each of us manages meaning. According to Aronson and Cooper's revisions of *cognitive dissonance theory*, dissonance negatively impacts our self-image until we find a way to dissipate this distressing feeling (Ch. 16).

Three theories that address culture deal with the relationship between culture and identity. In her *face-negotiation theory*, Ting-Toomey defines face as our public self-image (Ch. 31). She says that people raised in individualistic cultures tend to have an *I-identity* and are concerned with saving face. People born into collectivistic cultures almost always have a *we-identity* and are mainly concerned with giving face to others. Giles' *communication accommodation theory* postulates that during intergroup encounters, people whose identity is tied to their membership in a social or cultural group will communicate in a way that diverges from the speaking style of out-group members (Ch. 30). Philipsen's study of Nacirema and Teamsterville *speech codes* illustrates Giles' contention. The ethnographer found that every Nacireman seeks to be a unique, independent self, whereas the Teamsterville code defines residents as bundles of social roles (Ch. 32).

Cause for pause: Self-concept is a major topic discussed within the field of communication. The accepted wisdom suggests that most of us have been put down by others and need to find ways to boost our self-esteem. As a counterpoint to this concern, social psychologists have identified a fundamental attribution error—a basic perceptual bias that we consistently show.[1] When we have success, we interpret it as the result of our hard work and ability, but when others have that same success, we tend to think of them as lucky. Conversely, when others fail, we consider it their own fault, but when we fail, we blame others or curse the fickle finger of fate. As a corrective to this biased perception we should consider giving others the benefit of the doubt while holding ourselves to a more rigorous standard of accountability.

3. CREDIBILITY

Our verbal and nonverbal messages are validated or discounted by others' perception of our competence and character.

Credibility
The intelligence, character, and goodwill that audience members perceive in a message source.

More than two thousand years ago, **The Rhetoric** of Aristotle used the term ethical proof (*ethos*) to describe the credibility of the speaker that increases the probability that the speech will be persuasive. Aristotle defined *ethos* as a combination of a speaker's perceived intelligence or competence, character or trustworthiness, and goodwill toward the audience (Ch. 21). Since ethical proof is in the eye of the beholder, audience perceptions of the speaker's ability, virtue, and concern for their well-being can change while he or she is speaking. Burke's *dramatism* suggests that persuasion hinges on whether the audience can identify with the character of the speaker. Without a perceived overlap of physical characteristics, talents, occupation, background, personality, beliefs, or values, there will be no persuasion (Ch. 22). Walther believes that computer-mediated communication (CMC) can give the impression of greater commonality than really exists. In his hyperpersonal extension of *social information processing theory*, he says that people who meet others in online chat rooms overestimate their similarities because all they have to go on initially is the common interest that brought them together (Ch. 11).

Two other interpersonal theories employ credibility as an explanation for changes in a relationship. Burgoon's *expectancy violations theory* identifies communicator reward valence as a key variable in predicting the effect of words or deeds that surprise the other person. This index is the sum total of all positive and negative attributes that the other person brings to the encounter plus the potential he or she has to reward or punish us in the future (Ch. 7).

Sherif's *social judgment theory* claims that a wide latitude of acceptance among listeners and readers increases the possibility of significant attitude change (Ch. 14). High source credibility is an effective way to expand the range of discrepant messages that they'll consider. Petty and Cacioppo's *elaboration likelihood model* is the theory of public and personal influence that claims that credibility facilitates persuasion, but ELM isn't optimistic about its long-term effects. That's because we usually process credibility cues through a peripheral route that leads to short-term attitude change that's vulnerable to challenge and doesn't predict behavior (Ch. 15). Harding and Wood's *standpoint theory* recognizes that women, racial minorities, and others on the margins of society have low credibility in the eyes of those who have status. Yet the irony of this negative judgment is that the powerless occupy a position that affords them a less false view of social reality than is available to the overprivileged who look down on them. The theorists contend that to be credible, research must start by examining the lives of women and members of other marginalized groups (Ch. 34).

Cause for pause: All of the theories cited in this thread regard perceived credibility as a valuable asset in the communication process. Yet as ELM points out, our focus on the source of a message may cause us to lose sight of the intrinsic value of what's being said. Before embracing the speaker's point of view we might ask ourselves, "Would I think that this is such a good idea if it was presented by someone else less attractive, sexy, or popular?" A parallel question is equally appropriate when we don't like or respect the message source: "Just because this idea is voiced by a low-life creep I can't stand, does that mean it's totally wrong and without merit?"

4. EXPECTATION

What we expect to hear or see will affect our perception, interpretation, and response during an interaction.

Expectation
In human interaction, our anticipation of how others will act or react toward us.

Burgoon's *expectancy violations theory* defines expectation as what we anticipate will happen rather than what we might desire (Ch. 7). In interpersonal encounters, our expectations are shaped by the cultural and situational context; communicator characteristics such as age, gender, appearance, personality, and style of speaking of the other person; and the nature of our relationship. When taken by surprise, we react. According to Burgoon's subsequent *interaction adaptation theory,* we also change our interaction position. That's forecast by the comparison level (CL) of Thibaut and Kelley's *social exchange theory* as well. Based on past experience, our CL is a benchmark of satisfaction that we can reasonably expect to get (Ch. 9). If we attain much more or much less than what we anticipated, the CL will change for future interactions.

Expectation is integral to other interpersonal theories. Self-fulfilling prophecy is a major implication of the looking-glass self described by Mead's *symbolic interactionism*. Others tend to behave the way we expect them to act; they become what we behold (Ch. 5). Berger's *uncertainty reduction theory* states that the expectation of future interaction increases our motivation to reduce uncertainty (Ch. 10). This prediction is echoed in Walther's *social information processing theory.* According to his *hyperpersonal perspective* extension of SIP, this anticipation of future interaction coupled with an exaggerated sense of similarity results in a self-fulfilling prophecy. The person who is perceived to be wonderful starts acting that way (Ch. 11).

Theories introduced in the media effects section invoke expectation as a crucial variable. Gerbner's *cultivation theory* maintains that a steady diet of symbolic violence on television creates an exaggerated fear that the viewer will be physically threatened, mugged, raped, or killed. This expectation causes heavy viewers to have a general mistrust of others and to urge more restrictions and the use of force against those whom they fear (Ch. 27). Noelle-Neumann believes that people expend a great deal of time and energy trying to figure out the direction public opinion is going. If they foresee it swinging away from them, they'll keep quiet about what they really think, thus contributing to the *spiral of silence* (Ch. 29).

As Burgoon indicated, culture strongly affects our expectations. According to Ting-Toomey's *face-negotiation theory*, interdependent people raised in a collectivistic culture expect others to support their public image—to give them "face"—while their independent counterparts reared in an individualistic culture have no such expectation (Ch. 31).

Cause for pause: Expectations are interpretations of experience that seem likely to happen in the future. Perceptions are interpretations of sensory experience occurring in the present. The two concepts are easy to confuse and both are tricky to measure. Since we never can know for sure what another person experiences, theories that appeal to the concept of expectation may sound more definitive than they really are.

The first four threads of motivation, self-image, credibility, and expectation that I've laid out are psychological variables that strongly affect communication. Yet they don't necessarily involve "creating and interpreting messages," the activity I suggested in Chapter 1 that sets the discipline of communication apart. The remaining six threads I discern running through multiple theories do have that message focus.

5. AUDIENCE ADAPTATION

By mindfully creating a person-centered message specific to the situation, we increase the possibility of achieving our communication goals.

Audience adaptation
The strategic creation or adjustment of a message in light of the audience characteristics and specific setting.

Person-centered messages described in Delia's **constructivism** are the epitome of adaptation to an audience of one. After selecting multiple goals, the communicator develops a message plan tailored to a particular person in a specific situation (Ch. 8). According to Delia, not everyone possesses the cognitive complexity to pull it off. But those who are able to draw upon a wide array of interpersonal constructs are more likely to achieve their goals.

In a somewhat similar *plan-based theory of strategic communication*, Berger describes how we construct message plans to reach our interpersonal goals by taking into account the probable response to our words (Ch. 10). Rather than dealing with individual differences in cognitive complexity, Berger addresses the extent of plan complexity. A highly detailed plan with built-in contingencies may seem promising, but if making adjustments on the fly takes our total concentration, our performance will deteriorate.

Sherif's *social judgment theory* predicts that those who want to influence another will be most successful if they first figure out the other's latitude of acceptance, and then craft a persuasive message that falls within it (Ch. 14). Petty and Cacioppo's *elaboration likelihood model* suggests that the persuader first assess whether the target audience is ready and able to think through issue-relevant arguments that support the advocate's position. If not, the persuader can still achieve a temporary change of attitude by focusing attention on peripheral cues (Ch. 15).

For those who are considering surprising another by what they say or do, Burgoon's *expectancy violations theory* (EVT) offers practical advice (Ch. 7). If you're sure the other person will like the violation, go ahead and do it. But if the violation is neutral or ambiguous, you need to assess how the other feels about you. When the person values you or what you have to offer, your unexpected act will probably have positive results. Otherwise, it's better to conform to his or her expectations. EVT offers no advice for what to do if the response to our unexpected move isn't what we wanted, but Burgoon's follow-up *interaction adaptation theory* suggests we adjust our future expectations and actions accordingly.

The idea of strategic or thoughtful adaptation to an audience isn't limited to theories of interpersonal communication. In a public address context Aristotle's *Rhetoric* recommends the *enthymeme* over the formal syllogism when the speaker knows that the audience already agrees with the major or minor premise (Ch. 21). In a cultural context, Ting-Toomey's *face-negotiation theory* stresses the importance of mindfulness throughout an intercultural interaction (Ch. 31). Giles' *communication accommodation theory* states that people seeking the approval of others from a different culture will tend to adapt their speaking style to match that of the other (Ch. 30).

Cause for pause: All of these theories suggest that for maximum effectiveness, we should consciously adapt our message to the attitudes, actions, or abilities of the audience. Makes sense. There is, however, a danger that by doing so we'll lose the authenticity of our message or the integrity of our own beliefs. Adjusting becomes pandering when we say whatever others want to hear. Raymond Bauer's article "The Obstinate Audience" suggests a third intriguing possibility—that audience adaptation ends up changing the speaker more than the speaker changing the audience.[2] If so, the counterattitudinal advocacy studies of Festinger's *cognitive dissonance theory* might explain this surprising prediction (Ch. 16).

6. SOCIAL CONSTRUCTION

Persons-in-conversation co-construct their own social realities and are simultaneously shaped by the worlds they create.

This statement of social construction is taken directly from Pearce and Cronen's **coordinated management of meaning** (Ch. 6). They see themselves as curious participants in a pluralistic world as opposed to social scientists who they describe as detached observers trying to discover singular Truth. Because CMM claims that people jointly create the social worlds in which they live, the theorists urge us to ask, "What are we doing? What are we making together? How can we make better social worlds?" Like CMM, Deetz' *critical theory of communication in organizations* challenges the traditional idea that communication is merely the transmission of information or that it describes an independent reality. Language is constitutive; it doesn't represent things that already exist (Ch. 20). Yet unlike CMM, Deetz' version of social construction focuses on the issue of power. He describes the covert way managers use language to gain workers' consent to practices that expand corporate control over their lives.

Social construction
The communal creation of the real and the good.

Other theories of language, relationships, group decision making, media, and gender regard communication as creating meaning rather than reflecting it. Mead's *symbolic interactionism* describes how our concept of self is formed by the verbal and nonverbal communication of significant others (Ch. 5). Baxter's second generation of *relational dialectics* states that communication is constitutive in that it creates the contradictions that all relational partners experience. But our communication also creates fleeting moments of mutual consummation, completion, or wholeness that support a close relationship in the midst of dialectical tension (Ch. 12). Watzlawick's *interactional view* sees every family as playing a one-of-a-kind game with homemade rules that create its own reality—one that's often destructive. He regards the function of therapy as helping members frame an alternative social reality in which they can survive, and perhaps even thrive (Ch. 13).

Three theories emphasize the subtle nature of social construction. Poole's *adaptive structuration theory* adopts Giddens' view of structuration as the production and reproduction of social systems by people's use of rules and resources in interaction (Ch. 18). This means that members in groups are creating the group as they act within it, but they may not realize they're doing it. Gerbner's *cultivation theory* describes how media depiction of violence affects the heavy viewer's creation of a mean and scary world (Ch. 27). This social construction develops over years rather than hours, so viewers are unaware of the powerful effect that watching television has on them. McLuhan's *media ecology* also claims that television and other electronic communication inventions change the environment we live in. But whereas Gerbner sees message content as the agent of change, McLuhan claimed that the form of communication is what changes our sensory environment. The medium is the message. We have shaped our communication tools and they are now shaping us (Ch. 24).

Cause for pause: The range of the theories just cited shows that the idea of social construction is well-established in the field of communication. In fact, Craig presents all seven different theoretical traditions in communication theory as socially constructed (Ch. 4). Yet is there a foundational reality that language can describe, however poorly? As my Questions to Sharpen Your Focus ask at the end of the chapter on *CMM* (Ch. 6), are you willing to give up the notion of a Truth you can count on for a linguistically created social reality that has no existence apart from how it's talked about?

7. SHARED MEANING

Our communication is successful to the extent that we share a common interpretation of the signs we use.

Shared meaning
People's common interpretation or mutual understanding of what a verbal or nonverbal message signifies.

Geertz and Pacanowsky's *cultural approach to organizations* describes culture as webs of significance, that is, systems of shared meaning. Because this is so, Geertz says we should concern ourselves not only with the structures of cultural webs, but also with the process of their spinning—communication. Applying Geertz' ideas to organizations, Pacanowsky focuses on the collective interpretation of stories, metaphors, and rituals (Ch. 19). Philipsen defines a *speech code* as a historically enacted, socially constructed system of terms, meanings, premises, and rules pertaining to communicative conduct (Ch. 32). He champions ethnography—participant observation within the community—as the way to determine what a speech code means to those who use it.

Mead and other adherents of *symbolic interactionism* note that humans act toward others on the basis of the meanings they assign to those people (Ch. 5). Symbolic interactionists agree with Geertz, Pacanowsky, and Philipsen that the only way to access meaning within a community is through ethnography. All of these theories are concerned with shared interpretation.

Unlike the theories just cited, others describe the road to mutual understanding as bumpy and contentious. As the title of their theory suggests, Pearce and Cronen's *coordinated management of meaning* insists that meaning is socially created and must be constantly managed. Shared interpretation does not, however, imply that those parties will see eye to eye. Pearce says that two people may coordinate their conversation and actions with each other even when they do not—and perhaps should not—agree (Ch. 6).

"You'll have to phrase it another way. They have no word for 'fetch.'"

Along with most interpretive theorists, Deetz regards meanings to be in people rather than in words, but he goes on to ask, "*Whose* meanings are in people?" His *critical theory of communication in organizations* condemns the corporate executive suite for seeking to impose their meanings on workers and other stakeholders through both overt and covert means. Deetz labels this imposition as corporate colonization (Ch. 20).

Hall's *cultural studies* levels the same charge against those who control the media, calling the practice hegemony. The theorist doesn't regard hegemony as a plot or conspiracy among media practitioners, yet the end result is that media conglomerates and other culture industries establish the meanings that shape society. Viewing culture from a Marxist perspective, Hall sees media as powerful ideological tools that frame interpretation of events for the benefit of the haves over the have-nots (Ch. 26). Barthes' *semiotics* describes how this works. The media take a denotative sign and use it as a signifier to be paired with a different signified. The image that results is a new connotative sign that borrowed the original sign but has now lost its historical meaning (Ch. 25).

Cause for pause: The idea that it's people rather than words that *mean* suggests that texts don't interpret themselves. If so, shared interpretation is an accomplishment of the audience rather than the clarity of the message. Pushed to an extreme, however, the meaning-in-persons idea implies that what is said face-to-face, written on a page, or portrayed on a screen makes little difference. Every text is wide open for any interpretation, no matter what the communicator intended. As an author, I'm uncomfortable with this notion. I take words and images seriously and try to pick them carefully. I regard successful communication as mutual understanding between author and reader, speaker and listener, director and audience, that's consistent with what the author/speaker/director had in mind. To the extent this takes place, I see communication as successful. Readers/listeners/viewers are then free to respond as they will.

8. NARRATIVE

Narrative
Story; words and deeds that have sequence and meaning for those who live, create, or interpret them.

We respond favorably to stories and dramatic imagery with which we can identify.

Fisher's *narrative paradigm* claims that people are essentially storytellers. We experience life as a series of ongoing narratives as conflicts, characters, beginnings, middles, and ends (Ch. 23). Almost all communication is story that we judge by its narrative coherence and fidelity. In other words, does a narrative hang together? Does it ring true? Three other theories adopt the concept of narrative as the organizing feature of what they describe.

Burke saw all life as drama. Yet, unlike Fisher, he believed it's difficult to discern the meaning behind the lines. His dramatism offers a toolbox of literary techniques, such as the dramatistic pentad, so that rhetorical critics can figure out the speaker or author's motivation (Ch. 22). He was convinced that the master plot of most public communication is the purging of guilt by blaming others for misfortune or failure.

Pearce and Cronen's *coordinated management of meaning* claims that the stories we tell are a way to manage meaning (Ch. 6). Our stories told are always framed by our identities, our relationships with others, the episodes they refer to, and the culture of which we are a part. Trying to coordinate our stories told with our stories lived is a lifetime project that will never be complete.

Gerbner's *cultivation theory* says that television has become the dominant force in our society because it tells most of the stories, most of the time. Because the stories that TV runs are filled with symbolic violence, the world it creates for heavy viewers is a mean and scary place. These stories gradually cultivate fear by slowly changing viewers' perception of their social environment (Ch. 27).

Three other theories refer to stories as a major means for creating a desired end. Bormann's *symbolic convergence theory* predicts that groups will become more cohesive when members latch on to the creative and imaginative interpretation of events in another time or place (Ch. 3). Most of these fantasies are described in the form of story. Geertz and Pacanowsky's *cultural approach to organizations* regards oft-repeated stories as a way to socialize new employees. For participant observers, the stories are lenses through which to view a unique corporate culture (Ch. 19). And Tannen observes that the disparity between men's and women's *genderlect styles* can be seen in how they tell a story. As the heroes of their own stories, men try to elevate their status. By telling stories about others, or downplaying their role in their narratives, women seek connection (Ch. 33).

Cause for pause: I believe stories are both fascinating and powerful. In most chapters I've used extended examples to make the theories come alive. But as Warnick reminds us in her commentary on the *narrative paradigm*, there are bad stories that can effectively lead people astray or destroy others. Unless we filter narratives through the values of justice, goodness, and integrity that Fisher and the National Communication Association (NCA) Credo for Ethical Communication advocate, we could embrace a lie or perpetuate error. Well-told tales are inherently attractive, but they may not all be good.

9. CONFLICT

Unjust communication stifles needed conflict; healthy communication can make conflict productive.

Deetz' *critical theory of communication in organizations* describes managerial efforts to suppress conflict through discursive closure rather than address legitimate disagreements through open discussion (Ch. 20). He believes that corporations and their stakeholders would be well served by more conflict rather than less. Yet the managerial quest for greater control counters any attempt to establish democracy in the workplace. Opportunities for employees to voice complaints offer a chance to let off steam but rarely lead to meaningful participation in the decisions that affect their lives. From a *cultural studies* perspective, Hall sees the same corporate control of communication in the way the mass media interpret current events. Disputes are discussed, but that discussion is framed in a way that furthers the ideology of those who already have power (Ch. 26). Money talks.

Theories of face-to-face interaction also deal with the use of power to quell conflict rather than work through differences. The *double bind* that Watzlawick describes in his *interactional view* is a classic case of the dominant person in a complementary relationship insisting that the low-power person act as if the relationship were symmetrical (Ch. 13). Kramarae's *muted group theory* claims that women are a marginalized group and are kept on the margins of society through unjust communication practices (Ch. 35). Pearce and Cronen's *coordinated management of meaning* refers to culture-war arguments as reciprocal diatribes that demonize the opponent rather than invite a response the speaker would honestly consider (Ch. 6). CMM offers an alternative model of communication that doesn't minimize differences, yet consciously seeks to move away from power-play politics. Pearce's model of the cosmopolitan communicator is one who speaks in a way that others will listen, and listens in a way that encourages others to speak.

Other theorists assert that those who hate conflict and have remained silent can actually make conflict productive by speaking out. Collins' *black feminist thought* version of *standpoint theory* maintains that any woman who refuses to join into the discussion is cheating, especially if she really disagrees with what's been said (Ch. 34). Baxter and Montgomery base their *relational dialectics* on Bakhtin's core belief that two voices are the minimum for life, the minimum for existence (Ch. 12). Most of the theorists mentioned in this section regard *dialogue*—the final thread—as the form of communication that makes conflict productive.

Cause for pause: Although Ting-Toomey doesn't advocate the kind of discursive closure that Deetz and Hall oppose, her *face-negotiation theory* warns that a free and open discussion of conflicting opinions and interests within a collectivistic culture would be counterproductive (Ch. 31). Confronting the problem but not the person is a well-accepted principle of conflict resolution in the West. But Ting-Toomey says that in societies where giving *face* to others is the cultural norm, straight talk creates embarrassment.

10. DIALOGUE

Dialogue is transparent conversation that often creates unanticipated relational outcomes due to parties' profound respect for disparate voices.

Drawing upon Bakhtin's conception of dialogue, Baxter's second generation of **relational dialectics** describes dialogue as an aesthetic accomplishment that produces fleeting moments of unity through a profound respect for disparate voices (Ch. 12). Baxter stresses that dialogue doesn't bring a resolution to the contradictions that parties experience in close relationships. Yet dialogue and relationship rituals that honor multiple voices provide assurance that living within changing tensions can be exhilarating, never boring.

In their *coordinated management of meaning*, Pearce and Cronen adopt Buber's view of dialogue, which is more optimistic than Bakhtin's. They agree that dia-

Conflict
The struggle between people who perceive they have incompatible values and goals or are contesting over scarce resources.

Dialogue
Transparent conversation that often creates unanticipated relational outcomes due to parties' profound respect for disparate voices.

logue can't be produced on demand, but they think we can experience it if we seek it and prepare for it. Buber says dialogue takes place only in I-Thou relationships where we regard our partner as the very one we are. We stand our own ground yet are profoundly open to the other. We meet in the "between" and the result is usually unanticipated. Dialogue is typically not a way to accomplish a task; what we get is an authentic relationship. Pearce believes that dialogic communication is learnable, teachable, and contagious (Ch. 6).

With his *phenomenological approach* to healthy relationships, Carl Rogers is even more confident that dialogue is within reach when people seek it. He lays out three necessary and sufficient conditions for us to fulfill before another will reciprocate. We must demonstrate (1) congruence between our words and who we genuinely are, (2) unconditional positive regard for the other, and (3) listening with empathic understanding (Ch. 4). To the extent that we fulfill these communication criteria, Rogers believes that others and our relationship with them will be healthier.

Most communication theorists who discuss dialogue focus on the openness or transparency that Rogers' first condition describes. According to Altman and Taylor's *social penetration theory*, the vulnerability of self-disclosure is the way close relationships develop (Ch. 9). Two gender theories describe this kind of openness as more characteristic of women than of men. In her analysis of *genderlect styles*, Tannen concludes that women's conversation reflects their overarching desire for connection, whereas men's talk shows their constant concern for status (Ch. 33). The feminine style facilitates dialogue, the masculine style inhibits it. And because women are a *muted group* in the public sphere, according to Kramarae, they've developed back-channel routes to openly share their experience with other females—again privileging dialogue (Ch. 35).

Habermas' *discourse ethics* imagines an ideal speech situation where people are free to speak their minds without fear or constraint (Ch. 17). He believes that any ethical conclusions they reach will be valid only when (1) everyone has a chance to participate regardless of their status, (2) all participants exchange their views in a spirit of reciprocity and mutual understanding, and (3) their ethical judgments apply equally to everyone. It's the kind of forum that Deetz in his *critical theory of communication in organizations* suggests that all corporate stakeholders deserve, that Hirokawa and Gouran's *functional perspective for group decision making* would applaud, and that Pearce's Public Dialogue Consortium works to create (Chs. 20, 17, 6).

Cause for pause: In the communication discipline, *dialogue* is a term that's often used and much in favor. Yet advocates have a tough time describing what it is or how to achieve it. The boldfaced statement at the beginning of the thread is my best effort to put the concept into words, but I'm not sure I've captured the essence of what many theorists mean when they use the term.

In practice, dialogue is also exceedingly rare. Whether we use the criteria set forth by Baxter, Pearce, Rogers, or Habermas, probably less than 1 in 1,000 conversations would qualify as dialogue. Scarcity doesn't negate the value of this authentic and supportive form of communication. But it does suggest that a full-blown theory of relational communication must also take into account legitimate authority, jealousy, boredom, insecurity, interruptions, distractions, time pressures, headaches, and all the other "stuff" that make everyday communication less than ideal. Even so, I look forward to being pleasantly surprised the next time I'm fortunate enough to take part in dialogic communication.

UNRAVELING THE THREADS

I hope these 10 threads have helped you integrate the theories covered this term in a new way. It's possible, however, that you are overwhelmed by the 75 connections I've drawn. The 10 threads could be tangled together in your mind like intertwined pieces of string in a drawer. If so, Figure 36–1 may help bring order out of chaos.

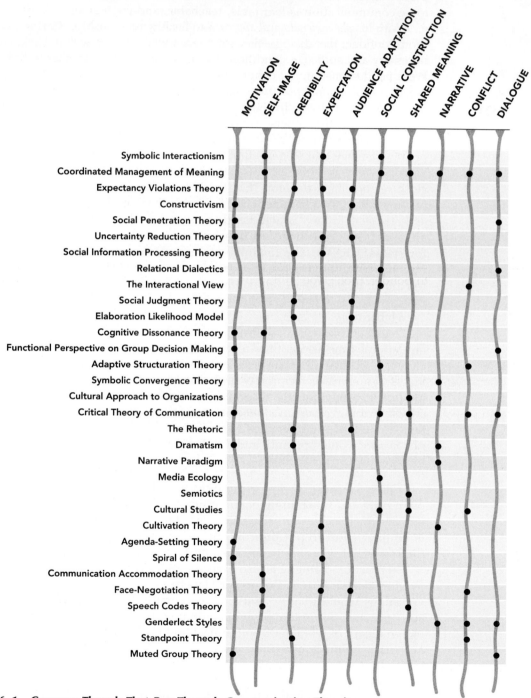

FIGURE 36–1   Common Threads That Run Through Communication Theories

In Figure 36–1, the labeled threads are separated and stretched out vertically. These threads are crosshatched horizontally with the 32 major theories featured in the text. Each marked intersection represents a link described in this chapter. You can let your eyes run down a thread and quickly review theories that draw upon that idea. This knowledge can help you when you study social construction, audience adaptation, dialogue, or any of the other principles in course work ahead. Conversely, you can select a given theory and scan across the page to see which principles it employs. These are the kinds of connections you'll want to review if you're writing a term paper or looking to the theory for practical advice. I also hope that you'll be intrigued by some links that didn't occur to you when you first studied the theories.

A FINAL NOTE

In the first chapter I compared this book to a collection of charts—a scenic atlas of communication maps that professionals in the field consider worth viewing. I hope you've found your first look intriguing and now have a desire to explore some particular areas. I urge you not to be content with watching other people's travel slides; the study of communication isn't an armchair activity. By all means, consider the perspectives of Burgoon, Baxter, Burke, and all the others. But also take a look for yourself. Unlike many academic disciplines, the study of communication is one in which we're all practitioners. Remember, however, that unexamined raw experience is not a substitute for true understanding. You need to ponder, probe, speculate, and follow your hunches if you wish to take advantage of the rich database that everyday talk provides.

Appendix B offers my recommendations for feature films that illustrate different aspects of the communication process. If you liked my extended references to *Nell, You've Got Mail, Bend It Like Beckham, Thank You for Smoking, Erin Brockovich, Blade Runner*, and *When Harry Met Sally*, you may want to rent a DVD and cull your own examples of theoretical principles at work.

The field is wide open for new ideas. There's no reason you have to stop with a first look at communication theory or settle for a secondhand glance. You've probably been mulling over an idea not suggested in these pages. Perhaps that notion could be developed and become the focus of a new chapter in a revised edition of this book. Choose the theoretical perspective or communication context that fascinates you, and switch from casual observation to an intensive gaze. Keep looking.

CALVIN AND HOBBES © 1987 Watterson. Reprinted with permission of Universal Press Syndicate. All rights reserved.

QUESTIONS TO SHARPEN YOUR FOCUS

1. Which *thread* most intrigues you? Are the theories it connects *objective* or *interpretive*? What *communication principle* that you've learned or discovered isn't represented in this chapter? Why do you think it's missing?

2. Which five theories presented in this book are your personal favorites? Do they tend to line up with a *thread* or *principle*, come out of a single *scholarly tradition*, or address a particular *communication context*?

3. In Figure 36–1, some theories appear in quite a few more threads than others. Can you spot a pattern that explains this uneven distribution?

4. What questions do you have about communication that weren't addressed by any of the theories covered in this book? Under what *communication contexts* would theories that speak to these issues best fit?

A SECOND LOOK

Motivation: David C. McClelland, *Human Motivation*, Cambridge University, Cambridge, UK, 1988.

Self-image: Bruce Bracken (ed.), *Handbook of Self-Concept: Developmental, Social, and Clinical Considerations*, Wiley, New York, 1995.

Credibility: Charles Self, "Credibility," in *An Integrated Approach to Communication Theory and Research*, Michael Salwen and Don Stacks (eds.), Lawrence Erlbaum, Mahwah, NJ, 1996, pp. 421–441.

Expectation: Robert Rosenthal, "Interpersonal Expectancy Effects: A 30-Year Perspective," *Current Directions in Psychological Science*, Vol. 3, No. 6, 1994, pp. 176–179.

Audience adaptation: Charles Berger, "Message Production Skill in Social Interaction," in *Handbook of Communication and Social Interaction Skills*, John O. Greene and Brant Burleson (eds.), Lawrence Erlbaum, Mahwah, NJ, 2003, pp. 257–289.

Social construction: Kenneth Gergen, *An Invitation to Social Construction*, Sage, Thousand Oaks, CA, 1999.

Shared meaning: Steve Duck, *Meaningful Relationships: Talking, Sense, and Relating*, Sage, Thousand Oaks, CA, 1994.

Narrative: Eric Peterson and Kristin M. Langellier, "Communication as Storytelling," in *Communication as . . . Perspectives on Theory*, Gregory Shepherd, Jeffrey St. John, and Ted Striphas (eds.), Sage, Thousand Oaks, CA, 2006, pp. 123–131.

Conflict: W. Barnett Pearce and Stephen Littlejohn, *Moral Conflict: When Social Worlds Collide*, Sage, Thousand Oaks, CA, 1997.

Dialogue: Rob Anderson, Leslie A. Baxter, and Kenneth Cissna (eds.), *Dialogue: Theorizing Difference in Communication Studies*, Sage, Thousand Oaks, CA, 2003.

APPENDIX A

Abstracts of Theories

What follows are brief summaries of the 33 theories featured in the book. There's a potential danger, of course, in trying to capture the gist of a theory in a few cryptic lines, but I didn't craft the abstracts to convey new concepts. Instead, these capsule statements are designed to jog your memory of ideas already considered. With the exception of Bormann's symbolic convergence theory (see Chapter 3), the abstracts are arranged in the same order as the theories appear in the text. At the end of each summary, I've made an attempt to label the communication theory tradition or traditions that undergird each theorist's thought. I hope you'll find both the summaries and their intellectual roots helpful.

Interpersonal Communication

Mead's symbolic interactionism: Humans act toward people, things, and events on the basis of the meanings they assign to them. Once people define a situation as real, it has very real consequences. Without language there would be no thought, no sense of self, and no socializing presence of society within the individual. (Socio-cultural tradition)

Pearce and Cronen's coordinated management of meaning: Persons-in-conversation co-construct their own social realities and are simultaneously shaped by the worlds they create. They can achieve coherence through common interpretation of their stories told. They can achieve coordination by meshing their stories lived. Dialogic communication, which is learnable, teachable, and contagious, improves the quality of life for everyone. (Socio-cultural and phenomenological traditions)

Burgoon's expectancy violations theory: Violating another person's interpersonal expectations can be a superior strategy to conformity. When the meaning of a violation is ambiguous, communicators with a high reward valence can enhance their attractiveness, credibility, and persuasiveness by doing the unexpected. When the violation valence or reward valence is negative, they should act in a socially appropriate way. (Socio-psychological tradition)

Delia's constructivism: Individuals who are more cognitively complex in their perceptions of others have the mental capacity to construct sophisticated message plans that pursue multiple goals. They then have the ability to deliver person-centered messages that achieve the outcomes they desire. (Socio-psychological and rhetorical traditions)

Altman and Taylor's social penetration theory: Interpersonal closeness proceeds in a gradual and orderly fashion from superficial to intimate levels of exchange as a function of anticipated present and future outcomes. Lasting intimacy requires continual and mutual vulnerability through breadth and depth of self-disclosure. (Socio-psychological tradition)

Berger's uncertainty reduction theory: When people meet, their primary concern is to reduce uncertainty about each other and their relationship. As verbal

Reproduced by permission of Punch Limited

output, nonverbal warmth, self-disclosure, similarity, and shared communication networks increase, uncertainty decreases—and vice versa. Information seeking and reciprocity are positively correlated with uncertainty. (Socio-psychological tradition)

Walther's social information processing theory: Based solely on the linguistic content of computer-mediated communication (CMC), parties who meet online can develop relationships just as close as those formed face-to-face—though it takes longer. Because online senders select, receivers magnify, channels promote, and feedback enhances favorable impressions, CMC may create hyperpersonal relationships. (Socio-psychological tradition)

Baxter and Montgomery's relational dialectics: Social life is a dynamic knot of contradictions, a ceaseless interplay between contradictory or opposing tendencies such as integration-separation, stability-change, and expression-nonexpression. Quality relationships are constituted through dialogue, which is an aesthetic accomplishment that produces fleeting moments of unity through a profound respect for the disparate voices. (Phenomenological tradition)

Watzlawick's interactional view: Relationships within a family system are interconnected and highly resistant to change. Communication among members has a content component and a relationship component that centers on issues of control. The system can be transformed only when members receive outside help to reframe their metacommunication. (Cybernetic tradition)

Sherif's social judgment theory: The larger the discrepancy between a speaker's position and a listener's point of view, the greater the change in attitude—as long as the message is within the hearer's latitude of acceptance. High ego-involvement usually indicates a wide latitude of rejection. Messages that fall there may have a boomerang effect. (Socio-psychological tradition)

Petty and Cacioppo's elaboration likelihood model: Message elaboration is the central route of persuasion that produces major positive attitude change. It occurs when unbiased listeners are motivated and able to scrutinize arguments that they consider strong. Message-irrelevant factors hold sway on the peripheral path, a more common route that produces fragile shifts in attitude. (Socio-psychological tradition)

Festinger's cognitive dissonance theory: Cognitive dissonance is an aversive drive that causes people to (1) avoid opposing viewpoints, (2) seek reassurance after making a tough decision, and (3) change private beliefs to match public behavior when there is minimal justification for an action. Self-consistency, a sense of personal responsibility, or self-affirmation can explain dissonance reduction. (Socio-psychological tradition)

Group and Public Communication

Hirokawa and Gouran's functional perspective on group decision making: Groups make high-quality decisions when members fulfill four requisite functions: (1) problem analysis, (2) goal setting, (3) identification of alternatives, and (4) evaluation of positive and negative consequences. Most group communication disrupts progress toward accomplishing these functional tasks, but counteractive communication can bring people back to rational inquiry. (Socio-psychological and cybernetic traditions)

Poole's adaptive structuration theory: Structuration is the production and reproduction of social systems by people's use of rules and resources in interaction. Communication matters when groups make decisions. Duality of structure means that the rules and resources members use will affect decisions, and in turn those structures will be affected by those decisions. (Socio-cultural and cybernetic traditions)

Bormann's symbolic convergence theory: Sharing common fantasies transforms a collection of individuals into a cohesive group. Symbolic convergence occurs when group members spontaneously create fantasy chains that display an energized, unified response to common themes. A fantasy theme analysis across groups can reveal a rhetorical vision that contains motives to enact the joint fantasy. (Rhetorical and socio-psychological traditions)

Geertz and Pacanowsky's cultural approach to organizations: Humans are animals suspended in webs of significance that they themselves have spun. An organization doesn't have a culture, it is a culture—a unique system of shared meanings. A nonintrusive ethnographic approach interprets stories, rites, and other symbolism to make sense of corporate culture. (Socio-cultural tradition)

Deetz' critical theory of communication in organizations: The naïve notion that communication is merely the transmission of information perpetuates managerialism, discursive closure, and the corporate colonization of everyday life. Language is the principal medium through which social reality is produced and reproduced. Managers can further a company's health and democratic values by coordinating stakeholder participation in corporate decisions. (Critical and phenomenological traditions)

Aristotle's rhetoric: Rhetoric is the art of discovering all available means of persuasion. A speaker supports the probability of a message by logical, ethical, and emotional proofs. Accurate audience analysis results in effective invention; arrangement; style; delivery; and, presumably, memory. (Rhetorical tradition)

Burke's dramatism: Life is drama. The dramatistic pentad of act, scene, agent, agency, and purpose is the critic's tool to discover a speaker's motives. The ultimate motive of rhetoric is the purging of guilt. Without audience identification with the speaker, there is no persuasion. (Rhetorical and semiotic traditions)

Fisher's narrative paradigm: People are storytelling animals; almost all forms of human communication are fundamentally narrative. Listeners judge a story by whether it hangs together and rings true with the values of an ideal audience. Thus, narrative rationality is a matter of coherence and fidelity. (Rhetorical tradition)

Mass Communication

McLuhan's media ecology: The media must be understood ecologically. Changes in communication technology alter the symbolic environment—the socially constructed, sensory world of meanings. We shaped our tools—the phonetic alphabet, printing press, and telegraph—and they in turn have shaped our perceptions, experiences, attitudes, and behavior. Thus the medium is the message. (Sociocultural tradition)

Barthes' semiotics: The significant visual sign systems of a culture affirm the status quo by suggesting that the world as it is today is natural, inevitable, and eternal. Mythmakers do this by co-opting neutral denotative signs to become signifiers without historical grounding in second-order connotative semiotic systems. (Semiotic tradition)

Hall's cultural studies: The mass media function to maintain the ideology of those who already have power. Corporately controlled media provide the dominant discourse of the day that frames interpretation of events. Critics should seek not only to interpret culture, but to change it. Media audiences do have the capacity to resist hegemonic influence. (Critical tradition)

Gerbner's cultivation theory: Television has become society's storyteller. Heavy television viewers see a vast quantity of dramatic violence, which cultivates an exaggerated belief in a mean and scary world. Mainstreaming and resonance are two of the processes that create a homogeneous and fearful populace. (Sociocultural and socio-psychological traditions)

McCombs and Shaw's agenda-setting theory: The media tell us (1) what to think about, and (2) how to think about it. The first process (agenda setting) transfers the salience of items on their news agenda to our agenda. The second process (framing) transfers the salience of selected attributes to prominence among the pictures in our heads. (Socio-psychological tradition)

Noelle-Neumann's spiral of silence: People live in perpetual fear of isolating themselves and carefully monitor public opinion to see which views are acceptable. When their opinions appear out of favor, they keep silent. Television's constant repetition of a single point of view biases perception of public opinion and accelerates the spiral of silence. (Socio-psychological tradition)

Cultural Context

Giles' communication accommodation theory: People in intercultural encounters who see themselves as unique individuals will adjust their speech style and content to mesh with others whose approval they seek. People who want to reinforce a strong group identification will interact with those outside the group in a way that accentuates their differences. (Socio-psychological tradition)

Ting-Toomey's face-negotiation theory: People from collectivistic cultures with an interdependent self-image are concerned with giving other-face or mutual face, so they adopt a conflict style of avoiding or integrating. People from individualistic cultures with an independent self-image are concerned with protecting self-face, so they adopt a conflict style of dominating. (Socio-cultural and socio-psychological traditions)

Philipsen's speech codes theory: Through ethnography of communication we know all cultures have multiple speech codes that involve a distinctive psychology, sociology, and rhetoric. The meaning of a speech code is determined by speakers and listeners, and is woven into speech itself. Artful use of the code can explain, predict, and control talk about talk. (Socio-cultural tradition)

Tannen's genderlect styles: Male-female conversation is cross-cultural communication. Masculine and feminine styles of discourse are best viewed as two distinct cultural dialects rather than as inferior or superior ways of speaking. Men's report talk focuses on status and independence; women's rapport talk seeks human connection. (Semiotic and socio-cultural traditions)

Harding and Wood's standpoint theory: Different locations within the social hierarchy affect what is seen. The standpoints of marginalized people provide less false views of the world than do the privileged perspectives of the powerful. Strong objectivity requires that scientific research start from the lives of women, the poor, gays and lesbians, and racial minorities. (Critical tradition)

Kramarae's muted group theory: Man-made language aids in defining, depreciating, and excluding women. Women are less articulate in public because the words and the norms for their use have been devised by men. As women cease to be muted, men will no longer maintain their position of dominance in society. (Critical phenomenological traditions)

APPENDIX B

Feature Films That Illustrate Communication Theories

(With a strong assist from my cinematic colleagues Russ Proctor and Ron Adler)

Interpersonal Messages
The Miracle Worker (general)
Pygmalion / My Fair Lady (symbolic interactionism)
Nell (symbolic interactionism)
Ghost World* (symbolic interactionism)
Black Like Me (symbolic interactionism)
The Color Purple (symbolic interactionism)
Mask (symbolic interactionism)
Stand and Deliver (symbolic interactionism)
She's All That (symbolic interactionism)
Chocolat (coordinated management of meaning)
Don Juan DeMarco (coordinated management of meaning)
Life Is Beautiful (coordinated management of meaning)
Anger Management (coordinated management of meaning)
The African Queen (expectancy violations theory)
Almost Famous* (expectancy violations theory)
How to Lose a Guy in 10 Days (expectancy violations theory)
Crash (expectancy violations theory)
The Sting (expectancy violations theory)
Hotel Rwanda (constructivism)
Dead Man Walking* (constructivism)
To Kill a Mockingbird (constructivism)
Anne of Green Gables (constructivism)

Relationship Development
Four Weddings and a Funeral* (general)
Good Will Hunting* (general)
Annie Hall (general)
Guess Who's Coming to Dinner (general)
Brothers McMullen* (general)
Bridget Jones's Diary* (general)
Before Sunrise* / Before Sunset* (social penetration theory)
Shrek (social penetration theory)
Coming Home* (social penetration theory)
The Breakfast Club* (social penetration theory)
Driving Miss Daisy (uncertainty reduction theory)
My Big Fat Greek Wedding (uncertainty reduction theory)
Witness* (uncertainty reduction theory)
Down in the Delta (uncertainty reduction theory)
Sideways* (uncertainty reduction theory)
The Chosen [1982] (uncertainty reduction theory)
You've Got Mail (social information processing theory)
Sleepless in Seattle (social information processing theory)

Relationship Maintenance
Breaking Away (general)
Children of a Lesser God* (relational dialectics)

*Asterisk indicates movie is rated R

Beaches (relational dialectics)
Bend It Like Beckham (relational dialectics)
The Story of Us* (relational dialectics)
Mr. Holland's Opus (relational dialectics)
Whale Rider (relational dialectics)
Little Miss Sunshine* (interactional view)
Soul Food* (interactional view)
Ordinary People* (interactional view)
Pieces of April (interactional view)
Parenthood* (interactional view)
What's Eating Gilbert Grape (interactional view)
When a Man Loves a Woman* (interactional view)
One True Thing* (interactional view)

Influence
Norma Rae (general)
Dead Man Walking* (social judgment theory)
A Civil Action (social judgment theory)
Schindler's List* (social judgment theory)
An Inconvenient Truth (elaboration likelihood model)
12 Angry Men (elaboration likelihood model)
My Cousin Vinny* (elaboration likelihood model)
Swing Kids (cognitive dissonance theory)
Thank You For Smoking* (cognitive dissonance theory)
10 Things I Hate About You (cognitive dissonance theory)
Casablanca (cognitive dissonance theory)

Group Decision Making
O Brother, Where Art Thou? (general)
Stagecoach [1939] (general)
Apollo 13 (functional perspective)
Flight of the Phoenix (functional perspective)
Poseidon [2006] (functional perspective)
Alien* (functional perspective)
The Dream Team (adaptive structuration theory)
Lord of the Flies* (adaptive structuration theory)
The 40-Year-Old Virgin* (symbolic convergence theory)
Dead Poets Society (symbolic convergence theory)
Paper Clips (symbolic convergence theory)

Organizational Communication
Office Space* (general)
Gung Ho (cultural approach)
Good Morning, Vietnam* (cultural approach)
Up the Down Staircase (cultural approach)
The Firm* (cultural approach)
A Few Good Men* (cultural approach)
Erin Brockovich* (critical theory)
Roger & Me* (critical theory)
The Insider* (critical theory)
Silkwood* (critical theory)

Public Rhetoric

Clarence Darrow (general)
Inherit the Wind (general)
Judgment at Nuremberg (general)
Julius Caesar (rhetoric)
The Apostle (rhetoric)
*My Cousin Vinny** (rhetoric)
*The Verdict** (rhetoric)
*Amistad** (rhetoric)
*Nixon** (dramatism)
Malcolm X (dramatism)
Julius Caesar (dramatism)
*Hurricane** (dramatism)
Snow Falling on Cedars (dramatism)
*The Widow of St. Pierre** (dramatism)
*Smoke** (narrative paradigm)
Big Fish (narrative paradigm)
Forrest Gump (narrative paradigm)

Media and Culture

*Blade Runner** (media ecology)
*Network** (media ecology)
*Broadcast News** (media ecology)
*Medium Cool** (media ecology)
Being There (media ecology)
*Donnie Darko** (semiotics)
*Amarcord** (semiotics)
The Manchurian Candidate [1962] (semiotics)
Stardust Memories (semiotics)
*The Seventh Seal** (semiotics)
The Year of Living Dangerously (cultural studies)
*Bamboozled** (cultural studies)
Good Night and Good Luck (cultural studies)
*Blood Diamond** (cultural studies)
*Fahrenheit 9/11** (cultural studies)

Media Effects

*Network** (general)
*Bob Roberts** (general)
The Candidate (general)
Avalon (cultivation theory)

Being There (cultivation theory)
All the President's Men (agenda-setting theory)
*Wag the Dog** (agenda-setting theory)
Absence of Malice (agenda-setting theory)
Quiz Show (agenda-setting theory)
*Mississippi Burning** (spiral of silence)

Intercultural Communication

A Passage to India (general)
*Do the Right Thing** (general)
*Tsotsi** (general)
Lone Star (general)
The Right Stuff (communication accommodation theory)
Zelig (communication accommodation theory)
*The Joy Luck Club** (face-negotiation theory)
Iron and Silk (face-negotiation theory)
Antz (face-negotiation theory)
Gung Ho (face-negotiation theory)
Shall We Dance? [1997] (face-negotiation theory)
Dances with Wolves (speech codes theory)
Kramer vs. Kramer (speech codes theory)
Hoop Dreams (speech codes theory)
Billy Elliot (speech codes theory)
Mean Girls (speech codes theory)
Clueless (speech codes theory)

Gender and Communication

*When Harry Met Sally** (genderlect styles)
Sleepless in Seattle (genderlect styles)
*Diner** (genderlect styles)
Steel Magnolias (genderlect styles)
The Cider House Rules (standpoint theory)
*Beloved** (standpoint theory)
*Waiting to Exhale** (standpoint theory)
*White Man's Burden** (standpoint theory)
*North Country** (muted group theory)
The Little Mermaid (muted group theory)
Fried Green Tomatoes (muted group theory)
*Maria Full of Grace** (muted group theory)
Tootsie (muted group theory)

APPENDIX C

NCA Credo for Communication Ethics

Questions of right and wrong arise whenever people communicate. Ethical communication is fundamental to responsible thinking, decision making, and the development of relationships and communities within and across contexts, cultures, channels, and media. Moreover, ethical communication enhances human worth and dignity by fostering truthfulness, fairness, responsibility, personal integrity, and respect for self and others. We believe that unethical communication threatens the quality of all communication and consequently the well-being of individuals and the society in which we live. Therefore, we, the members of the National Communication Association, endorse and are committed to practicing the following principles of ethical communication.

> **We advocate truthfulness, accuracy, honesty, and reason as essential to the integrity of communication.**

> **We endorse freedom of expression, diversity of perspective, and tolerance of dissent to achieve the informed and responsible decision making fundamental to a civil society.**

> **We strive to understand and respect other communicators before evaluating and responding to their messages.**

> **We promote access to communication resources and opportunities as necessary to fulfill human potential and contribute to the well-being of families, communities, and society.**

> **We promote communication climates of caring and mutual understanding that respect the unique needs and characteristics of individual communicators.**

> **We condemn communication that degrades individuals and humanity through distortion, intimidation, coercion, and violence and through the expression of intolerance and hatred.**

> **We are committed to the courageous expression of personal convictions in pursuit of fairness and justice.**

> **We advocate sharing information, opinions, and feelings when facing significant choices while also respecting privacy and confidentiality.**

> **We accept responsibility for the short- and long-term consequences of our own communication and expect the same of others.**

CALVIN AND HOBBES © 1989 Watterson. Reprinted with permission of Universal Press Syndicate. All rights reserved.

ENDNOTES

Chapter 1: Launching Your Study of Communicaton Theory

1 Judee Burgoon, "Expectancy Violations Theory," in *Conversations with Communication Theorists*, 2.0, McGraw-Hill, 2006. (DVD) Band 2.
2 Ernest Bormann, *Communication Theory*, Sheffield, Salem, WI, 1989, p. 25.
3 Burgoon, *Conversations. . .*
4 Fred Casmir, *Building Communication Theories: A Socio/Cultural Approach*, Lawrence Erlbaum, Hillsdale, NJ, 1994, p. 27.
5 Sir Karl Popper, *The Logic of Scientific Discovery*, Hutchinson, London, 1959, p. 59.
6 See "General Semantics of Alfred Korzibski" in the Theory Archive at www.afirstlook.com.
7 Frank E. X. Dance, "The Concept of Communication," *Journal of Communication*, Vol. 20, 1970, pp. 201–210.
8 Dance, p. 210.
9 Jennifer Daryl Slack, "Communication as Articulation," in *Communication as . . . Perspectives on Theory*, Gregory Shepherd, Jeffrey St. John, and Ted Striphas (eds.), Sage, Thousand Oaks, CA, 2006, p. 223.
10 Robert T. Craig, "Communication as a Practice," in *Communication as . . . Perspectives on Theory*, p. 39.
11 For a further discussion of Blumer and this statement, see Chapter 5.
12 Wendell Johnson, *People in Quandaries*, Harper, New York, 1946, p. 26.
13 Celeste Condit, "Communication as Relationality," in *Communication as . . . Perspectives on Theory*, p. 3.
14 *Cool Hand Luke*, Warner Brothers, 1967.

Chapter 2: Talk About Theory

1 "Best Spots," *Adweek*, December 11, 2006, http://www.vnuemedia.com/aw/creative/best_spots_06/1106_06.jsp.
2 Carl Hovland and Walter Weiss, "The Influence of Source Credibility on Communication Effectiveness," *Public Opinion Quarterly*, Vol. 15, 1951, pp. 635–650.
3 Herbert Kelman, "Processes of Opinion Change," *Public Opinion Quarterly*, Vol. 25, 1961, pp. 57–78.
4 Kenneth Burke, *A Grammar of Motives*, Prentice-Hall, Englewood Cliffs, NJ, 1945, p. xv.
5 Kenneth Burke, *The Philosophy of Literary Form: Studies in Symbolic Action*, 3rd ed., University of California, Berkeley, 1973, p. 71.
6 James A. Anderson, *Communication Theory: Epistemological Foundations*, Guilford, New York, 1996, p. 27.
7 *Conversations with Communication Theorists* may be viewed at www.mhhe.com/griffin7.
8 Anderson, p. 120.
9 Philosophers call this a question of *ontology*—the study of existence.
10 Poet William Henley, "Invictus," in *The Home Book of Verse*, 9th ed., Burton E. Stevenson (ed.), Holt, Rinehart and Winston, New York, p. 3501.
11 Anderson, p. 133.
12 C. S. Lewis, *The Abolition of Man*, Macmillan, New York, 1944, p. 309.
13 Philosophers call this a question of *axiology*—the study of ethical criteria.

14 George C. Homans, *The Nature of Social Science*, Harcourt, New York, 1967, p. 4.
15 William Melody and Robin Mansell, "The Debate over Critical vs. Administrative Research: Circularity or Challenge," *Journal of Communication*, Vol. 33, No. 3, 1983, p. 112.
16 Stan Deetz, "Fundamental Issues in Communication Studies," unpublished paper distributed to students enrolled in his communication theory class.
17 Robert Ivie, "The Social Relevance of Rhetorical Scholarship," *Quarterly Journal of Speech*, Vol. 81, No. 2, 1995, p. 138a.
18 Lawrence R. Frey, Carl H. Botan, and Gary L. Kreps, *Investigating Communication: An Introduction to Research Methods*, 2nd ed., Allyn and Bacon, Boston, 2000. The authors label their fourth method *naturalistic inquiry*. Since the types of naturalistic inquiry they describe are all forms of ethnography, I choose to use the label *ethnography* in accordance with accepted usage in the research community.
19 James McCroskey and Jason Teven, "Goodwill: A Reexamination of the Construct and Its Measurement," *Communication Monographs*, Vol. 66, 1999, pp. 90–103.
20 *Dances with Wolves*, TIG Productions, 1990.
21 Clifford Geertz, "Thick Description: Toward an Interpretive Theory of History," in *The Interpretation of Culture*, Basic Books, New York, 1973, p. 5.

Chapter 3: Weighing the Words

1 Richard Rodgers and Oscar Hammerstein II, "The Farmer and the Cowman," from *Oklahoma!* Rodgers & Hammerstein Library, New York, 1943, pp. 140–142.
2 Ernest Bormann, *Small Group Communication: Theory and Practice*, 3rd ed., Harper & Row, New York, 1990, p. 122.
3 Ernest Bormann, *The Force of Fantasy: Restoring the American Dream*, Southern Illinois University, Carbondale, IL, 2001, p. 5.
4 Alan D. DeSantis, "Smoke Screen: An Ethnographic Study of a Cigar Shop's Collective Rationalization," *Health Communication*, 2002, Vol. 14, p. 185.
5 Alan D. DeSantis, "Sometimes a Cigar [Magazine] Is More Than Just a Cigar [Magazine]: Pro-Smoking Arguments in *Cigar Aficionado*, 1992–2000," *Health Communication*, Vol. 15, 2003, pp. 457–480.
6 Alan D. DeSantis, "A Couple of White Guys Sitting Around Talking: The Collective Rationalization of Cigar Smokers," *Journal of Contemporary Ethnography*, Vol. 32, 2003, p. 462.
7 Abraham Kaplan, *The Conduct of Inquiry*, Chandler, San Francisco, 1964, p. 295.
8 Ernest Bormann, "Fantasy and Rhetorical Vision: The Rhetorical Criticism of Social Reality," *Quarterly Journal of Speech*, Vol. 58, 1972, p. 399.
9 Bormann attributes this insight to Harvard psychologist Robert Bales. I present Bales' interaction categories for analyzing group discussion in the introduction to group decision making (see pages 219–220). Bales changed his original category of "shows tension release" to "dramatizes" when he discovered that group members typically use verbal imagery to dispel discord.
10 DeSantis, "Smoke Screen," p. 193.

11 Francis Heylighen, "Occam's Razor," *Principia Cybernetica Web*, http://pespmc1.vub.ac.be/OCCAMRAZ.html, accessed March 12, 2007.

12 Ernest Bormann, *Small Group Communication*, p. 122.

13 Karl Popper, *Conjectures and Refutations: The Growth of Scientific Knowledge*, Harper & Row, New York, 1965, pp. 36–37.

14 John Cragan and Donald Shields, *Symbolic Theories in Applied Communication Research*, Hampton, Cresskill, NJ, 1995, p. 42.

15 Ibid., pp. 40–47.

16 Ernest G. Bormann, *Communication Theory*, Sheffield, Salem, WI, 1989, p. 214.

17 Klaus Krippendorff, "The Ethics of Constructing Communication," in *Rethinking Communication, Vol. 1: Paradigm Issues*, Brenda Dervin, Lawrence Grossberg, Barbara J. O'Keefe, and Ellen Wartella (eds.), Sage, Newbury Park, CA, 1989, p. 83.

18 Bormann, *The Force of Fantasy*, p. ix.

19 Eric Rothenbuhler, "Communication as Ritual," in *Communication as . . . Perspectives on Theory*, Gregory Shepherd, Jeffrey St. John, and Ted Striphas (eds.), Sage, Thousand Oaks, CA, 2006, p. 19.

20 Krippendorff, "The Ethics of Constructing Communication," p. 88.

21 William H. Melody and Robert Mansell, "The Debate over Critical vs. Administrative Research: Circularity or Challenge," *Journal of Communication*, Vol. 33, No. 3, 1983, p. 103.

22 Bormann, *The Force of Fantasy*, pp. 223–242.

23 DeSantis, "Smoke Screen," p. 168.

24 From Robert Frost, *A Masque of Reason*, cited in Ernest Bormann, "Symbolic Convergence Theory: A Communication Formulation," *Journal of Communication*, Vol. 35, No. 4, 1985, p. 135.

25 Barbara Warnick, "Left in Context: What Is the Critic's Role?" *Quarterly Journal of Speech*, Vol. 78, 1992, pp. 232–237.

26 Leigh Arden Ford, "Fetching Good out of Evil in AA: A Bormannean Fantasy Theme Analysis of *The Big Book* of Alcoholics Anonymous," *Communication Quarterly*, Vol. 37, 1989, pp. 1–15.

27 David Zarefsky, "Approaching Lincoln's Second Inaugural Address," in *The Practice of Rhetorical Criticism*, 2nd ed., James R. Andrews (ed.), Longman, New York, 1990, p. 69.

28 John Stewart, "A Postmodern Look at Traditional Communication Postulates," *Western Journal of Speech Communication*, Vol. 55, 1991, p. 374.

29 Ernest Bormann, John Cragan, and Donald Shields, "In Defense of Symbolic Convergence Theory: A Look at the Theory and Its Criticisms After Two Decades," *Communication Theory*, Vol. 4, 1994, pp. 259–294.

30 See Burke's dramatism and Fisher's narrative paradigm, Chapters 22 and 23.

31 Kenneth Gergen, *Toward Transformation in Social Knowledge*, Springer-Verlag, New York, 1982, p. 109.

32 Ernest Bormann, "Fantasy Theme Analysis and Rhetorical Theory," in *The Rhetoric of Western Thought*, 5th ed., James Golden, Goodwin Berquist, and William Coleman (eds.), Kendall/Hunt, Dubuque, IA, 1992, p. 379.

Chapter 4: Mapping the Territory

1 Robert T. Craig, "Communication Theory as a Field," *Communication Theory*, Vol. 9, 1999, p. 122.

2 Robert T. Craig, "Communication as a Practical Discipline," in *Rethinking Communication, Vol. 1: Paradigm Issues*, Brenda Dervin, Lawrence Grossberg, Barbara J. O'Keefe, and Ellen Wartella (eds.), Sage, Newbury Park, CA, 1989, pp. 97–122.

3 Craig, "Communication Theory as a Field," p. 120.

4 Ibid., p. 130.

5 The identification and titles of the seven traditions are taken from Craig (see note 3). I have altered his order of presentation to match the conceptual plan of Figure 4–3. The boldface minidefinitions of communication within each tradition are a paraphrase of, and consistent with, Craig's conception. The selection of pioneer figures for each tradition was my decision and reflects the features of each tradition I chose to emphasize.

6 Wilbur Schramm, director of the Stanford Institute for Communication Research, named four social scientists as founding fathers of communication research: Harold Lasswell, Kurt Lewin, Paul Lazarsfeld, and Carl Hovland. See Wilbur Schramm, "Communication Research in the United States," in *The Science of Human Communication*, Wilbur Schramm (ed.), Basic Books, New York, 1963, pp. 1–16.

7 Carl Hovland, Irving Janis, and Harold Kelley, *Communication and Persuasion*, Yale University, New Haven, CT, 1953, p. 17.

8 Norbert Wiener, *The Human Use of Human Beings*, Avon, New York, 1967, p. 23.

9 This all-inclusive definition is attributed to Wilbur Schramm by former student Donald Roberts, now a professor at the Institute for Communication Research at Stanford University. See note 6 above.

10 Claude Shannon and Warren Weaver, *The Mathematical Theory of Communication*, University of Illinois, Urbana, 1949, p. 66.

11 Cicero, *De Oratore*, E. W. Sutton and H. Rackham (trans.), Harvard University, Cambridge, MA, 1942, p. 25.

12 V. F. Ray, "Human Color Perception and Behavioral Response," Transactions of the New York Academy of Sciences, Vol. 16, No. 2, 1953; reproduced in Nancy Hickerson, *Linguistic Anthropology*, Holt, Rinehart and Winston, New York, 1980, p. 122.

13 Paul Kay and Willet Kempton, "What Is the Sapir–Whorf Hypothesis?" *American Anthropologist*, Vol. 86, 1984, pp. 65–79.

14 Edward Sapir, "The Status of Linguistics as a Science," in *Selected Writings*, David Mandelbaum (ed.), University of California, Berkeley, 1951 (1929), p. 160.

15 James Carey, *Communication as Culture*, Unwin Hyman, Boston, 1989, p. 23.

16 For an extended discussion of this socio-cultural concept, see Chapter 6, Coordinated Management of Meaning of W. Barnett Pearce & Vernon Cronen.

17 John Torpey, "Ethics and Critical Theory: From Horkheimer to Habermas," *Telos*, Vol. 19, No. 3, 1986, p. 73.

18 Herbert Marcuse, "Philosophy and Critical Theory," in *Negations: Essays in Critical Theory*, Free Association, London, 1988, p. 143.

19 Herbert Marcuse, "Repressive Tolerance," in *Critical Sociology*, Paul Connerton (ed.), Graham Bartram (trans.), Penguin, Middlesex, UK, 1978, pp. 310–311.

20 Theodor Adorno, "Sociology and Empirical Research," in *Critical Sociology*, p. 245.

21 Herbert Marcuse, cited in Tom Bottomore, *The Frankfurt School*, Routledge, London, 1989, p. 38.

22 Max Horkheimer, *Critical Theory: Selected Essays*, Herder & Herder, New York, 1972 (1937), p. 183.

23 Theodor Adorno, "Sociology and Empirical Research," in *Critical Sociology*, p. 256.

24 Theodor Adorno, "Cultural Criticism and Society," in *Critical Sociology*, p. 276.

25 Craig, "Communication Theory as a Field," p. 148.

26 Carl Rogers, "This Is Me," in *On Becoming a Person*, Houghton Mifflin, Boston, 1961, p. 24.

27 Carl Rogers, "The Necessary and Sufficient Conditions of Therapeutic Personality Change," *Journal of Consulting Psychology*, Vol. 21, 1957, pp. 95–103.

28 Rogers, "This Is Me," p. 16.

29 Carl Rogers, "The Characteristics of a Helping Relationship," in *On Becoming a Person*, p. 52.

30 Heidi L. Muller and Robert T. Craig (eds.), *Theorizing Communication: Readings Across Traditions*, Sage, Los Angeles, 2007, p. 499.

31 Richard L. Johannesen, "Communication Ethics: Centrality, Trends, and Controversies," in *Communication Yearbook 25*, William B. Gudykunst (ed.), Lawrence Erlbaum, Mahwah, NJ, 2001, pp. 201–235.

32 "NCA Credo for Communication Ethics," National Communication Association, Washington, DC, www.natcom.org/conferences/ethics/ethicsconfcredo99.html, accessed October 20, 2007.

33 Philosophers refer to these three approaches as (1) teleological ethics, (2) deontological ethics, and (3) virtue ethics.

Interpersonal Messages

1 An earlier version of these game metaphors appeared in Em Griffin, *Making Friends*, InterVarsity Press, Downers Grove, IL, 1987, pp. 12–18.

Chapter 5: Symbolic Interactionism

1 *Nell*, 1994, Egg Pictures, Twentieth-Century Fox.

2 The three premises are found in Herbert Blumer, *Symbolic Interactionism*, Prentice-Hall, Englewood Cliffs, NJ, 1969, p. 2. I have paraphrased the principles for stylistic consistency and to avoid gender-specific language.

3 See W. I. Thomas and Dorothy Thomas, *The Child in America*, Knopf, New York, 1928.

4 Jane Wagner, *The Search for Signs of Intelligent Life in the Universe*, Harper Perennial, New York, 1990, pp. 15, 18.

5 For a fascinating account of a gorilla that developed these symbolic associations with the word kitten, see Francine Patterson, *Koko's Kitten*, Scholastic, New York, 1985. Mead wouldn't have been troubled by the existence of an animal that can communicate hundreds of symbols in American Sign Language. He regarded the symbol-using difference between humans and other primates as one of great magnitude—a quantitative rather than a qualitative distinction.

6 Peter M. Hall, "Structuring Symbolic Interaction: Communication and Power" in *Communication Yearbook 4*, Dan Nimmo (ed.), Transaction, New Brunswick, NJ, 1980, p. 50.

7 Douglas Hofstadter, "Changes in Default Words and Images Engendered by Rising Consciousness" in *The Production of Reality*, 3rd ed., Jodi O'Brien and Peter Kollock (eds.), Pine Forge, Thousand Oaks, CA, 2001, p. 158.

8 George Herbert Mead, *Mind, Self, and Society*, University of Chicago, 1934, p. 43.

9 Peter Kollock and Jodi O'Brien, *The Production of Reality*, Pine Forge, Thousand Oaks, CA, 1994, p. 63.

10 Kingsley Davis, "Final Note on a Case of Extreme Isolation," in Jodi O'Brien (ed.), *The Production of Reality*, 4th ed., Pine Forge, Thousand Oaks, CA, 2006, pp. 89–95.

11 Harper Lee, *To Kill a Mockingbird*, Warner, New York, 1982, p. 282.

12 Ralph Waldo Emerson, "Astraea," *The Works of Ralph Waldo Emerson*, Vol. III, Nottingham Society, Philadelphia, n. d., p. 121.

13 Greg Shepherd, "Transcendence," *Communication as . . . Perspectives on Theory*, Gregory Shepherd, Jeffrey St. John, and Ted Striphas (eds.), Sage, Thousand Oaks, CA, 2006, p. 24.

14 George Herbert Mead, "The Social Self," *Journal of Philosophy, Psychology and Scientific Methods*, Vol. 10, 1913, p. 375.

15 Mead, *Mind, Self, and Society*, p. 174.

16 Their interpretation is open to question. As we learn later in the film, Nell's phonetic "may" is also the way she refers to her dead sister. When Nell reached toward the mirror, she might have seen her reflection as an image of her twin rather than of herself. If so, the psychologists' interpretation provides added support for Blumer's first premise. They responded to Nell's communication on the basis of the meaning it had for them.

17 Kollock and O'Brien, p. 63.

18 William Shakespeare, *As You Like It*, Act II, Scene VII, line 139, in *The Riverside Shakespeare*, G. Blakemore Evans (ed.), Houghton Mifflin, Boston, 1974, p. 381.

19 Erving Goffman, *The Presentation of Self in Everyday Life*, Doubleday Anchor, Garden City, NY, 1959.

20 Ibid., p. 56.

21 Joan P. Emerson, "Behavior in Private Places: Sustaining Definitions of Reality in Gynecological Examinations," in *The Production of Reality*, 4th ed., pp. 201–214.

22 Jean Mizer, "Cipher in the Snow," *Today's Education*, Vol. 53, November 1964, pp. 8–10.

23 George Bernard Shaw, "Pygmalion," *Selected Plays*, Dodd, Mead, New York, 1948, p. 270.

24 Saul Alinsky, *Reveille for Radicals*, Vintage, New York, 1969 (1946), pp. 77–78.

25 Randall Collins, "Toward a Neo-Meadian Sociology of Mind," *Symbolic Interaction*, Vol. 12, 1989, p. 1.

Chapter 6: Coordinated Management of Meaning (CMM)

1 W. Barnett Pearce, "The Coordinated Management of Meaning (CMM)" in *Theorizing About Intercultural Communication*, William B. Gudykunst (ed.), Sage, Thousand Oaks, CA, 2004, pp. 35–54.

2 Vernon Cronen, "Practical Theory, Practical Art, and the Pragmatic-Systemic Account of Inquiry," *Communication Theory*, Vol. 11, 2001, pp. 14–35. See also Kevin Barge, "Articulating CMM as a Practical Theory," *Human Systems*, Vol. 15, 2004, pp. 193–203.

3 W. Barnett Pearce, *Making Social Worlds: A Communication Perspective*, Blackwell, Malden, MA, 2008, p. 220.

4 Edited and paraphrased from Jonathan G. Shailor, "The Meaning and Use of 'Context' in the Theory of the Coordinated Management of Meaning," in *Context and Communication Behavior*, James Owen (ed.), Reno, NV, 1997, pp. 102–103.

5 Edited and paraphrased from John Burnham, "CMM: Report from Users," W. Barnett Pearce (ed.), unpublished manuscript.

6 www.publicdialogue.org.

7 Kimberly A. Pearce, *Making Better Social Worlds: Engaging in and Facilitating Dialogic Communication*, Pearce Associates, Redwood City, CA, 2002.

8 Edited and paraphrased from W. Barnett Pearce and Kimberly A. Pearce, "Extending the Theory of the Coordinated Management of Meaning (CMM) Through a Community Dialogue Process," *Communication Theory*, Vol. 10, 2000, pp. 405–423; and W. Barnett Pearce and Kimberly A. Pearce, "Combining Passions and Abilities: Toward Dialogic Virtuosity," *Southern Communication Journal*, Vol. 65, 2000, pp. 161–175.

9   W. Barnett Pearce, "'Listening for the Wisdom in the Public's Whining' or 'Working to Construct Patterns of Public Communication,'" unpublished manuscript.

10 W. Barnett Pearce and Kimberly A. Pearce, "Transcendent Storytelling: Abilities for Systemic Practitioners and Their Clients," *Human Systems: The Journal of Systemic Consultation & Management*, Vol. 9, 1998, pp. 178–179.

11 W. Barnett Pearce, *Interpersonal Communication: Making Social Worlds*, HarperCollins, New York, 1994, p. 71.

12 Naomi Eisenberger, Matthew Lieberman, and Kipling Williams, "Does Rejection Hurt? An fMRI Study of Social Exclusion," *Science*, Vol. 302, 2003, pp. 290–292.

13 Ibid., p. 75.

14 Ernest T. Stringer, *Action Research*, 2nd ed., Sage, Thousand Oaks, CA, 1999. Pearce's reference to Stringer's model of action research made during the taping of *Conversations with Communication Theorists* at the International Communication Association convention, San Francisco, May 1999.

15 Pearce and Pearce, "Transcendent Storytelling."

16 Hierarchy model: W. Barnett Pearce, Vernon Cronen, and Forrest Conklin, "On What to Look at When Studying Communication: A Hierarchical Model of Actors' Meanings," *Communication*, Vol. 4, 1979, pp. 195–220; Serpentine model: W. Barnett Pearce, *Interpersonal Communication: Making Social Worlds*, HarperCollins, New York, 1994, p. 32.

17 Ibid., p. 123. Pearce credits communication theorist John Shotter for this strategy.

18 W. Barnett Pearce, *Communication and the Human Condition*, Southern Illinois University, Carbondale, 1989, pp. 32–33.

19 Victoria Chen, "The Possibility of Critical Dialogue in the Coordinated Management of Meaning," *Human Systems*, Vol. 15, 2004, pp. 179–192.

20 Vernon Cronen, "Coordinated Management of Meaning: The Consequentiality of Communication and the Recapturing of Experience," in *The Consequentiality of Communication*, Stuart Sigman (ed.), Lawrence Erlbaum, Hillsdale, NJ, 1995, p. 38.

21 W. Barnett Pearce, Stephen W. Littlejohn, and Alison Alexander, "The Quixotic Quest for Civility: Patterns of Interaction Between the New Christian Right and Secular Humanists," in *Secularization and Fundamentalism Reconsidered*, Jeffrey K. Hadden and Anson Shupe (eds.), Paragon, New York, 1989, pp. 152–177.

22 See the analysis of the presentencing conversation between Judge Joseph Duffy and defendant Ramzi Ahmed Yousef in W. Barnett Pearce, "The Coordinated Management of Meaning," in *Theorizing About Intercultural Communication*.

23 Pearce, *Making Social Worlds*, p. 12.

24 The entire alternative speech and Pearce's rationale for it are in Pearce, *Making Social Worlds*, pp. 12-25.

25 Pearce, *Interpersonal Communication*, p. 366.

26 Pearce, *Communication and the Human Condition*, pp. 167–195.

27 Pearce and Pearce, "Combining Passions and Abilities," p. 172.

28 W. Barnett Pearce and Stephen W. Littlejohn, *Moral Conflict: When Social Worlds Collide*, Sage, Thousand Oaks, 1997, p. 37.

29 Pearce and Pearce, "Combining Passions and Abilities," p. 173.

30 Martin Buber, *I and Thou*, 2nd ed., R. G. Smith (trans.), Scribner's, New York, 1958, pp. 60, 69.

31 Martin Buber, *Between Man and Man*, Macmillan, New York, 1965, p. 204.

32 Ronald Arnett, *Communication and Community*, Southern Illinois University, Carbondale, 1986, p. 37.

33 Pearce, *Making Social Worlds*, p. x.

34 Edited and paraphrased from Gabrielle Parker, "CMM: Report from Users," W. Barnett Pearce (ed.), unpublished manuscript.

Chapter 7: Expectancy Violations Theory

1   Judee K. Burgoon, "A Communication Model of Personal Space Violations: Explication and an Initial Test," *Human Communication Research*, Vol. 4, 1978, pp. 129–142.

2   Ibid., p. 130.

3   Edward T. Hall, *The Hidden Dimension*, Doubleday, Garden City, NY, 1966, p. 1.

4   W. H. Auden, "Prologue: The Birth of Architecture," in *About the House*, Random House, New York, 1966, p. 14.

5   Judee K. Burgoon and Jerold Hale, "Nonverbal Expectancy Violations: Model Elaboration and Application to Immediacy Behaviors," *Communication Monographs*, Vol. 55, 1988, p. 58.

6   *Random House Webster's Electronic Dictionary and Thesaurus*, College Edition, WordPerfect, Orem, UT, 1994.

7   Judee K. Burgoon, "Cross-Cultural and Intercultural Applications of Expectancy Violations Theory," in *Intercultural Communication Theory*, Richard Wiseman (ed.), Sage, Thousand Oaks, CA, 1995, pp. 194–214.

8   Judee K. Burgoon and Joseph Walther, "Nonverbal Expectancies and the Evaluative Consequences of Violations," *Human Communication Research*, Vol. 17, 1990, p. 236.

9   Edward Hall, "A System of Notation of Proxemic Behavior," *American Anthropologist*, Vol. 41, 1963, pp. 1003–1026.

10 Cited in Judee K. Burgoon, Valerie Manusov, Paul Mineo, and Jerold Hale, "Effects of Gaze on Hiring, Credibility, Attraction, and Relational Message Interpretation," *Journal of Nonverbal Behavior*, Vol. 9, 1985, p. 133.

11 Douglas Kelley and Judee K. Burgoon, "Understanding Marital Satisfaction and Couple Type as Functions of Relational Expectations," *Human Communication Research*, Vol. 18, 1991, pp. 40–69.

12 Beth A. LePoire and Judee K. Burgoon, "Two Contrasting Explanations of Involvement Violations: Expectancy Violations Theory Versus Discrepancy Arousal Theory," *Human Communication Research*, Vol. 20, 1994, pp. 560–591.

13 Graham Chapman, John Cleese, Terry Gilliam, Eric Idle, Terry Jones, and Michael Palin, *The Complete Monty Python's Flying Circus: All the Words*, Volume One, Pantheon, New York, 1989, p. 40.

14 Judee K. Burgoon, "Nonverbal Violations of Expectations," in *Nonverbal Interaction*, John Wiemann and Randall P. Harrison (eds.), Sage, Beverly Hills, CA, 1983, p. 101.

15 Paul A. Mongeau, Colleen Carey, and Mary Lynn Williams, "First Date Initiation and Enactment: An Expectancy Violation Approach," in *Sex Differences and Similarities in Communication*, Daniel J. Canary and Kathryn Dindia (eds.), Lawrence Erlbaum, Mahwah, NJ, 1998, pp. 413–426.

16 Judee K. Burgoon, Lesa Stern, and Leesa Dillman, *Interpersonal Adaptation: Dyadic Interaction Patterns*, Cambridge University, Cambridge, UK, 1995.

17 For Em Griffin's treatment of Abraham Maslow's hierarchy of needs, go to *www.afirstlook.com* and click on Theory Archive.

18 Burgoon, "Cross-Cultural and Intercultural Applications," p. 209.

19 Peter A. Andersen, Laura K. Guerrero, David B. Buller, and Peter F. Jorgensen, "An Empirical Comparison of Three Theories of Nonverbal Immediacy Exchange,"

Human Communication Research, Vol. 24, 1998, pp. 501–535.

20 Immanuel Kant, "On a Supposed Right to Lie from Altruistic Motives," in *Critique of Practical Reason and Other Writings in Moral Philosophy*, Lewis White Beck (trans. and ed.), University of Chicago, 1964, p. 346.

21 Immanuel Kant, *Groundwork of the Metaphysics of Morals*, H. J. Paton (trans.), Harper Torchbooks, New York, 1964, p. 88.

Chapter 8: Constructivism

1 Walter H. Crockett, "Cognitive Complexity and Impression Formation," in *Progress in Experimental Personality Research*, Vol. 2, B. A. Maher (ed.), Academic Press, New York, 1965, pp. 47–90.

2 Ann Mayden Nicotera, "The Constructivist Theory of Delia, Clark, and Associates," in *Watershed Research Traditions in Human Communication Theory*, Donald Cushman and Branislav Kovačić (eds.), State University of New York, Albany, 1995, p. 52.

3 Brant R. Burleson, "Constructivism: A General Theory of Communication Skill," in *Explaining Communication: Contemporary Theories and Exemplars*, Bryan Whaley and Wendy Samter (eds.), Lawrence Erlbaum, Mahwah, NJ, 2007, pp. 105–128.

4 Brant R. Burleson and Michael S. Waltman, "Cognitive Complexity: Using the Role Category Questionnaire Measure," in A *Handbook for the Study of Human Communication*, Charles Tardy (ed.), Ablex, Norwood, NJ, 1988, p. 15.

5 Ruth Ann Clark and Jesse Delia, "Cognitive Complexity, Social Perspective-Taking, and Functional Persuasive Skills in Second-to-Ninth-Grade Students," *Human Communication Research*, Vol. 3, 1977, pp. 128–134.

6 Jesse Delia, Barbara J. O'Keefe, and Daniel O'Keefe, "The Constructivist Approach to Communication," in *Human Communication Theory*, Frank E. X. Dance (ed.), Harper & Row, New York, 1982, p. 163.

7 See Shereen Bingham and Brant R. Burleson, "Multiple Effects of Messages with Multiple Goals: Some Perceived Outcomes of Responses to Sexual Harassment," *Human Communication Research*, Vol. 16, 1989, p. 192.

8 James Price Dillard, "The Goals-Plans-Action Model of Interpersonal Influence," in *Perspectives on Persuasion, Social Influence, and Compliance Gaining*, John Seiter and Robert Gass (eds.), Pearson, Boston, 2003, pp. 185–206.

9 Bingham and Burleson, p. 192.

10 Dillard, p. 188.

11 Burleson, "Constructivism," p. 116.

12 John O. Greene, "Action Assembly Theory: Metatheoretical Commitments, Theoretical Propositions, and Empirical Allocations," in *Rethinking Communication*, Vol. 2, Brenda Dervin, Lawrence Grossberg, Barbara J. O'Keefe, and Ellen Wartella (eds.), Sage, Newbury Park, CA, 1989, pp. 117–128; for Em Griffin's chapter on Greene's action assembly theory from a previous edition of this text, click on Theory Archive at *www.afirstlook.com*.

13 Dillard, "The Goals-Plans-Action Model."

14 Bingham and Burleson, p. 193.

15 These three examples of comforting communication are from Brant R. Burleson, "Comforting Messages: Significance, Approaches, and Effects," in *Communication of Social Support*, Brant R. Burleson, Terrance Albrecht, and Irwin Sarason (eds.), Sage, Thousand Oaks, CA, 1994, p. 12.

16 Ibid., p. 22.

17 Brant R. Burleson and Wendy Samter, "A Social Skills Approach to Relationship Maintenance," in *Communication and Relationship Maintenance*, Daniel Canary and Laura Stafford (eds.), Academic Press, San Diego, 1994, pp. 61–90.

18 Comments expressed in a student's journal.

19 Beverly Davenport Sypher and Theodore Zorn, "Communication-Related Abilities and Upward Mobility: A Longitudinal Investigation," *Human Communication Research*, Vol. 12, 1986, pp. 420–431.

20 Brant R. Burleson, Jesse Delia, and James Applegate, "The Socialization of Person-Centered Communication: Parental Contributions to the Social-Cognitive and Communication Skills of Their Children," in *Perspectives in Family Communication*, Mary Anne Fitzpatrick and Anita Vangelisti (eds.), Sage, Thousand Oaks, CA, 1995, pp. 34–76.

21 Burleson, "Constructivism," p. 124.

22 Delia, O'Keefe, and O'Keefe, p. 167.

Relationship Development

1 Harold H. Kelley, Ellen Berscheid, Andrew Christensen, John Harvey, Ted Huston, George Levinger, Evie McClintock, Letitia Anne Peplau, and Donald Peterson, *Close Relationships*, W. H. Freeman, New York, 1983, p. 38.

2 See Jacqueline Wiseman, "Friendship: Bonds and Binds in a Voluntary Relationship," *Journal of Social and Personal Relationships*, Vol. 3, 1986, pp. 191–211; and Robert Hays, "Friendship," in *Handbook of Personal Relationships*, Steve Duck (ed.), John Wiley & Sons, New York, 1988, pp. 391–408.

3 Robert Sternberg, "A Triangular Theory of Love," *Psychological Review*, Vol. 9, 1986, pp. 119–135.

4 Robert Frost, "The Death of the Hired Man," in *The Poetry of Robert Frost*, Edward Lathem (ed.), Holt, Rinehart, and Winston, New York, 1969, pp. 34–36.

5 Keith Davis and Michael Todd, "Friendship and Love Relationships" in *Advances in Descriptive Psychology*, Vol. 2, Keith Davis (ed.), JAI, Greenwich, CT, 1982, pp. 79–122.

6 See Ron Adler and Neal Towne, *Looking Out/Looking In*, 10th ed., Wadsworth, Belmont, CA, 2002; and John Stewart, *Bridges Not Walls*, 9th ed., McGraw-Hill, New York, 2005.

Chapter 9: Social Penetration Theory

1 Dalmas Taylor and Irwin Altman, "Communication in Interpersonal Relationships: Social Penetration Processes," in *Interpersonal Processes: New Directions in Communications Research*, Michael Roloff and Gerald Miller (eds.), Sage, Newbury Park, CA, 1987, p. 259.

2 C. Arthur VanLear, "The Formation of Social Relationships: A Longitudinal Study of Social Penetration," *Human Communication Research*, Vol. 13, 1987, pp. 299–322.

3 Harold H. Kelley and John W. Thibaut, *Interpersonal Relationships*, John Wiley & Sons, New York, 1978.

4 John Stuart Mill, *A System of Logic*, J. W. Parker, London, 1843, Book VI, Chapter XII.

5 J. M. Rist, *Epicurus: An Introduction*, Cambridge University, Cambridge, England, 1972, p. 124.

6 Epicurus, "Leading Doctrines, 8," cited in R. D. Hicks, *Stoic and Epicurean*, Charles Scribner's Sons, New York, 1910, p. 183.

7 Ayn Rand, *The Fountainhead*, Signet, New York, 1971, p. x.

8 Irwin Altman, Anne Vinsel, and Barbara Brown, "Dialectic Conceptions in Social Psychology: An Application to Social Penetration and Privacy Regulation," in *Advances in Experimental Social Psychology*, Vol. 14, Leonard Berkowitz (ed.), Academic Press, New York, 1981, p. 139.

9 Sandra Petronio, *Boundaries of Privacy: Dialectics of Disclosure*, State University of New York, Albany, 2002, p. 10.

10 Ibid., p. 203.
11 Ibid., p. xv.
12 Paul H. Wright, "Self-Referent Motivation and the Intrinsic Quality of Friendship," *Journal of Social and Personal Relationships,* Vol. 1, 1984, pp. 115–130.
13 Richard Conville, *Relational Transitions: The Evolution of Personal Relationships,* Praeger, New York, 1991, pp. 19–40.
14 From John 15:13, *The New American Bible,* J. P. Kennedy & Sons, New York, 1970.

Chapter 10: Uncertainty Reduction Theory

1 Charles R. Berger, "Uncertainty and Information Exchange in Developing Relationships," in *Handbook of Personal Relationships,* Steve Duck (ed.), Wiley, New York, 1988, p. 244.
2 Charles R. Berger and Richard Calabrese, "Some Explorations in Initial Interaction and Beyond: Toward a Developmental Theory of Interpersonal Communication," *Human Communication Research,* Vol. 1, 1975, p. 100.
3 Charles R. Berger, "Beyond Initial Interaction: Uncertainty, Understanding, and the Development of Interpersonal Relationships," in *Language and Social Psychology,* H. Giles and R. St. Clair (eds.), Basil Blackwell, Oxford, UK, 1979, pp. 122–144.
4 Charles R. Berger and William B. Gudykunst, "Uncertainty and Communication," in *Progress in Communication Sciences,* Vol. X, Brenda Dervin and Melvin Voigt (eds.), Ablex, Norwood, NJ, 1991, p. 23.
5 For an excellent introduction to attribution theory, see Kelly Shaver, *An Introduction to Attribution Processes,* Lawrence Erlbaum, Hillsdale, NJ, 1983. Heider's theory is also described in the first two editions of this text (1991, 1994); click on Theory Archive at *www.afirstlook.com.*
6 Berger and Calabrese, pp. 99–112.
7 Joseph Cappella, "Mutual Influence in Expressive Behavior: Adult-Adult and Infant-Adult Dyadic Interaction," *Psychological Bulletin,* Vol. 89, 1981, pp. 101–132.
8 Berger and Gudykunst, p. 25.
9 Malcolm Parks and Mara Adelman, "Communication Networks and the Development of Romantic Relationships: An Extension of Uncertainty Reduction Theory," *Human Communication Research,* Vol. 10, 1983, pp. 55–79.
10 Ellen Berscheid and Elaine Walster, *Interpersonal Attraction,* 2nd ed., Addison-Wesley, Reading, MA, 1978, pp. 61–89.
11 Charles R. Berger, *Planning Strategic Interaction,* Lawrence Erlbaum, Mahwah, NJ, 1997, p. 17.
12 Charles R. Berger, "Goals, Plans, and Mutual Understanding in Relationships," in *Individuals in Relationships,* Steve Duck (ed.), Sage, Newbury Park, CA, 1993, p. 34.
13 Charles R. Berger, "Message Production Under Uncertainty," in *Developing Communication Theories,* Gerry Philipsen and Terrance Albrecht (eds.), State University of New York, Albany, 1997, p. 39.
14 Charles R. Berger, "Producing Messages Under Uncertainty," in *Message Production: Advances in Communication Theory,* John O. Greene (ed.), Lawrence Erlbaum, Mahwah, NJ, 1997, p. 222.
15 Personal correspondence from Charles Berger.
16 Berger, "Message Production Under Uncertainty," p. 39.
17 Charles R. Berger, "Inscrutable Goals, Uncertain Plans, and the Production of Communicative Action," in *Communication and Social Influence Processes,* Charles R. Berger and Michael Burgoon (eds.), Michigan State University, East Lansing, 1995, p. 17.
18 Berger, *Planning Strategic Interaction,* pp. 132–135.
19 Proverbs 15:22, New Revised Standard Version of the Bible.
20 William B. Gudykunst, "Uncertainty and Anxiety," in *Theories in Intercultural Communication,* Young Yun Kim and William B. Gudykunst (eds.), Sage, Newbury Park, CA, 1988, pp. 125–128.
21 William B. Gudykunst, *Bridging Differences: Effective Intergroup Communication,* Sage, Newbury Park, CA, 1991, p. 13.
22 William B. Gudykunst and Robin Shapiro, "Communication in Everyday Interpersonal and Intergroup Encounters," *International Journal of Intercultural Relations,* Vol. 20, 1996, pp. 19–45.
23 William B. Gudykunst, "An Anxiety/Uncertainty Management (AUM) Theory of Effective Communication: Making the Mesh of the Net Finer," in *Theorizing About Intercultural Communication,* William B. Gudykunst (ed.), Sage, Thousand Oaks, CA, 2005, p. 289.
24 William B. Gudykunst, "Toward a Theory of Effective Interpersonal and Intergroup Communication: An Anxiety/Uncertainty Management (AUM) Perspective," in *Intercultural Communication Competence,* R. L. Wiseman and J. Koester (eds.), Sage, Newbury Park, CA, 1993, p. 70, note 4.
25 Ibid., p. 286.
26 Ellen Langer, *The Power of Mindful Learning,* Addison-Wesley, Reading, MA, 1997.
27 Charles R. Berger, "Communicating Under Uncertainty," in *Interpersonal Processes: New Directions in Communication Research,* Michael Roloff and Gerald Miller (eds.), Sage, Newbury Park, CA, 1987, p. 40.
28 Kathy Kellermann and Rodney Reynolds, "When Ignorance Is Bliss: The Role of Motivation to Reduce Uncertainty in Uncertainty Reduction Theory," *Human Communication Research,* Vol. 17, 1990, p. 7.
29 Ibid., p. 71.
30 Michael Sunnafrank, "Predicted Outcome Value During Initial Interaction: A Reformulation of Uncertainty Reduction Theory," *Human Communication Research,* Vol. 13, 1986, pp. 3–33.
31 Charles R. Berger, "Communication Theories and Other Curios," *Communication Monographs,* Vol. 58, 1991, p. 102.
32 Berger, "Communicating Under Uncertainty," p. 58.

Chapter 11: Social Information Processing Theory

1 John Short, Ederyn Williams, and Bruce Christie, *The Social Psychology of Telecommunications,* John Wiley, London, 1976.
2 Richard Daft, Robert Lengel, and Linda K. Trevino, "Message Equivocality, Media Selection, and Manager Performance: Implications for Information Systems," *MIS Quarterly,* Vol. 11, 1987, pp. 355–368.
3 Lee Sproull and Sara Kiesler, "Reducing Social Context Cues: Electronic Mail in Organizational Communication," *Managerial Science,* Vol. 32, 1986, pp. 1492–1512.
4 Mary J. Culnan and M. Lynne Markus, "Information Technologies," in *Handbook of Organizational Communication,* Fredric Jablin, Linda L. Putnam, Karlene H. Roberts, and Lyman Porter (eds.), Sage, Newbury Park, CA, 1987, pp. 420–443.
5 Joseph B. Walther, "Interpersonal Effects in Computer-Mediated Interaction: A Relational Perspective," *Communication Research,* Vol. 19, 1992, pp. 52–90.
6 The fluid dynamics analogy was suggested by University of Washington communication professor Malcolm Parks at the National Communication Association meeting at Miami Beach, November 2003, on the occasion of Walther receiving the 2002 Woolbert Award.
7 Joseph B. Walther, Tracy Loh, and Laura Granka, "The Interchange of Verbal and Nonverbal Cues in Computer-Mediated and Face-to-Face Affinity," *Journal of Language and Social Psychology,* Vol. 24, 2005, pp. 36–65.
8 For a brief synthesis of the impact of nonverbal cues, see Judee Burgoon, "Nonverbal Signals," in *Handbook of Inter-*

personal Communication, 2nd ed., Mark Knapp and Gerald Miller (eds.), Sage, Thousand Oaks, CA, 1994, pp. 234–236.

9 Joseph B. Walther, "Relational Aspects of Computer-Mediated Communication: Experimental Observations Over Time," *Organization Science*, Vol. 6, 1995, pp. 186–202; Joseph B. Walther, "Time Effects in Computer-Mediated Groups: Past, Present, and Future," in *Distributed Work*, Pamela J. Hinds and Sara Kiesler (eds.), MIT, Cambridge, MA, 2002, pp. 235–257.

10 Walther, "Time Effects," p. 248.

11 Joseph B. Walther and Lisa C. Tidwell, "Nonverbal Cues in Computer-Mediated Communication, and the Effect of Chronomics on Relational Communication," *Journal of Organizational Computing*, Vol. 5, 1995, p. 362.

12 Joseph B. Walther and Lisa C. Tidwell, "Computer-Mediated Communication: Interpersonal Interaction On-Line," in *Making Connections: Readings in Relational Communication*, 2nd ed., Kathleen M. Galvin and Pamela J. Cooper (eds.), Roxbury, Los Angeles, 2000, p. 326.

13 Joseph B. Walther, Celeste L. Slovacek, and Lisa C. Tidwell, "Is a Picture Worth a Thousand Words? Photographic Images in Long-Term and Short-Term Computer-Mediated Communication," *Communication Research*, Vol. 28, 2001, p. 110.

14 Ibid., p. 122.

15 Martin Lea and Russell Spears, "Paralanguage and Social Perception in Computer-Mediated Communication," *Journal of Organizational Computing*, Vol. 2, 1992, pp. 321–341; Russell Spears and Martin Lea, "Social Influence and the Influence of the Social," in *Contexts of Computer-Mediated Communication*, Martin Lea (ed.), Harvester-Wheatsheaf, London, 1992, pp. 30–65.

16 Joseph B. Walther and Shawn Boyd, "Attraction to Computer-Mediated Social Support," in *Communication Technology and Society*, C. A. Lin and D. Atkin (eds.), Hampton, Cresskill, NJ, 2002, pp. 153–188.

17 Joseph B. Walther, "Computer-Mediated Communication: Impersonal, Interpersonal, and Hyperpersonal Interaction," *Communication Research*, Vol. 23, 1996, p. 26.

18 Walther and Tidwell, "Computer Mediated Communication," p. 325

19 Joseph B. Walther and Judee K. Burgoon, "Relational Communication in Computer-Mediated Interaction," *Human Communication Research*, Vol. 19, 1992, pp. 50–88; Joseph B. Walther, "Anticipated Ongoing Interaction Versus Channel Effects on Relational Communication in Computer-Mediated Interaction," *Human Communication Research*, Vol. 20, 1994, pp. 473–501.

20 Walther, "Relational Aspects of Computer-Mediated Communication," p. 197.

21 Walther, "Anticipated Ongoing Interaction," p. 494.

22 Joseph B. Walther and Malcolm R. Parks, "Cues Filtered Out, Cues Filtered In: Computer-Mediated Communication and Relationships" in *Handbook of Interpersonal Communication*, 3rd ed., Mark Knapp and J. A. Daly (eds.), Sage, Thousand Oaks, CA, 2002, p. 542.

23 Joseph B. Walther, "Group and Interpersonal Effects in International Computer-Mediated Collaboration," *Human Communication Research*, Vol. 23, 1997, p. 350.

24 Walther and Parks, p. 551.

25 Walther and Tidwell, "Computer-Mediated Communication," p. 329.

Relationship Maintenance

1 John Stewart, "Interpersonal Communication: Contact Between Persons," *Bridges Not Walls*, 5th ed., John Stewart (ed.), McGraw-Hill, New York, 1990, pp. 13–30.

2 Daniel Canary and Laura Stafford, "Maintaining Relationships throuh Strategic and Routing Interaction," in *Communication and Relational Maintenance*, Daniel Canary and Laura Stafford (eds.), Academic Press, San Diego, CA, 1994, pp. 3–22.

3 Laura Stafford and Daniel Canary, "Maintenance Strategies and Romantic Relationship Type, Gender and Relational Characteristics," *Journal of Social and Personal Relationships*, Vol. 8, 1991, p. 224.

4 Ibid., pp. 217–242.

Chapter 12: Relational Dialectics

1 Leslie A. Baxter, "Interpersonal Communication as Dialogue: A Response to the 'Social Approaches' Forum," *Communication Theory*, Vol. 2, 1992, p. 330.

2 Ibid., p. 335.

3 Leslie A. Baxter and Barbara Montgomery, *Relating: Dialogues and Dialectics*, Guilford, New York, 1996, p. 3.

4 Baxter and Montgomery, p. 8.

5 Leslie A. Baxter, "A Dialectical Perspective on Communication Strategies in Relationship Development," in *A Handbook of Personal Relationships*, Steve Duck (ed.), John Wiley & Sons, New York, 1988, p. 258.

6 Baxter and Montgomery, p. 43.

7 Leslie A. Baxter, "Relationships as Dialogues," *Personal Relationships*, Vol. 11, 2004, p. 14.

8 Baxter, "Dialectical Perspective," p. 259.

9 Irwin Altman, Anne Vinsel, and Barbara Brown, "Dialectic Conceptions in Social Psychology: An Application to Social Penetration and Privacy Regulation," in *Advances in Experimental Social Psychology*, Vol. 14, Leonard Berkowitz (ed.), Academic Press, New York, 1981, pp. 107–160.

10 Leslie A. Baxter, "A Tale of Two Voices," of *Family Communication*, Vol. 4, 2004, p. 188.

11 Baxter, "Relationships as Dialogues," p. 3.

12 Leslie A. Baxter and Lee West, "Couple Perceptions of Their Similarities and Differences: A Dialectical Perspective," *Journal of Social and Personal Relationships*, Vol. 20, 2003, pp. 491–514.

13 Mikhail Bakhtin, *Four Essays by M. M. Bakhtin*, M. Holquist (ed.), C. Emerson and M. Holquist (trans.), University of Texas, Austin, 1981, p. 272.

14 Baxter, "Relationships as Dialogues," p. 11.

15 Ibid., p. 12.

16 Ibid., p. 13.

17 Leslie A. Baxter and Dawn O. Braithwaite, "Performing Marriage: The Marriage Renewal Ritual as Cultural Performance," *Southern Communication Journal*, Vol. 67, 2002, pp. 94–109.

18 Mikhail Bakhtin, *Speech Genres and Other Late Essays*, C. Emerson and M. Holquist (eds.), V. McGee (trans.), University of Texas, Austin, 1986, p. 94.

19 Mikhail Bakhtin, *Problems of Dostoevsky's Poetics*, C. Emerson (ed. and trans.), University of Minnesota, Minneapolis, 1981

20 Mikhail Bakhtin, *Rabelais and His World*, H. Iswolsky (trans.), Indiana University, Bloomington, 1984.

21 G. Morson and C. Emerson, *Mikhail Bakhtin: Creation of a Prosaics*, Stanford University, Palo Alto, CA, 1990, p. 443.

22 Leslie A. Baxter and Carma Byland, "Social Influence in Close Relationships," in *Perspectives on Persuasion, Social Influence, and Compliance Gaining*, John Seiter and Robert Gass (eds.), Pearson, Boston, 2004, pp. 317–336.

23 *FLM Magazine*, Landmark Theatres, 2003.

24 Sissela Bok, *Lying: Moral Choice in Public and Private Life*, Vintage, New York, 1979, p. 48.

25 Ibid., p. 32.
26 Ibid., p. 263.
27 Baxter and Montgomery, "Rethinking Communication," p. 326.
28 Baxter, "Relationships as Dialogues," p. 17.
29 Baxter, "A Tale of Two Voices," p. 189.
30 Em Griffin and Glenn Sparks, "Friends Forever: A Longitudinal Exploration of Intimacy in Same-Sex Friends and Platonic Pairs," *Journal of Social and Personal Relationships,* Vol. 7, 1990, pp. 29–46; Andrew Ledbetter, Em Griffin, and Glenn Sparks, "Forecasting 'Friends Forever': A Longitudinal Investigation of Predictors of Relational Closeness," *Personal Relationships,* Vol. 14, 2007, pp. 343–350.
31 Barbara Montgomery, "Relationship Maintenance Versus Relationship Change: A Dialectical Dilemma," *Journal of Social and Personal Relationships,* Vol 10, 1993, p. 221.

Chapter 13: The Interactional View

1   Alan Watts, *The Book,* Pantheon, New York, 1966, p. 65. For other examples of Watts' use of the life-as-a-game metaphor, see Alan Watts, "The Game of Black-and-White," *The Book,* pp. 22–46; and Alan Watts, "The Counter Game," *Psychology East & West,* Ballantine, New York, 1969, pp. 144–185.
2   Paul Watzlawick, "The Construction of Clinical 'Realities,'" in *The Evolution of Psychotherapy: The Second Conference,* Jeffrey Zeig (ed.), Brunner/Mazel, New York, 1992, p. 64.
3   Watzlawick, Beavin, and Jackson list five axioms rather than four. I have omitted one stating that human beings communicate both digitally and analogically because the distinction has proved to be meaningless for most readers and I have been unable to explain why it is important to grasp.
4   Paul Watzlawick, *The Language of Change,* W. W. Norton, New York, 1978, p. 11.
5   Paul Watzlawick, Janet Beavin, and Don Jackson, *Pragmatics of Human Communication,* W. W. Norton, New York, 1967, p. 54.
6   L. Edna Rogers, "Relational Communication Theory: An Interactional Family Theory," in *Engaging Theories in Family Communication: Multiple Perspectives,* Dawn O. Braithwaite and Leslie A. Baxter (eds.), Sage, Thousand Oaks, CA, 2006, p. 119.
7   R. D. Laing, *Knots,* Pantheon, New York, 1970, p. 27.
8   Watzlawick, Beavin, and Jackson, p. 99.
9   L. Edna Rogers and Frank E. Millar III, "Domineeringness and Dominance: A Transactional View," *Human Communication Research,* Vol. 5, 1979, pp. 238–245.
10 Paul Watzlawick, John H. Weakland, and Richard Fisch, *Change,* W. W. Norton, New York, 1974, p. 95.
11 Watzlawick, *Language of Change,* p. 122.
12 Watzlawick, "The Construction of Clinical 'Realities,'" p. 61.
13 "Helping," Families Anonymous, Inc., Van Nuys, CA, n. d.
14 Janet Beavin Bavelas, "Research into the Pragmatics of Human Communication," *Journal of Strategic and Systemic Therapies,* Vol. 11, No. 2, 1992, pp. 15–29.

Influence

1   Kathy Kellermann and Tim Cole, "Classifying Compliance Gaining Messages: Taxonomic Disorder and Strategic Confusion," *Communication Theory,* Vol. 4, 1994, pp. 3–60.

Chapter 14: Social Judgment Theory

1   Muzafer Sherif and Carolyn Sherif, *Social Psychology,* Harper, New York, 1969.
2   Muzafer Sherif, "Experiments in Group Conflict," *Scientific American,* Vol. 195, 1956, pp. 54–58.
3   Carolyn Sherif, Muzafer Sherif, and Roger Nebergall, *Attitude and Attitude Change: The Social Judgment-Involvement Approach,* W. B. Saunders, Philadelphia, 1965, p. 222.
4   Ibid., p. 225.
5   Ibid., p. 214.
6   Gian Sarup, Robert Suchner, and Gitanjali Gaylord, "Contrast Effects and Attitude Change: A Test of the Two-Stage Hypothesis of Social Judgment Theory," *Social Psychology Quarterly,* Vol. 54, 1991, pp. 364–372.
7   Kathryn Greene, Roxanne Parrott, and Julianne M. Serovich, "Privacy, HIV Testing, and AIDS: College Students' Versus Parents' Perspectives," *Health Communication,* Vol. 5, 1993, pp. 59–74.
8   Stephen Bochner and Chester Insko, "Communicator Discrepancy, Source Credibility and Opinion Change," *Journal of Personality and Social Psychology,* Vol. 4, 1966, pp. 614–621.
9   Interview on *Morning Edition,* National Public Radio, May 31, 1995.
10 Hee Sun Park, Timothy Levine, Catherine Y. K. Westerma, Tierney Oregen, and Sarah Foregger, "The Effects of Argument Quality and Involvement Type on Attitude Formation and Attitude Change," *Human Communication Research,* Vol. 33, 2007, pp. 81-102.

Chapter 15: Elaboration Likelihood Model

1   Richard E. Petty and John T. Cacioppo, *Communication and Persuasion: Central and Peripheral Routes to Attitude Change,* Springer-Verlag, New York, 1986, p. 7.
2   Richard E. Petty and John T. Cacioppo, *Attitudes and Persuasion: Classic and Contemporary Approaches,* Wm. C. Brown, Dubuque, IA, 1981, p. 256.
3   Robert B. Cialdini, *Influence: Science and Practice,* 4th ed., Allyn and Bacon, Needham Heights, MA, 2001.
4   Richard E. Petty and Duane Wegener, "The Elaboration Likelihood Model: Current Status and Controversies," in *Dual Process Theories in Social Psychology,* Shelly Chaiken and Yaacov Trope (eds.), Guilford, New York, 1999, pp. 44–48.
5   John T. Cacioppo et al., "Dispositional Differences in Cognitive Motivation: The Life and Times of Individuals Varying in Need for Cognition," *Psychological Bulletin,* Vol. 119, 1996, pp. 197–253.
6   Richard E. Petty and John T. Cacioppo, "The Elaboration Likelihood Model of Persuasion," in *Advances in Experimental Social Psychology,* Vol. 19, Leonard Berkowitz (ed.), Academic Press, Orlando, FL, 1986, p. 129.
7   Louis Penner and Barbara Fritzsche, "Magic Johnson and Reactions to People with AIDS: A Natural Experiment," *Journal of Applied Social Psychology,* Vol. 23, 1993, pp. 1035–1050.
8   Ibid., p. 1048.
9   Michael Hawthorne, "Madigan: Video Busts Band's Bus in Dumping," *Chicago Tribune,* August 25, 2004, sec. 1, p. 1.
10 Petty and Wegener, pp. 51–52.
11 Duane Wegener and Richard E. Petty, "Understanding Effects of Mood Through the Elaboration Likelihood and Flexible Correction Models," in *Theories of Mood and Cognition: A User's Guidebook,* L. L. Martin and G. L. Clore (eds.), Lawrence Erlbaum, Mahwah, NJ, 2001, pp. 177–210.
12 Thomas R. Nilsen, *Ethics of Speech Communication,* Bobbs-Merrill, Indianapolis, 1966, p. 38.
13 Ibid., p. 35.
14 John Milton, *Areopagitica,* John Hales (ed.), with introduction and notes, 3rd ed., revised, Clarendon, Oxford, UK, 1882.

15 John Stuart Mill, *On Liberty*, Gateway, Chicago, 1955.

16 Søren Kierkegaard, *Philosophical Fragments*, Princeton University, Princeton, NJ, pp. 17–28.

17 Em Griffin, *The Mind Changers*, Tyndale, Carol Stream, IL, 1976, pp. 27–41; Em Griffin, *Getting Together*, Inter-Varsity, Downers Grove, IL, 1982, pp. 159–167.

18 Petty and Wegener, p. 46.

19 Paul Mongeau and James Stiff, "Specifying Causal Relationships in the Elaboration Likelihood Model," *Communication Theory*, Vol. 3, 1993, pp. 67–68.

20 Petty and Cacioppo, *Communication and Persuasion*, p. 32.

Chapter 16: Cognitive Dissonance Theory

1 Aesop, "The Fox and the Grapes," in *Aesop, Five Centuries of Illustrated Fables*, Metropolitan Museum of Art, New York, 1964, p. 12.

2 Leon Festinger, *A Theory of Cognitive Dissonance*, Stanford University, Stanford, CA, 1957, p. 4.

3 "Smoke! Smoke! Smoke! (That Cigarette)," Merle Travis, performed by Tex Williams, Capitol Records, 1947.

4 Leon Festinger, "Social Communication and Cognition: A Very Preliminary and Highly Tentative Draft," in *Cognitive Dissonance: Progress on a Pivotal Theory in Social Psychology*, Eddie Harmon-Jones and Judson Mills (eds.), American Psychological Association, Washington, DC, 1999, p. 361.

5 Festinger, *A Theory of Cognitive Dissonance*, pp. 5–6.

6 Ibid., pp. 84–97.

7 Dave D'Alessio and Mike Allen, "Selective Exposure and Dissonance After Decisions," *Psychological Reports*, Vol. 91, 2002, pp. 527-532.

8 Festinger, *A Theory of Cognitive Dissonance*, pp. 153-156.

9 D'Alessio and Allen, pp. 527–532.

10 Jeffrey Kluger, "Hollywood's Smoke Alarm," *Time Magazine*, April 12, 2007, http://www.time.com/time/magazine/article/09171,1009773,00.html, accessed October 22, 2007.

11 American Legacy Foundation, www.dontpassgas.org; "I Will Not Pass Gas," http://www.adcouncil.org/default.aspx?id=58, accessed May 1, 2007.

12 Dieter Frey, "Recent Research on Selective Exposure to Information," in *Advances in Experimental Social Psychology*, Vol. 19, Leonard Berkowitz (ed.), Academic Press, Orlando, FL, 1986, pp. 41–80.

13 Festinger, *A Theory of Cognitive Dissonance*, pp. 32-47.

14 Alan DeSantis and Susan E. Morgan, "Sometimes a Cigar [Magazine] Is More Than Just a Cigar [Magazine]: Pro-Smoking Arguments in *Cigar Aficionado*, 1992-2000," *Health Communication*, Vol. 15, 2003, p. 460.

15 Festinger, *A Theory of Cognitive Dissonance*, p. 95.

16 Leon Festinger and James Carlsmith, "Cognitive Consequences of Forced Compliance," *Journal of Abnormal and Social Psychology*, Vol. 58, 1959, pp. 203–210.

17 Elliot Aronson, "The Theory of Cognitive Dissonance: A Current Perspective," in *Advances in Experimental Social Psychology*, Vol. 4, Leonard Berkowitz (ed.), Academic Press, New York, 1969, p. 27.

18 Ibid., pp. 26–27.

19 Lynn R. Kahle, "Dissonance and Impression Management as Theories of Attitude Change," *Journal of Social Psychology*, Vol. 105, 1978, pp. 53–64.

20 Joel Cooper, "Unwanted Consequences and the Self: In Search of the Motivation for Dissonance Reduction," in *Cognitive Dissonance*, Harmon-Jones and Mills (eds.), p. 153.

21 Ibid., p. 151.

22 Richard Heslin and Michael Amo, "Detailed Test of the Reinforcement-Dissonance Controversy in the Counterat-

titudinal Advocacy Situation," *Journal of Personality and Social Psychology*, Vol. 23, 1972, pp. 234–242.

23 Anne E. Kornblut, "But Will They Love Him Tomorrow," *The New York Times*, Nation, March 19, 2006, sec. 4, p. 1.

24 Jeff Stone and Joel Cooper, "A Self-Standards Model of Cognitive Dissonance," *Journal of Experimental Social Psychology*, Vol. 37, 2001, p. 231.

25 R. B. Zajonc, "Leon Festinger (1919–1989)," *American Psychologist*, Vol. 45, 1990, p. 661.

26 Daryl Bem, "Self-Perception: An Alternative Interpretation of Cognitive Dissonance Phenomena," *Psychological Review*, Vol. 74, 1967, pp. 183–200.

Group Decision Making

1 Robert Bales, *Interaction Process Analysis*, Addison-Wesley, Reading, MA, 1950.

2 Irving Janis, *Groupthink*, 2nd ed., Houghton Mifflin, Boston, 1982. See also Em Griffin, *A First Look at Communication Theory*, 3rd ed., McGraw-Hill, New York, 1997, pp. 235–246. Also available in the theory archive of *www.afirstlook.com*.

3 Randy Hirokawa and Abran J. Salazar, "An Integrated Approach to Communication and Group Decision Making," in *Managing Group Life: Communicating in Decision-Making Groups*, Lawrence Frey and J. Kevin Barge (eds.), Houghton Mifflin, Boston, 1996, pp. 156–181.

Chapter 17: Functional Perspective on Group Decision Making

1 Some scholars also question the efficacy of communication in group decision making. See Dean Hewes, "A Socio-Egocentric Model of Group Decision-Making," in *Communication and Group Decision-Making*, Randy Hirokawa and Marshall Scott Poole (eds.), Sage, Beverly Hills, CA, 1986, pp. 265–291.

2 Randy Hirokawa, "Avoiding Camels: Lessons Learned in the Facilitation of High-Quality Group Decision Making Through Effective Discussion," the Van Zelst Lecture in Communication, Northwestern University School of Speech, Evanston, IL, May 24, 1993.

3 Dennis Gouran, "Group Decision Making: An Approach to Integrative Research," in *A Handbook for the Study of Human Communication*, Charles Tardy (ed.), Ablex, Norwood, NJ, 1988, pp. 247–267.

4 Proverbs 15:22, Revised Standard Version of the Bible.

5 Dennis Gouran, Randy Hirokawa, Kelly Julian, and Geoff Leatham, "The Evolution and Current Status of the Functional Perspective on Communication in Decision-Making and Problem-Solving Groups," in *Communication Yearbook 16*, Stanley Deetz (ed.), Sage, Newbury Park, CA, 1993, p. 591.

6 Randy Hirokawa and Dirk Scheerhorn, "Communication in Faulty Group Decision-Making," in *Communication and Group Decision-Making*, Randy Hirokawa and Marshall Scott Poole (eds.), Sage, Beverly Hills, CA, 1986, p. 69.

7 Hirokawa bases the distinction between rational and political logics on the work of Peter Senge, *The Fifth Discipline*, Doubleday, New York, 1990, p. 60.

8 Dennis Gouran and Randy Hirokawa, "The Role of Communication in Decision-Making Groups: A Functional Perspective" in *Communications in Transition*, Mary Mander (ed.), Praeger, New York, 1983, p. 174.

9 Randy Hirokawa, "Understanding the Relationship between Group Communication and Group Decision-Making Effectiveness from a Functional Perspective: Why 'It's Not All Bad' Isn't Quite 'Good Enough,'" Thomas M. Scheidel Lecture, University of Washington, Seattle, April 24, 1998.

ndy Hirokawa, "Functional Approaches to the Study of roup Discussion," *Small Group Research*, Vol. 25, 1994, p. 546.

11 Randy Hirokawa and Poppy McLeod, "Communication, Decision Development, and Decision Quality in Small Groups: An Integration of Two Approaches," paper presented at the annual meeting of the Speech Communication Association, Miami, November 18–21, 1993.

12 Marc Orlitzky and Randy Hirokawa, "To Err Is Human, to Correct for It Divine: A Meta-Analysis of the Functional Theory of Group Decision-Making Effectiveness," paper presented at the annual meeting of the National Communication Association, Chicago, November 19–23, 1997.

13 Andrea B. Hollingshead, Gwen Wittenbaum, et al., "A Look at Groups from the Functional Perspective," in *Theories of Small Groups: Interdisciplinary Perspectives*, Marshall Scott Poole and Andrea B. Hollingshead (eds.), Sage, London, 2005, pp. 21–62.

14 See, for example, J. Richard Hackman, "Work Teams in Organizations: An Orienting Framework," in *Groups That Work (and Those That Don't)*, J. Richard Hackman (ed.), Jossey-Bass, San Francisco, 1990, pp. 1–14.

15 Ivan Steiner, *Group Process and Productivity*, Academic Press, New York, 1972, p. 9.

16 Randy Hirokawa, "Avoiding Camels," p. 8.

17 Dennis Gouran and Randy Hirokawa, "Counteractive Functions of Communication in Effective Group Decision-Making," in Randy Hirokawa and Marshall Scott Poole (eds.), *Communication and Group Decision-Making*, Sage, Beverly Hills, CA, 1986, p. 82.

18 Randy Hirokawa, "Group Communication and Problem-Solving Effectiveness I: A Critical Review of Inconsistent Findings," *Communication Quarterly*, Vol. 30, 1982, p. 139.

19 Cited in Randy Hirokawa, "Researching the Role of Communication in Group Decision-Making: A Functional Theory Perspective," paper presented at the annual meeting of the Central States Communication Association, Chicago, April 11–14, 1991, p. 19.

20 Randy Hirokawa, "From the Tiny Pond to the Big Ocean: Studying Communication and Group Decision-Making Effectiveness from a Functional Perspective," 1999 B. Aubrey Fisher Memorial Lecture, Department of Communication, University of Utah, Salt Lake City.

21 Randy Hirokawa, "Group Communication and Decision-Making Performance: A Continued Test of the Functional Perspective," *Human Communication Research*, Vol. 14, 1988, p. 512.

22 Hirokawa, "From the Tiny Pond to the Big Ocean," p. 6.

23 Ibid.

24 Hirokawa, "Understanding the Relationship."

25 Hirokawa, "From the Tiny Pond to the Big Ocean," p. 11.

26 Gouran, Hirokawa, Julian, and Leatham, pp. 574–579.

27 Robert Craig, "Treatments of Reflective Thought in John Dewey and Hans-Georg Gadamer," paper presented at the 1994 Convention of the International Communication Association, Sydney, Australia, July 11–15, 1994.

28 John Dewey, *How We Think*, Heath, New York, 1910.

29 My analysis of Habermas' discourse ethics has been greatly informed by Theodore Glasser and James Ettema, "Ethics and Eloquence in Journalism: A Study of the Demands of Press Accountability," presented to the Media Ethics Division of the Association for Education in Journalism and Mass Communication, Miami Beach, FL, August 2002.

30 Sonja Foss, Karen Foss, and Robert Trapp, *Contemporary Perspectives on Rhetoric*, Waveland Press, Prospect Heights,

IL, 1991, pp. 241–272. (Like all interpreters of Habermas, Foss, Foss, and Trapp refer to his dense writing style. For that reason, all citations in this ethical reflection are from secondary sources. For an overview of Habermas' thinking, see Jane Braaten, *Habermas's Critical Theory of Society*, State University of New York, Albany, 1991. For a primary source, see Jürgen Habermas, "Discourse Ethics: Notes on a Program of Philosophical Justification," Shierry Weber Nicholsen and Christian Lenhardt (trans.), in *Communicative Ethics Controversy*, Seyla Benhabib and Fred Dallmayr (eds.), MIT Press, Cambridge, MA, 1990, pp. 60–110.

31 Theodore Glasser, "Communicative Ethics and the Aim of Accountability in Journalism," *Social Responsibility: Business, Journalism, Law, Medicine*, Vol. 21, Louis Hodges (ed.), Washington & Lee University, Lexington, VA, 1995, pp. 41–42.

32 Ibid., p. 49.

33 John Cragan and David Wright, "Small Group Communication Research of the 1980s: A Synthesis and Critique," *Communication Studies*, Vol. 41, 1990, pp. 212–236.

34 Cynthia Stohl and Michael Holmes, "A Functional Perspective for Bona Fide Groups," in *Communication Yearbook 16*, Stanley Deetz (ed.), Sage, Newbury Park, CA, 1993, p. 601.

35 See John Cragan and David Wright, "The Functional Theory of Small Group Decision-Making: A Replication," *Journal of Social Behavior and Personality*, Vol. 7, 1992 (Special Issue). Reprinted in John Cragan and David Wright (eds.), *Theory and Research in Small Group Communication*, Burgess, 1993, pp. 87–95.

36 B. Aubrey Fisher, "Decision Emergence: Phases in Group Decision Making," *Speech Monographs*, Vol. 37, 1970, pp. 53–66.

37 B. Aubrey Fisher, *Small Group Decision Making*, 2nd ed., McGraw-Hill, New York, 1980, p. 149.

38 Dennis Gouran, "Reflections on the Type of Question as a Determinant of the Form of Interaction in Decision-Making and Problem-Solving Discussions," *Communication Quarterly*, Vol. 53, 2003, pp. 111–125.

Chapter 18: Adaptive Structuration Theory

1 Marshall Scott Poole, "Adaptive Structuration Theory," *Conversations with Communication Theorists* (video), Em Griffin (ed.), McGraw-Hill, New York, 2000. The order of the second and third sentences is inverted.

2 Marshall Scott Poole, "Decision Development in Small Groups I: A Comparison of Two Models," *Communication Monographs*, Vol. 48, 1981, p. 4.

3 Marshall Scott Poole and Jonelle Roth, "Decision Development in Small Groups IV: A Typology of Group Decision Paths," *Human Communication Research*, Vol. 15, 1989, pp. 323–356.

4 Poole, "Decision Development in Small Groups I," p. 4.

5 Anthony Giddens, *The Constitution of Society: Outline of the Theory of Structuration*, University of California, Berkeley, 1984, p. 14.

6 Robert Boynton, "The Two Tonys: Why Is the Prime Minister So Interested in What Anthony Giddens Thinks?" *The New Yorker*, October 6, 1997, p. 67.

7 Giddens, *Constitution of Society*, p. xvi.

8 Marshall Scott Poole, "Group Communication and the Structuring Process," in *Small Group Communication*, 7th ed., Robert Cathcart, Larry Samovar, and Linda Henman (eds.), Brown & Benchmark, Madison, WI, 1996, p. 87. Definition based on Anthony Giddens, *Central Problems in Social The-*

ory: Action, Structure and Contradiction in Social Analysis, University of California, Berkeley, 1979, pp. 64–76.

9 Giddens, *Central Problems,* p. 5; *Constitution of Society,* p. 6.

10 Giddens, *Constitution of Society,* pp. 19–22.

11 Marshall Scott Poole, David Seibold, and Robert McPhee, "The Structuration of Group Decisions," in *Communication and Group Decision Making,* 2nd ed., Sage, Thousand Oaks, CA, 1996, p. 115.

12 For an example of an ethnographic study of structuration, see Lisa A. Howard and Patricia Geist, "Ideological Positioning in Organizational Change: The Dialectic of Control in a Merging Organization," *Communication Monographs,* Vol. 62, 1995, pp. 110–131.

13 Poole, "Group Communication," p. 86.

14 Poole, Seibold, and McPhee, "Structuration of Group Decisions," p. 119.

15 Marshall Scott Poole, David Seibold, and Robert McPhee, "Group Decision-Making as a Structurational Process," *Quarterly Journal of Speech,* Vol. 71, 1985, p. 79.

16 Poole, "Group Communication," p. 90.

17 Poole, Seibold, and McPhee, "Structuration of Group Decisions," p. 141.

18 Poole, "Group Communication," p. 87.

19 Ibid.

20 Poole, Seibold, and McPhee, "Structuration of Group Decisions," p. 122.

21 Marshall Scott Poole and Gerardine DeSanctis, "Understanding the Use of Group Decision Support Systems: The Theory of Adaptive Structuration," in *Organization and Communication Technology,* Sage, Newbury Park, CA, 1990, p. 179.

22 Wynne W. Chin, Abhijit Gopal, and W. David Salisbury, "Advancing the Theory of Adaptive Structuration: The Development of a Scale to Measure Faithfulness of Appropriation," *Information Systems Research,* Vol. 8, 1997, pp. 342–367.

23 Giddens, *Central Problems,* p. 71.

24 Marshall Scott Poole and Gerardine DeSanctis, "Microlevel Structuration in Computer-Supported Group Decision Making," *Human Communication Research,* Vol. 19, 1992, p. 7.

25 Marshall Scott Poole, "Do We Have Any Theories of Group Communication?" *Communication Studies,* Vol. 41, 1990, p. 243.

26 Poole, Seibold, and McPhee, "Structuration of Group Decisions," p. 120.

27 Poole, "Group Communication," p. 94.

28 John Cragan and David Wright, "Small Group Communication Research of the 1980s: A Synthesis and Critique," *Communication Studies,* Vol. 41, 1990, pp. 212–236.

29 Poole, "Do We Have Any Theories of Group Communication?" p. 240.

30 Kenneth Chase, "A Spiritual and Critical Revision of Structuration Theory," *Journal of Communication and Religion,* Vol. 16, No. 1, 1993, p. 8.

31 Poole, "Do We Have Any Theories of Group Communication?" p. 246.

Chapter 19: Cultural Approach to Organizations

1 Clifford Geertz, "Thick Description: Toward an Interpretive Theory of Culture," in *The Interpretation of Cultures,* Basic Books, New York, 1973, p. 5.

2 Michael Pacanowsky and Nick O'Donnell-Trujillo, "Organizational Communication as Cultural Performance," *Communication Monographs,* Vol. 50, 1983, p. 129. (Pacanowsky's early work was co-authored with Nick O'Donnell-Trujillo from the communication department at Southern Methodist University. Because Pacanowsky was the lead author in these

articles and Nick Trujillo's scholarship has taken a critical turn, I refer in the text of this chapter only to Pacanowsky. For critical ethnography, see Nick Trujillo, "Interpreting November 22: A Critical Ethnography of an Assassination Site," *Quarterly Journal of Speech,* Vol. 79, 1993, pp. 447–466.)

3 Michael Pacanowsky and Nick O'Donnell-Trujillo, "Communication and Organizational Cultures," *Western Journal of Speech Communication,* Vol. 46, 1982, p. 121.

4 Pacanowsky and O'Donnell-Trujillo, "Organizational Communication," p. 146.

5 Ibid., p. 131.

6 Pacanowsky and O'Donnell-Trujillo, "Communication and Organizational Cultures," p. 116.

7 Clifford Geertz, "Deep Play: Notes on the Balinese Cockfight," in *Myth, Symbol, and Culture,* Norton, New York, 1971, p. 29.

8 Geertz, "Thick Description," p. 5.

9 Gareth Morgan, *Images of Organization,* Sage, Newbury Park, CA, 1986, pp. 130–131.

10 Clifford Geertz, *A Life of Learning* (ACLS Occasional Paper No. 45), American Council of Learned Societies, New York, 1999, p. 14.

11 Pacanowsky and O'Donnell-Trujillo, "Communication and Organizational Cultures," p. 127.

12 Michael Pacanowsky, "Communication in the Empowering Organization," in *Communication Yearbook 11,* James Anderson (ed.), Sage, Newbury Park, CA, 1988, pp. 357, 362–364; for an update on the culture of W. L. Gore & Associates two decades later, see Alan Deutschman, "The Fabric of Creativity," *Fast Company,* December 2004, pp. 54–62.

13 Ibid., p. 357.

14 Ibid., p. 358.

15 Ibid., pp. 366–368.

16 Ibid., p. 123.

17 Michael Pacanowsky, "Slouching Towards Chicago," *Quarterly Journal of Speech,* Vol. 74, 1988, p. 454.

18 Bryan Taylor and Nick Trujillo, "Qualitative Research Methods," in *The New Handbook of Organizational Communication,* Fredric Jablin and Linda L. Putnam (eds.), Sage, Thousand Oaks, CA, 2001, pp. 161–194

19 Geertz, "Deep Play," pp. 5, 26.

20 Pacanowsky and O'Donnell-Trujillo, "Organizational Communication," p. 137.

21 Linda Smircich, "Concepts of Culture and Organizational Analysis," *Administrative Science Quarterly,* Vol. 28, 1983, pp. 339–358.

22 Taylor and Trujillo, p. 169.

23 T. M. Luhrmann, "The Touch of the Real," *London Times Literary Supplement,* January 12, 2001, p. 3.

Chapter 20: Critical Theory of Communication in Organizations

1 *Erin Brockovich,* Universal, 2000.

2 Stanley Deetz, *Transforming Communication, Transforming Business. Building Responsive and Responsible Workplaces,* Hampton, Cresskill, NJ, 1995, p. 33.

3 Stanley Deetz, *Democracy in an Age of Corporate Colonization: Developments in Communication and the Politics of Everyday Life,* State University of New York, Albany, 1992, p. 349.

4 *Time Magazine,* February 5, 1996, p. 45.

5 Deetz, *Democracy,* p. 43.

6 Deetz, *Transforming Communication,* p. 68.

7 Deetz, *Democracy,* p. 129.

8 Deetz, *Transforming Communication,* p. 4.

9 Stanley Deetz, "Future of the Discipline: The Challenges, the Research, and the Social Contribution," in *Communica-*

tion Yearbook 17, Stanley Deetz (ed.), Sage, Newbury Park, CA, 1994, p. 577.

10 Deetz, *Democracy*, p. 222.

11 Ibid., p. 217

12 Ibid., p. 235.

13 Ibid., p. 310.

14 Deetz, *Transforming Communication*, p. 114.

15 Ibid., p. xv.

16 Used by permission. As with other references to students, I've changed her name to protect confidentiality. To read student application logs for other theories, see *www.afirstlook.com*.

17 Deetz, *Transforming Communication*, p. 85.

18 Stan Deetz, personal correspondence, 2001.

19 Deetz, *Democracy*, p. 47.

20 Deetz, "Future of the Discipline," p. 587.

21 Deetz, *Transforming Communication*, p. 3.

22 Ibid., pp. 50–51.

23 Ibid., p. 2.

24 Deetz, *Democracy*, p. 169.

25 Deetz, *Transforming Communication*, pp. 175–184.

26 Donna Fenn, "The Power of Conviction," *The American Benefactor*, Winter 1998, p. 43.

27 George Cheney et al., "Democracy, Participation, and Communication at Work: A Multidisciplinary Review," in *Communication Yearbook 21*, Michael Roloff (ed.), Sage, Thousand Oaks, CA, 1998, p. 79.

28 Jack Stack, *The Great Game of Business*, Bantam, New York, 1994, p. 4.

29 Jack Stack, as quoted by Shel Horowitz, "'Stacked' for Success in the Game of Business," www.umass.edu/fambiz/great_game.html, accessed December 12, 2004.

30 Cornel West, *The American Evasion of Philosophy: A Geneology of Pragmatism*, University of Wisconsin, Madison, 1989, p. 86.

31 Ibid., p. 239.

32 Reinhold Niebuhr, *Christian Realism and Political Problems*, Charles Scribner's Sons, New York, 1953, pp. 1–14. See also Niebuhr's *Moral Man and Immoral Society*.

33 See Cornel West, *Prophecy Deliverance*, Westminster Press, Philadelphia, 1982, pp. 95–127.

34 West, *American Evasion*, p. 233.

35 The Good Samaritan, Luke 10:25–37.

36 Cornel West, "Why I'm Marching in Washington," *The New York Times*, October 14, 1995, p. 19.

37 Robert McPhee, "Comments on Stanley Deetz' *Democracy in an Age of Corporate Colonization*," paper presented at the 1995 Annual Convention of the Speech Communication Association, San Antonio, November 15–18, 1995.

38 Deetz, "Future of the Discipline," p. 581.

39 Stanley Deetz, "Critical Theory," in *Engaging Organizational Communication Theory: Multiple Perspectives*, S. May and Dennis Mumby (eds.), Sage, Thousand Oaks, CA, 2004, p. 101.

40 Ibid., p. 103.

Public Rhetoric

1 Aristotle, *On Rhetoric: A Theory of Civil Discourse*, George A. Kennedy (ed. and trans.), Oxford University Press, New York, 1991, p. 36.

2 Plato, *Gorgias*, Lane Cooper (trans.), Oxford University Press, New York, 1948, p. 122.

3 1 Corinthians 2:4, New Revised Standard Version of the Bible.

4 1 Corinthians 9:22, New Revised Standard Version of the Bible.

5 Hugh C. Dick (ed.), *Selected Writings of Francis Bacon*, Modern Library, New York, 1955, p. x.

Chapter 21: The Rhetoric

1 Clarke Rountree, "Sophist," in *Encyclopedia of Rhetoric and Composition: Communication from Ancient Times to the Information Age*, Theresa Enos (ed.), Garland, New York, 1996, p. 681

2 Aristotle, *On Rhetoric: A Theory of Civil Discourse*, George A. Kennedy (ed. and trans.), Oxford University Press, New York, 1991, p. 35.

3 David J. Garrow, *Bearing the Cross*, William Morrow, New York, 1986, p. 284.

4 Aristotle, 1991, p. 33.

5 Lloyd Bitzer, "Aristotle's Enthymeme Revisited," *Quarterly Journal of Speech*, Vol. 45, 1959, p. 409.

6 Attributed to Ralph Waldo Emerson by Dale Carnegie, *How to Win Friends and Influence People*, Pocket Books, New York, 1982, p. 29.

7 James McCroskey and Jason Teven, "Goodwill: A Reexamination of the Construct and Its Measurement," *Communication Monographs*, Vol. 66, 1999, pp. 90–103.

8 Jeffrey Walker, "*Pathos* and *Katharsis* in 'Aristotelian' Rhetoric: Some Implications," in *Rereading Aristotle's Rhetoric*, Alan Gross and Arthur Walzer (eds.), Southern Illinois University, Carbondale, 2000, pp. 74–92.

9 Aristotle, p. 122.

10 Lane Cooper, *The Rhetoric of Aristotle*, Appleton-Century-Crofts, New York, 1932, introduction.

11 Aristotle, p. 258.

12 Ibid., p. 244.

13 Ibid., p. 223.

14 Sara Newman, "Aristotle's Notion of 'Bringing-Before-the-Eyes': Its Contributions to Aristotelian and Contemporary Conceptualizations of Metaphor, Style, and Audience," *Rhetorica*, Vol. 20, 2002, pp. 1–23.

15 Amos 5:24, Revised Standard Version of the Bible.

16 Theodore White, *The Making of the President, 1964*, Atheneum, New York, 1965, p. 288.

17 Aristotle, *Nicomachean Ethics*, H. Rackham (trans.), Harvard University, Cambridge, MA, 1934, book 4, chapter 7.

18 Alan Gross and Marcelo Dascal, "The Conceptual Unity of Aristotle's Rhetoric," *Philosophy and Rhetoric*, Vol. 34, 2001, p. 288.

19 Voltaire, *Dictionnaire Philosophique*, "Aristotle," Oeuvres Complètes de Voltaire, Vol. 17, Librairie Garnier, Paris, p. 372.

Chapter 22: Dramatism

1 Marie Hochmuth Nichols, "Kenneth Burke and the New Rhetoric," *Quarterly Journal of Speech*, Vol. 38, 1952, pp. 133–144.

2 Kenneth Burke, "Rhetoric—Old and New," *The Journal of General Education*, Vol. 5, 1951, p. 203.

3 See, for example, Marshall Prisbell and Janis Anderson, "The Importance of Perceived Homophily, Levels of Uncertainty, Feeling Good, Safety, and Self-Disclosure in Interpersonal Relationships," *Communication Quarterly*, Vol. 28, 1980, No. 3, pp. 22–33.

4 Ruth 1:16, Revised Standard Version of the Bible.

5 Kenneth Burke, *A Grammar of Motives*, Prentice-Hall, Englewood Cliffs, NJ, 1945, p. xv.

6 Kenneth Burke, *Language as Symbolic Action: Essays on Life, Literature, and Method*, University of California, Berkeley, 1966, pp. 44–52.

7 Kenneth Burke, "Definition of Man," in *Language as Symbolic Action*, University of California, Berkeley, 1966, p. 16.

8 Paul Dickson, *The Official Rules*, Dell, New York, 1978, p. 165.

9 Kenneth Burke, *Permanence and Change: An Anatomy of Purpose*, Bobbs-Merrill, Indianapolis, 1965, pp. 69–70, also entire Part II; Burke, *Attitudes Toward History*, Hermes, Los Altos, CA, 1959, pp. 308–314.
10 Burke, *Permanence and Change*, p. 283.
11 Malcolm X, "The Ballot or the Bullet," in *Great Speakers and Speeches*, 2nd ed., John Lucaites and Lawrence Bernabo (eds.), Kendall/Hunt, Dubuque, IA, 1992, pp. 277–286.
12 Nichols, p. 144.

Chapter 23: Narrative Paradigm

1 Walter R. Fisher, *Human Communication as Narration: Toward a Philosophy of Reason, Value, and Action*, University of South Carolina, Columbia, 1987, p. 24.
2 Ibid., p. xi.
3 Walter R. Fisher, "Toward a Logic of Good Reasons," *Quarterly Journal of Speech*, Vol. 64, 1978, pp. 376–384; Walter R. Fisher, "Narration as a Human Communication Paradigm: The Case of Public Moral Argument," *Communication Monographs*, Vol. 51, 1984, pp. 1–22.
4 See the book of Ruth in the Old Testament.
5 Frederick Buechner, *Peculiar Treasures*, HarperCollins, New York, 1979, pp. 166–168.
6 Fisher, *Human Communication as Narration*, p. 58.
7 Walter R. Fisher, "Clarifying the Narrative Paradigm," *Communication Monographs*, Vol. 56, 1989, pp. 55–58.
8 Thomas Kuhn, *The Structure of Scientific Revolutions*, University of Chicago, 1962.
9 Fisher, *Human Communication as Narration*, p. 194.
10 Ibid., p. 20.
11 Ibid., pp. 59–62.
12 Ibid., p. 62–69.
13 Ibid, pp. 105–123.
14 Ibid., p. 109.
15 Ibid., pp. 187–188.
16 Ibid., p. 188.
17 Ruth 1:16, New Living Translation of the Bible.
18 Fisher, *Human Communication as Narration*, p. 76.
19 Barbara Warnick, "The Narrative Paradigm: Another Story," *Quarterly Journal of Speech*, Vol. 73, 1987, p. 176.
20 Walter R. Fisher, "The Narrative Paradigm: An Invitation, Not a Demand; A Proposal, Not a Panacea," paper presented at the Speech Communication Association Annual Meeting, San Francisco, 1989.

Media and Culture

1 *Blade Runner*, The Ladd Company, 1982.
2 David Lyon, *Postmodernity*, 2nd ed., University of Minnesota, Minneapolis, 1999, p. 1.
3 Jean Baudrillard, "On Nihilism," *On the Beach*, Vol. 6, Spring 1984, pp. 38–39.
4 Marshall McLuhan and Quentin Fiore, *The Medium Is the Massage*, Random House, New York, 1967, pp. 26–40.
5 Jean-Francois Lyotard, *The Postmodern Condition: A Report on Knowledge*, University of Minnesota, Minneapolis, 1984, p. xxiv.
6 Jean Baudrillard, *America*, Verso, London, 1988, p. 166.
7 Lyotard, *The Postmodern Condition*, p. 76.
8 Fredric Jameson, "Postmodernism and Consumer Society," in *The Anti-Aesthetic: Essays on Postmodern Culture*, H. Foster (ed.), Bay Press, Port Townsend, WA, 1983, p. 113.

Chapter 24: Media Ecology

1 See Richard S. Lindzen, "There Is No 'Consensus' on Global Warming," *The Wall Street Journal*, June 26, 2006, p. A14.
2 Marshall McLuhan, *Understanding Media: The Extensions of Man*, Gingko, Corte Madera, CA, 2003, p. 31.
3 Marshall McLuhan and Quentin Fiore, *The Medium Is the Massage: An Inventory of Effects*, Touchstone, New York, 1989, p. 26.
4 Ibid., pp. 84–85.
5 Ibid., p. 50.
6 John 8:32, New International Version of the Bible.
7 McLuhan and Fiore, *The Medium Is the Massage*, p. 40.
8 Maurice Charland, "McLuhan and the Problematic of Modernity: Riding the Maelstrom of Technological Mediation," unpublished manuscript.
9 Neil Postman, *Amusing Ourselves to Death*, Penguin, New York, 1985, p. 6.
10 Ibid., p. 7.
11 Neil Postman, "The Humanism of Media Ecology," Keynote Address, Inaugural Media Ecology Association Convention, Fordham University, New York, June 2000. Available at http://www.media-ecology.org/publications/proceedings/v1/humanism_of_media_ecology.html.
12 Neil Postman, "Informing Ourselves to Death," German Informatics Society, Stuttgart, Germany, October 11, 1990. Available at: http://www.eff.org/Net_culture/Criticisms/informing_ourselves_to_death.paper.
13 Neil Postman, *The Disappearance of Childhood*, Vintage, NewYork, 1994, p. 73.
14 McLuhan, *Understanding Media*, p. 17.
15 Dan M. Davin in *McLuhan: Hot & Cool*, Gerald Stearn (ed.), Dial, New York, 1967, p. 185.
16 Dwight Macdonald in *McLuhan: Hot & Cool*, p. 203.
17 Christopher Ricks in *McLuhan: Hot & Cool*, p. 211.
18 George N. Gordon, "An End to McLuhanacy," *Educational Technology*, January 1982, p. 42.
19 Tom Wolfe in *McLuhan: Hot & Cool*, p. 31.
20 Kenneth Boulding in *McLuhan: Hot & Cool*, p. 57.
21 Robert Putnam, "Bowling Alone: America's Declining Social Capital," *Journal of Democracy*, Vol. 6, No. 1, 1995, pp. 65–78.

Chapter 25: Semiotics

1 James R. Beniger, "Who Are the Most Important Theorists of Communication?" *Communication Research*, Vol. 17, 1990, pp. 698–715.
2 Umberto Eco, *A Theory of Semiotics*, Indiana University, Bloomington, 1976, p. 7.
3 Ferdinand de Saussure, *Course in General Linguistics*, Wade Baskin (trans.), McGraw-Hill, New York, 1966, p. 16.
4 Roland Barthes, "The World of Wrestling," in *Mythologies*, Annette Lavers (trans.), Hilland Wang, New York, 1972, p. 17.
5 Ibid., pp. 19, 24.
6 See Barthes' use of this phrase in *The Semiotic Challenge*, p. 85. Barthes used these words to describe rhetoricians' efforts to categorize figures of speech—alliteration, hyperbole, irony, etc. The phrase is even more appropriate to characterize *Elements of Semiology*.
7 Donald Fry and Virginia Fry, "Continuing the Conversation Regarding Myth and Culture: An Alternative Reading of Barthes," *American Journal of Semiotics*, Vol. 6, No. 2/3, 1989, pp. 183–197.
8 Irwin Levine and L. Russell Brown, "Tie a Yellow Ribbon Round the Ole Oak Tree," Levine and Brown Music, Inc., 1973.
9 Barthes, "Myth Today," in *Mythologies*, p. 118.
10 W. Thomas Duncanson, "Issues of Transcendence and Value in a Semiotic Frame," paper presented to a joint session of the Religious Speech Communication Association

and the Speech Communication Association Convention, San Francisco, November 19, 1989, p. 29.

11 Barthes, "The World of Wrestling," p. 25.

12 Kyong Kim, *Caged in Our Own Signs: A Book about Semiotics,* Ablex, Norwood, NJ, 1996, p. 189.

13 Anne Norton, *Republic of Signs: Liberal Theory and American Popular Culture,* University of Chicago Press, Chicago, 1993, p. 60.

14 Douglas Kellner, "Cultural Studies, Multiculturalism, and Media Culture," in *Gender, Race and Class in Media: A Text-Reader,* Gail Dines and Jan M. Humez (eds.), Sage, Thousand Oaks, CA, 1996, p. 15.

15 Dick Hebdige, *Subculture: The Meaning of Style,* Methuen, London, 1979, p. 130.

16 Stuart Hall, "The Work of Representation," in *Representation: Cultural Representations and Signifying Practices,* Stuart Hall (ed.), Sage, London, pp. 13–74.

Chapter 26: Cultural Studies

1 Stuart Hall, "Ideology and Communication Theory," in *Rethinking Communication Theory, Vol. 1: Paradigm Issues,* Brenda Dervin, Lawrence Grossberg, Barbara J. O'Keefe, and Ellen Wartella (eds.), Sage, Newbury Park, CA, 1989, p. 52.

2 Jorge Larrain, "Stuart Hall and the Marxist Concept of Ideology," in *Stuart Hall: Critical Dialogues in Cultural Studies,* David Morley and Kuan-Hsing Chen (eds.), Routledge, New York, 1996, p. 49.

3 Ibid., p. 48.

4 Theodor W. Adorno, "The Culture Industry: Enlightenment as Mass Deception," in *The Dialectic of the Enlightenment,* Max Horkheimer and Theodor W. Adorno (eds.), Continuum, New York, 1995, pp. 120–167.

5 Antonio Gramsci, *Selections from the Prison Notebooks of Antonio Gramsci,* ed. and trans. by Quintin Hoare and Geoffrey Nowell Smith, International Publishers, New York, 1971.

6 Michel Foucault, *The Archaeology of Knowledge,* Tavistock, London, 1982, p. 80.

7 Stuart Hall, *Representations: Cultural Representations and Signifying Practices:* Sage, London, 1997, p. 6.

8 Ibid., p. 2.

9 Michel Foucault, *Madness and Civilization: A History of Insanity in the Age of Reason,* Random House, New York, 1965.

10 Foucault, *The Archaelogy of Knowledge,* p. 46.

11 Douglas Kellner, *Media Culture: Cultural Studies, Identity and Politics Between the Modern and the Postmodern,* Routledge, New York, 1995, pp. 198–228.

12 Ibid., p. 210.

13 Ibid., p. 218.

14 Stuart Hall, "The Whites of Their Eyes: Racist Ideologies and the Media," in *Silver Linings,* George Bridges and Rosalind Brunt (eds.), Lawrence and Wishart, London, 1981, pp. 31–33.

15 Quoted and discussed, "On the Media," National Public Radio, September 22, 2001; www.wnyc.org/new/talk/onthemedia/transcripts_092201_bob.html.

16 Quoted and discussed, "On the Media," National Public Radio, December 15, 2001; www.wnyc.org/new/talk/onthemedia/transcripts_121501_president.html.

17 Helen Davis, *Understanding Stuart Hall,* Sage, Thousand Oaks, CA, 2004, p. 42.

18 Alexander Cockburn, "Redwoods, Tutus and Power," *Los Angeles Times,* June 21, 2001; www.latimes.com/news/comment/20010621/t000051554.html.

19 Robert Frost, "Stopping by Woods on a Snowy Evening," *Poetry of Robert Frost,* Holt, Rinehart and Winston, New York, 1969, p. 224.

20 Cited by Davis, *Understanding Stuart Hall,* p. 128.

21 *Parekh Report of the Commission on the Future of Multi-Ethnic Britain,* Profile/The Runnymede Trust, London, 2000, p. 169.

22 Clifford Christians, "Normativity as Catalyst," in *Rethinking Communication Theory, Vol. 1: Paradigm Issues,* Brenda Dervin, Lawrence Grossberg, Barbara J. O'Keefe, and Ellen Wartella (eds.), Sage, Newbury Park, CA, 1989, p. 148.

23 Samuel Becker, "Communication Studies: Visions of the Future," in *Rethinking Communication Theory,* Vol. 1, p. 126.

Media Effects

1 Paul Lazarsfeld, Bernard Berelson, and Hazel Gaudet, *The People's Choice,* Duell, Sloan and Pearce, New York, 1944.

2 A. W. van den Ban, "A Review of the Two-Step Flow of Communication Hypothesis," in *Speech Communication Behavior,* Larry L. Barker and Robert Kiebler (eds.), Prentice-Hall, Englewood Cliffs, NJ, 1971, pp. 193–205.

3 Fredric Wertham, *Seduction of the Innocent,* Rinehart, New York, 1954.

4 Dolf Zillmann, "Excitation Transfer in Communication-Mediated Aggressive Behavior," *Journal of Experimental Social Psychology,* Vol. 7, 1971, pp. 419–434.

5 Albert Bandura, *Social Learning Theory,* Prentice-Hall, Englewood Cliffs, NJ, 1977.

6 Tony Schwartz, *The Responsive Chord,* Doubleday, New York, 1973.

Chapter 27: Cultivation Theory

1 George Gerbner and Larry Gross, "Living with Television: The Violence Profile," *Journal of Communication,* Vol. 26, 1976, No. 2, p. 76.

2 Ibid., p. 77.

3 Jerome H. Skolnick, *The Politics of Protest,* Simon and Schuster, New York, 1969, pp. 3–24.

4 George Gerbner, Larry Gross, Nancy Signorielli, Michael Morgan, and Marilyn Jackson-Beeck, "The Demonstration of Power: Violence Profile No. 10," *Journal of Communication,* Vol. 29, No. 3, 1979, p. 180.

5 Albert Bandura, *Social Learning Theory,* Prentice-Hall, Englewood Cliffs, NJ, 1977.

6 George Gerbner, Larry Gross, Michael Morgan, and Nancy Signorielli, "The 'Mainstreaming' of America: Violence Profile No. 11," *Journal of Communication,* Vol. 30, No. 3, 1980, p. 11.

7 George Gerbner, Larry Gross, Michael Morgan, and Nancy Signorielli, "Charting the Mainstream: Television's Contributions to Political Orientations," *Journal of Communication,* Vol. 32, No. 2, 1982, p. 103.

8 Ibid., p. 117.

9 Gerbner, Gross, Morgan, and Signorielli, "The 'Mainstreaming' of America," p. 15.

10 Gerbner, Gross, Signorielli, Morgan, and Jackson-Beeck, p. 196.

11 Cees Koolstra, "Social Confusion as an Explanation of Cultivation: A Test of the Mechanism Underlying Confusion of Fiction with Reality on Television," *Perception and Motor Skills,* Vol. 104, 2007, pp. 102–110.

12 International Communication Association Newsletter, Jan/Feb 2006, George Gerbner Obituary.

13 Michael Morgan and James Shanahan, "Two Decades of Cultivation Research: An Appraisal and a Meta-Analysis," in *Communication Yearbook 20,* Brant R. Burleson (ed.), Sage, Thousand Oaks, CA, 1997, pp. 1–45.

4 Ibid., p. 20.
5 Ibid., pp. 27–28.
6 I'm grateful to Purdue University media effects researcher Glenn Sparks for this analogy.
7 Morgan and Shanahan, p. 5.

Chapter 28: Agenda-Setting Theory

1 Maxwell McCombs, "News Influence on Our Pictures of the World," in *Media Effects: Advances in Theory and Research,* Jennings Bryant and Dolf Zillmann (eds.), Lawrence Erlbaum, Hillsdale, NJ, 1994, p. 4.
2 Maxwell McCombs and Donald Shaw, "A Progress Report on Agenda-Setting Research," paper presented to the Association for Education in Journalism and Mass Communication, Communication Theory and Methodology Division, San Diego, CA, April 18–27, 1974, p. 28.
3 Walter Lippmann, *Public Opinion,* Macmillan, New York, 1922, p. 3.
4 Bernard C. Cohen, *The Press and Foreign Policy,* Princeton University, Princeton, NJ, 1963, p. 13.
5 Theodore White, *The Making of the President, 1972,* Bantam, New York, 1973, p. 245.
6 Paul Lazarsfeld, Bernard Berelson, and Hazel Gaudet, *The People's Choice,* Duell, Sloan and Pearce, New York, 1944.
7 Maxwell McCombs and Donald Shaw, "The Agenda-Setting Function of the Mass Media," *Public Opinion Quarterly,* Vol. 36, 1972, pp. 176–187.
8 David Weaver, D. A. Graber, Maxwell McCombs, and C. H. Eyal, *Media Agenda-Setting in a Presidential Election: Issues, Images, and Interests,* Praeger, New York, 1981.
9 Ray Funkhouser, "The Issues of the Sixties: An Exploratory Study in the Dynamics of Public Opinion," *Public Opinion Quarterly,* Vol. 37, 1973, pp. 62–75.
10 Shanto Iyengar, Mark Peters, and Donald Kinder, "Experimental Demonstrations of the 'Not-So-Minimal' Consequences of Television News Programs," *American Political Science Review,* Vol. 76, 1982, pp. 848–858. The experiment reported is only one of a series of studies conducted by Iyengar and Kinder at Yale and the University of Michigan.
11 McCombs, "News Influence," p. 11.
12 Maxwell McCombs and Tamara Bell, "The Agenda-Setting Role of Mass Communication," in *An Integrated Approach to Communication Theory and Research,* Michael Salwen and Donald Stacks (eds.), Lawrence Erlbaum, Hillsdale, NJ, 1996, p. 100.
13 James Tankard et al., "Media Frames: Approaches to Conceptualization and Measurement," paper presented at the annual meeting of the Association for Education in Journalism and Mass Communication, Boston, August 1991.
14 Maxwell McCombs, "New Frontiers in Agenda Setting: Agendas of Attributes and Frames," *Mass Communication Review,* Vol. 24, 1997, pp. 4–24.
15 Robert Entman, "Framing: Toward Clarification of a Fractured Paradigm," *Journal of Communication,* Vol. 43, No. 3, 1993, p. 52.
16 Toshiro Takeshita and Shunji Mikami, "How Did Mass Media Influence the Voters' Choice in the 1993 General Election in Japan? A Study of Agenda Setting," *Communication Review,* Vol. 17, 1995, pp. 27–41.
17 Esteban Lopez Escobar, Juan Pablo Llamas, and Maxwell McCombs, "The Spanish General Election in 1996: A Further Inquiry into Second-Level Agenda-Setting Effects," paper presented to the World Association for Public Opinion Research, Edinburgh, Scotland, September 1997.

18 Salma Ghanem, "Media Coverage of Crime and Public Opinion: An Explanation of the Second Level of Agenda Setting," unpublished doctoral dissertation, University of Texas at Austin, 1996. The study is also described in McCombs, "New Frontiers in Agenda Setting," pp. 11–12.
19 McCombs, "New Frontiers in Agenda Setting."
20 Bloj'o fear of flying study is excerpted in Maxwell McCombs and Donald Shaw, "A Progress Report on Agenda-Setting Research," paper presented at the Association for Education in Journalism and Mass Communication meeting, San Diego, CA, August 1974.
21 Deborah Blood and Peter Phillips, "Economic Headline News on the Agenda: New Approaches to Understanding Causes and Effects," in *Communication and Democracy: Exploring the Intellectual Frontiers in Agenda-Setting Theory,* Maxwell McCombs, Donald Shaw, and David Weaver (eds.), Lawrence Erlbaum, Mahwah, NJ, 1997, pp. 111–112.
22 John Fortunato, *The Ultimate Assist: The Relationship and Broadcasting Strategies of the NBA and Television Networks,* Hampton, Cresskill, NJ, 2001.
23 Maxwell McCombs, *Setting the Agenda,* Polity, Cambridge, UK, 2004, p. 140.
24 Scott Althaus and David Tewksbury, "Agenda Setting and the 'New' News: Patterns of Issue Importance Among Readers of the Paper and Online Versions of *The New York Times,*" *Communication Research,* Vol. 29, 2002, pp. 180–207.
25 Ibid., p. 197.
26 Clifford Christians, John Ferré, and Mark Fackler, *Good News: Social Ethics and the Press,* Oxford University Press, New York, 1993.
27 Richard Rorty, *Philosophy and the Mirror of Nature,* Princeton University, Princeton, NJ, 1979, p. 373.
28 Christians, Ferré, and Fackler, p. 192.
29 Martin Buber, *I and Thou,* 2nd ed., R. G. Smith (trans.), Scribner's, New York, 1958, pp. 60, 69.
30 Christians, Ferré, and Fackler, pp. 69, 73.
31 Ibid., p. 89.
32 Ibid., pp. 78, 111–113.
33 Clifford Christians and Kaarle Nordenstreng, "Social Responsibility Worldwide," *Journal of Mass Media Ethics,* Vol. 19, 2004, pp. 3–28.
34 Christians, Ferré, and Fackler, p. 92.
35 McCombs, "News Influence," p. 6.
36 Gerald Kosicki, "Problems and Opportunities in Agenda-Setting Research," *Journal of Communication,* Vol. 43, No. 2, 1993, p. 113.
37 Donald Shaw and Maxwell McCombs (eds.), *The Emergence of American Political Issues,* West, St. Paul, MN, 1977, p. 12.
38 McCombs, "New Frontiers in Agenda Setting," p. 9.

Chapter 29: Spiral of Silence

1 Elisabeth Noelle-Neumann, *The Spiral of Silence: Public Opinion—Our Social Skin,* 2nd ed., University of Chicago Press, Chicago, 1993, pp. 70–71.
2 Ibid., p. 178.
3 Ibid., p. 19.
4 Ibid., p. 9.
5 Ibid., p. 41.
6 Solomon E. Asch, "Effects of Group Pressure upon the Modification and Distortion of Judgments," in *Group Dynamics: Research and Theory,* Dorwin Cartwright and Alvin Zander (eds.), Row, Peterson, Evanston, IL, 1953, pp. 151–162.
7 Stanley Milgram, "Nationality and Conformity," *Scientific American,* Vol. 205, 1961, pp. 45–51.

8   Noelle-Neumann, *The Spiral of Silence*, 2nd ed., p. 182.
9   Ibid., pp. 216–217.
10 Elisabeth Noelle-Neumann, "Return to the Concept of Powerful Mass Media," *Studies of Broadcasting*, Vol. 9, 1973, p. 77.
11 Elisabeth Noelle-Neumann, "The Theory of Public Opinion: The Concept of the Spiral of Silence," in *Communication Yearbook 14*, James A. Anderson (ed.), Sage, Newbury Park, CA, 1991, p. 276.
12 Elisabeth Noelle-Neumann, "Turbulences in the Climate of Opinion: Methodological Applications of the Spiral of Silence Theory," *Public Opinion Quarterly*, Vol. 41, 1977, p. 139.
13 Elisabeth Noelle-Neumann, *The Spiral of Silence: Public Opinion—Our Social Skin*, University of Chicago, Chicago, 1984, pp. 17–18.
14 Noelle-Neumann, *The Spiral of Silence*, 2nd ed., p. 26.
15 Elisabeth Noelle-Neumann, "Mass-Media and Social Change in Developed Societies," in *Mass Media and Social Change*, Elihu Katz and Tamas Szecsko (eds.), Sage, London, 1981, p. 139.
16 Noelle-Neumann, "The Theory of Public Opinion," p. 274.
17 Noelle-Neumann, *The Spiral of Silence*, 2nd ed., p. 218.
18 Ibid.
19 Elisabeth Noelle-Neumann, "Public Opinion and the Classical Tradition: A Re-Evaluation," *Public Opinion Quarterly*, Vol. 43, 1979, p. 155.
20 Serge Moscovici, "Silent Majorities and Loud Minorities," in *Communication Yearbook 14*, James A. Anderson (ed.), Sage, Newbury Park, CA, 1991, pp. 298–308.
21 Mihaly Csikszentmihal, "Reflections on the 'Spiral of Silence,'" in *Communication Yearbook 14*, p. 297.
22 Carroll Glynn, Andrew Hayes, and James Shanahan, "Perceived Support for One's Opinions and Willingness to Speak Out: A Meta-Analysis of Survey Studies on the 'Spiral of Silence,'" *Public Opinion Quarterly*, Vol. 61, 1997, pp. 452–467.
23 Noelle-Neumann, *The Spiral of Silence*, 2nd ed., pp. 214–215.
24 Patricia Moy, David Domke, and Keith Stamm, "The Spiral of Silence and Public Opinion on Affirmative Action," *Journalism and Mass Communication Quarterly*, Vol. 78, 2001, pp. 7–25.
25 Dietram Scheufele, James Shanahan, and Eunjung Lee, "Real Talk: Manipulating the Dependent Variable in Spiral of Silence Research," *Communication Research*, Vol. 28, 2001, pp. 304–324.
26 Alexis de Tocqueville, *L'Ancien Régime et la Révolution*, Michel Lévy Frères, Paris, 1856, p. 259.
27 Noelle-Neumann, *The Spiral of Silence*, 1984, p. 184.

Intercultural Communication

1   Gerry Philipsen, *Speaking Culturally: Exploration in Social Communication*, State University of New York, Albany, 1992, p. 7.
2   Gerry Philipsen, "Speaking 'Like a Man' in Teamsterville: Cultural Patterns of Role Enactment in an Urban Neighborhood," *Quarterly Journal of Speech*, Vol. 61, 1975, pp. 13–22.
3   Donal Carbaugh, "Communication Rules in *Donahue* Discourse," in *Cultural Communication and Intercultural Contact*, Donal Carbaugh (ed.), Lawrence Erlbaum, Hillsdale, NJ, 1990, pp. 119–149.
4   See chapter on cultural variability in William B. Gudykunst and Stella Ting-Toomey, *Culture and Interpersonal Communication*, Sage, Newbury Park, CA, 1988, pp. 39–59.

5   Edward T. Hall, *Beyond Culture*, Anchor, New York, 1977, p. 91.
6   Ibid., pp. 85–128.

Chapter 30: Communication Accommodation Theory

1   Howard Giles, "Accent Mobility: A Model and Some Data," *Anthropological Linguistics*, Vol. 15, 1973, pp. 87–109.
2   Cindy Gallois, Tania Ogay, and Howard Giles, "Communication Accommodation Theory: A Look Back and a Look Ahead," in *Theorizing About Intercultural Communication*, William B. Gudykunst (ed.), Sage, Thousand Oaks, CA, 2005, p. 123.
3   Richard Bourhis, "Cross-Cultural Communication in Montreal: Two Field Studies Since Bill 101," *International Journal of the Sociology of Language*, Vol. 46, 1984, pp. 33–47.
4   Nikolas Coupland, Justine Coupland, Howard Giles, and Karen Henwood, "Accommodating the Elderly: Invoking and Extending a Theory," *Language and Society*, Vol. 17, 1988, p. 3.
5   Angie Williams and Howard Giles, "Intergenerational Conversations: Young Adults' Retrospective Accounts," *Human Communication Research*, Vol. 23, 1996, p. 237.
6   Ibid., p. 239.
7   Howard Giles, Kimberly Noels, et al., "Intergenerational Communication Across Cultures: Young People's Perceptions of Conversations with Family Elders, Non-Family Elders and Same-Age Peers," *Journal of Cross-Cultural Gerontology*, Vol. 18, 2003, p. 4.
8   Howard Giles, Nikalos Coupland, and Justine Coupland, "Accommodation Theory: Communication, Context, and Consequence," in *Contexts of Accommodation: Developments in Applied Sociolinguistics*, Howard Giles, Justine Coupland, and Nikalos Coupland (eds.), Cambridge University Cambridge, England, 1991, p. 10.
9   Howard Giles, Kimberly Noels, et al., "Intergenerational Communication," p. 9.
10 Coupland, Coupland, et al., "Accommodating the Elderly," p. 24.
11 Williams and Giles, "Intergenerational Conversations," p. 233.
12 Giles, Coupland, and Coupland, "Accommodation Theory," p. 46.
13 Ibid., p. 42.
14 Henri Tajfel and John C. Turner, "The Social Identity Theory of Intergroup Behavior," in *The Psychology of Intergroup Relations*, L. Worchel and W. Austin (eds.), Nelson Hall, Chicago, 1986, pp. 7–24.
15 Jake Harwood, "Communication as Social Identity," in *Communication as . . . Perspectives on Theory*, Gregory Shepherd, Jeffrey St. John, and Ted Striphas (eds.), Sage, Thousand Oaks, CA, 2006, p. 89.
16 Giles, Noels, et al., "Intergenerational Communication," p. 24.
17 Williams and Giles, "Intergenerational Conversations," p. 238.
18 Ibid., p. 221.
19 Cynthia Gallois and Victor Callan, "Interethnic Accommodation: The Role of Norms," in *Contexts of Accommodation*, p. 249.
20 Cynthia Gallois, Arlene Franklyn Stokes, et al., "Communication Accommodation in Intercultural Encounters," in *Theories in Intercultural Communication*, Young Yun Kim and William B. Gudykunst (eds.), Sage, Newbury Park, CA, 1988, p. 166.
21 Gallois, Ogay, and Giles, "Communication Accommodation Theory," p. 128.

22 Giles, Coupland, and Coupland, "Accommodation Theory," p. 28.

23 Gallois, Ogay, and Giles, "Communication Accommodation Theory," p. 126.

24 Fritz Heider, *The Psychology of Interpersonal Relations*, John Wiley, New York, 1958; Harold Kelley, "The Process of Causal Attribution," *American Psychologist*, Vol. 28, 1973, pp. 107–128.

25 Ellen B. Ryan, Ann P. Anas, and Melissa Vuckovich, "The Effects of Age, Hearing Loss, and Communication Difficulty on First Impressions," *Communication Research Reports*, Vol. 24, 2007, pp. 13–19.

26 Howard Giles, Anthony Mulac, James Bradac, and Patricia Johnson, "Speech Accommodation Theory: The First Decade and Beyond," in *Communication Yearbook 10*, Margaret L. McLaughlin (ed.) Sage, Newbury Park, CA, 1987, p. 26.

27 Jake Harwood, Priya Raman, and Miles Hewstone, "The Family and Communication Dynamics of Group Salience," *Journal of Family Communication*, Vol. 6, 2006, pp. 181–200.

28 Karen Henwood and Howard Giles, "An Investigation of the Relationship Between Stereotypes of the Elderly and Interpersonal Communication Between Young and Old," Final Report to the Nuffield Foundation, London, 1985.

29 Williams and Giles, "Intergenerational Conversations," p. 223.

30 Giles and Ogay, "Communication Accommodation Theory," p. 302.

31 Harwood, Raman, and Hewstone, "The Family and Communication Dynamics," p. 191.

32 Williams and Giles, "Intergenerational Conversations," p. 222.

33 Ibid., p. 239.

34 Gallois, Ogay, and Giles, "Communication Accommodation Theory," p. 134.

35 Ibid., p. 130.

36 Cindy Gallois and Howard Giles, "Accommodating Mutual Influence in Intergroup Encounters," in *Progress in Communication Sciences*, Vol. 14, M. T. Palmer and G. A. Barnett (eds.), Ablex, Stamford, UK, 1998, p. 158.

37 Gallois, Ogay, and Giles, "Communication Accommodation Theory," p. 134.

Chapter 31: Face-Negotiation Theory

1 Stella Ting-Toomey and Atsuko Kurogi, "Facework Competence in Intercultural Conflict: An Updated Face-Negotiation Theory," *International Journal of Intercultural Relations*, Vol. 22, 1998, p. 190.

2 Harry C. Triandis, *Individualism & Collectivism*, Westview, Boulder, CO, 1995, pp. 10–11.

3 Ting-Toomey and Kurogi, p. 190.

4 Ibid., p. 196.

5 Hazel Markus and Shinobu Kitayama, "Culture and the Self: Implications for Cognition, Emotion, and Motivation," *Psychological Review*, Vol. 2, pp. 224–253.

6 John Oetzel, "The Effects of Self-Construals and Ethnicity on Self-Reported Conflict Styles," *Communication Reports*, Vol. 11, 1998, p. 140; see also William B. Gudykunst et al., "The Influence of Cultural Individualism—Collectivism, Self-Construals, and Individual Values on Communication Styles Across Cultures," *Human Communication Research*, Vol. 22, 1996, pp. 510–540.

7 Ting-Toomey and Kurogi, p. 218.

8 John Oetzel and Stella Ting-Toomey, "Face Concerns in Interpersonal Conflict: A Cross-Cultural Empirical Test of the Face-Negotiation Theory," *Communication Research*, Vol. 30, 2003, p. 619.

9 Ting-Toomey and Kurogi, p. 187.

10 Penelope Brown and Stephen Levinson, "Universals in Language Usage: Politeness Phenomenon," in *Questions and Politeness: Strategies in Social Interaction*, Esther N. Goody (ed.), Cambridge University Press, Cambridge, UK, 1978, p. 66.

11 Lin Yutang, *My Country and My People*, John Day, Taipai, Republic of China, 1968, p. 199.

12 Stella Ting-Toomey, "Intercultural Conflict Styles: A Face-Negotiation Theory," in *Theories in Intercultural Communication*, Young Yun Kim and William B. Gudykunst (eds.), Sage, Newbury Park, CA, 1988, p. 215.

13 Ting-Toomey and Kurogi, p. 192.

14 M. A. Rahim, "A Measure of Styles of Handling Interpersonal Conflict," *Academy of Management Journal*, Vol. 26, 1983, pp. 368–376.

15 Robert Blake and Jane Mouton, *The Managerial Grid*, Gulf, Houston, 1964; Ralph Kilmann and Kenneth Thomas, "Developing a Forced-Choice Measure of Conflict-Handling Behavior: The 'Mode' Instrument," *Educational and Psychological Measurement*, Vol. 37, 1977, pp. 309–325.

16 Stella Ting-Toomey, John Oetzel, and Kimberlie Yee-Jung, "Self-Construal Types and Conflict Management Styles," *Communication Reports*, Vol. 14, 2002, pp. 87–104.

17 Stella Ting-Toomey, "Translating Conflict Face-Negotiation Theory into Practice," in Dan Landis, Jane Bennett, and Milton Bennett (eds.), *Handbook of Intercultural Training*, 3rd ed., Sage, Thousand Oaks, 2004, pp. 229–230.

18 Ibid., p. 230.

19 Ting-Toomey, Oetzel, and Yee-Jung, pp. 87–104.

20 Stella Ting-Toomey, "The Matrix of Face: An Updated Face-Negotiation Theory," in *Theorizing About Intercultural Communication*, William B. Gudykunst (ed.), Sage, Thousand Oaks, CA, 2004, p. 86.

21 Roger Fisher, William Ury, and Bruce Patton, *Getting to Yes: Negotiating Agreement Without Giving In*, 2nd ed., Penguin, New York, 1991.

22 Ting-Toomey and Kurogi, p. 194.

23 Stella Ting-Toomey, *Communicating Across Cultures*, Guilford, New York, 1999, p. vii.

24 Oetzel and Ting-Toomey, pp. 599–624.

25 Ibid., p. 617.

Chapter 32: Speech Codes Theory

1 Gerry Philipsen, "Speaking 'Like a Man' in Teamsterville: Culture Patterns of Role Enactment in an Urban Neighborhood," *Quarterly Journal of Speech*, Vol. 61, 1975, pp. 13–22; Gerry Philipsen, "Places for Speaking in Teamsterville," *Quarterly Journal of Speech*, Vol. 62, 1976, pp. 15–25.

2 Clifford Geertz, "Thick Description: Toward an Interpretive Theory of History," in *The Interpretation of Culture*, Basic Books, New York, 1973, p. 5.

3 Dell Hymes, "The Ethnography of Speaking," in T. Gladwin and W. C. Sturtevant (eds.), *Anthropology and Human Behavior*, Anthropological Society of Washington, Washington, DC, 1962, pp. 13–53.

4 Gerry Philipsen, "Cultural Communication," in *Handbook of International and Intercultural Communication*, 2nd ed., William B. Gudykunst and Bella Mody (eds.), Sage, Thousand Oaks, CA, 2002, p. 56.

5 Ibid., p. 60.

6 Donal Carbaugh, "Deep Agony: 'Self' vs. 'Society' in a *Donahue* Discourse," *Research on Language and Social Interaction*, Vol. 22, 1988/89, pp. 179–212.

7 Tamar Katriel and Gerry Philipsen, "'What We Need Is Communication': Communication as a Cultural Category in Some American Speech," *Communication Monographs*, Vol. 48, 1981, pp. 302–317.

8 Gerry Philipsen, *Speaking Culturally: Explorations in Social Communication*, State University of New York, Albany, 1992, p. 7.

9 Ibid., p. 4.

10 Ibid., p. 6.

11 Gerry Philipsen, "A Theory of Speech Codes," in *Developing Communication Theory*, Gerry Philipsen and Terrance Albrecht (eds.), State University of New York, Albany, 1997, pp. 119–156.

12 Gerry Philipsen, Lisa M. Coutu, and Patricia Covarrubias, "Speech Codes Theory: Restatement, Revisions, and Response to Criticisms," in *Theorizing About Intercultural Communication*, William B. Gudykunst (ed.), Sage, Thousand Oaks, CA, 2005, p. 59.

13 Dell Hymes, "Ways of Speaking," in *Explorations in the Ethnography of Speaking*, Richard Bauman and Joel Sherzer (eds.), Cambridge University, London, 1974, pp. 433–451.

14 Lisa M. Coutu, "Communication Codes of Rationality and Spirituality in the Discourse of and About Robert S. McNamara's *In Retrospect*," *Research on Language and Social Interaction*, Vol. 33, 2000, pp. 179–211.

15 Robert S. McNamara (with Brian VanDeMark), *In Retrospect: The Tragedy and Lessons of Vietnam*, Times Books, New York, 1995, p. 183.

16 Philipsen, "A Theory of Speech Codes," in *Developing Communication Theory*, Gerry Philipsen and Terrance Albrecht (eds.), State University of New York, Albany, 1996, p. 139.

17 Philipsen, *Speaking Culturally*, p. 110.

18 Ibid., p. 113, citing P. Berger, B. Berger, and H. Kellner, *The Homeless Mind: Modernization and Consciousness*, Vintage, New York, 1973, p. 89.

19 Ibid., p. 76. See also Katriel and Philipsen, "'What We Need Is Communication,'" p. 308.

20 Philipsen, "A Theory of Speech Codes," p. 140.

21 Tamar Katriel, *Talking Straight: Dugri Speech in Israeli Sabra Culture*, Cambridge University Press, Cambridge, UK, 1986.

22 Philipsen, "Mayor Daley's Council Speech," in *Speaking Culturally*, pp. 43–61.

23 Philipsen, *Speaking Culturally*, pp. 77–80.

24 Philipsen, "A Theory of Speech Codes," p. 148.

25 Dwight Conquergood, "Poetics, Play, Process, and Power: The Performance Turn in Anthropology," *Text and Performance Quarterly*, Vol. 1, 1989, pp. 82–95.

26 James Clifford, *Predicament of Culture*, Harvard University Press, Cambridge, MA, p. 49.

27 Conquergood, "Poetics, Play, Process, and Power," p. 87.

28 Dwight Conquergood, "Ethnography, Rhetoric, and Performance," *Quarterly Journal of Speech*, Vol. 78, 1992, p. 90.

29 Robin Wilson, "A Professor's Commitment to 'Shattered Cultures,'" *The Chronicle of Higher Education*, Vol. 40, No. 20, 1994, p. A6.

30 Philipsen, Coutu, and Covarrubias, p. 65.

Gender and Communication

1 Robin Lakoff, *Language and Women's Place*, Harper & Row, New York, 1975.

2 Kathryn Dindia, "Men Are from North Dakota, Women Are from South Dakota," paper presented at the National Communication Association convention, November 19–23, 1997.

3 Julia T. Wood and Kathryn Dindia, "What's the Difference? A Dialogue About Differences and Similarities Between Women and Men," in *Sex Differences and Similarities in Communication*, Daniel Canary and Kathryn Dindia (eds.), Lawrence Erlbaum, Mahwah, NJ, 1998, pp. 19–38.

4 Sandra L. Bem, "Androgyny vs. the Tight Little Lives of Fluffy Women and Chesty Men," *Psychology Today*, Vol. 9, 1975, pp. 58–62.

5 Cheris Kramarae, "Gender and Dominance," in *Communication Yearbook 15*, Stanley Deetz (ed.), Sage, Newbury Park, CA, 1992, pp. 469–474.

Chapter 33: Genderlect Styles

1 Deborah Tannen, *You Just Don't Understand*, Ballantine, New York, 1990, p. 42.

2 Deborah Tannen, *Conversational Style: Analyzing Talk Among Friends*, Ablex, Norwood, NJ, 1984.

3 Ibid., p. vii.

4 Tannen, *You Just Don't Understand*, p. 259.

5 Ibid., p. 279.

6 Ibid., p. 16.

7 Ibid., p. 108.

8 Ibid., p. 48.

9 Ibid., p. 212.

10 Ibid., p. 62.

11 Ibid., p. 72.

12 Ibid., p. 150.

13 Ibid., pp. 120–121, 298.

14 Carol Gilligan, *In a Different Voice: Psychological Theory and Women's Development*, Harvard University, Cambridge, MA, 1982.

15 Summary statement of Seyla Benhabib, "The Generalized and the Concrete Other: The Kohlberg–Gilligan Controversy and Feminist Theory," in Seyla Benhabib and Drucilla Cornell (eds.), *Feminism as Critique*, University of Minnesota, Minneapolis, 1987, p. 78.

16 Lawrence Kohlberg, *Essays on Moral Development, Volume One: The Philosophy of Moral Development*, Harper & Row, San Francisco, 1981, p. 12.

17 Gilligan, p. 18.

18 Carol Gilligan, "In a Different Voice: Women's Conceptions of Self and Morality," *Harvard Educational Review*, Vol. 47, 1977, p. 484.

19 Tannen, *Conversational Style*, p. 38.

20 J. W. Santrock, A. M. Minnett, and B. D. Campbell, *The Authoritative Guide to Self-Help Books*, Guilford, New York, 1994.

21 Ken Burke, Nancy Burroughs-Denhart, and Glen McClish, "Androgyny and Identity in Gender Communication," *Quarterly Journal of Speech*, Vol. 80, 1984, pp. 482–497.

22 Julia T. Wood and Christopher Inman, "In a Different Mode: Masculine Styles of Communicating Closeness," *Journal of Applied Communication Research*, Vol. 21, 1993, pp. 279–295.

23 Adrianne W. Kunkel and Brant R. Burleson, "Social Support and the Emotional Lives of Men and Women: An Assessment of the Different Cultures Perspective," in *Sex Differences and Similarities in Communication*, Daniel Canary and Kathryn Dindia (eds.), Lawrence Erlbaum, Mahwah, NJ, 1998, p. 116.

24 Senta Troemel-Ploetz, "Review Essay: Selling the Apolitical," *Discourse & Society*, Vol. 2, 1991, p. 497.

25 Ibid., p. 491.

26 Ibid., p. 495.

Chapter 34: Standpoint Theory

1 Julia T. Wood, *Communication Theories in Action*, Wadsworth, Belmont, CA, 1997, p. 250.
2 Sandra Harding, "Comment on Hekman's 'Truth and Method: Feminist Standpoint Theory Revisited': Whose Standpoint Needs the Regimes of Truth and Reality?" *Signs: Journal of Women in Culture and Society*, Vol. 22, 1997, p. 384.
3 Sandra Harding, *Whose Science? Whose Knowledge? Thinking from Women's Lives*, Cornell University Press, Ithaca, NY, 1991, pp. 269–270.
4 Meenakshi Gigi Durham, "On the Relevance of Standpoint Epistemology to the Practice of Journalism: The Case for 'Strong Objectivity,'" *Communication Theory*, Vol. 8, 1998, p. 117.
5 Julia T. Wood, "Gender and Moral Voice: Moving from Woman's Nature to Standpoint Epistemology," *Women's Studies in Communication*, Vol. 15, 1993, p. 13.
6 Julia T. Wood, "Feminist Standpoint Theory and Muted Group Theory: Commonalities and Divergences," *Women and Language*, Vol. 28, 2005, pp. 61–64.
7 Julia T. Wood, "Feminist Scholarship and the Study of Relationships," *Journal of Social and Personal Relationships*, Vol. 12, 1995, p. 110.
8 Georg Wilhelm Friedrich Hegel, *The Phenomenology of Mind*, Macmillan, New York, 1910, pp. 182–188.
9 Friedrich Engels, "Socialism: Utopian and Scientific," and "The Origin of the Family, Private Property, and the State," in *The Marx-Engels Reader*, Robert Tuckeer (ed.), W. W. Norton, New York, 1978, pp. 701–702, 734–736. See also Sandra Harding, "The Instability of the Analytical Categories of Feminist Theory," in *Sex and Scientific Inquiry*, Sandra Harding and Jean O'Barr (eds.), University of Chicago Press, Chicago, 1987, p. 292.
10 Harding, "Comment on Hekman's 'Truth and Method,'" p. 389.
11 Wood, "Feminist Scholarship," p. 111.
12 Jean-Francois Lyotard, *The Postmodern Condition: A Report on Knowledge*, University of Minnesota Press, Minneapolis, 1984, p. xxiv.
13 Wood, "Engendered Relations: Interaction, Caring, Power and Responsibility in Intimacy," in *Social Context and Relationships*, Steve Duck (ed.), Sage, Newbury Park, CA, 1993, p. 37.
14 Wood, "Feminist Scholarship," p. 112.
15 Toni Morrison, *Beloved*, Alfred Knopf, New York, 1987, pp. 67–68.
16 Wood, *Communication Theories*, p. 251. See also Harding, *Whose Science? Whose Knowledge?* p. 59.
17 Wood, "Gender and Moral Voice," p. 8.
18 Morrison, p. 190.
19 Harding, *Whose Science? Whose Knowledge?* p. 192.
20 Ibid., p. 269; Donna Haraway, "Situated Knowledges: The Science Question in Feminism and the Privilege of Partial Perspective," *Feminist Studies*, Vol. 14, 1988, p. 3.
21 Harding, *Whose Science? Whose Knowledge?* pp. 159, 58.
22 Ibid., p. 59.
23 Morrison, p. 23.
24 Wood, *Communication Theories*, p. 257.
25 Harding, *Whose Science? Whose Knowledge?* pp. 149–152.
26 Ibid., p. 270.
27 Wood, *Communication Theories*, p. 254.
28 Ibid.
29 Morrison, pp. 163–164.
30 Harding, *Whose Science? Whose Knowledge?* p. 167.
31 Julia T. Wood, *Who Cares? Women, Care, and Culture*, Southern Illinois University Press, Carbondale, 1994, p. 4.
32 Ibid., p. 6.
33 Ibid., pp. 8–9.
34 Ibid., p. 163.
35 Patricia Hill Collins, *Black Feminist Thought: Knowledge, Consciousness, and the Politics of Empowerment*, 2nd ed., Routledge, New York, 2000, p. 24.
36 Pearl Cleage, *Deals with the Devil and Other Reasons to Riot*, Ballantine, New York, 1993, p. 55.
37 The wording of the four criteria of black feminist epistemology and the quotations that accompany them are from Collins, *Black Feminist Thought*, pp. 257–266.
38 Seyla Benhabib, *Situating the Self: Gender, Community and Postmodernism in Contemporary Ethics*, Routledge, New York, 1992, p. 4.
39 Ibid., p. 2.
40 Jean-Francois Lyotard, *The Postmodern Condition: A Report on Knowledge*, Geoff Bennington and Brian Massumi (trans.), University of Minnesota, Minneapolis, 1984.
41 Benhabib, *Situating the Self*, p. 209.
42 Ibid., p. 229.
43 Ibid., p. 14.
44 Benhabib's critique of Habermas draws on Nancy Fraser, "Rethinking the Public Sphere," *Justice Interruptus*, Routledge, New York, 1997, pp. 69–98.
45 Benhabib, *Situating the Self*, p. 3.
46 Benhabib, "The Generalized and the Concrete Other: The Kohlberg-Gilligan Controversy and Feminist Theory," in *Situating the Self*, pp. 148–177.
47 Patricia Hill Collins, *Fighting Words: Black Women and the Search for Justice*, University of Minnesota, Minneapolis, 1998, p. xvii.
48 Susan Hekman, "Truth and Method: Feminist Standpoint Theory Revisited," *Signs*, Vol. 22, 1997, pp. 341–365; Nancy Hirschmann, "Feminist Standpoint as Postmodern Strategy," *Women and Politics*, Vol. 18, No. 3, 1997, pp. 73–92.
49 John Michael, "Making a Stand: Standpoint Epistemologies, Political Positions, Proposition 187," *Telos*, Vol. 108, 1996, pp. 93–103.
50 Lynn Worsham, "Romancing the Stones: My Movie Date with Sandra Harding," *Journal of Advanced Composition*, Vol. 15, 1995, p. 568.

Chapter 35: Muted Group Theory

1 Cheris Kramarae, *Women and Men Speaking*, Newbury House Publishers, Rowley, MA, 1981, p. 1.
2 Barrie Thorne, Cheris Kramarae, and Nancy Henley (eds.), *Language, Gender and Society*, Newbury House Publishers, Rowley, MA, 1983, p. 9.
3 Cheris Kramarae, "Folklinguistics," *Psychology Today*, Vol. 8, June 1974, pp. 82–85.
4 Edwin Ardener, "Belief and the Problem of Women," in *Perceiving Women*, 1975, p. 2.
5 Edwin Ardener, "The 'Problem' Revisited," in *Perceiving Women*, p. 22.
6 Ibid., p. 25.
7 Shirley Ardener, "The Nature of Women in Society," in *Defining Females*, Halsted, New York, 1978, p. 21.
8 Kramarae, *Women and Men Speaking*, p. 3.
9 Simone de Beauvoir, *The Second Sex*, H. M. Parshley (ed. and trans.), Bantam, New York, 1964, p. xv.
10 Kramarae, *Women and Men Speaking*, p. 3.
11 Julia P. Stanley, "Paradigmatic Women: The Prostitute," in *Papers in Language Variation*, David L. Shores and Carole P. Hines (eds.), University of Alabama, Tuscaloosa, 1977, p. 7.
12 Kramarae, *Women and Men Speaking*, p. 1.

13   Virginia Woolf, *A Room of One's Own*, Hogarth (Penguin edition), 1928, p. 45.

14   Dorothy Smith, "A Peculiar Eclipsing: Women's Exclusion from Man's Culture," *Women's Studies International Quarterly*, Vol. 1, 1978, p. 281.

15   Candace West, Michelle M. Lazar, and Cheris Kramarae, "Gender in Discourse," in *Discourse as Social Interaction*, Vol. 2, Teun van Dijk (ed.), Sage, Thousand Oaks, CA, 1997, p. 137.

16   Cheris Kramarae, "Feminist Fictions of Future Technology," in *Cybersociety 2.0: Revisiting Computer-Mediated Communication and Community*, Stephen Jones (ed.), Sage, Thousand Oaks, CA, p. 109.

17   Jana Kramer and Cheris Kramarae, "Women's Political Webs: Global Electronic Networks," in *Gender, Politics and Communication*, Annabele Sreberny and Liesbet van Zoonen (eds.), Hampton, Cresskill, NJ, 2000, pp. 214–215.

18   Ibid., p. 212.

19   Women's Leadership Network to Use the Internet to Fight Conservative Policies, *KJEnglish@aol.com*, April 8, 1995.

20   Kramarae, "Feminist Fictions of Future Technology," p. 111.

21   H. Jeanie Taylor and Cheris Kramarae, "Creating Cybertrust: Illustrations and Guidelines," in *Computing in the Social Sciences and Humanities*, Orville Vernon Burton (ed.), University of Illinois Press, Urbana, 2004, pp. 141–158.

22   Kramarae, *Women and Men Speaking*, p. 3.

23   Tillie Olsen, *Silences*, Delacorte/Seymour Lawrence, New York, 1978, p. 23.

24   Kramarae, *Women and Men Speaking*, p. 19.

25   Ibid., p. 12.

26   Ibid., p. 4.

27   Cheris Kramarae and Paula Treichler, *A Feminist Dictionary*, 2nd ed., Pandora, London, 1992, p. 17.

28   Anita Diamant, *The Red Tent*, St. Martins, New York, 1997; Susannah Meadows, "Meeting Under a Big 'Tent': How a Biblical Tale Became a Word-of-Mouth Phenom," *Newsweek*, February 5, 2001, p. 61.

29   Kramarae and Treichler, p. 4.

30   Dale Spender, *Man Made Language*, Routledge & Kegan, London, 1980, p. 87.

31   Cheris Kramarae, "Punctuating the Dictionary," *International Journal of the Sociology of Language*, Vol. 94, 1992, p. 135.

32   Kramarae and Treichler, p. 4.

33   Cheris Kramarae, "Harassment and Everyday Life," in *Women Making Meaning: New Feminist Directions in Communication*, Lana Rakow (ed.), Routledge, New York, 1992, p. 102.

34   Julia T. Wood (ed.), "Special Section—'Telling Our Stories' Sexual Harassment in the Communication Discipline," *Journal of Applied Communication Research*, Vol. 20, 1992, pp. 383–384.

35   Karen A. Foss and Sonja K. Foss, "Incorporating the Feminist Perspective in Communication Scholarship: A Research Commentary," in *Doing Research on Women's Communication: Perspectives on Theory and Method*, K. Carter and C. Spitzack (eds.), Ablex, Norwood, NJ, 1989, p. 72.

36   Deborah Tannen, *Conversational Style: Analyzing Talk Among Friends*, Ablex, Norwood, NJ, 1984, p. 43.

37   Kramarae, "Punctuating the Dictionary," p. 146.

Communication Theory

1   Karl Weick, *The Social Psychology of Organizing*, 2nd ed., Addison-Wesley, Reading, MA, 1979, pp. 35–42.

2   Warren Thorngate, "'In General' vs. 'It Depends': Some Comments on the Gergen-Schlenker Debate," *Personality and Social Psychology Bulletin*, Vol. 2, 1976, p. 406.

3   Ibid.

4   C. David Mortensen, "Communication Postulates," in *Contexts*, Jean N. Civikly (ed.), Holt, Rinehart and Winston, New York, 1975, p. 21.

5   Kanl Weick, p. 39.

6   Graham Chapman, John Cleese, Terry Gilliam, Eric Idle, Terry Jones, and Michael Palin, *The Complete Monty Python's Flying Circus: All the Words, Volume Two*, Pantheon, New York, 1989, p. 119.

Chapter 36: Common Threads in Comm Theories

1   To access a chapter on Heider's attribution theory that appeared in a previous edition, click on Theory Archive at *www.afirstlook.com*.

2   Raymond Bauer, "The Obstinate Audience," *American Psychologist*, Vol. 19, 1964, pp. 319–328.

CREDITS AND ACKNOWLEDGMENTS

Chapter 2

Page 13: Quoted from "Best Spots of November 2006," *Ad Week*, December 11, 2006. Nielsen Business Media, Inc.

Chapter 3

Page 27: Lyrics from "The Farmer and The Cowman" by Richard Rodgers and Oscar Hammerstein II. Copyright 1943 by Williamson Music. Copyright Renewed International Copyright Secured. All rights reserved. Reprinted by permission.

Page 36: Robert Frost, *A Masque of Reason*, copyright 1945 by Henry Holt and Company, copyright 1945 by Robert Frost. Reprinted by arrangement with Henry Holt and Co.

Chapter 4

Page 44 (Fig. 4-1): Claude E. Shannon and Warren Weaver's Model of Communication adapted from *The Mathematical Theory of Communication*. Copyright 1949, 1998 by Board of Trustees of the University of Illinois Press. Used by permission of the University of Illinois Press.

Page 46 (Fig. 4-2): Adapted from C. K. Ogden and I. A. Richards, Richards' Semantic Triangle, *The Meaning of Meaning*. Harcourt Brace, 1946, pp. 1–23. Used by permission of Cengage Learning Services Ltd. on behalf of Taylor & Francis Routledge.

Page 52: "Credo for Communication Ethics" reprinted by permission of National Communication Association, Washington, DC.

Interpersonal Messages

Page 56: Em Griffin, "Game Metaphors" from *Making Friends (& Making Them Count)*, pp. 12–18. Copyright © 1987 Em Griffin. Used by permission of InterVarsity Press, P.O. Box 1400, Downers Grove, IL, 60515, www.ivpress.com.

Chapter 5

Page 60: Jane Wagner, *The Search For Signs of Intelligent Life in the Universe*. Copyright © 1986 by Jane Wagner Inc. Reprinted by permission of HarperCollins Publishers, and by the author.

Chapter 6

Page 73: W. Barnett Pearce and Kimberly A. Pearce, "Transcendent Storytelling: Abilities for Systemic Practitioners and Their Clients." *Human Systems: The Journal of Systemic Consultation & Management*, Vol. 9, 1998, pp. 178–179. Used by permission of the KCC Foundation and the Leeds Family Therapy.

Page 76 (Fig. 6-3): W. Barnett Pearce, *Interpersonal Communication: Making Social Worlds* (East Brunswick, NJ: University Publishing Solutions, 2007), p. 32. Reproduced by permission of the publisher.

Page 80: W. Barnett Pearce as accessed on http://www.pearceassociates.com/essays/our_response.htm. Reprinted by permission of the author.

Chapter 7

Page 86: W.H. Auden, "Prologue: The Birth of Architecture," *About the House*, copyright © 1976 by Edward Mendelson, William Meredith, and Monroe K. Spears, Executors of the Estate of W.H. Auden, from *Collected Poems* by W.H. Auden. Used by permission of Random House, Inc., and by Faber and Faber Ltd.

Chapter 8

Pages 101, 103: Shereen Bingham and Brant R. Burleson, "Multiple Effects of Messages with Multiple Goals: Some Perceived Outcomes of Responses to Sexual Harassment," *Human Communication Research*, Vol. 16, 1989, pp. 192–193. Used by permission of Blackwell Publishing.

Chapter 10

Pages 126–128: Axioms from Charles R. Berger and Richard Calabrese, "Some Explorations in Initial Interaction and Beyond: Toward a Developmental Theory of Interpersonal Communication," *Human Communication Research*, Vol. 1, 1975, pp. 99–112. Used by permission of Blackwell Publishing.

Page 129 (Fig. 10-1): Theorems of Uncertainty Reduction Theory adapted from Charles R. Berger and Richard Calabrese, "Some Explorations in Initial Interaction and Beyond: Toward a Developmental Theory of Interpersonal Communication," *Human Communication Research*, Vol. 1, 1975, p. 100. Used by permission of Blackwell Publishing.

Page 135: Kathy Kellermann and Rodney Reynolds, "When Ignorance Is Bliss: The Role of Motivation to Reduce Uncertainty in Uncertainty Reduction Theory," *Human Communication Research*, Vol. 17, 1990, pp. 7, 71. Used by permission of Blackwell Publishing.

Chapter 11

Pages 141, 142, 145, 147: Nora Ephron and Delia Ephron, *You've Got Mail*. Reprinted by permission from International Creative Management, Inc., and from Industry Entertainment, Los Angeles, CA. Copyright © 1998 by Nora Ephron and copyright © 1998 by Delia Ephron.

Chapter 12

Pages 155, 158–165: Gurinder Chadha, Guljit Bindra, and Paul Mayeda Berges, *Bend It Like Beckham*, 2002, Kintop Pictures. Used by permission.

Pages 156, 161–163: Leslie A. Baxter, "Relationships as Dialogues," *Personal Relationships*, 2004. Used by permission of Blackwell Publishing.

Page 164: Gurinder Chadha, director and co-writer of *Bend It Like Beckham*. *FLM Magazine*, 2003. Courtesy of Landmark Theatres / FLM Magazine.

Page 166: Barbara Montgomery, "Relationship Maintenance Versus Relationship Change: A Dialectical Dilemma," *Journal of Social and Personal Relationships*, Vol. 10, 1993. Sage Publications.

Chapter 30

Pages 389, 391, 396: Angie Williams and Howard Giles, "Intergenerational Conversations: Young Adults' Retrospective Accounts," *Human Communication Research,* Vol. 23, 1996, pp. 223, 233, 237, 239. Used by permission of Blackwell Publishing.

Chapter 31

Pages 401, 403: Stella Ting-Toomey and Atsuko Kurogi, "Facework Competence in Intercultural Conflict: An Updated Face-Negotiation Theory," *International Journal of Intercultural Relations,* Vol. 22, 1998, pp. 190, 196, 218. Reprinted with permission from Elsevier.

Page 407 (Fig. 31-2): A Cultural Map of "An Eight-Style Conflict Grid: An Intercultural Approach," adapted from Stella Ting-Toomey and John Oetzel, *Managing Intercultural Conflict Effectively,* 2001. Reprinted by permission of Sage Publications via Copyright Clearance Center.

Chapter 33

Pages 429–430, 432, 434–435: Deborah Tannen, *You Just Don't Understand.* Copyright © 1990 by Deborah Tannen. Reprinted by permission of HarperCollins Publishers Inc., William Morrow; by Time Warner Book Group UK; and by the author.

Pages 430–431, 433–436: Nora Ephron, *When Harry Met Sally.* Copyright © 1989 by Nora Ephron. Reprinted with permission of International Creative Management, Inc.

Page 439: Senta Troemel-Ploetz, "Review Essay: Selling the Apolitical," *Discourse & Society,* Vol. 2, 1991. Sage Publications.

Chapter 34

Pages 442–443: Julia T. Wood, "Feminist Scholarship and the Study of Relationships," *Journal of Social and Personal Relationships,* Vol. 12, 1995. Sage Publications.

Pages 443–448: Toni Morrison, *Beloved.* Copyright © 1987 by Toni Morrison. Used by permission of Alfred A. Knopf, a division of Random House, Inc. and by International Creative Management, Inc.

Page 452: Lynn Worsham, "Romancing the Stones: My Movie Date with Sandra Harding," *Journal of Advanced Composition,* Vol. 15, 1995, p. 568. Used with permission.

Chapter 35

Pages 457: Dorothy Smith, "A Peculiar Eclipsing: Women's Exclusion from Man's Culture," *Women's Studies International Quarterly,* 1978. Reprinted with permission from Elsevier via Copyright Clearance Center.

Pages 461–462: Cheris Kramarae and Paula Treichler, with assistance from Ann Russo, *The Feminist Dictionary* 2e, Pandora Press Routledge & Kegan Paul plc, London 1992. Used by permission of the authors.

Pages 462–463: "Special Section–'Telling Our Stories': Sexual Harassment in the Communication Discipline," Julia T. Wood (ed.), *Journal of Applied Communication Research,* Vol. 20, 1992. Reprinted by permission of Taylor & Francis Ltd., www.informaworld.com.

Communication Theory

Page 469: Photo courtesy of Python (Monty) Pictures Ltd.

Appendix C

Page A-8: "Credo for Communication Ethics" reprinted by permission of National Communication Association, Washington, DC.

INDEX